This is ou

Christian themes from the Bible

Acknowledgments

The editor gratefully wishes to thank the Consultants of the *NIV Thematic Study Bible*: Alister McGrath, Donald J. Wiseman, J. I. Packer, Stephen Travis, Gordon McConville, and all those who compiled and edited the Thematic Section of the *NIV Thematic Study Bible*, on which this work is based.

THIS IS OUR
FAITH

*Christian themes
from the Bible*

Edited by Martin H. Manser

Hodder & Stoughton
LONDON SYDNEY AUCKLAND

Scripture quotations taken from the HOLY BIBLE, NEW
INTERNATIONAL VERSION. Copyright © 1973, 1978,
1984 by International Bible Society. First published in Great
Britain, 1979. Inclusive language version 1995, 1996. Used by
permission of Hodder & Stoughton, a member of the Hodder
Headline Group.

10 9 8 7 6 5 4 3 2 1

A CIP catalogue record for this title is
available from the British Library

ISBN 0 340 65650 6

Typeset by Hewer Text Composition Services, Edinburgh
Printed and bound in Great Britain by
Mackays of Chatham PLC, Chatham, Kent

Hodder and Stoughton Ltd
A Division of Hodder Headline PLC
338 Euston Road
London NW1 3BH

Contents

Introduction

The study of Scripture lies at the heart of the Christian faith. It is therefore important that readers of Scripture are given every means of help so that they will derive as much benefit and enjoyment as possible out of reading the Bible. *This is our Faith* is a selection of some 300 themes from the acclaimed *NIV Thematic Study Bible* published by Hodder and Stoughton.

Thematic study of the Bible is important because it draws together from different parts of the Bible what Scripture says on a particular subject. *This is our Faith* is a selection of themes relating to the key truths of Christianity: through God's *revelation* comes the *gospel* of Jesus Christ, centring on the *cross* and *resurrection*, showing God's *love, mercy* and *grace*. *Salvation* is considered from different aspects including *forgiveness, redemption* and *justification*. Salvation is not only individual so the themes of *the church, adoption* and *fellowship* are also included.

The ultimate aim of thematic study is not simply to group together truths intellectually but to respond to God in *repentance* and *faith*. *Assurance, spiritual growth, obedience* and *sanctification* as well as the devotional themes of *prayer, praise* and *worship* are all explored.

A thematic study is different from a lexical study in that the former is based on related ideas, the latter on individual words. The difference between them can be appreciated by considering the theme of "assurance". A word-based approach would be limited to identifying biblical passages in which the word "assurance" appears. A thematic approach, however, goes far beyond this and explores all the various elements of the theme. It identifies its basic concepts, its presuppositions and its consequences, in order that the theme in all its fulness can be unfolded to the reader. For example the material that deals with assurance covers the *basis of assurance* (e.g., the knowledge of

God, the certainty of his word, the work of the Holy Spirit), the *nature of assurance* (a relationship with God, salvation, eternal life and a future hope) and *the relationship between assurance and the life of faith*.

In this selection the actual text of key verses is quoted from the inclusive-language (gender-neutral) NIV Bible text. Many other verse references are also included to provide a wealth of biblical material.

A thorough system of cross-references allows the interrelationship of biblical themes to be understood and explored. For example, from "assurance" the reader is referred to the following: faith, forgiveness; hope; life of faith; obedience; peace, experience; predestination; resurrection; salvation.

Martin H. Manser
Aylesbury 1997

How to study a theme

Themes in this edition are arranged alphabetically by title. Each theme consists of a precise summary of the nature and importance of the theme, followed by a detailed analysis of its main parts. The text of Scripture for the main references appears in full, and many other scriptural references document each of the theme's aspects. At the end of the themes cross-references are provided to related themes included in this book.

Theme name ———————

Holy Spirit, indwelling
The Holy Spirit dwells within Jesus Christ and his

Introduction gives a concise definition of the theme
to show its contents and importance
→ disciples. Recognisable results in believers' lives
include Christlikeness and the fruit of the Spirit.

Major headings set out clearly the key aspects of
the theme
→ **The indwelling of the Holy Spirit in the OT**
Ge 41:38 So Pharaoh asked them [his

Main verse reference printed in bold type
(e.g., Ge 41:38)
officials], "Can we find anyone like this man
[Joseph], one in whom is the spirit of God?"
Ex 35:31 ". . . and he [the LORD] has filled him

Scripture text given for main references ———
→ [Bezalel] with the Spirit of God, with skill, ability
and knowledge in all kinds of crafts—" *See
also* **Nu** 27:18; **1Sa** 10:6–7; **Isa** 59:21; **Hag** 2:5

Comment or explanation is in reduced type. If it
relates to a single verse reference it follows it; if
it relates to a group of references it proceeds
them
The Holy Spirit indwells believers
2Ti 1:14 . . . the Holy Spirit who lives in us.
→ Believers are described as the temple of the Holy Spirit:
1Co 3:16; 6:19

If there are further secondary references after
such a group, they start on a new line
Eph 2:22; **1Jn** 2:27; 3:24

Parallel passages are preceded by "pp" and are not
in bold type
**Results of the Holy Spirit's indwelling in
believers**
→**Preaching and public testimony is aided** **Mt**

Subheadings
10:20▸pp **Mk** 13:11 pp **Lk** 12:12; **Ac** 4:8–12;
5:29–32
The fruit of the Spirit is displayed

Secondary verses support the main verse, preceded
by See also. The Bible book name only is
printed in bold type
(e.g., **Ro** 5:5)
Gal 5:22–23 . . . the fruit of the Spirit is
love, joy, peace, patience, kindness, goodness,
faithfulness, gentleness and self-control . . .
→ *See also* **Ro** 5:5; 14:17; 15:13,30

Cross-references to other themes are in italics.
These enable you to look up related material
**Those without the Holy Spirit's
indwelling are not Christlike**
Gal 5:17; **Jude** 18–19 *See also Christlikeness;
Holy Spirit in life of Jesus Christ; Holy Spirit, filling with;*

Abbreviations

A.D.	since the birth of Jesus Christ
B.C.	before the birth of Jesus Christ
c.	about
fn	footnote
NT	New Testament
OT	Old Testament
pp	parallel passage

The Old Testament

Genesis	Ge	2 Chronicles	2Ch	Daniel	Da
Exodus	Ex	Ezra	Ezr	Hosea	Hos
Leviticus	Lev	Nehemiah	Ne	Joel	Joel
Numbers	Nu	Esther	Est	Amos	Am
Deuteronomy	Dt	Job	Job	Obadiah	Ob
Joshua	Jos	Psalms	Ps	Jonah	Jnh
Judges	Jdg	Proverbs	Pr	Micah	Mic
Ruth	Ru	Ecclesiastes	Ecc	Nahum	Na
1 Samuel	1Sa	Song of Songs	SS	Habakkuk	Hab
2 Samuel	2Sa	Isaiah	Isa	Zephaniah	Zep
1 Kings	1Ki	Jeremiah	Jer	Haggai	Hag
2 Kings	2Ki	Lamentations	La	Zechariah	Zec
1 Chronicles	1Ch	Ezekiel	Eze	Malachi	Mal

The New Testament

Matthew	Mt	Ephesians	Eph	Hebrews	Heb
Mark	Mk	Philippians	Php	James	Jas
Luke	Lk	Colossians	Col	1 Peter	1Pe
John	Jn	1 Thessalonians	1Th	2 Peter	2Pe
Acts	Ac	2 Thessalonians	2Th	1 John	1Jn
Romans	Ro	1 Timothy	1Ti	2 John	2Jn
1 Corinthians	1Co	2 Timothy	2Ti	3 John	3Jn
2 Corinthians	2Co	Titus	Tit	Jude	Jude
Galatians	Gal	Philemon	Phm	Revelation	Rev

BIBLE THEMES

adoption

The deliberate action by which a family gives to a person all the privileges of being a member of that family.

adoption, descriptions

The words used by the NT to describe believers point to their status and privileges as the adopted children of God.

Believers are no longer slaves but children

Gal 4:7–9 So you are no longer slaves, but God's children; and since you are his children, he has made you also heirs. Formerly, when you did not know God, you were slaves to those who by nature are not gods. But now that you know God—or rather are known by God . . .   See also **Jn** 8:34–36; **Ro** 8:15; **Phm** 16

Believers are children of God

Ro 8:14 because those who are led by the Spirit of God are children of God.
1Jn 3:1–2 How great is the love the Father has lavished on us, that we should be called children of God! And that is what we are! . . . Dear friends, now we are children of God . . . See also **Lk** 20:36; **Ro** 8:21, 9:26; **Gal** 3:26; **Php** 2:15; **1Jn** 3:2; 5:2

Believers are children of the resurrection

Lk 20:36

Believers are children of light

Jn 12:36; **Eph** 5:8; **1Th** 5:5

Believers are heirs of God

Ro 8:17 Now if we are children, then we are heirs—heirs of God and co-heirs with Christ . . .   See also **Gal** 3:29; 4:7; **Tit** 3:7; **Heb** 6:17

Believers are brothers and sisters of Jesus Christ

Heb 2:11–12 Both the one who makes people holy and those who are made holy are of the same family. So Jesus is not ashamed to call them brothers and sisters. He says, "I will declare your name to my brothers and sisters . . ."
See also **Mt** 12:48–50; **Ro** 8:29; **Heb** 2:17

Believers are brothers and sisters of other believers

1Jn 3:14 We [believers] know that we have passed from death to life, because we love each other.   See also **1Jn** 4:19–20; **Rev** 12:10; 19:10

Believers are members of God's household, his family

Eph 2:19 . . . you are no longer foreigners and aliens, but fellow-citizens with God's people and members of God's household,   See also **Gal** 6:10; **Heb** 3:2–6   See also knowing God.

adoption, nature of

The giving by God of the status and privileges of being his children. God adopts those who believe in him and grants them the benefits of his salvation.

A family adopts a child

Ge 15:3 . . . Abram said, "You have given me no children; so a servant [Eliezer of Damascus] in my household will be my heir."
See also **Ge** 48:5; **Ex** 2:10; **Est** 2:7

God adopts the nation of Israel
Dt 14:2 . . . Out of all the peoples on the face of the earth, the LORD has chosen you to be his treasured possession.   *See also* **Dt** 7:7; **Isa** 63:16; **Am** 3:1–2; **Ro** 9:4

God is Israel's father
Jer 31:9 ". . . I [the LORD] am Israel's father, and Ephraim is my firstborn son."   *See also* **Mal** 1:6

Israel is God's son
Hos 11:1 "When Israel was a child, I [the LORD] loved him, and out of Egypt I called my son."   *See also* **Dt** 14:1

God adopts believers as his children
Jn 1:12–13 Yet to all who received him, to those who believed in his name, he gave the right to become children of God—children born not of natural descent, nor of human decision or a husband's will, but born of God.

God is the Father of believers
2Co 6:18 "I [the LORD] will be a Father to you, and you will be my sons and daughters, says the Lord Almighty."   *See also* **Mt** 6:9 pp **Lk** 11:2

Believers are adopted as an outcome of predestination
Eph 1:5 he [God the Father] predestined us to be adopted as his children through Jesus Christ, in accordance with his pleasure and will . . .

Believers are adopted as an outcome of redemption
Gal 4:5 to redeem those under law, that we might receive adoption as God's children.

Believers are adopted as an outcome of justification
Gal 3:24–26 . . . the law was put in charge to lead us to Christ that we might be justified by faith. Now that faith has come, we are no longer under the supervision of the law. You are all children of God through faith in Christ Jesus, *See also* **Jn** 1:12–13

Believers are adopted by grace
Eph 1:3–6 Praise be to the God and Father of our Lord Jesus Christ, who has blessed us in the heavenly realms with every spiritual blessing in Christ. For he chose us in him before the creation of the world to be holy and blameless in his sight. In love he predestined us to be adopted as his children through Jesus Christ, in accordance with his pleasure and will—to the praise of his glorious grace, which he has freely given us in the One he loves.   *See also* **Eze** 16:3–6; **Ro** 4:16; **Eph** 1:11

The final adoption of believers will occur at the resurrection
Ro 8:23 . . . we [believers] wait eagerly for our adoption, the redemption of our bodies. *See also* **Eph** 1:13–14; **1Jn** 3:2   *See also election; justification; last things; predestination; reconciliation; redemption; salvation.*

---

adoption, privileges and duties
As adopted members of the family of God, believers receive both the privileges and responsibilities of being children of God.

The privileges received by believers through adoption
Believers are given the Spirit of adoption
Gal 4:6 Because you are his children, he sent the Spirit of his Son into our hearts, the Spirit who calls out, "*Abba*, Father."   *See also* **Ro** 8:15

Believers have access to their heavenly Father
Eph 2:18 For through him we both have access to the Father by one Spirit.   *See also* **Eph** 3:12; **Heb** 4:16

Believers become heirs with Christ of heaven
Ro 8:17 Now if we are children, then we are heirs—heirs of God and co-heirs with Christ . . .   *See also* **Gal** 3:29; 4:7; **Col** 1:12; **1Pe** 1:4

The benefits God gives to those he adopts
Believers are pitied by him
Ps 103:13 As a father has compassion on his children, so the LORD has compassion on those who fear him;

Believers are protected
Pr 14:26 Those who fear the LORD have a secure fortress, and for their children it will be a refuge.

Believers are provided for
Mt 6:31–33 "So do not worry, saying, 'What shall we eat?' or 'What shall we drink?' or 'What shall we wear?' For the pagans run after all these things, and your heavenly Father knows that you need them. But seek first his kingdom and his righteousness, and all these things will be given to you as well."

Believers receive loving discipline
Heb 12:6 "because the Lord disciplines those he loves, and he punishes everyone he accepts as a child."

Believers are never forsaken
Ps 94:14 For the Lord will not reject his people; he will never forsake his inheritance.

Believers are assured by the Spirit
Ro 8:16 The Spirit himself testifies with our spirit that we are God's children.

The responsibilities of God's adopted children
Believers are to walk in the light Jn 12:35–36; Eph 5:8; 1Th 5:4–5
Believers are to shun evil 2Co 6:17–18; Php 2:15
Believers are to purify themselves 2Co 7:1; 1Jn 3:2–3
Believers are to live obediently Mt 12:50; 1Pe 1:14; 1Jn 5:2–3
Believers are to live in peace Mt 5:9; Ro 14:19
Believers are to live in love Gal 5:13; 1Pe 4:8; 1Jn 3:18
Believers are to be watchful 1Th 5:5–6
See also assurance; obedience.

---

assurance
Certainty of a present relationship with God through Jesus Christ and a secure future hope which is based upon divine revelation, centred on the person, promises and action of God and confirmed by the Holy Spirit.

---

assurance, and life of faith
The completeness of conviction and confidence expressed in the life of the believer, worked by the Holy Spirit. It derives from a reliance upon God and his promises alone, and results in boldness and steadfastness in service and in the face of difficulties.

Assurance and faith
Dt 9:3 But be assured today that the Lord your God is the one who goes across ahead of you [Israel] like a devouring fire. He will destroy them; he will subdue them [the Anakites] before you. And you will drive them out and annihilate them quickly, as the Lord has promised you.

Heb 10:22 let us draw near to God with a sincere heart in full assurance of faith, having our hearts sprinkled to cleanse us from a guilty conscience and having our bodies washed with pure water.   *See also* Dt 1:21; Jos 1:9; 2Ch 20:17; Jn 17:8; Heb 11:1; 12:5

Assurance and hope
Heb 6:11 We want each of you to show this same diligence to the very end, in order to make your hope sure.   *See also* Pr 23:18; Heb 6:19

Assurance expressed by believers
Assurance in adversity
Heb 13:6 So we say with confidence, "The Lord is my helper; I will not be afraid. What can human beings do to me?"   *See also* Ps 118:6–7; 3:6; 27:3–5; 46:1–3; 71:5–6; 73:26; Ro 8:38–39; 2Co 4:16

Assurance of God's promises
Jos 23:14 "Now I [Joshua] am about to go the way of all the earth. You know with all your heart and soul that not one of all the good promises the Lord your God gave you has failed. Every promise has been fulfilled; not one has failed."   *See also* 1Ki 8:56; Ro 4:20–21; 2Co 1:20

Assurance in ministry
Ro 1:16 I [Paul] am not ashamed of the gospel, because it is the power of God for the salvation of everyone who believes: first for the Jew, then for the Gentile.

1Ti 3:13 Those who have served well gain an excellent standing and great assurance in their faith in Christ Jesus. *See also* **2Co** 3:4; 4:1; 5:14; **1Th** 1:5; **2Pe** 1:12

Assurance in prayer
1Jn 5:14 This is the confidence we have in approaching God: that if we ask anything according to his will, he hears us. *See also* **1Jn** 3:21–22

Assurance of God's will
Ro 14:5 Some consider one day more sacred than another; others consider every day alike. Everybody should be fully convinced in their own minds. *See also* **Ro** 14:14,23; **1Co** 8:9–11

Assurance may be strengthened
Examples of believers asking for assurance
Ge 15:8; **Ex** 33:16; **Jdg** 6:17; **Lk** 1:18
Assurance through understanding
Col 2:2 My [Paul's] purpose is that they may be encouraged in heart and united in love, so that they may have the full riches of complete understanding, in order that they may know the mystery of God, namely, Christ,
Assurance through waiting on God
Ps 46:10 "Be still, and know that I am God; I will be exalted among the nations, I will be exalted in the earth." *See also* **Ps** 27:14; 33:20; **Isa** 30:15; 32:17–18
Assurance strengthened by others **2Ch** 32:6–8; **2Ti** 3:14; **Col** 4:12; **1Th** 3:2–3
False teaching weakens assurance **2Th** 2:2; **2Ti** 2:18

The delusion of false assurance
The danger of self-assurance **Lk** 18:9–14; **2Co** 10:12; **Php** 3:3–4
Such assurance proved false by conduct
1Jn 1:6 If we claim to have fellowship with him yet walk in the darkness, we lie and do not live by the truth. *See also* **1Jn** 2:9–11; 3:6; 4:20; **2Jn** 9; **3Jn** 11 *See also* faith; hope; life, of faith; obedience; peace, experience.

---

assurance, basis of
The assurance of believers is based upon the certain knowledge of God revealed in creation and his mighty acts in history, upon the certainty of his promises, the vindication and resurrection of Christ and the inward testimony and outward demonstration of the power of the Holy Spirit.

Assurance is based upon the certain knowledge of God
Assurance comes from knowing God through creation
Ro 1:19–20 . . . since the creation of the world God's invisible qualities—his eternal power and divine nature—have been clearly seen, being understood from what has been made, so that they are without excuse. *See also* **Ps** 19:1–4; **Ac** 14:17
Assurance comes from knowing God through his mighty acts
Ex 6:7 "I will take you [Israel] as my own people, and I will be your God. Then you will know that I am the LORD your God, who brought you out from under the yoke of the Egyptians.'"

Eze 37:13–14 "Then you, my people, will know that I am the LORD, when I open your graves and bring you up from them . . .'"
See also **Ex** 16:12; 29:46; **Jos** 3:10–13; **1Ki** 20:13; **Isa** 49:23; 60:16; **Eze** 20:42; 28:26

Assurance is based upon the certainty of God's word
Jn 17:8; **1Jn** 5:9–10
Assurance because of God's oath
Heb 6:17 Because God wanted to make the unchanging nature of his purpose very clear to the heirs of what was promised, he confirmed it with an oath. *See also* **Ge** 50:24; **Dt** 4:31; 7:7–9; **Ac** 2:30; **Heb** 7:21
Assurance because of God's promise
Jos 1:9 "Have I not commanded you? Be strong and courageous. Do not be terrified; do not be discouraged, for the LORD your God will be with you wherever you go."

Ro 4:20–21 Yet he [Abraham] did not waver through unbelief regarding the promise of God, but was strengthened in his faith and gave glory to God, being fully persuaded that God had power to do what he had promised. *See also* **Jos** 23:10,14; **2Sa** 7:25–26 pp **1Ch** 17:23–24;

1Ki 8:56; Ps 145:13; Isa 33:6; Heb 13:5; Jas 1:12; 2:5

Assurance is based upon God's vindication of his Son
Assurance because of the resurrection of Jesus Christ
Ac 2:32 "God has raised this Jesus to life, and we are all witnesses of the fact."

Ac 17:31 "For he [God] has set a day when he will judge the world with justice by the man he has appointed. He has given proof of this to everyone by raising him from the dead." *See also* **Ac** 1:3,22; 10:39–41; 13:30–31; **Ro** 1:4; **1Co** 15:3–7; **1Pe** 1:3
Assurance because of the miracles of Jesus Christ Mt 11:2–6 pp Lk 7:18–23; **Jn** 4:48; 10:38; 14:11; 20:30–31

Assurance comes through the work of the Holy Spirit
The Holy Spirit assures believers by enabling outward demonstrations of God's power
Heb 2:4 God also testified to it [salvation] by signs, wonders and various miracles, and gifts of the Holy Spirit distributed according to his will. *See also* **Mk** 16:17–18; **2Co** 3:2–3; **1Th** 1:5
The Holy Spirit assures believers by giving inward conviction
Ro 8:16 The Spirit himself testifies with our spirit that we are God's children.

1Jn 4:13 We know that we live in him [God] and he in us, because he has given us of his Spirit. *See also* **Jn** 15:26; 16:8–11; **Ac** 5:32; **Gal** 4:6
The Holy Spirit assures believers by sealing God's promise
Eph 1:13–14 . . . Having believed, you were marked in him with a seal, the promised Holy Spirit, who is a deposit guaranteeing our inheritance until the redemption of those who are God's possession—to the praise of his glory. *See also* **Ac** 15:8; **Ro** 5:5; **2Co** 1:22; 5:5; **Eph** 4:30; **1Jn** 3:24

Assurance based upon the testimony of God's people
Assurance because of the testimony of eye-witnesses
2Pe 1:16–19 We did not follow cleverly invented stories when we told you about the power and coming of our Lord Jesus Christ, but we were eye-witnesses of his majesty . . . *See also* **Ex** 10:2; **Lk** 1:2–4; **Jn** 1:32–34; 15:27; 19:35; **Ac** 1:22; 4:20; **1Pe** 5:1
Assurance because of the testimony of the apostles Ac 22:14–15; **1Co** 1:6; 2:1; **1Th** 2:13; **1Ti** 2:5–7; **Rev** 1:2

Assurance is based upon godly living
1Jn 2:3–5 We know that we have come to know him if we obey his commands . . . *See also* **1Jn** 2:23,29
Not continuing in sin: **1Jn** 3:9; 5:18
1Jn 3:14–20; 5:1

---

assurance, nature of
The God-given security which believers have in the blessings of divine grace. Believers are assured of the unfailing love of God and of their relationship with him as Father, the salvation and eternal life which he offers and the sure hope of one day sharing his glory.

Assurance of a relationship with God
Assurance of God's unfailing love
Ps 13:5 But I trust in your [the Lord's] unfailing love; my heart rejoices in your salvation. *See also* **Ex** 15:13; **Ps** 51:1; 130:7–8; **Isa** 54:10; **Jn** 13:1; **1Jn** 4:9
Assurance of acceptance by God Ac 15:8; **Ro** 5:1; 14:3; 15:7
Assurance of adoption as God's children
1Jn 3:1–3 How great is the love the Father has lavished on us, that we should be called children of God! And that is what we are! . . . *See also* **Jn** 1:12–13; **Ro** 8:14–17; **Gal** 4:6; **Jas** 1:18; **1Jn** 4:7; 5:1
Assurance of God's presence
Dt 31:8 "The Lord himself goes before you and will be with you; he will never leave you nor forsake you. Do not be afraid; do not be

discouraged." *See also* **Ge** 28:15; **Jos** 3:7; **Isa** 41:10; **Jer** 1:8; **Mt** 28:20; **Jn** 14:18; **Ac** 18:10

Assurance of access to God

Eph 3:12 In him [Christ Jesus] and through faith in him we may approach God with freedom and confidence. *See also* **Ro** 5:2; **Eph** 2:8; **Heb** 4:16; 10:19–22

Assurance of salvation

Isa 12:2 "Surely God is my salvation; I will trust and not be afraid. The LORD, the LORD, is my strength and my song; he has become my salvation." *See also* **Ps** 69:13

Assurance of redemption Job 19:25; **Ps** 111:9; **Ro** 3:24; **Eph** 1:14; **Heb** 9:12

Assurance of justification Ro 3:26; 5:16; 8:33–34; **1Co** 6:11

Assurance of forgiveness

1Jn 1:9 If we confess our sins, he [God] is faithful and just and will forgive us our sins and purify us from all unrighteousness. *See also* **2Ch** 7:14; **Ps** 32:5; 103:12; **Isa** 43:25; **Jer** 31:34; 36:3; **Mic** 7:18–19; **Lk** 24:47; **Ac** 2:38; 3:19; **Col** 2:13–14

Assurance of election

Isa 43:1 But now, this is what the LORD says—he who created you, O Jacob, he who formed you, O Israel: "Fear not, for I have redeemed you; I have summoned you by name; you are mine."

Eph 1:4 For he [God] chose us in him [Christ] before the creation of the world to be holy and blameless in his sight . . . *See also* **Isa** 44:1–2; **Ro** 8:28–30; 11:29; **1Co** 1:9; **2Ti** 1:9; **1Pe** 2:9–10

Assurance of preservation

2Ti 1:12 That is why I [Paul] am suffering as I am. Yet I am not ashamed, because I know whom I have believed, and am convinced that he is able to guard what I have entrusted to him for that day.

Jude 24 To him [God] who is able to keep you from falling and to present you before his glorious presence without fault and with great joy— *See also* **Jn** 6:39; **Ro** 8:38–39; **2Co** 4:14; **Php** 1:6; **Heb** 7:25; **2Pe** 1:10

Assurance of eternal life

Jn 3:15–16 ". . . For God so loved the world that he gave his one and only Son, that whoever believes in him shall not perish but have eternal life."

1Jn 5:11–13 . . . I [John] write these things to you who believe in the name of the Son of God so that you may know that you have eternal life. *See also* **Mt** 19:29 pp **Mk** 10:30 pp **Lk** 18:30; **Jn** 5:24; 6:40; 11:25–26; 17:2; **1Jn** 1:2; 5:20

Assurance of a future hope

Assurance of confidence at Jesus Christ's return Mt 24:30–31 pp **Mk** 13:26–27 pp **Lk** 21:27–28; **1Th** 4:13–17

Assurance on the day of judgment 1Co 1:8; **1Th** 3:13; **1Jn** 4:17

Assurance in the hope of resurrection Jn 6:40; **1Co** 15:42–44; **Php** 3:21

Assurance in the hope of glory

Ro 8:18 I [Paul] consider that our present sufferings are not worth comparing with the glory that will be revealed in us. *See also* **Ro** 5:2; **Col** 3:4; **1Th** 2:12; **1Pe** 5:10; **Rev** 5:10

Assurance in the hope of an eternal inheritance

Ro 8:17 Now if we are children, then we are heirs—heirs of God and co-heirs with Christ, if indeed we share in his sufferings in order that we may also share in his glory. *See also* **Mt** 25:34; **Gal** 4:7; **Heb** 9:15; **1Pe** 1:3–5

Assurance in the hope of an eternal reward Mt 5:12 pp **Lk** 6:23; **2Ti** 4:7–8; **Jas** 1:12 *See also election; forgiveness; predestination; resurrection; salvation.*

atonement

Reconciliation; sin has alienated humanity from God and provoked God's anger. God has responded by providing the means of restoring this broken relationship, bringing both sides to a place where they are at one again ("at-one-ment").

atonement, in New Testament

In dying for the sins of the world, Jesus Christ fulfilled and replaced the OT sacrificial system, so that all who believe in him are restored to fellowship with God. Christ is the true high priest, who finally liberates his people from the guilt of sin, by offering himself as the supreme sacrifice.

The atoning purpose of Jesus Christ's death

Jesus Christ's death on behalf of others

Jn 10:11 "I am the good shepherd. The good shepherd lays down his life for the sheep." *See also* **Jn** 10:14–18; **2Co** 5:15; **Heb** 2:9; **1Jn** 3:16

Jesus Christ's atoning death for sin

1Co 15:3 . . . that Christ died for our sins according to the Scriptures, *See also* **Ro** 4:25; 8:3; **Gal** 1:4; **1Pe** 3:18

The atoning significance of Jesus Christ's death is expressed by references to his blood . . .

Ro 5:9 Since we have now been justified by his blood, how much more shall we be saved from God's wrath through him!

Rev 5:9 . . . "You [the Lamb] are worthy to take the scroll and to open its seals, because you were slain, and with your blood you purchased for God members of every tribe and language and people and nation." *See also* **Eph** 2:13; **1Pe** 1:18–19; **1Jn** 1:7; **Rev** 7:14

Jesus Christ's atoning death is commemorated in the Lord's Supper

1Co 11:23–25 For I [Paul] received from the Lord what I also passed on to you: The Lord Jesus, on the night he was betrayed, took bread, and when he had given thanks, he broke it and said, "This is my body, which is for you; do this in remembrance of me." In the same way, after supper he took the cup, saying, "This cup is the new covenant in my blood; do this, whenever you drink it, in remembrance of me." *See also* **Mt** 26:26–28 pp **Mk** 14:22–24 pp **Lk** 22:19–20

Explanations of the atonement

Jesus Christ's death as an atoning sacrifice

Ro 3:25 God presented him as a sacrifice of atonement, through faith in his blood. *See also* **1Co** 5:7; **Eph** 5:2; **1Jn** 4:10; **Rev** 5:6

Jesus Christ's atoning death as redemption

Mk 10:45 "For even the Son of Man did not come to be served, but to serve, and to give his life as a ransom for many." pp **Mt** 20:28 *See also* **Ac** 20:28; **Gal** 3:13–14; **Eph** 1:7; **Col** 1:13–14

The atonement is effective because of Jesus Christ's sinlessness

2Co 5:21 God made him who had no sin to be sin for us, so that in him we might become the righteousness of God. *See also* **Heb** 4:15; **1Pe** 2:22–24; **1Jn** 3:5

Jesus Christ's death fulfils and replaces the Day of Atonement

Jesus Christ makes atonement as the new high priest Heb 7:26–28

Jesus Christ is the mediator of the new and better covenant Heb 8:6–7; 9:15

Jesus Christ has made atonement in the true heavenly sanctuary Heb 8:1–2; 9:24

Jesus Christ's atoning blood brings effective cleansing Heb 9:12–14

Jesus Christ's single sacrifice replaces the many required under the old covenant Heb 10:11–14

Access to the heavenly sanctuary is now open Heb 10:19–20

By dying with Christ, believers are released from this age into the life of the age to come

Ro 6:1–7 . . . We were therefore buried with him through baptism into death in order that, just as Christ was raised from the dead through the glory of the Father, we too may live a new life . . . *See also* **Ro** 7:4–6; **Gal** 2:19–20; 6:14; **Eph** 2:6–7; **Col** 2:11–13

God the Father and the atoning death of his Son

God's sending of his Son to make atonement
1Jn 4:14 And we have seen and testify that the Father has sent his Son to be the Saviour of the world.   *See also* **Jn** 3:16; **Ro** 8:32; **2Co** 5:18; **Gal** 4:4–5

God's grace displayed in making atonement for the ungodly
Eph 2:4–5 But because of his great love for us, God, who is rich in mercy, made us alive with Christ even when we were dead in transgressions—it is by grace you have been saved.   *See also* **Ro** 5:6–8; **Eph** 2:8–9; **Tit** 3:4–5

The worldwide scope of Jesus Christ's atoning death

1Jn 2:2 He is the atoning sacrifice for our sins, and not only for ours but also for the sins of the whole world.   *See also* **Jn** 1:29; **2Co** 5:19; **1Ti** 2:5

The appropriate response to the atonement

The response of repentance
Ac 3:19 "Repent, then, and turn to God, so that your sins may be wiped out . . ."   *See also* **Ac** 2:38; 17:30; 20:21

The response of faith
Ac 10:43 "All the prophets testify about him that everyone who believes in him receives forgiveness of sins through his name."   *See also* **Jn** 3:14–15; **Ac** 16:31; **Ro** 3:22; **Gal** 2:16

The response of baptism
Ac 22:16 " 'And now what are you waiting for? Get up, be baptised and wash your sins away, calling on his name.' "   *See also* **Ac** 2:38; **1Pe** 3:21   *See also* cross; faith; human race, and redemption; justification; regeneration; sin, remedy for.

---

atonement, in Old Testament

The OT laid down complex regulations by which the guilt of sin could be removed through the sacrificial system. Particular emphasis was placed upon the role of the high priest, who was required to make annual atonement for the sins of the people.

The covenantal framework of atonement

As God's covenant partners, the Israelites undertook to keep his laws
Ex 24:3 When Moses went and told the people all the Lord's words and laws, they responded with one voice, "Everything the Lord has said we will do."   *See also* **Dt** 26:17; **Jos** 24:24

The sin offering made atonement for unintentional sins under the covenant
Lev 9:7 Moses said to Aaron, "Come to the altar and sacrifice your sin offering and your burnt offering and make atonement for yourself and the people; sacrifice the offering that is for the people and make atonement for them, as the Lord has commanded."   *See also* **Lev** 4:13–14; **Nu** 15:22–26

The guilt offering atoned for sins where reparation was required
Lev 19:20–22 " '. . . With the ram of the guilt offering the priest is to make atonement for him before the Lord for the sin he has committed, and his sin will be forgiven.' "   *See also* **Lev** 6:1–7

Deliberate flouting of God's law could not be atoned for
Nu 15:30–31 " 'But those who sin defiantly, whether native-born or alien, blaspheme the Lord, and must be cut off from their people. Because they have despised the Lord's word and broken his commands, they must surely be cut off; their guilt remains on them.' "   *See also* **Nu** 35:33; **1Sa** 3:14

The Day of Atonement provided for the removal of the nation's sin
Lev 16:34 "This is to be a lasting ordinance for you: Atonement is to be made once a year for all the sins of the Israelites." . . .   *See also* **Ex** 30:10; **Lev** 16:1–33; **Heb** 9:7

The atonement cover
Ex 25:17–22 " '. . . There, above the cover between the two cherubim that are over the ark of the Testimony, I [the Lord] will meet with you [Moses] and give you all my commands for the Israelites." *See also* **Ex** 30:6; **Lev** 16:2; **Nu** 7:89

Atonement was effected by the blood of the sacrifice

Lev 17:11 " 'For the life of a creature is in the blood, and I have given it to you to make atonement for yourselves on the altar; it is the blood that makes atonement for one's life.' " *See also* **Heb** 9:22

The role of priests in making atonement

Priests were dedicated to God in order to make atonement for others

Ex 29:44 "So I will consecrate the Tent of Meeting and the altar and will consecrate Aaron and his sons to serve me as priests." *See also* **Lev** 8:22–30

The priests had to make atonement for their own sins

Heb 5:1–3 Every high priest . . . has to offer sacrifices for his own sins, as well as for the sins of the people. *See also* **Lev** 9:8–11

The priests represented the people before God to atone for their sin

Heb 5:1 Every high priest is selected from among human beings and is appointed to represent them in matters related to God, to offer gifts and sacrifices for sins. *See also* **Ex** 28:36–38; **Lev** 10:16–17

The people had constant reminders of the need for atonement

Rituals of cleansing included an atoning offering Lev 12:7–8; 14:18–22,53; 15:15

Atonement was a feature of Israel's festivals Nu 28:22,30; 29:5,11

Abuses of the system of atonement

The sinful conduct of the priests who made atonement

Hos 4:7–8 "The more the priests increased, the more they sinned against me; they exchanged their Glory for something disgraceful. They feed on the sins of my people and relish their wickedness." *See also* **1Sa** 2:12–17; **Jer** 6:13–14; **Eze** 22:26; **Mal** 1:6–8

The sinful conduct of the people who sought atonement without repenting of their sins

Hos 8:11–13 "Though Ephraim built many altars for sin offerings, these have become altars for sinning . . ." *See also* **Isa** 1:10–17; 66:3; **Jer** 7:21–24; **Am** 4:4

The need for repentance for a relationship of atonement

Pr 16:6 Through love and faithfulness sin is atoned for; through the fear of the LORD evil is avoided. *See also* **1Sa** 15:22; **Ps** 51:16–17; **Mic** 6:6–8

The prophets foretold a renewing of God's relationship with Israel, involving atonement for sin

Isaiah's message about the obedient servant Isa 53:4–12

Jeremiah's prophecy of a new covenant Jer 31:31–34

Ezekiel's vision of a new temple Eze 43:18–27 *See also* covenant; propitiation; sacrifice, in Old Testament; worship.

---

atonement, necessity

Scripture stresses the seriousness and reality of human sin, and that human beings are unable to atone for their own sins. In his grace, God provides a means by which the situation can be remedied.

Atonement is necessary because of human sinfulness

Atonement is necessary because sin cuts people off from God

Isa 59:2 But your iniquities have separated you from your God; your sins have hidden his face from you, so that he will not hear. *See also* **Isa** 64:7; **Eze** 39:23; **Hab** 1:13; **Jn** 9:31

Atonement is necessary because sin provokes God's wrath

Eph 2:1–3 . . . All of us also lived among them at one time, gratifying the cravings of our sinful nature and following its desires and thoughts. Like the rest, we were by nature objects of wrath. *See also* **Ge** 6:5–7; **Ex** 32:30–35; **Ro** 1:18–20; 2:8

God's gracious nature is the basis for atonement

Atonement is grounded in God's reluctance to punish sinners

Eze 18:32 "For I take no pleasure in the death of anyone, declares the Sovereign LORD. Repent and live!"　*See also* **Eze** 33:11; **1Ti** 2:1–4; **2Pe** 3:9

Atonement is grounded in God's readiness to forgive sin

Ex 34:6–7 And he [the LORD] passed in front of Moses, proclaiming, "The LORD, the LORD, the compassionate and gracious God, slow to anger, abounding in love and faithfulness, maintaining love to thousands, and forgiving wickedness, rebellion and sin. Yet he does not leave the guilty unpunished; he punishes the children and their children for the sin of the parents to the third and fourth generation."　*See also* **Ps** 145:8; **Da** 9:9; **Jnh** 4:2

Atonement is grounded in God's covenant love

Nu 14:19 "In accordance with your great love, forgive the sin of these people, just as you have pardoned them from the time they left Egypt until now."　*See also* **Ps** 25:6–7; 103:8–12; **Joel** 2:13

God's provision of atonement is a means of dealing with sin

Atonement through sacrifice

Lev 9:7 Moses said to Aaron, "Come to the altar and sacrifice your sin offering and your burnt offering and make atonement for yourself and the people; sacrifice the offering that is for the people and make atonement for them, as the LORD has commanded."　*See also* **Ex** 30:10; **Nu** 15:22–26

God's promised new covenant of forgiveness was fulfilled in Jesus Christ's atoning death

Heb 10:16–17 "This is the covenant I will make with them after that time, says the Lord. I will put my laws in their hearts, and I will write them on their minds." Then he adds: "Their sins and lawless acts I will remember no more."　*See also* **Jer** 31:33–34; **Mt** 26:28; **Heb** 9:15; 12:24

Images used to portray the at-one-ment, or restored relationship, between God and humanity

Atonement as forgiveness of sins

Eph 1:7–8 In him [Jesus Christ] we have redemption through his blood, the forgiveness of sins, in accordance with the riches of God's grace that he lavished on us with all wisdom and understanding.　*See also* **Lev** 19:22; **Ac** 13:38; **Col** 2:13–14

Atonement as cleansing and purification

Lev 16:30 ". . . on this day [the Day of Atonement] atonement will be made for you, to cleanse you. Then, before the LORD, you will be clean from all your sins."　*See also* **Isa** 6:6–7; **Tit** 2:14; **1Jn** 1:7; **Rev** 7:14

Atonement as reconciliation

2Co 5:19 . . . God was reconciling the world to himself in Christ, not counting people's sins against them . . .　*See also* **Ro** 5:9–11; **Eph** 2:14–16

Atonement as healing

1Pe 2:24 He himself bore our sins in his body on the tree, so that we might die to sins and live for righteousness; by his wounds you have been healed.　*See also* **2Ch** 7:14; **Ps** 103:2–3; **Isa** 53:5

Atonement as God buying people back for himself

Rev 5:9 . . . "You [the Lamb] are worthy to take the scroll and to open its seals, because you were slain, and with your blood you purchased for God members of every tribe and language and people and nation."　*See also* **Mt** 20:28 pp **Mk** 10:45; **Ac** 20:28; **1Pe** 1:18–19

Atonement as making holy: creating a relationship of consecrated nearness to God

Heb 10:10 And by that will, we have been made holy through the sacrifice of the body of Jesus Christ once for all.　*See also* **Col** 1:22; **Heb** 13:12　*See also* blood; forgiveness, divine; holiness; reconciliation, world to God; redemption; salvation; sin, and God's character.

---

baptism

A washing with water, which symbolises the

cleansing of believers from the stain and dirt of sin through the grace of God. Jesus Christ submitted to baptism as an example to believers. Through the work of the Holy Spirit, baptism is linked with union with the risen Jesus Christ.

baptism, in Gospels

In the Gospels baptising is based on the symbolic practice in the OT and Judaism of cleansing with water.

Washing was the means of achieving ritual purity
Ex 30:19–20; **Mk** 7:3–4

Sprinkling with water symbolises spiritual cleansing
Eze 36:25 "I will sprinkle clean water on you, and you will be clean; I will cleanse you from all your impurities and from all your idols." *See also* **Zec** 13:1; **Heb** 10:22

Being baptised by John was a confession that cleansing was needed
Mt 3:11 "I baptise you with water for repentance . . ." *See also* **Mt** 3:6; **Mk** 1:4–5 pp **Lk** 3:3; **Ac** 19:1–4

John promised that the Messiah would cleanse with the baptism of the Holy Spirit
Mt 3:11 ". . . He will baptise you with the Holy Spirit and with fire." pp **Mk** 1:8 pp **Lk** 3:16 *See also* **Isa** 44:3; **Eze** 36:25–26

Baptism involves both water and the Holy Spirit
Jn 3:5 ". . . no-one can enter the kingdom of God without being born of water and the Spirit."

The disciples of Jesus Christ baptised like John's
Jn 3:22–23; 4:1

Jesus Christ was baptised by John
Mt 3:13–17 pp **Mk** 1:9–11 pp **Lk** 3:21–22 pp **Jn** 1:32–33 *See also kingdom of God.*

baptism, of Jesus Christ

In obedience to God's will Jesus Christ was baptised in the River Jordan by John. The event was sealed by the descent of the Holy Spirit and the Father's voice of approval.

John tries to prevent Jesus Christ from being baptised
Mt 3:13–14 . . . Jesus came from Galilee to the Jordan to be baptised by John. But John tried to deter him, saying, "I need to be baptised by you, and do you come to me?"

The necessity of Jesus Christ's baptism
Mt 3:15 Jesus replied, "Let it be so now; it is proper for us to do this to fulfil all righteousness." Then John consented. *See also* **Mk** 10:38; **Lk** 12:50

The events surrounding Jesus Christ's baptism
The baptism itself
Mk 1:9 . . . Jesus came from Nazareth in Galilee and was baptised by John in the Jordan. pp **Mt** 3:13 pp **Lk** 3:21
Jesus Christ prays while being baptised
Lk 3:21 . . . Jesus was baptised too. And as he was praying, heaven was opened
The Holy Spirit descends on Jesus Christ
Mk 1:10 As Jesus was coming up out of the water, he saw heaven being torn open and the Spirit descending on him like a dove. pp **Mt** 3:16 pp **Lk** 3:22 *See also* **Jn** 1:32–34
The voice of the Father is heard
Mt 3:17 . . . a voice from heaven said, "This is my Son, whom I love; with him I am well pleased." pp **Mk** 1:11 pp **Lk** 3:22 *See also* **Mt** 17:5 pp **Mk** 9:7 pp **Lk** 9:35 *See also obedience, of Jesus Christ.*

baptism, practice

Baptism is associated with repenting of sin, believing the gospel message and becoming a member of Christ's body.

Baptism is ordained by Jesus Christ himself

Mt 28:19 "Therefore go and make disciples of all nations, baptising them in the name of the Father and of the Son and of the Holy Spirit." *See also* **Ac** 9:17–18; 16:14–15

Baptism is linked with repentance

Ac 2:38 Peter replied, "Repent and be baptised, every one of you, in the name of Jesus Christ for the forgiveness of your sins . . ." *See also* **Heb** 6:1–2

Baptism follows the decision to believe

Ac 2:41 Those who accepted his [Peter's] message were baptised . . .

Ac 18:8 . . . many of the Corinthians who heard him [Paul] believed and were baptised. *See also* **Ac** 8:12–13; 16:31–33

Baptism in the name of God or Jesus Christ

Baptism in or into the name of Jesus Christ
Ac 19:5 . . . they [a group of believers] were baptised into the name of the Lord Jesus. *See also* **Ac** 2:38; 8:16; 10:48

Baptism in the name of the Trinity Mt 28:18–20

Baptism was by immersion

Ro 6:4 We were therefore buried with him [Christ] through baptism . . . *See also* **Ac** 8:38

Baptism is linked with the gift of the Holy Spirit

Mk 1:8 "I [John the Baptist] baptise you with water, but he [Jesus] will baptise you with the Holy Spirit."

Ac 1:5 ". . . in a few days you [the apostles] will be baptised with the Holy Spirit." *See also* **Ac** 2:4; 11:16

1Co 12:13 . . . we were all baptised by one Spirit into one body . . .

Manifestations of the Holy Spirit may follow or precede water baptism

Ac 8:12–17; 9:17–18; 10:44–48

The person who baptises is of little importance

1Co 1:14 I [Paul] am thankful that I did not baptise any of you [members of the church at Corinth] except Crispus and Gaius,

Baptism "for the dead"

1Co 15:29 Now if there is no resurrection, what will those do who are baptised for the dead? . . .

Passages which may imply infant baptism

The "households" (not merely individuals) may well have included children: **Ac** 16:15,33; 18:8; **1Co** 1:16 **Mk** 10:13–16; **1Co** 7:14; **Col** 2:11–12

Passages apparently negating infant baptism

Ac 2:38–41; **Gal** 3:7   *See also repentance.*

---

baptism, significance

The NT uses a variety of images to explain the meaning of baptism, such as dying and rising with Christ, sharing in his death and being cleansed from sin.

Baptism is a symbol of the death of Jesus Christ

Lk 12:50 ". . . I [Jesus] have a baptism to undergo, and how distressed I am until it is completed!" *See also* **Ps** 42:7; 69:1–2; 88:7; **Mk** 10:38–39

Baptism is a symbol of the burial of Jesus Christ

Ro 6:3–4 . . . We were therefore buried with him [Jesus] through baptism into death in order that, just as Christ was raised from the dead through the glory of the Father, we too may live a new life.

Dying to sin and sharing Jesus Christ's sufferings, symbolised by baptism, is a lifelong process: **Ro** 8:13; **Col** 3:5

Baptism is a symbol of being saved from the flood

1Pe 3:21 and this water [of Noah's flood] symbolises baptism that now saves you also— not the removal of dirt from the body but the pledge of a good conscience towards God . . . *See also* **Ge** 7:6–7

Baptism is the gospel equivalent of circumcision

Col 2:11–12 In him [Christ] you were also circumcised, in the putting off of the sinful nature, not with a circumcision done by human hands but with the circumcision done by Christ, having been buried with him in baptism . . . *See also* **Dt** 10:16

Baptism recalls the exodus

1Co 10:1–2 . . . They [the Israelites] were all baptised into Moses in the cloud [that guided the Israelites] and in the sea [the Red Sea or the Sea of Reeds]. *See also* **Ex** 14:19–24

Baptism symbolises washing from sin

Ac 22:16 "'. . . Get up, be baptised and wash your sins away, calling on his name.'" *See also* **1Co** 6:11; **Tit** 3:5; **1Pe** 3:21

Baptism is a symbol of putting on Christ

Gal 3:27 for all of you who were baptised into Christ have clothed yourselves with Christ.

Baptism as a symbol of unity

Eph 4:5 one Lord, one faith, one baptism; *See also* **1Co** 12:13 *See also* cross; regeneration; sin, forgiveness of.

---

baptism, with Holy Spirit

A divine act, promised by John the Baptist and by Jesus Christ, whereby the Holy Spirit initiates Christians into realised union and communion with the glorified Jesus Christ, thus equipping and enabling them for sanctity and service.

Baptism with the Holy Spirit promised

John the Baptist anticipates baptism with the Spirit

Jn 1:33 ". . . 'The man on whom you see the Spirit come down and remain is the one who will baptise with the Holy Spirit.'" pp **Mt** 3:11 pp **Mk** 1:8 pp **Lk** 3:16

Jesus Christ promises baptism with the Spirit

Ac 1:4–5 ". . . wait for the gift my Father promised, which you have heard me speak about. For John baptised with water, but in a few days you will be baptised with the Holy Spirit." *See also* **Lk** 24:49; **Ac** 1:8

The gift of the Holy Spirit followed Jesus Christ's glorification

Ac 2:33 "Exalted to the right hand of God, he [Jesus] has received from the Father the promised Holy Spirit and has poured out what you now see and hear." *See also* **Jn** 7:39

Instances of baptism with the Holy Spirit

Ac 2:2–4

After Pentecost: **Ac** 8:15–17; 10:44–47; 19:6

A work of God recognised by Jewish Christians as experienced by Gentiles: **Ac** 10:46–47; 11:15–17; 15:8

The gift of the Holy Spirit is for all believers at the outset of their Christian lives

Ac 2:38–39 . . . "Repent and be baptised, every one of you, in the name of Jesus Christ for the forgiveness of your sins. And you will receive the gift of the Holy Spirit. The promise is for you and your children and for all who are far off— for all whom the Lord our God will call." *See also* **Ac** 2:16–18; **Joel** 2:28–29; **Gal** 3:2–5

This gift of the Holy Spirit links believers together in the one body of Christ

1Co 12:13 For we were all baptised by one Spirit into one body—whether Jews or Greeks, slave or free—and we were all given the one Spirit to drink.

blood

The symbol of life, which thus plays an especially important role in the sacrificial system of the OT. The shedding of the blood of a sacrificial animal represents the giving up of its life. The "blood of Christ" refers to Jesus Christ's obedient giving of his life, in order to achieve redemption and forgiveness.

blood, basis of life

Scripture treats blood as the basis of life, and regards the shedding of blood as representing the end of life.

Blood symbolises life

Lev 17:10–14 " 'I will set my face against any Israelites or any aliens living among them who eat blood and I will cut them off from their people. For the life of a creature is in the blood, and I have given it to you to make atonement for yourselves on the altar; it is the blood that makes atonement for one's life . . . the life of every creature is its blood. That is why I have said to the Israelites, "You must not eat the blood of any creature, because the life of every creature is its blood; anyone who eats it must be cut off." ' " *See also* **Ge** 9:4–6; **Dt** 12:20–25; **2Sa** 23:15–17; **Ps** 72:14; **Jer** 2:34; **Eze** 33:1–6; **Mt** 27:3–4; **Lk** 11:50–51 pp Mt 23:35–36

Blood indicating violent death

Ge 4:8–11 Now Cain said to his brother Abel, "Let's go out to the field." And while they were in the field, Cain attacked his brother Abel and killed him. Then the LORD said to Cain, "Where is your brother Abel?" "I don't know," he replied. "Am I my brother's keeper?" The LORD said, "What have you done? Listen! Your brother's blood cries out to me from the ground. Now you are under a curse and driven from the ground, which opened its mouth to receive your brother's blood from your hand." *See also* **Ge** 9:6; **Jdg** 9:22–24; **1Ki** 2:5–6,28–34; **2Ki** 9:30–33

Shedding blood as a sin

Ex 20:13 "You shall not murder."

pp Dt 5:17   *See also* **Ge** 42:21–22; **Dt** 21:1–9; **2Ki** 21:16; **Pr** 1:10–19; **Isa** 26:21; **Mt** 15:18–19 pp Mk 7:20–21; **Ro** 1:28–29

The eating of blood forbidden

Lev 3:17 " 'This is a lasting ordinance for the generations to come, wherever you live: You must not eat any fat or any blood.' " *See also* **Lev** 7:26–27; 17:10–14; **Dt** 12:23; **1Sa** 14:31–34; **Ac** 15:19–20,29 *See also* life.

blood, of Jesus Christ

The shedding of the blood of Jesus Christ is seen as representing the giving of his life as an atoning sacrifice for the sins of humanity.

The blood of Jesus Christ as part of his humanity

Jn 19:33–34 But when they came to Jesus and found that he was already dead, they did not break his legs. Instead, one of the soldiers pierced Jesus' side with a spear, bringing a sudden flow of blood and water. *See also* **Lk** 22:44; **Ac** 5:28; **1Jn** 5:6

The blood of Jesus Christ as a sacrifice

Heb 9:12–14,23–26; 10:3–14; 13:11–12

The blood of Jesus Christ as a symbol of atonement

Ro 3:25 God presented him as a sacrifice of atonement, through faith in his blood. He did this to demonstrate his justice, because in his forbearance he had left the sins committed beforehand unpunished *See also* **Eph** 1:7; **Rev** 7:14

The effects of the blood of Jesus Christ
The institution of the new covenant

1Co 11:25 In the same way, after supper he [Jesus] took the cup, saying, "This cup is the new covenant in my blood; do this, whenever you drink it, in remembrance of me." pp Mt 26:27–28 pp Mk 14:23–24 pp Lk 22:20 *See also* **Heb** 9:11–15; 12:24; 13:20

Redemption Ac 20:28; 1Pe 1:1–2,18–19; Rev 5:9–10

Forgiveness and justification
Ro 5:9 Since we have now been justified by his blood, how much more shall we be saved from God's wrath through him!   *See also* Mt 26:28 pp Mk 14:24 pp Lk 22:20; Ro 3:25–26
Victory over evil and Satan Rev 7:14–17; 12:10–11
Liberation from sin Rev 1:5–6
The promise of total restoration Col 1:19–20

The blood of Jesus Christ and believers
Believers are cleansed from all sin Heb 9:14; 10:22; 13:12; 1Jn 1:6–9
Believers have a new confidence before God Eph 2:13; Col 1:19–22; Heb 10:19–22

The blood of Jesus Christ and the Lord's Supper
Invitations to share in the blood of Jesus Christ
1Co 10:16 Is not the cup of thanksgiving for which we give thanks a participation in the blood of Christ? And is not the bread that we break a participation in the body of Christ?   *See also* Jn 6:53–57
Warnings about sinning against the blood of Jesus Christ
1Co 11:27 Therefore, whoever eats the bread or drinks the cup of the Lord in an unworthy manner will be guilty of sinning against the body and blood of the Lord.   *See also* Heb 10:28–31   *See also atonement; covenant, the new; cross; forgiveness; justification; Lord's Supper; peace; redemption; Satan, defeat of.*

---

blood, Old Testament sacrifices

The pouring out of animals' blood in sacrifice was God's provision, under the old covenant, for the atonement of sin.

God's provision of blood sacrifice to establish the old covenant
Ex 24:4–8 . . . Moses then took the blood, sprinkled it on the people and said, "This is the blood of the covenant that the LORD has made with you in accordance with all these words."   *See also* Heb 9:18–20

God's provision of blood sacrifices within the old covenant
Blood sacrifices and the priesthood Ex 29:10–21 pp Lev 8:14–24; Lev 9:8–14; 16:1–14
Blood sacrifices and various offerings Lev 1:1–17; 3:1–17; 4:1–35; 5:14–19; 16:15–22
Blood sacrifices and the Passover
Ex 12:1–14 ". . . On that same night I will pass through Egypt and strike down every firstborn—both people and animals—and I will bring judgment on all the gods of Egypt. I am the LORD. The blood will be a sign for you on the houses where you are; and when I see the blood, I will pass over you . . ."   *See also* 2Ch 30:15–20; 35:1–19; Ezr 6:19–21; Mk 14:12 pp Lk 22:7–8

Blood sacrifices must come from animals without defect
Lev 22:17–25 ". . . you must present a male without defect from the cattle, sheep or goats in order that it may be accepted on your behalf. Do not bring anything with a defect, because it will not be accepted on your behalf . . ."   *See also* Ex 12:5; Lev 1:3; 3:1; 4:3; 5:15; Nu 28:9,11; Dt 15:21; Eze 43:22–27

Blood sacrifices must not come from human beings
2Ki 23:10 He [Josiah] desecrated Topheth, which was in the Valley of Ben Hinnom, so no-one could use it to sacrifice son or daughter in the fire to Molech.   *See also* 2Ki 17:17; 21:1–6; Eze 20:25–26; Mic 6:7

The limited effect of blood sacrifices
They can become mere external ritual
Isa 1:11–13 "The multitude of your sacrifices—what are they to me?" says the LORD. "I have more than enough of burnt offerings, of rams and the fat of fattened animals; I have no pleasure in the blood of bulls and lambs and goats. When you come to appear

before me, who has asked this of you, this trampling of my courts? Stop bringing meaningless offerings! . . ."   *See also* **Isa** 66:2–4

They are worthless without obedience to God
Hos 6:6 "For I desire mercy, not sacrifice, and acknowledgement of God rather than burnt offerings."   *See also* **1Sa** 15:22–23; **Ps** 40:6–8; **Am** 4:4–5; 5:21–27

They are unable to cleanse the conscience
Heb 9:9–10 This is an illustration for the present time, indicating that the gifts and sacrifices being offered were not able to clear the conscience of the worshipper. They are only a matter of food and drink and various ceremonial washings—external regulations applying until the time of the new order.   *See also* **Heb** 10:1–4
See also covenant; sacrifice, in Old Testament; sin.

blood, symbol of guilt

Blood is often used as an image of people's sin and guilt, and the judgment which follows. Blood-guilt is ascribed to those who are responsible for the shedding of innocent blood.

Blood as an image of sin and guilt
Isa 59:2–3 But your iniquities have separated you from your God; your sins have hidden his face from you, so that he will not hear. For your hands are stained with blood, your fingers with guilt . . .   *See also* **Lev** 20:9–13,27; **2Sa** 1:14–16; **Isa** 1:15–18; **Na** 3:1; **Ac** 18:6

Blood as an image of judgment
Isa 34:5–6 My sword has drunk its fill in the heavens; see, it descends in judgment on Edom, the people I have totally destroyed. The sword of the LORD is bathed in blood . . .   *See also* **Ex** 7:14–21; **Ps** 78:44; 105:29; **Ac** 2:19–20; **Joel** 2:30–31

Blood as a sign of the end times
Ac 2:19–20 "'I will show wonders in the heaven above and signs on the earth below, blood and fire and billows of smoke. The sun will be turned to darkness and the moon to blood before the coming of the great and glorious day of the Lord.'"   *See also* **Joel** 2:30–31; **Rev** 6:12–15; 8:7–9; 16:3–6

Blood-guilt, the result of shedding innocent blood

Examples of blood-guilt

Ge 4:8–11 Now Cain said to his brother Abel, "Let's go out to the field." And while they were in the field, Cain attacked his brother Abel and killed him. Then the LORD said to Cain, "Where is your brother Abel?" "I don't know," he replied. "Am I my brother's keeper?" The LORD said, "What have you done? Listen! Your brother's blood cries out to me from the ground. Now you are under a curse and driven from the ground, which opened its mouth to receive your brother's blood from your hand."   *See also* **2Sa** 1:14–16; 4:5–12; **Eze** 35:5–9; **Hab** 2:12; **Mt** 27:3–8,24; **Ac** 5:28

The right to avenge blood-guilt under the law

Dt 19:11–13 But if out of hate someone lies in wait, assaults and kills a neighbour, and then flees to one of these cities, the killer shall be sent for by the town elders, be brought back from the city, and be handed over to the avenger of blood to die. Show no pity. You must purge from Israel the guilt of shedding innocent blood, so that it may go well with you.   *See also* **Nu** 35:16–28

Restraint to avoid further blood-guilt

Dt 4:41–42 Then Moses set aside three cities east of the Jordan, to which those who had killed a person could flee if they had unintentionally killed a neighbour without malice aforethought. They could flee into one of these cities and save their lives.   *See also* **Ge** 4:15; **Nu** 35:6–34; **Dt** 19:4–10; **Jos** 20:1–9

Blood-guilt cannot be forgotten

Ge 9:5–6 "And for your lifeblood I will surely demand an accounting. I will demand an accounting from every animal. And from each human being, too, I will demand an accounting for the life of another human being. Whoever sheds human blood, by human beings shall their blood be shed; for in the image of God has God made all people."   *See also* **Ge** 4:10–16; 42:22; **1Ki** 2:28–33; **Isa** 26:21; **Mt** 23:30–31   *See also judgment, God's; last things.*

Christlikeness

The process by which believers are conformed to the likeness of Jesus Christ, especially in relation to obedience to and trust in God. Through the Holy Spirit, God refashions believers in the image of his Son, who is set before them as a model of the form of the redeemed life.

Believers are to become Christlike

1Co 11:1 Follow my [Paul's] example, as I follow the example of Christ.

Php 2:5 Your attitude should be the same as that of Christ Jesus: *See also* **Jn** 13:15; **Ro** 8:29; **Eph** 4:11–13; **Php** 3:8–11,20–21; **1Jn** 2:6

The Holy Spirit makes believers Christlike

2Co 3:18 And we, who with unveiled faces all reflect the Lord's glory, are being transformed into his likeness with ever-increasing glory, which comes from the Lord, who is the Spirit. *See also* **Ro** 8:5–9; **Gal** 5:22–23; **1Th** 1:6

Christlikeness is the aim of discipleship

Mt 10:25 "It is enough for students to be like their teachers, and the servants like their masters . . ." *See also* **Lk** 6:40; **1Jn** 2:6

Christlikeness is based on total commitment to Jesus Christ

Lk 9:57–62 As they were walking along the road, someone said to him [Jesus], "I will follow you wherever you go." Jesus replied, "Foxes have holes and birds of the air have nests, but the Son of Man has nowhere to lay his head." He said to another man, "Follow me." But he replied, "Lord, first let me go and bury my father." Jesus said to him, "Let the dead bury their own dead, but you go and proclaim the kingdom of God." Still another said, "I will follow you, Lord; but first let me go back and say good-bye to my family." Jesus replied, "No-one who takes hold of the plough and looks back is fit for service in the kingdom of God." *See also* **Mt** 9:9 pp **Mk** 2:14 pp **Lk** 5:27; **Mt** 19:21 pp **Lk** 18:22; **Jn** 1:43; 10:27; 12:26; 15:10; **2Jn** 9

The demonstration of Christlikeness

In costly sacrifice

Mk 8:34–35 Then he [Jesus] called the crowd to him along with his disciples and said: "Those who would come after me must deny themselves and take up their cross and follow me. For those who want to save their lives will lose them but those who lose their lives for me and for the gospel will save them." pp **Mt** 16:24 pp **Lk** 9:23–24

1Pe 2:21–23 To this you were called, because Christ suffered for you, leaving you an example, that you should follow in his steps. "He committed no sin, and no deceit was found in his mouth." When they hurled their insults at him, he did not retaliate; when he suffered, he made no threats. Instead, he entrusted himself to him who judges justly. *See also* **Mt** 10:38; **Lk** 14:26–27; **Jn** 12:26; 21:19; **Php** 3:10; **1Pe** 4:1

In humility and service

Mt 20:26–28 [Jesus said] ". . . whoever wants to become great among you must be your servant, and whoever wants to be first must be your slave—just as the Son of Man did not come to be served, but to serve, and to give his life as a ransom for many." pp **Mk** 10:43–45 *See also* **Mt** 11:29; **Mk** 9:35; **Lk** 22:24–26; **Jn** 13:14–15; **Php** 2:4–5

In love for other believers

Jn 15:12 [Jesus said] "My command is this: Love each other as I have loved you."

1Jn 3:16 This is how we know what love is: Jesus Christ laid down his life for us. And we ought to lay down our lives for one another. *See also* **Jn** 13:34; 15:17; **Eph** 5:2,25

In a readiness to forgive others

Col 3:13 Bear with each other and forgive whatever grievances you may have against one another. Forgive as the Lord forgave you. *See also* **Mt** 6:12 pp **Lk** 11:4

In sharing Jesus Christ's mission to the world

Mt 4:19 "Come, follow me," Jesus said, "and I will make you fishers of men and women." pp **Mk** 1:17 *See also* **Jn** 20:21

By following godly examples that imitate Jesus Christ
1Co 11:1 Follow my [Paul's] example, as I follow the example of Christ. *See also* **Eph** 5:1; **1Th** 1:5–6; 2:14; **Heb** 6:12; 13:7–8; **3Jn** 11

Christlikeness is part of God's re-creation
Ge 1:26–27 Then God said, "Let us make human beings in our image, in our likeness, and let them rule over the fish of the sea and the birds of the air, over the livestock, over all the earth, and over all the creatures that move along the ground." So God created human beings in his own image, in the image of God he created them; male and female he created them.

2Co 4:4 The god of this age [the devil] has blinded the minds of unbelievers, so that they cannot see the light of the gospel of the glory of Christ, who is the image of God.

Eph 4:24 and to put on the new self, created to be like God in true righteousness and holiness.

Col 3:10 and have put on the new self, which is being renewed in knowledge in the image of its Creator.

The process of becoming Christlike
It is the purpose for which believers are saved
Ro 8:28–29 And we know that in all things God works for the good of those who love him, who have been called according to his purpose. For those God foreknew he also predestined to be conformed to the likeness of his Son, that he might be the firstborn among many brothers and sisters. *See also* **Eph** 2:10; **2Pe** 1:4
It continues in the experience of believers
2Co 3:18 And we, who with unveiled faces all reflect the Lord's glory, are being transformed into his likeness with ever-increasing glory, which comes from the Lord, who is the Spirit.
It will be complete when believers finally share Jesus Christ's glory
1Jn 3:2–3 Dear friends, now we are children of God, and what we will be has not yet been made known. But we know that when he appears, we shall be like him, for we shall see him as he is. All who have this hope in them purify themselves, just as he is pure. *See also* **Ps** 17:15; **Jn** 17:24; **1Co** 15:49–53; **Gal** 4:19; **Php** 3:20–21; **Col** 3:4; **1Jn** 4:17 *See also faith; holiness; obedience; sanctification; spiritual growth.*

church
The community of faithful believers, of whom Jesus Christ is the head, called out from the world to serve God down the ages. Scripture emphasises that the church is the body of Christ whose members are intended to be filled with the Holy Spirit. Scriptural understanding of the church is corporate, rather than solitary or individual.

church, and Holy Spirit
The church depends upon the activity of the Holy Spirit, without which its effective and faithful service is impossible.

The Holy Spirit forms the church
1Co 12:13 For we were all baptised by one Spirit into one body—whether Jews or Greeks, slave or free—and we were all given the one Spirit to drink. *See also* **Ac** 2:1–4,16–18; **Joel** 2:28–29; **Ac** 10:44–48; **Eph** 2:21–22

The Holy Spirit indwells the church
1Co 3:16 Don't you know that you yourselves are God's temple and that God's Spirit lives in you? *See also* **Eze** 10:4; **Jn** 16:14; **1Co** 6:19; **2Co** 6:16; **1Pe** 4:14

The Holy Spirit enables the church to function as the body of Christ
1Co 12:7 Now to each one the manifestation of the Spirit is given for the common good. *See also* **Ex** 31:1–5; **Nu** 11:24–27; **1Sa** 10:5–11; **Ro** 12:5; **1Co** 12:8–11

The Holy Spirit enables Christian unity
Eph 4:3–4; **Php** 2:1

The church worships, serves and speaks by the Holy Spirit

The church worships by the Spirit

Ac 2:11 ". . . Cretans and Arabs—we hear them declaring the wonders of God in our own tongues!"   *See also* Jn 4:24; Ac 10:45–46; Ro 8:15; 1Co 14:26–33; Php 3:3

The church serves by the Spirit

Ro 12:6–8 We have different gifts according to the grace given us . . .   *See also* 1Co 12:7–11; Eph 4:7–13

The church speaks by the Spirit

Ac 6:10 but they could not stand up against his [Stephen's] wisdom or the Spirit by whom he spoke.   *See also* Ac 4:8; 1Co 14:24–25

The Holy Spirit communicates Jesus Christ's message to the church

Rev 2:7 "Those who have ears, let them hear what the Spirit says to the churches . . ."   *See also* Jn 14:26; 16:13; Rev 2:11,17,29; 3:6,13,22

The Holy Spirit and the church's mission

The church fulfils its mission by the Spirit

Ac 1:8 "But you will receive power when the Holy Spirit comes on you; and you will be my witnesses in Jerusalem, and in all Judea and Samaria, and to the ends of the earth."   *See also* Jn 15:26–27; 20:21–23; Ac 4:31; Gal 3:3

The Spirit directs the church's missionary enterprise Ac 13:2–3; 15:28; 16:6   *See also* baptism, with Holy Spirit; Scripture; spiritual gifts; worship.

church, and Jesus Christ

Jesus Christ rules and governs his people and directs them towards the fulfilment of God's purposes. All power and authority within the church derive from Jesus Christ as the head.

Jesus Christ rules the universe in the interest of the church

Eph 1:22–23 And God placed all things under his feet and appointed him to be head over everything for the church, which is his body . . .   *See also* Eph 1:10; Col 1:18

All power and authority within the church derive from Jesus Christ as the head

Jesus Christ is recognised as head of the church

Eph 4:15 . . . we will in all things grow up into him who is the Head, that is, Christ.   *See also* Eph 5:23; Col 2:19

Within the church Jesus Christ alone rules with authority

Mt 23:8–10 "But you are not to be called 'Rabbi', for you have only one Master . . . Nor are you to be called 'teacher', for you have one Teacher, the Christ."   *See also* Jn 13:13; 2Co 4:5

The church owes obedience to its head

Jn 14:15 "If you love me, you will obey what I command."   *See also* Jn 14:21,23; Eph 5:24; 1Jn 3:24

All human authority in the church derives from its head

Eph 4:11 It was he [Christ] who gave some to be apostles, some to be prophets, some to be evangelists, and some to be pastors and teachers,   *See also* Gal 1:1

Jesus Christ is the cornerstone and builder of the church

Eph 2:20–22 . . . In him [Christ Jesus] the whole building is joined together and rises to become a holy temple in the Lord. And in him you too are being built together . . .   *See also* Mt 16:18; Ac 4:11; Ps 118:22; 1Pe 2:4–6

Jesus Christ's role as head of the church

He loves the church

Eph 5:25 . . . Christ loved the church and gave himself up for her   *See also* Jn 10:11; Eph 5:2,23; 1Jn 3:16

He cares for the church

Rev 7:17 "For the Lamb at the centre of the throne will be their shepherd; he will lead them to springs of living water. And God will wipe away every tear from their eyes."   *See also* Jn 10:14–15,27–28; 17:12; Eph 5:29–30

He provides for the growth of the church

Col 2:19 . . . the Head, from whom the whole body, supported and held together by its ligaments and sinews, grows as God causes it to grow.   *See also* **Eph** 4:15–16

He prays for the church Jn 17:20–26; **Ro** 8:34; **Heb** 7:25

He judges the church

Rev 2:23 ". . . all the churches will know that I [the Son of God] am he who searches hearts and minds, and I will repay each of you according to your deeds."   *See also* **Ro** 14:10–12; **2Co** 5:10; **Eph** 6:8

He will present the church blameless before God

Eph 5:27 . . . to present her [the church] to himself as a radiant church, without stain or wrinkle or any other blemish, but holy and blameless.   *See also* **2Co** 4:14; **Col** 1:22; **Jude** 24

---

church, leadership

Jesus Christ is the absolute head of the church. He sets leaders in the church to enable the whole church to grow into maturity. Christ's authority in the church is acknowledged more by the church's obedience to God than through any particular form of government.

Jesus Christ alone is head of the church

Col 1:18 And he [Christ] is the head of the body, the church; he is the beginning and the firstborn from among the dead, so that in everything he might have the supremacy.   *See also* **Mt** 23:8–10; **Eph** 1:22; 4:15; 5:23; **Col** 2:19; **Heb** 3:3

The Holy Spirit directs the church

Ac 13:2 While they [prophets and teachers] were worshipping the Lord and fasting, the Holy Spirit said, "Set apart for me Barnabas and Saul for the work to which I have called them." *See also* **Ac** 15:28; 16:6–7; 20:28; **Ro** 8:14; **1Co** 12:11; **Rev** 2:7,11

The appointment of leaders in the church

God calls and equips leaders

Eph 4:11 It was he [Christ] who gave some to be apostles, some to be prophets, some to be evangelists, and some to be pastors and teachers,   *See also* **Mt** 16:18; **Ac** 1:24–26; 9:15–16; 20:28; 26:16–18; **1Co** 12:28; **Gal** 1:15–17

Delegated leadership Ac 6:3–6; 14:23; **Tit** 1:5

The appointment of apostles

Mk 3:13–19 . . . He [Jesus] appointed twelve—designating them apostles—that they might be with him and that he might send them out to preach and to have authority to drive out demons . . . pp **Mt** 10:1–4 pp **Lk** 6:12–16

As founders of the church: **1Co** 9:1–2; **2Co** 3:3; **Eph** 2:20; **Rev** 21:14

As leaders of the church: **Ac** 2:42; 15:6,22–23; **1Th** 2:6; **2Pe** 3:2; **Jude** 17

Prophets as leaders

Ac 15:32 Judas and Silas, who themselves were prophets, said much to encourage and strengthen the believers.   *See also* **Ac** 11:27–30; 13:1–2; **Ro** 12:6; **1Co** 12:28; 14:29–30; **Eph** 3:5

Evangelists as leaders

Ac 21:8 Leaving the next day, we reached Caesarea and stayed at the house of Philip the evangelist, one of the Seven.   *See also* **Eph** 4:11; **2Ti** 4:5

Pastors and teachers as leaders

Ac 20:28 "Keep watch over yourselves and all the flock of which the Holy Spirit has made you overseers. Be shepherds of the church of God, which he bought with his own blood."   *See also* **Jn** 21:15–17; **Ac** 13:1; **Ro** 12:7; **1Co** 12:28; **1Ti** 3:2; **Tit** 1:9; **Jas** 3:1; **1Pe** 5:2

Elders as leaders

1Ti 3:1 Here is a trustworthy saying: Whoever aspires to be an overseer desires a noble task. *See also* **Ac** 11:30; 14:23; 15:2,22; 20:17; **1Ti** 5:17; **Tit** 1:5; **Jas** 5:14; **2Jn** 1

Deacons as leaders

Php 1:1 Paul and Timothy, servants of Christ Jesus, To all the saints in Christ Jesus at Philippi, together with the overseers and deacons: *See also* **Ac** 6:5–6; **1Ti** 3:8

Qualifications for church leadership

The first apostles were witnesses of Jesus Christ's life and resurrection: **Ac** 1:21–22; 10:41; **1Co** 9:1–2; 15:7–8; **2Pe** 1:16

Qualifications for elders and deacons: **Ac** 6:3; **1Ti** 3:1–12; 5:17; **Tit** 1:6–9; **1Pe** 5:1–4

Responsibilities of church leaders

To preach the gospel Ro 1:15; **1Co** 1:17; **Gal** 2:8; **Eph** 3:8; **1Ti** 2:7

To teach sound doctrine 1Ti 4:6,13; 5:17; **Heb** 13:7

To give direction in church life Ac 15:2,6,22–23; 16:4; 20:28–31; **1Ti** 5:17; **1Pe** 5:2

To be an example in loving service Mt 20:26–28 pp **Mk** 10:43–45; **Mk** 9:35; **Jn** 13:13–15; **Heb** 13:7; **1Pe** 5:3

To train and appoint other leaders Ac 14:23; **1Ti** 4:14; **2Ti** 2:2; **Tit** 1:5

To pray for the sick Jas 5:14

To exercise discipline in the church 2Co 13:10; **1Th** 5:12; **1Ti** 1:20; 5:20; **Tit** 3:10; **3Jn** 10

The church's responsibilities to its leaders

Ac 16:4

To respect and submit to its leaders 1Th 5:12–13; **1Ti** 5:19; **Heb** 13:17

To pray for its leaders Eph 6:19; **1Th** 5:25

To support its leaders financially 1Co 9:7–14; **Php** 4:15–19; **1Ti** 5:17–18

The corporate government of the church

In choosing leaders Ac 6:3–6

In implementing decisions Ac 15:22–29

In building up the church Ro 12:4–8; **1Co** 12:4–12,27; **Eph** 4:3,7–16; **1Pe** 4:10–11

In discerning true and false teachings 1Jn 4:1–3; **2Jn** 10; **Rev** 2:2

In exercising discipline Mt 18:15–20; **1Co** 5:4–5; **2Co** 2:6–8; **2Th** 3:14–15

The structure of the church

The pattern of church life

Ac 2:42 They devoted themselves to the apostles' teaching and to the fellowship, to the breaking of bread and to prayer. *See also* **Ac** 2:46; 5:42

The house church Ac 1:13–14; 12:12; 16:40; **Ro** 16:5; **1Co** 16:19; **Col** 4:15; **Phm** 2

The local church Ac 13:1; **Ro** 16:1; **1Co** 1:2; **1Th** 1:1

Churches in a region Ac 9:31; 15:41; **1Co** 16:1; **2Co** 8:1; **Gal** 1:2,22; **Rev** 1:4

The universal church

Mt 16:18 "And I [Jesus] tell you that you are Peter, and on this rock I will build my church, and the gates of Hades will not overcome it."

Referring to the local as well as the universal church: **1Co** 12:28; **Eph** 1:22; 3:10; 5:25 *See also teaching.*

---

church, life of

The church lives its life in union with Christ and in the power of the Holy Spirit. It is called to mutual love, holy living, and to worship.

The church lives its life in union with Christ

The church lives in Christ and Christ lives in the church

1Co 1:30 It is because of him [God] that you are in Christ Jesus . . . *See also* **Mt** 18:20; **Jn** 15:5; 17:21; **1Co** 8:6; **Gal** 2:20; **Col** 1:27; 2:6; **1Jn** 4:13

Believers are united with Christ in baptism

Gal 3:27 for all of you who were baptised into Christ have clothed yourselves with Christ. *See also* **Ac** 2:38; 19:5; **Ro** 6:3–4; **Col** 2:12

The church lives its life in the power of the Holy Spirit

The church lives in the Spirit, and the Spirit lives in the church

Ro 8:9–11 You, however, are controlled not by the sinful nature but by the Spirit, if the Spirit of God lives in you. And if anyone does not have the Spirit of Christ, that person does not belong to Christ . . . *See also* **1Co** 3:16; **Gal** 5:16,25; **Eph** 2:22; **2Ti** 1:14; **1Jn** 2:27

The Spirit is given to the church

Ac 1:4–5 . . . "Do not leave Jerusalem, but wait for the gift my [Jesus'] Father promised, which you have heard me speak about. For John baptised with water, but in a few days you will be baptised with the Holy Spirit." *See also* **Jn** 20:22; **Ac** 2:4; 15:8; **Ro** 7:6; 15:16; **1Co** 6:11; **Gal** 3:3; **1Pe** 1:1–2

The Spirit seals the church
Eph 1:13 . . . Having believed, you were marked in him [Christ] with a seal, the promised Holy Spirit, *See also* **2Co** 1:22; 5:5; **Eph** 4:30

The Spirit guides the church
Rev 2:7 "Those who have ears, let them hear what the Spirit says to the churches . . ." *See also* **Ac** 8:29; 10:19; 11:12; 13:2; 20:23; 21:4

The Spirit teaches the church
1Co 2:13 . . . we speak, not in words taught us by human wisdom but in words taught by the Spirit . . . *See also* **Jn** 16:13; **Eph** 1:17

The Spirit sanctifies the church
Ro 15:16 . . . so that the Gentiles might become an offering acceptable to God, sanctified by the Holy Spirit. *See also* **1Co** 6:11; **2Th** 2:13; **1Pe** 1:2

The Spirit endows the church with gifts
1Co 12:7 Now to each one the manifestation of the Spirit is given for the common good. *See also* **Ro** 12:6–8; **1Co** 12:8–11,28; **Eph** 4:11

The church as a fellowship
As a fellowship of mutual love
1Th 5:11 Therefore encourage one another and build each other up, just as in fact you are doing. *See also* **Ro** 15:2; **1Co** 14:12; **Gal** 6:10; **1Th** 4:18; **Heb** 10:25

As a fellowship of ordinary people
1Co 1:26–27 . . . But God chose the foolish things of the world to shame the wise; God chose the weak things of the world to shame the strong. *See also* **Lk** 6:20; **Jas** 2:5

The distinctiveness of the church
The church as a chosen people
1Pe 2:9 But you are a chosen people, a royal priesthood, a holy nation, a people belonging to God . . . *See also* **Eph** 1:4; **Col** 3:12

The church as a holy people
Heb 12:14 Make every effort . . . to be holy; without holiness no-one will see the Lord. *See*

also **Ro** 11:16; 15:16; **1Co** 1:2; **Eph** 2:21; 5:3; **1Th** 3:13; **Heb** 2:11; **1Pe** 1:15–16; **2Pe** 3:11

The church as a people set apart
2Co 7:1 Since we have these promises, dear friends, let us purify ourselves from everything that contaminates body and spirit, perfecting holiness out of reverence for God. *See also* **1Co** 5:9–12; **2Co** 6:14–18; **Eph** 5:7; **2Th** 3:14; **2Ti** 3:1–5; **Tit** 3:10–11

The church as a heavenly people
Jn 17:14–16 ". . . They [the disciples] are not of the world, even as I [Jesus] am not of it." *See also* **Lk** 10:20; **1Co** 15:48; **Gal** 4:26; **Eph** 2:6; **Php** 3:20; **Col** 3:1–4; **Heb** 11:16; 12:22–23

The church and worship
Praise in the life of the church
Heb 13:15 Through Jesus, therefore, let us continually offer to God a sacrifice of praise—the fruit of lips that confess his name. *See also* **Ac** 2:47; **1Co** 14:26; **Eph** 5:18–20; **Php** 3:3; **Col** 3:16

Prayer in the life of the church
Corporate prayer in the church: **Ac** 1:14; 2:42; 4:24–31; 12:5,12; 20:36; 21:5
Prayer for church leaders: **Ro** 15:30; **Eph** 6:19–20; **Col** 4:2–4; **1Th** 5:25; **2Th** 3:1; **Heb** 13:18
Eph 6:18; **1Ti** 2:1–2

Baptism in the life of the church
Ac 2:38; **1Co** 1:13; **Gal** 3:26–27; **Eph** 4:4–5; **Col** 2:11–12; **1Pe** 3:21

The Lord's Supper in the life of the church
1Co 10:16–17 Is not the cup of thanksgiving for which we give thanks a participation in the blood of Christ? And is not the bread that we break a participation in the body of Christ? Because there is one loaf, we, who are many, are one body, for we all partake of the one loaf. *See also* **Ac** 2:42,46; 20:7; **1Co** 10:21; 11:17–34

The suffering of the church
Suffering persecution from a hostile world
Jn 16:33 "I [Jesus] have told you these things, so that in me you may have peace. In this world you will have trouble. But take heart! I have overcome the world." *See also* **Mt** 5:10–12;

1Co 4:12; 2Co 4:9; 1Th 3:4; 2Ti 3:12
Sharing in the sufferings of Christ
Php 3:10 I [Paul] want to know Christ and the
power of his resurrection and the fellowship of
sharing in his sufferings, becoming like him in his
death,   *See also* Jn 15:20; Ro 8:17; 2Co
4:10–11; 1Pe 4:13
Suffering as the road to glory
Jas 1:12 Blessed are those who persevere under
trial, because when they have stood the test, they
will receive the crown of life that God has
promised to those who love him.   *See also* Ro
5:3; 8:18; 2Co 4:17; 2Ti 2:11–12; 1Pe 5:10
*See also holiness; life, spiritual; praise; prayer, in the
church; prophecy, in New Testament; spiritual gifts;
worship.*

church, nature of
The church is the people called by God, who are
united by their faith in Christ and by their
common life in him. Various descriptions and
metaphors emphasise the continuity between the
people of God in the OT and NT.

NT images of the church
The body of Christ
Ro 12:4–5 Just as each of us has one body
with many members, and these members do not
all have the same function, so in Christ we who
are many form one body, and each member
belongs to all the others.   *See also* 1Co
12:12,27; Eph 3:6; 5:23; Col 1:18,24; 2:19; 3:15
God's building or temple
1Co 3:16–17 Don't you know that you
yourselves are God's temple and that God's Spirit
lives in you? . . .   *See also* 1Co 3:10; 2Co
6:16; Eph 2:21–22; Heb 3:6; 10:21; 1Pe 2:5
A plant or vine
Jn 15:1–8 ". . . I [Jesus] am the vine; you
[the disciples] are the branches . . ."   *See also*
Ro 11:17–24; 1Co 3:6–8
Jesus Christ's flock
Jn 10:14–16 "I [Jesus] am the good
shepherd; I know my sheep and my sheep know
me . . . there shall be one flock and one
shepherd."   *See also* Mt 25:33; Lk 12:32; Ac
20:28–29; 1Pe 5:2–4

The bride of Christ
Rev 21:2 I [John] saw the Holy City, the new
Jerusalem, coming down out of heaven from God,
prepared as a bride beautifully dressed for her
husband.   *See also* Eph 5:25–27,31–32; Rev
19:7; 22:17
God's household or family
Eph 2:19 . . . you [Gentile believers] are no
longer foreigners and aliens, but fellow-citizens
with God's people and members of God's
household,   *See also* Jn 8:35–36; Gal 6:10; Eph
3:15; 1Ti 3:15; Heb 2:11; 1Pe 2:17; 4:17

NT descriptions of the church
Emphasising continuity with the OT church
Abraham's offspring: Ro 4:16; Gal 3:7,29
The people of God: Ro 9:25; 2Co 6:16; Heb 13:12;
1Pe 2:9–10
The new Jerusalem: Gal 4:26; Heb 12:22; Rev 3:12;
21:2,9–10
Gal 6:16
**Emphasising God's call and authority in the
church**
Children of God: Mt 5:9; Jn 1:12; Ro 8:15–16; 2Co
6:18; Gal 3:26; 4:5–6; 1Jn 3:10
The elect: Mt 24:22; Ro 11:7; 2Ti 2:10; 1Pe 1:1
Heirs of God and God's inheritance: Ro 8:17; Gal
3:29; 4:7; Tit 3:7; Heb 1:14; 6:17; 1Pe 1:4
A priesthood: 1Pe 2:5,9; Rev 1:6; 5:10; 20:6
Descriptions applied to the church by outsiders
Followers of the Way: Ac 9:2; 19:9,23; 22:4; 24:14
Ac 11:26; 24:5
Descriptions used by Christians
The believers. All these titles are seldom in the singular,
emphasising the corporateness of Christian life: Ac 1:15;
2:44; 5:12; Gal 6:10; 1Ti 4:12; 1Pe 2:17
The disciples: Ac 6:1–2; 9:19; 11:26; 14:22; 20:1
The "saints" is the most frequently used NT term for
Christians. It means "set apart for God", "made holy":
Ro 1:7; 15:25; 1Co 6:1; 14:33; Eph 1:1; Php
4:21; Col 1:12; Jude 3
Other NT descriptions of the church 1Ti 3:15;
Heb 12:23

The foundation of the church
Jesus Christ as the church's foundation-stone
1Co 3:11 For no-one can lay any foundation

other than the one already laid, which is Jesus Christ.   *See also* **Mt** 7:24–25; 21:42 pp **Mk** 12:10 pp **Lk** 20:17; **Ac** 4:11; **Eph** 2:20; **1Pe** 2:6; **Isa** 28:16; **1Pe** 2:7; **Ps** 118:22

Apostles and prophets as founders of the church

Eph 2:19–20 . . . God's household, built on the foundation of the apostles and prophets, with Christ Jesus himself as the chief cornerstone. *See also* **Mt** 16:18–19; **Rev** 21:14

The church as God's people

A people chosen by God

1Pe 2:9 But you are a chosen people, a royal priesthood, a holy nation, a people belonging to God, that you may declare the praises of him who called you out of darkness into his wonderful light.   *See also* **Jn** 15:16; **Ro** 8:33; **Eph** 1:4; **Col** 3:12; **2Th** 2:13; **Jas** 2:5; **1Pe** 1:2

A people called by God

Ro 1:6 And you also [Christians in Rome] are among those who are called to belong to Jesus Christ.   *See also* **Ac** 2:39; **1Co** 1:2,9; **Gal** 1:6; **2Th** 2:14; **2Ti** 1:9; **Jude** 1

A people loved by God

1Pe 2:10 Once you were not a people, but now you are the people of God; once you had not received mercy, but now you have received mercy.   *See also* **Eph** 2:1–5; **Tit** 3:4–7

God's covenant people

Heb 8:8–10 ". . . This is the covenant I will make with the house of Israel after that time, declares the Lord. I will put my laws in their minds and write them on their hearts. I will be their God, and they will be my people."   *See also* **Ro** 11:27; **Isa** 59:20–21; **Heb** 10:16; **Jer** 31:31–33   *See also* election.

---

church, Old Testament anticipations

As the people of God, the Christian church is continuous with Israel. The OT provides important anticipations of the church.

OT terms for the people of God

The descendants of Abraham **2Ch** 20:7; **Isa** 41:8–9; **Ro** 4:16; **Gal** 3:7

The saints

The term for "saints" means "set apart for God", "made holy", and is the most frequently used NT term for Christians: **1Sa** 2:9; **2Ch** 6:41 pp **Ps** 132:9; **Ps** 16:3; 31:23; **Da** 7:18

The assembly

"assembly" means "a community gathered together in response to God's call to serve and worship him". Its NT equivalents include the synagogue and the church: **Ps** 1:5; 107:32; 149:1

The scope of the OT people of God

Israel as God's people

Ex 6:7 "I [God] will take you [the Israelites] as my own people, and I will be your God . . . '"   *See also* **Ex** 19:5–6; **Lev** 26:12; **Jer** 30:22; **Eze** 36:28; **Hos** 2:23

Not all Israelites are God's people

Ro 9:6–7 . . . For not all who are descended from Israel are Israel. Nor because they are his descendants are they all Abraham's children. On the contrary, "It is through Isaac that your offspring will be reckoned."   *See also* **Ezr** 9:8; **Isa** 1:9; 11:11,16; **Jer** 23:3; **Eze** 14:22; **Mic** 2:12

God's people included non-Israelites

Isa 2:2–3 . . . Many peoples will come and say, "Come, let us go up to the mountain of the LORD, to the house of the God of Jacob. He will teach us his ways, so that we may walk in his paths." The law will go out from Zion, the word of the LORD from Jerusalem. pp **Mic** 4:1–2 *See also* **Ex** 12:38,48–49; **Dt** 31:12; **Ru** 4:10–11

The formation of the OT people of God

God's people are formed through God's promises

Ge 12:2 "I [God] will make you [Abraham] into a great nation and I will bless you; I will make your name great, and you will be a blessing."   *See also* **Ge** 15:5; 17:5–6; 22:17–18; **Ex** 1:7

God's people are chosen and called

Dt 7:6 . . . The LORD your God has chosen you [Israel] out of all the peoples on the face of the earth to be his people, his treasured possession.   *See also* **1Ch** 16:13 pp **Ps** 105:6; **Ps** 33:12; **Eze** 20:5

God's people have been redeemed
Dt 5:6 "I am the LORD your God, who brought you out of Egypt, out of the land of slavery." pp **Ex** 20:2   *See also* **Ex** 6:6; 19:4; **Eze** 20:6

God formed a covenant with his people
Ex 24:8 Moses then took the blood, sprinkled it on the people and said, "This is the blood of the covenant that the LORD has made with you in accordance with all these words."   *See also* **Ex** 19:5; 34:10,27; **Dt** 4:13; **Jdg** 2:1; **Jer** 31:31

OT images of the people of God
As God's bride
Jer 2:2 ". . . 'I remember the devotion of your youth, how as a bride you loved me and followed me through the desert, through a land not sown.'"   *See also* **Isa** 62:5; **Hos** 2:16,19–20; **Eph** 5:25–27; **Rev** 21:2

As God's vine
Isa 5:1–7 . . . The vineyard of the LORD Almighty is the house of Israel, and the people of Judah are the garden of his delight . . .
These passages form the background to Jesus Christ's claim to be the true vine (Jn 15:1): **Ps** 80:8; **Jer** 2:21; **Eze** 17:5–6; 19:10; **Hos** 10:1

As God's flock
Ps 95:7 for he is our God and we are the people of his pasture, the flock under his care . . .   *See also* **Ps** 74:1; 77:20; 100:3; **Isa** 40:11; **Zec** 9:16; **Mt** 26:31; **Zec** 13:7; **Lk** 12:32; **Jn** 10:16
The NT church is also described as a flock: **Ac** 20:28–29; **1Pe** 5:2–3

As God's inheritance
Dt 4:20 But as for you [Israel], the LORD took you and brought you out of the iron-smelting furnace, out of Egypt, to be the people of his inheritance, as you now are.   *See also* **Ps** 28:9; 33:12; **Isa** 19:25; **Mal** 3:17

As God's family
Am 3:1–2 . . . O people of Israel . . . the whole family I brought up out of Egypt: "You only have I chosen of all the families of the earth . . ."   *See also* **Ex** 4:22–23; **Dt** 1:31;

32:6; **Ps** 103:13; **Isa** 1:2; 30:9; **Hos** 11:1; **Mal** 2:10

Requirements of the people of God
To obey God's word
Dt 5:1 Moses summoned all Israel and said: Hear, O Israel, the decrees and the laws I declare in your hearing today. Learn them and be sure to follow them.   *See also* **Ex** 24:3; **Dt** 6:1–3; 13:4; **Jos** 1:7; **1Sa** 15:22

To remember their redemption
Dt 5:15 "Remember that you were slaves in Egypt and that the LORD your God brought you out of there with a mighty hand and an outstretched arm . . ."   *See also* **Dt** 7:18; 15:15; 16:12; **Ps** 105:5

To commemorate their redemption
Ex 12:25–27 ". . . when your children ask you, 'What does this ceremony mean to you?' then tell them, 'It is the Passover sacrifice to the LORD, who passed over the houses of the Israelites in Egypt and spared our homes when he struck down the Egyptians.'" . . .   *See also* **Nu** 9:2–3; **Dt** 16:1; **Lk** 22:14–20

To love God wholeheartedly
Dt 6:5 Love the LORD your God with all your heart and with all your soul and with all your strength.   *See also* **Dt** 10:12; 11:1; 19:9; **Jos** 23:11

The marks of the people of God
Circumcision as a mark of God's people Ge 17:10–14; **Lev** 12:3
Circumcision had to be internal as well as external, as a sign of spiritual commitment to God: **Dt** 10:16; 30:6; **Jer** 4:4; **Ro** 2:27; **Col** 2:11
The presence of God Ex 25:8; 33:15–16; 40:35; **Nu** 10:33–36; **2Ch** 5:14   *See also covenant; Israel, people of God; redemption.*

church, purpose
The church is called to praise and glorify God, to establish Jesus Christ's kingdom, and to proclaim the gospel throughout the world.

God's purposes for the church
To praise God
1Pe 2:9 But you are a chosen people, a royal priesthood, a holy nation, a people belonging to God, that you may declare the praises of him who called you out of darkness into his wonderful light.   *See also* **Eph** 1:5–6,11–12,14; **Heb** 13:15; **1Pe** 2:5

To share God's glory
Ro 8:29–30 For those God foreknew he also predestined to be conformed to the likeness of his Son, that he might be the firstborn among many brothers and sisters. And those he predestined, he also called; those he called, he also justified; those he justified, he also glorified.   *See also* **Mt** 13:43; **Jn** 17:24; **Ro** 9:23; **1Co** 2:7; **Php** 3:21; **Col** 3:4; **2Th** 2:14; **Rev** 2:26–27; 3:4–5,21

God will build his church
Mt 16:18–19 "And I [Jesus] tell you that you are Peter, and on this rock I will build my church, and the gates of Hades will not overcome it. I will give you the keys of the kingdom of heaven; whatever you bind on earth will be bound in heaven, and whatever you loose on earth will be loosed in heaven."   *See also* **Mt** 27:40 pp **Mk** 15:29; **Jn** 2:19–22; **1Co** 3:9; **Eph** 2:21–22; 4:11–13; **Heb** 3:3–6; **1Pe** 2:5

To challenge Satan's dominion
Eph 3:10–11 His [God's] intent was that now, through the church, the manifold wisdom of God should be made known to the rulers and authorities in the heavenly realms . . .   *See also* **Mt** 16:18; **Eph** 6:12; **1Jn** 2:14

To go into the world in mission
2Co 5:18 All this is from God, who reconciled us to himself through Christ and gave us the ministry of reconciliation.   *See also* **Mt** 5:13–16; 28:19–20; **Mk** 16:15; **Lk** 24:48; **Jn** 20:21; **Ac** 1:8; **Php** 2:15–16; **Col** 1:27

The church's mission
To preach the gospel to the world
Mk 13:10 "And the gospel must first be preached to all nations." pp **Mt** 24:14   *See also* **Mt** 28:19; **Lk** 24:47; **Jn** 10:16; **Ac** 13:47

To do good to all
Gal 6:10 Therefore, as we have opportunity, let us do good to all people, especially to those who belong to the family of believers.   *See also* **Mt** 25:37–40; **Lk** 6:35; **Ac** 9:36; **Eph** 2:10; **1Ti** 6:18; **Jas** 1:27; **1Pe** 2:12

Images of the church's mission
Mt 5:13–16 "You are the salt of the earth . . . You are the light of the world . . ."

Jn 15:5–8 "I [Jesus] am the vine; you are the branches. If you remain in me and I in you, you will bear much fruit . . ."

A fruitful plant in a fruitless world: **Mt** 7:18–19; **Ro** 7:4; **Eph** 5:9–10; **Php** 1:11; **Col** 1:6,10; **Jas** 3:17

Salt in an insipid world: **Mk** 9:50; **Lk** 14:34–35

Light in a dark world: **Ro** 13:12–14; **Eph** 5:8; **Php** 2:15; **1Th** 5:5–6

The growth of the church
Numerical growth among the first Christians
Ac 11:21 The Lord's hand was with them, and a great number of people believed and turned to the Lord.   *See also* **Ac** 2:41,47; 4:4; 5:14; 6:1,7; 9:31,42; 11:24; 12:24; 13:49; 16:5; 17:4; 18:8; 19:20

The church is to grow to maturity
Eph 4:12–13 . . . so that the body of Christ may be built up until we all reach unity in the faith and in the knowledge of the Son of God and become mature, attaining to the whole measure of the fulness of Christ.   *See also* **Php** 1:6; 3:13–15; **2Th** 1:3

Aspects of growth
Growth in character: **2Co** 9:10; **1Th** 3:12

Growth into Christ: **Eph** 4:15; **Col** 1:10; **2Pe** 3:18 **Heb** 6:1

Prayers for the growth of the church
Eph 3:14–19 . . . And I [Paul] pray that you, being rooted and established in love, may have power, together with all the saints, to grasp how wide and long and high and deep is the love of Christ, and to know this love that surpasses knowledge—that you may be filled to the measure of all the fulness of God.   *See also* **Eph** 1:17–19; **Php** 1:9–11; **Col** 1:9–12; **1Th** 3:11–13; **2Th** 1:11–12

Visions of the church's final destiny

Rev 7:9–10 After this I looked and there before me was a great multitude that no-one could count, from every nation, tribe, people and language, standing before the throne and in front of the Lamb . . .   *See also* **Mt** 24:31; **Jn** 10:16; **Eph** 1:10; **1Th** 4:16–17; **Heb** 12:22–23; **Rev** 21:2   *See also evangelism; kingdom of God; mission, of church; preachers and preaching; reconciliation; spiritual growth; spiritual warfare.*

---

church, unity

The church is one in essence, because it is founded on one gospel, united to one Lord and indwelt by one Spirit. Its unity is under constant threat because of the tendency to division that is inherent in fallen humanity, and needs to be continually maintained and actively expressed in fellowship.

The unity of the church
The church is one
Ro 12:5 . . . in Christ we who are many form one body, and each member belongs to all the others.   *See also* **1Co** 12:12,20; **Eph** 4:25
The church transcends all barriers
Col 3:11 Here there is no Greek or Jew, circumcised or uncircumcised, barbarian, Scythian, slave or free, but Christ is all, and is in all. *See also* **Jn** 10:16; **Ac** 10:28–29,47; 15:8–9; **Gal** 3:28; **Eph** 2:14–16; 3:6
The church's unity reflects the unity within the Trinity
Eph 4:4–6 There is one body and one Spirit— just as you were called to one hope when you were called—one Lord, one faith, one baptism; one God and Father of all, who is over all and through all and in all.   *See also* **Jn** 17:11; **Ro** 3:29–30; 10:12–13; **Gal** 3:27–28
The church's unity is the work of the Trinity
Eph 2:16–18 . . . in this one body to reconcile both of them to God through the cross, by which he [Christ] put to death their hostility . . . For through him we both have access to the Father by one Spirit.   *See also* **Jn** 11:52; **Ac** 10:45–47; **1Co** 12:13; **Eph** 2:22; 4:3

The purpose of the church's unity
To lead others to faith
Jn 17:23 ". . . May they [all believers] be brought to complete unity to let the world know that you sent me [Jesus] and have loved them even as you have loved me."   *See also* **Jn** 17:21
To lead believers to maturity
Eph 4:13 until we all reach unity in the faith and in the knowledge of the Son of God and become mature, attaining to the whole measure of the fulness of Christ.

The nature of the church's unity
Php 2:1–2 . . . then make my [Paul's] joy complete by being like-minded, having the same love, being one in spirit and purpose.   *See also* **2Co** 13:11; **Php** 1:27; **Col** 2:2

Appeals for unity in the church
Eph 4:3 Make every effort to keep the unity of the Spirit through the bond of peace.   *See also* **Ro** 12:10; 15:5,7; **1Co** 12:25; **Col** 3:14; **1Pe** 3:8

The church's unity is expressed in fellowship
Fellowship with God
1Co 1:9 God, who has called you into fellowship with his Son Jesus Christ our Lord, is faithful. *See also* **2Co** 13:14; **Php** 2:1; **2Pe** 1:4; **1Jn** 1:3,6–7
Fellowship expressed by meeting together
Ac 2:46 Every day they continued to meet together in the temple courts. They broke bread in their homes and ate together with glad and sincere hearts,   *See also* **Ac** 2:1,42; 5:12; 6:2; **1Co** 14:26; **Heb** 10:25
Fellowship expressed through sharing resources
Ac 2:44–45 All the believers were together and had everything in common. Selling their possessions and goods, they gave to anyone who had need.   *See also* **Ac** 4:32,34–37; 11:27–30; **Ro** 15:26; **1Co** 16:1–2; **2Co** 8:2–5,13–14; 9:13; **Php** 4:14–18
Fellowship through suffering
Rev 1:9 I, John, your brother and companion in

the suffering and kingdom and patient endurance
that are ours in Jesus . . .   *See also* **Ro** 8:17;
2Co 1:7; **Php** 3:10; 4:14; **Heb** 10:33–34; 13:3
Fellowship through shared spiritual blessings
1Co 9:23 I [Paul] do all this for the sake of
the gospel, that I may share in its blessings.
See also **Ro** 11:17; **Php** 1:7; **2Th** 2:14; **1Pe** 5:1;
Jude 3

**Specific actions which express
fellowship and unity in the church**
Sharing in the Lord's Supper
1Co 10:16–17 Is not the cup of thanksgiving
for which we give thanks a participation in the
blood of Christ? And is not the bread that we
break a participation in the body of
Christ? . . .   *See also* **Ac** 2:46; 20:7; **1Co** 11:33
Baptism as an expression of unity
Eph 4:4–6 There is one body and one Spirit—
just as you were called to one hope when you
were called—one Lord, one faith, one baptism;
one God and Father of all, who is over all and
through all and in all.   *See also* **1Co** 12:13
Extending hospitality **Ac** 28:7; **Ro** 12:13; 16:23;
1Ti 5:10; **Tit** 1:8; **1Pe** 4:9; **3Jn** 8
Greeting one another **Ac** 18:27; **Ro** 16:3–16;
1Co 16:19–20; **Col** 4:10; **Phm** 17
Welcoming former opponents **Ac** 9:26–27; **Gal**
2:9; **2Co** 2:5–8

Divisions in the church
Causes of division in the NT church
Personal ambition: **Mk** 9:34; 10:35–41 pp **Mt** 20:20–24
Ethnic tension: **Ac** 6:1
Differences of opinion: **Ac** 15:37–40; **Php** 4:2
Troublesome heretical leaders: **Ro** 16:17; **Jude** 19
Partisan spirit: **1Co** 1:11–12; 3:3–4
1Co 6:1–6
Greed: **1Co** 11:18,20–21; **Jas** 4:1–3
Warnings against divisions in the church
1Co 1:10 I [Paul] appeal to you, brothers and
sisters, in the name of our Lord Jesus Christ, that
all of you agree with one another so that there
may be no divisions among you and that you
may be perfectly united in mind and thought.
See also **Ro** 12:16; 16:17; **2Co** 12:20; **Eph** 4:31;
Jas 4:11

Acceptable differences in the church
In secondary matters of conscience, Christians are to
respect rather than judge each other. These things need
not impair the essential unity that is in Christ: **Ro**
14:1–3,5–6; **1Co** 8:9–13
In varieties of spiritual gifts: **1Co** 12:4–6,14–25; **Gal**
2:7
Necessary divisions in the church
Between the true gospel and heretical alternatives: **2Co**
11:2–6,13–15; **Gal** 1:6–9; **Col** 2:8,16–19; **1Ti**
4:1–6; **1Jn** 2:18–19; **2Jn** 9–11; **Jude** 18–20
Between those truly committed to Jesus Christ, and
those apparently part of the church but living sinful lives:
1Co 5:9–10; **2Th** 3:6; **1Ti** 6:3–5; **2Ti** 3:2–9; **2Pe**
1:20–21; 2:1–3; **Rev** 2:20,24; 3:1,4
Over essential gospel principles: **Ac** 15:2,5–6,19; **Gal**
2:11   *See also* fellowship; love.

---

conversion
Turning or returning to God in repentance, faith
and obedience by those who do not know God or
who have turned from him. Although conversion
can be seen as a human act or decision, Scripture
stresses that the work of God lies behind this
human decision, guiding and motivating it.

---

conversion, examples
Scripture gives examples of individuals and peoples
who have turned to God in conversion.

Examples of conversion in the OT
Peoples who turned to God **Isa** 19:22; **Jnh**
3:5–10

Individuals who turned to God
2Ki 5:15; **2Ch** 33:12–13; **Da** 4:34–37; **Jnh**
1:16

Examples of conversion in the NT
Examples of people in general **Jn** 4:42; **Ac** 2:41;
8:12; 9:35; 15:3
Examples of individual converts **Lk** 15:18;
19:8–9; **Ac** 8:35–38
Paul: **Ac** 9:3–18 pp **Ac** 22:6–11 pp **Ac** 26:12–18
Ac 10:44–48; 13:12; 16:14–15,29–34

The prophetic vision of the future conversion of Israel and the nations

Israel's turning back to God

Hos 3:5 Afterwards the Israelites will return and seek the LORD their God and David their king. They will come trembling to the LORD and to his blessings in the last days.   *See also* **Jer** 50:4–5; **Hos** 11:10–11; **Ro** 11:26

The conversion of the nations

Jer 16:19 O LORD, my strength and my fortress, my refuge in time of distress, to you the nations will come from the ends of the earth and say, "Our ancestors possessed nothing but false gods, worthless idols that did them no good."   *See also* **Ps** 22:27–28; **Isa** 2:3 pp **Mic** 4:2; **Zec** 14:16   *See also gospel, responses; preaching, effects.*

---

conversion, God's demand

Through his servants, God calls people to turn to him. He wants to save the world which is alienated from him, and to restore those of his backslidden people who return to him and renew their commitment to the covenant.

The need for conversion

The world is alienated from God

Ro 1:21–23 For although they [humankind] knew God, they neither glorified him as God nor gave thanks to him, but their thinking became futile and their foolish hearts were darkened . . .   *See also* **Ro** 1:28; 3:11–12; **Ps** 14:3

The world does not know God

Gal 4:8 Formerly, when you [believers in Galatia] did not know God, you were slaves to those who by nature are not gods.   *See also* **1Co** 1:21; 15:34; **1Th** 4:5; **2Th** 1:8

God's people have turned away from him

Mal 3:7 "Ever since the time of your ancestors you [the people of Israel] have turned away from my decrees and have not kept them. Return to me, and I will return to you," says the LORD Almighty . . .   *See also* **Nu** 14:43; **Dt** 9:12; **1Sa** 15:11; **1Ki** 11:9; **2Ch** 25:27; **Jer** 8:5; **Eze** 6:9; **Da** 9:11; **Ac** 7:39

God's demands for the conversion of all people

Isa 45:22 "Turn to me and be saved, all you ends of the earth; for I am God, and there is no other."

Ac 17:30 "In the past God overlooked such ignorance, but now he commands all people everywhere to repent."   *See also* **Ps** 65:5; **Jnh** 4:11; **Zec** 9:10

God's demands for the conversion of his own people

God's desire to save his people

Eze 33:11 ". . . 'As surely as I live, declares the Sovereign LORD, I take no pleasure in the death of the wicked, but rather that they turn from their ways and live. Turn! Turn from your evil ways! Why will you die, O house of Israel?'"   *See also* **Jer** 3:22; **Joel** 2:12–13; **Zec** 1:3

God's faithfulness to his people

Jer 3:14 "Return, faithless people," declares the LORD, "for I am your husband. I will choose you—one from a town and two from a clan—and bring you to Zion."   *See also* **Lev** 26:40–42; **2Ch** 30:9; **Hos** 3:5; 6:1–3

God's promise of restoration

2Ch 7:13–14 ". . . if my [God's] people, who are called by my name, will humble themselves and pray and seek my face and turn from their wicked ways, then will I hear from heaven and will forgive their sin and will heal their land."   *See also* **1Ki** 8:48–49 pp **2Ch** 6:38–39; **Ne** 1:9

The call to conversion through God's servants

The encouragement of his leaders **Jos** 24:14–15; **2Ki** 11:17

Josiah: **2Ki** 23:24–25; **2Ch** 34:31–33

2Ch 15:11–15; 19:4; 29:6–10; **Ps** 51:13

The ministry of his prophets

Jer 35:15 "'Again and again I [the LORD] sent all my servants the prophets to you. They said, "Each of you must turn from your wicked ways and reform your actions; do not follow other gods to serve them. Then you shall live in the land I

have given to you and your ancestors." But you have not paid attention or listened to me.' "
See also **2Ch** 24:19; **Jer** 25:4; **Hos** 14:1–2; **Jnh** 3:2

The preaching of believers
Ac 26:16–18 " ' . . . I [Jesus] am sending you [Paul] to them [the Gentiles] to open their eyes and turn them from darkness to light, and from the power of Satan to God, so that they may receive forgiveness of sins and a place among those who are sanctified by faith in me.' "   *See also* **Ac** 2:38; **Ro** 10:14–15; **Isa** 52:7

Rejection of God's call to conversion
Isa 9:13 But the people have not returned to him who struck them, nor have they sought the Lord Almighty.   *See also* **Jer** 3:10; **Hos** 5:4; 7:10; **Am** 4:6–11   *See also preachers and preaching.*

---

conversion, nature of
True repentance results in a turning from sin and an inner renewal which can only be brought about by God, who draws people to himself and who, through Jesus Christ, gives forgiveness and new life.

Conversion as turning to God
Turning back to God
Dt 4:30–31 When you [the people of Israel] are in distress and all these things have happened to you, then in later days you will return to the Lord your God and obey him . . .

Lk 1:16–17 "Many of the people of Israel will he [John the Baptist] bring back to the Lord their God . . ."   *See also* **Dt** 30:2–3,10; **Lk** 22:32; **Jas** 5:19–20
Turning from idolatry
Ac 14:15 " . . . We [Barnabas and Paul] are bringing you [people of Lystra] good news, telling you to turn from these worthless things to the living God, who made heaven and earth and sea and everything in them."   *See also* **1Sa** 7:3; **Jer** 3:12–13; 4:1–2; **1Th** 1:9–10
Turning from sinful ways
2Ki 17:13–14 The Lord warned Israel and

Judah through all his prophets and seers: "Turn from your evil ways. Observe my commands and decrees, in accordance with the entire Law that I commanded your ancestors to obey and that I delivered to you through my servants the prophets." . . .

Isa 55:6–7 . . . Let the wicked forsake their ways and the unrighteous their thoughts. Let them turn to the Lord, and he will have mercy on them, and to our God, for he will freely pardon.   *See also* **2Ki** 13:11; 14:24; 15:9; **Jer** 18:11; 25:5; **Eze** 18:23; **Da** 9:13

Conversion as a turning away from unbelief to faith
It is linked to repentance
Ac 3:19 "Repent, then, and turn to God, so that your sins may be wiped out, that times of refreshing may come from the Lord,"   *See also* **Eze** 14:6; 18:30; **Ac** 26:20
It is linked to coming to faith
Ac 11:21 The Lord's hand was with them [believers from Cyprus and Cyrene], and a great number of people believed and turned to the Lord.

Conversion brings new life
It results in a transformed life
2Co 5:17 Therefore, if anyone is in Christ, there is a new creation: the old has gone, the new has come!   *See also* **Ro** 12:2; **2Co** 3:18; **Gal** 6:14–15
It is symbolised in baptism
Ro 6:3–4 . . . We were therefore buried with him through baptism into death in order that, just as Christ was raised from the dead through the glory of the Father, we too may live a new life.   *See also* **Col** 2:12; 3:1–3
It demands a new lifestyle
Hos 12:6 But you must return to your God; maintain love and justice, and wait for your God always.

Mt 18:3–4 And he [Jesus] said: "I tell you the truth, unless you change and become like little children, you will never enter the kingdom of heaven . . ."   *See also* **Gal** 5:22–24; **Eph** 4:1;

5:8–11; **1Pe** 2:11–12

Conversion brings a new relationship with God
It brings a new status
Gal 4:7 So you are no longer slaves, but God's children; and since you are his children, he has made you also heirs.   *See also* **Gal** 3:26–29; **1Jn** 3:1; **1Pe** 2:9–10
It brings a new understanding
2Co 3:15–16 . . . whenever anyone turns to the Lord, the veil is taken away.   *See also* **Jer** 31:34; **Heb** 8:11

Conversion is a work of God
God turns people to himself
Jer 24:7 " 'I will give them a heart to know me, that I am the LORD. They will be my people, and I will be their God, for they will return to me with all their heart.' "

La 5:21 Restore us to yourself, O LORD, that we may return; renew our days as of old   *See also* **1Ki** 8:58; **Jer** 31:18; **Eze** 36:26–27; **Jn** 6:44; 15:16; **Eph** 2:12–13
God gives new birth
Jas 1:17–18 . . . He [God] chose to give us birth through the word of truth, that we might be a kind of firstfruits of all he created.   *See also* **Jn** 3:3–6; **Tit** 3:4–5; **1Pe** 1:23   *See also baptism, practice; faith; grace; knowing God, nature of; regeneration; repentance.*

---

covenant
God's commitment to, and requirement of, his people expressed in promise, law, judgment, faithfulness and mercy. Also used of commitment within human relationships based upon agreements.

---

covenant, at Sinai
God's faithful commitment, made in pursuance of his promises to Abraham, to acknowledge the newly-redeemed Israel as his own special people. Israel's required response to the grace of God in election was to be holiness and obedience to the law.

The occasion of the covenant
The covenant fulfilled God's promises to Abraham
Dt 29:12–13 You [the Israelites] are standing here in order to enter into a covenant with the LORD your God, a covenant the LORD is making with you this day and sealing with an oath, to confirm you this day as his people, that he may be your God as he promised you and as he swore to your fathers, Abraham, Isaac and Jacob.   *See also* **Ex** 2:24; 6:4–8; **Dt** 7:8
The covenant followed Israel's redemption from slavery
Jer 34:13 "This is what the LORD, the God of Israel, says: I made a covenant with your ancestors when I brought them out of Egypt, out of the land of slavery . . ."   *See also* **Ex** 20:2 pp **Dt** 5:6; **Lev** 26:45
The covenant was mediated through Moses **Ex** 34:27; **Lev** 26:46; **Dt** 29:1; **Jn** 1:17
The covenant was accompanied by signs of God's presence **Ex** 19:18–19; 20:18–19; 24:16; **Ps** 68:8

Sealing the covenant
Sharing a meal **Ex** 24:11
Offering a sacrifice **Ex** 24:5–8; **Ps** 50:5
God's oath **Dt** 28:9; 29:14; **Eze** 16:8
Israel's promise **Ex** 19:8; 24:3,7

The covenant relationship
Israel as God's people
Dt 7:6 For you [Israel] are a people holy to the LORD your God. The LORD your God has chosen you out of all the peoples on the face of the earth to be his people, his treasured possession.   *See also* **Ex** 19:5–6; **Lev** 26:12; **Dt** 14:2; **Jer** 13:11
Israel adopted into God's family
Hos 11:1 "When Israel was a child, I [the LORD] loved him, and out of Egypt I called my son."   *See also* **Dt** 1:30–31; 8:5; **Isa** 63:16; **Mal** 2:10
Israel as God's bride
Jer 2:2 ". . . 'I [the LORD] remember the devotion of your [Israel's] youth, how as a bride you loved me and followed me through the

desert, through a land not sown.' "   *See also* Isa 54:5–8; Jer 31:32; Eze 16:8; Hos 2:14–16

The blessings of the covenant
Inheriting God's promises Dt 6:3; 26:18–19; 28:9; Jos 23:5
Provision and protection Lev 26:3–13; Dt 28:1–14

The requirements of the covenant
Obedience to the law
Ex 24:7 Then he [Moses] took the Book of the Covenant and read it to the people [Israel]. They responded, "We will do everything the LORD has said; we will obey."

Ex 34:27–28 Then the LORD said to Moses, "Write down these words, for in accordance with these words I have made a covenant with you and with Israel." . . . And he wrote on the tablets the words of the covenant—the Ten Commandments.   *See also* Dt 4:13; Jos 8:31; Ne 8:1
Holiness
Dt 14:2 for you [Israel] are a people holy to the LORD your God. Out of all the peoples on the face of the earth, the LORD has chosen you to be his treasured possession.
Lev 11:45 " 'I am the LORD who brought you [the people of Israel] up out of Egypt to be your God; therefore be holy, because I am holy.' "   *See also* Lev 20:26
Wholehearted devotion
Ex 34:14 "Do not worship any other god, for the LORD, whose name is Jealous, is a jealous God."

Dt 10:12 And now, O Israel, what does the LORD your God ask of you but to fear the LORD your God, to walk in all his ways, to love him, to serve the LORD your God with all your heart and with all your soul.   *See also* Ex 23:32; Dt 4:23; 6:5; 10:20; Jos 24:14–15

Breaking the covenant
The consequences of breaking the covenant
Disease: Lev 26:15–16; Dt 28:21–22

Drought and crop failure: Lev 26:19–20; Dt 28:23–24
Defeat by enemies: Lev 26:17,25; Dt 28:25
Exile from the land: Lev 26:32–33; Dt 28:36–37; Jos 23:16; Eze 17:19–20
Israel's unfaithfulness to the covenant
Ps 78:37 their [the people of Israel's] hearts were not loyal to him [God], they were not faithful to his covenant.   *See also* 2Ki 18:12; 1Ch 5:25; Jer 3:8; 11:10; Eze 16:32; Hos 6:7

God's commitment to the covenant
God's covenant of love
Dt 7:9 Know therefore that the LORD your God is God; he is the faithful God, keeping his covenant of love to a thousand generations of those who love him and keep his commands.   *See also* Ne 1:5; Da 9:4
The everlasting covenant
Eze 16:60 " 'Yet I [the LORD] will remember the covenant I made with you [Israel] in the days of your youth, and I will establish an everlasting covenant with you.' "   *See also* Isa 61:8; Jer 32:40

Renewing the covenant
Lev 26:40–45; Dt 29:1; Jos 24:22–25; 2Ki 23:3 pp 2Ch 34:31   *See also* law, Ten Commandments; sin.

---

covenant, nature of
A solemn agreement or promise, sometimes confirmed by sacrifice or by sharing in a meal, by which two or more parties commit themselves to the rights and responsibilities demanded by their relationship and their agreed course of action, and accept the serious consequences of breaking faith.

Kinds of covenant relationship
The relationship between king and people
2Sa 5:3 When all the elders of Israel had come to King David at Hebron, the king made a compact with them at Hebron before the LORD, and they anointed David king over Israel. pp 1Ch 11:3   *See also* 2Sa 3:21; 2Ki 11:17; 2Ch 23:3
Terms for peace granted to a weaker party
Jos 9:15 Then Joshua made a treaty of peace with them [the Gibeonites] to let them live, and

the leaders of the assembly ratified it by oath.
See also **1Sa** 11:1; **1Ki** 15:19–20; 20:34; **Eze**
17:13–14

A mutual commitment to peaceful relations
1Ki 5:12 The LORD gave Solomon wisdom, just
as he had promised him. There were peaceful
relations between Hiram and Solomon, and the
two of them made a treaty.   *See also* **Ge**
21:27; 26:28–29; 31:44; **Am** 1:9

An agreement on a common course of action
Jer 34:8 The word came to Jeremiah from the
LORD after King Zedekiah had made a covenant
with all the people in Jerusalem to proclaim
freedom for the slaves.   *See also* **2Ki** 11:4 pp
2Ch 23:1; **Ezr** 10:3; **Ne** 9:38; **Ps** 83:5

The relationship between husband and wife Pr
2:17; **Mal** 2:14

God's covenant with Israel is likened to a marriage: **Jer**
2:2; **Eze** 16:8

An expression of friendship
1Sa 18:3 And Jonathan made a covenant with
David because he loved him as himself.   *See*
also **1Sa** 20:16–17

Sealing a covenant
By sharing a meal Ge 26:30; 31:53–54
The meal Jesus Christ shared with his disciples is an
important part of the institution of the new covenant:
Mt 26:26–29 pp **Mk** 14:22–25 pp **Lk** 22:17–20;
1Co 11:23–25

By offering a sacrifice Jer 34:18–19; **Ge**
15:9–18; **Ex** 24:4–8; **Ps** 50:5; **Heb** 12:24

By making an oath Ge 21:31; 26:31; **Jos** 9:15;
2Ki 11:4; **Ne** 10:28–29

The obligations of a covenant
Covenant responsibilities must be honoured
Nu 30:2 "When a man makes a vow to the
LORD or takes an oath to bind himself by a
pledge, he must not break his word but must do
everything he said."

1Sa 20:8 "As for you [Jonathan], show
kindness to your servant [David], for you have
brought him into a covenant with you before the
LORD . . ."   *See also* **Jos** 9:18; **Mt** 5:33–37;
Gal 3:15

Covenant obligations are watched over by God

1Sa 20:42 Jonathan said to David, "Go in
peace, for we have sworn friendship with each
other in the name of the LORD, saying, 'The LORD
is witness between you and me, and between
your descendants and my descendants for
ever.' " . . .   *See also* **Ge** 31:48–54; **Jos** 9:19;
Jer 34:15–16; **Mal** 2:14–16

The consequences of breaking covenant faith

Jos 9:20 "This is what we [Israel's leaders] will
do to them [the Gibeonites]: We will let them
live, so that wrath will not fall on us for breaking
the oath we swore to them."   *See also* **Jer**
34:18–22; **Eze** 17:16–18; **Am** 1:9

**Covenants with other nations are
forbidden**

Ex 34:12 "Be careful not to make a treaty
with those who live in the land where you are
going, or they will be a snare among you
[Israel]."   *See also* **Dt** 23:6; **Jos** 9:7

**Covenants with other nations lead to a
commitment to foreign gods** Ex 23:32–33;
34:15–16; **Dt** 7:2–4

**Covenants with other nations lead to a denial
of faith in God** Isa 28:15,18; 30:1–2; 31:1; **Hos**
12:1

---

covenant, the new

The fulfilment of God's purposes of salvation
expressed in the covenants of the OT, mediated
by Jesus Christ and sealed in his blood. It is a
covenant of grace, the benefits of which include
forgiveness, a renewed relationship with God and,
through the Holy Spirit, an inward transformation
that enables obedience to its demands and so
ensures that it will not again be broken.

Jer 31:31 "The time is coming," declares the
LORD, "when I will make a new covenant with
the house of Israel and with the house of
Judah." *See also* **Heb** 8:8

The new covenant fulfils the OT covenants

God's covenant with Noah Isa 54:9–10; Hos 2:18

God's covenant with Abraham Lk 1:72–73; Ac 3:25–26; Gal 3:14–16

God's covenant at Sinai Eze 16:60,62; 20:37

God's covenant with David Isa 55:3; Eze 34:24–26; 37:25–26; Lk 1:69

Jesus Christ, the mediator of the new covenant

The new covenant fulfilled in the Messiah

Mal 3:1 ". . . suddenly the Lord you are seeking will come to his temple; the messenger of the covenant, whom you desire, will come," says the Lord Almighty.　*See also* Isa 42:6; 49:8

The new covenant effected through Jesus Christ's death

Heb 9:15 For this reason Christ is the mediator of a new covenant, that those who are called may receive the promised eternal inheritance—now that he has died as a ransom to set them free from the sins committed under the first covenant.　*See also* Heb 9:16–17

The new covenant sealed in Jesus Christ's blood

Lk 22:20 In the same way, after the supper he [Jesus] took the cup, saying, "This cup is the new covenant in my blood, which is poured out for you." pp Mt 26:28 pp Mk 14:24　*See also* Ex 24:8; Jn 6:54; 1Co 10:16; 11:25; Heb 10:29

The ministry of the Holy Spirit

2Co 3:6 He [God] has made us competent as ministers of a new covenant—not of the letter but of the Spirit; for the letter kills, but the Spirit gives life.

2Co 3:18 And we, who with unveiled faces all reflect the Lord's glory, are being transformed into his likeness with ever-increasing glory, which comes from the Lord, who is the Spirit.　*See also* Isa 59:21; Eze 36:26–27; Ro 8:2–4; 2Co 3:8

The superior blessings of the new covenant

God's grace and mercy

Heb 12:24 to Jesus the mediator of a new covenant, and to the sprinkled blood that speaks a better word than the blood of Abel.

A complete forgiveness

Heb 8:12 "For I [the Lord] will forgive their wickedness and will remember their sins no more."　*See also* Jer 31:34; Ro 11:27; Heb 10:17

Release from the law's condemnation 2Co 3:9; Gal 3:13–14

An inward enabling to obey God's laws

Jer 31:32–33 "It [the new covenant] will not be like the covenant I made with their ancestors when I took them by the hand to lead them out of Egypt, because they broke my covenant, though I was a husband to them," declares the LORD. "This is the covenant that I will make with the house of Israel after that time," declares the LORD. "I will put my law in their minds and write it on their hearts. I will be their God, and they will be my people."　*See also* Jer 32:38–40; Eze 11:19–20; 2Co 3:3; Heb 8:9–10; 9:14; 10:16

A new knowledge of God

Heb 8:11 "No longer will they teach their neighbours, or say to one another, 'Know the Lord,' because they will all know me, from the least of them to the greatest."　*See also* Jer 31:34; 2Co 3:15–16

A renewed relationship with God

Eze 37:26–27 "'I [the LORD] will make a covenant of peace with them [a re-united Israel]; it will be an everlasting covenant . . . I will put my sanctuary among them for ever. My dwelling-place will be with them; I will be their God, and they will be my people.'"　*See also* Jer 24:7; 31:1; Eze 34:30–31; Hos 2:19–23

A superior priesthood

Heb 8:6 But the ministry Jesus has received is as superior to theirs [the OT priests] as the covenant of which he is mediator is superior to the old one, and it is founded on better promises.　*See also* Heb 7:22; 9:24–25

A superior sacrifice

Heb 9:14 How much more, then, will the blood

of Christ, who through the eternal Spirit offered himself unblemished to God, cleanse our consciences from acts that lead to death, so that we may serve the living God!   *See also* Heb 9:20–23,26–28; 10:4,8–14

A lasting covenant
Isa 61:8 "For I, the LORD, love justice; I hate robbery and iniquity. In my faithfulness I will reward them and make an everlasting covenant with them."

2Co 3:11 And if what was fading away came with glory, how much greater is the glory of that which lasts!   *See also* Jer 50:5; Heb 8:7,13; 13:20   *See also blood, of Jesus Christ; forgiveness; grace; law, and gospel; Lord's Supper; sacrifice, New Testament fulfilment of; sanctification.*

---

covenant, with Abraham

God's gracious promise made to Abraham, and repeated to his descendants, to bless both them and, through them, the whole world. In response God calls for faithful obedience, expressed particularly in the outward sign of circumcision.

Features of the Abrahamic covenant
The covenant is based upon God's gracious promise
Gal 3:18 For if the inheritance depends on the law, then it no longer depends on a promise; but God in his grace gave it to Abraham through a promise.   *See also* Ge 15:4–7; 17:4–8; 18:10,14; Heb 6:13–15
The covenant was confirmed by sacrifice Ge 15:9–18
The covenant was given in perpetuity
Ge 17:7 "I [God] will establish my covenant as an everlasting covenant between me and you [Abraham] and your descendants after you for the generations to come . . ."   *See also* Ge 17:13,19; 1Ch 16:15–17 pp Ps 105:8–10; Jer 33:23–25

God's promises to Abraham
Ge 12:2–3 "I [the LORD] will make you [Abraham] into a great nation and I will bless you; I will make your name great, and you will

be a blessing. I will bless those who bless you, and whoever curses you I will curse; and all peoples on earth will be blessed through you."
God promised the land of Canaan
Ge 17:8 "The whole land of Canaan, where you [Abraham] are now an alien, I [God] will give as an everlasting possession to you and your descendants after you . . ."   *See also* Ge 12:7; 15:18–21; Ex 6:4; Jos 1:3; Ne 9:8; Ac 7:5
God promised that Abraham would be the father of a nation
Ge 15:5 He [God] took him [Abraham] outside and said, "Look up at the heavens and count the stars—if indeed you can count them." Then he said to him, "So shall your offspring be."   *See also* Ge 12:2; 17:4–6,16; 22:17; Heb 11:11–12
God promised a relationship with himself
Ge 17:8 ". . . I will be their God."   *See also* Ge 26:24; Dt 29:13; Mt 22:32 pp Mk 12:26; Ex 3:6; Ac 7:32

The requirements of the covenant
Obedience
Ge 17:9–14 Then God said to Abraham, "As for you, you must keep my covenant, you and your descendants after you for the generations to come . . ."
Ge 22:18 ". . . through your offspring all nations on earth will be blessed, because you [Abraham] have obeyed me [the LORD]."   *See also* Ge 26:5; Nu 32:11; Heb 11:8,17–19
Faith
Ge 15:6 Abram believed the LORD, and he credited it to him as righteousness.

Ne 9:8 "You [God] found his [Abraham's] heart faithful to you, and you made a covenant with him to give to his descendants the land of the Canaanites, Hittites, Amorites, Perizzites, Jebusites and Girgashites . . ."   *See also* Ro 4:3,11–12,18; Gal 3:6–7; Heb 11:8–12; Jas 2:23

God's faithfulness to the covenant
God remembers his promise
Ps 105:42 For he [the LORD] remembered his holy promise given to his servant Abraham.   *See also* Ge 21:2; 50:24; Ex 33:1; Ac 7:17; Heb 6:15

God shows compassion for his people
2Ki 13:23 But the LORD was gracious to them [Israel] and had compassion and showed concern for them because of his covenant with Abraham, Isaac and Jacob. To this day he has been unwilling to destroy them or banish them from his presence.   *See also* **Ex** 2:24–25; 32:13–14; **Dt** 9:27; **Lk** 1:72–73

The scope of the covenant
The covenant continued through Isaac, not Ishmael
Ge 17:19–21 ". . . your wife Sarah will bear you a son, and you [Abraham] will call him Isaac. I [God] will establish my covenant with him as an everlasting covenant for his descendants after him . . ."   *See also* **Ge** 21:12; **Ro** 9:7–8; **Gal** 4:28

The covenant confirmed through Abraham, Isaac and Jacob
Lev 26:42 "I [the LORD] will remember my covenant with Jacob and my covenant with Isaac and my covenant with Abraham, and I will remember the land."   *See also* **Ge** 26:24
Jacob: **Ge** 28:13–14; 32:12
Ex 3:6; **Dt** 1:8; **Ac** 7:8

The people of Israel are heirs to the covenant
Dt 29:12–13 You [the people of Israel] are standing here in order to enter into a covenant with the LORD your God, a covenant the LORD is making with you this day and sealing with an oath, to confirm you this day as his people, that he may be your God as he promised you and as he swore to your fathers, Abraham, Isaac and Jacob.   *See also* **Ac** 3:25

All nations will be blessed through Abraham
Ge 18:18 "Abraham will surely become a great and powerful nation, and all nations on earth will be blessed through him."   *See also* **Ge** 26:4; **Ac** 3:25; **Gal** 3:8–9,14,29   *See also* election; faith; necessity; obedience.

---

covenant, with David

God's promise to establish David and his descendants on Israel's throne for ever. It provided Israel with a basis for the hope of deliverance and restoration, and became a focus for the Messianic

expectation which was fulfilled, ultimately, in Jesus Christ.

God's promise to establish David's line
God's election of David
Ps 78:70 He [the LORD] chose David his servant and took him from the sheep pens;   *See also* **2Sa** 6:21; **1Ki** 8:16 pp **2Ch** 6:6

God's covenant is everlasting
Ps 89:3–4 You [the LORD] said, "I have made a covenant with my chosen one, I have sworn to David my servant, 'I will establish your line for ever and make your throne firm through all generations.'" . . .   *See also* **2Sa** 7:11–16; 23:5; **1Ki** 2:45; **2Ch** 13:5; **Ps** 18:50; 89:28–29,35–37; **Jer** 33:17

God's covenant is inherited through obedience
Ps 132:11–12 The LORD swore an oath to David, a sure oath that he will not revoke: "One of your own descendants I will place on your throne—if your sons keep my covenant and the statutes I teach them, then their sons shall sit on your throne for ever and ever."   *See also* **1Ki** 8:25–26 pp **2Ch** 6:16–17; **1Ki** 9:4–5 pp **2Ch** 7:17–18

God's covenant blessings are forfeited through disobedience
Jer 22:4–5 "'For if you [the king and leaders of Judah] are careful to carry out these commands, then kings who sit on David's throne will come through the gates of this palace, riding in chariots and on horses, accompanied by their officials and their people. But if you do not obey these commands, declares the LORD, I swear by myself that this palace will become a ruin.'"
See also **1Ki** 9:6–9 pp **2Ch** 7:19–22; **1Ki** 11:11–13,31–33; **Jer** 7:24–26; 22:6–9; 36:30–31

God's promise is fulfilled by grace
2Ch 21:7 Nevertheless, because of the covenant the LORD had made with David, the LORD was not willing to destroy the house of David. He had promised to maintain a lamp for him and his descendants for ever. pp **2Ki** 8:19   *See also* **1Ki** 11:34–36,39; 15:4; **Ps** 89:30–34

The Davidic covenant as a basis for hope

God's election of Jerusalem

2Ki 21:7 . . . the LORD had said to David and to his son Solomon, "In this temple and in Jerusalem, which I have chosen out of all the tribes of Israel, I will put my Name for ever." pp 2Ch 33:7 *See also* 1Ki 8:20–21 pp 2Ch 6:10–11; 1Ki 11:32,36; 1Ch 23:25; 2Ch 6:41–42 pp Ps 132:8–10

God's promise to defend Jerusalem

Isa 37:35 "I [the LORD] will defend this city [Jerusalem] and save it, for my sake and for the sake of David my servant!" pp 2Ki 19:34 *See also* 2Ki 19:20; Zec 12:7–9

God's promise to restore David's house

Am 9:11 "In that day I [the LORD] will restore David's fallen tent. I will repair its broken places, restore its ruins, and build it as it used to be," *See also* Ac 15:16; Jer 33:25–26

Hopes expressed in the Davidic covenant are focused in the Messiah

The Messiah fulfils the Davidic hope

Jer 23:5–6 "The days are coming," declares the LORD, "when I will raise up to David a righteous Branch, a King who will reign wisely and do what is just and right in the land. In his days Judah will be saved and Israel will live in safety. This is the name by which he will be called: The LORD Our Righteousness." *See also* Ps 110:1–2; Isa 9:7; 11:1–2; 16:5; 55:3; Eze 34:23–25; Zec 3:8; Jn 7:42

God's promise to David fulfilled in Jesus Christ

Lk 1:32–33 "He [Jesus] will be great and will be called the Son of the Most High. The Lord God will give him the throne of his father David, and he will reign over the house of Jacob for ever; his kingdom will never end."

Rev 22:16 "I, Jesus, have sent my angel to give you [John] this testimony for the churches. I am the Root and the Offspring of David, and the bright Morning Star." *See also* Mt 1:1; 22:41–46 pp Mk 12:35–37 pp Lk 20:41–44 Many Jews in Jesus Christ's day were expecting a literal

fulfilment of God's promise to restore the Davidic empire. The true hope expressed in the Davidic covenant and fulfilled in Christ is the coming of the kingdom of God: Mk 11:10 pp Mt 21:9; Lk 24:21; Ac 1:6 Ac 2:29–31; 13:34; Ro 1:3; 2Ti 2:8 *See also kingdom of God, coming.*

covenant, with Noah

God's confirmation of, and commitment to maintain, his relationship with the natural order—implicit in the act of creation—whereby he promised never again to destroy the earth with a flood. This divine pledge, given unconditionally to Noah and to every living creature on earth, was accompanied by the sign of the rainbow.

The occasion of the covenant

The flood as divine judgment

Ge 6:17 "I [God] am going to bring floodwaters on the earth to destroy all life under the heavens, every creature that has the breath of life in it. Everything on earth will perish." *See also* Ge 6:5–7,11–13; 2Pe 2:5

God's promise of salvation to Noah and his family

Ge 6:18 "But I [God] will establish my covenant with you [Noah], and you will enter the ark—you and your sons and your wife and your sons' wives with you." *See also* Ge 7:23; 8:1,15–17; Heb 11:7; 1Pe 3:20

God's promise never again to destroy the earth with a flood

Ge 9:11 "I [God] establish my covenant with you [Noah and his sons]: Never again will all life be cut off by the waters of a flood; never again will there be a flood to destroy the earth." *See also* Ge 8:21; Isa 54:9

The sign of the covenant

Ge 9:13 "I [God] have set my rainbow in the clouds, and it will be the sign of the covenant between me and the earth." *See also* Ge 9:14–17

A universal covenant

God's relationship with every living creature

Ge 9:8–10 Then God said to Noah and to his

sons with him: "I now establish my covenant with you and with your descendants after you and with every living creature that was with you—the birds, the livestock and all the wild animals, all those that came out of the ark with you—every living creature on earth." *See also* **Ge** 7:1–3; **Eze** 34:25; **Hos** 2:18; **Zec** 11:10

God's relationship with the natural order

Ge 8:22 "As long as the earth endures, seedtime and harvest, cold and heat, summer and winter, day and night will never cease."

Jer 33:25–26 "This is what the LORD says: 'If I have not established my covenant with day and night and the fixed laws of heaven and earth, then I will reject the descendants of Jacob and David my servant and will not choose one of his sons to rule over the descendants of Abraham, Isaac and Jacob. For I will restore their fortunes and have compassion on them.'" *See also* **Ge** 1:14,31–2:1; **Ps** 74:16–17; **Jer** 5:24; 33:20–21

An everlasting covenant

Ge 9:16 "Whenever the rainbow appears in the clouds, I [God] will see it and remember the everlasting covenant between God and all living creatures of every kind on the earth." *See also* **Ge** 9:12

Isa 24:5 The earth is defiled by its people; they have disobeyed the laws, violated the statutes and broken the everlasting covenant. *See also* **Ge** 9:6; **Nu** 35:33; **Isa** 26:21 *See also creation; promises, divine.*

creation

The created order, established as a sovereign decision on the part of God. The creation is dependent upon and under the authority of its Creator. Scripture affirms the role of both Jesus Christ and the Holy Spirit in the work of creation.

creation, and God

The natural world is sustained by God and speaks of God.

God sustains the creation
He upholds the natural order

Heb 1:3 The Son is the radiance of God's glory and the exact representation of his being, sustaining all things by his powerful word. After he had provided purification for sins, he sat down at the right hand of the Majesty in heaven. *See also* **Job** 38:33–37; **Ps** 104:1–35; 135:6–7; 145:16–17; **Mt** 10:29–30; **Col** 1:17

He sustains humanity

Ac 17:28 "'For in him we live and move and have our being.' As some of your own poets have said, 'We are his offspring.'" *See also* **Job** 33:4; **Ps** 36:6; **Da** 4:34–35; **1Co** 8:6

Creation is upheld for the good of humanity

Ge 8:22 "As long as the earth endures, seedtime and harvest, cold and heat, summer and winter, day and night will never cease." *See also* **Ge** 9:12–16; **Mt** 6:11

God's sustaining power reserves the world for judgment

2Pe 3:7 By the same word the present heavens and earth are reserved for fire, being kept for the day of judgment and destruction of the ungodly. *See also* **2Pe** 3:9–12

God has given humanity responsibility to preserve creation

Ge 1:28 God blessed them and said to them [male and female], "Be fruitful and increase in number; fill the earth and subdue it. Rule over the fish of the sea and the birds of the air and over every living creature that moves on the ground." *See also* **Ge** 2:15; 9:1–3; **Ps** 8:6–8; 115:16; **Heb** 2:8; **Jas** 3:7

Creation is spoilt by sin

Ge 3:17–19 To Adam he [the LORD God] said, "Because you listened to your wife and ate from the tree about which I commanded you, 'You must not eat of it,' Cursed is the ground because of you; through painful toil you will eat of it all the days of your life. It will produce thorns and thistles for you, and you will eat the plants of the field. By the sweat of your brow you will eat your food until you return to the ground, since from it you were taken; for dust you are and to dust you will return." *See also* Ro 8:20–22; Heb 6:8

Creation speaks of God's nature and character
His revelation of himself
Job 12:7–10 "But ask the animals, and they will teach you, or the birds of the air, and they will tell you; or speak to the earth, and it will teach you, or let the fish of the sea inform you. Which of all these does not know that the hand of the LORD has done this? In his hand is the life of every creature and the breath of all people."
His eternal power and divine nature
Ro 1:20 For since the creation of the world God's invisible qualities—his eternal power and divine nature—have been clearly seen, being understood from what has been made, so that they are without excuse. *See also* Jer 32:17
His authority Job 38:4–39:30; Jer 33:2
His glory and majesty
Ps 19:1–2 The heavens declare the glory of God; the skies proclaim the work of his hands. Day after day they pour forth speech; night after night they display knowledge. *See also* Ps 8:1–9
His love and faithfulness
Ps 36:5 Your love, O LORD, reaches to the heavens, your faithfulness to the skies. *See also* Mt 6:30
His power
Isa 40:25–28 "To whom will you compare me? Or who is my equal?" says the Holy One. Lift your eyes and look to the heavens: Who created all these? He who brings out the starry host one by one, and calls them each by name. Because of his great power and mighty strength, not one of them is missing. Why do you say, O Jacob, and complain, O Israel, "My way is hidden from the LORD; my cause is disregarded by my God"? Do you not know? Have you not heard? The LORD is the everlasting God, the Creator of the ends of the earth. He will not grow tired or weary, and his understanding no-one can fathom.
His wisdom
Ps 136:5 who by his understanding made the heavens . . . *See also* Pr 8:27–29

His unchangeableness and eternity
Ps 102:25–27 "In the beginning you laid the foundations of the earth, and the heavens are the work of your hands. They will perish, but you remain; they will all wear out like a garment. Like clothing you will change them and they will be discarded. But you remain the same, and your years will never end." *See also* Ps 90:1–2; Heb 1:11
His spiritual work in believers' lives Mt
13:3–43 *See also providence; revelation, creation; sin.*

creation, and Holy Spirit
The Holy Spirit was active with the Father and the Word in creation. He is the active power of God present within creation.

The Holy Spirit is involved in creative activity
Ge 1:2 Now the earth was formless and empty, darkness was over the surface of the deep, and the Spirit of God was hovering over the waters. *See also* Job 26:13; Ps 33:6

The Holy Spirit is the breath of life throughout creation
Ge 2:7 the LORD God formed a man from the dust of the ground and breathed into his nostrils the breath of life, and the man became a living being. *See also* Job 12:10; 32:8; 33:4; 34:14–15; Ps 104:30

The Holy Spirit is present everywhere in creation
Ps 139:7–8 Where can I go from your Spirit? Where can I flee from your presence? If I go up to the heavens, you are there; if I make my bed in the depths, you are there.

The Holy Spirit controls nature and history
Isa 34:16 Look in the scroll of the LORD and read: None of these will be missing, not one will lack her mate. For it is his mouth that has given the order, and his Spirit will gather them together. *See also* Isa 40:7

The Holy Spirit enables creative achievement

Ex 31:1–5 Then the LORD said to Moses, "See I have chosen Bezalel son of Uri, the son of Hur, of the tribe of Judah, and I have filled him with the Spirit of God, with skill, ability and knowledge in all kinds of crafts . . .   *See also* **Ex** 35:30–35

---

creation, and Jesus Christ

Scripture identifies the pre-existent Jesus Christ as involved in the work of creation, and relates this to his work in redemption, by which a new creation is brought out of the ruins of the old.

Jesus Christ's creation of the present world

Jesus Christ created all things

Jn 1:3 Through him [Jesus] all things were made; without him nothing was made that has been made.   *See also* **Jn** 1:10; **Ac** 3:15; **1Co** 8:6; **Col** 1:15–16; **Heb** 1:2

Jesus Christ sustains the created universe

Heb 1:3 The Son is the radiance of God's glory . . . sustaining all things by his powerful word . . .   *See also* **1Co** 8:6; **Col** 1:17; **Rev** 3:14

Jesus Christ will bring the entire work of creation to perfection

Eph 1:9–10 And he made known to us the mystery of his will according to his good pleasure, which he purposed in Christ, to be put into effect when the times will have reached their fulfilment—to bring all things in heaven and on earth together under one head, even Christ. *See also* **Ro** 8:19–22; **Col** 1:20

Jesus Christ makes a new creation possible

Jesus Christ recreates people through a new birth

2Co 5:17 Therefore, if anyone is in Christ, there is a new creation: the old has gone, the new has come!   *See also* **Jn** 1:12–13; 3:5–6; **Gal** 6:15; **Jas** 1:18

Jesus Christ's work of new creation should be evident in believers' lives

Eph 4:24 . . . put on the new self, created to be like God in true righteousness and holiness. *See also* **Eph** 3:15; **Col** 3:10

Through Jesus Christ a new heaven and earth will be created

2Pe 3:13 But in keeping with his promise we are looking forward to a new heaven and a new earth, the home of righteousness.   *See also* **Rev** 21:1,4–5   *See also* redemption, in New Testament; regeneration.

---

creation, origin

The free act of God based on his own wisdom and power, forming the whole natural order by his word.

God is Creator of the universe and everything in it

Ne 9:6 "You alone are the LORD. You made the heavens, even the highest heavens, and all their starry host, the earth and all that is on it, the seas and all that is in them . . ."   *See also* **Ge** 1:1; 2:1; **Ps** 24:1–2; **Pr** 8:22–31; **Ecc** 3:11; 11:5; **Isa** 66:1–2; **Jer** 10:16; 51:19; **Jn** 1:3; **Ac** 4:24; 7:50; 14:15; 17:24

Light and darkness

Ge 1:3–5 And God said, "Let there be light," and there was light . . . God called the light "day", and the darkness he called "night" . . .   *See also* **Isa** 45:7

The heavens

Ps 136:5 who by his understanding made the heavens . . .   *See also* **Ge** 1:6–8; **Ps** 33:6; 96:5; **Am** 5:8; **Rev** 14:7

The land

Ge 1:9–10 God said, "Let the water under the sky be gathered to one place, and let dry ground appear." And it was so. God called the dry ground "land" . . .   *See also* **Ps** 95:5; 102:25; 104:5–6; **Ge** 1:14; **Ex** 20:11; **Ps** 74:17; 118:24

The sea and sea creatures

Ps 95:5 The sea is his, for he made it . . . *See also* **Ge** 1:20–22

Birds

Ge 1:20–22 . . . God said, ". . . let birds fly

above the earth across the expanse of the sky." . . .

Land animals

Ge 1:24–25 . . . God said, "Let the land produce living creatures according to their kinds: livestock, creatures that move along the ground, and wild animals, each according to its kind." And it was so . . . *See also* **Job 40:15**

The human race

Ge 1:26–27 Then God said, "Let us make human beings in our image, in our likeness . . ." So God created human beings in his own image, in the image of God he created them; male and female he created them. *See also* **Ge** 2:7,21–22; 5:1–2; **Dt** 32:6; **Ps** 100:3; 139:14; **Pr** 14:31; 17:5; 22:2; **Ecc** 12:1,7

The role of Jesus Christ in creation

Jn 1:3 Through him [Christ] all things were made; without him nothing was made that has been made. *See also* **Jn** 1:10; **1Co** 8:6; **Col** 1:16; **Heb** 1:2

The role of the Spirit in creation

Job 33:4 "The Spirit of God has made me; the breath of the Almighty gives me life." *See also* **Ge** 1:2; **Ps** 104:30; **Isa** 40:12–13

The creation of the world

Ge 1:1 In the beginning God created the heavens and the earth.

Heb 11:3 By faith we understand that the universe was formed at God's command, so that what is seen was not made out of what was visible. *See also* **Ps** 33:9; 148:5; **Ro** 4:17

The original creation was complete and perfect

Its completion

Ge 2:1 Thus the heavens and the earth were completed in all their vast array. *See also* **Ge** 2:2–3; **Ex** 20:11; **Isa** 48:12–13; **Heb** 4:3

Its perfection

Ge 1:31 God saw all that he had made, and it was very good . . . *See also* **Ge** 1:10,12,18,21,25; **Ecc** 7:29; **Isa** 45:18; **1Ti** 4:4

The witness of creation

Creation should cause people to worship God

Rev 4:11 "You are worthy, our Lord and God, to receive glory and honour and power, for you created all things, and by your will they were created and have their being." *See also* **Ne** 9:6; **Ps** 19:1–4; 95:6; 148:5,13; **Ro** 1:20

Sinners refuse the witness of creation

Ro 1:18–20 The wrath of God is being revealed from heaven against all the godlessness and wickedness of those who suppress the truth by their wickedness, since what may be known about God is plain to them, because God has made it plain to them. For since the creation of the world God's invisible qualities—his eternal power and divine nature—have been clearly seen, being understood from what has been made, so that they are without excuse.

Believers receive the witness of creation by faith

Heb 11:3 By faith we understand that the universe was formed at God's command, so that what is seen was not made out of what was visible. *See also* **Ge** 6:6 *See also human race, and creation; life; world, God's creation.*

---

creation, renewal

God's creation, spoilt by sin, will one day be completely renewed. The old order will pass away and a new everlasting order established.

The renewal of creation

The passing away of the old order

2Pe 3:10–12 But the day of the Lord will come like a thief. The heavens will disappear with a roar; the elements will be destroyed by fire, and the earth and everything in it will be laid bare. Since everything will be destroyed in this way, what kind of people ought you to be? You ought to live holy and godly lives as you look forward to the day of God and speed its coming. That day will bring about the destruction of the heavens by fire, and the elements will melt in the heat. *See also* **Ps** 102:25–26; **Isa** 34:4; 51:6; **Mt** 5:18; 24:35; **Rev** 6:14; 21:4

The expectancy of nature

Ro 8:19–22 The creation waits in eager

expectation for the children of God to be revealed. For the creation was subjected to frustration, not by its own choice, but by the will of the one who subjected it, in hope that the creation itself will be liberated from its bondage to decay and brought into the glorious freedom of the children of God. We know that the whole creation has been groaning as in the pains of childbirth right up to the present time.   *See also* **Ge** 3:17-19; 5:29

Jesus Christ's destruction of all his enemies
1Co 15:24-28 Then the end will come, when he [Christ] hands over the kingdom to God the Father after he has destroyed all dominion, authority and power. For he must reign until he has put all his enemies under his feet. The last enemy to be destroyed is death. For he "has put everything under his feet". Now when it says that "everything" has been put under him, it is clear that this does not include God himself, who put everything under Christ. When he has done this, then the Son himself will be made subject to him who put everything under him, so that God may be all in all.   *See also* **Ps** 110:1; **Ac** 2:34-35; **Heb** 1:13; 10:13

The new heavens and new earth
Rev 21:1-2 Then I [John] saw a new heaven and a new earth, for the first heaven and the first earth had passed away, and there was no longer any sea. I saw the Holy City, the new Jerusalem, coming down out of heaven from God, prepared as a bride beautifully dressed for her husband.   *See also* **Isa** 65:17; 66:22; **Ac** 3:21; **Heb** 11:10,16; 12:22; **2Pe** 3:13; **Rev** 3:12; 21:3-5,10

The purity of the new creation
Rev 21:27 Nothing impure will ever enter it [the heavenly city], nor will anyone who does what is shameful or deceitful, but only those whose names are written in the Lamb's book of life.   *See also* **Ps** 37:20; **Isa** 52:1; **Joel** 3:17; **Rev** 20:10; 22:14-15

The creation of the new humanity
The new birth
2Co 5:17 Therefore, if anyone is in Christ, there is a new creation: the old has gone, the new has

come!   *See also* **Jn** 3:3,5-8; **Ro** 6:4; **Gal** 6:15; **Eph** 2:15; **Tit** 3:5

Renewal in God's image
Col 3:10 . . . put on the new self, which is being renewed in knowledge in the image of its Creator.   *See also* **Eph** 4:24

A new heart and a new spirit
Eze 36:26 "'I [the LORD] will give you a new heart and put a new spirit in you; I will remove from you your heart of stone and give you a heart of flesh.'"   *See also* **Ps** 51:10; **Jer** 31:33; **Eze** 11:19; 18:31; **2Co** 4:16; **Col** 3:1

A new mind
Eph 4:23 . . . be made new in the attitude of your minds;   *See also* **Ro** 12:1-2

A new song
Rev 5:9-10 . . . they [the four living creatures and the 24 elders] sang a new song: "You [the Lamb] are worthy to take the scroll and to open its seals, because you were slain, and with your blood you purchased for God members of every tribe and language and people and nation. You have made them to be a kingdom and priests to serve our God, and they will reign on the earth."   *See also* **Ps** 33:3; 40:3; 144:9; 149:1; **Isa** 42:10; **Rev** 14:3; 15:3-4

The future glorification of humanity
The desire for a new body
Ro 8:23-25 . . . we ourselves, who have the firstfruits of the Spirit, groan inwardly as we wait eagerly for our adoption, the redemption of our bodies. For in this hope we were saved. But hope that is seen is no hope at all. Who hopes for what one already has? But if we hope for what we do not yet have, we wait for it patiently. *See also* **Ro** 8:17-18; **2Co** 5:1-5

The resurrection of a new body
Ro 8:11 And if the Spirit of him who raised Jesus from the dead is living in you, he who raised Christ from the dead will also give life to your mortal bodies through his Spirit, who lives in you.   *See also* **Job** 19:25-27; **Da** 12:2-3; **Jn** 5:28-29; **Ac** 24:15

The nature of the resurrection body
1Co 15:42-54 . . . The body that is sown is perishable, it is raised imperishable; it is sown in

dishonour, it is raised in glory; it is sown in weakness, it is raised in power; it is sown a natural body, it is raised a spiritual body. If there is a natural body, there is also a spiritual body . . .   *See also* **Php** 3:21

The absence of sorrow and pain
Rev 21:4 "He [God] will wipe every tear from their eyes. There will be no more death or mourning or crying or pain, for the old order of things has passed away."   *See also* **Isa** 25:7–8; 35:10; 51:11; 60:20; 65:19; **Rev** 7:17

A new name
Isa 56:5 ". . . I will give them an everlasting name that will not be cut off."   *See also* **Isa** 62:2; 65:15; **Rev** 2:17; 3:12

A new home
Jn 14:2 "In my Father's house are many rooms; if it were not so, I [Jesus] would have told you. I am going there to prepare a place for you."   *See also* **2Co** 5:1

God will dwell with his people
Rev 21:3 And I [John] heard a loud voice from the throne saying, "Now the dwelling of God is with human beings, and he will live with them. They will be his people, and God himself will be with them and be their God.   *See also* **Eze** 48:35; **Zec** 2:10   *See also heaven; hope; redemption; regeneration; resurrection.*

---

cross

An instrument of execution, used especially by the Roman authorities for putting criminals to death. The sufferings of Jesus Christ on the cross, foreshadowed in the OT, are related in the NT gospel accounts. Scripture sees the death of Christ as central to the Christian faith. Through the cross and resurrection of Christ, God achieved the redemption of believers.

---

cross, accounts of

Each of the four Gospels provides a detailed account of Jesus Christ's death on the cross.

The way to the cross
Simon is compelled to carry the cross
Mk 15:21 A certain man from Cyrene, Simon, the father of Alexander and Rufus, was passing by on his way in from the country, and they forced him to carry the cross. pp Mt 27:32 pp Lk 23:26
Women follow the cross and Jesus Christ is offered relief from pain
Lk 23:27–31 A large number of people followed him, including women who mourned and wailed for him . . .   *See also* **Mt** 27:34 pp **Mk** 15:23

The crucifixion of Jesus Christ
Jesus Christ crucified between two criminals
Mk 15:22–27 They brought Jesus to the place called Golgotha (which means The Place of the Skull) . . . And they crucified him . . . They crucified two robbers with him, one on his right and one on his left. pp Mt 27:33–38 pp Lk 23:32–43
The humiliation of Jesus Christ on the cross
Mk 15:29–32 Those who passed by hurled insults at him, shaking their heads and saying, "So! You who are going to destroy the temple and build it in three days, come down from the cross and save yourself!" . . . pp Mt 27:39–44 pp Lk 23:35–39
The words of Jesus Christ on the cross
Jn 19:30 . . . "It is finished." . . .   *See also* **Mt** 27:46 pp **Mk** 15:34; **Mt** 27:50; **Mk** 15:37; **Lk** 23:28–31,34,43,46; **Jn** 19:26–28
The death of Jesus Christ
Mk 15:33–37 . . . And at the ninth hour Jesus cried out in a loud voice . . . With a loud cry, Jesus breathed his last. pp Mt 27:45–50 pp Lk 23:44–46   *See also* **Jn** 19:28–35

Supernatural events at the cross
Mk 15:38 The curtain of the temple was torn in two from top to bottom. pp Mt 27:51–53 pp Lk 23:45

Witnesses of the crucifixion
Mk 15:39–41 And when the centurion, who stood there in front of Jesus, heard his cry and saw how he died, he said, "Surely this man was the Son of God!" . . . pp Mt 27:54–56 pp Lk 23:47–49   *See also resurrection.*

cross, centrality

The death of Jesus Christ on the cross is central to the Christian faith. Through the cross and resurrection of Christ, God achieved the redemption of believers and brought hope to the world.

The gospel as the "message of the cross"

1Co 2:2 For I resolved to know nothing while I was with you except Jesus Christ and him crucified.   *See also* **1Co** 1:17–18,23; **Gal** 3:1

The cross redeems from the curse of the law

Gal 3:13 Christ redeemed us from the curse of the law by becoming a curse for us, for it is written: "Cursed is everyone who is hung on a tree."   *See also* **Ro** 6:14; 7:4; **2Co** 5:21; **Gal** 2:19–21; **Eph** 1:7; 2:13–16; **Col** 2:13–14; **Tit** 2:14; **1Pe** 1:18–19

The cross brings reconciliation and justification

Ro 4:25 He [Jesus the Lord] was delivered over to death for our sins and was raised to life for our justification.

Ro 5:10 For if, when we were God's enemies, we were reconciled to him through the death of his Son, how much more, having been reconciled, shall we be saved through his life!   *See also* **Ro** 5:8–9; **1Co** 15:3–4; **Eph** 2:16; **Col** 1:20–22

The cross destroys the power of Satan

Col 2:13–15 . . . He [Christ] forgave us all our sins, having cancelled the written code, with its regulations, that was against us and that stood opposed to us; he took it away, nailing it to the cross. And having disarmed the powers and authorities, he made a public spectacle of them, triumphing over them by the cross.   *See also* **Jn** 12:31; 14:30; **Gal** 1:4; **Heb** 2:14–15; **1Pe** 3:21–22

The cross as a stumbling-block or offence

1Co 1:22–24 Jews demand miraculous signs and Greeks look for wisdom, but we preach Christ crucified: a stumbling-block to Jews and foolishness to Gentiles, but to those whom God has called, both Jews and Greeks, Christ the power of God and the wisdom of God.   *See also* **Gal** 5:11; 6:12

The cross unites believers with Jesus Christ

Ro 6:4–7 . . . If we [Christians] have been united with him like this in his death, we will certainly also be united with him in his resurrection. For we know that our old self was crucified with him so that the body of sin might be done away with, that we should no longer be slaves to sin . . .   *See also* **Ro** 6:2; 8:36; **1Co** 15:30–31; **2Co** 4:10–12; 5:14–15; **Gal** 2:20; **Eph** 2:14–16; **Col** 2:20; 3:1–3; **2Ti** 2:11

The cross as a symbol of discipleship

Mt 16:24 Then Jesus said to his disciples, "Those who would come after me must deny themselves and take up their cross and follow me." pp Mk 8:34 pp Lk 9:23–24

Php 2:5–8 Your attitude should be the same as that of Christ Jesus: Who, being in very nature God, did not consider equality with God something to be grasped, but made himself nothing, taking the very nature of a servant, being made in human likeness. And being found in appearance as a human being, he humbled himself and became obedient to death—even death on a cross! *See also* **Mt** 10:38; **Lk** 14:27; **Jn** 12:23–25; **Ro** 8:13; **Gal** 5:24; 6:14; **Eph** 5:25–26; **Col** 3:5; **1Pe** 2:21,24   *See also* atonement; blood, of Jesus Christ; justification; propitiation; reconciliation; redemption; salvation.

cross, predictions

The death of Jesus Christ fulfils OT predictions and was clearly anticipated in his teaching.

The cross foreshadowed in the OT

Ps 22:1 My God, my God, why have you forsaken me? Why are you so far from saving

me, so far from the words of my groaning?
See also **Ge** 3:15; **Ps** 22:6–7,16–18; 31:5; 69:21;
Isa 52:12–13; **Zec** 12:10; 13:7

Jesus Christ predicts his death on the cross
Jesus Christ's first announcement of his death
Mt 16:21 From that time on Jesus began to
explain to his disciples that he must go to
Jerusalem and suffer many things at the hands of
the elders, chief priests and teachers of the law,
and that he must be killed and on the third day
be raised to life. pp **Mk** 8:31 pp **Lk** 9:22
Jesus Christ's second announcement of his death
Mt 17:22–23 . . . he [Jesus] said to them
[the disciples], "The Son of Man is going to be
betrayed into human hands. People will kill him,
and on the third day he will be raised to
life." . . .   *See also* **Mk** 9:31
Jesus Christ's third announcement of his death
Mt 20:18–19 "We [Jesus and his disciples]
are going up to Jerusalem, and the Son of Man
will be betrayed to the chief priests and the
teachers of the law. They will condemn him to
death and will turn him over to the Gentiles to be
mocked and flogged and crucified. On the third
day he will be raised to life!" pp **Mk** 10:33–34
pp **Lk** 18:31–33

Other allusions to the cross
In the teaching of Jesus Christ
Mt 26:31 . . . " 'I [the Lord Almighty] will
strike the shepherd, and the sheep of the flock
will be scattered.' "   *See also* **Mt** 20:22 pp **Mk**
10:38; **Mt** 26:2; **Mk** 2:19–20; 10:45; **Lk** 9:44;
22:42
"lifted up" is used in John's Gospel as a reference to
the crucifixion: **Jn** 3:14; 8:28; 12:32–33
Jn 18:11
In history
Mt 17:9–13 ". . . In the same way the Son
of Man is going to suffer at their hands." . . .
In the experience of Jesus Christ
Mt 26:12 "When she poured this perfume on
my body, she did it to prepare me for burial." pp
Mk 14:8

In the Lord's Supper
Mt 26:26–28 While they [the disciples] were
eating, Jesus took bread, gave thanks and broke
it, and gave it to his disciples, saying, "Take and
eat; this is my body." Then he took the cup,
gave thanks and offered it to them, saying,
"Drink from it, all of you. This is my blood of
the covenant, which is poured out for many for
the forgiveness of sins." pp **Mk** 14:22–25 pp **Lk**
22:19–20

God's perfect timing for Jesus Christ's death on the cross
Jn 2:4 "Dear woman, [Jesus' mother] why do
you involve me?" Jesus replied. "My time has
not yet come."   *See also* **Jn** 7:6,8,30; 8:20;
13:1; 17:1

The curse of the cross
Dt 21:22–23 If anyone guilty of a capital
offence is put to death and the body is hung on
a tree, you must not leave the body on the tree
overnight. Be sure to bury it that same day,
because anyone who is hung on a tree is under
God's curse. You must not desecrate the land the
LORD your God is giving you as an inheritance.
See also **Ac** 5:30; **Gal** 3:10–13; **1Pe** 2:24   *See
also forgiveness; Lord's Supper; prophecy, concerning
Jesus Christ.*

election
Scripture affirms that God chooses a people as his
own, not on account of their numerical strength or
moral merits, but on account of his love for them.
Election is on the basis of divine grace, not
human merit.

election, privileges
God chose a people to enjoy a unique relationship
with him which entailed the privilege of belonging
to him, sharing in all his inheritance, serving him,
praising him and proclaiming him.

God elected Israel out of all the nations of the world
Dt 7:6 For you [Israel] are a people holy to the

LORD your God. The LORD your God has chosen you out of all the peoples on the face of the earth to be his people, his treasured possession.   *See also* **Dt** 14:1–2; **1Ki** 3:8; **1Ch** 16:13; **Ps** 105:6,43; 135:4; **Isa** 41:8–9; **Eze** 20:5–6

The election of the nation is anticipated in the election of the patriarchs
Dt 4:37–38 Because he [the LORD] loved your ancestors and chose their descendants after them, he brought you out of Egypt by his Presence and his great strength, to drive out before you nations greater and stronger than you and to bring you into their land to give it to you for your inheritance, as it is today.   *See also* **Dt** 10:15; **Ac** 13:17–19

Election was not based on merit
Dt 7:7–8 The LORD did not set his affection on you [Israel] and choose you because you were more numerous than other peoples, for you were the fewest of all peoples. But it was because the LORD loved you and kept the oath he swore to your ancestors that he brought you out with a mighty hand and redeemed you from the land of slavery, from the power of Pharaoh king of Egypt.   *See also* **Dt** 9:4–6; **Eze** 16:1–14

God conferred privileges on the people he elected
Election meant that God dwelled in their midst
2Ch 6:6 " '. . . I [the LORD] have chosen Jerusalem for my Name to be there, and I have chosen David to rule my people Israel.' "   *See also* **1Ki** 14:21 pp 2Ch 12:13; **2Ki** 21:7 pp 2Ch 33:7; **2Ch** 6:34–35; 7:12,16; **Ne** 1:9; **Ps** 132:13
Election meant that God showed divine favour
Ps 33:12 Blessed is the nation whose God is the LORD, the people he chose for his inheritance.   *See also* **Ps** 65:4; 106:4–5; **Isa** 14:1; 43:1,20; 44:1–5; 45:4; **Zec** 1:17

God gave responsibilities to the people he elected
Election calls for obedient and holy living
Lev 20:26 " 'You [Israel] are to be holy to me because I, the LORD, am holy, and I have set you

apart from the nations to be my own.' "   *See also* **Ex** 19:5–6
Election means increased accountability
Am 3:2 "You [Israel] only have I [the LORD] chosen of all the families of the earth; therefore I will punish you for all your sins."   *See also* **2Ki** 23:26

God's choice of Israel does not automatically imply election to salvation
Ro 9:6–8 It is not as though God's word had failed. For not all who are descended from Israel are Israel. Nor because they are his descendants are they all Abraham's children. On the contrary, "It is through Isaac that your offspring will be reckoned." In other words, it is not the natural children who are God's children, but it is the children of the promise who are regarded as Abraham's offspring.   *See also* **Ro** 11:7–8   *See also adoption; church; covenant; Israel, people of God.*

---

election, responsibilities

God's election lays responsibilities upon those who have been chosen. Election to salvation has the natural consequence of election to service.

Election to leadership
Jer 1:5 "Before I formed you [Jeremiah] in the womb I knew you, before you were born I set you apart; I appointed you as a prophet to the nations."   *See also* **Jdg** 13:2–5; **Ps** 105:26; 106:23

Election to religious service
Dt 21:5 The priests, the sons of Levi, shall step forward, for the LORD your God has chosen them to minister and to pronounce blessings in the name of the LORD and to decide all cases of dispute and assault.   *See also* **Dt** 18:3–5; **1Sa** 2:27–28; **1Ch** 15:2; **2Ch** 29:11

Election to build the house of God
Election to build the tabernacle
Ex 31:2–5 "See I [the LORD] have chosen Bezalel son of Uri, the son of Hur, of the tribe of Judah, and I have filled him with the Spirit of

God, with skill, ability and knowledge in all kinds of crafts . . ."   *See also* **Ex** 35:30–33; 31:6–11; 35:34–36:2

Election to build the temple
1Ch 28:6 "He [the Lord] said to me [David], 'Solomon your son is the one who will build my house and my courts, for I have chosen him to be my son, and I will be his father.'"   *See also* **1Ch** 28:10; 29:1

Election of foreign kings as instruments of discipline
Isa 45:1 "This is what the Lord says to his anointed, to Cyrus, whose right hand I take hold of to subdue nations before him and to strip kings of their armour, to open doors before him so that gates will not be shut:"
Cyrus: **Isa** 44:28; 48:14–15
The king of Assyria: **Isa** 7:17,20
Nebuchadnezzar: **Jer** 25:9; 27:6; 43:10

Election to kingship
1Ch 28:4 "Yet the Lord, the God of Israel, chose me [David] from my whole family to be king over Israel for ever. He chose Judah as leader, and from the house of Judah he chose my family, and from my father's sons he was pleased to make me king over all Israel."
David: **1Sa** 16:1–13; **Ps** 78:70–71; 89:3–4
1Sa 10:20–24; **1Ch** 28:5–7

Election of the Messiah
The OT predicts the coming of a "chosen one"
Isa 42:1–7 "Here is my servant, whom I uphold, my chosen one in whom I delight; I will put my Spirit on him and he will bring justice to the nations . . ."   *See also* **Isa** 9:6–7; 49:5–7
The NT identifies Jesus Christ as God's chosen Messiah
Lk 9:35 A voice came from the cloud, saying, "This is my Son, whom I have chosen; listen to him." pp **Mt** 3:16–17   *See also* **Mt** 12:15–21; **Isa** 42:1–4; **1Pe** 1:18–21; 2:4–6

Election to apostleship
Lk 6:13–16 When morning came, he [Jesus] called his disciples to him and chose twelve of

them, whom he also designated apostles . . .
pp **Mk** 3:14–19   *See also* **Jn** 6:70; 13:18; 15:16,19; **Ac** 1:2,21–26; 9:15–16; 22:14–15; **Ro** 1:1; **1Co** 1:1

---

election, to salvation
God chooses to bring individuals to salvation through faith in Jesus Christ.

Election is part of God's eternal decree
Election is from eternity
Eph 1:4 For he [God] chose us [believers] in him [Christ] before the creation of the world to be holy and blameless in his sight . . .   *See also* **2Th** 2:13; **2Ti** 1:9
Election is God's sovereign prerogative
Ro 9:15–24 For he says to Moses, "I will have mercy on whom I have mercy, and I will have compassion on whom I have compassion." . . .

Ro 11:1–6 I ask then: Did God reject his people? By no means! I am an Israelite myself, a descendant of Abraham, from the tribe of Benjamin. God did not reject his people, whom he foreknew. Don't you know what the Scripture says in the passage about Elijah—how he appealed to God against Israel: "Lord, they have killed your prophets and torn down your altars; I am the only one left, and they are trying to kill me"? And what was God's answer to him? "I have reserved for myself seven thousand who have not bowed the knee to Baal." So too, at the present time there is a remnant chosen by grace. And if by grace, then it is no longer by works; if it were, grace would no longer be grace.   *See also* **Ex** 33:19; **Isa** 65:1; **Jer** 18:1–12; **Jn** 15:16; 17:6; **Ro** 9:10–13; **Eph** 2:10
God's election places individuals within the covenant of grace
Ne 9:7–8 "You are the Lord God, who chose Abram and brought him out of Ur of the Chaldeans and named him Abraham. You found his heart faithful to you, and you made a covenant with him . . ."   *See also* **Ge** 15:7–8,18–21; 18:19; **Gal** 3:29

Election is not on the basis of merit
1Co 1:26–31 . . . But God chose the foolish things of the world to shame the wise; God chose the weak things of the world to shame the strong. He chose the lowly things of this world and the despised things—and the things that are not—to nullify the things that are, so that no-one may boast before him . . . *See also* **Dt** 7:7–8; 9:4–6; **Jas** 2:5

God's election of his people is the foundation of his saving action
Election does not suspend God's use of the means of salvation
2Th 2:13–14 . . . "God chose you [Thessalonian Christians] . . . to be saved through the sanctifying work of the Spirit and through belief in the truth. He called you to this through our gospel, that you might share in the glory of our Lord Jesus Christ. *See also* **Mt** 1:21; **Eph** 2:8–10; **Jas** 1:18; **1Pe** 1:2

Election works in tandem with the call of the gospel
Mt 22:14 "For many are invited, but few are chosen." *See also* **Ro** 8:29–30

Election is evidenced through a positive response to the gospel
1Th 1:4–5 For we [Paul, Silas and Timothy] know, brothers and sisters loved by God, that he has chosen you, because our gospel came to you not simply with words, but also with power, with the Holy Spirit and with deep conviction . . . *See also* **Jn** 6:37–40

Election is a motive for praise
Ro 11:28–36 As far as the gospel is concerned, they [Israel] are enemies on your account; but as far as election is concerned, they are loved on account of the patriarchs, for God's gifts and his call are irrevocable. Just as you who were at one time disobedient to God have now received mercy as a result of their disobedience, so they too have now become disobedient in order that they too may now receive mercy as a result of God's mercy to you. For God has bound everyone over to disobedience so that he may have mercy on them all. Oh, the depth of the riches of the wisdom and knowledge of God! How unsearchable his judgments, and his paths beyond tracing out! "Who has known the mind of the Lord? Or who has been his counsellor?" "Who has ever given to God, that God should repay the gift?" For from him and through him and to him are all things. To him be the glory for ever! Amen.

Eph 1:3–14 Praise be to the God and Father of our Lord Jesus Christ, who has blessed us in the heavenly realms with every spiritual blessing in Christ. For he chose us in him before the creation of the world to be holy and blameless in his sight. In love he predestined us to be adopted as his children through Jesus Christ, in accordance with his pleasure and will—to the praise of his glorious grace, which he has freely given us in the One he loves . . . *See also* **1Th** 1:2–4

Election is a source of practical comfort
Ro 8:31–39 . . . Who will bring any charge against those whom God has chosen? It is God who justifies . . . *See also* **Jn** 10:27–29; 17:2

Election is an incentive for righteous behaviour
Col 3:12–14 Therefore, as God's chosen people, holy and dearly loved, clothe yourselves with compassion, kindness, humility, gentleness and patience. Bear with each other and forgive whatever grievances you may have against one another. Forgive as the Lord forgave you. And over all these virtues put on love, which binds them all together in perfect unity. *See also* **Jn** 15:16–17; **Php** 2:12–13; **2Th** 2:13–15; **2Pe** 1:3–11

Election is a stimulus to the preaching of the gospel
2Ti 2:10 Therefore I endure everything for the sake of the elect, that they too may obtain the salvation that is in Christ Jesus, with eternal glory. *See also assurance; evangelism; grace, and salvation; predestination.*

evangelism

The proclamation of the good news of Jesus Christ, which arises naturally from believers' love for God and appreciation of all that God has done for them. The NT stresses the importance of evangelism, and provides guidance as to how it should be carried out.

evangelism, kinds of

Scripture recognises that evangelism takes place in a variety of contexts, and offers models for evangelism in today's church.

Public evangelism
Preaching in synagogues
Ac 14:1 At Iconium Paul and Barnabas went as usual into the Jewish synagogue. There they spoke so effectively that a great number of Jews and Gentiles believed.
In Pisidian Antioch: **Ac** 13:14–16,42–44 **Ac** 17:2,10,17; 18:4; 19:8
Preaching in recognised meeting-places
Ac 17:19–23 . . . Paul then stood up in the meeting of the Areopagus and said: "People of Athens! I see that in every way you are very religious . . ."   *See also* **Ac** 5:25; 10:27–28; 16:13; 19:9
Making a public defence to accusers
Ac 21:37–22:1 . . . Paul answered, "I am a Jew, from Tarsus in Cilicia, a citizen of no ordinary city. Please let me speak to the people." . . .   *See also* **Ac** 4:7–12; 7:1–2; 24:10; 26:1

Personal evangelism
Giving personal testimony
1Jn 1:1–3 . . . We proclaim to you what we have seen and heard, so that you also may have fellowship with us. And our fellowship is with the Father and with his Son, Jesus Christ.   *See also* **Mk** 5:19; **Jn** 4:39; **Ac** 26:9–18; **1Co** 7:16; **1Pe** 3:1–2
Evangelism in homes
Ac 10:24–25 The following day he [Peter] arrived in Caesarea. Cornelius was expecting them and had called together his relatives and close friends. As Peter entered the house, Cornelius met him and fell at his feet in reverence.
Believers invite others into their homes: **Lk** 5:29; **Ac** 18:26; 28:30–31
Believers visit the homes of others: **Ac** 9:17 pp Ac 22:12; **Ac** 16:32–34

Evangelism in strategic areas
Going to major centres Ac 16:12; 17:1,15; 18:1,19
Rome: **Ac** 23:11; 28:14
Going into new territories Ro 15:20,23–24; **2Co** 10:15–16

Evangelism among strategic people
Speaking to prominent people
Ac 18:8 Crispus, the synagogue ruler, and his entire household believed in the Lord; and many of the Corinthians who heard him believed and were baptised.   *See also* **Ac** 13:7; 24:24; 25:8–9,11–12; 26:2–3; 28:7–8
Evangelising households
Ac 16:34 The jailer brought them [Paul and Silas] into his house and set a meal before them; he was filled with joy because he had come to believe in God—he and his whole family.   *See also* **Jn** 4:53; **Ac** 11:14; 18:8

Using literature in evangelism
Jn 20:30–31 Jesus did many other miraculous signs in the presence of his disciples, which are not recorded in this book. But these are written that you may believe that Jesus is the Christ, the Son of God, and that by believing you may have life in his name.   *See also* **Lk** 1:1–4; **Ac** 1:1–2

Appealing to Scripture in evangelism
Ac 26:22–23 ". . . I [Paul] stand here and testify to small and great alike. I am saying nothing beyond what the prophets and Moses said would happen . . ."   *See also* **Ac** 8:35; 10:43; 13:22–23; **Ro** 1:2–3; 16:25–26; **1Co** 15:3–4

Signs and wonders in evangelism
Miracles confirm the message
Ac 8:6 When the crowds heard Philip and saw the miraculous signs he did, they all paid close

attention to what he said.   *See also* **Mk**
16:17–20; **Ac** 4:14; 19:10–12; **1Co** 2:4–5; **Heb**
2:3–4

Miracles give opportunity for preaching
Ac 3:9–16 . . . While the beggar held on to
Peter and John, all the people were astonished
and came running to them in the place called
Solomon's Colonnade. When Peter saw this, he
said to them: "People of Israel, why does this
surprise you? Why do you stare at us as if by
our own power or godliness we had made this
man walk? . . ."   *See also* **Ac** 2:5–14;
14:8–11; 16:26–31

Miracles result in people believing
Ac 9:40–42 . . . He [Peter] took her
[Tabitha] by the hand and helped her to her feet.
Then he called the believers and the widows and
presented her to them alive. This became known
all over Joppa, and many people believed in the
Lord.   *See also* **Jn** 7:31; 11:45; **Ac** 9:33–35;
13:10–12

The response to evangelism
Acceptance of the message
Ac 2:37–41 . . . Those who accepted his
[Peter's] message were baptised, and about three
thousand were added to their number that day.
See also **Ac** 4:4; 17:4,34; 19:17–20; **1Th** 2:13

Rejection of the message
Heb 4:2 For we also have had the gospel
preached to us, just as they did; but the message
they heard was of no value to them, because
those who heard did not combine it with faith.
See also **Ro** 10:16; **Ac** 13:50–51; 17:32; 18:6
See also mission.

---

evangelism, motivation

Evangelism arises from a natural response to the
grace of God, a concern for those who have yet
to hear the good news and a desire to be faithful
to the great commission to bring the good news
to the ends of the earth. Evangelism is guided
and directed by the Holy Spirit.

Motives for evangelism
Recognising God's call
2Ti 1:11 And of this gospel I [Paul] was

appointed a herald and an apostle and a
teacher.   *See also* **Isa** 6:8–9; **Jnh** 1:1–2; **Ac**
22:14–15; **2Co** 4:1; **1Ti** 2:7

A divine compulsion
1Co 9:16–17 Yet when I [Paul] preach the
gospel, I cannot boast, for I am compelled to
preach. Woe to me if I do not preach the
gospel! . . .   *See also* **Jer** 20:9; **Am** 3:8; **Ac**
4:20

A God-given responsibility
Eze 3:17–20 ". . . When I [the LORD] say to
the wicked, 'You will surely die,' and you do not
warn them or speak out to dissuade them from
their evil ways in order to save their lives, those
wicked people will die for their sins, and I will
hold you accountable for their blood . . ."   *See
also* **Eze** 33:7–9; **1Co** 3:10–15; **2Co** 5:10–11

A desire to win the lost
Ro 10:1 Brothers and sisters, my [Paul's]
heart's desire and prayer to God for the Israelites
is that they may be saved.

1Co 9:19–23 . . . To the weak I [Paul]
became weak, to win the weak. I have become
all things to all people so that by all possible
means I might save some . . .   *See also* **Ac**
20:19–20; **Ro** 1:14–15; 9:1–3; 11:14; 15:17–20;
2Co 5:20

A recognition of coming judgment
Jude 23 snatch others from the fire and save
them . . .   *See also* **Jas** 5:20; **2Pe** 3:9

Responding to God's grace
2Co 5:14–15 For Christ's love compels us,
because we are convinced that one died for all,
and therefore all died . . .   *See also* **2Co**
5:18–19; **Eph** 3:7; **1Ti** 1:12–16

Confidence in the gospel
Ro 1:16–17 I [Paul] am not ashamed of the
gospel, because it is the power of God for the
salvation of everyone who believes: first for the
Jew, then for the Gentile . . .   *See also* **Isa**
55:10–11; **1Co** 1:17–18; **2Co** 10:4–5; **2Ti** 1:8–9

God directs and guides evangelism
Divine guidance in evangelism
Ac 8:26–29 . . . The Spirit told Philip, "Go to
that chariot and stay near it."

Ac 16:6–10 . . . After Paul had seen the vision, we got ready at once to leave for Macedonia, concluding that God had called us to preach the gospel to them.   *See also* **Ac** 5:19–20; 9:10–11; 10:19–20; 11:12; 13:2; 18:9–11

God opens the door for evangelism

2Co 2:12 Now when I [Paul] went to Troas to preach the gospel of Christ and found that the Lord had opened a door for me,   *See also* **Ac** 14:27; **1Co** 16:9; **Col** 4:3; **Rev** 3:8

Areas of ministry assigned by God

Gal 2:7–9 . . . For God, who was at work in the ministry of Peter as an apostle to the Jews, was also at work in my [Paul's] ministry as an apostle to the Gentiles . . .   *See also* **Ac** 9:15

The Holy Spirit empowers evangelism

Ac 1:8 "But you will receive power when the Holy Spirit comes on you; and you will be my [Jesus'] witnesses in Jerusalem, and in all Judea and Samaria, and to the ends of the earth." *See also* **Mt** 10:19–20 pp **Mk** 13:11 pp **Lk** 12:11–12; **Jn** 15:26–27; **1Th** 1:5

Evangelism as a result of persecution

Ac 8:4–5 Those who had been scattered preached the word wherever they went . . . *See also* **Ac** 11:19–21; 13:50–51; 14:6–7; 18:2

evangelism, nature of

Evangelism focuses on the proclaiming of the good news of the coming of the kingdom of God in Christ, including the forgiveness of sins and the hope of eternal life, through the death and resurrection of Jesus Christ.

Evangelism as the proclamation of good news

Isa 52:7 How beautiful on the mountains are the feet of those who bring good news, who proclaim peace, who bring good tidings, who proclaim salvation, who say to Zion, "Your God reigns!"

Mk 16:15 He [Jesus] said to them [the disciples], "Go into all the world and preach the good news to all creation."   *See also* **2Sa**

18:31; **2Ki** 7:9; **Isa** 40:9; 41:27; **Na** 1:15; **Ac** 14:7,15; **Ro** 10:15; 15:16; **1Ti** 2:7; **2Ti** 1:11

Jesus Christ as the focus of evangelism

The gospel message is revealed by God

Gal 1:11–12 . . . I [Paul] did not receive it [the gospel] from any human source, nor was I taught it; rather, I received it by revelation from Jesus Christ.   *See also* **Ro** 16:25–26; **Gal** 1:15–16; **Eph** 3:3–6

The gospel message centres on Jesus Christ

Mk 1:1 The beginning of the gospel about Jesus Christ, the Son of God.

Eph 3:8 Although I [Paul] am less than the least of all God's people, this grace was given me: to preach to the Gentiles the unsearchable riches of Christ,   *See also* **Lk** 1:19; 2:10; 3:16–18; **Ac** 11:20; **Ro** 1:9; **2Co** 4:4

The announcement of God's kingdom

Ac 28:31 Boldly and without hindrance he [Paul] preached the kingdom of God and taught about the Lord Jesus Christ.   *See also* **Mt** 24:14; **Mk** 1:14–15; **Lk** 4:43; 8:1; 9:2; **Ac** 8:12

God's promises are fulfilled in Jesus Christ

Lk 4:18–19 "The Spirit of the Lord is on me [Jesus], because he has anointed me to preach good news to the poor. He has sent me to proclaim freedom for the prisoners and recovery of sight for the blind, to release the oppressed, to proclaim the year of the Lord's favour."   *See also* **Isa** 61:1–2; **Mt** 11:3–5 pp **Lk** 7:20–22; **Ac** 5:42; 8:35; 9:22; 13:32–33; **Ro** 1:2–4

Jesus Christ's death and resurrection

1Co 15:3–4 For what I [Paul] received I passed on to you as of first importance: that Christ died for our sins according to the Scriptures, that he was buried, that he was raised on the third day according to the Scriptures,   *See also* **Ac** 2:22–24; 3:15; 17:18; **1Co** 15:14; 1:23; **2Ti** 2:8

The announcement of God's salvation

Ro 1:16–17 I [Paul] am not ashamed of the gospel, because it is the power of God for the salvation of everyone who believes: first for the Jew, then for the Gentile . . .   *See also* **Ps** 40:10; 96:2–3 pp **1Ch** 16:23–24; **1Co** 1:21; 15:1–2; **Eph** 1:13; **2Th** 2:13–14

The call to repentance for the forgiveness of sins

Lk 24:47 "and repentance and forgiveness of sins will be preached in his [Jesus'] name to all nations, beginning at Jerusalem." *See also* **Mt** 4:17; 12:41 pp Lk 11:32; **Mk** 1:4 pp Mt 3:2 pp Lk 3:3; **Ac** 2:38

The announcement of peace with God

Ac 10:36 "You know the message God sent to the people of Israel, telling the good news of peace through Jesus Christ, who is Lord of all." *See also* **Eph** 2:17–18; 6:15

Evangelism and miracles

Mt 4:23 Jesus went throughout Galilee, teaching in their synagogues, preaching the good news of the kingdom, and healing every disease and sickness among the people.

1Co 2:4–5 My [Paul's] message and my preaching were not with wise and persuasive words, but with a demonstration of the Spirit's power, so that your faith might not rest on human wisdom, but on God's power. *See also* **Mt** 9:35; 10:7–8; **Lk** 9:6; 11:20; **Ro** 15:18–19; **1Th** 1:5; **Heb** 2:3–4 *See also church; purpose; forgiveness; gospel; transmission; kingdom of God; peace; preachers and preaching; revelation; salvation.*

---

evil

The presence of corruption, malevolence and depravity in the world, opposed to God's nature and will. Scripture stresses that evil is a force in its own right, rather than the mere absence of good, and describes its origins and the manner in which God deals with its continuing presence and power in his world.

---

evil, origins of

Although Scripture does not reveal the ultimate origin of evil, it identifies a number of intermediate sources.

Satan as a source of evil

Ge 3:1 Now the serpent was more crafty than any of the wild animals the Lord God had made. He said to the woman, "Did God really say, 'You

must not eat from any tree in the garden'?"

Mt 4:1 Then Jesus was led by the Spirit into the desert to be tempted by the devil. pp Mk 1:13 pp Lk 4:2

Jn 8:44 [Jesus said] "You belong to your father, the devil, and you want to carry out your father's desire. He was a murderer from the beginning, not holding to the truth, for there is no truth in him. When he lies, he speaks his native language, for he is a liar and the father of lies."

1Jn 3:8 The one who does what is sinful is of the devil, because the devil has been sinning from the beginning. The reason the Son of God appeared was to destroy the devil's work.

Rev 12:9 The great dragon was hurled down—that ancient serpent called the devil, or Satan, who leads the whole world astray. He was hurled to the earth, and his angels with him. *See also* **1Ch** 21:1; **Job** 1:11; 2:5; **Mt** 5:37; 6:13; 13:38–39; **Lk** 13:16; **Jn** 13:2; 17:15; **Ac** 5:3; **2Co** 4:4; 12:7; **Eph** 2:2; 6:11; **1Th** 2:18–; **1Pe** 5:8; **1Jn** 3:12; 5:19; **Rev** 2:10; 20:2

Other evil powers

Lk 9:39 "A spirit seizes him and he suddenly screams; it throws him into convulsions so that he foams at the mouth. It scarcely ever leaves him and is destroying him." pp Mk 9:17–18

Eph 6:12 For our struggle is not against flesh and blood, but against the rulers, against the authorities, against the powers of this dark world and against the spiritual forces of evil in the heavenly realms.

1Ti 4:1 The Spirit clearly says that in later times some will abandon the faith and follow deceiving spirits and things taught by demons. *See also* **Jdg** 9:23; **1Sa** 16:14; 18:10–11; 19:9–10; **Mt** 12:45 pp Lk 11:26; **Rev** 12:7; 16:13–14

Fallen human nature as a source of evil

Ge 6:5 The Lord saw how great the wickedness of the human race had become on the earth, and that every inclination of the thoughts of their hearts was only evil all the time.

Mt 15:19 [Jesus said] "For out of the heart come evil thoughts, murder, adultery, sexual immorality, theft, false testimony, slander." pp Mk 7:21–22

Jas 1:13–14 When tempted, no-one should say, "God is tempting me." For God cannot be tempted by evil, nor does he tempt anyone; but each of you is tempted when, by your own evil desire, you are dragged away and enticed.   *See also* **Ge** 8:21; **Pr** 6:18; **Ecc** 8:11; 9:3; **Isa** 59:7; **Jer** 4:14; 17:9; 18:12

The hypocrisy of the Pharisees and teachers of the law: **Mt** 23:25 pp **Lk** 11:39; **Mt** 23:27–28

Ro 1:24; 7:14–23; **1Ti** 6:10; **Jas** 3:6; 4:1

Physical evil is a consequence of moral evil

Ge 3:17 To Adam he [God] said, "Because you listened to your wife and ate from the tree about which I commanded you, 'You must not eat of it,' Cursed is the ground because of you; through painful toil you will eat of it all the days of your life."

Ro 5:12 Therefore, just as sin entered the world through one man, and death through sin, and in this way death came to all people, because all sinned—   *See also* **Dt** 28:20–24,58–59; **Ps** 90:8–9; **Pr** 14:30; **Mal** 4:6; **Ro** 6:23; 8:19–21; **Rev** 16:1,5–6   *See also* Satan; sin.

---

evil, responses to

Scripture outlines several ways in which believers should respond to evil.

Evil is to be avoided

Ps 1:1 Blessed are those who do not walk in the counsel of the wicked or stand in the way of sinners or sit in the seat of mockers.

Pr 4:14 Do not set foot on the path of the wicked or walk in the way of evildoers.

1Th 5:22 Avoid every kind of evil.   *See also* **Job** 28:28; **Ps** 119:115; **Pr** 4:27; 14:16; **Isa** 52:11; **Ac** 2:40; **Ro** 12:9; 13:14

Evil likened to yeast: **1Co** 5:6–7; **Gal** 5:9

2Co 6:14–18; **Eph** 4:27; 5:3,6–7; **2Th** 3:6; **1Pe** 3:11; **Ps** 34:14

Evil is to be hated

Pr 8:13 "To fear the Lord is to hate evil; I hate pride and arrogance, evil behaviour and perverse speech."   *See also* **Ps** 97:10; **Am** 5:15; **Jn** 3:20; **Ro** 12:9

Evil is to be rebuked

Mt 16:23 Jesus turned and said to Peter, "Get behind me, Satan! You are a stumbling-block to me; you do not have in mind the concerns of God, but human concerns." pp Mk 8:33

2Ti 4:2 Preach the Word; be prepared in season and out of season; correct, rebuke and encourage—with great patience and careful instruction.   *See also* **1Sa** 2:29; 13:13; 15:22; **2Sa** 12:9; **1Ki** 18:18; **2Ch** 16:9; 24:20; 26:18; **Ezr** 10:10; **Ps** 141:5; **Da** 4:27; 5:22; **Mt** 14:4 pp Mk 6:18; **Lk** 23:40; **Ac** 5:3–4,9; **1Ti** 1:3; 5:20; **Tit** 1:13; 2:15

Evil is to be resisted

Pr 1:10 My son, if sinners entice you, do not give in to them.

Gal 2:11 When Peter came to Antioch, I [Paul] opposed him to his face, because he was clearly in the wrong.

Eph 6:11 Put on the full armour of God so that you can take your stand against the devil's schemes.

Jas 4:7 Submit yourselves, then, to God. Resist the devil, and he will flee from you.   *See also* **1Co** 5:13; **Eph** 5:11; **Heb** 12:1; **1Pe** 2:1; 5:9

Evil is to be repaid with good

Lk 6:35 "But love your enemies, do good to them, and lend to them without expecting to get anything back. Then your reward will be great, and you will be sons of the Most High, because he is kind to the ungrateful and wicked."

Ro 12:20–21 . . . "If your enemies are

hungry, feed them; if they are thirsty, give them something to drink. In doing this, you will heap burning coals on their heads." Do not be overcome by evil, but overcome evil with good. *See also* **Pr** 25:21–22; **Ex** 23:5; **Lev** 19:18; **Mt** 5:44 pp Lk 6:27; **1Th** 5:15; **1Pe** 3:9

Believers should pray in response to evil
Mt 6:13 "And lead us not into temptation, but deliver us from the evil one." pp Lk 11:4
Ac 4:29 "Now, Lord, consider their threats and enable your servants to speak your word with great boldness."

Heb 4:16 Let us then approach the throne of grace with confidence, so that we may receive mercy and find grace to help us in our time of need. *See also* **Ex** 17:4; **1Ki** 18:36; **2Ki** 19:19; **2Ch** 20:12; **Ezr** 8:23; **Ne** 1:4; **Mt** 26:41 pp Mk 14:38 pp Lk 22:46; **Ac** 12:5; **Jas** 5:13

Believers should trust God in the face of evil
Ps 23:4 Even though I walk through the valley of the shadow of death, I will fear no evil, for you [Lord] are with me; your rod and your staff, they comfort me.

Mt 26:39 . . . [Jesus prayed] "My Father, if it is possible, may this cup be taken from me. Yet not as I will, but as you will." pp Mk 14:36 pp Lk 22:42 *See also* **Ps** 4:8; 20:7; 27:1; **Isa** 12:2; **Da** 3:17–18; **Hab** 3:17–18; **2Ti** 1:12; **Heb** 13:6; **Ps** 118:6–7

---

evil, victory over
Although evil continues to be present and active in the world, Scripture gives an assurance that God will finally triumph over evil in all its forms.

Satan's power is already limited by God
Job 1:12 The Lord said to Satan, "Very well, then, everything he [Job] has is in your hands, but on the man himself do not lay a finger." . . . *See also* **Ge** 3:14–15; **Job** 2:6; **Zec** 3:2; **Rev** 12:9

Evil spirits are subject to God's control
1Sa 16:14 Now the Spirit of the Lord had departed from Saul, and an evil spirit from the Lord tormented him. *See also* **Jdg** 9:23; **1Sa** 18:10; 19:9; **1Ki** 22:23; **Col** 2:13–15; **Jude** 6

Jesus Christ's triumph over evil powers
1Jn 3:8 . . . The reason the Son of God appeared was to destroy the devil's work. *See also* **Mt** 12:25–29 pp Mk 3:23–27 pp Lk 11:17–22; **Mk** 1:27 pp Lk 4:36; **Lk** 4:13; 10:18; **Jn** 12:31; 14:30; **Heb** 2:14–15; **1Jn** 4:4; **Rev** 3:21

God's transforming power reverses the effects of evil in human lives
2Co 3:18 And we [Christians], who with unveiled faces all reflect the Lord's glory, are being transformed into his likeness with ever-increasing glory, which comes from the Lord, who is the Spirit.

1Jn 3:2 Dear friends, now we are children of God, and what we will be has not yet been made known. But we know that when he appears, we shall be like him, for we shall see him as he is. *See also* **Jnh** 3:10; **Mk** 5:15 pp Lk 8:35; **Lk** 19:8; **Ac** 26:17–18; **Ro** 6:14; 12:2; **1Co** 15:10; **2Co** 12:9; **Col** 3:10

God brings good out of evil
Ge 50:20 [Joseph to his brothers] "You intended to harm me, but God intended it for good to accomplish what is now being done, the saving of many lives."

Ro 8:28 And we know that in all things God works for the good of those who love him, who have been called according to his purpose. *See also* **Ge** 45:8; **Job** 23:10; **Jn** 9:3; 12:24; **Ac** 2:36; 3:13–16; 5:30–31; **Php** 1:12–14,17–18; **Jas** 1:2–3; **1Pe** 1:6–7

The removal of the curse on creation
Ro 8:20–21 For the creation was subjected to frustration, not by its own choice, but by the will of the one who subjected it, in hope that the creation itself will be liberated from its bondage to

decay and brought into the glorious freedom of the children of God.   *See also* **Mt** 19:28; **Ac** 3:21; **Rev** 21:1,5; 22:3

Jesus Christ's victory over evil is expressed in his thousand-year reign with believers, during which Satan is bound
Rev 20:4 . . . They came to life and reigned with Christ for a thousand years.   *See also* **Rev** 20:2

The final defeat of all evil powers
Rev 20:4 . . . They came to life and reigned with Christ for a thousand years.

Ro 16:20 The God of peace will soon crush Satan under your feet. The grace of our Lord Jesus be with you.

Rev 20:10 And the devil . . . was thrown into the lake of burning sulphur, where the beast and the false prophet had been thrown. They will be tormented day and night for ever and ever.
See also **Mal** 4:1; **Mt** 13:41–42; 25:41; **1Co** 15:25; **2Th** 2:8; **Rev** 19:20; 21:8

Evil will be excluded from the new heaven and earth
2Pe 3:13 But in keeping with his [God's] promise we are looking forward to a new heaven and a new earth, the home of righteousness.
See also **Isa** 65:17; **Rev** 21:4,27; 22:15   *See also heaven; hope; last things; Satan, defeat of.*

---

faith
A constant outlook of trust towards God, whereby human beings abandon all reliance on their own efforts and put their full confidence in him, his word and his promises.

---

faith, and blessings
Confidence in the ability and willingness of God to act in supernatural power to advance his kingdom, and a commitment, expressed in prayer and action, to being the means by which he does so.

God's power is released through faith
Mt 17:20 He [Jesus] replied, "Because you have so little faith. I tell you the truth, if you have faith as small as a mustard seed, you can say to this mountain, 'Move from here to there' and it will move. Nothing will be impossible for you."   *See also* **Mk** 9:23; **Lk** 17:6

Praying in faith
Mt 21:21–22 Jesus replied, "I tell you the truth, if you have faith and do not doubt, not only can you do what was done to the fig-tree, but also you can say to this mountain, 'Go, throw yourself into the sea,' and it will be done. If you believe, you will receive whatever you ask for in prayer." pp Mk 11:22–24   *See also* **Jas** 1:5–7; 5:14–15

Praying in Jesus Christ's name
Jn 14:12–14 "I [Jesus] tell you the truth, all who have faith in me will do what I have been doing, and they will do even greater things than these, because I am going to the Father. And I will do whatever you ask in my name, so that the Son may bring glory to the Father. You may ask me for anything in my name, and I will do it."

In the OT, faith in God's power
Heb 11:32–34 . . . who through faith conquered kingdoms, administered justice, and gained what was promised; who shut the mouths of lions, quenched the fury of the flames, and escaped the edge of the sword; whose weakness was turned to strength; and who became powerful in battle and routed foreign armies.   *See also* **Heb** 11:11–12; **Jos** 14:6–14; **1Sa** 14:6; 17:32–47; **2Ch** 20:20; 32:7–8; **Da** 6:23

In the NT, healing in response to faith
Mt 9:22 Jesus turned and saw her [the woman with a severe haemorrhage]. "Take heart, daughter," he said, "your faith has healed you." And the woman was healed from that moment. pp Mk 5:34 pp Lk 8:48   *See also* **Mt** 9:29–30; **Mk** 10:52 pp Lk 18:42; **Lk** 17:19; **Ac** 3:16; 14:8–10

Powerful ministries marked by faith
Ac 11:24 He [Barnabas] was a good man, full of the Holy Spirit and faith, and a great number of people were brought to the Lord.   *See also* **Ac** 6:5–10; **1Co** 12:9

Faith and spiritual warfare
Eph 6:16 In addition to all this, take up the shield of faith, with which you can extinguish all the flaming arrows of the evil one.   *See also* **1Th** 5:8; **1Jn** 5:4–5

The importance of love accompanying faith
1Co 13:2 . . . if I have a faith that can move mountains, but have not love, I am nothing.
See also evil, victory over; prayer, and faith; spiritual warfare.

---

faith, and salvation

Both in the OT and in the NT faith is the only basis of salvation. Faith is the means by which God's grace in Christ, and with him the blessings of salvation, is received. Paul's doctrine of justification by faith emphasises the centrality of faith in the Christian life.

Salvation by faith in the OT
Hab 2:4 ". . . the righteous will live by their faith . . ."
The faith of Abraham and other individuals
Ge 15:6 Abram believed the LORD, and he credited it to him as righteousness.   *See also* **Ro** 4:9–16; **Heb** 11:4–5,7

Salvation by faith in the NT
Ro 1:16–17 . . . in the gospel a righteousness from God is revealed, a righteousness that is by faith from first to last, just as it is written: "The righteous will live by faith."   *See also* **1Co** 1:21; **Php** 3:8–9
Salvation through faith alone
Eph 2:8–9 For it is by grace you have been saved, through faith—and this not from yourselves, it is the gift of God—not by works, so that no-one can boast.   *See also* **Ro** 3:27–28; 4:1–8; **Ps** 32:1–2; **Ro** 9:30–32; **Gal** 3:10–14; **Dt** 27:26

Salvation is by faith in Jesus Christ
Jn 3:14–16 "Just as Moses lifted up the snake in the desert, so the Son of Man must be lifted up, that everyone who believes in him may have eternal life. For God so loved the world that he gave his one and only Son, that whoever believes in him shall not perish but have eternal life."
Ro 10:9–10 . . . if you confess with your mouth, "Jesus is Lord," and believe in your heart that God raised him from the dead, you will be saved . . .   *See also* **Jn** 8:24; **Ac** 8:37 fn; 13:38–39; **Ro** 3:21–26; 4:24; **2Co** 4:13–14; **Gal** 3:22
Salvation is for all who believe
Ro 10:4 Christ is the end of the law so that there may be righteousness for everyone who believes.   *See also* **Ac** 15:7–9; **Ro** 3:29–30
Salvation is for those who persevere in their faith
Col 1:21–23 . . . if you continue in your faith, established and firm, not moved from the hope held out in the gospel . . .   *See also* **Heb** 3:14; 6:11–12
Saving faith shows itself in action
Jas 2:14 What good is it, my brothers and sisters, if people claim to have faith but have no deeds? Can such faith save them?
Blessings of salvation received through faith
Justification and peace with God Ro 5:1–2; **Gal** 2:15–16; 5:5
Forgiveness Lk 7:48–50; **Ac** 10:43
Adoption into God's family Jn 1:12; **Gal** 3:26
The gift of the Holy Spirit Jn 7:38–39; **Gal** 3:2; **Eph** 1:13
Jesus Christ in the heart Eph 3:17
Protection through God's power 1Pe 1:5
Access to God Eph 3:12; **Heb** 10:22
Sanctification Ac 26:17–18
New life Gal 2:20
Eternal life Jn 3:16,36; 5:24; 6:40,47
Victory over death Jn 11:25–27   *See also adoption; conversion; forgiveness; justification; regeneration; righteousness; salvation; sanctification.*

---

faith, body of beliefs
That body of essential truth to which Christians hold. It is revealed by God and is to be passed

on by faithful teachers. Believers are urged to remain true to the faith and to contend for it.

Faith as the truth that Christians believe
Gal 1:23 They [the Christians in Judea] only heard the report: "The man [Paul] who formerly persecuted us is now preaching the faith he once tried to destroy."

1Ti 2:7 And for this purpose I [Paul] was appointed a herald and an apostle—I am telling the truth, I am not lying—and a teacher of the true faith to the Gentiles.   *See also* **Ac** 6:7; **Eph** 4:5; **1Ti** 1:2; **Tit** 3:15
Terms equivalent to "the faith"
The truth: **Jn** 14:6; **1Ti** 3:15; **3Jn** 3
Ac 2:42
The gospel: **Gal** 1:6–9; **Php** 1:7
2Ti 1:13–14
Aspects of "the faith" summarised Ac 2:22–24,32–33; **1Co** 15:1–4; **Php** 2:5–11; **Col** 1:15–20; **1Ti** 1:15; 3:16; **2Ti** 2:11–13; **Heb** 6:1–2

The source and transmission of the faith
The faith has been given by God
Gal 1:11–12 I want you to know, brothers and sisters, that the gospel I [Paul] preached is not of human origin. I did not receive it from any human source, nor was I taught it; rather, I received it by revelation from Jesus Christ.   *See also* **Jn** 1:17; 8:40; **1Co** 11:23; **2Ti** 3:16; **2Pe** 1:21
The faith is passed on by apostles and teachers
Tit 1:9 He [one who is an elder] must hold firmly to the trustworthy message as it has been taught, so that he can encourage others by sound doctrine and refute those who oppose it.   *See also* **Jn** 15:20; **Ac** 4:20; **2Ti** 2:2; **2Pe** 1:16

Christians must remain true to the faith
Ac 14:21–22 . . . Then they [Paul and Barnabas] returned to Lystra, Iconium and Antioch, strengthening the disciples and encouraging them to remain true to the faith. "We must go through many hardships to enter the kingdom of God," they said.

1Co 16:13 Be on your guard; stand firm in the faith; be courageous; be strong.   *See also* **Heb** 4:14–16
Being strengthened in the faith
Php 1:25 . . . I [Paul] know that I will remain, and I will continue with all of you for your progress and joy in the faith,

Col 2:6–7 So then, just as you received Christ Jesus as Lord, continue to live in him, rooted and built up in him, strengthened in the faith as you were taught, and overflowing with thankfulness.
See also **Eph** 4:11–13; **Jude** 20
The danger of turning from the faith
Mt 24:10 "At that time many will turn away from the faith and will betray and hate each other,"

Heb 6:6 if they fall away, to be brought back to repentance, because to their loss they are crucifying the Son of God all over again and subjecting him to public disgrace.   *See also* **Ac** 13:8; **2Co** 13:5–6; **1Ti** 5:8; 6:10,20–21; **Heb** 2:1; 3:12; 10:35; 12:25

Christians must contend for the faith
Php 1:27 Whatever happens, conduct yourselves in a manner worthy of the gospel of Christ. Then, whether I come and see you or only hear about you in my absence, I will know that you stand firm in one spirit, striving together with one accord for the faith of the gospel.

Jude 3 Dear friends, although I was very eager to write to you about the salvation we share, I felt I had to write and urge you to contend for the faith that was once for all entrusted to the saints.
Refuting false teachers 1Ti 4:1–6; **2Ti** 3:6–8; **Tit** 1:10–13; **2Jn** 7
Witnessing to the truth 1Pe 3:15
Contending for the faith is a responsibility of leaders
Apostles: **Php** 1:7,15–16; **2Ti** 4:7
1Ti 3:2,9; 6:12   *See also gospel, basics of; revelation; spiritual warfare; teaching; truth.*

faith, nature of

Confidence in and commitment to God and Jesus Christ. These attitudes remain sure even though the objects of faith are unseen. True faith is seen in obedient action, love and continuing good works.

The object of faith
God as the object of faith
Heb 11:6 And without faith it is impossible to please God, because anyone who comes to him must believe that he exists and that he rewards those who earnestly seek him. *See also* **Ps** 25:1–2; 26:1; **Pr** 29:25; **1Pe** 1:21
Jesus Christ as the object of faith
Jn 14:1 "Do not let your [the disciples'] hearts be troubled. Trust in God; trust also in me [Jesus]." *See also* **Jn** 3:16,18,36; 6:68–69
False objects of faith
Human resources: **Ps** 20:7; **Hos** 10:13
Ps 118:9; **Pr** 28:26; **Isa** 42:17

Faith is personal trust in God
2Sa 22:31 "As for God, his way is perfect; the word of the LORD is flawless. He is a shield for all who take refuge in him." *See also* **Ps** 18:2–6; 27:13–14; **1Pe** 2:23
True faith cannot be second-hand
2Ti 1:5 I [Paul] have been reminded of your [Timothy's] sincere faith, which first lived in your grandmother Lois and in your mother Eunice and, I am persuaded, now lives in you also. *See also* **Jn** 4:42

Faith and assurance
Assurance accompanies faith
Heb 11:1 Now faith is being sure of what we hope for and certain of what we do not see. *See also* **Ro** 4:19–21; **1Ti** 3:13; **Heb** 10:22
Faith may be mixed with doubt Mt 14:31; **Mk** 9:24; **Jn** 20:24–28

Faith and sight
2Co 5:7 We live by faith, not by sight.
Faith as trust in what is unseen
Jn 20:29 Then Jesus told him [Thomas],

"Because you have seen me, you have believed; blessed are those who have not seen and yet have believed." *See also* **2Co** 4:18; **Heb** 11:1–3,7,27
Faith looks towards an unseen future
Heb 11:13–14 All these people [Abel, Enoch, Noah, Abraham] were still living by faith when they died. They did not receive the things promised; they only saw them and welcomed them from a distance. And they admitted that they were aliens and strangers on earth. People who say such things show that they are looking for a country of their own. *See also* **Heb** 11:8–10,20–22,24–26

Faith and obedience
True faith is demonstrated in obedience
Ro 1:5 Through him [Jesus] and for his name's sake, we received grace and apostleship to call people from among all the Gentiles to the obedience that comes from faith.

Heb 4:2 For we also have had the gospel preached to us, just as they did; but the message they heard was of no value to them, because those who heard did not combine it with faith. *See also* **Ro** 16:26; **2Co** 9:13; **1Pe** 1:2
Examples of obedient faith
Noah builds the ark: **Ge** 6:22; **Heb** 11:7
Abraham leaves Haran: **Ge** 12:4; **Heb** 11:8
Abraham offers Isaac: **Ge** 22:1–10; **Heb** 11:17
Ex 14:15–16
Caleb and Joshua: **Nu** 13:30; 14:8–9
Jos 3:5–13; 6:2–5; **Heb** 11:30 **Jn** 21:4–6; **Ac** 26:19

Faith and works
True faith is demonstrated in good deeds
Jas 2:14–26 . . . faith by itself, if it is not accompanied by action, is dead. But someone will say, "You have faith; I have deeds." Show me your faith without deeds, and I will show you my faith by what I do . . . *See also* **Php** 2:17; **1Th** 1:3; **Tit** 1:1; **2Pe** 1:5
True faith issues in love
Gal 5:6 For in Christ Jesus neither circumcision nor uncircumcision has any value. The only thing

that counts is faith expressing itself through love.　*See also* **Eph** 1:15; 6:23; **1Th** 3:6; 5:8; **1Ti** 1:5,14; 4:12

True faith is constantly productive
Lk 8:15 "But the seed on good soil stands for those with a noble and good heart, who hear the word, retain it, and by persevering produce a crop." pp **Mt** 13:23 pp **Mk** 4:20　*See also* **Jn** 15:1–5　*See also assurance; hope; life, of faith; love; obedience, to God.*

faith, necessity

A fundamental duty for all people and the necessary response to God's self-revelation. The only channel through which God's blessings may be received, and the only means by which life may be made meaningful, in relationship with God.

The call to faith
In the OT
Ps 37:3–5 Trust in the LORD and do good; dwell in the land and enjoy safe pasture. Delight yourself in the LORD and he will give you the desires of your heart. Commit your way to the LORD; trust in him and he will do this:　*See also* **Pr** 3:5–6; **Isa** 26:4; 50:10
In the NT
Jn 6:28–29 . . . Jesus answered, "The work of God is this: to believe in the one he has sent."　*See also* **Mk** 1:15; **Ac** 16:30–31; 19:4; 20:21; **Ro** 1:5; **1Jn** 3:23

God's self-revelation leaves no excuse for unbelief
Jn 14:8–11 . . . Jesus answered: "Don't you know me, Philip, even after I have been among you such a long time? Anyone who has seen me has seen the Father. How can you say, 'Show us the Father'? . . ."

Ro 10:17–18 Consequently, faith comes from hearing the message, and the message is heard through the word of Christ. But I ask: Did they not hear? Of course they did: "Their voice has gone out into all the earth, their words to the ends of the world."　*See also* **Ps** 19:4;

Jn 1:10–12; **Ro** 1:18–21; 3:1–4; **Ps** 51:4; **Ro** 16:25–27

The need for faith in God
The LORD is the only true God
Hab 2:18–20 "Of what value is an idol, since someone has carved it? Or an image that teaches lies? For those who make them trust in their own creations; they make idols that cannot speak . . . But the LORD is in his holy temple; let all the earth be silent before him."　*See also* **Ps** 115:2–11
God alone can be trusted absolutely
Ps 9:10 Those who know your name will trust in you, for you, LORD, have never forsaken those who seek you.　*See also* **Ps** 91:1–4; **Isa** 12:2; **Na** 1:7
Faith in God is the basis for peace
Isa 26:3 You will keep in perfect peace those whose minds are steadfast, because they trust in you.　*See also* **Ps** 42:11; **Jn** 14:1; **Ro** 15:13; **2Pe** 1:1–2
Faith is necessary to receive God's blessing
Heb 11:6 And without faith it is impossible to please God, because anyone who comes to him must believe that he exists and that he rewards those who earnestly seek him.　*See also* **Ps** 40:4; **Jer** 17:7–8; **Jn** 5:24
Faith is necessary to avoid God's judgment
Jn 3:36 "Those who believe in the Son have eternal life, but those who reject the Son will not see life, for God's wrath remains on them."　*See also* **Jn** 3:18; **2Th** 2:12; **1Pe** 2:6–8; **Isa** 28:16; **Ps** 118:22; **Isa** 8:14

Actions not springing from faith are sinful
Ro 14:23 . . . and everything that does not come from faith is sin.　*See also* **Ro** 14:5–8,14

Unbelief challenged
Heb 3:12–18; **Ps** 95:7–8; **Isa** 7:9; **Jer** 17:5–6; **Mk** 16:14　*See also gospel, transmission; repentance; revelation; salvation, necessity of.*

faith, origins of
Faith is a gift from God himself and is not to be

seen as the result of human striving or achievement. Faith is inspired by the word and works of God.

Faith is a gift from God

Jn 6:63–65 "The Spirit gives life; the flesh counts for nothing. The words I have spoken to you are spirit and they are life. Yet there are some of you who do not believe." For Jesus had known from the beginning which of them did not believe and who would betray him. He went on to say, "This is why I told you that no-one can come to me unless the Father has enabled them."

Eph 2:8–9 For it is by grace you have been saved, through faith—and this not from yourselves, it is the gift of God—not by works, so that no-one can boast. *See also* **Mt** 16:15–17; **Mk** 9:24; **Lk** 17:5; **Ac** 3:16; 14:27; 18:27; **Ro** 12:3; **1Co** 4:7; 12:9; **Php** 1:29; **Jas** 2:5

Faith comes through God's word

Faith following a direct word from God Heb 11:29–30; **Ex** 14:15; **Jos** 6:2–5; **Ac** 27:23–25
Faith through the Scriptures Jn 2:22; 20:30–31; **2Ti** 3:15
Faith comes through hearing God's word preached
Ro 10:14–17 How, then, can they call on the one they have not believed in? And how can they believe in the one of whom they have not heard? And how can they hear without someone preaching to them? And how can they preach unless they are sent? As it is written, "How beautiful are the feet of those who bring good news!" . . . Consequently, faith comes from hearing the message, and the message is heard through the word of Christ. *See also* **Isa** 52:7; 53:1; **Jn** 1:7; 4:41–42; 17:20; **Ac** 11:19–21; **1Co** 2:4–5

Faith comes through a personal encounter with Jesus Christ

Jn 9:35–38; 20:26–28

Faith comes through witnessing miracles

Jn 14:11 "Believe me [Jesus] when I say that I am in the Father and the Father is in me; or at least believe on the evidence of the miracles themselves." *See also* **Jn** 2:11; 4:53
The raising of Lazarus: **Jn** 11:45; 12:11
Ac 9:42

Faith based on knowledge of God

Knowledge of God's faithfulness leads to faith Ps 46:1–3; **La** 3:19–24; **Na** 1:7; **Ac** 2:25–26
Knowledge of God's achievements leads to faith Dt 3:21–22; **1Sa** 17:34–37; **Jer** 14:22
See also grace, and salvation; preachers and preaching; promises, divine; Scripture.

---

fellowship

Association based upon the sharing of something in common. Believers have fellowship with one another on the basis of their common fellowship with God, their participation in the blessings of the gospel and their common task of mission. True fellowship is demonstrated in concern for, and practical commitment to, one another.

fellowship, among believers

The fellowship that believers share as a result of their common union with God through Jesus Christ is expressed in life together. It is evident in worship together, in a love for one another which reflects God's own love and in a practical commitment to one another which is demonstrated in concern for the weak and readiness to share with the poor and needy.

Sharing in the fellowship of God's love

1Jn 4:10–12 . . . Dear friends, since God so loved us, we also ought to love one another . . . *See also* **Jn** 13:34; 15:12; **Eph** 5:1–2; **1Jn** 3:10

Sharing in the fellowship of a common devotional life

Ac 2:42 They [the believers] devoted themselves to the apostles' teaching and to the fellowship, to the breaking of bread and to prayer.

Worshipping together
Ps 55:14 with whom I once enjoyed sweet fellowship as we walked with the throng at the house of God.   *See also* **Ps** 42:4; **1Co** 14:26; **Eph** 5:19; **Col** 3:16

Praying together
Ac 1:14 They [the believers] all joined together constantly in prayer, along with the women and Mary the mother of Jesus, and with his brothers.   *See also* **Ac** 4:24; 12:12; **Jas** 5:16
Breaking bread together 1Co 10:16–17; **2Pe** 2:13; **Jude** 12

True fellowship means sharing with those in need
Heb 13:16 And do not forget to do good and to share with others, for with such sacrifices God is pleased.   *See also* **Ac** 20:34–35; **Eph** 4:28
Showing hospitality
Ro 12:13 Share with God's people who are in need. Practise hospitality.   *See also* **Isa** 58:7; **Heb** 13:1–2; **1Pe** 4:9; **3Jn** 8
Sharing money and possessions
Dt 15:10–11 . . . There will always be poor people in the land. Therefore I command you to be open-handed towards those of your people who are poor and needy in your land.

Ac 2:44–45 All the believers were together and had everything in common. Selling their possessions and goods, they gave to anyone who had need.   *See also* **Dt** 10:18–19; **Mt** 25:35–36; **Lk** 3:11; **Ac** 4:32–35; **2Co** 8:13–15; **1Ti** 6:17–18; **Jas** 1:27; 2:15–16
Examples of sharing with the needy Job 31:16–20; **Ac** 6:1; 9:36
The collection for believers in Judea: **Ac** 11:29–30; **Ro** 15:26; **2Co** 8:3–4

Strengthening one another in fellowship together
Bearing with the weak
Gal 6:1–2 . . . Carry each other's burdens, and in this way you will fulfil the law of Christ.   *See also* **Isa** 42:3; **Ro** 14:1; 15:1; **1Th** 5:14

Strengthening the weak
Isa 35:3–4 Strengthen the feeble hands, steady the knees that give way . . .   *See also* **Job** 4:3–4
Encouraging one another
Heb 10:24–25 And let us consider how we may spur one another on towards love and good deeds. Let us not give up meeting together, as some are in the habit of doing, but let us encourage one another—and all the more as you see the Day approaching.   *See also* **1Sa** 23:16; **Ro** 1:12; **1Th** 5:11; **Heb** 13:3
Putting the needs of others first
Ro 15:2 We should all please our neighbours for their good, to build them up.   *See also* **1Co** 10:24,32–33

True fellowship means living in harmony
1Pe 3:8 Finally, all of you, live in harmony with one another; be sympathetic, love one another, be compassionate and humble.   *See also* **Ro** 12:16; **Eph** 4:2–3; **Php** 2:1–4; **Col** 3:12–14
Showing equal concern for all Ac 10:34; **1Co** 12:25; **Jas** 2:1–4
Examples of fellowship Nu 10:31–32; **1Sa** 18:3; **2Ki** 10:15–16
Failure to exhibit true fellowship 1Sa 30:22; **1Co** 1:11–12; 11:17–22   *See also* **church, life of; church, unity; love, for one another; peace, experience; prayer; worship.**

fellowship, in gospel

A mutual participation in the blessings of God's grace. Believers are united with one another on the basis of their common reception of the benefits of salvation.

Fellowship and the community of God's people
God calls out a community of people, for fellowship with himself
Dt 7:6 For you [Israel] are a people holy to the LORD your God. The LORD your God has chosen you out of all the peoples on the face of the earth to be his people, his treasured possession.   *See also* **Ex** 19:5–6; **1Pe** 2:5,9–11

God will bless a people united in fellowship
Mt 18:19–20; 2Ch 7:14; Jer 31:23–25; 1Co 11:29–34

God will restore fellowship with his scattered people
Mic 2:12 "I [the LORD] will surely gather all of you, O Jacob; I will surely bring together the remnant of Israel. I will bring them together like sheep in a pen, like a flock in its pasture; the place will throng with people."   *See also* Isa 11:12–13; Jer 3:18; 31:1; 50:4–5

Sharing in God's grace
Fellowship in a common blessing
Ps 106:4–5 . . . that I may enjoy the prosperity of your chosen ones, that I may share in the joy of your [the LORD'S] nation and join your inheritance in giving praise.   *See also* Nu 10:32; Jos 22:19

Fellowship in a common salvation
Jude 3 Dear friends, although I was very eager to write to you about the salvation we share, I felt I had to write and urge you to contend for the faith that was once for all entrusted to the saints.   *See also* 1Co 9:23; Php 1:7; Tit 1:4; Heb 3:1; 1Pe 5:1; 2Pe 1:4; 1Jn 1:7

Fellowship in a common inheritance
Col 1:12 giving thanks to the Father, who has qualified you to share in the inheritance of the saints in the kingdom of light.   *See also* Ro 8:17; 1Pe 3:7

Fellowship in God's family
Heb 2:11 Both the one who makes people holy and those who are made holy are of the same family. So Jesus is not ashamed to call them brothers and sisters.   *See also* Mal 2:10; Mt 6:9 pp Lk 11:2; Mt 12:49–50 pp Mk 3:34–35 pp Lk 8:21; Mt 23:8–9

Fellowship between Jew and Gentile
Eph 3:6 This mystery is that through the gospel the Gentiles are heirs together with Israel, members together of one body, and sharers together in the promise in Christ Jesus.   *See also* Ro 11:17; 15:27; Eph 2:16–18

Fellowship in holding a common truth
2Th 2:15 So then, brothers and sisters, stand firm and hold to the teachings we passed on to you, whether by word of mouth or by letter.   *See also* Ps 119:63; 1Co 11:2; 15:2–3; 2Ti 2:2; 3:14; Tit 2:15

Fellowship in union with Christ
1Co 10:16–17 Is not the cup of thanksgiving for which we give thanks a participation in the blood of Christ? And is not the bread that we break a participation in the body of Christ? Because there is one loaf, we, who are many, are one body, for we all partake of the one loaf.

Eph 2:19–22 . . . And in him [Christ Jesus] you too are being built together to become a dwelling in which God lives by his Spirit.   *See also* Ro 12:5; 1Co 12:12,27; Eph 4:4–5; Col 1:15; 1Pe 2:4–5

Fellowship through the Holy Spirit
1Co 12:13 For we were all baptised by one Spirit into one body—whether Jews or Greeks, slave or free—and we were all given the one Spirit to drink.   *See also* Eze 36:27–28; 2Co 13:14; Eph 4:3; Php 2:1   *See also* baptism; Lord's Supper; salvation; sanctification; truth.

fellowship, in service
Partnership in a common enterprise. God's people are called to work together especially in the task of mission, to recognise one another's gifts and to give support to one another's ministries.

Fellowship in mission
Partnership in preaching the gospel
Gal 2:9 James, Peter and John, those reputed to be pillars, gave me [Paul] and Barnabas the right hand of fellowship when they recognised the grace given to me. They agreed that we should go to the Gentiles, and they to the Jews.   *See also* Mk 10:7; Lk 10:1–2; Php 1:5

Supporting the work of others
Ac 14:26 From Attalia they [Paul and Barnabas] sailed back to Antioch, where they had been committed to the grace of God for the work they had now completed.

Php 4:14–16 . . . as you Philippians know, in the early days of your acquaintance with the gospel, when I [Paul] set out from Macedonia, not one church shared with me in the matter of giving and receiving, except you only . . . *See also* Ac 13:2–3; 15:40; 2Co 11:9; 3Jn 5–8

Standing together in adversity
Heb 10:32–34 . . . Sometimes you [Hebrew Christians] were publicly exposed to insult and persecution; at other times you stood side by side with those who were so treated . . . *See also* 2Co 1:7; Php 1:27–30; 4:14; Heb 11:25

Fellowship between Paul and his co-workers
Php 4:3 . . . I [Paul] ask you, true companion, help these women [Euodia and Syntyche] who have contended at my side in the cause of the gospel, along with Clement and the rest of my co-workers, whose names are in the book of life.
Barnabas: Ac 11:26–30; 13:42–50; 14:1–23; 15:22–29
Ro 16:3,9,21; 2Co 8:23; Php 2:25; Phm 1,24

In fellowship different gifts are combined for effective service
1Co 12:12 The body is a unit, though it is made up of many parts; and though all its parts are many, they form one body. So it is with Christ. *See also* 1Co 12:4–6

Spiritual gifts are given to all to share
1Co 12:7 Now to each one the manifestation of the Spirit is given for the common good. *See also* Ro 12:4–8; 1Co 12:14–20; 1Pe 4:10

Recognising one another's gifts
1Co 12:21–26 The eye cannot say to the hand, "I don't need you!" And the head cannot say to the feet, "I don't need you!" . . .

Accepting one another's ministries
Gal 2:7–8 . . . For God, who was at work in the ministry of Peter as an apostle to the Jews, was also at work in my ministry as an apostle to the Gentiles. *See also* 1Co 12:27–31; 16:15–18; 2Pe 3:15–16

Examples of sharing in different roles
Ne 4:16–22 From that day on, half of my men did the work, while the other half were equipped with spears, shields, bows and armour . . .

1Co 3:5–8 . . . The one who plants and the one who waters have one purpose, and they will each be rewarded according to their own labour. *See also* Ex 4:15–16; 17:10–13; 1Co 12:8–11

Examples of working together in fellowship
Ecc 4:9–12 Two are better than one, because they have a good return for their work: If they fall down, one can help the other up. But pity those who fall and have no friend to help them up . . . *See also* Dt 3:18–20; Jdg 20:11; Ezr 3:8–10; Ne 4:6; Lk 5:7–10 *See also evangelism; gospel; mission, of church; spiritual gifts.*

---

fellowship, with God
The relationship with God, disrupted by sin yet established through Jesus Christ, which provides the only proper basis for true human fellowship. God's desire for fellowship with humanity is made known through his calling of a people to be his own and to reflect his holiness and love.

God's fellowship with his people is shown by his presence
God's presence with Israel
Lev 26:12 "'I will walk among you [Israel] and be your God, and you will be my people.'" *See also* Ex 33:14; Isa 63:9; Hag 1:13

God's presence in the tabernacle
Ex 25:8 "Then have them [the Israelites] make a sanctuary for me, and I [the LORD] will dwell among them." *See also* Ex 29:45–46; 40:34–36; Lev 26:11; Dt 12:11

God's presence in the temple
1Ki 6:12–13 ". . . I [the LORD] will live among the Israelites and will not abandon my people Israel." *See also* 1Ki 8:29 pp 2Ch 6:20; 2Ch 7:1–2; Isa 6:1

God's presence in the new Jerusalem
Zec 2:10–13 "Shout and be glad, O Daughter of Zion. For I am coming, and I will live among you," declares the LORD . . . *See also* Eze 37:26–28; 43:4–7; 48:35; Rev 21:3

The church's fellowship with God
Fellowship with the Father, Son and Holy Spirit
Jn 14:23 Jesus replied, "Those who love me will obey my teaching. My Father will love them, and we will come to them and make our home with them."   *See also* **Jn** 14:7,16–17
Fellowship is made possible through Jesus Christ
Eph 2:18–19 For through him [Christ Jesus] we both have access to the Father by one Spirit . . .   *See also* **Ro** 5:10; **2Co** 5:18–19; **Col** 1:20–22; **Heb** 10:19–22
Fellowship with Jesus Christ
1Co 1:9 God, who has called you into fellowship with his Son Jesus Christ our Lord, is faithful.
See also **Mt** 28:20; **Jn** 15:4–5; **Ro** 6:4–5; **1Co** 10:15–16; **Php** 3:10
Fellowship with God is inseparable from fellowship with one another
1Jn 1:3 We [the apostles] proclaim to you what we have seen and heard, so that you also may have fellowship with us. And our fellowship is with the Father and with his Son, Jesus Christ.   *See also* **Mt** 18:20; **Mk** 9:37; **Jn** 17:21; **2Co** 13:11

The demands of fellowship with God
Holiness
Lev 20:26 " 'You [Israel] are to be holy to me because I, the LORD, am holy, and I have set you apart from the nations to be my own.' "

2Co 6:14–18 . . . What agreement is there between the temple of God and idols? For we are the temple of the living God. As God has said: "I will live with them and walk among them, and I will be their God, and they will be my people." "Therefore come out from them and be separate, says the Lord. Touch no unclean thing, and I will receive you." . . .   *See also* **Ex** 34:12–14; **Ezr** 6:21; **1Co** 5:11; **Eph** 5:8–11; **Jas** 4:4
Obedience to God's will
1Jn 3:24 Those who obey his [God's] commands live in him, and he in them. And this is how we know that he lives in us: We know it by the Spirit he gave us.   *See also* **Isa** 57:15;

Mt 12:49–50 pp **Mk** 3:34–35 pp **Lk** 8:21; **Jn** 14:21

Sin separates people from fellowship with God
Isa 59:2 But your iniquities have separated you from your God; your sins have hidden his face from you, so that he will not hear.

1Jn 1:5–6 . . . If we claim to have fellowship with him [God] yet walk in the darkness, we lie and do not live by the truth.   *See also* **Ge** 3:8; **Eze** 39:23

Examples of fellowship with God
Ge 5:22; 6:9; **2Ch** 20:7
Moses: **Ex** 33:11; **Nu** 12:3
Jos 1:9; **Mal** 2:6   *See also covenant, nature of; forgiveness; heaven, community of redeemed; holiness; prayer, response to God; reconciliation; sin.*

---

forgiveness
The freeing of a person from guilt and its consequences, including punishment; usually as an act of favour, compassion or love, with the aim of restoring a broken personal relationship. Forgiveness can involve both the remission of punishment and the cancellation of debts.

---

forgiveness, application
God's forgiveness of believers' sins leads them to pray for his forgiveness of others and to be forgiving in their dealings with other people.

Prayers for forgiveness on behalf of others
For God's own people
Ex 32:30–32 The next day Moses said to the people, "You have committed a great sin. But now I will go up to the LORD; perhaps I can make atonement for your sin." So Moses went back to the LORD and said, "Oh, what a great sin these people have committed! They have made themselves gods of gold. But now, please forgive their sin—but if not, then blot me out of the book you have written."   *See also* **Ne** 1:4–11; **Da** 9:4–19; **Am** 7:1–6

For other human beings

Ge 18:20–33 . . . but Abraham remained standing before the LORD. Then Abraham approached him and said: "Will you sweep away the righteous with the wicked? What if there are fifty righteous people in the city? Will you really sweep it away and not spare the place for the sake of the fifty righteous people in it? Far be it from you to do such a thing—to kill the righteous with the wicked, treating the righteous and the wicked alike. Far be it from you! Will not the Judge of all the earth do right?" . . .

For one's persecutors

Lk 23:33–34 When they came to the place called the Skull, there they crucified him, along with the criminals—one on his right, the other on his left. Jesus said, "Father, forgive them, for they do not know what they are doing." . . . *See also* **Mt** 5:43–44; **Ac** 7:59–60

Prayers for forgiveness for oneself

Lk 11:4 " 'Forgive us our sins, for we also forgive everyone who sins against us . . . ' " pp **Mt** 6:12 *See also* **Ne** 9:1–3; **Ps** 51:1–17

Examples of forgiveness given

Ps 32:1–5 Blessed are those whose transgressions are forgiven, whose sins are covered. Blessed are those whose sin the LORD does not count against them and in whose spirit is no deceit. When I kept silent, my bones wasted away through my groaning all day long. For day and night your hand was heavy upon me; my strength was sapped as in the heat of summer. *Selah* Then I acknowledged my sin to you and did not cover up my iniquity. I said, "I will confess my transgressions to the LORD" and you forgave the guilt of my sin . . . *See also* **Isa** 6:1–7; **Jn** 8:3–11

The call to exercise forgiveness
As a principle of life

Lk 6:37 "Do not judge, and you will not be judged. Do not condemn, and you will not be condemned. Forgive, and you will be forgiven." *See also* **Mt** 5:38–48 pp Lk 6:27–36

Within the church

Col 3:12–13 Therefore, as God's chosen people, holy and dearly loved, clothe yourselves with compassion, kindness, humility, gentleness and patience. Bear with each other and forgive whatever grievances you may have against one another. Forgive as the Lord forgave you. *See also* **2Co** 2:5–11; **Eph** 4:32; **1Pe** 3:8–9
Forgiving enemies Pr 24:17; 25:21–22; **Mt** 5:44; **Ro** 12:20

Being forgiven is dependent on forgiving others

Mk 11:25 "And when you stand praying, if you hold anything against anyone, forgive him, so that your Father in heaven may forgive you your sins." *See also* **Mt** 6:12 pp Lk 11:4; **Mt** 6:14–15; 18:21–35; **Lk** 6:37

Forgiveness is to be without limits

Lk 17:3–4 . . . "Rebuke a brother or sister who sins, and if they repent, forgive them. If anyone sins against you seven times in a day, and seven times comes back to you and says, 'I repent,' you must forgive them." *See also* **Mt** 18:21–22

Examples of human forgiveness

Ac 7:59–60 While they were stoning him, Stephen prayed, "Lord Jesus, receive my spirit." Then he fell on his knees and cried out, "Lord, do not hold this sin against them." When he had said this, he fell asleep. *See also* **Ge** 50:15–21; **2Sa** 16:5–11 *See also prayer, for others; sin, forgiveness of.*

forgiveness, divine

God forgives the sins of believers on the basis of the once for all sacrifice offered by Jesus Christ on the cross. Believers' sins are no longer held against them, on account of the atoning death of Jesus Christ.

God's nature and forgiveness

Ex 34:5–7 Then the LORD came down in the cloud and stood there with him and proclaimed his name, the LORD. And he passed in front of

Moses, proclaiming, "The LORD, the LORD, the compassionate and gracious God, slow to anger, abounding in love and faithfulness, maintaining love to thousands, and forgiving wickedness, rebellion and sin . . ." *See also* **Nu** 14:17–20; **Ne** 9:16–17; **Ps** 103:1–18; **Isa** 43:25; **Mic** 7:18–20; **1Jn** 1:8–9

God's promise of forgiveness
Jer 31:31–34 "The time is coming," declares the LORD, "when I will make a new covenant with the house of Israel and with the house of Judah. It will not be like the covenant I made with their ancestors when I took them by the hand to lead them out of Egypt, because they broke my covenant, though I was a husband to them," declares the LORD. "This is the covenant that I will make with the house of Israel after that time," declares the LORD. "I will put my law in their minds and write it on their hearts. I will be their God, and they will be my people. No longer will they teach their neighbours, or say to one another, 'Know the LORD,' because they will all know me, from the least of them to the greatest," declares the LORD. "For I will forgive their wickedness and will remember their sins no more." *See also* **2Ch** 7:14; **Isa** 55:6–7; **Heb** 8:8–12

People's need of forgiveness
1Jn 1:8–10 If we claim to be without sin, we deceive ourselves and the truth is not in us. If we confess our sins, he is faithful and just and will forgive us our sins and purify us from all unrighteousness. If we claim we have not sinned, we make him out to be a liar and his word has no place in our lives. *See also* **Ps** 51:1–5; **Isa** 6:1–5; **Ro** 3:9,23

The means of forgiveness
Under the old covenant
Heb 9:22 In fact, the law requires that nearly everything be cleansed with blood, and without the shedding of blood there is no forgiveness. *See also* **Lev** 4:27–31; 5:17–18
Under the new covenant
Mt 26:27–28 Then he [Jesus] took the cup, gave thanks and offered it to them, saying, "Drink from it, all of you. This is my blood of the covenant, which is poured out for many for the forgiveness of sins." *See also* **Jn** 1:29; **Eph** 1:7–8; **Col** 2:13–15

The assurance of forgiveness
1Jn 1:8–9 If we claim to be without sin, we deceive ourselves and the truth is not in us. If we confess our sins, he is faithful and just and will forgive us our sins and purify us from all unrighteousness. *See also* **Ps** 51:7; 103:8–12; 130:3–4; **Pr** 28:13; **Isa** 1:18; **Ac** 2:38; **Jas** 5:13–16; **1Jn** 2:1–2 *See also assurance; atonement; blood; conversion, nature of; grace; mercy; reconciliation; repentance; sin, remedy for.*

---

forgiveness, Jesus Christ's ministry
A central feature of Jesus Christ's ministry was his declaration that believers' sins were forgiven through their faith in him.

Jesus Christ's ministry of forgiveness was foretold
Mt 1:20–21 . . . "Joseph son of David, do not be afraid to take Mary home as your wife, because what is conceived in her is from the Holy Spirit. She will give birth to a son, and you are to give him the name Jesus, because he will save his people from their sins."

Jn 1:29 The next day John saw Jesus coming towards him and said, "Look, the Lamb of God, who takes away the sin of the world!"

Jesus Christ's exercise of forgiveness
Lk 23:33–34 When they came to the place called the Skull, there they crucified him, along with the criminals—one on his right, the other on his left. Jesus said, "Father, forgive them, for they do not know what they are doing." . . . *See also* **Jn** 8:3–11

Jesus Christ has authority on account of his divinity to forgive sins
Mt 9:1–8 Jesus stepped into a boat, crossed

over and came to his own town. Some people brought to him a paralytic, lying on a mat. When Jesus saw their faith, he said to the paralytic, "Take heart, son; your sins are forgiven." At this, some of the teachers of the law said to themselves, "This fellow is blaspheming!" Knowing their thoughts, Jesus said, "Why do you entertain evil thoughts in your hearts? Which is easier: to say, 'Your sins are forgiven,' or to say, 'Get up and walk'? But so that you may know that the Son of Man has authority on earth to forgive sins . . . ." Then he said to the paralytic, "Get up, take your mat and go home." And the man got up and went home. When the crowd saw this, they were filled with awe; and they praised God, who had given such authority to human beings. pp Mk 2:1–12 pp Lk 5:17–26

People's offence at Jesus Christ's exercise of forgiveness
Mk 2:5–7 When Jesus saw their faith, he said to the paralytic, "Son, your sins are forgiven." Now some teachers of the law were sitting there, thinking to themselves, "Why does this fellow talk like that? He's blaspheming! Who can forgive sins but God alone?" pp Mt 9:2–3 pp Lk 5:20–21

Parables of forgiveness
Mt 18:23–35; **Lk** 7:36–50; 15:11–32

The church's ministry of forgiveness in Jesus Christ's name
Jn 20:21–23 Again Jesus said, "Peace be with you! As the Father has sent me, I am sending you." And with that he breathed on them and said, "Receive the Holy Spirit. If you forgive the sins of anyone, their sins are forgiven; if you do not forgive them, they are not forgiven." *See also* Ac 2:38; 13:38; 26:15–18 *See also covenant, the new; gospel, promises.*

gospel
The good news of God's redemption of sinful humanity through the life, death and resurrection of his Son Jesus Christ.

gospel, basics of
The chief characteristic and fundamental doctrine of the gospel is that Jesus Christ is both Lord and Saviour.

Jesus Christ as Lord
The universal lordship of Jesus Christ
Mt 28:18 Then Jesus came to them and said, "All authority in heaven and on earth has been given to me." *See also* Da 7:13–14; Lk 10:22; Jn 3:35; 17:2; Ac 10:36; Ro 14:9; 1Co 15:27; Eph 1:20–22; Php 2:9–10; Col 1:15–20

Personal implications of the lordship of Jesus Christ
Lk 12:8–9 "I tell you, those who acknowledge me before others the Son of Man will also acknowledge before the angels of God. But those who disown me before others will be disowned before the angels of God."

Ro 10:9 . . . if you confess with your mouth, "Jesus is Lord," and believe in your heart that God raised him from the dead, you will be saved. *See also* Mt 7:21–27 pp Lk 6:46–49; Jn 13:13–14

The lordship of Jesus Christ can only be acknowledged through divine inspiration and revelation
1Co 12:3 . . . I tell you that no-one who is speaking by the Spirit of God says, "Jesus be cursed," and no-one can say, "Jesus is Lord," except by the Holy Spirit. *See also* Jn 16:13–15; 1Jn 4:2–3

Jesus Christ as Saviour
Lk 2:11 "Today in the town of David a Saviour has been born to you; he is Christ the Lord." *See also* Jn 1:29; 4:42; Ac 5:31; 1Ti 2:5–6; Tit 2:11–14; 1Jn 4:14

Jesus Christ is the promised Messiah
Mt 1:20–23 ". . . and you are to give him the name Jesus, because he will save his people from their sins." All this took place to fulfil what the Lord had said through the prophet: "The virgin will be with child and will give birth to a son, and they will call him Immanuel"——which

means, "God with us."   *See also* **Isa** 7:14; **Ps** 130:8; **Isa** 53:11; **Ac** 13:23

Jesus Christ did everything that was required to save his people

Jn 19:30 When he had received the drink, Jesus said, "It is finished." With that, he bowed his head and gave up his spirit.   *See also* **Mt** 3:15; **Jn** 4:34; 17:4; **1Co** 15:20–22

Salvation comes only through Jesus Christ

Jn 14:6 . . . "I [Jesus] am the way and the truth and the life. No-one comes to the Father except through me."   *See also* **Ac** 4:12; 10:43; 16:30–31; **1Ti** 2:5

Jesus Christ will return to judge the world and bring his people to glory

Mt 16:27 "For the Son of Man is going to come in his Father's glory with his angels, and then he will reward everyone according to what they have done."   *See also* **Jn** 14:3; **Ac** 1:11; 17:31; **1Th** 4:16–17; **2Ti** 4:1; **Rev** 1:7; 22:7,12,20   *See also cross, centrality; grace; law, and gospel; salvation.*

---

gospel, descriptions

The beauty, authority and importance of the gospel can be seen from the way it is described in Scripture.

In the Gospels
As good and joyful news

Mt 4:23 Jesus went throughout Galilee, teaching in their synagogues, preaching the good news of the kingdom, and healing every disease and sickness among the people.   *See also* **Mk** 1:14; 16:15; **Lk** 2:10–11

As being of heavenly origin

Jn 17:16–18 "They are not of the world, even as I [Jesus] am not of it. Sanctify them by the truth; your word is truth. As you sent me into the world, I have sent them into the world."   *See also* **Jn** 8:28; 12:49–50; 14:10,24

As words of life

Jn 6:63 ". . . The words I [Jesus] have spoken to you are spirit and they are life."   *See also* **Jn** 3:11–15

As being complete and gloriously rich

Col 1:25–27 I [Paul] have become its servant by the commission God gave me to present to you the word of God in its fulness—the mystery that has been kept hidden for ages and generations, but is now disclosed to the saints. To them God has chosen to make known among the Gentiles the glorious riches of this mystery, which is Christ in you, the hope of glory.   *See also* **Ro** 10:12–13; **Eph** 3:8

In the OT

Isa 52:7–10 How beautiful on the mountains are the feet of those who bring good news, who proclaim peace, who bring good tidings, who proclaim salvation, who say to Zion, "Your God reigns!" Listen! Your watchmen lift up their voices; together they shout for joy. When the LORD returns to Zion, they will see it with their own eyes. Burst into songs of joy together, you ruins of Jerusalem, for the LORD has comforted his people, he has redeemed Jerusalem. The LORD will lay bare his holy arm in the sight of all the nations, and all the ends of the earth will see the salvation of our God.   *See also* **Isa** 40:9; 41:27; 61:1; **Na** 1:15

In the NT

1Ti 1:11 . . . the glorious gospel of the blessed God, which he entrusted to me [Paul].   *See also* **Ac** 20:24; **Ro** 1:16–17; 10:15; **Isa** 52:7; **Ro** 15:18–19; **Eph** 1:13; **Rev** 14:6   *See also truth; word of God.*

---

gospel, foundation

The gospel rests upon the history of Jesus Christ: his birth, obedient life, atoning death, physical resurrection from the dead and his ascension into heaven.

The incarnation of Jesus Christ
The historical facts

Lk 2:4–7 So Joseph also went up from the town of Nazareth in Galilee to Judea, to Bethlehem the town of David, because he belonged to the house and line of David. He went there to register with Mary, who was pledged to be married to him and was expecting a child. While they were there, the time came for the baby to be born, and she gave birth to her firstborn, a son. She wrapped him in cloths and placed him in a manger, because there was no room for them in the inn.   *See also* **Lk 2:10–12; Mt 1:20–21; Lk 1:30–35**

Its theological significance
Jn 1:14 The Word became flesh and made his dwelling among us. We have seen his glory, the glory of the One and Only, who came from the Father, full of grace and truth.   *See also* **Jn 1:9; Ro 8:3; 2Co 8:9; Gal 4:4–5; Php 2:6–7; 1Ti 3:16; Heb 2:14; 1Jn 1:1–2**

The sinless life of Jesus Christ
1Pe 2:22 "He [Jesus] committed no sin, and no deceit was found in his mouth."   *See also* **Isa 53:9; 2Co 5:21; Heb 4:15; 7:26–28; 1Jn 3:5**

The death of Jesus Christ
An historical event
Php 2:8 And being found in appearance as a human being, he [Jesus] humbled himself and became obedient to death—even death on a cross!   *See also* **Mt 27:50 pp Mk 15:37 pp Lk 23:46 pp Jn 19:30**

Its redemptive significance
Ro 5:8–11 But God demonstrates his own love for us in this: While we were still sinners, Christ died for us . . .   *See also* **Lk 12:49–50; 24:26; Jn 17:4; Ac 2:23; Ro 5:19; 1Co 1:23–24; 1Pe 2:24**

The resurrection of Jesus Christ
Its historical reality
1Co 15:3–8 For what I [Paul] received I passed on to you as of first importance: that Christ died for our sins according to the Scriptures, that he was buried, that he was raised on the third day according to the Scriptures, and that he appeared to Peter, and then to the Twelve. After that, he appeared to more than five hundred of the brothers and sisters at the same time . . .   *See also* **Mt 28:1–8 pp Mk 16:1–8 pp Lk 24:1–10 pp Jn 20:1–9; 2Ti 2:8–10**

Its implication for believers
1Co 15:14 And if Christ has not been raised, our [the apostles'] preaching is useless and so is

your [believers'] faith.   *See also* **Ro 4:25; 6:1–14; 1Co 15:21,42–49**

The ascension of Jesus Christ
Ac 1:9 After he [Jesus] said this, he was taken up before their very eyes, and a cloud hid him from their sight.   *See also* **Mk 16:19; Lk 24:50–51; Ac 1:1–2; 2:33; Ro 8:34; Col 3:1; 1Ti 3:16; Heb 1:3; 12:2   *See also* atonement; kingdom of God; redemption.**

---

gospel, promises
To all who believe and submit to its demands, the promises of the gospel include forgiveness of sins, new life in Jesus Christ and adoption into the family of God.

Forgiveness of sins
The sin of God's people is imputed to God's Son
Jn 1:29 . . . John saw Jesus coming towards him and said, "Look, the Lamb of God, who takes away the sin of the world!"   *See also* **Isa 53:4–6; Lk 24:46–47; Ac 5:30–32; 13:38; Tit 2:13–14; Heb 9:28; 1Pe 2:24**
The righteousness of God's Son is imputed to God's people
Ro 1:16–17 . . . For in the gospel a righteousness from God is revealed, a righteousness that is by faith from first to last, just as it is written: "The righteous will live by faith."   *See also* **Ro 3:21–26; 9:30; Php 3:7–9**

Peace with God
Ro 5:1–2 Therefore, since we [believers] have been justified through faith, we have peace with God through our Lord Jesus Christ, through whom we have gained access by faith into this grace in which we now stand. And we rejoice in the hope of the glory of God.   *See also* **Jn 14:27; Ro 8:1–4,31–35**

New birth
1Pe 1:23–25 For you have been born again, not of perishable seed, but of imperishable, through the living and enduring word of God . . .   *See also* **Jn 1:12–13; 3:5–8; Jas 1:18**

Eternal life

Jn 3:14–16 "Just as Moses lifted up the snake in the desert, so the Son of Man must be lifted up, that everyone who believes in him may have eternal life. For God so loved the world that he gave his one and only Son, that whoever believes in him shall not perish but have eternal life."
See also **Jn** 1:4; 6:68–69; 10:10; 20:31; **1Jn** 1:1–2; 5:12

The gift of the Holy Spirit

Ac 2:38 Peter replied, "Repent and be baptised, every one of you, in the name of Jesus Christ for the forgiveness of your sins. And you will receive the gift of the Holy Spirit." *See also* **Joel** 2:28–32; **Jn** 7:37–39; **Ac** 8:14–17; 19:1–7

Adoption into God's family

Ro 8:12–17 . . . For you did not receive a spirit that makes you a slave again to fear, but you received the Spirit of adoption. And by him we cry, "*Abba*, Father." The Spirit himself testifies with our spirit that we are God's children . . .
See also **Jn** 1:12–13; **Gal** 3:26; 4:4–6; **Eph** 1:5
See also adoption; assurance; forgiveness; justification; peace, experience; regeneration; righteousness.

gospel, requirements

The gospel demands an obedient response to all that God has done for humanity in Jesus Christ. This includes faith in God, trust in the work of Jesus Christ, the repenting of sin, being baptised, and becoming like Christ through discipleship.

The requirement of faith
Belief in God

Heb 11:6 And without faith it is impossible to please God, because anyone who comes to him must believe that he exists and that he rewards those who earnestly seek him. *See also* **Jn** 10:38; 11:25–27; 14:8–11

Trust in Jesus Christ

Jn 3:14–16 "Just as Moses lifted up the snake in the desert, so the Son of Man must be lifted up, that everyone who believes in him may have eternal life. For God so loved the world that he gave his one and only Son, that whoever believes

in him shall not perish but have eternal life."
See also **Jn** 1:12–13; 3:36; 7:37–39; 20:31; **Ac** 13:38–39; 16:31; **Ro** 3:22

The requirement of repentance
A conscious change of mind and heart

Ac 3:17–20 ". . . Repent, then, and turn to God, so that your sins may be wiped out . . ." *See also* **Ps** 51:17; **Jer** 3:12–13; 6:16; **Lk** 18:13–14; **Ac** 17:30

Turning away from sin

Ac 8:22 "Repent of this wickedness and pray to the Lord. Perhaps he will forgive you [Simon the sorcerer] for having such a thought in your heart." *See also* **2Ch** 7:14; **Ps** 34:14; **Isa** 59:20; **Jer** 25:4–6

Turning towards God

Ac 20:21 "I [Paul] have declared to both Jews and Greeks that they must turn to God in repentance and have faith in our Lord Jesus."
See also **Dt** 4:29–31; 30:8–10; **Isa** 44:21–22; 55:6–7; **Hos** 14:1–2; **Jas** 4:8–10

The requirement of baptism

Ac 2:38 Peter replied, "Repent and be baptised, every one of you, in the name of Jesus Christ for the forgiveness of your sins . . ." *See also* **Mt** 28:18–20; **Ac** 8:12,36–38; 10:47–48; 19:1–5; 22:16

The requirement of public confession of Jesus Christ

Ro 10:9–10 . . . if you confess with your mouth, "Jesus is Lord," and believe in your heart that God raised him from the dead, you will be saved. For it is with your heart that you believe and are justified, and it is with your mouth that you confess and are saved. *See also* **Mt** 10:32 pp Lk 12:8–9

The requirement of discipleship
Willingness to learn from Jesus Christ

Mt 11:28–30 ". . . Take my yoke upon you and learn from me, for I am gentle and humble in heart, and you will find rest for your souls. For my yoke is easy and my burden is light." *See also* **Jn** 13:14–15; **Php** 2:5; **1Pe** 2:21

Willingness to obey Jesus Christ
Jn 14:15 "If you love me [Jesus], you will obey what I command." *See also* **Jn** 14:21,23; 15:10; **1Jn** 2:3–6; 3:21–24; 5:3; **2Jn** 6

Willingness to suffer for the sake of Jesus Christ
Mt 16:24 Then Jesus said to his disciples, "Those who would come after me must deny themselves and take up their cross and follow me." pp Mk 8:34 pp Lk 9:23 *See also* **Ac** 14:21–22; **Php** 1:29; **2Ti** 3:10–12; **Jas** 1:2; **1Pe** 3:14; 4:12–19 *See also baptism; faith; obedience, to God; repentance.*

---

gospel, responses
The gospel cannot be subscribed to half-heartedly or in part; it must be either accepted or rejected.

The gospel calls for a positive response
Ro 10:5–13 . . . if you confess with your mouth, "Jesus is Lord," and believe in your heart that God raised him from the dead, you will be saved. For it is with your heart that you believe and are justified, and it is with your mouth that you confess and are saved. As the Scripture says, "Anyone who trusts in him will never be put to shame." . . . *See also* **Ac** 13:38–39; 16:29–32; **Ro** 3:21–26; **Jn** 6:41–52; **1Jn** 5:1,5,10–12

The command to accept the gospel
Mt 11:28 "Come to me [Jesus], all you who are weary and burdened, and I will give you rest."

Ac 17:30 "In the past God overlooked such ignorance, but now he commands all people everywhere to repent." *See also* **Mt** 6:19–24 pp Lk 11:34–36; **Mt** 7:7–12 pp Lk 11:9–13; **Mt** 7:24–27 pp Lk 6:47–49; **Jn** 4:13–14; 6:35–40; 8:31–32,36; 10:9–10; 11:25–26; 12:44–46

Examples of people who accepted the gospel
Mk 1:16–18 As Jesus walked beside the Sea of Galilee, he saw Simon and his brother Andrew casting a net into the lake, for they were fishermen. "Come, follow me," Jesus said, "and I will make you fishers of men and women." At once they left their nets and followed him. pp Mt 4:18–22 *See also* **Mk** 1:19–20; **Mt** 9:9 pp Mk 2:14 pp Lk 5:27–28; **Ac** 2:41; 11:19–21; 13:46–48; 16:13–15

Rejection of the gospel
Through lack of perception
Jn 12:37–41 Even after Jesus had done all these miraculous signs in their presence, they still would not believe in him . . . *See also* **Mt** 13:13–15 pp Mk 4:10–12 pp Lk 8:9–10; **Isa** 6:9; **Ro** 11:8; **Eph** 4:17–19

Through worldly distractions
Mt 13:22 "Those who received the seed that fell among the thorns are the people who hear the word, but the worries of this life and the deceitfulness of wealth choke it, making it unfruitful." pp Mk 4:18–19 pp Lk 8:14 *See also* **Mt** 6:24 pp Lk 16:13; **2Ti** 4:10; **Jas** 4:4; **1Jn** 2:15

Through indifference
Mt 12:30 "Whoever is not with me [Jesus] is against me, and whoever does not gather with me scatters." pp Lk 11:23

Through hostility to God
Ro 8:6–8 . . . the sinful mind is hostile to God. It does not submit to God's law, nor can it do so. Those controlled by the sinful nature cannot please God. *See also* **Jn** 7:13–20; 10:24–33; **Ac** 4:15–18; 5:17–28; 7:51–53; 19:8–9; 21:27–32; **1Th** 2:14–16

Warnings against rejecting the gospel
Heb 2:1–4 . . . how shall we escape if we ignore such a great salvation? . . . *See also* **Mk** 8:36–38; **Lk** 12:5,16–21; 13:22–30; **Jn** 12:47–50; **Heb** 6:4–6; 10:29–31; 12:25; **2Pe** 2:17–22

Examples of people who rejected the gospel
Mt 19:16–22 . . . Jesus answered, "If you want to be perfect, go, sell your possessions and give to the poor, and you will have treasure in heaven. Then come, follow me." When the young man heard this, he went away sad, because he

had great wealth. pp Mk 10:17—22 pp Lk 18:18—23 *See also* Ac 5:29—33; 7:51—58; 17:32; 13:44—47; 19:23—28; 24:24—25; 26:24—28

The gospel evokes opposition
Jn 17:14 "I have given them your word and the world has hated them, for they are not of the world any more than I am of the world."

Ac 17:13 When the Jews in Thessalonica learned that Paul was preaching the word of God at Berea, they went there too, agitating the crowds and stirring them up. *See also* Ac 13:8; 17:5—9; 1Th 2:14—16

The gospel evokes persecution
Ac 8:1—3 And Saul was there, giving approval to his death. On that day a great persecution broke out against the church at Jerusalem, and all except the apostles were scattered throughout Judea and Samaria. Godly men buried Stephen and mourned deeply for him. But Saul began to destroy the church. Going from house to house, he dragged off both men and women and put them in prison.

1Th 3:7 Therefore, brothers and sisters, in all our distress and persecution we were encouraged about you because of your faith. *See also* Ac 13:49—50; 2Th 1:4

---

gospel, transmission
The gospel has been passed down through the NT witness to Jesus Christ, through the proclamation of the good news about Jesus Christ, and through the providential guidance of the Holy Spirit.

The NT witness to Jesus Christ
The events of Jesus Christ's life were carefully recorded
Lk 1:1—4 Many have undertaken to draw up an account of the things that have been fulfilled among us, just as they were handed down to us by those who from the first were eye-witnesses and servants of the word. Therefore, since I [Luke] myself have carefully investigated everything from the beginning, it seemed good

also to me to write an orderly account . . . *See also* Jn 21:24; Ac 1:1—2

The apostles bore witness to the gospel
1Co 15:3—8 For what I received I passed on to you as of first importance: that Christ died for our sins according to the Scriptures, that he was buried, that he was raised on the third day according to the Scriptures, and that he appeared to Peter, and then to the Twelve. After that, he appeared to more than five hundred of the brothers and sisters at the same time, most of whom are still living, though some have fallen asleep. Then he appeared to James, then to all the apostles, and last of all he appeared to me also, as to one abnormally born.

2Pe 1:16 We did not follow cleverly invented stories when we told you about the power and coming of our Lord Jesus Christ, but we were eye-witnesses of his majesty.

1Jn 1:1—4 That which was from the beginning, which we have heard, which we have seen with our eyes, which we have looked at and our hands have touched—this we proclaim concerning the Word of life. The life appeared; we have seen it and testify to it, and we proclaim to you the eternal life, which was with the Father and has appeared to us. We proclaim to you what we have seen and heard, so that you also may have fellowship with us. And our fellowship is with the Father and with his Son, Jesus Christ. We write this to make our joy complete. *See also* Lk 24:45—48; Jn 15:27; Ac 1:8,21—22; 2:32; 4:1—20; 5:32; 13:30—31; Heb 2:3—4; 1Pe 5:1; 1Jn 4:14

The proclamation of the gospel
Ac 5:42 Day after day, in the temple courts and from house to house, they never stopped teaching and proclaiming the good news that Jesus is the Christ.

Ro 10:14—15 How, then, can they call on the one they have not believed in? And how can they believe in the one of whom they have not heard? And how can they hear without someone preaching to them? And how can they preach unless they are sent? As it is written, "How beautiful are the feet of those who bring good news!"

1Co 15:1–2 Now, brothers and sisters, I want to remind you of the gospel I preached to you, which you received and on which you have taken your stand. By this gospel you are saved, if you hold firmly to the word I preached to you. Otherwise, you have believed in vain.

Eph 3:8–9 Although I am less than the least of all God's people, this grace was given me: to preach to the Gentiles the unsearchable riches of Christ, and to make plain to everyone the administration of this mystery, which for ages past was kept hidden in God, who created all things.   *See also* **Ac** 8:12; **1Co** 1:21; **Gal** 1:23; **2Ti** 4:2; **Heb** 13:7

The guidance of the Holy Spirit in the transmission of the gospel
Jn 14:26 But the Counsellor, the Holy Spirit, whom the Father will send in my [Jesus'] name, will teach you all things and will remind you of everything I have said to you.

Jn 15:26 "When the Counsellor comes, whom I [Jesus] will send to you from the Father, the Spirit of truth who goes out from the Father, he will testify about me."   *See also* **Jn** 16:12–15; **Ac** 5:32; **Heb** 2:3–4; **1Jn** 5:6   *See also church, purpose; evangelism, nature of; mission, of church; preachers and preaching; teaching.*

---

grace
The unmerited favour of God, made known through Jesus Christ, and expressed supremely in the redemption and full forgiveness of sinners through faith in Jesus Christ.

---

grace, and Christian life
The Christian life, from its beginning to its end, is totally dependent upon the grace of God.

God's grace compensates for human weaknesses
2Co 12:8–9 Three times I pleaded with the Lord to take it away from me. But he said to me, "My grace is sufficient for you, for my power is made perfect in weakness." Therefore I will boast all the more gladly about my weaknesses, so that Christ's power may rest on me.

1Pe 5:10 And the God of all grace, who called you to his eternal glory in Christ, after you have suffered a little while, will himself restore you and make you strong, firm and steadfast.   *See also* **1Co** 2:1–5; **2Co** 9:8; **Heb** 2:14; 4:15; 5:2; **Jas** 4:6; **2Pe** 3:17–18

Believers are to pray for grace
Heb 4:16 Let us then approach the throne of grace with confidence, so that we may receive mercy and find grace to help us in our time of need.   *See also* **Ps** 25:16; **Hos** 14:1–2; **Col** 1:9; 4:12

Christian experience may be summed up in terms of grace
1Co 15:10 . . . by the grace of God I [Paul] am what I am, and his grace to me was not without effect. No, I worked harder than all of them [the other apostles]—yet not I, but the grace of God that was with me.   *See also* **Ac** 18:27; **Ro** 5:2; **Gal** 1:15; **Php** 1:7

Believers should go on to experience more of God's grace
Ac 20:32 "Now I [Paul] commit you [the Ephesian elders] to God and to the word of his grace, which can build you up and give you an inheritance among all those who are sanctified."   *See also* **Ac** 13:43; **Col** 1:3–6; **Heb** 13:9; **1Pe** 5:12; **2Pe** 3:18

Believers are enabled to serve Jesus Christ by his grace
1Pe 4:10 Each of you should use whatever gift you have received to serve others, faithfully administering God's grace in its various forms. *See also* **Ac** 15:39–40; **Ro** 5:17; 12:6; 15:15;

1Co 3:10; 2Co 12:9; Gal 2:9; Eph 3:7–9

God's grace is seen in Christian character, especially in generosity
2Co 8:6–7 . . . we [Paul and Timothy] urged Titus, since he had earlier made a beginning, to bring also to completion this act of grace on your part. But just as you excel in everything—in faith, in speech, in knowledge, in complete earnestness and in your love for us—see that you also excel in this grace of giving.   *See also* Ac 4:33; 11:22–23; 2Co 9:13–14; Col 4:6

An ongoing experience of God's grace requires the believer's co-operation
2Co 6:1 As God's co-workers we [Paul and Timothy] urge you not to receive God's grace in vain.   *See also* Php 2:12–13; Heb 12:15; 1Pe 5:5; Jas 4:6   *See also spiritual growth.*

---

grace, and Holy Spirit
The Holy Spirit is both an expression of God's grace and the means by which it is experienced.

The Holy Spirit is himself a gracious gift of God
Ac 2:38 Peter replied [to the crowd at Pentecost], "Repent and be baptised, every one of you, in the name of Jesus Christ for the forgiveness of your sins. And you will receive the gift of the Holy Spirit."

Ac 6:5–8 . . . Stephen, a man full of faith and of the Holy Spirit . . . a man full of God's grace and power . . .

Tit 3:4–7 . . . when the kindness and love of God our Saviour appeared, he saved us, not because of righteous things we had done, but because of his mercy. He saved us through the washing of rebirth and renewal by the Holy Spirit, whom he poured out on us generously through Jesus Christ our Saviour, so that, having been justified by his grace, we might become heirs having the hope of eternal life.

1Jn 3:24 Those who obey his [God's]

commands live in him, and he in them. And this is how we know that he lives in us: We know it by the Spirit he gave us.   *See also* Jn 6:63; 20:21–22; Ac 5:32; 11:15–17; 15:6–8; 1Co 2:12; Gal 3:14

Through the Holy Spirit God brings believers out of slavery and into his family
Ro 8:15–16 For you did not receive a spirit that makes you a slave again to fear, but you received the Spirit of adoption. And by him we cry, "*Abba*, Father." The Spirit himself testifies with our spirit that we are God's children.   *See also* Gal 4:6–7; Eph 2:17–18

Through the Holy Spirit God equips believers to serve him
1Co 12:4–7 There are different kinds of gifts, but the same Spirit. There are different kinds of service, but the same Lord. There are different kinds of working, but the same God works all of them in everyone. Now to each one the manifestation of the Spirit is given for the common good.   *See also* Jn 7:37–39; Ac 1:8; 2:4; 4:31; Ro 5:5; Gal 3:5; Heb 2:4

The Holy Spirit in God's gracious work of redemption
Ro 8:1–2 . . . there is now no condemnation for those who are in Christ Jesus, because through Christ Jesus the law of the Spirit of life set me free from the law of sin and death.   *See also* 1Co 2:4–5,13; 1Th 1:4–5; 1Pe 1:12

The Holy Spirit in God's gracious work of sanctifying and sustaining his people
2Co 3:17–18 Now the Lord is the Spirit, and where the Spirit of the Lord is, there is freedom. And we, who with unveiled faces all reflect the Lord's glory, are being transformed into his likeness with ever-increasing glory, which comes from the Lord, who is the Spirit.

2Th 2:13 . . . we ought always to thank God for you, brothers and sisters loved by the Lord, because from the beginning God chose you to be saved through the sanctifying work of the Spirit and through belief in the truth.   *See also* Ac 9:31; Ro 8:26–27; 14:17–18; 15:13;

Gal 5:4–5,22–23; 6:8; **Eph** 2:22; 3:16–20; **Php** 1:18–19; **2Ti** 1:14; **Heb** 10:29; **Jas** 4:4–6　See also sanctification; spiritual gifts.

---

grace, and Jesus Christ

Grace is demonstrated pre-eminently in Jesus Christ and the work he came to do.

God's promise of grace has been fulfilled in Jesus Christ

Jn 1:14 The Word became flesh and made his dwelling among us. We have seen his glory, the glory of the One and Only, who came from the Father, full of grace and truth.

Jn 1:16–17 From the fulness of his grace we have all received one blessing after another. For the law was given through Moses; grace and truth came through Jesus Christ.

2Ti 1:8–10 . . . God, who has saved us and called us to a holy life—not because of anything we have done but because of his own purpose and grace. This grace was given us in Christ Jesus before the beginning of time, but it has now been revealed through the appearing of our Saviour, Christ Jesus . . .　See also **Jn** 3:16–17; **Ac** 13:38; **Ro** 1:1–5; 5:8,16–17; **Eph** 1:3–8; **Tit** 2:11–14; 3:4–5; **1Pe** 1:3–5

Grace was expressed in Jesus Christ's life and ministry

Mt 9:36 When he [Jesus] saw the crowds, he had compassion on them, because they were harassed and helpless, like sheep without a shepherd. pp Mk 6:34

2Co 8:9 For you [Corinthian Christians] know the grace of our Lord Jesus Christ, that though he was rich, yet for your sakes he became poor, so that you through his poverty might become rich.　See also **Mt** 9:10–13 pp Mk 2:15–17 pp Lk 5:27–32; **Mt** 11:4–5; 19:13–15 pp Mk 10:13–16 pp Lk 18:15–17; **Lk** 2:40; 4:22; 19:9–10; 23:34; **Jn** 10:11; **Ac** 10:37–38; **Heb** 2:9; **1Jn** 3:16

Grace is demonstrated in Jesus Christ's atoning death on the cross

Jn 1:16–17 From the fulness of his [Christ's] grace we have all received one blessing after another. For the law was given through Moses; grace and truth came through Jesus Christ.

Eph 2:4–5 . . . because of his great love for us, God, who is rich in mercy, made us alive with Christ even when we were dead in transgressions—it is by grace you have been saved.

1Pe 2:10 Once you [Gentile believers] were not a people, but now you are the people of God; once you had not received mercy, but now you have received mercy.　See also **Jn** 3:16; **Ro** 3:22–24; 5:1–2; 8:32; **1Co** 1:4–6; **2Co** 5:18–19; **Gal** 2:21; **Eph** 4:7; **2Th** 2:16–17; **1Ti** 1:13–14; **1Pe** 1:3–5; **1Jn** 4:10　See also atonement, necessity; forgiveness, Jesus Christ's ministry; justification; predestination.

---

grace, and salvation

Deliverance through Jesus Christ is the result of accepting God's undeserved favour.

Salvation is all God's doing

Ro 5:6–8 . . . at just the right time, when we were still powerless, Christ died for the ungodly. Very rarely will anyone die for a righteous person, though for a good person someone might possibly dare to die. But God demonstrates his own love for us in this: While we were still sinners, Christ died for us.

Ro 9:14–16 What then shall we say? Is God unjust? Not at all! For he says to Moses, "I will have mercy on whom I have mercy, and I will have compassion on whom I have compassion." It does not, therefore, depend on human desire or effort, but on God's mercy.

Eph 1:7 In him we have redemption through his blood, the forgiveness of sins, in accordance with the riches of God's grace

1Ti 1:15–16 Here is a trustworthy saying that

deserves full acceptance: Christ Jesus came into the world to save sinners—of whom I [Paul] am the worst. But for that very reason I was shown mercy so that in me, the worst of sinners, Christ Jesus might display his unlimited patience as an example for those who would believe on him and receive eternal life.   *See also* **Ex** 33:19; **Ac** 4:12; 20:24; **Ro** 5:15–17; **2Co** 6:2; **Col** 1:13–14; **2Th** 2:16; **Tit** 2:11; **Heb** 7:23–25; **Rev** 7:10

There is nothing human beings can do to save themselves

Tit 3:4–7 . . . when the kindness and love of God our Saviour appeared, he saved us, not because of righteous things we had done, but because of his mercy. He saved us through the washing of rebirth and renewal by the Holy Spirit, whom he poured out on us generously through Jesus Christ our Saviour, so that, having been justified by his grace, we might become heirs having the hope of eternal life.   *See also* **Lk** 18:9–14; **Ro** 11:5–6

Salvation is not by keeping God's law

Gal 5:4 You who are trying to be justified by law have been alienated from Christ; you have fallen away from grace.   *See also* **Ro** 5:20–21; 6:14; 8:1–4; **Gal** 2:21; 3:17–18; **1Ti** 1:9

Salvation must be accepted as a free gift by faith

Eph 2:4–9 . . . because of his great love for us, God, who is rich in mercy, made us alive with Christ even when we were dead in transgressions—it is by grace you have been saved. And God raised us up with Christ and seated us with him in the heavenly realms in Christ Jesus, in order that in the coming ages he might show the incomparable riches of his grace, expressed in his kindness to us in Christ Jesus. For it is by grace you have been saved, through faith—and this not from yourselves, it is the gift of God—not by works, so that no-one can boast.   *See also* **Ac** 15:7–11; 16:30–31; **Ro** 3:21–24; 4:14–16; 5:1–2; **Heb** 4:16   *See also conversion; faith; law; life, spiritual; redemption; salvation.*

grace, in Old Testament

In the OT, grace is evident in the special relationship between God and his people.

God's grace was expressed in the covenant relationship

Dt 7:7–9 The LORD did not set his affection on you [the Israelites] and choose you because you were more numerous than other peoples, for you were the fewest of all peoples. But it was because the LORD loved you and kept the oath he swore to your ancestors that he brought you out with a mighty hand and redeemed you from the land of slavery, from the power of Pharaoh king of Egypt. Know therefore that the LORD your God is God; he is the faithful God, keeping his covenant of love to a thousand generations of those who love him and keep his commands.

2Ki 13:22–23 Hazael king of Aram oppressed Israel throughout the reign of Jehoahaz. But the LORD was gracious to them and had compassion and showed concern for them because of his covenant with Abraham, Isaac and Jacob. To this day he has been unwilling to destroy them or banish them from his presence.   *See also* **Ge** 9:8–11; 17:1–8; **Ex** 6:2–8; **Dt** 8:17–18; **Ne** 1:5–6; **Isa** 55:1–3; **Eze** 16:1–8

God's grace affirmed
God's grace shown in his compassion
Ps 86:15 But you, O Lord, are a compassionate and gracious God, slow to anger, abounding in love and faithfulness.

La 3:22 Because of the LORD's great love we [his people] are not consumed, for his compassions never fail.

Joel 2:13 Return to the LORD your God, for he is gracious and compassionate, slow to anger and abounding in love, and he relents from sending calamity.   *See also* **Ex** 33:19; **Dt** 13:17–18; **2Ch** 30:9; **Ezr** 8:22; **Ps** 103:13; **Eze** 39:25; **Hos** 2:19; **Jnh** 4:1–2; **Mic** 7:18–20; **Zec** 10:6; **Mal** 3:17

God's grace shown in his readiness to forgive
Isa 55:7 Let the wicked forsake their ways and
the unrighteous their thoughts. Let them turn to
the LORD, and he will have mercy on them, and
to our God, for he will freely pardon.

Jer 33:6–9 "'. . . I will bring Judah and
Israel back from captivity and will rebuild them as
they were before. I will cleanse them from all the
sin they have committed against me and will
forgive all their sins of rebellion against
me . . .'"   *See also* **Da** 9:9–10; **Mic** 7:18–20

**God's grace shown in his favour, provision
and healing**
Lev 26:9 "'I will look on you with favour and
make you fruitful and increase your numbers, and
I will keep my covenant with you.'"

Jer 32:40–41 "I will make an everlasting
covenant with them: I will never stop doing good
to them, and I will inspire them to fear me, so
that they will never turn away from me. I will
rejoice in doing them good and will assuredly
plant them in this land with all my heart and
soul."   *See also* **Nu** 10:29; **Dt** 13:17–18; **2Sa**
22:28; **Ps** 30:4–5; **Isa** 49:8; **Jer** 9:23–24; 33:6–9;
Na 1:7; **Zec** 12:10

**God made his grace known to
individuals**
Ne 9:16–20 "But they, our ancestors, became
arrogant and stiff-necked, and did not obey your
commands . . . But you are a forgiving God,
gracious and compassionate, slow to anger and
abounding in love. Therefore you did not desert
them . . . Because of your great compassion you
did not abandon them in the desert . . . You
gave your good Spirit to instruct them. You did
not withhold your manna from their mouths, and
you gave them water for their thirst."
Job 10:12 [Job said] "You [God] gave me life
and showed me kindness, and in your providence
watched over my spirit."   *See also* **Ge**
24:35–36; 32:9–10; 39:20–21; **Ex** 33:12–13; **Dt**
33:23; **Jdg** 2:18; **1Sa** 2:21; **1Ki** 3:6; **Ezr** 7:27–28;
Ne 2:8; **Ps** 6:9; **Isa** 26:10

God's grace implored
2Ch 33:12 In his [Manasseh's] distress he
sought the favour of the LORD his God and
humbled himself greatly before the God of his
ancestors.

Ps 51:1 When the prophet Nathan came to him
after David had committed adultery with
Bathsheba. [David prayed] "Have mercy on me,
O God, according to your unfailing love; according
to your great compassion blot out my
transgressions."

Isa 33:2 O LORD, be gracious to us [his
people]; we long for you. Be our strength every
morning, our salvation in time of distress.   *See
also* **Ge** 24:12; **Ex** 32:11; **1Ki** 8:28–30; **2Ki** 13:4;
Ne 9:32; **Ps** 25:16; 69:13; **Da** 9:17–19; **Hos** 14:2;
Hab 3:2; **Zec** 1:12   *See also covenant.*

---

heaven
God's habitation where he is worshipped and
served by angels. Solely on account of the
sacrifice of Jesus Christ on the cross, believers will
inherit a place in heaven and there for ever enjoy
perfect fellowship with God in his worship and
service.

---

heaven, community of
redeemed
The community of the redeemed in heaven will
represent all peoples and languages. They will owe
this solely to the sacrifice of Jesus Christ. They
will share in the divine life in perfect fellowship
with God, free for ever from suffering and death.

Heaven as a divine gift
Ro 6:23 . . . the gift of God is eternal life in
Christ Jesus our Lord.   *See also* **Lk** 12:32;
22:28–30; **Jn** 17:2

**Divine preparations made for believers
in heaven**
Jn 14:2 "In my Father's house are many
rooms . . . I [Jesus] am going there to prepare
a place for you."   *See also* **2Co** 5:1; **Heb** 11:16

The redeemed in heaven come from all peoples

Rev 7:9–10 After this I [John] looked and there before me was a great multitude that no-one could count, from every nation, tribe, people and language, standing before the throne and in front of the Lamb . . .   *See also* **Isa** 59:19; **Mal** 1:11; **Mt** 8:11 pp **Lk** 13:29; **Rev** 5:9

The redeemed owe their place in heaven solely to Jesus Christ

Rev 7:14 . . . "These are they who have come out of the great tribulation; they have washed their robes and made them white in the blood of the Lamb."   *See also* **1Pe** 1:18–19; **Rev** 22:14

The redeemed are identified with Jesus Christ

Jesus Christ acknowledges the redeemed as his own

Lk 12:8 "I [Jesus] tell you, those who acknowledge me before others the Son of Man will also acknowledge before the angels of God."   *See also* **Mt** 7:21–23

Believers possess the family likeness to Jesus Christ

1Co 15:49 . . . just as we have borne the likeness of the earthly, so shall we bear the likeness of the heavenly.   *See also* **2Co** 3:18; **Php** 3:21; **1Jn** 3:2

Believers share divine life

2Pe 1:4 Through these he has given us his very great and precious promises, so that through them you may participate in the divine nature . . . *See also* **Rev** 2:7; 3:21

Believers on earth at the second coming will be taken up to heaven

Rev 11:12 Then they heard a loud voice from heaven saying to them, "Come up here." And they went up to heaven in a cloud, while their enemies looked on.   *See also* **Jn** 11:26; **1Th** 4:16–17

Conditions in heaven for the redeemed
Perpetual and perfect fellowship with the Lord

Rev 21:3 And I heard a loud voice from the throne saying, "Now the dwelling of God is with human beings, and he will live with them. They will be his people, and God himself will be with them and be their God."   *See also* **Ps** 17:15; **Mt** 5:8; **Jn** 14:3; **1Th** 4:17; **Rev** 22:4

Joy in the immediate presence of God

Ps 16:11 You have made known to me the path of life; you will fill me with joy in your presence, with eternal pleasures at your right hand.   *See also* **Isa** 51:11; **Mt** 25:21; **Lk** 15:7,10; **Jn** 15:11; **1Th** 2:19–20; **Heb** 12:2,22; **Jude** 24

Restfulness

2Th 1:5–7 . . . God is just: He will pay back trouble to those who trouble you and give relief to you who are troubled, and to us as well. This will happen when the Lord Jesus is revealed from heaven . . .   *See also* **Heb** 4:3,9; **Rev** 14:13

There will no longer be any need for the marriage relationship

Mt 22:30 "At the resurrection people will neither marry nor be given in marriage; they will be like the angels in heaven." pp **Mk** 12:25 pp **Lk** 20:35–36

Heaven is filled with the light of God's glory

Rev 21:23 The city does not need the sun or the moon to shine on it, for the glory of God gives it light, and the Lamb is its lamp.   *See also* **Da** 12:3; **Mt** 13:43; **2Co** 4:17; **1Pe** 2:9

Believers will share Jesus Christ's glory

Col 3:4 When Christ, who is your life, appears, then you also will appear with him in glory. *See also* **Jn** 17:24; **1Th** 2:12; **1Pe** 5:4,10

Divine glory will banish the memory of earthly troubles

Ro 8:18 I [Paul] consider that our present sufferings are not worth comparing with the glory that will be revealed in us.   *See also* **2Co** 4:17; **1Pe** 5:1

There will be no more death or suffering in heaven

Rev 21:4 "He [God] will wipe every tear from their eyes. There will be no more death or mourning or crying or pain, for the old order of

things has passed away."   *See also* **Isa** 25:8;
35:10; 51:11; **Lk** 20:35–36; **Rev** 7:17

Believers are citizens of the heavenly Jerusalem

Php 3:20 But our citizenship is in heaven. And
we eagerly await a Saviour from there, the Lord
Jesus Christ,   *See also* **Ps** 87:5; **Isa** 35:9–10;
51:11; **Gal** 4:26; **Heb** 11:16; **Rev** 21:2

Their names are enrolled as citizens of heaven

Lk 10:20 "However, do not rejoice that the
spirits submit to you, but rejoice that your names
are written in heaven."   *See also* **Php** 4:3; **Heb**
12:23; **Rev** 3:5; 13:8; 14:1; 17:8; 20:12; 21:27
See also redemption.

---

heaven, inheritance

Heaven is the secure inheritance, of priceless
value, awaiting the redeemed. There, faithful
service will be rewarded and the redeemed will be
given resurrection bodies for service in the
heavenly realm.

Believers inherit the kingdom of heaven

Their inheritance is secure

Mt 25:34 "Then the King will say to those on
his right, 'Come, you who are blessed by my
Father; take your inheritance, the kingdom
prepared for you since the creation of the
world.'"   *See also* **Lk** 12:32; 22:28–29; **Jas** 2:5

**The value of their inheritance is beyond human
calculation**

1Co 2:9–10 However, as it is written: "No eye
has seen, no ear has heard, no mind has
conceived what God has prepared for those who
love him"—but God has revealed it to us by his
Spirit . . .   *See also* **Ac** 20:32; **Eph** 1:18; 2:6–7

**As those adopted into God's family they are
heirs of God and Christ**

Ro 8:17 Now if we are children, then we are
heirs—heirs of God and co-heirs with Christ, if
indeed we share in his sufferings in order that we
may also share in his glory.   *See also* **Gal** 4:7;
Tit 3:7; **Heb** 6:17

The nature of the heavenly inheritance
It is inviolable

1Pe 1:3–5 . . . an inheritance that can never
perish, spoil or fade—kept in heaven for
you . . .   *See also* **Rev** 21:25,27

It is a response to faith and love

Jas 2:5 . . . Has not God chosen those who
are poor in the eyes of the world to be rich in
faith and to inherit the kingdom he promised
those who love him?   *See also* **Col** 1:12; 3:24;
Heb 11:7

It is for overcomers

Rev 21:7 "Those who overcome will inherit all
this, and I will be their God and they will be my
children."   *See also* **1Jn** 4:4; 5:3–5; **Rev**
2:7,11,17,26–28; 3:5,12,21

The heavenly treasure is to be sought

Mt 6:19–21 "Do not store up for yourselves
treasures on earth . . . But store up for
yourselves treasures in heaven . . . For where
your treasure is, there your heart will be also."
See also **Mt** 13:44; 19:21; **Lk** 12:33; **2Co** 4:18;
Php 3:8; **1Ti** 6:18–19; **Rev** 3:18

Heavenly rewards
Service will be rewarded in heaven

1Co 3:11–14 . . . If the building survives, the
builder will receive a reward.   *See also* **Mt** 5:12
pp Lk 6:23; **Rev** 22:12

**The prospect of heavenly rewards should be a
spur to present service**

Php 3:14 I [Paul] press on towards the goal to
win the prize for which God has called me
heavenwards in Christ Jesus.   *See also* **Heb**
11:26

Rewards will vary

Mt 16:27 "For the Son of Man is going to
come in his Father's glory with his angels, and
then he will reward everyone according to what
they have done."   *See also* **Da** 12:3; **Mt**
25:20–23 pp Lk 19:15–19; **1Co** 3:8; **2Co** 9:6; **Rev**
22:12

**Endurance for Jesus Christ's sake will be
specially rewarded**

Mt 5:10–12 ". . . Rejoice and be glad,
because great is your reward in heaven, for in the
same way they persecuted the prophets who were

before you." pp Lk 6:22–23

Rewards for service include crowns signifying position and authority
1Pe 5:4 And when the Chief Shepherd appears, you [faithful elders] will receive the crown of glory that will never fade away. *See also* **1Th 2:19; 2Ti 4:8**

The redeemed will share Jesus Christ's position in glory
Eph 2:6 And God raised us up with Christ and seated us with him in the heavenly realms in Christ Jesus, *See also* **Jn 14:3; 17:24; 1Jn 3:2; Rev 22:4**

The resurrection body as a heavenly inheritance
Php 3:20–21 But our citizenship is in heaven. And we eagerly await a Saviour from there, the Lord Jesus Christ, who . . . will transform our lowly bodies so that they will be like his glorious body. *See also* **1Co 15:42–44; 2Co 5:1–4** *See also kingdom of God; resurrection.*

heaven, nature of

Scripture refers to heaven as God's habitation but also uses the term as an alternative for God himself.

Heaven as God's habitation
It is the place where he dwells
Dt 26:15 "Look down from heaven, your holy dwelling-place . . ." *See also* **Ge 28:17; 2Ch 6:21; Ecc 5:2; Rev 13:6**
It is insufficient as God's dwelling-place
1Ki 8:27 "But will God really dwell on earth? The heavens, even the highest heaven, cannot contain you . . ." pp **2Ch 6:18** *See also* **Ps 113:5–6**

Heaven as the place of God's throne
Ps 11:4 The Lord is in his holy temple; the Lord is on his heavenly throne . . . *See also* **Ex 24:9–11; 1Ki 22:19; Isa 6:1; 63:15; Da 7:9; Mt 5:34; 23:22; Ac 7:49; Isa 66:1; Heb 8:1; Rev 4:1–6; 20:11**

Heaven as God's vantage point
Ps 33:13 From heaven the Lord looks down and sees all humanity; *See also* **Ps 53:2; 102:19–20; Ecc 5:2**

Heaven as an alternative term for God
Lk 15:18 "'I will set out and go back to my father and say to him: Father, I [the younger son] have sinned against heaven and against you.'" *See also* **Mt 8:11; 13:11; 16:19; 18:18; 21:25** pp **Mk 11:30** pp **Lk 20:4; Jn 3:27; 17:1**

Heaven and the sovereignty of God
Heaven is the place of God's rule
Da 4:26 "The command to leave the stump of the tree with its roots means that your kingdom will be restored to you [Nebuchadnezzar] when you acknowledge that Heaven rules." *See also* **Ps 45:6; 103:19; Ac 17:24**
God's voice from heaven speaks with divine authority
Dt 4:36 From heaven he [God] made you hear his voice to discipline you . . . *See also* **Da 4:31; Jn 12:28; 1Th 4:16; 2Pe 1:17–18**

Heaven glimpsed by human eyes
At the baptism of Jesus Christ
Mk 1:10 As Jesus was coming up out of the water, he saw heaven being torn open and the Spirit descending on him like a dove. pp **Mt 3:16** pp **Lk 3:21–22** *See also* **Jn 1:32**
In visions
Ac 7:56 "Look," he [Stephen] said, "I see heaven open and the Son of Man standing at the right hand of God." *See also* **2Co 12:2–4; Rev 4:1**

Prayer addressed to God in heaven
1Ki 8:30 "Hear the supplication of your servant and of your people Israel when they pray towards this place. Hear from heaven, your dwelling-place, and when you hear, forgive." *See also* **Dt 26:15; 2Ch 30:27; Ne 1:4; Ps 20:6; Rev 5:8**

The association of oaths with heaven
Mt 23:22 "And anyone who swears by heaven swears by God's throne and by the one who sits

on it."   *See also* **Ge** 24:3; **Da** 12:7; **Mt** 5:34;
Jas 5:12

The place of Jesus Christ in heaven
His pre-existence in heaven
Jn 6:38 "For I [Jesus] have come down from
heaven not to do my will but to do the will of
him who sent me."   *See also* **Jn** 3:13
His ascension into heaven after his resurrection
Lk 24:51 While he [Jesus] was blessing them,
he left them and was taken up into heaven. pp
Mk 16:19   *See also* **Eph** 1:20
His place is now with God the Father
Heb 9:24 . . . he [Christ] entered heaven
itself, now to appear for us in God's presence.
See also **Col** 3:1
His second coming will be from heaven
1Th 4:16 For the Lord himself will come down
from heaven, with a loud command, with the
voice of the archangel and with the trumpet call
of God . . .   *See also* **Mt** 25:31; **Ac** 1:11; **1Th**
1:10

The new heaven
The new heaven completely replaces the old
Rev 21:1 Then I saw a new heaven and a
new earth, for the first heaven and the first earth
had passed away, and there was no longer any
sea.   *See also* **Isa** 65:17; 66:22; **2Pe** 3:13
The new Jerusalem is divinely created in heaven
Rev 21:2 I saw the Holy City, the new
Jerusalem, coming down out of heaven from God,
prepared as a bride beautifully dressed for her
husband.   *See also* **Isa** 2:2–5; **Heb** 11:16; 13:14;
Rev 3:12; 21:10
Fulness of life in heaven is wholly sustained by God
Rev 21:22–23 I did not see a temple in the
city, because the Lord God Almighty and the Lamb
are its temple. The city does not need the sun or
the moon to shine on it, for the glory of God
gives it light, and the Lamb is its lamp.

Rev 22:1–2 Then the angel showed me the
river of the water of life, as clear as crystal,

flowing from the throne of God and of the Lamb
down the middle of the great street of the city.
On each side of the river stood the tree of life,
bearing twelve crops of fruit, yielding its fruit every
month. And the leaves of the tree are for the
healing of the nations.   *See also* **Isa** 55:1; **Eze**
47:8–9,12; **Jn** 7:38–39; **Rev** 2:7   *See also last
things; prayer.*

---

heaven, worship and service
All in heaven engage continuously in the worship
of God, while they perfectly carry out his will.

All heaven worships God
The multitude in heaven and the twenty-four elders
Rev 19:6–7 Then I heard what sounded like a
great multitude, like the roar of rushing waters
and like loud peals of thunder, shouting:
"Hallelujah! For our Lord God Almighty reigns. Let
us rejoice and be glad and give him
glory! . . ."   *See also* **Ne** 9:6; **Rev** 4:6–11;
7:11–12; 11:16; 22:8–9
The redeemed
1Pe 2:9 But you are a chosen people, a royal
priesthood, a holy nation, a people belonging to
God, that you may declare the praises of him
who called you out of darkness into his wonderful
light.   *See also* **Isa** 51:11; **Rev** 19:5–7
The angels Lk 2:13–14; **Rev** 5:11–12; 7:11
God is worshipped in song
Rev 15:2–3 . . . They [victorious believers]
held harps given them by God and sang the song
of Moses the servant of God and the song of the
Lamb: "Great and marvellous are your deeds, Lord
God Almighty. Just and true are your ways, King
of the ages."   *See also* **Rev** 14:3
Jesus Christ is worshipped in heaven
Php 2:10–11 that at the name of Jesus every
knee should bow, in heaven and on earth and
under the earth, and every tongue confess that
Jesus Christ is Lord, to the glory of God the
Father.   *See also* **Da** 7:14; **Heb** 1:6; **Rev** 5:8–14

All heaven serves God
God's will is perfectly done in heaven
Mt 6:10 "'. . . your will be done on earth as

it is in heaven.'" *See also* Mt 12:50

The redeemed will serve God
Rev 22:3 . . . The throne of God and of the
Lamb will be in the city, and his servants will
serve him. *See also* Rev 5:10; 7:13–15

**The redeemed will reign with Jesus Christ and
share his authority** Mt 19:28; 25:34; 1Co 6:3;
2Ti 2:12; Heb 12:28; Rev 2:26–27; 3:21; 20:6

The divine service of angels
They have divine authority Rev 8:2; 18:1; 20:1
They serve Jesus Christ Mt 25:31; 26:53; Lk
4:10; 22:43; 2Th 1:7–8; Heb 1:6; 1Pe 3:22
They serve believers 1Ki 19:5–8; Mt 24:31;
Heb 1:14
They serve by encouraging Ge 21:17; Lk 22:43;
Ac 27:23–24
They serve by guarding Ex 14:19; 2Ki 6:15–17;
Ps 91:11; Mt 18:10; Rev 7:2–3
They serve by instructing Ge 22:11,15; Zec 6:5;
Mt 1:20; 2:13; 28:5–7; Lk 1:13,19; Ac 8:26;
10:3–5
They serve by delivering believers in trouble
Da 6:22; Ac 5:19; 12:7
Their service is continuous Ge 28:12; Jn 1:51
See also praise; worship, places.

---

hell
A term used in English translations of the Bible to
represent the Hebrew word "Sheol" (the place of
the departed) and the Greek word "Gehenna",
which came to refer to the place of punishment
for the wicked after death. The Valley of Hinnom
(Hebrew "Ge Hinnom", from which "Gehenna" is
derived) on the south side of Jerusalem became a
symbol of all that is hateful to God, on account
of its use for human sacrifice.

---

hell, as incentive to action
The reality of hell should affect the way people
live.

The importance of making the right
choice
Mt 7:13–14 "Enter through the narrow gate.
For wide is the gate and broad is the road that

leads to destruction, and many enter through it.
But small is the gate and narrow the road that
leads to life, and only a few find it." *See also*
Dt 30:19; Jer 21:8; Lk 13:23–25

A personal spiritual life is vital
**It is more important than short-term worldly
gain**
Mt 16:26 What good will it be for you to gain
the whole world, yet forfeit your soul? Or what
can you give in exchange for your soul? pp Mk
8:36 pp Lk 9:25 *See also* Lk 12:20; 16:19–25
It is not just outward appearance
Mt 3:7–10 ". . . Produce fruit in keeping with
repentance. And do not think you [Pharisees and
Sadducees] can say to yourselves, 'We have
Abraham as our father' . . ." pp Lk 3:7–9
**Religious activity alone is not only valueless
but perilous**
Mt 7:21–23 "Not everyone who says to me,
'Lord, Lord,' will enter the kingdom of heaven,
but only those who do the will of my Father who
is in heaven . . ." *See also* Pr 14:12; Jer
23:11–12; Lk 13:26–28; Jn 15:6

Believers must maintain their loyalty to
God
Mt 10:28 "Do not be afraid of those who kill
the body but cannot kill the soul. Rather, be
afraid of the One who can destroy both soul and
body in hell." pp Lk 12:4–5 *See also* Dt
4:23–24; Isa 8:12–13

Temptations to sin must be dealt with
drastically
Mt 5:29–30 "If your right eye causes you to
sin, gouge it out and throw it away. It is better
for you to lose one part of your body than for
your whole body to be thrown into hell . . ."
See also Mt 18:8–9; Mk 9:43–48

Some attitudes and practices that lead
to hell
Deliberately continuing in sin
Heb 10:26–27 If we deliberately keep on
sinning after we have received the knowledge of
the truth, no sacrifice for sins is left, but only a

fearful expectation of judgment and of raging fire . . . *See also* **Nu** 15:30; **Heb** 6:4–6; **2Pe** 2:20

Lack of spiritual response Mt 22:13; 24:51; 25:30

Wilfully ignoring divine activity
Mt 11:20–24 ". . . And you, Capernaum, will you be lifted up to the skies? No, you will go down to the depths. If the miracles that were performed in you had been performed in Sodom, it would have remained to this day . . ." pp **Lk** 10:13–15　*See also* **Mt** 23:33; 25:41–46

Contempt for fellow humans
Mt 5:22 ". . . But anyone who says, 'You fool!' will be in danger of the fire of hell."
See also **Jas** 3:6　*See also* heaven.

---

hell, experience
The state of final separation from God, and so from all light, love, peace, pleasure and fulfilment.

Hell is separation from God
2Th 1:8–10 . . . They [those hostile to believers] will be punished with everlasting destruction and shut out from the presence of the Lord and from the majesty of his power on the day he comes to be glorified in his holy people and to be marvelled at among all those who have believed . . .　*See also* **Mt** 7:23; 8:12; 25:32; **Rev** 21:8

The final state of the wicked is one of eternal punishment
Mt 25:41–46 "Then he [the King] will say to those on his left, 'Depart from me, you who are cursed, into the eternal fire prepared for the devil and his angels . . .' . . . Then they will go away to eternal punishment . . ."　*See also* **Jude** 7

Biblical expressions for final punishment
God's wrath
Jn 3:36 "Those who believe in the Son have eternal life, but those who reject the Son will not see life, for God's wrath remains on them."
See also **Dt** 32:22; **Zep** 1:18; **Mt** 3:7; **Ro** 2:5;

1Th 1:10; **Rev** 19:15–16
Torment
Lk 16:23–24 In hell, where he [the rich man] was in torment, he looked up and saw Abraham far away, with Lazarus by his side . . .　*See also* **Mt** 8:29; **Rev** 14:11; 20:10
Corruption Ps 55:23; **2Pe** 1:4
Destruction
Gal 6:8 Those who sow to please their sinful nature, from that nature will reap destruction . . .　*See also* **Dt** 7:10; **Ps** 88:11; **Jn** 17:12; **Ro** 9:22; **Php** 3:18–19; **2Th** 2:3; **Rev** 17:8
Unquenchable fire
Jude 7 . . . They [Sodom and Gomorrah] serve as an example of those who suffer the punishment of eternal fire.　*See also* **Isa** 66:24; **Mt** 3:12; 18:8–9; **Heb** 10:27; **Rev** 19:20
Intense darkness, emphasising utter isolation
Jude 13 They [godless people] are wild waves of the sea, foaming up their shame; wandering stars, for whom blackest darkness has been reserved for ever.　*See also* **Mt** 22:13; **2Pe** 2:17; **Jude** 6
Death
Jn 8:21 Once more Jesus said to them [the Pharisees], "I am going away, and you will look for me, and you will die in your sin. Where I go, you cannot come."　*See also* **Job** 28:22; **Pr** 15:11; **Isa** 28:15; **Hos** 13:14; **Ro** 6:23; **1Co** 15:26,54–55
The second death
Rev 20:14–15 Then death and Hades were thrown into the lake of fire. The lake of fire is the second death . . .　*See also* **Rev** 20:6; 21:8

The finality of hell
Lk 16:26 " 'And besides all this, between us and you a great chasm has been fixed, so that those who want to go from here to you cannot, nor can anyone cross over from there to us.' "
See also **Heb** 6:4–6; 10:26–27; **Rev** 16:11　*See also* last things.

---

hell, place of punishment
The place of eternal punishment in fire and darkness intended for Satan and his angels, but also for human beings who choose to reject God.

Hell was originally created for the devil and his angels
Mt 25:41 "Then he [the King] will say to those on his left, 'Depart from me, you who are cursed, into the eternal fire prepared for the devil and his angels.'" *See also* **Lk** 8:31; **2Pe** 2:4; **Rev** 20:1–3,10

Hell is a consequence of rejecting God
Mt 13:40–42 ". . . They [the angels] will throw them [sinners] into the fiery furnace, where there will be weeping and gnashing of teeth." *See also* **Dt** 32:22; **Mk** 9:42–48; **Jn** 3:36; **Ro** 2:8; **1Th** 5:9; **Heb** 10:26–29; **2Pe** 3:7; **Rev** 20:15; 21:8

Jesus Christ possesses authority over hell
Mt 16:18 "And I tell you that you are Peter, and on this rock I will build my church, and the gates of Hades will not overcome it."

Rev 1:18 "I am the Living One; I was dead, and behold I am alive for ever and ever! And I hold the keys of death and Hades." *See also* **Jn** 5:27; **Ac** 10:42; 17:31

The Valley of Hinnom as a figure of hell
The Valley of Hinnom as a geographical feature Jos 15:8; 18:16
The Valley of Hinnom as a place of child sacrifice
2Ch 28:3 He [Ahaz] burned sacrifices in the Valley of Ben Hinnom and sacrificed his children in the fire, following the detestable ways of the nations that the LORD had driven out before the Israelites. pp 2Ki 16:3 *See also* **2Ki** 23:10; **2Ch** 33:6 pp 2Ki 21:6; **Jer** 32:35
The Valley of Hinnom as a place of God's judgment
Jer 7:30–32 "The people of Judah have done evil in my eyes, declares the LORD. They have set up their detestable idols in the house that bears my Name and have defiled it. They have built the high places of Topheth in the Valley of Ben Hinnom to burn their sons and daughters in the

fire—something I did not command, nor did it enter my mind. So beware, the days are coming, declares the LORD, when people will no longer call it Topheth or the Valley of Ben Hinnom, but the Valley of Slaughter, for they will bury the dead in Topheth until there is no more room.'" *See also* Jer 19:1–15
The Valley of Hinnom as a synonym for hell
Mt 10:28 "Do not be afraid of those who kill the body but cannot kill the soul. Rather, be afraid of the One who can destroy both soul and body in hell." pp Lk 12:4–5 *See also* **Mt** 5:29–30; 18:8–9 pp Mk 9:43–48 *See also human race; judgment, God's; Satan.*

---

holiness
The quality of God that sets him utterly apart from his world, especially in terms of his purity and sanctity. The holiness of God is also manifested in the persons and work of Jesus Christ and the Holy Spirit. Believers are called upon to become like God in his holiness.

---

holiness, believers' growth in
Believers are enabled to grow in holiness on account of the sacrificial death of Jesus Christ, foreshadowed by the OT sacrificial system, and through the sanctifying work of the Holy Spirit.

Holiness begins with God's initiative
God chooses who and what is to be holy
2Ch 7:16 "I [the LORD] have chosen and consecrated this temple so that my Name may be there for ever. My eyes and my heart will always be there." pp 1Ki 9:3 *See also* **Ex** 20:11; **Nu** 16:7; **2Ch** 29:11; **Zec** 2:12
God chooses and calls his people to holiness
Dt 7:6 For you [Israel] are a people holy to the LORD your God. The LORD your God has chosen you out of all the peoples on the face of the earth to be his people, his treasured possession.

Eph 1:4 For he [God] chose us [Christians] in him [Christ] before the creation of the world to be holy and blameless in his sight . . . *See also* **Dt** 14:2; **Ro** 1:7; **Col** 3:12; **1Pe** 1:2,15

Holiness is conferred by the holy God
Holiness is conferred by the presence of God
Ex 29:42–43 "For the generations to come this burnt offering is to be made regularly at the entrance to the Tent of Meeting before the Lord. There I [the Lord] will meet you and speak to you; there also I will meet with the Israelites, and the place will be consecrated by my glory."
See also **Ex** 3:4–5; 19:23; **2Ch** 7:1–2
Holiness is conferred through covenant relationship with God
Ex 19:5–6 " 'Now if you obey me [the Lord] fully and keep my covenant, then out of all nations you will be my treasured possession. Although the whole earth is mine, you will be for me a kingdom of priests and a holy nation.' . . ." *See also* **Dt** 28:9; **Eze** 37:26–28; **1Pe** 2:9
Holiness is conferred by the sovereign action of God
1Th 5:23 May God himself, the God of peace, sanctify you through and through. May your whole spirit, soul and body be kept blameless at the coming of our Lord Jesus Christ. *See also* **Lev** 20:8; **Isa** 4:3–4; **Eze** 36:25; **Zep** 1:7; **Ac** 15:9; **Heb** 2:11

Holiness through the OT rituals
Cleansing from what is unclean
Nu 8:6–7 "Take the Levites from among the other Israelites and make them ceremonially clean. To purify them, do this: Sprinkle the water of cleansing on them; then make them shave their whole bodies and wash their clothes, and so purify themselves." *See also* **Ex** 19:14; **Nu** 19:9; **Ne** 12:30
Purification and atonement through sacrifice
Nu 8:12–14 "After the Levites lay their hands on the heads of the bulls, use the one for a sin offering to the Lord and the other for a burnt offering, to make atonement for the Levites. Make the Levites stand in front of Aaron and his sons and then present them as a wave offering to the Lord. In this way you are to set the Levites apart from the other Israelites, and the Levites will be mine." *See also* **Ex** 29:35–37; **Lev** 8:14–15; 16:5–10,15–22,29–30

Consecration by anointing
Lev 8:10–12 Then Moses took the anointing oil and anointed the tabernacle and everything in it, and so consecrated them. He sprinkled some of the oil on the altar seven times, anointing the altar and all its utensils and the basin with its stand, to consecrate them. He poured some of the anointing oil on Aaron's head and anointed him to consecrate him. *See also* **Ex** 29:21; 40:9

Holiness through Jesus Christ
Through the sacrifice of Jesus Christ
Heb 10:10 . . . we have been made holy through the sacrifice of the body of Jesus Christ once for all. *See also* **Eph** 5:25–27; **Col** 1:22; **Heb** 1:3; 9:13–14,23–28; 10:14,19–22; 13:12; **1Jn** 1:7; 2:2; 4:10
Through relationship with Jesus Christ
1Co 1:2 To the church of God in Corinth, to those sanctified in Christ Jesus and called to be holy, together with all those everywhere who call on the name of our Lord Jesus Christ—their Lord and ours: *See also* **1Co** 1:30

Holiness through the sanctifying work of the Holy Spirit
2Th 2:13 But we ought always to thank God for you, brothers and sisters loved by the Lord, because from the beginning God chose you to be saved through the sanctifying work of the Spirit and through belief in the truth. *See also* **Jn** 3:5–8; **Ro** 15:16; **1Co** 6:11; **1Th** 4:7–8; **Tit** 3:5; **1Pe** 1:2

The human response to holiness
Repentance
1Jn 1:9 If we confess our sins, he is faithful and just and will forgive us our sins and purify us from all unrighteousness. *See also* **Ezr** 9:1–7; 10:1–4; **Ps** 51:1–10; **Ac** 2:38; **Ro** 6:11–13; **Jas** 4:8
Faith
Gal 5:5 But by faith we eagerly await through the Spirit the righteousness for which we hope. *See also* **Ro** 1:17–18; **2Th** 2:13
Obedience
1Pe 1:22 Now that you have purified yourselves

by obeying the truth so that you have sincere mutual affection, love one another deeply, from the heart.   *See also* Ps 119:9; Jn 17:17; Ro 6:16—19   *See also atonement; faith; obedience; repentance; sanctification; spiritual growth.*

---

holiness, in behaviour

Behaviour that reflects the holy character of God himself is to be expressed in both social and personal dimensions of life.

Holiness in practice is a reflection of God's own character

1Pe 1:15—16 . . . just as he who called you is holy, so be holy in all you do; for it is written: "Be holy, because I am holy."   *See also* Lev 11:44—45; 19:2; 20:7; Eph 4:24; 1Jn 3:3

Holiness demands a different way of life

Shunning practices that defile

Lev 18:1—3 The LORD said to Moses, "Speak to the israelites and say to them: 'I am the LORD your God. You must not do as they do in Egypt, where you used to live, and you must not do as they do in the land of Canaan, where I am bringing you. Do not follow their practices.'"

Eph 5:11—12 Have nothing to do with the fruitless deeds of darkness, but rather expose them . . .

1Ti 5:22 Do not be hasty in the laying on of hands, and do not share in the sins of others. Keep yourself pure.   *See also* Lev 18:21—24, 29—30; 20:1—3,6—7,23—26; 21:7; 2Co 6:17—7:1; Gal 5:19—21,24; Eph 5:3—7; Col 3:5—10

Obedience to God's law

Lev 20:7—8 "'Consecrate yourselves and be holy, because I am the LORD your God. Keep my decrees and follow them. I am the LORD, who makes you holy.'"   *See also* Lev 18:4—5; 19:37; Dt 6:25; 28:9; Ps 119:9; Ro 7:12; 1Pe 1:22

Holiness is expressed in social behaviour

Care for the disadvantaged

Lev 19:9—10 "'When you reap the harvest of your land, do not reap to the very edges of your field or gather the gleanings of your harvest. Do not go over your vineyard a second time or pick up the grapes that have fallen. Leave them for the poor and the alien. I am the LORD your God.'"   *See also* Lev 19:14,33—34; 1Ti 5:3—4,8; Jas 1:27

A concern for truth and justice

Lev 19:15—16 "'Do not pervert justice; do not show partiality to the poor or favouritism to the great, but judge your neighbour fairly. Do not go about spreading slander among your people. Do not do anything that endangers your neighbour's life. I am the LORD.'"   *See also* Lev 19:11—13,35—37

Loving one's neighbour

Lev 19:18 "'Do not seek revenge or bear a grudge against one of your people, but love your neighbour as yourself. I am the LORD.'"   *See also* Lev 19:16—17

Holiness is expressed in family and sexual relations

1Th 4:3—7 It is God's will that you should be sanctified: that you should avoid sexual immorality; that each of you should learn to control your own body in a way that is holy and honourable, not in passionate lust like the heathen, who do not know God; and that in this matter no-one should wrong or take advantage of a brother or sister. The Lord will punish those who commit all such sins, as we have already told you and warned you. For God did not call us to be impure, but to live a holy life.   *See also* Lev 18:5—20,22—23; 19:3; 20:9; Eph 5:3; 1Co 6:13—15,18—19

Holiness is seen in personal character

Col 3:12 . . . as God's chosen people, holy and dearly loved, clothe yourselves with compassion, kindness, humility, gentleness and patience.   *See also* Eph 4:23—24,32—5:2; 2Ti 2:22

holiness, of God

The moral excellence of God that unifies his attributes and is expressed through his actions, setting him apart from all others. Believers are called to be holy as God is holy.

God's nature is holy
He is perfect
Dt 32:4 He is the Rock, his works are perfect, and all his ways are just. A faithful God who does no wrong, upright and just is he.

Isa 6:3 And they were calling to one another: "Holy, holy, holy is the LORD Almighty; the whole earth is full of his glory."

Rev 4:8 ... "Holy, holy, holy is the Lord God Almighty, who was, and is, and is to come." *See also* **2Sa** 22:31; **Job** 6:10; **Ps** 18:30; 22:3; 71:22; 78:41; **Isa** 41:14; 43:15; **Hab** 1:13; **Jn** 17:11; **Rev** 6:10
He is uniquely holy
1Sa 2:2 "There is no-one holy like the LORD; there is no-one besides you . . ." *See also* **Ex** 15:11; **Ps** 77:13; **Isa** 40:25; **Rev** 15:4

God's name is holy
Eze 36:21–23 "'. . . I will show the holiness of my great name . . .'" *See also* **Lev** 22:32; **1Ch** 16:35; 29:16; **Ps** 33:21; 97:12; **Isa** 57:15; **Eze** 39:25; **Lk** 1:49

God's dwelling-place is holy
Isa 57:15 ... "I live in a high and holy place . . ." *See also* **2Ch** 8:11; 30:27; **Ps** 2:6; 3:4; 5:7; 11:4; 15:1; 20:6; 47:8; 48:1; 65:4; **Isa** 63:15; **Joel** 3:17; **Ob** 16–17; **Jnh** 2:4; **Mic** 1:2; **Hab** 2:20; **Zec** 2:13; **Ac** 21:28; **Eph** 2:21–22; **Heb** 10:19–22; **Rev** 22:19

God's holiness is revealed in his righteous activity
Isa 5:16 ... the holy God will show himself holy by his righteousness. *See also* **Jdg** 5:11; **1Sa** 12:7; **Ps** 77:13; 145:17; **Da** 9:14,16; **Zep** 3:5

God's holiness affects worship
It is celebrated in worship
Ps 99:5 Exalt the LORD our God and worship at his footstool; he is holy. *See also* **1Ch** 16:29; **Ps** 29:2; 99:5; 103:1; 105:3; 145:21; **Isa** 6:3
Coming before a holy God requires preparation
Ex 3:5 "Do not come any closer," God said. "Take off your sandals, for the place where you are standing is holy ground." *See also* **Ex** 29:37; **Ps** 24:3–4; **1Co** 11:28; **Heb** 10:1–2,22
Special requirements and tasks are given to worship leaders Lev 21:7–8,10–15
Aaron and his family: **Ex** 28:1–43; **Lev** 21:16–23
2Ch 29:5

God's holiness is to be seen in his people
God's people are to be holy because he is holy
Lev 19:2 "Speak to the entire assembly of Israel and say to them: 'Be holy because I, the LORD your God, am holy.'"

2Ti 1:9 [God] who has saved us and called us to a holy life—not because of anything we have done but because of his own purpose and grace ... *See also* **Ex** 19:6; 22:31; **Lev** 11:44; **Mt** 5:48; **Ro** 12:1; **1Co** 1:2; **2Co** 11:2; **Eph** 1:4; 5:3; **Php** 4:8; **Col** 1:22; 3:12; **1Th** 3:13; 4:3–7; **Tit** 1:8; **Heb** 2:11; 3:1; 12:10; **1Pe** 1:15–16
Becoming holy involves striving after God
2Pe 3:14 ... make every effort to be found spotless, blameless and at peace with him. *See also* **2Co** 7:1; 13:11; **Eph** 4:22–24; **1Ti** 5:22; **Heb** 12:14; **Jas** 1:20–21; **2Pe** 3:11–12
The holiness of believers originates from God
Ex 31:13 "Say to the Israelites, 'You must observe my Sabbaths. This will be a sign between me and you for the generations to come, so that you may know that I am the LORD, who makes you holy.'" *See also* **Lev** 22:9; **Dt** 28:9; **Ps** 4:3; **1Jn** 3:1–3
Jesus Christ purifies Christian believers
1Jn 1:7 But if we walk in the light, as he is in the light, we have fellowship with one another, and the blood of Jesus, his Son, purifies us from all sin. *See also* **Heb** 7:26–28; 9:26–28;

10:10,14; **1Jn** 3:4–6

God's holiness makes sin objectionable to him

Hab 1:13 Your eyes are too pure to look on evil; you cannot tolerate wrong . . .   *See also* **Jos** 24:19–20; **Jer** 50:29

God's holiness necessitates dependence upon him for forgiveness

Ps 51:1–17 . . . Against you, you only, have I sinned and done what is evil in your sight, so that you are proved right when you speak and justified when you judge . . . Cleanse me with hyssop, and I shall be clean; wash me, and I shall be whiter than snow . . . Do not cast me from your presence or take your Holy Spirit from me . . .   *See also* **Da** 9:4–19; **1Jn** 1:9   *See also Christlikeness; fellowship, with God; forgiveness; righteousness, of God; sanctification; worship.*

holiness, of Jesus Christ

The holiness of Jesus Christ is seen in his divine nature and work, as he stands apart from and above the created world with divine power, authority and purity. Recognition of the holiness of Jesus Christ leads both to a realisation of sin and unworthiness and to worship and adoration.

The holy character of Jesus Christ
Its divine origin
Lk 1:35 . . . "The Holy Spirit will come upon you [Mary], and the power of the Most High will overshadow you. So the holy one to be born will be called the Son of God."   *See also* **Jn** 1:1–2; 3:31; 8:23; 13:3; 17:14,16

Its divine nature
Col 2:9 For in Christ all the fulness of the Deity lives in bodily form,   *See also* **Jn** 1:14; 10:30,38; 14:10; **Php** 2:6; **Heb** 1:3

Its divine purity
Heb 7:26 Such a high priest meets our need—one who is holy, blameless, pure, set apart from sinners, exalted above the heavens. *See also* **2Co** 5:21; **Heb** 4:15; **1Pe** 1:19; 2:22; **1Jn** 3:3,5

Its divine power
Ac 4:30 "Stretch out your hand to heal and perform miraculous signs and wonders through the name of your holy servant Jesus."   *See also* **Ac** 10:38

The holy work of Jesus Christ
He is set apart as God's servant
Ac 4:27 ". . . Herod and Pontius Pilate met together with the Gentiles and the people of Israel in this city [Jerusalem] to conspire against your holy servant Jesus, whom you [God] anointed."   *See also* **Mk** 10:45 pp **Mt** 20:28; **Jn** 14:31; **Ac** 3:26; **Php** 2:7–8; **Heb** 10:7

His life is consecrated to the will and purpose of God
Mt 26:39 . . . he [Jesus] fell with his face to the ground and prayed, "My Father, if it is possible, may this cup be taken from me. Yet not as I will, but as you will." pp **Mk** 14:35–36 pp **Lk** 22:42   *See also* **Mt** 26:42; **Jn** 12:49–50; 14:31

He is appointed as the judge of sinners **Jn** 5:22,26–27; **Ac** 17:31; **2Co** 5:10
He makes God's people holy
Heb 13:12 . . . Jesus also suffered outside the city gate to make the people holy through his own blood.   *See also* **Jn** 17:19; **Eph** 5:25–27; **Heb** 2:11; 10:10,14; **1Pe** 2:4–5,9–10

Declarations of the holiness of Jesus Christ
By David: **Ps** 16:10; **Ac** 2:27; 13:35
Mk 1:24 pp **Lk** 4:34; **Lk** 1:35
By Peter: **Jn** 6:69; **Ac** 3:14
Rev 3:7

Results of recognising the holiness of Jesus Christ
Awareness of sin and unworthiness
Lk 5:8 When Simon Peter saw this, he fell at Jesus' knees and said, "Go away from me, Lord; I am a sinful man!"   *See also* **Mt** 8:8 pp **Lk** 7:6–7

Fear Mt 8:28–34 pp Mk 5:9–17 pp Lk 8:26–37;
Rev 1:17

Adoration and worship Rev 5:8–14   *See also
obedience, of Jesus Christ; righteousness, of Jesus Christ.*

holiness, purpose

God in his holiness desires a holy people amongst
whom he can dwell, and who can effectively
worship, witness to and serve him as they prepare
for a future with God and to be like God.

The goal of holiness is to be like God
Lev 19:2 "Speak to the entire assembly of
Israel and say to them: 'Be holy because I, the
LORD your God, am holy.'"

Mt 5:48 [Jesus said to his disciples] "Be
perfect, therefore, as your heavenly Father is
perfect."   *See also* Ro 8:29; Heb 12:10; 1Pe
1:15–16; 1Jn 3:2–3

God dwells with holy people
God dwelt with the people of Israel
Dt 23:14 . . . the LORD your God moves
about in your camp to protect you and to deliver
your enemies to you. Your camp must be holy, so
that he will not see among you anything indecent
and turn away from you.   *See also* Ex
29:42–46; Nu 5:1–3; 1Ki 9:3; Eze 37:26–28; Zec
2:10–12
God dwells with Christians
Eph 2:19–22 . . . you are no longer
foreigners and aliens, but fellow-citizens with God's
people and members of God's household, built on
the foundation of the apostles and prophets, with
Christ Jesus himself as the chief cornerstone. In
him the whole building is joined together and rises
to become a holy temple in the Lord. And in him
you too are being built together to become a
dwelling in which God lives by his Spirit.   *See
also* 1Co 3:16–17

Holiness is required for acceptable
worship
Heb 10:19–22 Therefore, brothers and sisters,
since we have confidence to enter the Most Holy
Place by the blood of Jesus, by a new and living
way opened for us through the curtain, that is,
his body, and since we have a great priest over
the house of God, let us draw near to God with
a sincere heart in full assurance of faith, having
our hearts sprinkled to cleanse us from a guilty
conscience and having our bodies washed with
pure water.   *See also* Lev 22:17–22; 2Ch
29:15–31; Isa 56:6–7; Mt 15:7–9 pp Mk 7:6; Isa
29:13; Ro 12:1

Holiness is needed for effective witness
1Pe 2:9–12 . . . you are a chosen people, a
royal priesthood, a holy nation, a people belonging
to God, that you may declare the praises of him
who called you out of darkness into his wonderful
light. Once you were not a people, but now you
are the people of God; once you had not received
mercy, but now you have received mercy. Dear
friends, I urge you, as aliens and strangers in the
world, to abstain from sinful desires, which war
against your soul. Live such good lives among the
pagans that, though they accuse you of doing
wrong, they may see your good deeds and glorify
God on the day he visits us.   *See also* Eze
20:41; 36:20; 39:7; 1Pe 3:1–2

Holiness is needed for godly service
Heb 9:13–14 The blood of goats and bulls and
the ashes of a heifer sprinkled on those who are
ceremonially unclean sanctify them so that they
are outwardly clean. How much more, then, will
the blood of Christ, who through the eternal Spirit
offered himself unblemished to God, cleanse our
consciences from acts that lead to death, so that
we may serve the living God!   *See also*
Ex 28:41; Lev 21:6–8; 2Ch 35:3; Zep 3:9; Lk
1:74–75; 2Ti 2:20–21; Tit 2:14

Holiness leads to a future hope
Holy people will see God
Heb 12:14 Make every effort to live in peace
with everyone and to be holy; without holiness
no-one will see the Lord.   *See also* Mt 5:8; 1Th
3:13; 2Th 1:10
Holy people will receive eternal life
Ro 6:22 . . . now that you have been set free
from sin and have become slaves to God, the

benefit you reap leads to holiness, and the result is eternal life.   *See also* **2Pe** 3:11

Holy people will inherit the kingdom
Col 1:12 giving thanks to the Father, who has qualified you to share in the inheritance of the saints in the kingdom of light.   *See also* **Da** 7:18,22,27; **Eph** 1:18; **Rev** 20:6
Holy people will judge the world 1Co 6:2
Believers' ultimate destiny is to share God's holiness for ever
Eph 5:25–27 . . . Christ loved the church and gave himself up for her to make her holy, cleansing her by the washing with water through the word, and to present her to himself as a radiant church, without stain or wrinkle or any other blemish, but holy and blameless.

Rev 21:2–3 I [John] saw the Holy City, the new Jerusalem, coming down out of heaven from God, prepared as a bride beautifully dressed for her husband. And I heard a loud voice from the throne saying, "Now the dwelling of God is with human beings, and he will live with them. They will be his people, and God himself will be with them and be their God."   *See also Christlikeness; fellowship, with God; heaven; hope; righteousness; worship.*

---

holiness, separation from worldly

God's people are called to holiness, which involves being distinct from other people. In the OT, this is seen in the command to separate from other nations and from everything that can compromise commitment to the LORD. In the NT believers are called to distance themselves from the ways and values of the world, which can be dishonouring to God and destructive to obedience to him.

Israel is to be set apart from other nations
Lev 20:23–26 [God said] " 'You must not live according to the customs of the nations I am going to drive out before you. Because they did all these things, I abhorred them . . . I am the LORD your God, who has set you apart from the nations . . . You are to be holy to me because

I, the LORD, am holy, and I have set you apart from the nations to be my own.' "   *See also* **Ex** 33:15–16; **Lev** 15:31; 18:29–30; **Dt** 7:1–6; 23:9–14; **Ezr** 9:1–2,10–12; **Isa** 52:11

Common things are designated clean or unclean by ritual law
Clean and unclean animals
Lev 11:46–47 [God said] " 'These are the regulations concerning animals, birds, every living thing that moves in the water and every creature that moves about on the ground. You must distinguish between the unclean and the clean, between living creatures that may be eaten and those that may not be eaten.' "   *See also* **Lev** 11:1–23 pp Dt 14:3–20; **Mk** 7:14–19; **Ac** 10:14
Infectious skin diseases Lev 13:2–3; 14:2
Mildew Lev 13:47–49; 14:33–36
Bodily discharges Lev 12:2; 15:2
Corpses Lev 5:2–3; 11:31–40; 21:1,11

What is holy must be kept separate
The Israelites must distinguish between the holy and the common Lev 10:10–11; Eze 44:23
Contact with the profane desecrates the holy
Ac 21:28 [Some Jews shouted] "People of Israel, help us! This is the man [Paul] who teaches everyone everywhere against our people and our law and this place. And besides, he has brought Greeks into the temple area and defiled this holy place."   *See also* **Jer** 51:51
Unclean people and things must be removed
Nu 5:1–3 The LORD said to Moses, "Command the Israelites to send away from the camp anyone who has an infectious skin disease or a discharge of any kind, or who is ceremonially unclean because of a dead body. Send away male and female alike; send them outside the camp so that they will not defile their camp, where I dwell among them."

Ezr 10:10–11 Then Ezra the priest stood up and said to them, "You have been unfaithful; you have married foreign women, adding to Israel's guilt. Now make confession to the LORD, the God of your ancestors, and do his will. Separate yourselves from the peoples around you and from

your foreign wives."   *See also* **Lev** 7:22–27;
13:45–46; 19:5–8; **Nu** 19:13,20; **Dt** 23:10–14;
2Ch 26:21

**Unclean people are not to approach what is
sacred Lev** 7:20–21; 22:3–6

The holy must be treated with respect
**Unintentional defilement of the holy carries a
penalty Lev** 5:14–16

Warnings against contempt for the holy
Lev 22:1–2 The LORD said to Moses, "Tell
Aaron and his sons to treat with respect the
sacred offerings the Israelites consecrate to me, so
that they will not profane my holy name. I am
the LORD."   *See also* **Ex** 19:10–13; 28:42–43;
30:18–21; 31:14–15; **Nu** 4:15,17–20; **Heb**
10:28–29

Examples of contempt for the holy Lev 10:1–2;
Nu 16:1–7,18–35; **1Sa** 6:19–20; **2Sa** 6:6–7; **Eze**
22:26,31; **Ac** 5:1–10

Christians are called to be separate from the ways of the world
Jn 15:19 [Jesus said] "If you belonged to the
world, it would love you as its own. As it is, you
do not belong to the world, but I have chosen
you out of the world. That is why the world
hates you."

Jas 4:4 You adulterous people, don't you know
that friendship with the world is hatred towards
God? Anyone who chooses to be a friend of the
world becomes an enemy of God.

1Pe 2:9–11 But you are a chosen people, a
royal priesthood, a holy nation, a people belonging
to God, that you may declare the praises of him
who called you out of darkness into his wonderful
light. Once you were not a people, but now you
are the people of God; once you had not received
mercy, but now you have received mercy. Dear
friends, I urge you, as aliens and strangers in the
world, to abstain from sinful desires, which war
against your soul.   *See also* **Jn** 17:14–16; **2Co**
6:14–7:1; **2Ti** 2:19; **Jas** 1:27   *See also* **world.**

holiness, set apart
Believers are holy, in that they are called to be
set apart from the world as God's own people.
Likewise certain days and articles are holy because
they are set apart for God alone.

Believers are called to be a holy people, set apart for God
The nation of Israel
Dt 7:6 For you are a people holy to the LORD
your God. The LORD your God has chosen you out
of all the peoples on the face of the earth to be
his people, his treasured possession.   *See also*
Ex 19:5–6; **Lev** 20:26; **Dt** 26:18–19

The priests
1Ch 23:13 . . . Aaron was set apart, he and
his descendants for ever, to consecrate the most
holy things, to offer sacrifices before the LORD, to
minister before him and to pronounce blessings in
his name for ever.   *See also* **Lev** 21:5–8

The Nazirites Nu 6:1–8

The apostles and prophets Lk 1:70; **Ac** 3:21;
Eph 3:5; **2Pe** 3:2

Christians
Eph 1:4 For he [God] chose us in him [Christ]
before the creation of the world to be holy and
blameless in his sight . . .

1Pe 1:15–16 But just as he who called you is
holy, so be holy in all you do; for it is written:
"Be holy, because I am holy."   *See also* **1Co**
1:2; **Col** 3:12; **2Ti** 1:9; **1Pe** 2:9

Consecration sets apart for holiness
God's people are consecrated
Lev 20:7–8 "'Consecrate yourselves and be
holy, because I am the LORD your God. Keep my
decrees and follow them. I am the LORD, who
makes you holy.'"   *See also* **Ex** 19:10–11,
14–15; **Lev** 11:44–45; **Jos** 3:5; 7:13; **1Sa** 16:5

Priests are consecrated for divine service
Ex 30:30 "Anoint Aaron and his sons and
consecrate them so they may serve me as
priests."   *See also* **Ex** 40:12–15; **1Sa** 7:1; **1Ch**
15:14; **2Ch** 23:6; 29:5; 35:3

Articles are consecrated for divine use
Ex 40:9–11 "Take the anointing oil and anoint
the tabernacle and everything in it; consecrate it
and all its furnishings, and it will be holy. Then
anoint the altar of burnt offering and all its
utensils; consecrate the altar, and it will be most
holy. Anoint the basin and its stand and
consecrate them." *See also* **Ex** 29:36–37;
30:25–29

Days and occasions set apart for God
The Sabbath
Lev 23:1–3 The LORD said to Moses, "Speak
to the Israelites and say to them: 'These are my
appointed feasts, the appointed feasts of the LORD,
which you are to proclaim as sacred assemblies.
There are six days when you may work, but the
seventh day is a Sabbath of rest, a day of sacred
assembly. You are not to do any work; wherever
you live, it is a Sabbath to the LORD.'" *See
also* **Ge** 2:3; **Ex** 16:23–25; 20:11

The Passover Lev 23:4–8; **Nu** 28:16,25
The Feast of Weeks Lev 23:15–16,21; **Nu** 28:26
The Feast of Trumpets Lev 23:23–25; **Nu** 29:1;
Ne 8:2,9–11
The Day of Atonement Lev 23:26–28,32; **Nu**
29:7
The Feast of Tabernacles Lev 23:33–36; **Nu**
29:12
The sabbath year Lev 25:1–5
The Year of Jubilee Lev 25:8–12

**Places identified with the presence of
God are made holy**
Holy ground Ex 3:5; **Jos** 5:15
Holy mountains Ex 19:18–23; **2Pe** 1:18
The tabernacle Ex 29:42–44; 40:9
The temple
1Ki 9:3 The LORD said to him [Solomon]: "I
have heard the prayer and plea you have made
before me; I have consecrated this temple, which
you have built, by putting my Name there for
ever. My eyes and my heart will always be
there." pp **2Ch** 7:16 *See also* **1Ki** 8:10–13;
Eze 42:14,20; **Mt** 24:15; **Ac** 6:13; 21:28

Jerusalem and the holy land Joel 3:17; **Zec**
2:12; **Mt** 4:5; 27:53

**Things associated with worship are
holy**
Bread Ex 29:32–33; **1Sa** 21:3–6; **Mt** 12:3–4 pp
Mk 2:25–26 pp **Lk** 6:3–4
Perfume Ex 30:34–38
Ritual offerings
Lev 6:24–29 The LORD said to Moses, "Say to
Aaron and his sons: 'These are the regulations for
the sin offering: The sin offering is to be
slaughtered before the LORD in the place where
the burnt offering is slaughtered; it is most
holy.'" *See also* **Lev** 6:17; 7:1,6; 10:12–13,
16–18
Offerings dedicated with a vow Lev
27:9,14,20–23,28
Tithes Lev 27:30–33
The firstborn Ex 13:2,11–12; **Lk** 2:22–23
See also Sabbath.

hope
In Scripture, a confident expectation for the future,
describing both the act of hoping and the object
hoped for. When grounded in God, hope provides
the motivation to live the Christian life even in
the face of trouble.

hope, as confidence
Hope means more than a vague wish that
something will happen. It is a sure and confident
expectation in God's future faithfulness and
presence. The horizon of Christian hope extends
beyond death into an eternity prepared by God
himself, the reality of which is guaranteed by
Jesus Christ.

God and Jesus Christ are the hope of
believers
Ps 71:5 For you have been my hope, O
Sovereign LORD, my confidence since my youth.

1Ti 1:1 Paul, an apostle of Christ Jesus by the
command of God our Saviour and of Christ Jesus
our hope, *See also* **Jer** 14:8; 17:13; **Mt** 12:21;

Isa 42:4; Ac 28:20; Ro 15:12–13; Isa 11:10; 1Ti 4:10; 1Pe 1:21

The hope of resurrection and eternal life
Ac 23:6 Then Paul, knowing that some of them were Sadducees and the others Pharisees, called out in the Sanhedrin, "My brothers, I am a Pharisee, the son of a Pharisee. I stand on trial because of my hope in the resurrection of the dead."
Tit 1:2 . . . the hope of eternal life, which God, who does not lie, promised before the beginning of time,   *See also* Ac 2:26–27; Ps 16:9; Ac 24:15; Ro 8:24; 1Co 15:19; Tit 3:7; Heb 6:11; 7:19; 1Pe 1:3

The hope of future glory
Ro 5:2 through whom [Christ] we have gained access by faith into this grace in which we now stand. And we rejoice in the hope of the glory of God.

Col 1:27 To them [the saints] God has chosen to make known among the Gentiles the glorious riches of this mystery, which is Christ in you, the hope of glory.

Tit 2:13 . . . we wait for the blessed hope— the glorious appearing of our great God and Saviour, Jesus Christ,   *See also* Ro 8:18–21; 2Co 3:10–12; Gal 5:5; Eph 1:12,18; 1Th 2:19; 5:8; 2Ti 4:8

Hope is a Christian virtue
Ro 5:3–4 Not only so, but we also rejoice in our sufferings, because we know that suffering produces perseverance; perseverance, character; and character, hope.

1Co 13:13 And now these three remain: faith, hope and love. But the greatest of these is love.   *See also* Ro 12:12; 15:13; 1Co 13:7; Eph 4:4; Col 1:23; Heb 3:6; 1Pe 3:15

The effect of future hope on living now
Col 1:4–5 . . . we [Paul and Timothy] have

heard of your faith in Christ Jesus and of the love you have for all the saints—the faith and love that spring from the hope that is stored up for you in heaven and that you have already heard about in the word of truth, the gospel . . .   *See also* Ro 8:22–23; 1Th 1:3; 5:8; Heb 6:19; 1Pe 1:13; 1Jn 3:1–3   *See also resurrection; salvation.*

hope, in God
A total grounding of one's confidence and expectation in God's goodness and providential care even in the face of trouble.

Hope in God is commanded
Ps 131:3 O Israel, put your hope in the LORD both now and for evermore.

1Ti 6:17 Command those who are rich in this present world not to be arrogant nor to put their hope in wealth, which is so uncertain, but to put their hope in God, who richly provides us with everything for our enjoyment.   *See also* Ps 31:24; 130:7; Ro 12:12; Heb 10:23

Hope can be placed in Scripture as the word of God
Ps 119:74 May those who fear you rejoice when they see me, for I have put my hope in your word.   *See also* Ps 119:43,49,81,114,147; 130:5; Isa 42:4; Ac 26:6; Ro 15:4; Col 1:5

Hope can be placed in God in the face of difficulty or trial
Ps 42:5 Why are you downcast, O my soul? Why so disturbed within me? Put your hope in God, for I will yet praise him, my Saviour . . .

2Co 1:10 He [God] has delivered us from such a deadly peril, and he will deliver us. On him we have set our hope that he will continue to deliver us,   *See also* Ezr 10:2; Job 5:16; 13:15; Ps 9:18; 25:19–21; 119:116; Jer 14:19; 1Ti 5:5

The outcome of hoping in God
It brings security and confidence
Ps 146:5 Blessed are those whose help is the

God of Jacob, whose hope is in the LORD their God, *See also* Job 11:18; Ps 25:3; 33:17–18, 20–22; 39:7; 52:9; 71:5; 147:11; Jer 14:22; La 3:21–22; Ac 24:15; Ro 15:12; 1Ti 4:10

It leads to specific results
Ps 37:9 For those who are evil will be cut off, but those who hope in the LORD will inherit the land.

Isa 40:31 but those who hope in the LORD will renew their strength. They will soar on wings like eagles; they will run and not grow weary, they will walk and not be faint.

Ro 15:13 May the God of hope fill you with all joy and peace as you trust in him, so that you may overflow with hope by the power of the Holy Spirit. *See also* Ps 33:22; 62:5; 71:14; Pr 24:14–16; Isa 51:5; Jer 29:11; La 3:25; Mic 7:7; Zec 9:12; Ro 4:18; 5:2,5; 2Co 1:7; 10:15; 1Th 1:3; 2Ti 2:25; Tit 1:2; 1Pe 3:5; 1Jn 3:3 *See also faith.*

hope, nature of
Hope, in its general sense, is the anticipation of a future outcome. It is a subjective expectation which may be either firmly based or misdirected.

Hope that an event will take place
1Co 9:10 . . . when farmers plough and thresh, they ought to do so in the hope of sharing in the harvest.

1Ti 3:14 . . . I [Paul] hope to come to you soon . . . *See also* Est 9:1; Lk 6:34; Ac 24:26; Ro 15:24; 1Co 9:15; 16:7; 2Co 1:13–14; 5:11; 11:1
Paul hopes to send Timothy to the Philippians: Php 2:19,23
Phm 22; 2Jn 12; 3Jn 14

Hope for a positive outcome
Ecc 9:4 Anyone who is among the living has hope—even a live dog is better off than a dead lion! *See also* Ru 1:12; 2Ki 4:28; Pr 19:18; Ro 11:14

Misplaced or vain hope
Ps 33:17 A horse is a vain hope for deliverance; despite all its great strength it cannot save.

Jer 23:16 This is what the LORD Almighty says: "Do not listen to what the prophets are prophesying to you; they fill you with false hopes. They speak visions from their own minds, not from the mouth of the LORD." *See also* Job 8:13–14; 11:20; Pr 26:12; 29:20; Jer 50:7; 1Ti 6:17

Hope removed or not satisfied
Job 30:26 "Yet when I hoped for good, evil came; when I looked for light, then came darkness."

Jer 8:15 "We hoped for peace but no good has come, for a time of healing but there was only terror." *See also* Job 6:19–20; 14:7–12; 19:10; 27:8; Isa 38:18; Jer 13:16; 14:19; La 3:18; Eze 37:11; Zec 9:5; Lk 24:21; 1Th 4:13

The malicious hope of the wicked
Pr 10:28 The prospect of the righteous is joy, but the hopes of the wicked come to nothing. *See also* Pr 11:7,23; 24:19–20; Lk 20:20; 23:8; Ac 16:19 *See also covenant.*

hope, results of
Hope gives believers confidence and reassurance in this present life, allowing them to lead effective lives for God. It also reassures them of the reality of eternal life, allowing them to face death with confidence.

Hope reassures believers in this present life
Hope reassures believers in their faith
Heb 3:6 But Christ is faithful as a son over God's house. And we are his house, if we hold on to our courage and the hope of which we boast. *See also* Eph 1:18–19; Heb 7:18–22; 10:23
Hope encourages believers
Ps 31:2 Turn your ear to me, come quickly to

my rescue; be my rock of refuge, a strong fortress to save me.   *See also* Isa 40:31; 49:23; Ro 5:3–5

Hope encourages believers to rejoice
Ro 12:12 Be joyful in hope, patient in affliction, faithful in prayer.   *See also* Ro 5:1–2

Hope encourages believers to look for restoration Ps 37:9; Jer 14:8; 31:17; La 3:29–31; Hos 2:15; Zec 9:12

Hope leads to more effective Christian living and witness

Hope encourages believers to be bold
2Co 3:12 Therefore, since we have such a hope, we are very bold.

Hope encourages believers to evangelise 1Pe 3:15

Hope leads to godly living Ps 25:21; Heb 6:10–12; 1Jn 3:2

Hope equips believers for spiritual warfare 1Th 5:8

Hope enables believers to face suffering with confidence
Ro 5:3–5 Not only so, but we also rejoice in our sufferings, because we know that suffering produces perseverance; perseverance, character; and character, hope. And hope does not disappoint us, because God has poured out his love into our hearts by the Holy Spirit, whom he has given us.   *See also* Ps 22:24; 147:11; Php 1:20

Hope enables believers to face the future with confidence

Hope assures believers of an eternal dimension to life
1Co 15:19 If only for this life we have hope in Christ, we are to be pitied more than all people.

Hope enables believers to face death with confidence
Ps 16:9–10 Therefore my heart is glad and my tongue rejoices; my body also will rest secure, because you will not abandon me to the grave, nor will you let your Holy One see decay.   *See also* Job 19:25–27; Ps 33:18; 1Co 6:14; 2Co 4:10–14; Php 1:3–6; Rev 1:17–18

Hope assures believers of their eternal life Ac 2:26–27; Ro 8:23–25; Tit 1:1–2; 3:7; 1Pe 1:3

Hope enables believers to face the coming wrath with confidence 1Th 1:10

Hope assures believers of their heavenly inheritance
1Pe 1:3–5 Praise be to the God and Father of our Lord Jesus Christ! In his great mercy he has given us new birth into a living hope through the resurrection of Jesus Christ from the dead, and into an inheritance that can never perish, spoil or fade—kept in heaven for you, who through faith are shielded by God's power until the coming of the salvation that is ready to be revealed in the last time.   *See also* Eph 1:18   *See also* assurance; heaven; inheritance; peace, experience.

---

human race

Human beings are the high point of God's creation. They alone are created in his image. As a result of sin they are alienated from God and from one another, and are unable by themselves to alter this situation. The salvation of humanity rests totally upon the atoning sacrifice of Jesus Christ, received by grace through faith.

---

human race, and creation

Although the human race is the pinnacle of God's creative work, it shares the inherent limitations of the physical realm. Human beings are nevertheless given responsibility to manage and steward the world.

The human race is an integral part of the physical creation

The human race was created from the ground
Ge 2:7 the LORD God formed the man from the dust of the ground and breathed into his nostrils the breath of life, and the man became a living being.   *See also* Ge 3:17–19; Job 10:8–9; Ps 103:13–14

The human race was created on the same day as the animals Ge 1:24–27

The human race was created from dust like the animals Ge 2:7,19

The human race is set apart from the rest of creation

The human race is uniquely created in God's image

Ge 5:1–2 . . . When God created human beings, he made them in the likeness of God. He created them male and female and blessed them. And when they were created, he called them "human beings". *See also* **Ge** 1:26–27; 9:6; **Jas** 3:9

The human race is given authority to take care of creation

Ge 1:26–28 Then God said, "Let us make human beings in our image, in our likeness, and let them rule over the fish of the sea and the birds of the air, over the livestock, over all the earth, and over all the creatures that move along the ground." So God created human beings in his own image, in the image of God he created them; male and female he created them. God blessed them and said to them, "Be fruitful and increase in number; fill the earth and subdue it. Rule over the fish of the sea and the birds of the air and over every living creature that moves on the ground." *See also* **Ge** 2:15; 9:1–3; **Ps** 8:3–8; **Heb** 2:5–8

The human race is created with the power of choice

Ge 2:16–17 And the LORD God commanded the man, "You are free to eat from any tree in the garden; but you must not eat from the tree of the knowledge of good and evil, for when you eat of it you will surely die." *See also* **Ge** 2:19

Human beings are created accountable to God for their actions

Mt 12:36 "But I tell you that people will have to give account on the day of judgment for every careless word they have spoken." *See also* **Eze** 18:20; **Jn** 3:18–19; **Ro** 2:14–15; **Rev** 2:23

The human race is created dependent upon God

Mt 4:4 Jesus answered, "It is written: 'People do not live on bread alone, but on every word that comes from the mouth of God.'"

2Co 3:5 Not that we are competent in ourselves to claim anything for ourselves, but our competence comes from God. *See also* **2Ch** 20:12; **Jer** 10:23; **Jas** 4:13–15

The human race comprises two complementary genders

Ge 2:18–24 The LORD God said, "It is not good for the man to be alone. I will make a helper suitable for him." . . . But for Adam no suitable helper was found. So the LORD God caused the man to fall into a deep sleep; and while he was sleeping, he took one of the man's ribs and closed up the place with flesh. Then the LORD God made a woman from the rib he had taken out of the man, and he brought her to the man. The man said, "This is now bone of my bones and flesh of my flesh; she shall be called 'woman', for she was taken out of man." For this reason a man will leave his father and mother and be united to his wife, and they will become one flesh. *See also* **Ge** 1:26–27; 5:1–2

The human race is one entity with a common ancestry in Adam

Ac 17:26 "From one man he made all the nations, that they should inhabit the whole earth; and he determined the times set for them and the exact places where they should live." *See also* **Ge** 9:18–19; 10:32–11:1 *See also creation.*

---

human race, and God

Though vastly superior to the human race, God nevertheless loves, sustains and governs it, sending his Son as a human being to redeem humanity.

God is incomparably superior to the human race

Isa 40:15–22 Surely the nations are like a drop in a bucket; they are regarded as dust on the scales; he weighs the islands as though they were fine dust . . . Before him all the nations are as nothing; they are regarded by him as worthless and less than nothing . . . He sits enthroned above the circle of the earth, and its people are like grasshoppers. He stretches out the heavens like a canopy, and spreads them out like a tent to live in.   *See also* **Job** 25:1–6; 38:1–7; **Ps** 8:3–4; **Isa** 31:1–3; **Ac** 17:24–25; **1Co** 1:20–25

The human race is dependent upon God
Job 34:14–15 "If it were his intention and he withdrew his spirit and breath, all people would perish together and they would return to the dust."   *See also* **Job** 12:10; **Ps** 36:5–6; **Ac** 17:24–28

The human race is valued and loved by God
The human race is the object of God's care and compassion
Ps 103:13 As a father has compassion on his children, so the LORD has compassion on those who fear him;   *See also* **Ps** 10:17–18; **La** 3:31–33; **Mt** 6:25–33 pp **Lk** 12:22–31
God wants to bless the human race **Ge** 12:1–3; **Ro** 10:12
God wants to save the human race
Jn 3:16–17 "For God so loved the world that he gave his one and only Son, that whoever believes in him shall not perish but have eternal life. For God did not send his Son into the world to condemn the world, but to save the world through him."   *See also* **1Ti** 2:1–4; **2Pe** 3:8–9
God highly values the human race and human life
Ge 9:6 "Whoever sheds human blood, by human beings shall their blood be shed; for in the image of God has God made all people."   *See also* **Ex** 20:13; **Mt** 16:26 pp **Mk** 8:36–37 pp **Lk** 9:25; **1Pe** 1:18–19

God is sovereign and watches over the human race
Ps 33:10–15 The LORD foils the plans of the nations; he thwarts the purposes of the peoples. But the plans of the LORD stand firm for ever, the purposes of his heart through all generations. Blessed is the nation whose God is the LORD, the people he chose for his inheritance. From heaven the LORD looks down and sees all humanity; from his dwelling-place he watches all who live on earth—he who forms the hearts of all, who considers everything they do.   *See also* **Ps** 9:7–8; **Pr** 5:21; **Da** 5:18–21

God will judge and punish the wickedness of the human race
Isa 2:12–17 The LORD Almighty has a day in store for all the proud and lofty, for all that is exalted (and they will be humbled) . . . The arrogance of all people will be brought low and human pride humbled . . .   *See also* **Mt** 13:40–43; **Ac** 17:29–31; **Ro** 2:5–11

God is to be feared and worshipped by the entire human race
Ps 33:8 Let all the earth fear the LORD; let all the people of the world revere him.

Ro 1:20–25 For since the creation of the world God's invisible qualities—his eternal power and divine nature—have been clearly seen . . . They exchanged the truth of God for a lie, and worshipped and served created things rather than the Creator . . .   *See also* **1Ch** 16:28–31; **Ps** 96:7–10   *See also atonement; cross; redemption; salvation.*

human race, and redemption
Through Jesus Christ's death on the cross and his redemption, human beings are offered a salvation that will give them spiritual life and freedom, reconcile them to God, and unite them to one another as part of a new humanity.

Salvation is offered to the human race through Jesus Christ
Jn 3:14–17 "Just as Moses lifted up the snake in the desert, so the Son of Man must be lifted up, that everyone who believes in him may have eternal life. For God so loved the world that he gave his one and only Son, that whoever believes in him shall not perish but have eternal life. For God did not send his Son into the world to condemn the world, but to save the world through him."   *See also* **Mt** 28:18–20; **Lk** 24:45–47;

Ac 2:38–39; 10:34–35,44–48; **1Ti** 2:1–7; **Tit** 2:11–14; **Rev** 14:6–7

The Saviour was himself a human being
Gal 4:4 But when the time had fully come, God sent his Son, born of a woman, born under law,

1Ti 2:5–6 For there is one God and one mediator between God and human beings, Christ Jesus, himself human, who gave himself as a ransom for all—the testimony given in its proper time.　*See also* **Mt** 1:1; **Ro** 1:3–4; 8:3; **Php** 2:8; **Heb** 2:17

The human race is reconciled to God through Jesus Christ's death on the cross
2Co 5:18–21 All this is from God, who reconciled us to himself through Christ and gave us the ministry of reconciliation: that God was reconciling the world to himself in Christ, not counting people's sins against them. And he has committed to us the message of reconciliation. We are therefore Christ's ambassadors, as though God were making his appeal through us. We implore you on Christ's behalf: Be reconciled to God. God made him who had no sin to be sin for us, so that in him we might become the righteousness of God.　*See also* **Ro** 5:1–2; **Eph** 2:14–18; **Col** 1:19–22; **Heb** 2:17; 10:19–22

The human race is united in Jesus Christ
Gal 3:26–28 You are all children of God through faith in Christ Jesus, for all of you who were baptised into Christ have clothed yourselves with Christ. There is neither Jew nor Greek, slave nor free, male nor female, for you are all one in Christ Jesus.　*See also* **Jn** 10:14–16; **1Co** 12:12–13; **Eph** 2:13–22; **Col** 3:9–11; **Rev** 5:9–14

The human race is renewed in Jesus Christ
Eph 2:15 . . . His purpose was to create in himself one new humanity out of the two, thus making peace,　*See also* **1Co** 15:47–49; **2Co** 5:17

In Jesus Christ the human race is given spiritual life and freedom
Eph 2:4–5 But because of his great love for us, God, who is rich in mercy, made us alive with Christ even when we were dead in transgressions . . .　*See also* **Ro** 5:17–18; 8:1–2,9–11; **2Co** 3:13–17　*See also atonement; church; cross; justification; propitiation; reconciliation; redemption; salvation.*

human race, and sin
As a result of the fall, human beings have become separated from God through sin, and are divided amongst themselves. All are in a condition of spiritual blindness, slavery and death, and are incapable of saving themselves from this situation.

All the human race is sinful
Ro 3:9–12 . . . Jews and Gentiles alike are all under sin. As it is written: "There is no-one righteous, not even one; there is no-one who understands, no-one who seeks God. All have turned away, they have together become worthless; there is no-one who does good, not even one."　*See also* **Ps** 14:1–3; 53:1–3; **Ge** 6:5–13; **Job** 15:14–16; **Ecc** 7:20; **Ro** 1:18–32; **Rev** 18:1–5

The human race is estranged from God
Isa 59:1–2 Surely the arm of the Lord is not too short to save, nor his ear too dull to hear. But your iniquities have separated you from your God; your sins have hidden his face from you, so that he will not hear.　*See also* **Ge** 3:8–10, 22–24; **Ps** 5:4–5; **Eph** 2:12; 4:17–18; **Col** 1:21

The human race is spiritually callous, blind, enslaved and dead
Eph 2:1–3 As for you, you were dead in your transgressions and sins, in which you used to live when you followed the ways of this world and of the ruler of the kingdom of the air, the spirit who is now at work in those who are disobedient. All of us also lived among them at one time, gratifying the cravings of our sinful nature and following its desires and thoughts. Like the rest, we were by nature objects of wrath.

Eph 4:17–19 So I tell you this, and insist on it in the Lord, that you must no longer live as the Gentiles do, in the futility of their thinking. They are darkened in their understanding and separated from the life of God because of the ignorance that is in them due to the hardening of their hearts. Having lost all sensitivity, they have given themselves over to sensuality so as to indulge in every kind of impurity, with a continual lust for more.   *See also* Ro 1:21; 5:12–14; 6:16–20; 2Co 4:4; 1Jn 5:19

The human race is divided
The human race is divided individual against individual Ge 4:3–9; Ro 1:28–29
The human race is divided man against woman Ge 3:8–12,16; Pr 21:9
The human race is divided nation against nation Ge 11:1–9; Mt 24:6–7
The human race is divided Jew against Gentile Ac 10:27–28; Eph 2:11–12
The human race is divided rich against poor Am 8:4–6; Jas 2:1–7

The human race has been weakened by sin
The human race has become subject to death Ge 2:16–17 And the LORD God commanded the man, "You are free to eat from any tree in the garden; but you must not eat from the tree of the knowledge of good and evil, for when you eat of it you will surely die."

Ro 6:23 For the wages of sin is death, but the gift of God is eternal life in Christ Jesus our Lord.   *See also* Ro 5:12; 1Co 15:21; Jas 1:15
Human beings have become weak and frail Isa 40:6–7 A voice says, "Cry out." And I said, "What shall I cry?" "All people are like grass, and all their glory is like the flowers of the field. The grass withers and the flowers fall, because the breath of the LORD blows on them. Surely the people are grass."   *See also* Job 14:1–12; Ps 90:3–6; 103:13–16; Ecc 12:1–7; 1Pe 1:24–25   *See also* sin, universality.

human race, destiny
All human beings must face judgment, when God will reward them according to their attitude towards him.

The human race will face final judgment
Mt 16:27 "For the Son of Man is going to come in his Father's glory with his angels, and then he will reward everyone according to what they have done."

1Co 4:5 Therefore judge nothing before the appointed time; wait till the Lord comes. He will bring to light what is hidden in darkness and will expose the motives of people's hearts. At that time each will receive praise from God.   *See also* Da 12:1–2; Mal 3:16–18; Mt 13:40–43; Jn 5:24–29; Ro 2:5–11

Unbelievers will be separated from God
2Th 1:8–10 He will punish those who do not know God and do not obey the gospel of our Lord Jesus. They will be punished with everlasting destruction and shut out from the presence of the Lord and from the majesty of his power on the day he comes to be glorified in his holy people . . .   *See also* Mt 25:31–46; Mk 9:42–48; Lk 13:22–28; 2Pe 3:7; Rev 20:11–15

Those who have faith will live in God's presence
Rev 21:1–3 Then I saw a new heaven and a new earth, for the first heaven and the first earth had passed away, and there was no longer any sea. I saw the Holy City, the new Jerusalem, coming down out of heaven from God, prepared as a bride beautifully dressed for her husband. And I heard a loud voice from the throne saying, "Now the dwelling of God is with human beings, and he will live with them. They will be his people, and God himself will be with them and be their God."

Jn 14:1–3 ". . . Trust in God; trust also in

me. In my Father's house are many rooms; if it were not so, I would have told you. I am going there to prepare a place for you. And if I go and prepare a place for you, I will come back and take you to be with me that you also may be where I am." *See also* **Zec** 2:10–13; **Rev** 7:13–17; 22:3–4

United in the praise of God

Rev 7:9–10 After this I looked and there before me was a great multitude that no-one could count, from every nation, tribe, people and language, standing before the throne and in front of the Lamb. They were wearing white robes and were holding palm branches in their hands. And they cried out in a loud voice: "Salvation belongs to our God, who sits on the throne, and to the Lamb." *See also* **Isa** 2:2–4 pp Mic 4:1–3; **Mt** 8:11 pp Lk 13:29; **Rev** 5:9–10; 21:22–27

Delivered from suffering, pain and death

Rev 21:3–4 And I heard a loud voice from the throne saying, "Now the dwelling of God is with human beings, and he will live with them. They will be his people, and God himself will be with them and be their God. He will wipe every tear from their eyes. There will be no more death or mourning or crying or pain, for the old order of things has passed away." *See also* **Isa** 25:6–8; 65:17–25; **Rev** 7:16–17; 22:1–3

Sharing in the glory of Jesus Christ

Col 3:4 When Christ, who is your life, appears, then you also will appear with him in glory.

1Pe 5:4 And when the Chief Shepherd appears, you will receive the crown of glory that will never fade away. *See also* **2Ti** 4:8 *See also heaven; hell; judgment; God's; last things.*

Israel, people of God

God called Israel out of Egypt to be his own treasured possession and his covenant faithfulness with them is maintained, despite their persistent disobedience.

God's election of Israel

The nation was founded upon God's promises to the patriarchs

Ge 12:1–3 . . . ". . . I [the LORD] will make you [Abraham] into a great nation and I will bless you . . ." *See also* **Ge** 17:1–8; 35:9–13

Israel as God's chosen possession

1Ki 8:53 "For you [the LORD] singled them [Israel] out from all the nations of the world to be your own inheritance, just as you declared through your servant Moses when you, O Sovereign LORD, brought our ancestors out of Egypt." *See also* **Ex** 19:3–6; **Dt** 7:6; 32:7–12; **Ps** 135:3–4

God redeemed Israel from Egypt

Ex 6:6–7 "Therefore, say to the Israelites: 'I am the LORD, and I will bring you out from under the yoke of the Egyptians. I will free you from being slaves to them, and I will redeem you with an outstretched arm and with mighty acts of judgment. I will take you as my own people, and I will be your God. Then you will know that I am the LORD your God, who brought you out from under the yoke of the Egyptians.'" *See also* **Ex** 3:7–10; **2Sa** 7:22–24 pp 1Ch 17:20–22

God enters into a special covenant relationship with Israel **Ex** 24:3–8

Israel's privileged status within the covenant

Ro 9:4–5 . . . Theirs [Israel's] is the adoption; theirs the divine glory, the covenants, the receiving of the law, the temple worship and the promises. Theirs are the patriarchs, and from them is traced the human ancestry of Christ, who is God over all, for ever praised! Amen. *See also* **Ro** 3:1–2; **Php** 3:4–6

Israel's disobedience to the covenant

Israel provoked God in the wilderness

Ps 78:40–41 How often they [Israel] rebelled against him [God] in the desert and grieved him in the wasteland! Again and again they put God to the test; they vexed the Holy One of Israel. *See also* **Ex** 32:1–10; **Nu** 11:1–6; 14:1–4

Israel's unfaithfulness in the promised land

Isa 1:4 Ah, sinful nation, a people loaded with guilt, a brood of evildoers, children given to corruption! They have forsaken the LORD; they have spurned the Holy One of Israel and turned their backs on him. *See also* **Jdg** 2:10–13; **Jer** 11:9–10; **Eze** 20:27–28

Israel exiled for her sins

2Ki 18:11–12 The king of Assyria deported Israel to Assyria and settled them in Halah, in Gozan on the Habor River, and in towns of the Medes. This happened because they had not obeyed the LORD their God, but had violated his covenant—all that Moses the servant of the LORD commanded. They neither listened to the commands nor carried them out. *See also* **2Ki** 25:8–12 pp Jer 39:8–10 pp Jer 52:12–16

God's promise to restore Israel

God's promise not to abandon Israel completely

Dt 4:31 For the LORD your God is a merciful God; he will not abandon or destroy you or forget the covenant with your ancestors, which he confirmed to them by oath. *See also* **Lev** 26:44–45; **Isa** 6:11–13; **Jer** 31:35–37

God's promise to bring Israel back to the land

Jer 30:3 " 'The days are coming,' declares the LORD, 'when I will bring my people Israel and Judah back from captivity and restore them to the land I gave to their ancestors to possess,' says the LORD." *See also* **Isa** 43:5–7; **Eze** 37:11–14

God's promise to reunite Israel

Jer 3:18 "In those days the house of Judah will join the house of Israel, and together they will come from a northern land to the land I [the LORD] gave your ancestors as an inheritance." *See also* **Eze** 37:15–23; **Hos** 1:10–11

The promise of a restored relationship between Israel and God

Jer 31:31–34 "The time is coming," declares the LORD, "when I will make a new covenant with the house of Israel and with the house of Judah . . ." *See also* **Isa** 40:1–2; **Eze** 36:24–28

Israel returns from exile Ezr 1:1–5 pp 2Ch 36:22–23

Jesus Christ, the Saviour of Israel

Jesus Christ's ministry was specifically to the nation of Israel

Mt 10:5–6 These twelve [the apostles] Jesus sent out with the following instructions: "Do not go among the Gentiles or enter any town of the Samaritans. Go rather to the lost sheep of Israel." *See also* **Mt** 15:21–28 pp Mk 7:24–30

Jesus accepts the title "Christ" (Messiah), God's anointed deliverer for Israel

Mt 16:16–17 Simon Peter answered, "You are the Christ, the Son of the living God." Jesus replied, "Blessed are you, Simon son of Jonah, for this was not revealed to you by flesh and blood, but by my Father in heaven." pp Mk 8:29 pp Lk 9:20

Jesus Christ declares to Israel the good news of God's reign

Mk 1:14–15 After John was put in prison, Jesus went into Galilee, proclaiming the good news of God. "The time has come," he said. "The kingdom of God is near. Repent and believe the good news!" *See also* **Mt** 4:23; 9:35; Lk 8:1

Israel's rejection of Jesus Christ

Israel warned that rejection of Christ means exclusion from the kingdom

Mt 8:11–12 "I [Jesus] say to you [Jesus' followers] that many will come from the east and the west, and will take their places at the feast with Abraham, Isaac and Jacob in the kingdom of heaven. But the subjects of the kingdom will be thrown outside, into the darkness, where there will be weeping and gnashing of teeth." *See also* **Mt** 21:33–46 pp Mk 12:1–12 pp Lk 20:9–19; **Mt** 22:1–10 pp Lk 14:16–24; **Lk** 13:28–30

Israel's rejection of the gospel

Ro 9:30–10:4 What then shall we say? That the Gentiles, who did not pursue righteousness, have obtained it, a righteousness that is by faith; but Israel, who pursued a law of righteousness, has not attained it. Why not? Because they pursued it not by faith but as if it were by works.

They stumbled over the "stumbling-stone". As it is written: "See, I lay in Zion a stone that causes people to stumble and a rock that makes them fall, and the one who trusts in him will never be put to shame." Brothers and sisters, my heart's desire and prayer to God for the Israelites is that they may be saved. For I can testify about them that they are zealous for God, but their zeal is not based on knowledge. Since they did not know the righteousness that comes from God and sought to establish their own, they did not submit to God's righteousness. Christ is the end of the law so that there may be righteousness for everyone who believes.   *See also* **Ac** 28:24–28; **Isa** 6:9–10; **1Th** 2:14–16

God's faithfulness to Israel maintained
Membership of the true Israel is based on
God's election, not merely on physical descent
from Abraham Ro 9:6–18
A remnant of Israel has been elected by grace
Ro 11:1–12
Paul declares that "all Israel" will be saved
Isa 59:20–21; **Ro** 11:25–32

The new Israel
The church as the new Israel
Gal 6:15–16 Neither circumcision nor uncircumcision means anything; what counts is a new creation. Peace and mercy to all who follow this rule, even to the Israel of God.

Php 3:3 For it is we [believers] who are the circumcision, we who worship by the Spirit of God, who glory in Christ Jesus, and who put no confidence in the flesh—   *See also* **1Pe** 2:9–10
The church described as the 12 tribes of Israel
Jas 1:1 James, a servant of God and of the Lord Jesus Christ, To the twelve tribes scattered among the nations: Greetings.   *See also* **Rev** 7:4–8; 21:12
The apostles as the 12 leaders of the new Israel
Mt 19:28 Jesus said to them [the 12 apostles], "I tell you the truth, at the renewal of all things, when the Son of Man sits on his

glorious throne, you who have followed me will also sit on twelve thrones, judging the twelve tribes of Israel."   *See also* **Lk** 22:29–30; **Rev** 21:14   *See also church; covenant; election.*

---

judgment, God's
God judges the world by identifying and condemning sin and by vindicating and rewarding the righteous. God exercises temporal judgment on the world and on his people; final judgment will take place when Jesus Christ returns.

The nature of God's judgment
Its certainty
Ecc 12:14 For God will bring every deed into judgment, including every hidden thing, whether it is good or evil.   *See also* **Ps** 7:11; **Ecc** 3:17; 11:9; **Jas** 5:9
Its righteousness
Ge 18:25 "Far be it from you [the Lord] to do such a thing—to kill the righteous with the wicked, treating the righteous and the wicked alike. Far be it from you! Will not the Judge of all the earth do right?"   *See also* **Ps** 9:7–8; 50:6; 96:13 pp 1Ch 16:33
Its impartiality
2Ch 19:7 ". . . Judge carefully, for with the Lord our God there is no injustice or partiality or bribery."   *See also* **Dt** 10:17; **Job** 34:19; **Ps** 98:9; **Ro** 2:11; **Eph** 6:9

The purpose of God's judgment
To display his glory
Isa 5:16 But the Lord Almighty will be exalted by his justice, and the holy God will show himself holy by his righteousness.   *See also* **Ex** 14:4; **Isa** 59:18–19; **Eze** 7:27; 38:23; **Rev** 14:7
To vindicate the righteous
1Sa 24:12–15 ". . . May the Lord be our judge and decide between us. May he consider my [David's] cause and uphold it; may he vindicate me by delivering me from your [Saul's] hand."   *See also* **Ps** 7:8–9; **Isa** 34:8; **Jer** 11:20; 51:9–10; **Rev** 16:5–7
To defend the weak
Ps 140:12 I know that the Lord secures justice

for the poor and upholds the cause of the needy.   *See also* Ps 82:1–4; Isa 11:4; Eze 34:16–22

To bring salvation to his people
Isa 30:18 Yet the LORD longs to be gracious to you [Israel]; he rises to show you compassion. For the LORD is a God of justice. Blessed are all who wait for him!   *See also* Ex 6:6; Dt 32:36; Ps 76:8–9; 105:5–7 pp 1Ch 16:12–14; Isa 33:22

To punish sin
Ro 2:12 All who sin apart from the law will also perish apart from the law, and all who sin under the law will be judged by the law.   *See also* Ps 1:4–6; Jn 12:48; Ro 5:16; Heb 10:26–30; 13:4

To turn people to God
Isa 19:22 The LORD will strike Egypt with a plague; he will strike them and heal them. They will turn to the LORD, and he will respond to their pleas and heal them.   *See also* 1Ki 8:33 pp 2Ch 6:24; 2Ch 7:13–14; Da 4:33–34; Hos 2:5–7; 1Co 11:29–32

God's judgment may be delayed
Job 24:1–4 "Why does the Almighty not set times for judgment? Why must those who know him look in vain for such days? . . ."

2Pe 3:9 The Lord is not slow in keeping his promise, as some understand slowness. He is patient with you, not wanting anyone to perish, but everyone to come to repentance.   *See also* Ps 74:10–11; 94:2–3; Hab 1:2–4,13; Ac 17:30; Ro 3:25; Rev 6:10

Examples of God's judgment
Judgment on ungodly individuals
Ac 12:23 Immediately, because Herod did not give praise to God, an angel of the Lord struck him down, and he was eaten by worms and died.   *See also* 2Ch 21:18–19; Da 5:26–28; Rev 2:22
Judgment following particular sins Ge 4:10–14; Nu 20:12; Lev 10:1–2; 1Sa 25:38–39; 2Sa 6:6–8; 2Ki 2:23–24; 5:27; 2Ch 26:19–20; Ac 5:1–10
Judgment on peoples and nations
Joel 3:12–13 "Let the nations be roused; let them

advance into the Valley of Jehoshaphat, for there I [the LORD] will sit to judge all the nations on every side . . ."   *See also* Ge 6:17; 19:24–25
Egypt: Ex 7:4–5; Nu 33:4
1Sa 2:10; 5:6
Assyria: Isa 10:12; 37:36 pp 2Ki 19:35
Isa 34:5
Babylon: Jer 25:12; 51:56
Jer 25:31–33
God's judgment on his enemies
Dt 32:41–43 "when I [the LORD] sharpen my flashing sword and my hand grasps it in judgment, I will take vengeance on my adversaries and repay those who hate me . . ."   *See also* Ps 45:3–6; Isa 1:24; Eze 38:21–22; Jn 12:31; Rev 20:7–10

God's judgment on Israel
God's warning of judgment
Dt 28:15–24 . . . The LORD will send on you [Israel] curses, confusion and rebuke in everything you put your hand to, until you are destroyed and come to sudden ruin because of the evil you have done in forsaking him . . .

Jer 1:16 "I [the LORD] will pronounce my judgments on my people because of their wickedness in forsaking me, in burning incense to other gods and in worshipping what their hands have made."   *See also* Lev 26:15–20,33; Jer 11:7–8
Plagues Nu 16:46–47; 21:5–9; 2Sa 24:15 pp 1Ch 21:14
Drought and famine 1Ki 17:1; Hag 1:10–11
Defeat by enemies Jos 7:1–7; Jdg 2:11–16; 2Ch 28:4–5
Exile 2Ki 17:23; Jer 11:17; La 1:5; Eze 39:23–24

God's final judgment on the whole earth
Ac 17:31 "For he [God] has set a day when he will judge the world with justice by the man he has appointed. He has given proof of this to everyone by raising him from the dead."   *See also* Da 12:2; Mt 25:31–32; Jn 12:48; Ro 2:16; 14:10; 1Co 4:5; 2Ti 4:1; 1Pe 4:5; Rev 20:11–15   *See also* last things; sin.

justice

A concern to act rightly, and to be seen by others to act rightly. Divine justice embraces every aspect of the right ordering of human society according to the will of God, its creator.

justice, believers' lives

God requires justice to be evident in the lives of his people. Through justification, believers are granted the status of being righteous in his sight, and are called upon to live out that righteousness in their lives.

God's law demands justice
The law is written on the conscience
Ro 2:14–15 . . . Indeed, when Gentiles, who do not have the law, do by nature things required by the law, they are a law for themselves, even though they do not have the law, since they show that the requirements of the law are written on their hearts . . . *See also* **Ge** 20:5–6; **Pr** 20:27
Isa 51:7 "Hear me, you who know what is right, you people who have my law in your hearts . . ." *See also* **Ecc** 8:5
The law in the OT
Ex 20:1–3 And God spoke all these words: "I am the LORD your God, who brought you out of Egypt, out of the land of slavery. You shall have no other gods before me."

Dt 6:4–5 Hear, O Israel: The LORD our God, the LORD is one. Love the LORD your God with all your heart and with all your soul and with all your strength. *See also* **Ex** 20:4–17 pp Dt 5:6–21; **Ps** 119:1,165 pp Mt 22:37–40
The law in the NT
Mt 5:17 "Do not think that I have come to abolish the Law or the Prophets; I have not come to abolish them but to fulfil them." *See also* **Ro** 7:7,12,22; 13:10; **1Ti** 1:8–11

Justification is by faith
Ro 1:17 For in the gospel a righteousness from God is revealed, a righteousness that is by faith from first to last, just as it is written: "The

righteous will live by faith." *See also* **Hab** 2:4; **Ge** 15:6; **Ro** 3:21–24; 4:24–25; 5:1; 9:30; **Gal** 3:6,24; **Php** 3:9

The marks of the just person
Jas 2:17 In the same way, faith by itself, if it is not accompanied by action, is dead. *See also* **Mt** 25:34–36; **Eph** 2:10; **1Jn** 3:7,9
Thinking justly
Ps 1:2 But their delight is in the law of the LORD, and on his law they meditate day and night. *See also* **Ps** 24:4; 40:8; 119:111–112; **Mt** 5:8; **Php** 4:8
Speaking justly
Ps 141:3 Set a guard over my mouth, O LORD; keep watch over the door of my lips. *See also* **Pr** 4:24; 8:6–8; **Eph** 4:25; **1Pe** 3:10
Behaving justly
Mic 6:8 He has showed you, O people, what is good. And what does the LORD require of you? To act justly and to love mercy and to walk humbly with your God. *See also* **Dt** 6:25; **Ps** 106:3; **Pr** 21:3; **Isa** 33:15–16; **Ac** 24:16

Examples of just people
Job 1:8 Then the LORD said to Satan, "Have you considered my servant Job? There is no-one on earth like him; he is blameless and upright, a man who fears God and shuns evil." *See also* **2Sa** 8:15; **1Ki** 3:11–12,28; **Lk** 23:50–51; **Ac** 25:8,11

The vindication of the just
2Ti 4:8 Now there is in store for me the crown of righteousness, which the Lord, the righteous Judge, will award to me on that day—and not only to me, but also to all who have longed for his appearing. *See also* **Ps** 86:17; **Da** 12:3; **Rev** 7:9–17 *See also justification; righteousness.*

justice, human

God created the world in justice, and expects that his creatures will deal fairly and justly with one another as a result. Sin brings injustice into the world, by disrupting the justice established by God at creation. As a result, human justice often falls short of God's standards.

God shows his concern for human justice

By commanding it
Isa 56:1 This is what the LORD says: "Maintain justice and do what is right . . ."

Mic 6:8 He has showed you, O people, what is good. And what does the LORD require of you? To act justly and to love mercy and to walk humbly with your God. *See also* **Ex** 23:1–9; **Dt** 24:17; **Ps** 82:3; **Pr** 21:3; **Hos** 12:6; **Ro** 13:7

By commending its maintenance
Ps 106:3 Blessed are those who maintain justice, who constantly do what is right. *See also* **Ge** 20:5–6; **1Ki** 3:11–12,28; **Job** 1:8; **Ps** 37:37; 112:5

By condemning its neglect
Mal 3:5 "So I will come near to you for judgment. I will be quick to testify against sorcerers, adulterers and perjurers, against those who defraud labourers of their wages, who oppress the widows and the fatherless, and deprive aliens of justice, but do not fear me," says the LORD Almighty. *See also* **Dt** 27:19; **Job** 31:13–14; **Isa** 3:14,15; 10:1; **Jer** 7:5–8,14; **Eze** 22:29–31

Justice in relationships within the family
Parents and children
Ex 20:12 "Honour your father and your mother, so that you may live long in the land the LORD your God is giving you." pp **Dt** 5:16 *See also* **Mt** 15:4; **Eph** 6:1–3; **Col** 3:20–21; **1Ti** 3:4
Brothers and sisters Ge 4:9–10
Husband and wife Mal 2:14; **1Co** 7:4–5; **Col** 3:18–19

Justice in the community
Pr 29:7 The righteous care about justice for the poor, but the wicked have no such concern.

Jas 1:27 Religion that God our Father accepts as pure and faultless is this: to look after orphans and widows in their distress . . . *See also* **Job** 29:16; **Ps** 82:3; **Pr** 29:14; 31:8–9; **Isa** 1:17; **Jer** 22:16

Justice in the business world
Col 4:1 Masters, provide your slaves with what is right and fair, because you know that you also have a Master in heaven. *See also* **Lev** 19:35–36; **Dt** 25:15; **Eph** 6:9; **Jas** 5:1–4

Justice in courts of law
Ex 23:6–8 "Do not deny justice to your poor people in their lawsuits. Have nothing to do with a false charge and do not put an innocent or honest person to death, for I will not acquit the guilty. Do not accept a bribe, for a bribe blinds those who see and twists the words of the righteous." *See also* **Lev** 19:15; **Dt** 1:16; 16:18–20; 17:6; 25:1–3; 27:25; **2Ch** 19:5–7
Partiality condemned: **Pr** 12:17; 18:5; 24:23–25; 28:21

Pr 18:17; **Jn** 18:23; **Ac** 23:3

Justice in rulers and governments
Pr 8:15 "By me [Wisdom] kings reign and rulers make laws that are just;" *See also* **1Ki** 10:9; **1Ch** 18:14; **Pr** 16:12–13; 29:26–27; 31:8–9; **Jer** 22:13–16; **Eze** 45:9; **Ro** 13:1–4; **1Pe** 2:13–14,17

Justice in the community of faith
Am 5:21–24 "I [God] hate, I despise your [Israel's] religious feasts; I cannot stand your assemblies . . . but let justice roll on like a river, righteousness like a never-failing stream!"

Lk 11:42 "Woe to you Pharisees, because you give God a tenth of your mint, rue and all other kinds of garden herbs, but you neglect justice and the love of God . . ." *See also* **Isa** 58:6–7; **Hos** 6:6; 12:6; **Mt** 23:23; **1Co** 6:1–8; **Jas** 2:1–4,12–13

Justice in a believer's life
Mic 6:8 He has showed you, O people, what is good. And what does the LORD require of you? To act justly and to love mercy and to walk humbly with your God. *See also* **Pr** 21:3; **Php** 4:8; **Tit** 2:12; **1Pe** 3:16 *See also* **law**.

justice, of God

The moral righteousness of God is revealed in his laws and expressed in his judicial acts. God's commands and judgments meet perfect standards of justice, and his apportioning of punishments and rewards is also perfectly just. God's justice is impartial. Special praise is his for vindicating the penitent and the needy who have no human champions. Ultimately, all God's ways will be seen as just and equitable.

God's justice declared
God the Father
Ps 92:15 ". . . The LORD is upright; he is my Rock, and there is no wickedness in him."

1Pe 1:17 Since you call on a Father who judges each person's work impartially, live your lives as strangers here in reverent fear. *See also* **Ge** 18:25; **Job** 36:3; **Ps** 11:7; 25:8; 33:5; 51:4; **Isa** 61:8; **Jer** 9:24; **Zep** 3:5; **Rev** 15:3
God the Son
1Jn 2:1 My [John's] dear children, I write this to you so that you will not sin. But if anybody does sin, we have one who speaks to the Father in our defence—Jesus Christ, the Righteous One. *See also* **Ps** 45:6; **Heb** 1:8–9; **Ps** 72:1–4 The righteousness of the coming Messiah: **Isa** 9:7; 11:3–5; 42:1,3; **Mal** 3:1–3
Ac 3:14; **1Co** 1:30; **Rev** 19:11
God the Spirit
Jn 16:8–11 "When he [the Counsellor] comes, he will convict the world of guilt in regard to sin and righteousness and judgment . . ." *See also* **Ac** 5:3,9; **Eph** 4:1,28,30

God's justice described
As impartial
1Pe 1:17 . . . a Father who judges each person's work impartially . . . *See also* **Dt** 10:17; **2Ch** 19:7; **Job** 34:19; **Da** 5:27; **Ac** 10:34; **Ro** 2:5,11; **Gal** 2:6; **Eph** 6:9; **Col** 3:25
As inescapable
Ro 2:3 So when you, a mere human being, pass judgment on them and yet do the same things, do you think you will escape God's

judgment? *See also* **Ps** 68:21–23; **Jer** 11:11; 16:16–18; 51:53; **La** 2:22; **Am** 9:1–4; **Ob** 4; **Heb** 2:2–3
As infallible
Heb 4:13 Nothing in all creation is hidden from God's sight. Everything is uncovered and laid bare before the eyes of him to whom we must give account. *See also* **1Sa** 2:3; **1Ch** 28:9; **Pr** 16:2; 21:2; 24:12; **Lk** 16:15; **Ro** 2:2,16

God's justice desired
By the oppressed
Ps 9:19 Arise, O LORD, let not mortals triumph; let the nations be judged in your presence. *See also* **Jdg** 3:9; **Ps** 7:6; 10:12–14
By those who are misrepresented
Ps 26:1 Vindicate me [David] O LORD, for I have led a blameless life . . . *See also* **1Sa** 24:15; **Ps** 35:23–24

God's justice doubted
Mal 2:17 You [Judah] have wearied the LORD with your words. "How have we wearied him?" you ask. By saying, "All who do evil are good in the eyes of the LORD, and he is pleased with them" or "Where is the God of justice?" *See also* **Job** 6:29; 27:2; 34:5; **Ps** 73:2–14; **Ecc** 8:11,14; **Isa** 40:27; **Ro** 9:14,19–20

God's justice demonstrated
In his demands for social justice
Mic 6:8 He has showed you, O people, what is good. And what does the LORD require of you? To act justly and to love mercy and to walk humbly with your God. *See also* **Dt** 16:18,20; **Isa** 1:16–17; **Am** 5:21–24; **Mal** 3:5; **Mt** 23:23; **Lk** 20:46–47
In his defence of the oppressed
Ps 103:6 The LORD works righteousness and justice for all the oppressed. *See also* **Ps** 72:2; 140:12; **Pr** 22:22–23; **Isa** 11:4; **Eze** 34:16; **Lk** 18:7–8
In his vindication of the righteous
Ro 8:33 Who will bring any charge against those whom God has chosen? It is God who justifies. *See also* **Ps** 17:1–2; 24:5; **Isa** 50:8–9; 54:17; 61:8

In the cross
Ro 3:25–26 God presented him [Jesus] as a sacrifice of atonement . . . to demonstrate his justice at the present time, so as to be just and the one who justifies those who have faith in Jesus. *See also* **2Co** 5:21; **Gal** 3:13
In the resurrection
Ac 17:31 "For he has set a day when he will judge the world with justice by the man he has appointed. He has given proof of this to everyone by raising him from the dead."
On the day of judgment
Ro 2:5 . . . for the day of God's wrath, when his righteous judgment will be revealed. *See also* **Ps** 9:8; **Ac** 17:31; **Rev** 16:5,7; 19:2 *See also atonement; cross; judgment, God's; propitiation.*

---

justification
The acquittal, or declaration of being righteous, before God as judge. It is a central aspect of Paul's understanding of what God achieved for believers through the death and resurrection of Jesus Christ.

---

justification, Jesus Christ's work
On account of the death and resurrection of Jesus Christ, the demands of the law of God are met, and believers are granted the status of being righteous in the sight of God.

Justification is grounded in the death of Jesus Christ
Jesus Christ's death shields believers from God's wrath
Ro 5:9 Since we have now been justified by his [Christ's] blood, how much more shall we be saved from God's wrath through him! *See also* **Ro** 3:24; 4:25; 5:18; **1Pe** 2:24
Jesus Christ's death fulfils the demands of the law of God
Ro 8:3–4 For what the law was powerless to do in that it was weakened by the sinful nature, God did by sending his own Son in the likeness of sinful humanity to be a sin offering. And so he condemned sin in our sinful nature, in order that

the righteous requirements of the law might be fully met in us, who do not live according to the sinful nature but according to the Spirit. *See also* **Ro** 3:25–26; **Gal** 3:13; **1Jn** 2:2

Justification is grounded in the resurrection of Jesus Christ
Ro 4:25 He [Jesus the Lord] was delivered over to death for our sins and was raised to life for our justification.

Ro 10:9–10 That if you confess with your mouth, "Jesus is Lord," and believe in your heart that God raised him from the dead, you will be saved. For it is with your heart that you believe and are justified, and it is with your mouth that you confess and are saved. *See also* **Ac** 2:22–39; 4:10–12; 17:30–31; **1Pe** 3:18–21

Justification means believers are reckoned as righteous through the death of Jesus Christ
Ro 5:19 For just as through the disobedience of the one man [Adam] the many were made sinners, so also through the obedience of the one man [Jesus Christ] the many will be made righteous.

1Co 1:30 It is because of him that you are in Christ Jesus, who has become for us wisdom from God—that is, our righteousness, holiness and redemption.

2Co 5:21 God made him [Jesus Christ] who had no sin to be sin for us, so that in him we might become the righteousness of God. *See also* **1Co** 6:9–11; **Php** 3:8–9

Justification is received by faith
Ro 1:17 For in the gospel a righteousness from God is revealed, a righteousness that is by faith from first to last, just as it is written: "The righteous will live by faith." pp **Gal** 3:11 *See also* **Hab** 2:4; **Ro** 5:1; **Eph** 2:8
The example of Abraham
Ge 15:6 Abram believed the LORD, and he [the LORD] credited it to him as righteousness. *See*

also **Ro** 4:1–5,9–22; **Gal** 3:6–9,16–18

The example of David Ro 4:6–8; **Ps** 32:1–2

Apostolic teaching on the need of faith for justification

Ac 13:39 "Through him [Jesus] everyone who believes is justified from everything you could not be justified from by the law of Moses." *See also* **Ro** 3:22,25,27–30; 4:5; 5:1; 9:30–32; 10:10; **1Co** 6:11; **Gal** 2:16; 3:8,14; **Eph** 2:8

Justification is a gift of God's grace

Ro 3:24 [all who believe] . . . are justified freely by his [God's] grace through the redemption that came by Christ Jesus. *See also* **Ro** 5:15–17; 8:33; **Tit** 3:7

Not by works or the law

Gal 3:11 Clearly no-one is justified before God by the law, because, "The righteous will live by faith." *See also* **Ro** 3:20; 4:5; **Gal** 2:16,21; 3:2–5,24; 5:4–6; **Eph** 2:8–9 *See also atonement; faith; reconciliation; redemption.*

---

justification, necessity

Sinful, law-breaking humanity needs a means of justification because of its failure to keep God's law and live up to God's requirements.

Justification in human relationships

The acquittal of the innocent

Dt 25:1 When people have a dispute, they are to take it to court and the judges will decide the case, acquitting the innocent and condemning the guilty. *See also* **Pr** 17:15; **Isa** 43:9,26; **Ro** 8:33

Justification of oneself

Job 32:2 But Elihu son of Barakel the Buzite, of the family of Ram, became very angry with Job for justifying himself rather than God. *See also* **Lk** 10:29; 16:15; 18:9–14

The need for justification

The reality of God's righteousness

Ps 11:7 For the LORD is righteous . . . *See also* **Ps** 33:5; 35:28; **Jer** 23:6; **Mt** 6:33; **Jn** 17:25; **Ro** 1:17; 3:22

The reality of God's justice

Ps 9:8 He [the LORD] will judge the world in righteousness; he will govern the peoples with justice. *See also* **Job** 36:3; **Ps** 11:7; 33:5; **Isa** 5:16; **Jer** 9:24; **Lk** 18:7; **Rev** 19:11

The reality of God's judgment

Ge 18:25 "Far be it from you to do such a thing—to kill the righteous with the wicked, treating the righteous and the wicked alike. Far be it from you! Will not the Judge of all the earth do right?" *See also* **Jdg** 11:27; **Ps** 51:4; **Mic** 6:2; **Mt** 12:36; **Ro** 2:16

The reality of God's law

Jas 4:12 There is only one Lawgiver and Judge, the one who is able to save and destroy. But you—who are you to judge your neighbour? *See also* **Ex** 20:2–17 pp **Dt** 5:6–21; **Ps** 19:7; **Isa** 33:22; **Ro** 7:12,16; 8:3–4; **1Ti** 1:8

Human guilt shows the need for justification

Ps 143:2 Do not bring your servant into judgment, for no-one living is righteous before you [the LORD]. *See also* **Ro** 3:23; **1Jn** 1:8,10

People are unable to justify themselves, even through the law

Isa 64:6 All of us have become like one who is unclean, and all our righteous acts are like filthy rags; we all shrivel up like a leaf, and like the wind our sins sweep us away.

Ro 3:20–21 Therefore no-one will be declared righteous in his sight by observing the law; rather, through the law we become conscious of sin . . .

Gal 2:15–16 "We . . . know that a person is not justified by observing the law, but by faith in Jesus Christ. So we, too, have put our faith in Christ Jesus that we may be justified by faith in Christ and not by observing the law, because by observing the law no-one will be justified." *See also* **Am** 4:4; **Mt** 5:20; **Lk** 10:29; 16:15; 18:9–14; **Ro** 1:17; 3:20; **Gal** 2:21; 3:2–3; 2:11; 5:4; **Php** 3:4–8 *See also judgment, God's; law; righteousness, of God; sin.*

---

justification, results

Justification brings a changed relationship with God

and a future hope. It will also bring a change in behaviour.

The results of justification
Peace with God, access to his presence and the hope of his glory
Ro 5:1–2 Therefore, since we have been justified through faith, we have peace with God through our Lord Jesus Christ, through whom we have gained access by faith into this grace in which we now stand. And we rejoice in the hope of the glory of God. *See also* **Ro** 8:30; **Tit** 3:7
Assurance of forgiveness Ro 5:9; **Eph** 1:13–14
Knowing Jesus Christ and participating in his resurrection
Php 3:10–11 I want to know Christ and the power of his resurrection and the fellowship of sharing in his sufferings, becoming like him in his death, and so, somehow, to attain to the resurrection from the dead. *See also* **Ro** 6:5
Freedom from condemnation
Ro 8:31–34 What, then, shall we say in response to this? If God is for us, who can be against us? He who did not spare his own Son, but gave him up for us all—how will he not also, along with him, graciously give us all things? Who will bring any charge against those whom God has chosen? It is God who justifies. Who then can condemn? Christ Jesus, who died—more than that, who was raised to life—is at the right hand of God and is also interceding for us. *See also* **Ro** 8:1–4; **Gal** 3:13–14
Freedom from domination by sin
Ro 6:14 For sin shall not be your master, because you are not under law, but under grace.

Ro 6:17–18 But thanks be to God that, though you used to be slaves to sin, you wholeheartedly obeyed the form of teaching to which you were entrusted. You have been set free from sin and have become slaves to righteousness. **Adoption into God's family Ro** 8:15–17; **Gal** 4:6–7
Righteousness in the sight of God
Ro 5:17 For if, by the trespass of the one man [Adam], death reigned through that one man, how much more will those who receive God's

abundant provision of grace and of the gift of righteousness reign in life through the one man, Jesus Christ.

Php 3:8–9 . . . I consider everything a loss compared to the surpassing greatness of knowing Christ Jesus my Lord, for whose sake I have lost all things. I consider them rubbish, that I may gain Christ and be found in him, not having a righteousness of my own that comes from the law, but that which is through faith in Christ— the righteousness that comes from God and is by faith. *See also* **Ro** 3:20–22; **1Co** 1:30

Justification must lead to good works
Jas 2:24 You see that people are justified by what they do and not by faith alone. *See also* **Ro** 6:15–18; **Gal** 5:13–16; **Jas** 2:14–26 *See also adoption; assurance; forgiveness; gospel; hope; knowing God; effects; peace; righteousness, as faith; sanctification.*

---

kingdom of God

Or, less frequently, "kingdom of heaven", the kingly rule of God in the lives of people and nations. It refers to the recognition of the authority of God, rather than a definite geographical area, and begins with the ministry of Jesus Christ.

---

kingdom of God, coming

The kingdom of God comes into being wherever the kingly authority of God is acknowledged. Although God is always sovereign, Scripture looks to a future "realm" or "reign" of salvation. This has come in Christ and yet will come in its fulness only when Jesus Christ returns.

God is sovereign over Israel and over the whole earth
Ps 47:7–8 For God is the King of all the earth . . . God reigns over the nations . . . *See also* **Ex** 15:18; **1Sa** 12:12; **1Ch** 16:31; 28:5; 29:11–12; **Ps** 9:7–8; 45:6; 93:1–2; 103:19; 145:11–13; **Isa** 37:16; **Da** 4:34–35

The coming reign of God
Its expectation
Isa 51:4–5 "Listen to me, my people; hear me, my nation: The law will go out from me; my justice will become a light to the nations. My righteousness draws near speedily, my salvation is on the way, and my arm will bring justice to the nations . . ."

Mk 15:43 Joseph of Arimathea . . . who was himself waiting for the kingdom of God . . . pp Lk 23:51   *See also* Isa 2:2–4 pp Mic 4:1–3; Isa 32:1; Jer 3:17; Da 2:44; 7:18,21–22,27; Zec 8:22; 14:9; Mk 11:10

Its association with the coming of the Messiah
Isa 9:6–7 For to us a child is born, to us a son is given, and the government will be on his shoulders. And he will be called Wonderful Counsellor, Mighty God, Everlasting Father, Prince of Peace. Of the increase of his government and peace there will be no end. He will reign on David's throne and over his kingdom, establishing and upholding it with justice and righteousness from that time on and for ever . . .

Da 7:14 "He [one like a son of man] was given authority, glory and sovereign power; all nations and peoples of every language worshipped him. His dominion is an everlasting dominion that will not pass away, and his kingdom is one that will never be destroyed."   *See also* Isa 11:1–9; Jer 23:5–6; Mic 5:2

The kingdom of God was central in the preaching of Jesus Christ and the apostles
Mt 24:14 "And this gospel of the kingdom will be preached in the whole world as a testimony to all nations, and then the end will come."

Lk 8:1 . . . Jesus travelled about from one town and village to another, proclaiming the good news of the kingdom of God . . .

Ac 28:31 Boldly and without hindrance he [Paul] preached the kingdom of God and taught about the Lord Jesus Christ.   *See also* Mt 4:17,23;

9:35; 10:7; Mk 1:13–14; Lk 4:43; 9:2,11; 10:9; Ac 1:3,6–8; 8:12; 19:8; 20:25; 28:23

The kingdom of God has come in Christ: it is present
Mt 11:12 "From the days of John the Baptist until now, the kingdom of heaven has been forcefully advancing . . ."   *See also* Mt 3:1–2; 4:17; 13:31–32 pp Mk 4:30–32 pp Lk 13:18–19; Mt 13:33 pp Lk 13:20–21; Mt 16:28 pp Mk 9:1 pp Lk 9:27; Lk 11:20; 16:16; 17:20–21

The kingdom of God will come in its fulness only when Jesus Christ returns: it is future
Lk 22:18 "For I [Jesus] tell you I will not drink again of the fruit of the vine until the kingdom of God comes." pp Mt 26:29 pp Mk 14:25   *See also* Mt 6:10 pp Lk 11:2; Mt 25:31,34; Lk 22:16; 1Co 15:24; 2Ti 4:18; Rev 11:15; 12:10   *See also* church; hope; last things; preachers and preaching.

kingdom of God, entry into
Entering or inheriting the kingdom of God is the privilege of those who acknowledge and live by the rule of God and have become part of the new order of salvation and righteousness in Christ.

Entry into the kingdom of God is of vital importance
It is costly
Mt 13:44 "The kingdom of heaven is like treasure hidden in a field. When a man found it, he hid it again, and then in his joy went and sold all he had and bought that field."

Ac 14:22 . . . "We must go through many hardships to enter the kingdom of God," . . .   *See also* Mt 8:19–20 pp Lk 9:57–58; Mt 13:45–46; Lk 18:29–30; 2Th 1:5; Rev 1:9
It is a matter of urgency
Lk 9:59–62 . . . "Let the dead bury their own dead, but you go and proclaim the kingdom of God." Still another said, "I will follow you, Lord; but first let me go back and say good-bye to my family." Jesus replied, "No-one who takes

hold of the plough and looks back is fit for service in the kingdom of God." pp Mt 8:21—22

Conditions of entry into the kingdom of God
Childlike trust
Mk 10:15 ". . . anyone who will not receive the kingdom of God like a little child will never enter it." pp Lk 18:17   *See also* **Mt** 18:3
To be born again of God's Spirit
Jn 3:3 ". . . "I [Jesus] tell you [Nicodemus] the truth, no-one can see the kingdom of God without being born again."   *See also* **Jn** 3:5; **1Co** 15:50
Obedience to God's will
Mt 7:21 "Not everyone who says to me [Jesus], 'Lord, Lord,' will enter the kingdom of heaven, but only those who do the will of my Father who is in heaven."

Warnings about entry into the kingdom of God
The way is narrow
Lk 13:24—28 "Make every effort to enter through the narrow door . . ."   *See also* **Mt** 7:13—14; 23:13
The wicked will not inherit the kingdom
1Co 6:9—10 Do you not know that the wicked will not inherit the kingdom of God? Do not be deceived: Neither the sexually immoral nor idolaters nor adulterers nor male prostitutes nor homosexual offenders nor thieves nor the greedy nor drunkards nor slanderers nor swindlers will inherit the kingdom of God.   *See also* **Mt** 5:20; **Mk** 9:43—47; **Gal** 5:19—21; **Eph** 5:5
The need for readiness and watchfulness
Mt 24:42—44 "Therefore keep watch, because you do not know on what day your Lord will come . . . So you also must be ready, because the Son of Man will come at an hour when you do not expect him."   *See also* **Mt** 24:37—39 pp Lk 17:26—27; **Mt** 25:13; **Lk** 12:35—40
Entry is not based on outward appearances nor granted to all who claim to know the Lord
Mt 7:21—23 ". . . Many will say to me [Jesus] on that day, 'Lord, Lord, did we not prophesy in your name, and in your name drive

out demons and perform many miracles?' Then I will tell them plainly, 'I never knew you. Away from me, you evildoers!' "   *See also* **Mt** 13:24—30,47—50; **Lk** 13:25—27

The kingdom of God is a kingdom of grace
It belongs to those qualified by God
Col 1:12—13 . . . who [the Father] has qualified you to share in the inheritance of the saints in the kingdom of light. For he has rescued us from the dominion of darkness and brought us into the kingdom of the Son he loves,   *See also* **Lk** 12:32; 22:29—30
It belongs to the poor and the poor in spirit
Lk 6:20 . . . "Blessed are you who are poor, for yours is the kingdom of God." pp Mt 5:3   *See also* **Mt** 11:5 pp Lk 7:22; **Mt** 19:23—24 pp Mk 10:23—25 pp Lk 18:24—25; **Jas** 2:5; 5:1
It belongs to the childlike
Mt 19:14 Jesus said, "Let the little children come to me, and do not hinder them, for the kingdom of heaven belongs to such as these." pp Mk 10:14 pp Lk 18:16
It belongs to sinners
Mk 2:17 . . . "It is not the healthy who need a doctor, but the sick. I have not come to call the righteous, but sinners." pp Mt 9:12—13 pp Lk 5:31—32   *See also* **Mt** 21:31
It belongs to those who are persecuted for Jesus Christ's sake
Mt 5:10 "Blessed are those who are persecuted because of righteousness, for theirs is the kingdom of heaven." pp Lk 6:22—23
It belongs to Gentiles as well as to Jews
Mt 8:11 "I say to you that many will come from the east and the west, and will take their places at the feast with Abraham, Isaac and Jacob in the kingdom of heaven."   *See also* **Mt** 21:43; 22:8—10; **Lk** 14:21—24   *See also grace; regeneration; righteousness; salvation.*

kingdom of God, qualities
Those who have entered the kingdom must live according to its values, anticipating the reign of peace which will come when Jesus Christ returns.

The kingdom of God does not conform to the standards of this world

Jn 18:36 Jesus said, "My kingdom is not of this world. If it were, my servants would fight to prevent my arrest by the Jews. But now my kingdom is from another place."

Ro 14:17 For the kingdom of God is not a matter of eating and drinking, but of righteousness, peace and joy in the Holy Spirit,

Those who inherit the kingdom of God are to bear its fruit

1Th 2:12 . . . urging you to live lives worthy of God, who calls you into his kingdom and glory.   *See also* **Mt** 25:34–36; **2Pe** 1:10–11

The kingdom of God is and will be a kingdom of peace
Peace between people

Isa 2:2–4 . . . They [the nations] will beat their swords into ploughshares and their spears into pruning hooks. Nation will not take up sword against nation, nor will they train for war any more. pp Mic 4:1–4

Jas 3:18 Peacemakers who sow in peace raise a harvest of righteousness.   *See also* **Isa** 9:5; 19:24–25; **Mic** 5:4–5; **Mt** 5:9

The peace and prosperity of all creation

Isa 11:6–9 The wolf will live with the lamb, the leopard will lie down with the goat, the calf and the lion and the yearling together; and a little child will lead them . . .   *See also* **Isa** 35:1–2,9; 41:17–19; **Eze** 47:9,12; **Hos** 2:21–22

The kingdom of God is a kingdom of forgiveness

Mt 6:12 pp Lk 11:4; **Mt** 18:21–35; **Lk** 17:3–4

Status in the kingdom of God

Mt 18:1–5 " . . . those who humble themselves like this child are the greatest in the kingdom of heaven . . ." pp Mk 9:33–37 pp Lk 9:46–48

Mt 20:25–28 . . . whoever wants to become great among you must be your servant . . . pp

Mk 10:42–45 pp Lk 22:25–27   *See also* **Mt** 5:19; 11:11 pp Lk 7:28; **Mt** 19:30 pp Mk 10:31 *See also Christlikeness; forgiveness; peace.*

---

knowing God
A faith-relationship and love-relationship with God involving mind, heart and will, and bringing experience of his presence and power. To know God is to worship him and be transformed by him. Human knowledge of God, which begins with knowledge about him, comes through God's self-revelation.

---

knowing God, effects
Knowing God has a transforming effect on a person spiritually and morally and makes that person bold in actions for God. Not knowing God in the present will result in dissatisfaction and degeneration into wickedness and in the future will bring eternal alienation from him.

The effects of knowing God
Spiritual transformation: from death to life

Col 1:9 For this reason, since the day we heard about you [Colossian believers], we [Paul and Timothy] have not stopped praying for you and asking God to fill you with the knowledge of his will through all spiritual wisdom and understanding.   *See also* **Jn** 17:3; **Gal** 4:8–9; **Eph** 1:17; 3:19; **Col** 2:2

Moral transformation: from evil to good

Pr 2:1–6 My son, if you accept my words and store up my commands within you . . . then you will understand the fear of the LORD and find the knowledge of God. For the LORD gives wisdom, and from his mouth come knowledge and understanding.

2Co 10:5 We [believers] demolish arguments and every pretension that sets itself up against the knowledge of God, and we take captive every thought to make it obedient to Christ.

1Th 4:3–5 It is God's will that you should be sanctified: that you should avoid sexual immorality; that each of you should learn to control your own body in a way that is holy and honourable, not in passionate lust like the heathen, who do not know God;　*See also* **Ro** 16:26; **Eph** 4:17–24; **Php** 1:9–11; **Col** 1:10; **1Jn** 3:10; 4:8

Boldness of action for God

Jer 32:38–39 "They [the people of Israel] will be my people, and I will be their God. I will give them singleness of heart and action, so that they will always fear me for their own good and the good of their children after them."

Da 11:32 "With flattery he [the king of the North] will corrupt those who have violated the covenant, but the people who know their God will firmly resist him."　*See also* **Ps** 138:3; **Pr** 28:1; **Ac** 6:8–10; **2Co** 3:12; **1Pe** 1:13

Biblical images of knowing God

Like parent and child

2Sa 7:14 " 'I [the LORD] will be his [David's offspring's] father, and he shall be my son. When he does wrong, I will punish him with a rod wielded by human beings, with floggings inflicted by human hands.' "　pp **1Ch** 17:13

1Jn 3:1 How great is the love the Father has lavished on us [believers], that we should be called children of God! And that is what we are! The reason the world does not know us is that it did not know him.

God disciplines like a parent: **Heb** 12:6; **Pr** 3:12; **Dt** 8:5

Ps 2:7; 27:10; 68:5; 89:26; 103:13; **Isa** 49:15; 66:12–13; **Hos** 11:1; **Mt** 5:45,48; 6:6–9,18,32; **Lk** 15:11–32; **Jn** 14:21; **1Co** 1:3

Like husband and wife

Isa 62:5 As a young man marries a young woman, so will your [Israel's] people marry you; as a bridegroom rejoices over his bride, so will your God rejoice over you.

Jer 3:14 "Return, faithless people," declares the LORD, "for I am your husband . . ."　*See also* **Isa** 54:5; **Jer** 2:2; 3:20; 31:32; **Hos** 2:16; **Eph** 5:25; **Rev** 19:7; 21:2

Like king and subject

Ps 97:1 The LORD reigns, let the earth be glad;

let the distant shores rejoice.　*See also* **1Sa** 8:7; **Ps** 5:2; 10:16; 29:10; 44:4; 84:3; 95:3; 99:1; 145:1; **Mt** 6:33 pp **Lk** 12:31; **1Ti** 1:17; 6:15

Like shepherd and sheep

Ge 48:15 Then he [Jacob] blessed Joseph and said, "May the God before whom my fathers Abraham and Isaac walked, the God who has been my shepherd all my life to this day,"

Ps 23:1–2 The LORD is my [David's] shepherd, I shall not be in want. He makes me lie down in green pastures, he leads me beside quiet waters,

Isa 40:11 He [the LORD] tends his flock like a shepherd: He gathers the lambs in his arms and carries them close to his heart; he gently leads those that have young.　*See also* **Ps** 28:9; 80:1; **Eze** 34:16; **Mic** 7:14; **Jn** 10:11; **Rev** 7:17

The peril of not knowing God

Lack of satisfaction and degeneration in the present

Ro 1:21–32 . . . Furthermore, since they did not think it worth while to retain the knowledge of God, he gave them over to a depraved mind, to do what ought not to be done . . .

Tit 1:15–16 To the pure, all things are pure, but to those who are corrupted and do not believe, nothing is pure. In fact, both their minds and consciences are corrupted. They claim to know God, but by their actions they deny him. They are detestable, disobedient and unfit for doing anything good.　*See also* **Ex** 5:2; **Jer** 4:22; **Ro** 10:2–3; **1Th** 4:3–5

Eternal punishment in the future

Mt 7:22–23 "Many will say to me [Jesus] on that day, 'Lord, Lord, did we not prophesy in your name, and in your name drive out demons and perform many miracles?' Then I will tell them plainly, 'I never knew you. Away from me, you evildoers!' "

Ro 1:18–19 The wrath of God is being revealed from heaven against all the godlessness and wickedness of those who suppress the truth by their wickedness, since what may be known about God is plain to them, because God has made it plain to them.   *See also* **Ro** 2:5; **2Th** 1:8   *See also judgment, God's; sin; spiritual growth.*

---

knowing God, nature of

To know God is not merely to know things about him, such as his character, but also to experience his presence and power. To know God is to be transformed by him. Human knowledge of God is as a result of God's revelation of himself.

The origin of knowing God
Knowing God depends on revelation
Ro 11:33—36 Oh, the depth of the riches of the wisdom and knowledge of God! How unsearchable his judgments, and his paths beyond tracing out! "Who has known the mind of the Lord? Or who has been his counsellor?" "Who has ever given to God, that God should repay the gift?" For from him and through him and to him are all things. To him be the glory for ever! Amen.   *See also* **Isa** 40:13; **Dt** 29:29; **Nu** 12:6; 23:3; **Job** 12:22; **Isa** 40:5; 65:1; **Eze** 20:5; **Da** 2:20—23,28

Am 4:13; **Mt** 11:25—27 pp **Lk** 10:21—22; **Ro** 16:25—26; **Gal** 1:12; **Eph** 3:4—5
God gives knowledge of his reality through creation
Ro 1:20 For since the creation of the world God's invisible qualities—his eternal power and divine nature—have been clearly seen, being understood from what has been made, so that they are without excuse.   *See also* **Ps** 8:1; 19:1—4; 97:6; **Ac** 14:17; 17:24—27
God gives knowledge of his mercy and his will through Scripture, both law and gospel
Ro 1:17 For in the gospel a righteousness from God is revealed, a righteousness that is by faith from first to last, just as it is written: "The righteous will live by faith."   *See also* **Dt** 31:13; **Ac** 10:36; **1Co** 1:20—21; **Heb** 8:10—11; **Jer** 31:33—34
God gives knowledge of himself through Jesus Christ
Mt 11:27 "All things have been committed to me [Jesus] by my Father. No-one knows the Son except the Father, and no-one knows the Father except the Son and those to whom the Son

chooses to reveal him." pp **Lk** 10:22   *See also* **Jn** 3:2; 8:19; 10:32; 14:7; 16:30; 17:3; **Col** 2:2; **2Ti** 1:9—10; **1Pe** 1:20—21
God gives knowledge of himself and his ways through the Spirit
Eph 1:17 I [Paul] keep asking that the God of our Lord Jesus Christ, the glorious Father, may give you the Spirit of wisdom and revelation, so that you may know him better.   *See also* **Isa** 11:2; **Jn** 14:16—17,26; 15:26; 16:12—15; **Ac** 4:31; **1Co** 2:9—11; 12:8; **Eph** 3:16—19; **1Pe** 1:12
God gives knowledge of his greatness and grace through experience of him, submission to him and in answer to prayer
Ps 56:9—11 Then my [David's] enemies will turn back when I call for help. By this I will know that God is for me. In God, whose word I praise, in the LORD, whose word I praise—in God I trust; I will not be afraid. What can human beings do to me?   *See also* **Ex** 9:29; **Ps** 17:6—7; 66:19—20; **Isa** 41:19—20; 45:3—6; 50:4; 60:16; **Jer** 22:16; 24:7; **Eze** 6:7

The nature of knowing God
Knowing his character
Jnh 4:2 He [Jonah] prayed to the LORD, "O LORD, is this not what I said when I was still at home? That is why I was so quick to flee to Tarshish. I knew that you are a gracious and compassionate God, slow to anger and abounding in love, a God who relents from sending calamity."   *See also* **Dt** 7:9; **Ps** 9:10; 36:10; 135:5; **1Th** 4:3—5; **1Jn** 4:8,16
Knowing his words and works
Am 3:7 Surely the Sovereign LORD does nothing without revealing his plan to his servants the prophets.   *See also* **Ge** 41:25; **Ex** 6:6—7; 7:5,17; 18:11; **Dt** 29:29
Samuel: **1Sa** 3:7,21
David: **1Sa** 17:46; **2Sa** 7:21 pp **1Ch** 17:19; **2Sa** 7:27 pp **1Ch** 17:25
2Ki 8:10; 19:19; **Ps** 147:19; **Eze** 20:9; **Lk** 2:26; **Jn** 17:8; **Ac** 2:22; 22:14
To know Jesus Christ is to know God
Jn 14:6 Jesus answered, "I am the way and the truth and the life. No-one comes to the Father except through me."

Col 1:15 He [Christ] is the image of the invisible God . . . *See also* **Mt** 16:16–17; **Jn** 8:19; 15:15; 16:15; 17:26; **Col** 2:2–3; **1Jn** 5:20
To know God is to experience his salvation
Jn 17:3 "Now this is eternal life: that they may know you, the only true God, and Jesus Christ, whom you have sent." *See also* **Ps** 17:6–7; **Isa** 25:9; 43:12; 52:10; 56:1; **1Jn** 5:13,20 *See also law; life, spiritual; revelation; Scripture.*

last things
The doctrine of the last things ("eschatology") includes the subjects of death, the second coming of Jesus Christ, the resurrection of the dead, the last judgment, heaven and hell.

Death
Physical death is universal
Job 30:23 "I know you [God] will bring me down to death, to the place appointed for all the living." *See also* **2Sa** 14:14; **Ro** 5:12
The timing of natural death is beyond human control
Ecc 8:8 No-one has power over the wind to contain it; so no-one has power over when death comes . . . *See also* **Ps** 90:10; **Mt** 6:27; **Jas** 4:14
Death is not to be feared by the believer
Ps 23:4 Even though I walk through the valley of the shadow of death, I will fear no evil, for you are with me; your rod and your staff, they comfort me. *See also* **Ps** 116:15; **Pr** 14:32; **Ro** 14:8; **Php** 1:21; **Rev** 14:13
For believers, death is likened to falling asleep
Jn 11:11–13 . . . "Our friend Lazarus has fallen asleep; but I am going there to wake him up." . . . Jesus had been speaking of his death, but his disciples thought he meant natural sleep. *See also* **Mk** 5:39; **Ac** 13:36; **1Co** 15:6
At the second coming, believers still living on earth will not experience death
1Th 4:15–17 . . . we who are still alive, who are left till the coming of the Lord, will certainly not precede those who have fallen asleep . . . the dead in Christ will rise first. After that, we who are still alive and are left will be caught up together with them in the clouds to meet the Lord in the air. And so we will be with the Lord for ever. *See also* **1Co** 15:51–52
Death is the penalty for unforgiven sin
Ro 6:23 . . . the wages of sin is death, but the gift of God is eternal life in Christ Jesus our Lord. *See also* **1Ch** 10:13; **Pr** 11:19; **Ro** 5:12

The second coming of Jesus Christ
The second coming is foretold
Mt 26:64 ". . . In the future you will see the Son of Man sitting at the right hand of the Mighty One and coming on the clouds of heaven." pp **Mk** 14:62 *See also* **Lk** 21:27; **Ac** 1:11; **Heb** 9:28
The timing of the second coming is known only to God the Father
Mt 24:36 "No-one knows about that day or hour, not even the angels in heaven, nor the Son, but only the Father." pp **Mk** 13:32 *See also* **Mal** 3:1; **Mt** 24:44 pp **Lk** 12:40; **Rev** 16:15
God's purpose at the second coming is to gather his people together, to reward the faithful and judge the wicked
Mt 16:27 "For the Son of Man is going to come in his Father's glory with his angels, and then he will reward everyone according to what they have done." *See also* **Da** 7:13–14; **Mt** 25:31–32; **Jn** 14:3; **1Co** 4:5; **1Th** 4:16–17; **1Pe** 5:4; **1Jn** 3:2; **Jude** 14–15
The right attitude towards the second coming
1Jn 2:28 And now, dear children, continue in him, so that when he appears we may be confident and unashamed before him at his coming. *See also* **Mk** 13:35; **Ac** 3:19–20; **1Ti** 6:13–14; **2Pe** 3:11

The resurrection of the dead
All will be raised
Jn 5:28–29 ". . . all who are in their graves will hear his voice and come out—those who have done good will rise to live, and those who have done evil will rise to be condemned." *See also* **Da** 12:2; **Ac** 24:15
Believers in Jesus Christ will be raised to eternal life
Jn 6:40 "For my Father's will is that all those

who look to the Son and believe in him shall
have eternal life, and I will raise them up at the
last day." *See also* Jn 11:25; 2Co 4:14; 1Th
4:16

Unbelievers will be condemned

Jn 5:29 ". . . those who have done evil will
rise to be condemned." *See also* Mt 25:46

Believers will be given resurrection bodies

1Co 15:42—44 So will it be with the
resurrection of the dead. The body that is sown is
perishable, it is raised imperishable . . . it is
sown a natural body, it is raised a spiritual body.
If there is a natural body, there is also a spiritual
body. *See also* 1Co 15:50–53

The last judgment

All face judgment after death

Heb 9:27 Just as people are destined to die
once, and after that to face judgment, *See also*
Ro 14:12; 1Pe 4:5; Rev 20:11–12

Judgment is entrusted to Jesus Christ

Jn 5:22 "Moreover, the Father judges no-one,
but has entrusted all judgment to the Son,"
See also Ac 10:42; 17:31; Rev 1:18

Those who have not responded to Christ will be condemned

Jn 12:48 "There is a judge for those who reject
me and do not accept my words; that very word
which I spoke will condemn them at the last
day." *See also* 2Th 1:7–8; 2Pe 3:7; Jude 15;
Rev 20:15

Believers will not be judged for sin

Jn 5:24 "I tell you the truth, those who hear
my word and believe him who sent me have
eternal life and will not be condemned; they have
crossed over from death to life." *See also* Jn
3:18; Ro 8:1–2,33–34

Believers will be judged on how they have lived their Christian lives

2Co 5:10 For we [Christians] must all appear
before the judgment seat of Christ, that everyone
may receive what is due to them for the things
done while in the body, whether good or bad.
See also 1Co 4:5; Heb 9:28; 1Jn 4:17

Heaven

God's throne is in heaven where he is continuously worshipped

Rev 4:9–10 Whenever the living creatures give
glory, honour and thanks to him who sits on the
throne and who lives for ever and ever, the
twenty-four elders fall down before him who sits
on the throne, and worship him who lives for
ever and ever . . . *See also* Isa 6:1–3

God's will is perfectly served in heaven

Mt 6:10 "'your kingdom come, your will be
done on earth as it is in heaven.'" pp Lk
11:2 *See also* 1Ki 22:19

At Jesus Christ's second coming, a new heaven and earth will replace the old

Rev 21:1 Then I saw a new heaven and a
new earth, for the first heaven and the first earth
had passed away . . .

The redeemed will enjoy life in the presence of God in the new heaven

1Th 4:17 . . . And so we will be with the
Lord for ever. *See also* Mt 5:8; Php 3:20; Jude
24; Rev 21:1–4

All life in heaven is sustained by God

Rev 22:1–2 Then the angel showed me the
river of the water of life, as clear as crystal,
flowing from the throne of God and of the Lamb
down the middle of the great street of the
city . . . *See also* Jn 6:58; Rev 2:7; 21:23

Hell

Hell is the destiny of human beings who reject God

Mt 25:41 "Then he [the King, Jesus] will say
to those on his left, 'Depart from me, you who
are cursed, into the eternal fire prepared for the
devil and his angels.'" *See also* Mt 13:41–42;
Ro 2:8; Heb 10:26–27; Jude 6; Rev 17:8

Those in hell are finally separated from God

2Th 1:9 They will be punished with everlasting
destruction and shut out from the presence of the
Lord . . . *See also* Mt 25:46

Hell is a place of fire, darkness and weeping

Rev 20:15 All whose names were not found
written in the book of life were thrown into the
lake of fire. *See also* Mt 8:12; 2Pe 3:7;
Jude 7

Jesus Christ himself frequently warned about the dangers of hell
Lk 12:5 "But I will show you whom you should fear. Fear him who, after the killing of the body, has power to throw you into hell . . ." *See also* **Mt** 5:29–30; 13:40 *See also heaven; hell; judgment, God's; redemption; resurrection.*

law

The God-given regulation of the life of the people of God in relationship with him. As the command of God, it enables and gives shape to the relationship between God and human beings on the one hand, and between fellow human beings on the other.

law, and gospel

The law, which bears witness to the grace of God, points ahead to its fulfilment and climax in the gospel of Jesus Christ. The gospel does not abolish the law, but fulfils it, by allowing it to be seen in its proper light.

Human beings cannot fulfil the law by their own efforts
Ro 3:20 Therefore no-one will be declared righteous in his [God's] sight by observing the law . . .

Gal 2:15–16 "We who are Jews by birth and not 'Gentile sinners' know that a person is not justified by observing the law, but by faith in Jesus Christ. So we, too, have put our faith in Christ Jesus that we may be justified by faith in Christ and not by observing the law, because by observing the law no-one will be justified." *See also* **Ac** 13:39; **Ro** 4:13–15

The law brings knowledge of human sin and the need for redemption
Ro 3:20 . . . through the law we become conscious of sin.

Ro 5:20 The law was added so that the trespass might increase . . . *See also* **1Ti** 1:9–10; **1Jn** 3:4

The law points to the coming of Jesus Christ
Gal 3:24 So the law was put in charge to lead us to Christ that we might be justified by faith.

Believers are not justified by works of the law, but through faith in the blood of Jesus Christ
Ro 3:28 For we maintain that a person is justified by faith apart from observing the law.

Gal 3:11 Clearly no-one is justified before God by the law, because, "The righteous will live by faith." *See also* **Hab** 2:4; **Ro** 4:1–5; **Gal** 3:10–14; **Eph** 2:15

The relationship between believers and the law
Dying to the law through Jesus Christ
Gal 2:19 For through the law I died to the law so that I might live for God.
The law remains valid for believers
Ro 7:11–12 For sin, seizing the opportunity afforded by the commandment, deceived me, and through the commandment put me to death. So then, the law is holy, and the commandment is holy, righteous and good.

1Ti 1:8 We know that the law is good if one uses it properly.

1Pe 1:15–16 But just as he who called you is holy, so be holy in all you do; for it is written: "Be holy, because I am holy." *See also* **Lev** 11:44–45; 19:2; 20:7; **Ro** 7:7–11; 13:8–10; **Jas** 2:8–11
The Holy Spirit enables believers to fulfil the law through Jesus Christ
Ro 8:3–4 For what the law was powerless to do in that it was weakened by the sinful nature, God did by sending his own Son in the likeness of sinful humanity to be a sin offering. And so he condemned sin in our sinful nature, in order that the righteous requirements of the law might be fully met in us, who do not live according to the sinful nature but according to the Spirit. *See also* **Jer** 31:31–34; **Eze** 11:19–20; **Gal** 5:13–18

See also *gospel; grace,* and *salvation; justification; life, spiritual; love; righteousness,* of *believers; sin.*

---

law, Jesus Christ's attitude
Jesus Christ accepted the authority of the OT law and saw himself as coming to fulfil its purpose.

Jesus Christ's disputes with the Pharisees and teachers of the law
The Pharisees and teachers of the law accuse Jesus Christ's disciples of not following tradition
Mk 7:5 So the Pharisees and teachers of the law asked Jesus, "Why don't your disciples live according to the tradition of the elders instead of eating their food with 'unclean' hands?" pp Mt 15:2
Jesus Christ accuses the Pharisees and teachers of the law of hypocrisy
Mk 7:6–8 He [Jesus] replied, "Isaiah was right when he prophesied about you hypocrites; as it is written: 'These people honour me with their lips, but their hearts are far from me. They worship me in vain; their teachings are merely human rules.' You have let go of the commands of God and are holding on to human traditions." pp Mt 15:7–9   See also **Isa 29:13**
Jesus Christ gives examples where human tradition is observed rather than God's law
Mk 7:10–13 pp Mt 15:3–6; Mt 23:1–36 pp Mk 12:38–39 pp Lk 20:45–46
The Pharisees accuse Jesus Christ of breaking the Sabbath
Mk 2:23–24 One Sabbath Jesus was going through the cornfields, and as his disciples walked along, they began to pick some ears of corn. The Pharisees said to him, "Look, why are they doing what is unlawful on the Sabbath?" pp Mt 12:1–2 pp Lk 6:1–2
Jesus Christ demonstrates his authority over the Sabbath
Mk 2:27–3:4 Then he [Jesus] said to them, "The Sabbath was made for people, not people for the Sabbath. So the Son of Man is Lord even of the Sabbath." Another time he went into the synagogue, and a man with a shrivelled hand was there. Some of them were looking for a reason to

accuse Jesus, so they watched him closely to see if he would heal him on the Sabbath. Jesus said to the man with the shrivelled hand, "Stand up in front of everyone." Then Jesus asked them, "Which is lawful on the Sabbath: to do good or to do evil, to save life or to kill?" But they remained silent. pp Mt 12:8–10 pp Lk 6:5–7
Jesus Christ challenges the religious leaders to think about principles not rules
Mk 3:4 Then Jesus asked them, "Which is lawful on the Sabbath: to do good or to do evil, to save life or to kill?" But they remained silent. pp Lk 6:9 pp Mt 12:11–12   See also **Lk 13:10–17**

Jesus Christ came to fulfil the law
Mt 5:17 [Jesus said] "Do not think that I have come to abolish the Law or the Prophets; I have not come to abolish them but to fulfil them."

Mt 5:21–22 "You have heard that it was said to the people long ago, 'Do not murder, and anyone who murders will be subject to judgment.' But I [Jesus] tell you that anyone who is angry with a brother or sister will be subject to judgment. Again, anyone who says to a brother or sister, 'Raca,' is answerable to the Sanhedrin. But anyone who says, 'You fool!' will be in danger of the fire of hell."   See also **Ex 20:13**
Mt 5:27–28 "You have heard that it was said, 'Do not commit adultery.' But I [Jesus] tell you that anyone who looks at a woman lustfully has already committed adultery with her in his heart."   See also **Ex 20:14**

Jesus Christ asserts the continuing validity of the law
Mt 5:18–19 "I [Jesus] tell you the truth, until heaven and earth disappear, not the smallest letter, not the least stroke of a pen, will by any means disappear from the Law until everything is accomplished. Anyone who breaks one of the least of these commandments and teaches others to do the same will be called least in the kingdom of heaven, but whoever practises and teaches these commands will be called great in the kingdom of heaven."

Lk 10:25–28 On one occasion an expert in the law stood up to test Jesus. "Teacher," he asked, "what must I do to inherit eternal life?" "What is written in the Law?" he replied. "How do you read it?" He answered: " 'Love the Lord your God with all your heart and with all your soul and with all your strength and with all your mind'; and, 'Love your neighbour as yourself.' " "You have answered correctly," Jesus replied. "Do this and you will live." pp Mt 22:37–39 pp Mk 12:29–34   *See also* Lk 10:29–37; 16:16

Jesus Christ himself was obedient to the law and its commands

In honouring his parents Lk 2:41–51

In being baptised

Mt 3:13–15 Then Jesus came from Galilee to the Jordan to be baptised by John. But John tried to deter him, saying, "I need to be baptised by you, and do you come to me?" Jesus replied, "Let it be so now; it is proper for us to do this to fulfil all righteousness." Then John consented.

In resisting temptation Lk 4:1–13

In observing the Passover

Lk 22:7–8 Then came the day of Unleavened Bread on which the Passover lamb had to be sacrificed. Jesus sent Peter and John, saying, "Go and make preparations for us to eat the Passover."

In submitting to the will of God

Mt 26:39 Going a little farther, he fell with his face to the ground and prayed, "My Father, if it is possible, may this cup be taken from me. Yet not as I will, but as you will." pp Mk 14:35–36 pp Lk 22:41–42   *See also obedience, of Jesus Christ.*

---

law, letter and spirit

A rigid adherence to the letter of the law often masks hypocrisy and neglect of its spirit, namely having God at the centre of one's life and putting others before oneself, or recognising that the law points to Jesus Christ.

The letter of the law
Overemphasis on keeping some parts of the law
Mk 7:1–8 . . . The Pharisees and all the Jews do not eat unless they give their hands a ceremonial washing, holding to the tradition of the elders. When they come from the market-place they do not eat unless they wash. And they observe many other traditions, such as the washing of cups, pitchers and kettles . . . pp Mt 15:1–2   *See also* Isa 29:13; Mt 9:10–13 pp Mk 2:15–17 pp Lk 5:29–32
Hypocrisy with regard to keeping the law
Mk 7:9–13 " . . . Moses said, 'Honour your father and your mother,' and, 'Anyone who curses father or mother must be put to death.' But you [Pharisees and teachers of the law] say that if anyone says to father or mother: 'Whatever help you might otherwise have received from me is Corban' (that is, a gift devoted to God), then you no longer let them do anything for their father or mother. Thus you nullify the word of God by your tradition that you have handed down. And you do many things like that." pp Mt 15:3–6   *See also* Mt 23:1–33; Lk 11:37–52; 18:9–14; Jn 9:1–16; Ro 2:17–24; Isa 52:5

The spirit of the law
Jesus Christ and the law
Mt 5:17–6:19 "Do not think that I [Jesus] have come to abolish the Law or the Prophets; I have not come to abolish them but to fulfil them. I tell you the truth, until heaven and earth disappear, not the smallest letter, not the least stroke of a pen, will by any means disappear from the Law until everything is accomplished. Anyone who breaks one of the least of these commandments and teaches others to do the same will be called least in the kingdom of heaven, but whoever practises and teaches these commands will be called great in the kingdom of heaven . . ."   *See also* Mt 19:16–30 pp Mk 10:17–30 pp Lk 18:18–30
Jesus Christ's attitude to the Sabbath
Mk 2:23–3:6 . . . he [Jesus] said to them [the Pharisees], "The Sabbath was made for people, not people for the Sabbath . . ." . . .

pp Mt 12:1–14 pp Lk 6:1–11   *See also* **Mk** 1:21–28 pp Lk 4:31–37; **Lk** 13:10–17; 14:1–6; **Jn** 5:1–16; 7:21–24

Jesus Christ's treatment of the woman taken in adultery

Jn 8:2–11 . . . The teachers of the law and the Pharisees brought in a woman caught in adultery. They made her stand before the group and said to Jesus, "Teacher, this woman was caught in the act of adultery. In the Law Moses commanded us to stone such women. Now what do you say?" . . . When they kept on questioning him, he straightened up and said to them, "Let anyone of you who is without sin be the first to throw a stone at her." . . . Jesus straightened up and asked her, "Woman, where are they? Has no-one condemned you?" "No-one, sir," she said. "Then neither do I condemn you," Jesus declared. "Go now and leave your life of sin."

The greatest commandment

Mt 22:34–40 . . . an expert in the law, tested him [Jesus] with this question: "Teacher, which is the greatest commandment in the Law?" Jesus replied: " 'Love the Lord your God with all your heart and with all your soul and with all your mind.' This is the first and greatest commandment. And the second is like it: 'Love your neighbour as yourself.' All the Law and the Prophets hang on these two commandments." pp Mk 12:28–34   *See also* **Mt** 25:31–46

The importance of obedience and right attitudes outweighs that of outward actions

Ro 2:25–29 . . . A person is not a Jew who is only one outwardly, nor is circumcision merely outward and physical. No, a person is a Jew who is one inwardly; and circumcision is circumcision of the heart, by the Spirit, not by the written code. Such a person's praise is not from others, but from God.   *See also* **1Sa** 15:22–23; **Ps** 51:16–17; **Pr** 21:3; **Isa** 1:11–17; **Jer** 7:21–23; **Hos** 6:6; **Am** 5:21–24; **Mic** 6:6–8; **Gal** 3:1–5

The spirit of the law is embodied in the new covenant

2Co 3:3–6 . . . He [God] has made us [apostles] competent as ministers of a new covenant—not of the letter but of the Spirit; for

the letter kills, but the Spirit gives life.   *See also* **Jn** 4:19–24; **Ro** 7:4–6; 8:1–11; **1Co** 15:45–46; **2Co** 3:13–18; **Gal** 5:18; **Heb** 7:18–22; 8:1–13; **Jer** 31:31–34   *See also* covenant, the new; righteousness; Sabbath; sin.

---

law, Old Testament

OT laws and legal traditions govern every aspect of the life of the covenant people of God.

Kinds of OT law

Criminal law

Ex 21:12–14 "Anyone who strikes someone a fatal blow shall surely be put to death. However, if it is not done intentionally, but God lets it happen, that person is to flee to a place I will designate. But if anyone schemes and kills someone deliberately, that person shall be taken from my altar and put to death."

Civil law

Dt 16:18–20 Appoint judges and officials for each of your tribes in every town the Lord your God is giving you, and they shall judge the people fairly. Do not pervert justice or show partiality. Do not accept a bribe, for a bribe blinds the eyes of the wise and twists the words of the righteous. Follow justice and justice alone, so that you may live and possess the land the Lord your God is giving you.   *See also* **Dt** 15:12–18

Social law

Ex 22:21–22 "Do not ill-treat or oppress an alien, for you were aliens in Egypt. Do not take advantage of a widow or an orphan."   *See also* **Dt** 24:19–22

Cultic law

Cultic law deals explicitly with the ritual or religious life of the people of God. Leviticus chapters 1–7 are totally devoted to this kind of law: **Lev** 1:10–13; 4:13–21; 7:11–18

Examples of OT law

Conditions for freeing servants

Ex 21:2–6 "If you buy a Hebrew servant, he is to serve you for six years. But in the seventh year, he shall go free, without paying anything . . ." pp Dt 15:12–18   *See also* **Ex** 21:3–11; **Lev** 25:39–55

Dealing with injuries

Ex 21:23–25 "But if there is serious injury, you are to take life for life, eye for eye, tooth for tooth, hand for hand, foot for foot, burn for burn, wound for wound, bruise for bruise."   *See also* **Mt 5:38**

Property is to be protected

Ex 22:1 "Whoever steals an ox or a sheep and slaughters it or sells it must pay back five head of cattle for the ox and four sheep for the sheep."   *See also* **Lev 6:1–7; Lk 19:8**

The rights of aliens must be respected

Ex 22:21 "Do not ill-treat or oppress an alien, for you were aliens in Egypt."   *See also* **Lev 19:33; Dt 10:19**

Justice must be universally respected

Ex 23:2–3 ". . . When you give testimony in a lawsuit, do not pervert justice by siding with the crowd, and do not show favouritism to the poor in a lawsuit."   *See also* **Lev 19:15**

The Sabbath must be observed by all

Ex 23:12 "Six days do your work, but on the seventh day do not work, so that your ox and your donkey may rest and the slave born in your household, and the alien as well, may be refreshed."   *See also* **Ex 20:8–11**

Three annual festivals are to be celebrated

Ex 23:15–16 "Celebrate the Feast of Unleavened Bread . . . Celebrate the Feast of Harvest with the firstfruits of the crops you sow in your field. Celebrate the Feast of Ingathering at the end of the year . . ."   *See also* **Ex 12:17; Dt 16:16**

Worship must be in accordance with God's will and must be kept pure Dt 12:1–7; 13:6–8

Certain foods are declared to be unclean Lev 11:1–23 pp Dt 14:3–20

A tenth of all produce must be given to God

Dt 14:22 Be sure to set aside a tenth of all that your fields produce each year.   *See also* **Lev 27:30**

Cultic laws are grounded in the holiness of God

Lev 11:44 "I am the LORD your God; consecrate yourselves and be holy, because I am holy . . ."

Lev 19:1–2 The LORD said to Moses, "Speak to the entire assembly of Israel and say to them: 'Be holy because I, the LORD your God, am holy.'"   *See also* **1Pe 1:16**

Full details were given for each type of offering: burnt, grain, fellowship, sin and guilt offerings. Only perfect animals were to be offered: **Lev 1:3; 2:1–2; 3:1–2; 4:27–28; 5:17–18**

Rules governing infectious or contagious diseases

Lev 13:2 "When anyone has a swelling or a rash or a bright spot on the skin that may become an infectious skin disease, they must be brought to Aaron the priest or to one of his sons who is a priest."

Lev 15:13 "'When people are cleansed from their discharge, they are to count off seven days for their ceremonial cleansing; they must wash their clothes and bathe themselves with fresh water, and they will be clean.'"

There must not be unlawful sexual relations

Lev 18:6 "'No-one is to approach any close relative to have sexual relations. I am the LORD.'"

A Day of Atonement must be held Lev 23:26–32 pp Lev 16:2–34 pp Nu 29:7–11 *See also atonement; sacrifice; worship.*

---

law, purpose of

The law covers and regulates every area of life of the covenant people of God in accordance with the commands of God. Although the laws may be divided into categories of civil, criminal, social and cultic (or ritual) law, these distinctions are not clear-cut, and occasionally overlap with one another.

The origins of the law

Law as God's command is found in the story of creation

Ge 2:16–17 And the LORD God commanded the man, "You are free to eat from any tree in the garden; but you must not eat from the tree of the knowledge of good and evil, for when you eat of it you will surely die."

The law expresses the covenant relation between God and his people
Dt 4:44–45 This is the law Moses set before the Israelites. These are the stipulations, decrees and laws Moses gave them when they came out of Egypt

Dt 5:1 Moses summoned all Israel and said: Hear, O Israel, the decrees and the laws I declare in your hearing today. Learn them and be sure to follow them.   *See also* **Ex** 20:1–17 pp **Dt** 5:6–21; **Dt** 10:12–13; 30:1–16

The purpose of the law
The law shows the proper response to the holiness of God
Lev 19:2 "Speak to the entire assembly of Israel and say to them: 'Be holy because I, the LORD your God, am holy.'"
The law ensures that the people continue to receive the blessings of the covenant promises
Dt 6:24–25 "The LORD commanded us to obey all these decrees and to fear the LORD our God, so that we might always prosper and be kept alive, as is the case today. And if we are careful to obey all this law before the LORD our God, as he has commanded us, that will be our righteousness."   *See also* **Ge** 22:17–18; **Ex** 20:12; **Dt** 6:3–7
Breaking the law leads to forfeiting the covenant blessings
Jer 11:9–11 Then the LORD said to me [Jeremiah], "There is a conspiracy among the people of Judah and those who live in Jerusalem. They have returned to the sins of their ancestors who refused to listen to my words. They have followed other gods to serve them. Both the house of Israel and the house of Judah have broken the covenant I made with their ancestors. Therefore this is what the LORD says: 'I will bring on them a disaster they cannot escape. Although they cry out to me, I will not listen to them.'"   *See also* **Ex** 32:1–4
The law deepens the believer's knowledge of God through meditation
Ps 1:1–2 Blessed are those who do not walk in the counsel of the wicked or stand in the way

of sinners or sit in the seat of mockers. But their delight is in the law of the LORD, and on his law they meditate day and night.   *See also* **Dt** 6:2; **Ps** 19:7–14; 119:25–32,105–120
The law will finally be written on believers' hearts
Jer 31:33 . . . "I will put my law in their minds and write it on their hearts. I will be their God, and they will be my people."   *See also* **Eze** 11:19–20

The general principles underlying the law
Justice
Dt 16:20 Follow justice and justice alone, so that you may live and possess the land the LORD your God is giving you.
Righteousness
Dt 16:18 Appoint judges and officials for each of your tribes in every town the LORD your God is giving you, and they shall judge the people fairly.
Holiness
Lev 19:2 ". . . 'Be holy because I, the LORD your God, am holy.'"
Love
Lev 19:18–19 "'Do not seek revenge or bear a grudge against one of your people, but love your neighbour as yourself. I am the LORD. Keep my decrees. Do not mate different kinds of animals. Do not plant your field with two kinds of seed. Do not wear clothing woven of two kinds of material.'"   *See also* covenant; holiness; justice; obedience; righteousness.

---

law, Ten Commandments
The basic laws given to Israel through Moses following the exodus from Egypt (Ex 20:1–17; Dt 5:6–21). The first four commandments safeguard Israel's special relation to God; the remaining six protect individuals within the community and promote their well-being.

The Ten Commandments are to govern the life of Israel as the people of God
Israel should obey God alone
Ex 20:2–3 "I am the LORD your God, who brought you out of Egypt, out of the land of

slavery. You shall have no other gods before me." pp Dt 5:6–7   *See also* **Dt** 6:13–15

Idolatry forbidden
Ex 20:4–6 "You shall not make for yourself an idol in the form of anything in heaven above or on the earth beneath or in the waters below. You shall not bow down to them or worship them . . ." pp Dt 5:8–10   *See also* **Ex** 32:1–8; **Lev** 19:4; **1Co** 10:7

God's name should not be misused
Ex 20:7 "You shall not misuse the name of the Lord your God, for the Lord will not hold anyone guiltless who misuses his name." pp Dt 5:11
See also **Mt** 7:21

A day of rest is commanded
Ex 20:8–11 "Remember the Sabbath day by keeping it holy. Six days you shall labour and do all your work, but the seventh day is a Sabbath to the Lord your God. On it you shall not do any work, neither you, nor your son or daughter, nor your male or female servant, nor your animals, nor the alien within your gates. For in six days the Lord made the heavens and the earth, the sea, and all that is in them, but he rested on the seventh day. Therefore the Lord blessed the Sabbath day and made it holy." pp Dt 5:12–15   *See also* **Ex** 16:23; **Lev** 19:3; **Isa** 56:2; **Jer** 17:21–22

Parents are to be honoured
Ex 20:12 "Honour your father and your mother, so that you may live long in the land the Lord your God is giving you." pp Dt 5:16   *See also* **Mt** 15:4; **Eph** 6:1–3

Murder is forbidden
Ex 20:13 "You shall not murder." pp Dt 5:17   *See also* **Ge** 4:8–16; **Mt** 5:21

Adultery is forbidden
Ex 20:14 "You shall not commit adultery." pp Dt 5:18   *See also* **Lev** 18:20; **2Sa** 11:2–5; **Mt** 5:27; **Heb** 13:4

Stealing is forbidden
Ex 20:15 "You shall not steal." pp Dt 5:19
See also **Lev** 19:11,13

False witness is forbidden
Ex 20:16 "You shall not give false testimony against your neighbour." pp Dt 5:20   *See also* **Lev** 19:11

Coveting is forbidden
Ex 20:17 "You shall not covet your neighbour's house. You shall not covet your neighbour's wife, or his male or female servant, his ox or donkey, or anything that belongs to your neighbour." pp Dt 5:21   *See also* **Lev** 19:17–18; **Job** 31:9–12; **Ro** 7:7

The circumstances surrounding the giving of the Ten Commandments
The Ten Commandments written on stone tablets
Ex 24:12 The Lord said to Moses, "Come up to me on the mountain and stay here, and I will give you the tablets of stone, with the law and commands I have written for their instruction."
See also **Dt** 4:13; 9:9–10

The stone tablets broken
Ex 32:19 When Moses approached the camp and saw the calf and the dancing, his anger burned and he threw the tablets out of his hands, breaking them to pieces at the foot of the mountain.   *See also* **Dt** 9:16–17

A second set of stone tablets made
Ex 34:1 The Lord said to Moses, "Chisel out two stone tablets like the first ones, and I will write on them the words that were on the first tablets, which you broke."

Ex 34:28 Moses was there with the Lord forty days and forty nights without eating bread or drinking water. And he wrote on the tablets the words of the covenant—the Ten Commandments.   *See also* **Dt** 10:1–2

The second set of stone tablets put in the ark of the covenant
Ex 40:20 He took the Testimony and placed it in the ark . . .   *See also* **Dt** 10:1–2   *See also* **Sabbath.**

life
The state of being alive, characterised by vitality, growth and development.

life, believers' experience
God is at work in all that happens to believers,

whether to warn them, to draw them to himself
or to do them good.

**God has a purpose in all the
experiences that believers have in life**
Ro 8:28 And we know that in all things God
works for the good of those who love him, who
have been called according to his purpose.

Eph 1:11 In him [Christ] we were also chosen,
having been predestined according to the plan of
him [God] who works out everything in conformity
with the purpose of his will,   *See also* **Ge**
21:22; 28:16; 39:20–21; 45:5–8; **1Sa** 2:6–9; **1Ch**
29:11–12; **Job** 42:10–13; **Ps** 75:6–7; **Ac** 17:28;
1Pe 4:12
Rejection of this conviction leads to despair
Ecc 1:1–2,16–17

**God uses every experience in the lives
of believers for good**
To warn and correct
Ps 119:67 Before I was afflicted I went astray,
but now I obey your word.   *See also* **Ge** 12:17;
2Ch 7:13–14; **Job** 5:17; **Isa** 38:17; 48:9–10; **Am**
4:10–11; **Ro** 2:4; **Heb** 12:5–11; **Rev** 9:20–21
To test and exercise believers' trust in God
Dt 8:15–16 He [the Lord] led you [Israelites]
through the vast and dreadful desert, that thirsty
and waterless land, with its venomous snakes and
scorpions. He brought you water out of hard rock.
He gave you manna to eat in the desert,
something your ancestors had never known, to
humble and to test you so that in the end it
might go well with you.   *See also* **Ex** 15:22–25;
Jdg 2:21–22; **Ps** 23:1–6; 81:7; **Isa** 43:1–2; **Na**
1:7; **Ro** 8:35–39; **Php** 4:12; **Heb** 11:17–19; 13:6
To purify and prepare believers for glory
2Co 4:16–17 Therefore we do not lose heart.
Though outwardly we are wasting away, yet
inwardly we are being renewed day by day. For
our light and momentary troubles are achieving for
us an eternal glory that far outweighs them
all.   *See also* **Job** 23:10; **Ps** 66:10; **Isa** 48:10;
Jer 9:7; **Zec** 13:8–9; **Ro** 5:3–5; 8:28–30; **1Pe**
1:6–7

To benefit others Est 4:14; **2Co** 1:3–6; 4:15;
Php 1:12–14; **2Ti** 2:10

**In all of life's experiences believers
should be thankful and trusting**
Php 4:6 Do not be anxious about anything, but
in everything, by prayer and petition, with
thanksgiving, present your requests to God.   *See
also* **Ge** 8:20; **Dt** 8:18; **Job** 1:20–21; **Ps** 103:1–2;
Pr 3:5–6; **Ac** 16:25; **Eph** 5:20; **1Ti** 4:4–5

**Believers do not merit the blessings
they receive**
Ps 103:10 he [the Lord] does not treat us as
our sins deserve or repay us according to our
iniquities.   *See also* **Ge** 32:10; 50:19–21; **Ezr**
9:13; **La** 3:22; **Lk** 7:6; **Ro** 6:23   *See also
Christlikeness; peace, experience; spiritual growth.*

life, human
Seen by Scripture as the climax of the work of
creation, life is a gift of God and is to be treated
with reverence and respect.

Life is from God
Ge 2:7 the Lord God formed a man from the
dust of the ground and breathed into his nostrils
the breath of life, and the man became a living
being.

Ac 3:15 You [the Jews] killed the author of
life . . .

Ac 17:25 ". . . he himself gives all life and
breath and everything else."   *See also* **1Sa** 2:6;
Job 33:4; **Ps** 139:13; **Da** 5:23; **Ac** 17:28; **Jas**
4:14–15

**The ultimate duration of life is
unknown to people**
Ps 39:4 "Show me, O Lord, my life's end and
the number of my days; let me know how
fleeting is my life."   *See also* **Ge** 27:2; **Jas**
4:13–14

Life is precious
Mt 10:31 "So don't be afraid; you are worth

more than many sparrows." *See also* **Ge 1:26–27; 9:5–6; Ps 49:7–9; 139:14; Mt 16:26 pp Lk 9:25**

God's presence in life
Dt 30:16 For I [the Lord] command you [his people] today to love the Lᴏʀᴅ your God, to walk in his ways, and to keep his commands, decrees and laws . . .

Ps 23:6 Surely goodness and love will follow me all the days of my life, and I will dwell in the house of the Lᴏʀᴅ for ever. *See also* **Ps 71:5–6,9**

Life is to be lived for God
Ecc 12:13; Jer 10:23; Mic 6:8; Mt 10:39; Php 1:21

The span of human life
Ecc 11:8–12:8 However many years people may live, let them enjoy them all. But let them remember the days of darkness, for there will be many. Everything to come is meaningless . . . *See also* **Ps 90:10**

Life is temporary
2Co 5:1 Now we know that if the earthly tent we live in is destroyed, we have a building from God, an eternal house in heaven, not built by human hands. *See also* **Ps 49:12; 103:15–16; Isa 38:12; 2Pe 1:13–14**

Life is short
1Ch 29:15 "We are aliens and strangers in your sight, as were all our ancestors. Our days on earth are like a shadow, without hope."

Job 14:1 "Mortals born of woman are of few days and full of trouble."

Jas 4:14 Why, you do not even know what will happen tomorrow. What is your life? You are a mist that appears for a little while and then vanishes. *See also* **Job 7:6–7; 8:9; 9:25; 14:2; Ps 39:4–6; 89:47; 90:12; 102:11; 144:4; Ecc 6:12; Isa 40:6–8**

The termination of life by death is due to sin
Ro 5:12 Therefore, just as sin entered the world

through one man, and death through sin, and in this way death came to all people, because all sinned— *See also* **Ge 2:17; 1Co 15:22**

Examples of long life **Ge 5:3–32; 9:29; 11:10–32**

A full span of years
Pr 3:16 Long life is in her [wisdom's] right hand . . . *See also* **Ex 20:12 pp Dt 5:16; Ex 23:25–26; 1Ki 3:14; Job 5:26; Pr 3:2; 9:11; 10:27**

Attitudes to life
Life loved
1Pe 3:10 For, "Whoever among you would love life and see good days must keep your tongue from evil and your lips from deceitful speech." *See also* **Ps 34:12–13; Job 8:21; Ps 91:16**

Life despised
Ecc 2:22–23 What do people get for all the toil and anxious striving with which they labour under the sun? All their days their work is pain and grief; even at night their minds do not rest. This too is meaningless. *See also* **Job 7:16; 10:1; Ecc 2:17; Jnh 4:8**

---

life, of faith
The way by which believers journey through this world and into the life to come. Jesus Christ himself is the way to life.

Life seen as travelling with God
Walking with God
Ge 17:1 When Abram was ninety-nine years old, the Lᴏʀᴅ appeared to him and said, "I am God Almighty; walk before me and be blameless." *See also* **Ge 5:22,24; 6:9; 48:15; Ps 56:13; 89:15; Mic 4:5; Zec 10:12**

Journeying from the old to the new
Isa 43:19 "See, I am doing a new thing! Now it springs up; do you not perceive it? I am making a way in the desert and streams in the wasteland." *See also* **Ex 18:8; Isa 40:3–5; Mic 2:13**

God's guidance along the way
Ex 13:21 By day the Lᴏʀᴅ went ahead of them in a pillar of cloud to guide them on their way and by night in a pillar of fire to give them light,

so that they could travel by day or night.   *See also* Ex 23:20; Dt 1:32–33; 8:2; Ne 9:12,19; Ps 25:9; Jer 2:17; Gal 5:25

God's ways
Walking in God's way
Isa 35:8 And a highway will be there; it will be called the Way of Holiness. The unclean will not journey on it; it will be for those who walk in that Way; wicked fools will not go about on it.

1Jn 2:6 Whoever claims to live in him [Jesus] must walk as Jesus did.   *See also* Ge 18:19; Ex 18:20; Dt 10:12–13; 13:5; 28:9; Jos 22:5; Job 23:10–12; Ps 1:1–2; 18:30; 2Ti 3:10
God teaches believers his way
Isa 48:17 This is what the LORD says—your Redeemer, the Holy One of Israel: "I am the LORD your God, who teaches you what is best for you, who directs you in the way you should go."   *See also* 1Sa 12:23; 1Ki 8:35–36 pp 2Ch 6:26–27; Ps 25:8–9,12; 86:11; 119:30; Pr 6:23; Isa 2:3; 30:20–21

Characteristics of the way of life include holiness, obedience, trust, humility, joy and peace: Ps 16:11; 23:2; Pr 8:20; Jer 6:16; Mic 6:8; Gal 5:22–23
Sinners refuse to follow God's way
Isa 53:6 We all, like sheep, have gone astray, each of us has turned to our own way . . .
See also Isa 56:11; Ac 14:16; 2Pe 2:15
All other routes end in death
Pr 14:12 There is a way that seems right to a person, but in the end it leads to death.   *See also* Dt 11:28; 31:29; Jdg 2:17; 2Ki 21:22; Ps 1:6; Pr 15:10; 16:25
Those who travel God's way are blessed
Pr 4:18 The path of the righteous is like the first gleam of dawn, shining ever brighter till the full light of day.   *See also* Dt 5:33; 1Ki 8:23; Pr 11:5; Isa 26:7–8; Mt 5:3–12

Jesus Christ is the way to life
Jn 14:6 . . . "I am the way and the truth and the life. No-one comes to the Father except through me."

Col 2:3 in whom [Christ] are hidden all the treasures of wisdom and knowledge.   *See also* Jn 8:12; Heb 12:2

"the Way" was an early designation of Christianity, suggestive of the content of the church's message that Jesus Christ is the way to life: Ac 9:2; 19:9,23; 22:4; 24:14,22

Entrance to the way to life
Entrance is restricted
Mt 7:13–14 "Enter through the narrow gate. For wide is the gate and broad is the road that leads to destruction, and many enter through it. But small is the gate and narrow the road that leads to life, and only a few find it."   *See also* Jn 10:9; 14:6
Entrance is by faith
Heb 11:8–10 By faith Abraham, when called to go to a place he would later receive as his inheritance, obeyed and went, even though he did not know where he was going . . .   *See also* Jn 3:15–16; 2Co 5:7; Heb 11:6,13–16   *See also assurance, and life of faith; faith.*

---

life, spiritual

Life embraces more than physical existence; it includes humanity's relationship with God. Human beings come to life spiritually only through faith in the redeeming work of God in Jesus Christ. This spiritual life is a foretaste of the life which believers will finally enjoy to the full in the new heaven and earth. Life in the Spirit means keeping in step with the promptings and guidance of the Holy Spirit, and always being open to his gifts and empowerment.

The nature of spiritual life
It is new life
Ac 5:20 "Go, stand in the temple courts," he [an angel of the Lord] said, "and tell the people the full message of this new life."   *See also* Ac 11:18; 2Pe 1:3; 1Jn 3:14
It is true life
1Ti 6:19 In this way they will lay up treasure for themselves as a firm foundation for the coming age, so that they may take hold of the life that is truly life.

It is eternal life
Ro 5:21 so that, just as sin reigned in death, so also grace might reign through righteousness to bring eternal life through Jesus Christ our Lord. *See also* **Da** 12:2; **Mt** 19:29; **Jn** 6:27; **1Jn** 5:11,20

It is abundant life
Ps 16:11 You have made known to me the path of life; you will fill me with joy in your presence, with eternal pleasures at your right hand.

Jer 17:8 "They will be like a tree planted by the water that sends out its roots by the stream. It does not fear when heat comes; its leaves are always green. It has no worries in a year of drought and never fails to bear fruit." *See also* **Ps** 1:3; **Jn** 10:10

The origins and nature of spiritual life
Spiritual life is the work of the Holy Spirit
Jn 3:6 "Flesh gives birth to flesh, but the Spirit gives birth to spirit."

Jn 3:8 "The wind blows wherever it pleases. You hear its sound, but you cannot tell where it comes from or where it is going. So it is with everyone born of the Spirit." *See also* **Eze** 36:26; **Jn** 3:3,5–7; **Ro** 8:11; **Tit** 3:5–7

Spiritual life unites believers to Jesus Christ
Eph 2:4–5 . . . God, who is rich in mercy, made us alive with Christ . . . *See also* **Ro** 6:3–5; 8:10; **1Co** 12:13; **Col** 2:13; **1Jn** 5:12

Spiritual life makes believers the children of God
Jn 1:12–13 Yet to all who received him, to those who believed in his name, he [God] gave the right to become children of God . . . *See also* **Dt** 30:20; **Mt** 6:9; **Ro** 8:15; **Jas** 1:18; **1Jn** 4:7; 5:1

Spiritual life brings people to know God
Jn 17:3 "Now this is eternal life: that they may know you, the only true God, and Jesus Christ, whom you have sent." *See also* **Mt** 11:27

Spiritual life brings about faith
Jn 3:15 ". . . everyone who believes in him may have eternal life."

Jn 20:31 But these are written that you may believe that Jesus is the Christ, the Son of God, and that by believing you may have life in his name. *See also* **Jn** 3:16,36; 5:24; 6:40; 11:25

Keeping in step with the Spirit
A new way of life is made possible
Gal 5:25 Since we live by the Spirit, let us keep in step with the Spirit. *See also* **Ro** 8:5–6,9–16; **Gal** 5:16–18,22–24

Bondage to the written law is ended
Ro 2:29 . . . circumcision is circumcision of the heart, by the Spirit, not by the written code . . . *See also* **Ro** 7:6; 8:2; **2Co** 3:6; **Gal** 5:17–18

Obedience to God is made possible
Ro 8:4 in order that the righteous requirements of the law might be fully met in us, who do not live according to the sinful nature but according to the Spirit. *See also* **Eze** 36:27; **Ro** 8:13; **Gal** 5:16; **1Th** 4:7–8

Deepening unity is encouraged
Eph 4:3 Make every effort to keep the unity of the Spirit through the bond of peace. *See also* **Col** 2:13; **Php** 2:1–4

Strength and encouragement are received Ac 9:31

Gifts for those living in the Spirit
Gifts are given for building up the church
1Co 12:4–11 . . . Now to each one the manifestation of the Spirit is given for the common good . . . *See also* **Ro** 12:6–8; **1Co** 12:27–30

Visions are given Ac 2:17; **Joel** 2:28; **Rev** 1:10,12–13; 4:2; 17:3; 21:10

Miracles are worked
Mt 12:28 "But if I [Jesus] drive out demons by the Spirit of God, then the kingdom of God has come upon you." *See also* **Ac** 10:38; **Ro** 15:19; **Gal** 3:5

Ministry is enhanced
2Co 3:6 He has made us competent as ministers of a new covenant—not of the letter but of the Spirit; for the letter kills, but the Spirit gives life. *See also* **2Co** 3:7–9

Those living in the Spirit receive revelation and guidance
God is revealed as Father
Gal 4:6 Because you are his children, he sent the Spirit of his Son into our hearts, the Spirit who calls out, "*Abba*, Father." *See also* **Ro 8:14–16**
God's purposes are revealed
1Co 2:9–10 . . . "No eye has seen, no ear has heard, no mind has conceived what God has prepared for those who love him"—but God has revealed it to us by his Spirit . . . *See also* **Ro 15:13; 2Co 5:2–5; Gal 5:5; Eph 1:17–18**
Guidance is given to believers
Ac 8:29 The Spirit told Philip, "Go to that chariot and stay near it." *See also* **Ac 10:19; 11:12; 13:2; 16:6–7; 20:22–23**
Help is given to pray Ro 8:26–27; Eph 6:18; Jude 20

The Holy Spirit sanctifies those in whom he lives
Through the Spirit, Jesus Christ lives in believers Eph 3:16–17
The Spirit transforms believers
2Co 3:18 And we, who with unveiled faces all reflect the Lord's glory, are being transformed into his likeness with ever-increasing glory, which comes from the Lord, who is the Spirit. *See also* **Ro 15:16; 2Th 2:13; 1Pe 1:2**
The fruit of the Spirit is seen in believers' lives Ac 13:52; Ro 5:5; 8:6; 14:17; 15:30; Gal 5:22–23; Col 1:8; 1Th 1:6
Examples of life in the Holy Spirit
Jesus Christ Mt 4:1 pp Mk 1:12 pp Lk 4:1; Mt 12:18,28; Lk 4:14,18; 10:21; Ac 10:38
Simeon Lk 2:25–27
Peter Ac 4:8; 10:19,44
Stephen Ac 6:5,10; 7:55
The first Christians Ac 4:31; 6:3–5; 11:24,27–29; 13:1–3; 15:28 *See also* **church,** and **Holy Spirit;** *knowing God; obedience; regeneration; resurrection; spiritual gifts.*

---

light
The brightness that enables sight in the darkness.

Scripture often uses light as a symbol of the saving presence of God in a fallen world, with darkness being used as a symbol of sin or the absence of God.

---

light, and people of God
Scripture often uses light as a symbol of the people of God, and especially the manner in which believers are able and required to reflect the glory of God in a dark world of sin.

The people of God as the light of the world
Mt 5:14–16 "You are the light of the world. A city on a hill cannot be hidden. Neither do people light a lamp and put it under a bowl. Instead they put it on its stand, and it gives light to everyone in the house. In the same way, let your light shine before others, that they may see your good deeds and praise your Father in heaven." *See also* **Ps 37:5–6; Pr 4:18; 13:9; Isa 58:8–10; 60:1–5; 62:1; Da 12:3; Lk 2:32; Ac 13:47**

Examples of believers acting as light to the world
Moses on Mount Sinai: **Ex 34:29–30,35**
2Sa 23:3–4; Job 29:21–25; Jn 5:35; Ac 6:15; Php 2:15

God is the source of the light of his people
God and his law as the source of light
Ps 27:1 The LORD is my light and my salvation—whom shall I fear? The LORD is the stronghold of my life—of whom shall I be afraid?

Ps 118:27 The LORD is God, and he has made his light shine upon us . . . *See also* **Jdg 5:31; Job 11:13–17; 22:27–28; Ps 19:8; 34:5; 56:13; 97:11; Pr 6:23; Ecc 8:1; Isa 60:19–20; Jn 1:5**
The gospel of forgiveness as a source of light
Ac 26:17–18 "'. . . I [Jesus] am sending you [Saul] to them to open their eyes and turn them from darkness to light, and from the power of Satan to God, so that they may receive

forgiveness of sins and a place among those who are sanctified by faith in me.'" *See also* Job 33:28–30; Ps 112:4; Isa 9:2; 29:18; Mt 4:16; Jn 3:19–21; Eph 1:18; 5:27; Heb 6:4; 10:32

The people of God are called to live in his light

Eph 5:8–14 For you were once darkness, but now you are light in the Lord. Live as children of light (for the fruit of the light consists in all goodness, righteousness and truth) and find out what pleases the Lord. Have nothing to do with the fruitless deeds of darkness, but rather expose them. For it is shameful even to mention what the disobedient do in secret. But everything exposed by the light becomes visible, for it is light that makes everything visible. This is why it is said: "Wake up, O sleeper, rise from the dead, and Christ will shine on you."

1Jn 1:7 But if we walk in the light, as he [God] is in the light, we have fellowship with one another, and the blood of Jesus, his Son, purifies us from all sin. *See also* Ps 36:9; 89:15; Isa 2:5; Lk 16:8; Jn 9:4; 12:35–36; Ro 13:12; 1Th 5:5–6; 1Jn 2:8–10 *See also adoption, descriptions; holiness; sanctification.*

---

light, natural

Scripture stresses that every source of light (sun, moon and stars) is created by God, and subject to him.

God is the source of natural light

Ge 1:3–5 And God said, "Let there be light," and there was light. God saw that the light was good, and he separated the light from the darkness . . . *See also* Ge 1:14–18; 2Sa 22:13–15; Job 41:18–21; Ps 8:3–4; 74:16; 97:4; 136:7–9; Isa 45:7; Jer 31:35; Jas 1:17

God controls natural light

Ps 104:19 The moon marks off the seasons, and the sun knows when to go down. *See also* Job 9:7; 36:30–32; Ps 121:5–6; Mt 5:45; 2Co 4:6

Miracles involving natural light

The pillars of cloud and fire Ex 13:21–22; 14:20; Dt 1:31; Ne 9:12,19; Ps 78:14; 105:39

Other miracles Ex 9:23–24; 10:23; Isa 38:8; Hab 3:11; Lk 23:44–45; Ac 9:3; 22:6,9,11; 26:13

Natural light associated with angels

Mt 28:3; Lk 24:4; Ac 12:7

Natural light used figuratively

The sun

Rev 1:16 . . . His [someone "like a son of man"] face was like the sun shining in all its brilliance. *See also* Isa 30:26; Lk 21:25; Rev 12:1

Lightning

Lk 9:29 As he [Jesus] was praying, the appearance of his face changed, and his clothes became as bright as a flash of lightning. pp Mt 17:2 pp Mk 9:2 *See also* Eze 1:4; Da 10:6; Hos 6:5; Lk 10:18; 17:24

Light

Ps 104:2 He [the LORD] wraps himself in light as with a garment; he stretches out the heavens like a tent . . . *See also* Eze 1:26–28 *See also creation.*

---

light, spiritual

Light is often used in Scripture as a symbol of the presence of God in the world. It is often especially associated with the word of God, the salvation brought about by God, or the person of Jesus Christ.

Light as a symbol of God

God's purity

1Jn 1:5 . . . God is light; in him there is no darkness at all. *See also* Job 25:4–6; Isa 5:20; 1Jn 1:7

God's glory

Rev 21:23 The city does not need the sun or the moon to shine on it, for the glory of God gives it light, and the Lamb is its lamp. *See also* Ps 76:4; 84:11; Isa 60:19–20; Hab 3:4; 1Ti 6:15–16

God's knowledge Ps 90:8; 139:11–12; **Da** 2:22; **1Co** 4:5

God's unchangeability

Jas 1:17 Every good and perfect gift is from above, coming down from the Father of the heavenly lights, who does not change like shifting shadows.

God's vengeance Ps 94:1; **Isa** 10:17

Satan as an imitator of light

2Co 11:14 And no wonder, for Satan himself masquerades as an angel of light.

Light as a symbol of God's favour towards his people

Ezr 9:8 "But now, for a brief moment, the LORD our God has been gracious in leaving us a remnant and giving us a firm place in his sanctuary, and so our God gives light to our eyes and a little relief in our bondage."   *See also* **Nu** 6:25; **Job** 3:20; 29:2–3; **Ps** 4:6; 31:16; 44:3; 67:1; 80:3,7; **Mic** 7:8–9; **Rev** 22:5

Light as a symbol of God's word

As perceived by believers

Ps 119:105 Your word is a lamp to my feet and a light for my path.   *See also* **Ps** 19:8; 119:130; **2Pe** 1:19

As perceived by unbelievers

Jn 3:20 "All those who do evil hate the light, and will not come into the light for fear that their deeds will be exposed."   *See also* **Job** 24:13–17; **Jn** 1:5

Light as a symbol of salvation

1Pe 2:9 . . . God . . . called you out of darkness into his wonderful light.   *See also* **Isa** 9:2; 51:4; **Ac** 26:23; **Eph** 5:14; **Col** 1:12; **1Jn** 2:8

Light as a symbol of Jesus Christ

Foretold in the OT

Nu 24:17 ". . . A star will come out of Jacob; a sceptre will rise out of Israel . . ."   *See also* **Isa** 9:2; 42:6–7; 49:6; 53:11; **Mal** 4:2

Revealed in the NT

Jn 8:12 . . . "I [Jesus] am the light of the world. Whoever follows me will never walk in darkness, but will have the light of life."   *See*

also **Mt** 4:16; 17:2; **Lk** 1:78–79; 2:32; **Jn** 1:4–9; 9:5; 12:35–36,46; **Ac** 13:47; **2Co** 4:6; **Heb** 1:3; **Rev** 1:16; 22:16   *See also holiness, of God; salvation.*

Lord's Day

As well as keeping the Sabbath, the first Christians assembled together on the first day of the week to commemorate Jesus Christ's resurrection through the Lord's Supper. The Lord's Day quickly became the focal point of the Christian week, eventually assuming the characteristics of the Jewish Sabbath, namely worship and rest.

The disciples continued to observe the Sabbath

Lk 23:56 . . . they [the women who had come with Jesus from Galilee] rested on the Sabbath in obedience to the commandment. *See also* **Ac** 13:14,42; 16:13; 17:2; 18:4

The Lord's Day commemorated Jesus Christ's resurrection

The resurrection took place on the first day of the week

Mk 16:9 When Jesus rose early on the first day of the week, he appeared first to Mary Magdalene, out of whom he had driven seven demons.   *See also* **Mt** 28:1–7 pp **Mk** 16:1–7 pp **Lk** 24:1–6 pp **Jn** 20:1

The disciples assembled together on the first day of the week

Ac 20:7 On the first day of the week we [the believers gathered at Troas] came together to break bread . . .   *See also* **Jn** 20:19–20,24–26

The Lord's Day took over the role of the Sabbath

1Co 16:2 On the first day of every week, each one of you should set aside a sum of money in keeping with your income, saving it up, so that when I come no collections will have to be made.   *See also* **Rev** 1:10   *See also Lord's Supper; Sabbath.*

Lord's Supper

The commemoration and remembrance of Jesus Christ's last supper, and all the benefits that result to believers. Other terms have been used subsequently by Christians, including "Communion" and "Eucharist".

Terms for the Lord's Supper in the NT
Ac 2:42; 1Co 10:16; 11:20,24

Jesus Christ's institution of the Lord's Supper
1Co 11:23–25 For I [Paul] received from the Lord [as being something Jesus himself ordained] what I also passed on to you: The Lord Jesus, on the night he was betrayed, took bread, and when he had given thanks, he broke it and said, "This is my body, which is for you; do this in remembrance of me." In the same way, after supper he took the cup, saying, "This cup is the new covenant in my blood; do this, whenever you drink it, in remembrance of me." pp Mt 26:26–28 pp Mk 14:22–24 pp Lk 22:17–20

Celebrating the Lord's Supper in the NT
As part of an ordinary meal
1Co 11:21 for as you eat, each of you goes ahead without waiting for anybody else. One remains hungry, another gets drunk.

On the Lord's day
Ac 20:7 On the first day of the week we came together to break bread . . .   See also Jn 20:26

The fourfold formula for breaking bread: taking, giving thanks, breaking, giving
Mt 26:26 . . . Jesus took bread, gave thanks and broke it, and gave it to his disciples . . . pp Mk 14:22 pp Lk 22:19   See also Lk 24:30; Jn 6:11; 1Co 11:24

The sharing of the cup
1Co 11:25 In the same way, after supper he [Jesus] took the cup, saying, "This cup is the new covenant in my blood; do this, whenever you drink it, in remembrance of me." pp Mt 26:27–28 pp Mk 14:23–24 pp Lk 22:20

Themes connected with the Lord's Supper
The Passover
1Co 5:7–8 . . . For Christ, our Passover lamb, has been sacrificed. Therefore let us keep the Festival, not with the old yeast, the yeast of malice and wickedness, but with bread without yeast, the bread of sincerity and truth.   See also Jn 11:50; Jn 13:1; 19:14,33,36; Ex 12:46; Nu 9:12

The new covenant
1Co 11:25 In the same way, after supper he [Jesus] took the cup, saying, "This cup is the new covenant in my blood . . ." pp Mt 26:27–28 pp Mk 14:23–24 pp Lk 22:20

Remembrance
1Co 11:24 and when he [Jesus] had given thanks, he broke it and said, "This is my body, which is for you; do this in remembrance of me." pp Lk 22:19

Thanksgiving, fellowship and unity
1Co 10:16 Is not the cup of thanksgiving for which we give thanks a participation in the blood of Christ? And is not the bread that we break a participation in the body of Christ?   See also Mt 26:26–27 pp Mk 14:22–23 pp Lk 22:19; 1Co 11:20–21

The Lord's return
1Co 11:26 For whenever you eat this bread and drink this cup, you proclaim the Lord's death until he comes.   See also Mt 26:29 pp Mk 14:25 pp Lk 22:16; 1Co 16:22; Rev 22:20

Separation from sin
1Co 10:21 You cannot drink the cup of the Lord and the cup of demons too; you cannot have a part in both the Lord's table and the table of demons.   See also 1Co 11:27–32

A foretaste of heaven
Mt 26:29 "I tell you, I will not drink of this fruit of the vine from now on until that day when I drink it anew with you in my Father's kingdom." pp Mk 14:25   See also covenant, the new; fellowship; forgiveness; heaven.

love

A caring commitment, in which affection and delight are shown to others, which is grounded in the nature of God himself. In his words and actions, and supremely in the death of Jesus Christ on the cross, God demonstrates the nature of love and defines the direction in which human love in all its forms should develop.

---

love, abuse of
Scripture warns that love can be misdirected and shows a number of examples.

Exaggerated love of self
Self-interest is condemned
Php 2:3–4 Do nothing out of selfish ambition or vain conceit, but in humility consider others better than yourselves. Each of you should look not only to your own interests, but also to the interests of others.   *See also* **Mt** 16:25 pp **Mk** 8:35 pp **Lk** 9:24; **Ro** 14:15; 15:1; **1Co** 8:9; 10:24; **Gal** 5:26; **Jas** 3:14–15

Examples of self-love Est 6:6; **Isa** 5:8; **Da** 4:30; **2Ti** 3:2; **Jas** 5:5

Love of prestige
Pride in one's position or reputation is condemned
Pr 25:27 It is not good to eat too much honey, nor is it honourable to seek one's own honour.

1Co 13:4 Love is patient, love is kind. It does not envy, it does not boast, it is not proud. *See also* **Pr** 21:4; 25:6–7; **Mt** 23:12 pp **Lk** 14:11; **Ro** 12:10; **Jas** 3:1

Examples of the love of prestige 2Sa 15:1; **1Ki** 1:5; **Isa** 14:13; **Jer** 46:5; **Eze** 28:2; **Mt** 20:21; 23:6–7 pp **Lk** 20:46; **Lk** 14:7; 22:24; **Jn** 12:43; **2Th** 2:4; **3Jn** 9

Love of the world
Love of the world is condemned
1Jn 2:15 Do not love the world or anything in the world. If you love the world, the love of the Father is not in you.   *See also* **Ex** 23:2; **Mt** 16:26 pp **Mk** 8:36–37 pp **Lk** 9:25; **Ro** 12:2; **Col** 3:2; **2Ti** 2:4; **Tit** 2:12; **Jas** 4:4

Examples of the love of the world Mt 24:38; **Lk** 14:18; **2Ti** 4:10

Love of money
Love of money is condemned
1Ti 6:9–10 Those who want to get rich fall into temptation and a trap and into many foolish and harmful desires that plunge people into ruin and destruction. For the love of money is a root of all kinds of evil. Some people, eager for money, have wandered from the faith and pierced themselves with many griefs.   *See also* **Ps** 62:10; **Pr** 28:20; **Ecc** 5:10; **Lk** 12:15

Examples of the love of riches Jos 7:21; **2Ki** 5:20; **Mic** 3:11; **Mt** 19:22 pp **Mk** 10:22 pp **Lk** 18:23; **Mt** 26:15; **Lk** 16:14; **Jn** 12:6; **Ac** 16:19; 24:26; **2Pe** 2:15

Love of sin
The love of sin is condemned
2Th 2:12 . . . all will be condemned who have not believed the truth but have delighted in wickedness.   *See also* **Job** 15:16; **Pr** 2:14; 17:19; **Ro** 1:32; **2Pe** 2:10

Examples of the love of sinning 1Ki 21:25; **Jer** 14:10; **Mic** 3:2; **2Pe** 2:13–14

Love of other gods
Idolatry is condemned
Dt 6:13–14 Fear the LORD your God, serve him only and take your oaths in his name. Do not follow other gods, the gods of the peoples around you;   *See also* **Ex** 20:3; **Lev** 26:1; **Dt** 12:30; **Ac** 17:29; **1Jn** 5:21

Examples of the love of idols Ex 32:4; **Jdg** 2:11–12; **2Ki** 17:15; **Da** 5:4; **Ac** 17:16; **Ro** 1:23   *See also sin.*

---

love, and enemies
God loves even those who oppose him and believers must follow his example in loving their enemies.

God's love for sinners
Isa 53:6 We all, like sheep, have gone astray, each of us has turned to our own way; and the LORD has laid on him the iniquity of us all.

Jn 3:16 "For God so loved the world that he gave his one and only Son, that whoever believes in him shall not perish but have eternal life."

2Pe 3:9 The Lord is not slow in keeping his promise, as some understand slowness. He is patient with you, not wanting anyone to perish, but everyone to come to repentance.　*See also* **Ge** 18:32; **La** 3:33; **Eze** 18:23; **Mt** 5:45; **Ro** 5:8; 8:32; **2Co** 5:19; **1Jn** 4:9–10

The example of Jesus Christ

Mt 23:37 "O Jerusalem, Jerusalem, you who kill the prophets and stone those sent to you, how often I have longed to gather your children together, as a hen gathers her chicks under her wings, but you were not willing." pp Lk 13:34
1Pe 3:18 For Christ died for sins once for all, the righteous for the unrighteous, to bring you to God. He was put to death in the body but made alive by the Spirit,　*See also* **Isa** 53:5; **Mt** 20:28 pp **Mk** 10:45; **Lk** 23:34; **Ro** 5:6; **2Co** 5:14; 8:9; **Heb** 3:12; **1Pe** 2:21,24; **1Jn** 2:2

God's people must love their enemies

Lev 19:18 " 'Do not seek revenge or bear a grudge against one of your people, but love your neighbour as yourself. I am the LORD.' "

Lk 6:35–36 "But love your enemies, do good to them, and lend to them without expecting to get anything back. Then your reward will be great, and you will be sons of the Most High, because he is kind to the ungrateful and wicked. Be merciful, just as your Father is merciful."　*See also* **Ex** 23:4; **Pr** 24:17; 25:21; **Mt** 5:44; **Lk** 6:27; **Col** 3:13; **1Th** 5:15; **2Ti** 2:25; **1Pe** 3:9

Examples of love for enemies

Ge 50:20–21; **Nu** 12:13; **1Sa** 24:17; 26:21; **2Sa** 19:23; **2Ki** 6:22; **Ac** 7:60; 9:17; **1Co** 4:12　*See also forgiveness.*

love, and the world

Scripture promotes the love of family, home and country and contains many examples of such love.

Parental love
Aspects of parental love

Pr 13:24 Those who spare the rod hate their children, but those who love them are careful to discipline them.

Eph 6:4 Fathers, do not exasperate your children; instead, bring them up in the training and instruction of the Lord.　*See also* **Dt** 6:7; **2Co** 12:14; **Col** 3:21; **1Ti** 3:4; **2Ti** 3:15
Examples of maternal love Ge 21:16; **Ex** 2:3; **Jdg** 5:28; **1Sa** 2:19; **2Sa** 21:10; **1Ki** 3:26; 17:18 The Shunammite: **2Ki** 4:20,27
Mt 15:22 pp **Mk** 7:26; **Lk** 2:48; 7:12–13; **Jn** 19:25
Examples of paternal love Ge 22:2; 31:28; 37:35; 42:38
David: **2Sa** 12:16; 13:39
Mk 5:23 pp **Lk** 8:41–42

Love for parents

Ex 20:12 "Honour your father and your mother, so that you may live long in the land the LORD your God is giving you."

1Ti 5:4 But if a widow has children or grandchildren, these should learn first of all to put their religion into practice by caring for their own family and so repaying their parents and grandparents, for this is pleasing to God.　*See also* **Ge** 46:29; **Lev** 19:3; **Jdg** 11:36; **1Sa** 22:3; **1Ki** 19:20; **Jer** 35:8; **Mt** 15:4 pp **Mk** 7:10; **Lk** 2:51; **Jn** 19:26–27; **Eph** 6:1; **Col** 3:20

Other instances of family love

Ge 34:7; 45:14–15; **Ru** 1:16–17; **2Sa** 13:22 Mordecai and Esther: **Est** 2:7,11

Love of home and country
Examples of love of home **Ge** 31:30; 49:29; 50:25; **Nu** 10:30; **Ru** 1:6; **2Sa** 10:12; 19:37; 23:15; **Ne** 4:14
Exhortations to patriotism

Ps 122:6 Pray for the peace of Jerusalem: "May those who love you be secure."

Ps 137:5–6 If I forget you, O Jerusalem, may

my right hand forget (its skill). May my tongue cling to the roof of my mouth if I do not remember you, if I do not consider Jerusalem my highest joy.   *See also* **2Sa** 1:20; **Est** 4:8; **Jer** 51:50

Examples of patriotism 1Sa 17:26; 27:8–10; **Ne** 1:3–4; 2:5; **Est** 8:6; **Ps** 137:1; **Jer** 51:51; **Ro** 9:3

love, for God

Scripture teaches believers to love God and shows how such love should be expressed in worship and practical service.

Believers' response to God's love
1Jn 4:19 We love because he first loved us. *See also* **Dt** 7:7–8; **Ps** 116:1; **Jn** 15:16; **Eph** 2:4–5; **1Jn** 4:10

Love for God is commanded
Mt 22:37–38 Jesus replied [to the expert in the law]: " 'Love the Lord your God with all your heart and with all your soul and with all your mind.' This is the first and greatest commandment." pp **Mk** 12:29–30   *See also* **Dt** 6:5; 10:12; 11:1; **Jos** 22:5; 23:11; **Ps** 31:23

Loving God involves loving Jesus Christ
Jn 8:42 Jesus said to them [the Jews], "If God were your Father, you would love me, for I came from God and now am here. I have not come on my own; but he sent me."   *See also* **Jn** 5:42; 15:23

Expressing love for God
Delight in worship and in God's house
Ps 27:4 One thing I ask of the LORD, this is what I seek: that I may dwell in the house of the LORD all the days of my life, to gaze upon the beauty of the LORD and to seek him in his temple.   *See also* **Ps** 26:8; 43:4; 65:4; 84:2; 122:1,6; **Ac** 2:46–47

Love for God's word
Ps 119:97 Oh, how I love your law! I meditate on it all day long.   *See also* **Ps** 1:2; 19:7–8,10; 119:16,35,72,163; **Jer** 15:16; **Eze** 3:3

Self-sacrifice
Lk 14:33 "In the same way, those of you who

do not give up everything you have cannot be my [Jesus'] disciples."   *See also* **Jn** 21:15–17; **Ro** 12:1; **Php** 3:8

Giving
1Ch 29:3 ". . . in my devotion to the temple of my God I now give my personal treasures of gold and silver for the temple of my God, over and above everything I have provided for this holy temple:"   *See also* **Ex** 25:2; 35:5; **1Ch** 29:6,9; **2Co** 8:4–5,8; 9:7

Obeying God
1Jn 5:3 This is love for God: to obey his commands. And his commands are not burdensome,   *See also* **Ps** 40:8; **Jn** 14:15,23; 15:14; **2Jn** 6

Loving others
1Jn 4:21 And he [God] has given us this command: Those who love God must also love one another.   *See also* **Jn** 13:35; 15:12; **1Jn** 4:11

The blessings of loving God
Jn 14:15–16 "If you love me [Jesus], you will obey what I command. And I will ask the Father, and he will give you another Counsellor to be with you for ever—"   *See also* **Jn** 14:23; 16:27; **1Pe** 1:8

Examples of love for God and Jesus Christ
Ps 18:1 I love you, O LORD, my strength. *See also* **Ps** 73:25; **Mt** 26:7 pp **Mk** 14:3; **Jn** 12:3; **Lk** 2:37; 7:47; 24:53; **Jn** 11:16; 21:16; **Ac** 21:13; **Heb** 6:10   *See also knowing God; obedience; prayer, relationship with God; worship, reasons.*

love, for one another

Scripture instructs God's people to love one another and illustrates what this means in practice.

Reasons for loving one another
God commands it
Gal 5:14 The entire law is summed up in a single command: "Love your neighbour as yourself."   *See also* **Lev** 19:18

Love for foreigners commanded: **Lev** 19:34; **Dt** 10:19 **Mt** 22:39 pp **Mk** 12:31; **Jn** 15:12; **Ro** 13:10;

1Th 4:9; Heb 13:1; Jas 2:8; 1Pe 1:22; 2:17; 1Jn 3:23; 4:21; 2Jn 5

God has taken the initiative in showing love
1Jn 4:11 Dear friends, since God so loved us, we also ought to love one another.   *See also* Mal 2:10; 1Co 8:11–13; 1Jn 3:16

God's people are known by their love
Jn 13:35 "By this everyone will know that you are my [Jesus'] disciples, if you love one another."   *See also* 1Jn 2:10; 3:14; 4:7,16,20

Love maintains fellowship
1Pe 4:8 Above all, love each other deeply, because love covers over a multitude of sins. *See also* Pr 10:12; 17:9; Eph 4:2

Love promotes sacrificial service
1Th 2:8 We loved you so much that we were delighted to share with you not only the gospel of God but our lives as well, because you had become so dear to us.   *See also* Pr 17:17; 2Co 12:15; Gal 5:13; Php 2:30; 4:10; 1Th 1:3

Expressing love for one another
In caring for the sick
Mt 25:36 "'I needed clothes and you clothed me, I was sick and you looked after me, I was in prison and you came to visit me.'"   *See also* Job 2:11; Gal 4:14

In meeting material needs
Mt 25:35 "'For I was hungry and you gave me something to eat, I was thirsty and you gave me something to drink, I was a stranger and you invited me in,'"   *See also* Dt 15:7–8; 1Jn 3:17

In affectionate greetings
2Co 13:12 Greet one another with a holy kiss.   *See also* Ge 33:4; 45:14–15; Ac 20:37; Ro 16:16; 1Co 16:20; 1Pe 5:14

Examples of the demonstration of love for one another
Ge 14:14–16; Ex 32:31–32; 1Sa 18:3; Lk 7:2–6; 10:29–37; Ac 4:32; 16:33; 20:38; Ro 16:4; 2Co 2:4; Eph 1:15; Php 1:8; 4:1; 2Ti 1:16–17; Phm 12; 3Jn 6

Paul's love for his churches
Corinth: 2Co 1:3–6; 2:4
Gal 4:19
Philippi: Php 1:3,7; 4:1

Thessalonica: 1Th 2:7–8; 3:7–10,12   *See also* church, life of; church, unity; fellowship, among believers; reconciliation, between believers.

---

love, in relationships
Human love is ennobled by being patterned on God's love for his people. It is also safeguarded by God's commands.

The love between husband and wife
Conjugal love is commanded
Col 3:18–19 Wives, submit to your husbands, as is fitting in the Lord. Husbands, love your wives and do not be harsh with them.   *See also* Ge 2:24; Dt 24:5; Pr 5:18–20; Ecc 9:9; Eph 5:22,28,33; 1Pe 3:7

It is patterned on God's love for his people
Isa 54:5 "For your Maker is your husband— the LORD Almighty is his name—the Holy One of Israel is your Redeemer; he is called the God of all the earth."

Eph 5:25–27 Husbands, love your wives, just as Christ loved the church and gave himself up for her to make her holy, cleansing her by the washing with water through the word, and to present her to himself as a radiant church, without stain or wrinkle or any other blemish, but holy and blameless.   *See also* Isa 62:5; Jer 3:14; Eze 16:8; Hos 2:19; 2Co 11:2; Rev 19:7

The power of human love
SS 8:6–7 Place me like a seal over your heart, like a seal on your arm; for love is as strong as death, its jealousy unyielding as the grave. It burns like blazing fire, like a mighty flame. Many waters cannot quench love; rivers cannot wash it away. If one were to give all the wealth of one's house for love, it would be utterly scorned.   *See also* Ge 29:20,30; Pr 6:34–35

Examples of love in courtship and marriage
Ge 24:67; 29:18; Jdg 16:4; 1Sa 1:5; Est 2:17; SS 1:2; 4:10; Hos 3:1; Mt 1:19

Safeguards on human love
Sexual immorality is condemned
1Co 7:2 . . . since there is so much immorality, each man should have his own wife, and each woman her own husband. *See also* **Lev** 18:22; 19:29; **Dt** 23:17–18; **Mt** 5:32; **Ac** 15:29; **Ro** 1:26–27; **1Co** 5:1; 6:18; 10:8; **Eph** 5:3; **Col** 3:5; **1Th** 4:3
Adultery is condemned
Ex 20:14 "You shall not commit adultery." *See also* **Lev** 20:10; **Dt** 5:18; **Pr** 6:24; **1Co** 6:9; **Heb** 13:4
Restrictions on divorce
Mt 19:9 "I [Jesus] tell you that anyone who divorces his wife, except for marital unfaithfulness, and marries another woman commits adultery." *See also* **Mal** 2:16; **Mt** 5:32; **Mk** 10:11–12; **Lk** 16:18; **1Co** 7:10–11
Lust is condemned
Mt 5:28 "But I [Jesus] tell you that anyone who looks at a woman lustfully has already committed adultery with her in his heart." *See also* **Job** 31:1; **Pr** 6:25; **1Co** 7:9; **Eph** 4:19; **1Th** 4:5
Polygamy is forbidden
1Ti 3:2 Now the overseer must be above reproach, the husband of but one wife . . . *See also* **Dt** 17:17; **Mal** 2:15; **1Ti** 3:12; **Tit** 1:6

---

love, nature of
Scripture offers an understanding of the source, character and value of love, based on the nature and actions of God.

God is the source of love
His very character is love
1Jn 4:7–8 Dear friends, let us love one another, for love comes from God. Everyone who loves has been born of God and knows God. Whoever does not love does not know God, because God is love. *See also* **1Th** 3:12; **2Ti** 1:7; **1Jn** 4:16,19
The love of God is revealed in the cross of Jesus Christ
1Jn 3:16 This is how we know what love is: Jesus Christ laid down his life for us. And we ought to lay down our lives for one another.

1Jn 4:10 This is love: not that we loved God, but that he loved us and sent his Son as an atoning sacrifice for our sins. *See also* **Jn** 15:13; **Eph** 5:2,25
Love is part of the Holy Spirit's fruit
Gal 5:22 But the fruit of the Spirit is love . . . *See also* **Ro** 5:5; 15:30; **Col** 1:8

The loving-kindness of God referred to in the OT
Jer 31:3 The Lord appeared to us in the past, saying: "I have loved you with an everlasting love; I have drawn you with loving-kindness." *See also* **Ex** 15:13; 34:6; **2Ch** 6:42; **Ps** 6:4; 32:10; 51:1; 107:43; **Isa** 54:10; 63:7; **La** 3:22; **Hos** 2:19

The love of God in the NT
To describe God's love for humanity
Jn 3:16 "For God so loved the world that he gave his one and only Son, that whoever believes in him shall not perish but have eternal life." *See also* **Jn** 5:42; 15:10; **Ro** 8:39; **2Co** 13:14; **Eph** 2:4; **Heb** 12:6; **1Jn** 3:1
To describe love for God **Lk** 10:27; **Jn** 14:21; 21:15; **Ro** 8:28; **1Th** 1:3; **Jas** 1:12; **1Pe** 1:8; **1Jn** 5:3
To describe brotherly love **Jn** 13:35; **Ro** 13:8; **1Co** 16:24; **2Co** 8:8; **Gal** 5:13; **Eph** 4:2; **Php** 1:9; **Col** 2:2; **Phm** 5
To describe love expressed by eating together **2Pe** 2:13 fn; **Jude** 12
To describe love in a negative sense **Lk** 11:43; **Jn** 3:19; 12:43; **2Ti** 4:10; **2Pe** 2:15; **1Jn** 2:15

Characteristics of love
1Co 13:4–8 Love is patient, love is kind. It does not envy, it does not boast, it is not proud. It is not rude, it is not self-seeking, it is not easily angered, it keeps no record of wrongs. Love does not delight in evil but rejoices with the truth. It always protects, always trusts, always hopes, always perseveres. Love never fails . . . *See also* **Ro** 12:9; **1Ti** 1:5; **1Pe** 1:22; **1Jn** 4:18

Love is shown by deeds
1Jn 3:17–18 If anyone of you has material possessions and sees a brother or sister in need

but has no pity on them, how can the love of God be in you? Dear children, let us not love with words or tongue but with actions and in truth.   *See also* **Jn** 14:15,23; **Ro** 5:8; 14:15; **Gal** 2:20; **1Jn** 4:9; 5:2–3; **2Jn** 6; **3Jn** 5–6

The pre-eminence of love
1Co 13:13 And now these three remain: faith, hope and love. But the greatest of these is love.   *See also* **Mt** 22:37–39 pp **Mk** 12:29–31; **Ro** 13:9–10; **1Co** 12:31–13:3; **Gal** 5:6; **Eph** 3:17–19; **Col** 3:14; **2Pe** 1:7; **1Jn** 2:10   *See also assurance, nature of; election; salvation, necessity of.*

mercy
A quality of compassion, especially as expressed in God's forgiveness of human sin. Scripture stresses God's forbearance towards sinners. In his mercy, God shields sinners from what they deserve and gives gifts that they do not deserve.

mercy, demonstration of God's
God demonstrates his mercy in his various dealings with his people.

God as a parent
Ps 103:13–14 As a father has compassion on his children, so the Lord has compassion on those who fear him; for he knows how we are formed, he remembers that we are dust.

Eph 1:4–6 For he chose us in him before the creation of the world to be holy and blameless in his sight. In love he predestined us to be adopted as his children through Jesus Christ, in accordance with his pleasure and will—to the praise of his glorious grace, which he has freely given us in the One he loves.   *See also* **Isa** 49:15; 63:7–8; 66:13; **Jer** 31:20; **Hos** 11:1–4; **Mal** 3:17; **2Co** 1:3

God's mercy and compassion to those in distress
Isa 49:13 Shout for joy, O heavens; rejoice, O earth; burst into song, O mountains! For the Lord comforts his people and will have compassion on

his afflicted ones.   *See also* **Ex** 2:23–24; **Ps** 91:14–16; 111:2–9; 113:7–9; 142:1–3; **Isa** 63:9; **Jnh** 2:2; **2Co** 4:1; **Heb** 4:16

In judgment, God's mercy is just and true
Dt 32:36 The Lord will judge his people and have compassion on his servants when he sees their strength is gone and no-one is left, slave or free.   *See also* **Ps** 143:1; **Isa** 11:3–5; 30:18; 54:7–8; 60:10; **Hab** 3:2; **Rev** 19:11

God may choose to show no mercy
Ps 59:5 O Lord God Almighty, the God of Israel, rouse yourself to punish all the nations; show no mercy to wicked traitors . . .   *See also* **Jos** 11:20; **Jer** 21:7; **Jas** 2:13

God's mercy shown in his actions
The act of salvation
Eph 2:4–5 . . . because of his great love for us, God, who is rich in mercy, made us alive with Christ even when we were dead in transgressions—it is by grace you have been saved.   *See also* **Ex** 15:13; **Jdg** 2:18; **Ps** 13:5; 28:6–8; 31:21–22

David appeals to God's mercy: **Ps** 40:10–11; 57:1; 69:16; 86:15–16

Ps 98:2–3; 116:4–6; **Ne** 9:27; **1Pe** 1:3; 2:10; **2Pe** 3:15

His forgiveness
Ps 51:1–2 Have mercy on me, O God, according to your unfailing love; according to your great compassion blot out my transgressions. Wash away all my iniquity and cleanse me from my sin.   *See also* **Nu** 14:18–19; **Ps** 25:6–7; 79:8; 130:1–4; **Isa** 55:7; **Hos** 14:1–4; **Mic** 7:18–19; **1Ti** 1:15–16; **1Jn** 1:9

His blessing
Dt 13:17–18 None of those condemned things shall be found in your hands, so that the Lord will turn from his fierce anger; he will show you mercy, have compassion on you, and increase your numbers, as he promised on oath to your forefathers, because you obey the Lord your God, keeping all his commands that I am giving you today and doing what is right in his eyes.   *See*

also **Dt** 7:12–13; 30:3   *See also justice; salvation; sin, and God's character.*

---

mercy, God's

A central aspect of God's character, expressed in his covenant relationships with undeserving people.

God is merciful

Da 9:9 "The Lord our God is merciful and forgiving, even though we have rebelled against him;"

Eph 2:4 . . . God, who is rich in mercy . . .   *See also* **2Sa** 24:14; **Ne** 9:31; **Ps** 5:7; 25:6; **Jer** 3:12; **Lk** 1:78; **1Ti** 1:2; **Jas** 5:11; **1Pe** 1:3; **2Jn** 3; **Jude** 2

God's mercy is expressed in his faithfulness to his covenant with his people

Mic 7:18–20 Who is a God like you, who pardons sin and forgives the transgression of the remnant of his inheritance? You do not stay angry for ever but delight to show mercy. You will again have compassion on us; you will tread our sins underfoot and hurl all our iniquities into the depths of the sea. You will be true to Jacob, and show mercy to Abraham, as you pledged on oath to our ancestors in days long ago.   *See also* **Dt** 4:31; 7:9; **1Ki** 8:23–24; **Ne** 1:5; 9:30–31; **Ps** 143:1; **Isa** 63:9; **Lk** 1:54–55,69–75

God's faithfulness and mercy are never-ending

Ps 103:17 But from everlasting to everlasting the LORD's love is with those who fear him, and his righteousness with their children's children—   *See also* **Ps** 25:6; 106:1; 119:132

God's mercy and grace are seen in Jesus Christ

Jn 1:14 The Word became flesh and made his dwelling among us. We have seen his glory, the glory of the One and Only, who came from the Father, full of grace and truth.   *See also* **Ro** 3:22–24; 5:15; **Eph** 1:7; **Heb** 4:16; **Jude** 21

God's mercy is not confined to the Jewish nation

Ro 3:29–30 Is God the God of Jews only? Is he not the God of Gentiles too? Yes, of Gentiles too, since there is only one God, who will justify the circumcised by faith and the uncircumcised through that same faith.   *See also* **Isa** 49:6; **Jnh** 4:2; **Ro** 10:12; 11:28–32; 15:8–12; **Gal** 3:14; **Eph** 3:6–8; **Col** 1:27

God chooses when and where to exercise his mercy

Ro 9:15–16 For he says to Moses, "I will have mercy on whom I have mercy, and I will have compassion on whom I have compassion." It does not, therefore, depend on human desire or effort, but on God's mercy.   *See also* **Ex** 33:19; **Dt** 7:7–8; **Ps** 33:12; **Jn** 15:16; **1Co** 1:27–29

God responds in mercy to those who call to him

Ps 6:9 The LORD has heard my cry for mercy; the LORD accepts my prayer.   *See also* **1Ki** 8:28; **2Ch** 6:19; **Job** 9:15; **Da** 9:18   *See also covenant; grace; love.*

---

mercy, human

Believers are urged to show the same qualities of mercy and compassion towards one another as God demonstrates to them. A lack of mercy is regarded as characteristic of godless people.

The need for human mercy

Pr 18:23 The poor plead for mercy, but the rich answer harshly.   *See also* **Dt** 28:49–50; **2Sa** 12:6; **1Ki** 3:26; **Job** 19:21; **Pr** 21:10; **Isa** 47:6; 49:15; **Zec** 7:9–11

Believers should be merciful

Mic 6:8 He has showed you, O people, what is good. And what does the LORD require of you? To act justly and to love mercy and to walk humbly with your God.

Mt 5:7 "Blessed are the merciful, for they will be shown mercy."

Lk 6:36 "Be merciful, just as your Father is merciful."   *See also* **Zec** 7:9; **Jas** 2:12–13; **1Pe** 3:9; **Jude** 22

Lack of mercy characterises the godless

Isa 13:18 Their bows will strike down the young men; they will have no mercy on infants nor will they look with compassion on children. *See also* Jer 6:23; 21:7; 50:42; **Am** 1:11–12; **Hab** 1:13–17; **Mt** 23:23

Lack of mercy on Israel's part was sometimes obedience to God

Dt 7:2 and when the Lord your God has delivered them over to you and you have defeated them, then you must destroy them totally. Make no treaty with them, and show them no mercy. *See also* **Dt** 13:6–9; 19:11–13,21; 28:53–54; **Jos** 6:17–19; **1Sa** 15:18–19

Mercy as a greeting and a blessing
As a greeting

1Ti 1:2 . . . Grace, mercy and peace from God the Father and Christ Jesus our Lord. *See also* **2Ti** 1:2; **2Jn** 3; **Jude** 2

As a blessing

Gal 6:16 Peace and mercy to all who follow this rule, even to the Israel of God. *See also* **2Ti** 1:16–18; **Jude** 21

mercy, of Jesus Christ

Jesus Christ displays the same attitude of grace and mercy towards men and women as his Father does.

Jesus Christ is merciful

Lk 4:16–21 . . . "The Spirit of the Lord is on me, because he has anointed me to preach good news to the poor. He has sent me to proclaim freedom for the prisoners and recovery of sight for the blind, to release the oppressed, to proclaim the year of the Lord's favour." . . . *See also* Isa 61:1–2

Jn 15:12–13 "My command is this: Love each other as I have loved you. Greater love has no-one than this, to lay down one's life for one's friends." *See also* **2Co** 8:9; 13:14; **Eph** 4:7; **Php** 2:1; **1Ti** 1:16; **2Ti** 1:18; 2:1; **Jude** 21

Jesus Christ's concern for people in need

Mt 9:36 When he [Jesus] saw the crowds, he had compassion on them, because they were harassed and helpless, like sheep without a shepherd. pp Mk 6:34 *See also* **Mt** 14:14; 15:32 pp Mk 8:2; **Mt** 23:37 pp Lk 13:34

Jesus Christ's response to appeals for mercy

Mt 20:30–34 Two blind men were sitting by the roadside, and when they heard that Jesus was going by, they shouted, "Lord, Son of David, have mercy on us!" The crowd rebuked them and told them to be quiet, but they shouted all the louder, "Lord, Son of David, have mercy on us!" . . . Jesus had compassion on them and touched their eyes. Immediately they received their sight and followed him. *See also* **Mt** 8:2–3 pp Mk 1:39–40 pp Lk 5:12–13; **Mt** 8:5–13; 9:18–30; 15:22; 17:14–18; **Jn** 11:6; **2Co** 12:8–9

Jesus Christ's mercy in response to judgment

Jn 12:47 "As for those who hear my words but do not keep them, I do not judge them. For I did not come to judge the world, but to save it."

Jesus Christ as high priest

Heb 2:17–18 For this reason he [Jesus] had to be made like his brothers and sisters in every way, in order that he might become a merciful and faithful high priest in service to God, and that he might make atonement for the sins of the people. Because he himself suffered when he was tempted, he is able to help those who are being tempted. *See also* **Heb** 4:15

Jesus Christ's mercy is shown in his actions
In salvation

Eph 5:2 . . . Christ loved us and gave himself up for us as a fragrant offering and sacrifice to God. *See also* Lk 19:10; **Gal** 2:20; **Eph** 5:25; **1Ti** 1:14–16; **Tit** 3:4–7

In forgiveness

Lk 23:34 Jesus said, "Father, forgive them, for

they do not know what they are doing." . . .
See also **Mk** 2:10

In blessing

Mk 10:13–16 People were bringing little children to Jesus to have him touch them, but the disciples rebuked them. When Jesus saw this, he was indignant. He said to them, "Let the little children come to me, and do not hinder them, for the kingdom of God belongs to such as these. I tell you the truth, anyone who will not receive the kingdom of God like a little child will never enter it." And he took the children in his arms, put his hands on them and blessed them. pp Mt 19:13–15   See also forgiveness, Jesus Christ's ministry.

mission

Specific actions that bear witness to the good news of what God has done for his people. Israel, Jesus Christ and the church all in their different ways bear witness to the saving acts of God in history. Christian mission is empowered by the Holy Spirit.

mission, of church

The continuation of Jesus Christ's mission through his followers. Believers are empowered by the Holy Spirit and sent out by Christ to bear witness to him and to preach, heal, teach, baptise and make disciples of all peoples.

The power and authority of the church's mission

Believers are sent out by Jesus Christ

Jn 15:16 "You [the disciples] did not choose me [Jesus], but I chose you and appointed you to go and bear fruit—fruit that will last . . ."   See also **Mt** 9:37–38; **Lk** 10:1–3; **Jn** 4:36–38

Believers are given authority by Jesus Christ

Lk 9:1 When Jesus had called the Twelve together, he gave them power and authority to drive out all demons and to cure diseases,   See also **Mt** 10:1; 28:18; **Mk** 6:7; 16:17–18; **Lk** 10:17–19

Believers continue Jesus Christ's mission

Jn 20:21 Again Jesus said, "Peace be with you [the disciples]! As the Father has sent me, I am sending you."   See also **Jn** 17:18

Believers are empowered by the Holy Spirit

Ac 1:8 "But you [the apostles] will receive power when the Holy Spirit comes on you; and you will be my [Jesus'] witnesses in Jerusalem, and in all Judea and Samaria, and to the ends of the earth."   See also **Lk** 24:49; **Jn** 20:22; **Ac** 4:31; **Heb** 2:4

The task of the church in mission

Making disciples

Mt 28:19–20 "Therefore go and make disciples of all nations, baptising them in the name of the Father and of the Son and of the Holy Spirit, and teaching them to obey everything I [Jesus] have commanded you. And surely I am with you always, to the very end of the age." See also **Ac** 2:41–42; 14:15; 16:14–15; 18:8; **Ro** 10:14–15; **1Jn** 1:2–3

Preaching and healing

Lk 9:2 and he [Jesus] sent them [the Twelve] out to preach the kingdom of God and to heal the sick.   See also **Mt** 10:7–8; **Mk** 16:20; **Lk** 9:6

Proclaiming the gospel

Ac 20:24 "However, I [Paul] consider my life worth nothing to me, if only I may finish the race and complete the task the Lord Jesus has given me—the task of testifying to the gospel of God's grace."   See also **Ac** 8:40; **Ro** 1:9; 15:20; **2Ti** 1:11

Bearing witness to Jesus Christ

Ac 5:30–32 ". . . We [the apostles] are witnesses of these things, and so is the Holy Spirit, whom God has given to those who obey him."   See also **Lk** 24:48; **Jn** 15:26–27; **Ac** 4:20

Bringing honour to God

Eph 3:10–11 His [God's] intent was that now, through the church, the manifold wisdom of God should be made known to the rulers and authorities in the heavenly realms . . .   See also **Jn** 15:8; **1Pe** 2:12

The universal scope of the church's mission

Lk 24:47 "and repentance and forgiveness of sins will be preached in his [Christ's] name to all nations, beginning at Jerusalem."   *See also* **Mt** 24:14 pp Mk 13:10; **Mk 16:15**

The church reaching out in mission
To the Jews

Mt 10:5–6 These twelve Jesus sent out with the following instructions: "Do not go among the Gentiles or enter any town of the Samaritans. Go rather to the lost sheep of Israel."   *See also* **Mt** 10:9–15 pp Mk 6:8–11 pp Lk 9:3–5 pp Lk 10:4–12; **Ac 11:19**

To the Samaritans

Ac 8:4–8 . . . Philip went down to a city in Samaria and proclaimed the Christ there . . . *See also* **Ac** 8:14–17,25

To the Gentiles

Paul as the apostle to the Gentiles: **Ac 9:15; Ro** 11:13; 15:16

Ac 10:34–35; 11:20–21; 13:1–3; 15:40–41; 16:9–10; 18:23; 28:31

Missions undertaken by church officials
Ac 11:22–23

Paul and Barnabas take gifts to Jerusalem: **Ac 11:30;** 12:25

Ac 15:22–23   *See also baptism; church, purpose; evangelism; gospel; preachers and preaching.*

mission, of Israel

God chose Israel to be his own people, and bring the good news of his salvation to the world. God's mission through Israel is fulfilled in the mission of his servant and continues through the mission of the church.

Israel as a channel of God's blessing
Blessings for all people through Abraham

Ge 18:18 "Abraham will surely become a great and powerful nation, and all nations on earth will be blessed through him."   *See also* **Ge** 12:2–3; 22:18; 26:4; 28:13–14; **Ac** 3:25; **Gal 3:8**

Israel's call to be a nation of priests

Ex 19:5–6 "'. . . you [Israel] will be for me [the LORD] a kingdom of priests and a holy nation.' . . ."   *See also* **Isa 61:6**

God's desire to display his glory
God's glory is to fill the earth

Hab 2:14 "For the earth will be filled with the knowledge of the glory of the LORD, as the waters cover the sea."   *See also* **Nu** 14:21; **Ps** 72:18–19; **Isa 6:3**

God's people display his glory

Isa 60:1–3 ". . . See, darkness covers the earth and thick darkness is over the peoples, but the LORD rises upon you [God's restored people] and his glory appears over you. Nations will come to your light, and kings to the brightness of your dawn."   *See also* **Isa** 46:13; 49:3; 55:5

God's people declare his glory among the nations

Ps 96:3 Declare his [the LORD's] glory among the nations, his marvellous deeds among all peoples.   *See also* **Ps** 57:9; 96:10; 105:1–2 pp 1Ch 16:8–9; **Ps 145:11–12**

The nations will be drawn to God's people
In recognition of God's presence among his people

Zec 8:20–23 . . . This is what the LORD Almighty says: "In those days ten people from all languages and nations will take firm hold of one Jew by the hem of his robe and say, 'Let us go with you, because we have heard that God is with you.'"   *See also* **1Ki** 10:1 pp 2Ch 9:1; **Isa** 45:14; **Jer** 16:19; **Eze** 37:27–28; **39:7**

To Jerusalem as the centre of universal worship

Isa 2:2–4 . . . Many peoples will come and say, "Come, let us go up to the mountain of the LORD, to the house of the God of Jacob. He will teach us his ways, so that we may walk in his paths." The law will go out from Zion, the word of the LORD from Jerusalem . . . pp Mic 4:1–3   *See also* **Isa** 11:9; 25:6–8; 27:13; 56:6–8; **Zec 14:16**

God made known through his mighty acts

God's deliverance of Israel

Ex 7:5 "And the Egyptians will know that I am the LORD when I stretch out my hand against Egypt and bring the Israelites out of it."   *See also* **Ps** 98:1–3; 102:15–16; **Isa** 49:26; **Eze** 38:23

God's action on behalf of Israel

Ex 34:10 Then the LORD said: "I am making a covenant with you [Israel]. Before all your people I will do wonders never before done in any nation in all the world. The people you live among will see how awesome is the work that I, the LORD, will do for you."   *See also* **Ex** 8:19; **Jos** 4:24; **1Ki** 8:41–43 pp **2Ch** 6:32–33; **Ps** 67:1–4; 126:2

God's renewal of Israel

Eze 36:23 "'I will show the holiness of my great name, which has been profaned among the nations, the name you [Israel] have profaned among them. Then the nations will know that I am the LORD, declares the Sovereign LORD, when I show myself holy through you before their eyes.'"   *See also* **Eze** 20:40–41; 28:24–25; 38:16

Israel as a witness to other nations

God's people sent to other nations

Isa 66:19 "I will set a sign among them, and I will send some of those who survive to the nations—to Tarshish, to the Libyans and Lydians (famous as archers), to Tubal and Greece, and to the distant islands that have not heard of my fame or seen my glory. They will proclaim my glory among the nations."   *See also* **1Ki** 17:9; **Jnh** 1:2; 3:2; **Mt** 23:15

Examples of God's people bearing witness to him **Ge** 41:16; **Ex** 7:16–17; **2Ki** 5:3; **Da** 2:44–47; 3:16–18

Israel's failure in mission

Isa 26:18 We [God's people] were with child, we writhed in pain, but we gave birth to wind. We have not brought salvation to the earth; we have not given birth to people of the world. *See also* **Eze** 36:20–21

The fulfilment of God's mission through Israel

The mission of God's Messiah

Isa 11:10 In that day the Root of Jesse will stand as a banner for the peoples; the nations will rally to him, and his place of rest will be glorious.   *See also* **Ro** 15:12; **Ps** 72:17; **Gal** 3:16

The mission of God's servant

Isa 49:6 he [the LORD] says: "It is too small a thing for you to be my servant to restore the tribes of Jacob and bring back those of Israel I have kept. I will also make you a light for the Gentiles, that you may bring my salvation to the ends of the earth."   *See also* **Isa** 42:1–6; 52:15

The mission of the church

1Pe 2:9 But you [the church] are a chosen people, a royal priesthood, a holy nation, a people belonging to God, that you may declare the praises of him who called you out of darkness into his wonderful light.   *See also* **Ro** 15:16

---

mission, of Jesus Christ

Jesus Christ came to reveal God, to announce the coming of God's kingdom and to redeem a fallen humanity through his death on the cross. Though he came first to the Jews, the scope of Christ's mission includes the whole human race and continues through the Spirit-empowered witness of the church.

Jesus Christ's mission originated with God

It was purposed by God

1Pe 1:18–20 . . . He [Jesus] was chosen before the creation of the world, but was revealed in these last times for your sake.   *See also* **Ac** 2:23; **Eph** 1:4–5

The Father sent the Son

Gal 4:4–5 But when the time had fully come, God sent his Son, born of a woman, born under law . . .   *See also* **Jn** 5:37–38; 7:29; 8:42; 10:36; 17:8; **1Jn** 4:14

Jesus Christ came in willing obedience to the Father **Jn** 6:38; **Php** 2:5–8

Jesus Christ's mission was motivated by God's love

Jn 3:16 "For God so loved the world that he

gave his one and only Son, that whoever believes in him shall not perish but have eternal life." *See also* **Ro** 5:8; **1Jn** 4:10

Jesus Christ's mission was to make God known
He reveals God in his own person
Jn 1:18 No-one has ever seen God, but God the One and Only, who is at the Father's side, has made him known. *See also* **Jn** 14:9; 17:26; **Col** 1:15; **Heb** 1:1–3
He reveals God through his teaching
Jn 18:37 . . . Jesus answered, ". . . for this reason I was born, and for this I came into the world, to testify to the truth . . ." *See also* **Mt** 7:28–29; **Jn** 3:11–13

Jesus Christ's mission was to announce God's kingdom
Lk 4:43 But he [Jesus] said, "I must preach the good news of the kingdom of God to the other towns also, because that is why I was sent." *See also* **Mt** 4:17; **Mk** 1:14–15; **Mt** 12:28 pp **Lk** 11:20

Jesus Christ's mission was to redeem humanity
He came to seek and save the lost
Lk 19:10 "For the Son of Man came to seek and to save what was lost." *See also* **Lk** 15:1–10
He came to save from sin
Mt 1:21 "She [Mary] will give birth to a son, and you [Joseph] are to give him the name Jesus, because he will save his people from their sins." *See also* **Ro** 3:25–26; **1Ti** 1:15
He came to break the devil's power
1Jn 3:8 . . . The reason the Son of God appeared was to destroy the devil's work. *See also* **Ge** 3:15; **Jn** 12:31; **Heb** 2:14–15
He came to bring eternal life
Jn 10:10 "The thief comes only to steal and kill and destroy; I [Jesus] have come that they may have life, and have it to the full." *See also* **Jn** 6:38–40; 17:2–3

He came to give access to God **Eph** 2:18; 3:12; **Heb** 10:19–20
He came to restore a fallen humanity **Ro** 5:17–18; **1Co** 15:21–22

Jesus Christ's mission was to establish the church
Mt 16:18 ". . . I [Jesus] tell you that you are Peter, and on this rock I will build my church, and the gates of Hades will not overcome it." *See also* **Eph** 2:17–19; 5:25–27; **1Pe** 2:4–5,9–10

The scope of Jesus Christ's mission
Jesus Christ came first to Israel **Mt** 10:5–6; 15:24; **Jn** 1:11
Jesus Christ's mission extends to all peoples **Isa** 49:6; **Mt** 8:11; **Jn** 10:16; **Mt** 8:10 pp **Lk** 7:9; **Mt** 15:28 pp **Mk** 7:29; **Ac** 1:8; 26:17–18

Jesus Christ's mission made the cross necessary
Mt 20:28 ". . . the Son of Man did not come to be served, but to serve, and to give his life as a ransom for many." pp **Mk** 10:45 *See also* **Mt** 16:21 pp **Mk** 8:31 pp **Lk** 9:22; **Lk** 12:50; **Col** 2:14–15; **Heb** 12:2

Jesus Christ's mission will be completed at his return
1Jn 3:2 Dear friends, now we are children of God, and what we will be has not yet been made known. But we know that when he [Jesus] appears, we shall be like him, for we shall see him as he is. *See also* **Mt** 24:31 pp **Mk** 13:27; **Col** 3:4; **1Th** 4:16–17

Jesus Christ's mission continues through the church
Jn 20:21–22 Again Jesus said, "Peace be with you [his disciples]! As the Father has sent me, I am sending you." . . . *See also* **Mt** 28:18–20; **Jn** 15:26–27 *See also* church, nature of; cross; kingdom of God, coming; redemption; salvation.

---

obedience
A willingness to submit to the authority of

someone else and to actually do what one is asked or told to do. Scripture lays particular emphasis upon the need for believers to obey God, stressing his trustworthiness. This obedience is especially clear in the life and death of Jesus Christ.

obedience, of Jesus Christ

The selfless obedience of Jesus Christ to the will of God his Father, through which the redemption of humanity is accomplished. Christ also shows himself willing to submit to earthly authorities and sets an example which believers are called to imitate.

Jesus Christ was totally obedient to his Father's will

Obedience was central to Jesus Christ's life and thought

Jn 4:34 "My food," said Jesus, "is to do the will of him who sent me and to finish his work."

Heb 10:9 . . . he [Jesus] said, "Here I am, I have come to do your [God's] will." . . . *See also* **Mt** 3:15; 8:9–10 pp Lk 7:8–9; **Jn** 5:30; 6:38; 14:31; **Heb** 10:7; **Ps** 40:7–8

Jesus Christ's obedience meant ultimate personal cost

Mt 26:39 . . . he [Jesus] fell with his face to the ground and prayed, "My Father, if it is possible, may this cup be taken from me. Yet not as I will, but as you will." pp Mk 14:36 pp Lk 22:42

Php 2:8 . . . he [Jesus] humbled himself and became obedient to death—even death on a cross! *See also* **Isa** 50:5–6; 53:10–12; **Mt** 16:21 pp Mk 8:31 pp Lk 9:22; **Jn** 10:18; 13:1; **Heb** 5:8

Jesus Christ's obedience was necessary for God's salvation plan

Ro 5:18–19 . . . through the obedience of the one man the many will be made righteous. *See also* **Mt** 27:40–42 pp Mk 15:30–31 pp Lk 23:35–37; **Lk** 24:26; **Jn** 17:2–4,26; 19:30

Jesus Christ's obedience was shown in his human relationships

He was obedient to his parents

Lk 2:51 . . . he [Jesus] went down to Nazareth with them [Mary and Joseph] and was obedient to them . . .

He was obedient to secular authorities Mt 17:24–27; 22:17–21 pp Mk 12:15–17 pp Lk 20:22–25

He was obedient to the Jewish law Mt 5:17–18; 22:37–40 pp Mk 12:29–31 pp Lk 10:26–28; **Mk** 2:23–28; **Jn** 7:19; 10:37–38

Believers should follow Jesus Christ's example of obedience

Obedience to God's will is paramount

Mt 19:17 ". . . If you want to enter life, obey the commandments." *See also* **Mt** 7:21; 12:50 pp Mk 3:35 pp Lk 8:21; **Jn** 15:10; **Eph** 6:6

Christlike obedience expresses love for God 2Jn 6 And this is love: that we walk in obedience to his [God's] commands. As you have heard from the beginning, his command is that you walk in love. *See also* **Jn** 14:15,20–21; 15:12

Obedience should characterise believers' lives Ro 1:5 . . . we [Paul and his fellow-workers] received grace and apostleship to call people from among all the Gentiles to the obedience that comes from faith. *See also* **Ac** 5:29; **2Co** 2:9 *See also baptism, of Jesus Christ; law, Jesus Christ's attitude.*

obedience, to authorities

Scripture teaches that all people, Christians included, should submit not only to God himself but also to divinely instituted secular authorities.

Obedience is owed to rulers

Ro 13:1–7 Let everyone be subject to the governing authorities, for there is no authority except that which God has established. The authorities that exist have been established by God. Consequently, whoever rebels against the authority is rebelling against what God has instituted, and those who do so will bring judgment on themselves . . . *See also* **1Ti**

2:1–3; **Tit** 3:1; **1Pe** 2:13–14,17
Jesus Christ expounds this principle
Mk 12:17 Then Jesus said to them, "Give to Caesar what is Caesar's and to God what is God's." . . .   pp Mt 22:21 pp Lk 20:25

Obedience is owed to church leaders
Heb 13:17 Obey your leaders and submit to their authority . . .   *See also* **1Pe** 5:5

Obedience is owed within the household
Eph 6:1–3 Children, obey your parents in the Lord, for this is right . . .   *See also* **Pr** 15:5; **Col** 3:20
Jesus Christ sets the example
Lk 2:51 Then he [Jesus] went down to Nazareth with them [his parents] and was obedient to them . . .

Obedience to secular authority is limited by obedience to God
Ac 5:29 Peter and the other apostles replied: "We must obey God rather than human beings!"   *See also* **Ac** 4:19   *See also justice; law.*

---

obedience, to God
A willingness to submit oneself to the will of God and to put it into effect. Scripture emphasises the necessity for God's laws to be followed, gives examples and reasons, and describes the rewards.

Obedience is demanded of God's people
Lev 25:18 " 'Follow my decrees and be careful to obey my laws, and you will live safely in the land.' "

1Sa 15:22 . . . ". . . To obey is better than sacrifice, and to heed is better than the fat of rams."   *See also* **Dt** 26:16; 32:46; **Ro** 6:16–18; **1Pe** 1:14–16
Examples of obedience in the OT
Jos 11:15 As the Lord commanded his servant Moses, so Moses commanded Joshua, and Joshua did it; he left nothing undone of all that the Lord

commanded Moses.   *See also* **Ge** 6:22; 12:1–4; 22:2–3; **Ex** 40:16; **Jnh** 3:3
The example of Jesus Christ
Mt 26:39 . . . "My Father, if it is possible, may this cup be taken from me. Yet not as I will, but as you will." pp Mk 14:36 pp Lk 22:42
Jn 14:31 "but the world must learn that I love the Father and that I do exactly what my Father has commanded me . . ."   *See also* **Jn** 17:4; **Ro** 5:19; **Php** 2:8; **Heb** 5:8

Jesus Christ is obeyed
By the wind and the waves
Mt 8:26–27 . . . he got up and rebuked the winds and the waves, and it was completely calm. The disciples were amazed and asked, "What kind of man is this? Even the winds and the waves obey him!" pp Mk 4:39–41 pp Lk 8:24–25
By evil spirits
Mk 1:27 The people were all so amazed that they asked each other, "What is this? A new teaching—and with authority! He even gives orders to evil spirits and they obey him." pp Lk 4:36

Obedience and love
Jn 14:15 "If you love me, you will obey what I command."

1Jn 5:3 This is love for God: to obey his commands. And his commands are not burdensome.   *See also* **Ps** 119:167; **1Jn** 2:5; 3:10; **2Jn** 6

Obedience and faith
Heb 11:8 By faith Abraham, when called to go to a place he would later receive as his inheritance, obeyed and went, even though he did not know where he was going.

Mt 7:21 "Not everyone who says to me, 'Lord, Lord,' will enter the kingdom of heaven, but only he who does the will of my Father who is in heaven."   *See also* **Ro** 1:5; **Jas** 2:14–26

God rewards those who obey him

Ex 19:5 " 'Now if you obey me fully and keep my covenant, then out of all nations you will be my treasured possession . . .' "

Jn 15:10 "If you obey my commands, you will remain in my love . . ."   *See also* **Dt** 5:29; **1Ki** 3:14; **2Ki** 18:5–7; **Mt** 7:21,24–25 pp **Lk** 6:47–48; **Mt** 12:50 pp **Mk** 3:35 pp **Lk** 8:21; **Jn** 12:26; 14:21,23; 21:4–6; **1Jn** 2:17

Obedience to the word of God

Mt 7:24–27 "Therefore everyone who hears these words of mine and puts them into practice is like a wise man who built his house on the rock. The rain came down, the streams rose, and the winds blew and beat against that house; yet it did not fall, because it had its foundation on the rock . . ."

Jas 1:22 Do not merely listen to the word, and so deceive yourselves. Do what it says.   *See also* **Ps** 119:9–11; **Jnh** 3:3; **Lk** 11:28; **Jn** 17:6; **Jas** 2:14–20

Examples of people who obeyed God

Ge 6:9

Abraham: **Ge** 12:1–4; 17:23

The psalmist: **Ps** 119:30,100–106

The apostles: **Ac** 4:19–20; 5:29

Php 3:7–14   *See also faith, nature of; gospel, requirements; holiness.*

---

peace

The state of harmony that is available to believers through having a right relationship with God and others and is especially associated with the presence of the Holy Spirit.

---

peace, destruction of

Because of human sinfulness, God's provision of peace is always under threat. Scripture shows that this breaking of peace has implications for the whole of creation.

Causes of the destruction of peace

Sin and self-centredness

Isa 57:21 "There is no peace," says my God, "for the wicked."   *See also* **Ge** 11:4–9; **Isa** 59:7–8; **Lk** 19:41–44

Idolatry

Zec 10:2 The idols speak deceit, diviners see visions that lie; they tell dreams that are false, they give comfort in vain. Therefore the people wander like sheep oppressed for lack of a shepherd.   *See also* **Ex** 32:7–10; **1Ti** 6:9–10

Fear and anxiety

Jn 20:19 On the evening of that first day of the week, when the disciples were together, with the doors locked for fear of the Jews, Jesus came and stood among them and said, "Peace be with you!"   *See also* **Jos** 7:3–5; **Pr** 29:25; **Jer** 30:10; 46:27; **Mt** 6:31–34 pp **Lk** 12:29–30

The sins of ancestors

Lev 26:36–42 " '. . . also because of their ancestors' sins they will waste away . . .' " *See also* **Ge** 3:16–19; **2Ki** 23:26–27; **Jer** 31:29; **Eze** 18:2

Friends

Jer 20:10 I hear many whispering, "Terror on every side! Report him! Let's report him!" All my friends are waiting for me to slip, saying, "Perhaps he will be deceived; then we will prevail over him and take our revenge on him."   *See also* **La** 1:1–2,19

Enemies

Ps 35:19–20 . . . They do not speak peaceably, but devise false accusations against those who live quietly in the land.   *See also* **2Ki** 9:14–28; **La** 1:16

The consequences of the human destruction of peace

Humanity suffers Dt 28:53–57; **1Ki** 2:5–6; **2Ki** 6:24–29; 25:2–3; **Eze** 13:10–16; **Rev** 6:3–8

Nations suffer

Jer 49:31–32 "Arise and attack a nation at ease, which lives in confidence," declares the LORD, "a nation that has neither gates nor bars; its people live alone. Their camels will become plunder, and their large herds will be booty. I will scatter to the winds those who are in distant places and will bring disaster on them from every side," declares the LORD.   *See also* **Eze 38:14–23**

The land suffers
Jer 25:37 The peaceful meadows will be laid waste because of the fierce anger of the LORD. *See also* **Ex 8:12–14; Lev 26:27–35; Isa 1:7; 36:16–20**

The whole creation suffers
Rev 6:3–4 When the Lamb opened the second seal, I heard the second living creature say, "Come!" Then another horse came out, a fiery red one. Its rider was given power to take peace from the earth and to make people slay each other. To him was given a large sword.   *See also* **Ge 6:5–7; Isa 24:1–5; Ro 8:22; Rev 8:7–13**   *See also Satan; sin.*

---

peace, divine in New Testament

God's ultimate provision of peace is discovered in the person and work of Jesus Christ. It is only through Christ that peace with God can be achieved and maintained.

Provision of peace through the Father
Peace in a believer's relationship with the Father
Ro 5:1 Therefore, since we have been justified through faith, we have peace with God through our Lord Jesus Christ,   *See also* **Ro 8:1,31–39; 1Co 1:2–3**

Peace through the Father's provision for the believer
1Ti 6:17 . . . God, who richly provides us with everything for our enjoyment.   *See also* **Mt 6:25–34** pp **Lk 12:22–31; Mt 7:7–11** pp **Lk 11:9–13**

Provision of peace through Jesus Christ
Through Jesus Christ's coming
Lk 2:10–14 But the angel said to them [the shepherds], "Do not be afraid. I bring you good news of great joy that will be for all the people. Today in the town of David a Saviour has been born to you; he is Christ the Lord . . ." Suddenly a great company of the heavenly host appeared

with the angel, praising God and saying, "Glory to God in the highest, and on earth peace to those on whom his favour rests."
These OT prophecies are fulfilled in the coming of Jesus Christ: **Isa 9:6–7; Mic 5:2–5; Zec 9:9–10 Lk 2:25–32; Eph 2:17**

Through Jesus Christ's teaching
Jn 16:33 "I have told you these things, so that in me you may have peace . . ."   *See also* **Jn 14:23–27; 15:3**

Through Jesus Christ's ministry
Ac 10:36 "You know the message God sent to the people of Israel, telling the good news of peace through Jesus Christ, who is Lord of all."   *See also* **Mk 4:35–41** pp **Mt 8:23–27** pp **Lk 8:22–25; Lk 4:33–35** pp **Mk 1:23–25; Lk 4:38–41** pp **Mt 8:14–17** pp **Mk 1:29–34**

Through Jesus Christ's death
Col 1:19–20 For God was pleased to have all his fulness dwell in him [Christ], and through him to reconcile to himself all things, whether things on earth or things in heaven, by making peace through his blood, shed on the cross.   *See also* **Isa 53:5; Mt 26:26–28** pp **Mk 14:22–24** pp **Lk 22:19–20; Gal 6:14–16; Eph 2:13–17**

Through Jesus Christ's resurrection
Lk 24:36 While they [the disciples] were still talking about this, Jesus himself stood among them and said to them, "Peace be with you." *See also* **Mk 16:4–6** pp **Lk 24:1–8; Jn 20:19–21,26–29; 2Co 4:14; Heb 13:20–21**

Through Jesus Christ's ascension
Ro 8:34 Who then can condemn? Christ Jesus, who died—more than that, who was raised to life—is at the right hand of God and is also interceding for us.   *See also* **Lk 24:51–53; Ac 2:33–39**

Provision of peace through the Holy Spirit
Through the Holy Spirit's inner witness
2Co 1:21–22 Now it is God who makes both us and you stand firm in Christ. He anointed us, set his seal of ownership on us, and put his Spirit in our hearts as a deposit, guaranteeing what is to come.   *See also* **Ro 8:14–17; Gal 4:6–7**

Through the Holy Spirit's presence
Ac 9:31 Then the church throughout Judea, Galilee and Samaria enjoyed a time of peace. It was strengthened; and encouraged by the Holy Spirit, it grew in numbers, living in the fear of the Lord. *See also* **Jn** 14:16–18; **Gal** 5:16–18; **Rev** 22:17

Peace as the Holy Spirit's fruit and gift
Gal 5:22 But the fruit of the Spirit is love, joy, peace . . . *See also* **Ro** 14:17 *See also cross; gospel, promises; kingdom of God, qualities; reconciliation.*

peace, divine in Old Testament

Providing peace for his creation is a characteristic of God. In the OT peace came through adherence to God's will as expressed in his spoken word, covenants and law. The Hebrew word "shalom" means "peace in all its fulness, in every aspect of life".

Peace provided for God's people
Through obedience to God's spoken word
Ge 2:16–17 And the LORD God commanded the man, "You are free to eat from any tree in the garden; but you must not eat from the tree of the knowledge of good and evil, for when you eat of it you will surely die." *See also* **2Ki** 5:13–19; **Job** 22:21–22; **Ps** 85:8; **Isa** 54:13; **Da** 10:15–19

Through obedience to God's covenants
Dt 29:9 Carefully follow the terms of this covenant, so that you may prosper in everything you do. *See also* **Dt** 30:15–16; **Mal** 2:1–6

Through obedience to God's laws
Ps 119:165 Great peace have they who love your law, and nothing can make them stumble. *See also* **Lev** 26:3–12; **Dt** 28:1–7; **2Ch** 14:2–7; **Ps** 37:34–38; **Pr** 3:13–17; **Isa** 48:18

Peace expressed in signs
Ge 9:13–16 "I have set my rainbow in the clouds, and it will be the sign of the covenant between me and the earth. Whenever I bring clouds over the earth and the rainbow appears in the clouds, I will remember my covenant between me and you and all living creatures of every kind.

Never again will the waters become a flood to destroy all life. Whenever the rainbow appears in the clouds, I will see it and remember the everlasting covenant between God and all living creatures of every kind on the earth." *See also* **Ex** 13:21–22; 40:36–38; **Jdg** 6:22–24

Peace provided for God's nation
Through provision of the land
Ps 37:11 But the meek will inherit the land and enjoy great peace. *See also* **1Sa** 7:13–14; **1Ch** 4:40; **Ps** 37:3

Through provision of a holy city
Isa 33:20–24 Look upon Zion, the city of our festivals; your eyes will see Jerusalem, a peaceful abode, a tent that will not be moved; its stakes will never be pulled up, nor any of its ropes broken . . . *See also* **Ps** 122:6–8; **Isa** 66:10–13; **Jer** 33:6–9; **Zec** 1:16–17

Through provision of a house of God
Hag 2:9 " 'The glory of this present house will be greater than the glory of the former house,' says the LORD Almighty. 'And in this place I will grant peace,' declares the LORD Almighty." *See also* **1Ch** 22:6–10; **Eze** 37:24–28

Through provision of the law
Isa 48:18 "If only you had paid attention to my commands, your peace would have been like a river . . ." *See also* **Dt** 6:1–3; 30:15–16

The benefits of peace
Peace and God's presence
Isa 41:10 "So do not fear, for I am with you . . ." *See also* **Nu** 6:22–26; **Jos** 1:9; **Ps** 23:1–4; 29:11; **Jer** 30:10–11

Peace in captivity
Jer 29:7 "Also, seek the peace and prosperity of the city to which I have carried you into exile. Pray to the LORD for it, because if it prospers, you too will prosper." *See also* **Ex** 1:6–12; **Jer** 31:1–2

Peace in suffering
Ps 119:50 My comfort in my suffering is this: Your promise preserves my life. *See also* **Isa** 61:1–4; **Jer** 34:1–5

Peace in poverty
Isa 14:30 The poorest of the poor will find

pasture, and the needy will lie down in safety . . .   *See also* **1Sa** 2:6–9; **Ps** 68:5–10; **Pr** 17:1

Peace with enemies
Pr 16:7 When people's ways are pleasing to the LORD, he makes even their enemies live at peace with them.   *See also* **1Ch** 22:7–9; **Jer** 29:4–7   *See also* covenant; law.

---

peace, experience
Peace is the birthright of every believer in all circumstances. It is found only in God and is maintained through having a close relationship with him.

Peace for believers in differing situations
In times of sickness, pressure and hardships
Ps 41:1–3 Blessed are those who have regard for the weak; the LORD delivers them in times of trouble. The LORD will protect them and preserve their lives; he will bless them in the land and not surrender them to the desire of their foes. The LORD will sustain them on their sick-bed and restore them from their bed of illness.

Mt 11:28 "Come to me, all you who are weary and burdened, and I will give you rest."   *See also* **Job** 1:13–22; 2:7–10; **Ac** 16:22–25; **2Co** 12:7–10; **2Ti** 4:16–18
In times of death and grief
Jn 14:1–3 "Do not let your hearts be troubled. Trust in God; trust also in me. In my Father's house are many rooms; if it were not so, I would have told you. I am going there to prepare a place for you. And if I go and prepare a place for you, I will come back and take you to be with me that you also may be where I am."   *See also* **Job** 19:25–26; **2Ki** 22:18–20; **Isa** 57:1–2; **1Th** 4:13–18

The effects of peace for believers
Forgiveness
Ac 7:60 Then he [Stephen] fell on his knees and cried out, "Lord, do not hold this sin against them." When he had said this, he fell asleep. *See also* **Ro** 12:17–19

Encouragement
2Co 1:3–6 Praise be to the God and Father of our Lord Jesus Christ, the Father of compassion and the God of all comfort, who comforts us in all our troubles, so that we can comfort those in any trouble with the comfort we ourselves have received from God . . .   *See also* **Php** 4:11–13
Health and healing
Pr 14:30 A heart at peace gives life to the body, but envy rots the bones.   *See also* **Isa** 57:18–19
Security
Pr 1:33 "but whoever listens to me will live in safety and be at ease, without fear of harm." *See also* **Ac** 27:21–26; **Ro** 8:28,35–39
Hope
Ro 15:13 May the God of hope fill you with all joy and peace as you trust in him, so that you may overflow with hope by the power of the Holy Spirit.   *See also* **Ro** 5:1–5

How believers maintain peace
Through remaining in Christ
Jn 15:4–7 "Remain in me, and I will remain in you. No branch can bear fruit by itself; it must remain in the vine. Neither can you bear fruit unless you remain in me. I am the vine; you are the branches. If you remain in me and I in you, you will bear much fruit; apart from me you can do nothing. If you do not remain in me, you are like a branch that is thrown away and withers; such branches are picked up, thrown into the fire and burned. If you remain in me and my words remain in you, ask whatever you wish, and it will be given you."   *See also* **Jn** 16:33; **Ro** 5:1–5
Through living by the Holy Spirit
Ro 8:6 . . . the mind controlled by the Spirit is life and peace;   *See also* **Ro** 14:17–19; **Gal** 5:22
Through obedience to God's word
Jos 1:8–9 "Do not let this Book of the Law depart from your mouth; meditate on it day and night, so that you may be careful to do everything written in it. Then you will be prosperous and successful. Have I not commanded you? Be strong and courageous. Do not be terrified; do not be discouraged, for the LORD your God will be with you wherever you go."   *See*

also **Ps** 119:165–167

Through prayer and meditation

Php 4:6–9 Do not be anxious about anything, but in everything, by prayer and petition, with thanksgiving, present your requests to God. And the peace of God, which transcends all understanding, will guard your hearts and your minds in Christ Jesus . . .   *See also* **Ps** 1:1–3; **Isa** 26:3; **1Ti** 2:1–2

Final peace in death for believers

Isa 57:2 Those who walk uprightly enter into peace; they find rest as they lie in death.

Rev 14:13 Then I heard a voice from heaven say, "Write: Blessed are the dead who die in the Lord from now on." "Yes," says the Spirit, "they will rest from their labour, for their deeds will follow them."   *See also* **2Ki** 22:19–20; **Lk** 2:29

Hope of future peace for believers

Peace in heaven

1Pe 1:4 . . . an inheritance that can never perish, spoil or fade——kept in heaven for you, *See also* **Jn** 14:1–3; **1Th** 4:13–14; **Rev** 7:9–17

Peace in God's new creation

Rev 21:1–4 . . . And I heard a loud voice from the throne saying, "Now the dwelling of God is with human beings, and he will live with them. They will be his people, and God himself will be with them and be their God. He will wipe every tear from their eyes. There will be no more death or mourning or crying or pain, for the old order of things has passed away."   *See also* **Isa** 11:6–9; **Ro** 8:18–23; **Rev** 22:3–5   *See also assurance; forgiveness; hope; life, of faith; prayer; Scripture.*

---

peace, search for

Scripture teaches that peace is only found in God, but people try to find it elsewhere. A person's desire for peace varies according to his or her circumstances.

The places where people search for peace

People search for peace in others

Ge 5:28–29 When Lamech had lived 182 years, he had a son. He named him Noah and said, "He will comfort us in the labour and painful toil of our hands caused by the ground the Lord has cursed."   *See also* **SS** 8:10

People search for peace in material possessions

Ecc 4:8 . . . There was no end to his toil, yet his eyes were not content with his wealth . . . *See also* **Job** 21:7–13; **Da** 4:4; **Mt** 19:16–22; **Lk** 12:16–19

People search for peace in God

Ps 4:8 I will lie down and sleep in peace, for you alone, O Lord, make me dwell in safety. *See also* **Job** 22:21; **Pr** 19:23; **Isa** 26:3; **Lk** 7:37–50

The dangers in searching for peace

It can lead to greed

Ecc 4:6 Better one handful with tranquillity than two handfuls with toil . . .   *See also* **Mt** 23:25

It can lead to suffering and bondage **Ge** 42:1–17; **Jos** 9:3–27; **Mk** 5:25–26

It can lead to destruction

1Th 5:3 While people are saying, "Peace and safety", destruction will come on them suddenly, as labour pains on a pregnant woman, and they will not escape.   *See also* **2Ki** 20:12–19; **Lk** 16:19–26

People's search for peace varies according to their circumstances

The desire can increase in times of suffering and difficulties

Ex 2:23 During that long period, the king of Egypt died. The Israelites groaned in their slavery and cried out, and their cry for help because of their slavery went up to God.   *See also* **Jer** 14:19; 47:2–6; **La** 3:7–24; **Eze** 7:23–27; **Mk** 5:24–34 pp **Mt** 9:18–22 pp **Lk** 8:42–48

The desire can diminish in times of comfort

Ex 8:12–15 After Moses and Aaron left Pharaoh, Moses cried out to the Lord about the frogs he had brought on Pharaoh. And the Lord did what Moses asked. The frogs died in the houses, in the courtyards and in the fields. They were piled into heaps, and the land reeked of them. But when Pharaoh saw that there was relief, he hardened his heart and would not listen to Moses and Aaron, just as the LORD had said. *See also* **Job** 12:5; **Hos** 10:1; **Am** 6:1

praise

The celebration, honouring and adoration of God, in the power of the Holy Spirit, whether by individual believers or communities of believers.

praise, examples

Scripture provides many examples of individuals who praised God. These examples illustrate the variety of ways and methods in which God can be praised, as well as the motivation for that praise.

OT examples of those who praised God

Melchizedek
Ge 14:18–20 Then Melchizedek king of Salem brought out bread and wine. He was priest of God Most High, and he blessed Abram, saying, "Blessed be Abram by God Most High, Creator of heaven and earth. And blessed be God Most High, who delivered your enemies into your hand." Then Abram gave him a tenth of everything.

Moses
Ex 15:1–2 Then Moses and the Israelites sang this song to the LORD: "I will sing to the LORD, for he is highly exalted. The horse and its rider he has hurled into the sea. The LORD is my strength and my song; he has become my salvation. He is my God, and I will praise him, my father's God, and I will exalt him."

Jethro
Ex 18:9–10 Jethro was delighted to hear about all the good things the LORD had done for Israel in rescuing them from the hand of the Egyptians. He said, "Praise be to the LORD, who rescued you [Moses] from the hand of the Egyptians and of Pharaoh, and who rescued the people from the hand of the Egyptians."

David
1Ch 29:10–13 David praised the LORD in the presence of the whole assembly, saying, "Praise be to you, O LORD, God of our father Israel, from everlasting to everlasting. Yours, O LORD, is the greatness and the power and the glory and the majesty and the splendour, for everything in heaven and earth is yours. Yours, O LORD, is the kingdom; you are exalted as head over all. Wealth and honour come from you; you are the ruler of all things. In your hands are strength and power to exalt and give strength to all. Now, our God, we give you thanks, and praise your glorious name."

Ezra
Ne 8:6 Ezra praised the LORD, the great God; and all the people lifted their hands and responded, "Amen! Amen!" Then they bowed down and worshipped the LORD with their faces to the ground.

NT examples of those who praised God

Jesus Christ
Lk 10:21 At that time Jesus, full of joy through the Holy Spirit, said, "I praise you, Father, Lord of heaven and earth, because you have hidden these things from the wise and learned, and revealed them to little children. Yes, Father, for this was your good pleasure."

Zechariah
Lk 1:67–68 His [John's] father Zechariah was filled with the Holy Spirit and prophesied: "Praise be to the Lord, the God of Israel, because he has come and has redeemed his people."

The shepherds
Lk 2:20 The shepherds returned, glorifying and praising God for all the things they had heard and seen, which were just as they had been told.

Simeon
Lk 2:28 Simeon took him [Jesus] in his arms and praised God . . .

The disciples
Lk 19:37 When he [Jesus] came near the place where the road goes down the Mount of Olives, the whole crowd of disciples began joyfully to praise God in loud voices for all the miracles they had seen:

Ac 2:46–47 Every day they [the believers] continued to meet together in the temple courts. They broke bread in their homes and ate together with glad and sincere hearts, praising God and enjoying the favour of all the people. And the Lord added to their number daily those who were being saved.   *See also* **Lk** 24:50–53; **Ac** 16:25

Those who were healed by Jesus Christ Lk 18:35–43; **Ac** 3:1–10

The citizens of heaven

Rev 15:2–3 And I saw what looked like a sea of glass mixed with fire and, standing beside the sea, those who had been victorious over the beast and his image and over the number of his name. They held harps given them by God and sang the song of Moses the servant of God and the song of the Lamb: "Great and marvellous are your deeds, Lord God Almighty. Just and true are your ways, King of the ages."   *See also heaven, worship and service; prayer, as praise and thanksgiving.*

---

praise, manner and methods

Praise is the natural response of believers to God at all times and in all places, involving adoration in music and song. God himself assists believers to praise him through his Spirit.

The manner of praise
God is praised in faith

Ps 28:7 The LORD is my strength and my shield; my heart trusts in him, and I am helped. My heart leaps for joy and I will give thanks to him in song.

Ps 106:12 Then they believed his promises and sang his praise.

God is praised through Jesus Christ

Heb 13:15 Through Jesus, therefore, let us continually offer to God a sacrifice of praise—the fruit of lips that confess his name.   *See also* **Php** 2:9–11

God can be praised at any time and in any place

Ps 104:33 I will sing to the LORD all my life; I will sing praise to my God as long as I live.

Ps 145:2 Every day I will praise you and extol

your name for ever and ever.   *See also* **Ps** 146:2

God helps believers to praise him

Ps 51:15 O Lord, open my lips, and my mouth will declare your praise.   *See also* **Ps** 40:3; **Isa** 61:3

The Holy Spirit moves believers to praise

Lk 1:67 His [John's] father Zechariah was filled with the Holy Spirit and prophesied:

Eph 5:18–20 Do not get drunk on wine, which leads to debauchery. Instead, be filled with the Spirit. Speak to one another with psalms, hymns and spiritual songs. Sing and make music in your heart to the Lord, always giving thanks to God the Father for everything, in the name of our Lord Jesus Christ.   *See also* **Lk** 10:21; **Ac** 2:11; 10:44–46; **Col** 3:16–17

The methods of praise
In singing

Eph 5:19 Speak to one another with psalms, hymns and spiritual songs. Sing and make music in your heart to the Lord,   *See also* **Ne** 12:46; **Ps** 149:1; **Isa** 42:10; **Lk** 1:46–47,68; **Ac** 16:25; **Col** 3:16

With musical instruments

Ps 150:3–5 Praise him with the sounding of the trumpet, praise him with the harp and lyre, praise him with tambourine and dancing, praise him with the strings and flute, praise him with the clash of cymbals, praise him with resounding cymbals.   *See also* **1Ch** 25:3; **2Ch** 7:6; **Ps** 33:2; 92:1–3; **Isa** 38:20

In dancing

Ps 149:3 Let them praise his name with dancing and make music to him with tambourine and harp.   *See also* **Ex** 15:19–20; **2Sa** 6:14; **Ps** 150:4

With thanksgiving

Ps 42:4 These things I remember as I pour out my soul: how I used to go with the multitude, leading the procession to the house of God, with shouts of joy and thanksgiving among the festive throng.

Ps 100:4 Enter his gates with thanksgiving and

his courts with praise; give thanks to him and praise his name. *See also* **2Ch** 5:13

Hallelujah as a frequent expression of praise to God

Ps 106:48 Praise be to the LORD, the God of Israel, from everlasting to everlasting. Let all the people say, "Amen!" Praise the LORD. *See also* **Ps** 111:1; 113:1; 135:1; 149:1; 150:1; **Rev** 19:3–4

Praise for his patient love

Ps 106:1 Praise the LORD. Give thanks to the LORD, for he is good; his love endures for ever. *See also* **Ps** 117:2

Praise for his election of Israel

Ps 135:3–4 Praise the LORD, for the LORD is good; sing praise to his name, for that is pleasant. For the LORD has chosen Jacob to be his own, Israel to be his treasured possession. *See also* **1Ch** 16:36; **Ps** 148:14

Praise for his sovereign rule

Ps 146:10 The LORD reigns for ever, your God, O Zion, for all generations. Praise the LORD.

Rev 19:6 Then I heard what sounded like a great multitude, like the roar of rushing waters and like loud peals of thunder, shouting: "Hallelujah! For our Lord God Almighty reigns." *See also* **Rev** 19:1

Hosanna as an acclamation of praise
At Jerusalem
Mt 21:9 The crowds that went ahead of him and those that followed shouted, "Hosanna to the Son of David!" "Blessed is he who comes in the name of the Lord!" "Hosanna in the highest!" pp **Mk** 11:9–10 pp **Jn** 12:13 *See also* **Mt** 21:5

The OT background

Ps 118:25–26 O LORD, save us; O LORD, grant us success. Blessed is he who comes in the name of the LORD. From the house of the LORD we bless you. *See also* **1Ch** 16:35–36; **Ps** 79:9; 106:47

"Selah" in the context of praise
Following the assurance of answered prayer
Ps 3:4 To the LORD I cry aloud, and he answers

me from his holy hill. *See also* **Ps** 21:2; 24:6; 32:5; 81:7; 84:8

Following an expression of deliverance

Ps 3:8 From the LORD comes deliverance. May your blessing be on your people. *Selah* *See also* **Ps** 32:7; 49:15; 57:3; 68:19; 76:9; **Hab** 3:13

After a statement comparing God's greatness with human insignificance

Ps 9:20 Strike them with terror, O LORD; let the nations know they are only mortals. *Selah* *See also* **Ps** 39:5,11; 47:4; 52:5; 55:19; 59:5; 67:4; 75:3; 89:37; **Hab** 3:3

After an affirmation of security in God

Ps 46:7 The LORD Almighty is with us; the God of Jacob is our fortress. *Selah* *See also* **Ps** 46:11; 48:8; 61:4

On reflection of evil opposition

Ps 54:3 Strangers are attacking me; ruthless people seek my life—people without regard for God. *Selah* *See also* **Ps** 62:4; 140:3,5

praise, reasons
Scripture treats praise as the natural response of believers to God's person and actions.

Praise is commanded of God's people
Ps 68:32 Sing to God, O kingdoms of the earth, sing praise to the Lord . . .

1Pe 2:9 But you are a chosen people, a royal priesthood, a holy nation, a people belonging to God, that you may declare the praises of him who called you out of darkness into his wonderful light.

Rev 19:5 Then a voice came from the throne, saying: "Praise our God, all you his servants, you who fear him, both small and great!" *See also* **Ps** 30:4; 150:6; **Isa** 42:10; **Php** 2:9–11

Praise is due to God alone
Dt 10:21 He is your praise; he is your God, who performed for you those great and awesome wonders you saw with your own eyes.
1Ch 16:25 For great is the LORD and most worthy of praise; he is to be feared above all gods.

Isa 42:8 "I am the LORD; that is my name! I will not give my glory to another or my praise to idols."   *See also* **Ps** 66:4; 118:15–21; 148:13; **Rev** 4:11

Praise is pleasing to God
Ps 69:30–31 I will praise God's name in song and glorify him with thanksgiving. This will please the LORD more than an ox, more than a bull with its horns and hoofs.   *See also* **Ps** 135:3; 147:1; **Isa** 43:20–21; 61:10–11; **Jer** 13:11

Praise as an act of witness
Ps 9:11 Sing praises to the LORD, enthroned in Zion; proclaim among the nations what he has done.   *See also* **2Sa** 22:50; **Ps** 34:1–3; **Isa** 42:12; **2Co** 9:13

Praise in response to God's nature
For his greatness
Dt 32:3 I will proclaim the name of the LORD. Oh, praise the greatness of our God!

Ps 150:2 Praise him for his acts of power; praise him for his surpassing greatness.   *See also* **1Ch** 16:25; **Ne** 8:6; **Ps** 104:1; **Mt** 9:8
For his righteousness
Ps 98:8–9 Let the rivers clap their hands, let the mountains sing together for joy; let them sing before the LORD, for he comes to judge the earth. He will judge the world in righteousness and the peoples with equity.   *See also* **Da** 4:37
For his faithfulness
Ps 57:9–10 I will praise you, O Lord, among the nations; I will sing of you among the peoples. For great is your love, reaching to the heavens; your faithfulness reaches to the skies.
Ps 138:2 I will bow down towards your holy temple and will praise your name for your love and your faithfulness, for you have exalted above all things your name and your word.   *See also* **1Ki** 8:15–20,56; **Ps** 89:1
For his strength
Ps 59:16 But I will sing of your strength, in the morning I will sing of your love; for you are my fortress, my refuge in times of trouble.   *See also* **Ps** 28:7; 81:1

Praise in response to God's deeds
For deliverance from enemies
Ex 18:10 He [Jethro] said, "Praise be to the LORD, who rescued you from the hand of the Egyptians and of Pharaoh, and who rescued the people from the hand of the Egyptians."

Ps 18:46–48 The LORD lives! Praise be to my Rock! Exalted be God my Saviour! He is the God who avenges me, who subdues nations under me, who saves me from my enemies. You exalted me above my foes; from violent people you rescued me.   *See also* **Ge** 14:20; **Jdg** 16:24; **Ps** 43:1–4; 124:1–7
For answered prayer
Ps 28:6 Praise be to the LORD, for he has heard my cry for mercy.   *See also* **Ps** 66:19–20
For sending his Son, Jesus Christ
Lk 1:68–69 "Praise be to the Lord, the God of Israel, because he has come and has redeemed his people. He has raised up a horn of salvation for us in the house of his servant David"

Eph 1:3 Praise be to the God and Father of our Lord Jesus Christ, who has blessed us in the heavenly realms with every spiritual blessing in Christ.   *See also* **Lk** 2:10–14,25–28; 24:53; **1Pe** 1:3–6   *See also church, purpose; worship, reasons.*

---

prayer
Fellowship with God through Jesus Christ, expressed in adoration, thanksgiving and intercession, through which believers draw near to God and learn more of his will for their lives. Scripture stresses the vital role of the Holy Spirit in stimulating and guiding prayer.

prayer, and faith
Effective prayer depends on faith, especially on a willingness to trust in God's faithfulness to his promises to his people.

Faith is necessary in order to approach God
Heb 11:6 And without faith it is impossible to please God, because anyone who comes to him

must believe that he exists and that he rewards those who earnestly seek him.

Faith is necessary to receive benefits from God

Mk 6:5–6 He [Jesus] could not do any miracles there, except lay his hands on a few sick people and heal them. And he was amazed at their lack of faith. Then Jesus went round teaching from village to village.

Jas 5:16–18 . . . The prayer of a righteous person is powerful and effective. Elijah was human just as we are. He prayed earnestly that it would not rain, and it did not rain on the land for three and a half years. Again he prayed, and the heavens gave rain, and the earth produced its crops.   *See also* **Eph** 3:12; **Heb** 10:22

Faith is necessary for effective prayer

Mt 21:21–22 Jesus replied, "I tell you the truth, if you have faith and do not doubt, not only can you do what was done to the fig-tree, but also you can say to this mountain, 'Go, throw yourself into the sea,' and it will be done. If you believe, you will receive whatever you ask for in prayer." pp **Mk** 11:22–24

Jas 1:5–8 If any of you lacks wisdom, you should ask God, who gives generously to all without finding fault, and it will be given to you. But when you ask, you must believe and not doubt, because the one who doubts is like a wave of the sea, blown and tossed by the wind. Those who doubt should not think they will receive anything from the Lord; they are double-minded and unstable in all they do.   *See also* **Jas** 5:14–15

Jesus Christ responded to people's need on the basis of faith

Mt 9:27–30 As Jesus went on from there, two blind men followed him, calling out, "Have mercy on us, Son of David!" When he had gone indoors, the blind men came to him, and he asked them, "Do you believe that I am able to do this?" "Yes, Lord," they replied. Then he touched their eyes and said, "According to your

faith will it be done to you"; and their sight was restored . . .   *See also* **Mt** 8:5–13 pp **Lk** 7:1–10; **Mt** 9:20–22 pp **Mk** 5:25–34 pp **Lk** 8:43–48; **Mt** 15:21–28 pp **Mk** 7:24–30

Examples of notable prayers of faith

1Ki 18:36–37; **Jas** 5:17–18; **1Ki** 17:19–22; **2Ki** 4:32–35   *See also faith.*

---

prayer, and God's will

Prayer is concerned not only with the well-being of the one who prays. A vital aspect of its purpose is to allow the will of God to be done, and to bring glory and honour to his name.

True motives for prayer

The desire that God's name be honoured

Mt 6:9–13 "This, then, is how you should pray: 'Our Father in heaven, hallowed be your name . . .'" pp **Lk** 11:2–4   *See also* **Nu** 14:13–16; **Jos** 7:7–9; **2Sa** 7:25–26; **1Ki** 18:36–37; **Ps** 115:1; **Jn** 17:1

The desire that God's will be fulfilled

Mt 6:9–13 "This, then, is how you should pray: '. . . your kingdom come, your will be done on earth as it is in heaven . . .'" pp **Lk** 11:2–4   *See also* **Mt** 26:39 pp **Mk** 14:36 pp **Lk** 22:42; **Mt** 26:42; **Heb** 10:7

God answers prayer that accords with his will

1Jn 5:14–15 This is the confidence we have in approaching God: that if we ask anything according to his will, he hears us. And if we know that he hears us—whatever we ask—we know that we have what we asked of him.

Petitioners may enquire of God to discover his will

Ps 143:10 Teach me to do your will, for you are my God . . .   *See also* **Ge** 25:22–23; **Jdg** 1:1–2; **2Sa** 2:1; **1Ch** 14:14–15

The Holy Spirit helps believers to pray in God's will

Ro 8:26–27 In the same way, the Spirit helps us in our weakness. We do not know what we ought to pray for, but the Spirit himself intercedes for us with groans that words cannot express. And he who searches our hearts knows the mind of the Spirit, because the Spirit intercedes for the saints in accordance with God's will.

God's response to prayers allows believers to discern his will

2Co 12:7–9 To keep me [Paul] from becoming conceited because of these surpassingly great revelations, there was given me a thorn in my flesh, a messenger of Satan, to torment me. Three times I pleaded with the Lord to take it away from me. But he said to me, "My grace is sufficient for you, for my power is made perfect in weakness." Therefore I will boast all the more gladly about my weaknesses, so that Christ's power may rest on me.   *See also* **Ex** 33:18–20; **2Sa** 12:15–18; **Job** 19:7–8; **Ps** 35:13–14

God does not respond to the prayers of the wicked

Jn 9:31 "We know that God does not listen to sinners. He listens to the godly person who does his will."   *See also* **Ps** 66:18; **Pr** 15:8; **Isa** 1:15; 59:1–2; **La** 3:44; **1Pe** 3:12

---

prayer, and worship

Worship is turning to God in awe, praise and joy, as his people realise how wonderful he is. Prayer is a natural part of worship: to know God is to want to worship him and pray to him.

Worship is a fundamental requirement of life

All nations are exhorted to worship God
1Ch 16:28–29 Ascribe to the Lord, O families of nations, ascribe to the Lord glory and strength, ascribe to the Lord the glory due to his name. Bring an offering and come before him; worship the Lord in the splendour of his holiness.   *See also* **Ps** 29:1–2; 96:9

Israel is commanded to worship God
2Ki 17:36 "But the Lord, who brought you up out of Egypt with mighty power and outstretched arm, is the one you must worship. To him you shall bow down and to him offer sacrifices."
See also **Ps** 95:6–7; 99:4–5

Right attitudes in worship are imperative
Reverence and humility characterise acceptable worship
Heb 12:28–29 Therefore, since we are receiving a kingdom that cannot be shaken, let us be thankful, and so worship God acceptably with reverence and awe, for our "God is a consuming fire."   *See also* **Ps** 5:7; 95:6; 138:2; **Ecc** 5:1
Honesty, without hypocrisy, characterises acceptable worship
Am 5:21–24 "I hate, I despise your religious feasts; I cannot stand your assemblies. Even though you bring me burnt offerings and grain offerings, I will not accept them. Though you bring choice fellowship offerings, I will have no regard for them. Away with the noise of your songs! I will not listen to the music of your harps. But let justice roll on like a river, righteousness like a never-failing stream!"   *See also* **Mt** 15:7–9 pp **Mk** 7:6–7; **Isa** 29:13; **Lk** 18:9–14; **Jn** 4:24

Prayer can focus on different aspects of God's character
Prayer can focus on God's holiness
Ex 15:11 "Who among the gods is like you, O Lord? Who is like you—majestic in holiness, awesome in glory, working wonders?"   *See also* **Ps** 77:13; 96:9; 99:5
Prayer can focus on God's glory
Ps 19:1–6 The heavens declare the glory of God; the skies proclaim the work of his hands . . .   *See also* **Ps** 29:1–2; 138:5; **Ro** 16:27; **Php** 4:20; **Jude** 25
Prayer can focus on God's majesty
Ps 104:1–4 . . . O Lord my God, you are very great; you are clothed with splendour and majesty . . .   *See also* **Ps** 8:1; 76:4; 96:4–6
Prayer can focus on God's kingship
Ps 97:1 The Lord reigns, let the earth be glad; let the distant shores rejoice.   *See also* **Ps** 9:7; 22:3; 93:1; 95:3; 102:12
Prayer can focus on God's love and compassion
Ps 103:1–18 . . . The Lord is compassionate and gracious, slow to anger, abounding in

love . . .   *See also* **Ps** 111:4; 118:1–4;
145:17–20

Prayer can focus on God's justice and righteousness
Ps 97:2 Clouds and thick darkness surround him
[the LORD]; righteousness and justice are the
foundation of his throne.   *See also* **Ps** 7:17; 9:8;
97:6; 111:3

Prayer can focus on God's creative activity
Ne 9:6 "You alone are the LORD. You made the
heavens, even the highest heavens, and all their
starry host, the earth and all that is on it, the
seas and all that is in them. You give life to
everything, and the multitudes of heaven worship
you."   *See also* **Ps** 90:2; 95:3–7; 102:25–27;
104:5–9,24–26   *See also holiness, of God; worship.*

prayer, answers
God has promised to answer prayer for personal
or corporate needs and for the needs of others.

God answers the prayers of individuals
God answers the psalmists' prayers
Ps 145:18–19 The LORD is near to all who
call on him, to all who call on him in truth. He
fulfils the desires of those who fear him; he hears
their cry and saves them.   *See also* **Ps** 3:4;
6:8–9; 30:2–3; 66:19–20; 116:1–2; 118:5; 138:3
God answers Moses' prayers Ex 15:23–25;
17:4–7; **Nu** 11:10–17
God answers Hannah's prayer for a son
1Sa 1:27 "I prayed for this child, and the LORD
has granted me what I asked of him."   *See
also* **1Sa** 1:10–20
God answers the prayers of the prophets
Ps 99:6 Moses and Aaron were among his
priests, Samuel was among those who called on
his name; they called on the LORD and he
answered them.   *See also* **1Sa** 7:9; **La** 3:55–57;
Jnh 2:1–2; **Jas** 5:17–18
**God answers the prayers of the kings of
Israel 1Ki** 9:3; **2Ch** 18:31

God answers corporate petition
**Answered prayer for deliverance from
hardship**
Dt 26:7–8 "Then we cried out to the LORD,

the God of our ancestors, and the LORD heard our
voice and saw our misery, toil and oppression. So
the LORD brought us out of Egypt with a mighty
hand and an outstretched arm, with great terror
and with miraculous signs and wonders."   *See
also* **Ex** 2:23–25; 3:7–9; **Nu** 20:16; **1Sa** 12:8; **Ps**
81:7

Answered prayer for deliverance from enemies
1Sa 12:10–11 "They cried out to the LORD
and said, 'We have sinned; we have forsaken the
LORD and served the Baals and the Ashtoreths.
But now deliver us from the hands of our
enemies, and we will serve you.' Then the LORD
sent Jerub-baal, Barak, Jephthah and Samuel, and
he delivered you from the hands of your enemies
on every side, so that you lived securely."   *See
also* **Jdg** 3:9,15; **2Ki** 19:19–20; **1Ch** 5:20

God answers the prayer of the oppressed
Jas 5:4 Look! The wages you failed to pay the
workers who mowed your fields are crying out
against you. The cries of the harvesters have
reached the ears of the Lord Almighty.   *See also*
Ex 22:22–23; **Job** 34:28

God answers prayer for healing
Jas 5:14–16 Is any one of you sick? Call the
elders of the church to pray over you and anoint
you with oil in the name of the Lord. And the
prayer offered in faith will make you well; the
Lord will raise you up. If you have sinned, you
will be forgiven. Therefore confess your sins to
each other and pray for each other so that you
may be healed. The prayer of a righteous person
is powerful and effective.   *See also* **Nu**
12:10–15; **1Ki** 17:21–22; **2Ki** 4:32–35; 20:1–6
pp 2Ch 32:24 pp Isa 38:1–6; **Mt** 8:2–3 pp Mk
1:40–42 pp Lk 5:12–13; **Ac** 9:40

God answers prayer for others
Dt 9:18–19 Then once again I [Moses] fell
prostrate before the LORD for forty days and forty
nights; I ate no bread and drank no water,
because of all the sin you [Israel] had committed,
doing what was evil in the LORD's sight and so
provoking him to anger. I feared the anger and

wrath of the LORD, for he was angry enough with you to destroy you. But again the LORD listened to me.   *See also* 1Sa 7:8–9; Ac 12:5–8

prayer, as praise and thanksgiving

Prayer embraces praising God for who he is, thanking him for what he has already done, and looking forward with joy to what he has promised to do in the future.

Scripture exhorts God's people to praise and thank him

Php 4:6 Do not be anxious about anything, but in everything, by prayer and petition, with thanksgiving, present your requests to God.   *See also* Ps 66:1; 68:4; 95:1–2; 105:1–3; **Eph** 5:19–20; **Col** 4:2; 1Th 5:16–18; **Heb** 13:15

Praise and thanksgiving in prayer for God's goodness towards his people
Praise and thanksgiving for deliverance and salvation
Ps 65:1–5 Praise awaits you, O God, in Zion; to you our vows will be fulfilled. O you who hear prayer, to you all people will come. When we were overwhelmed by sins, you forgave our transgressions . . .   *See also* Ps 66:5–6; 81:1–7; 124:1–8; Jnh 2:1–9
Praise and thanksgiving for provision of material needs
Mk 8:6 . . . When he [Jesus] had taken the seven loaves and given thanks, he broke them and gave them to his disciples to set before the people . . . pp Mt 15:36   *See also* Ps 65:9–13; **Mt** 26:26–27 pp Mk 14:22–23 pp Lk 22:19–20
Praise and thanksgiving for help in time of trouble
Ps 34:1–4 I will extol the LORD at all times; his praise will always be on my lips. My soul will boast in the LORD; let the afflicted hear and rejoice. Glorify the LORD with me: let us exalt his name together. I sought the LORD, and he answered me; he delivered me from all my fears.   *See also* Ps 30:1–12; 40:1–5; 103:1–5; 116:1–19

Praise and thanksgiving for the encouragement of other believers
Php 1:3–6 I thank my God every time I remember you. In all my prayers for all of you, I always pray with joy because of your partnership in the gospel from the first day until now, being confident of this, that he who began a good work in you will carry it on to completion until the day of Christ Jesus.   *See also* Ro 1:8; 2Co 8:1; **Eph** 1:16; **2Th** 1:3

Notable songs of praise and thanksgiving
Ex 15:1–18
David, on his deliverance from Saul: 2Sa 22:2–51; Ps 18:1–50

1Ch 16:8–36; **Lk** 1:46–55   *See also praise.*

prayer, asking God
God wants his people to turn to him in prayer, individually and corporately, in times of need or crisis, and to bring requests to him as a Father.

God's people are commanded to bring their requests to him
Php 4:6 Do not be anxious about anything, but in everything, by prayer and petition, with thanksgiving, present your requests to God.   *See also* 1Ch 16:11; **Mt** 7:7 pp Lk 11:9; **Jn** 16:24; **Eph** 6:18–20; 1Th 5:17; **Jas** 5:13

Prayer for deliverance from difficulty
Ps 4:1 Answer me when I call to you, O my righteous God. Give me relief from my distress; be merciful to me and hear my prayer.
Ps 107:6 Then they cried out to the LORD in their trouble, and he delivered them from their distress.   *See also* Ps 40:2–3; Jnh 2:1–3; Ac 12:5

Prayer for deliverance from enemies
Ps 17:8–9 Keep me as the apple of your eye; hide me in the shadow of your wings from the wicked who assail me, from my mortal enemies who surround me.
Ps 35:4 May those who seek my life be disgraced and put to shame; may those who plot

my ruin be turned back in dismay.   *See also* 2Ki 19:9–11; 2Ch 14:11

Prayers of individuals in time of crisis
Jacob's prayer **Ge 32:9–12**
David's prayers
Ps 28:1–9 To you I call, O LORD my Rock; do not turn a deaf ear to me. For if you remain silent, I shall be like those who have gone down to the pit. Hear my cry for mercy as I call to you for help, as I lift up my hands towards your Most Holy Place . . .   *See also* **Ps** 4:1; 5:1–3; 30:8–10; 142:1–7
Elijah's prayer
1Ki 19:4 . . . He [Elijah] came to a broom tree, sat down under it and prayed that he might die. "I have had enough, LORD," he said. "Take my life; I am no better than my ancestors."
Jeremiah's prayer Jer 15:15–18
Jesus Christ's prayers
Mt 26:39 Going a little farther, he [Jesus] fell with his face to the ground and prayed, "My Father, if it is possible, may this cup be taken from me. Yet not as I will, but as you will." pp Mk 14:35–36 pp Lk 22:42–44

Individual petition to God in prayer
Individual prayer for guidance
Ge 24:12–14 Then he [Abraham's servant] prayed, "O LORD, God of my master Abraham, give me success today, and show kindness to my master Abraham. See, I am standing beside this spring, and the daughters of the townspeople are coming out to draw water. May it be that when I say to a girl, 'Please let down your jar that I may have a drink,' and she says, 'Drink, and I'll water your camels too'—let her be the one you have chosen for your servant Isaac. By this I will know that you have shown kindness to my master."   *See also* **Jdg** 1:1–2; 6:36–40; **1Sa** 14:41; **2Sa** 2:1; **1Ch** 14:14–15
Individual prayer for healing
2Ki 20:1–11 . . . Hezekiah turned his face to the wall and prayed to the LORD, "Remember, O LORD, how I have walked before you faithfully and with wholehearted devotion and have done what is good in your eyes." And Hezekiah wept

bitterly . . . pp Isa 38:1–10
Individual prayer for the birth of a child
1Sa 1:10–11 In bitterness of soul Hannah wept much and prayed to the LORD. And she made a vow, saying, "O LORD Almighty, if you will only look upon your servant's misery and remember me, and not forget your servant but give her a son, then I will give him to the LORD for all the days of his life, and no razor will ever be used on his head."   *See also* **Ge** 25:21; 30:17

Corporate petition to God
Corporate prayer for deliverance
Ex 2:23 . . . The Israelites groaned in their slavery and cried out, and their cry for help because of their slavery went up to God.   *See also* **Nu** 20:15–16; **Dt** 26:6–8; **Jdg** 3:9; 4:3; 6:7–10; **1Sa** 12:8
Corporate prayer for restoration Ps 44:23–26; 79:8–9; 80:4–7; 85:4–7
Corporate prayer for protection, especially at times of crisis
Ezr 8:21–23 There, by the Ahava Canal, I [Ezra] proclaimed a fast, so that we might humble ourselves before our God and ask him for a safe journey for us and our children, with all our possessions . . . So we fasted and petitioned our God about this, and he answered our prayer.   *See also* **2Ch** 20:12–13; **Ezr** 10:1; **Est** 4:16; **Ps** 74:18–23; **Da** 2:17–18

The first Christians prayed together when they met
Ac 1:13–14 When they arrived, they went upstairs to the room where they were staying. Those present were Peter, John, James and Andrew; Philip and Thomas, Bartholomew and Matthew; James son of Alphaeus and Simon the Zealot, and Judas son of James. They all joined together constantly in prayer, along with the women and Mary the mother of Jesus, and with his brothers.   *See also* **Ac** 2:42,46–47; 16:13,16; 20:36; 21:5

The first Christians prayed together at times of crisis or important decisions
When threatened with punishment
Ac 4:24–31 When they [the Jerusalem believers] heard this [what the chief priests and elders had said to Peter and John], they raised their voices together in prayer to God . . . *See also* **Ac** 12:5,12
When Barnabas and Saul were sent off by the church at Antioch Ac 13:3
When Paul and Silas experienced persecution Ac 16:25

Prayers for mercy and grace
Ps 143:1 O LORD, hear my prayer, listen to my cry for mercy; in your faithfulness and righteousness come to my relief.

Heb 4:16 Let us then approach the throne of grace with confidence, so that we may receive mercy and find grace to help us in our time of need. *See also* **2Ch** 6:18–19; **Ps** 130:1–2; **Mt** 20:30–31

---

prayer, for others
Believers should pray, not only for their own needs, but for those of others. Scripture provides many examples of intercession, and commends it as pleasing to God.

Believers must value others
Php 2:3–4 Do nothing out of selfish ambition or vain conceit, but in humility consider others better than yourselves. Each of you should look not only to your own interests, but also to the interests of others.

Examples of praying for others
Moses prays for the Israelites
Dt 9:18–19 Then once again I fell prostrate before the LORD for forty days and forty nights; I ate no bread and drank no water, because of all the sin you [the Israelites] had committed, doing what was evil in the LORD's sight and so provoking him to anger. I feared the anger and wrath of the LORD, for he was angry enough with you to destroy you. But again the LORD listened

to me. *See also* **Ex** 32:9–14; 34:9; **Nu** 14:11–19; **Dt** 9:25–29
Samuel prays for Israel
1Sa 7:5–9 Then Samuel said, "Assemble all Israel at Mizpah and I will intercede with the LORD for you." . . . Then Samuel took a suckling lamb and offered it up as a whole burnt offering to the LORD. He cried out to the LORD on Israel's behalf, and the LORD answered him. *See also* **1Sa** 12:19–23
Job prays for his friends
Job 42:10 After Job had prayed for his friends, the LORD made him prosperous again and gave him twice as much as he had before.
Jeremiah prays for Judah
Jer 7:16 "So do not pray for this people nor offer any plea or petition for them; do not plead with me, for I will not listen to you." *See also* **Jer** 11:14; 14:11

Jesus Christ intercedes for believers
Ro 8:34 Who then can condemn? Christ Jesus, who died—more than that, who was raised to life—is at the right hand of God and is also interceding for us. *See also* **Isa** 53:12; **Heb** 7:25; **1Jn** 2:1

The Holy Spirit intercedes for believers
Ro 8:26–27 . . . the Spirit helps us in our weakness. We do not know what we ought to pray for, but the Spirit himself intercedes for us with groans that words cannot express. And he who searches our hearts knows the mind of the Spirit, because the Spirit intercedes for the saints in accordance with God's will.

Christians are to intercede for others
Christians are to pray for their enemies
Mt 5:44 "But I tell you: Love your enemies, and pray for those who persecute you," *See also* **Lk** 6:28; 23:34; **Ac** 7:60
Christians are to pray for one another
Eph 6:18 And pray in the Spirit on all occasions with all kinds of prayers and requests. With this in mind, be alert and always keep on praying for all the saints. *See also* **1Th** 5:25; **Phm** 22; **Heb** 13:18–19; **Jas** 5:14–16; **1Jn** 5:16

Christians are to prayer for rulers
1Ti 2:1–2 I urge, then, first of all, that requests, prayers, intercession and thanksgiving be made for everyone—for kings and all those in authority, that we may live peaceful and quiet lives in all godliness and holiness.

Examples of pleas made to Jesus Christ on behalf of others
Mt 8:5–13 pp Lk 7:1–10; **Mt** 15:21–28 pp Mk 7:24–30; **Mt** 17:14–20 pp Mk 9:14–29 pp Lk 9:37–42

Examples of notable prayers of intercession
2Ki 19:14–19 pp Isa 37:14–20; **Ezr** 8:21–23; **Da** 9:1–19; **Jn** 17:6–26
Paul for the believers in Ephesus: **Eph** 1:15–21; 3:14–21
Col 1:9–13   *See also forgiveness, application.*

prayer, God's promises
God promises to hear and respond to the prayers of his people, when they pray in the name of his Son and according to his will.

God expects his people to make requests of him in prayer
Mt 7:7–11 "Ask and it will be given to you; seek and you will find; knock and the door will be opened to you. For everyone who asks receives; everyone who seeks finds; and to everyone who knocks, the door will be opened. Which of you, if your children ask for bread, will give them a stone? Or if they ask for a fish, will give them a snake? If you, then, though you are evil, know how to give good gifts to your children, how much more will your Father in heaven give good gifts to those who ask him!" pp Lk 11:9–13   *See also* **Mt** 21:22

God promises to answer prayer in the name of Jesus Christ
Jn 14:13–14 "And I will do whatever you ask in my name, so that the Son may bring glory to the Father. You may ask me for anything in my name, and I will do it."

Jn 15:7 "If you remain in me [Jesus] and my words remain in you, ask whatever you wish, and it will be given you."   *See also* **Jn** 15:16; 16:23–24

God promises to respond to the prayers of his people in times of need
Ps 91:14–16 "Because you [who makes the Most High his dwelling] love me," says the LORD, "I will rescue you; I will protect you, for you acknowledge my name. You will call upon me, and I will answer you; I will be with you in trouble, I will deliver you and honour you. With long life will I satisfy you and show you my salvation."   *See also* **Ps** 50:14–15

God promises to hear the prayers of the oppressed
Ps 10:17 You hear, O LORD, the desire of the afflicted; you encourage them, and you listen to their cry.   *See also* **Ex** 22:22–23,26–27; **Ps** 102:19–20; **Isa** 41:17

God promises to hear the prayers of the truly penitent
2Ch 7:14 "if my people, who are called by my name, will humble themselves and pray and seek my face and turn from their wicked ways, then will I hear from heaven and will forgive their sin and will heal their land."   *See also* **Eze** 36:37; **Zec** 10:6; 13:8–9

God promises to hear the prayers of his obedient people
1Jn 3:22 and receive from him anything we ask, because we obey his commands and do what pleases him.

The need in prayer to have confidence in God's promises
Mk 11:24 "Therefore I tell you, whatever you ask for in prayer, believe that you have received it, and it will be yours."

1Jn 5:14 This is the confidence we have in approaching God: that if we ask anything according to his will, he hears us.   *See also* **Mt** 18:19   *See also faith, and blessings; promises, divine.*

prayer, in the church

The prayer life of the NT provides a pattern from which the modern church can learn, both in terms of the importance of prayer, and also matters for prayer.

Prayer was at the centre of the life of the early church

They prayed when they met together

Ac 1:14 They all joined together constantly in prayer, along with the women and Mary the mother of Jesus, and with his brothers.　*See also* **Ac** 2:42; 4:23–31; 12:12; 20:36; 21:5

They prayed about the selection and ordination of Christian leaders

Ac 13:2–3 While they [the leaders of the church at Antioch] were worshipping the Lord and fasting, the Holy Spirit said, "Set apart for me Barnabas and Saul for the work to which I have called them." So after they had fasted and prayed, they placed their hands on them and sent them off.　*See also* **Ac** 1:24–25; 6:6; 14:23

They prayed during persecution

Ac 12:5 So Peter was kept in prison, but the church was earnestly praying to God for him. *See also* **Ac** 7:59–60; 12:12; 16:22–25

They prayed for healing

Ac 9:40 Peter sent them all out of the room; then he got down on his knees and prayed. Turning towards the dead woman, he said, "Tabitha, get up." She opened her eyes, and seeing Peter she sat up.　*See also* **Ac** 28:7–8

The apostles' teaching on prayer in church life

The importance of prayer

Col 4:2 Devote yourselves to prayer, being watchful and thankful.　*See also* **Ro** 12:12; **Eph** 6:18; **1Th** 5:17; **1Ti** 2:1; **1Pe** 4:7

Prayer for the spread of the gospel

Col 4:3–4 And pray for us, too, that God may open a door for our message, so that we may proclaim the mystery of Christ, for which I am in chains. Pray that I may proclaim it clearly, as I should.　*See also* **Eph** 6:19–20; **2Th** 3:1

Prayer for the sick

Jas 5:14 Is any one of you sick? Call the elders of the church to pray over you and anoint you with oil in the name of the Lord.

Prayer for sinners

1Jn 5:16–17 If you see your brother or sister commit a sin that does not lead to death, you should pray and God will give them life. I refer to those whose sin does not lead to death. There is a sin that leads to death. I am not saying that you should pray about that. All wrongdoing is sin, and there is sin that does not lead to death. *See also* **Jas** 5:16

Prayer for God's servants

Ro 15:30 I urge you, brothers and sisters, by our Lord Jesus Christ and by the love of the Spirit, to join me in my struggle by praying to God for me.　*See also* **2Co** 1:11

Orderly conduct of public prayer

1Co 11:4–5 Every man who prays or prophesies with his head covered dishonours his head. And every woman who prays or prophesies with her head uncovered dishonours her head—it is just as though her head were shaved.　*See also* **1Co** 11:13–15

The practice of the apostles

Prayer was central to their ministry

Ac 6:3–4 ". . . We [the apostles] will turn this responsibility over to them [deacons] and will give our attention to prayer and the ministry of the word."

They prayed for the church

Col 1:9–10 For this reason, since the day we [Paul and Timothy] heard about you, we have not stopped praying for you and asking God to fill you with the knowledge of his will through all spiritual wisdom and understanding. And we pray this in order that you may live a life worthy of the Lord and may please him in every way: bearing fruit in every good work, growing in the knowledge of God.　*See also* **Eph** 1:16–21; 3:16–19; **Php** 1:9–11; **Col** 1:3; **1Th** 1:2; **2Th** 1:11–12　*See also* church, *life of.*

prayer, persistence

An answer to prayer may not come immediately.

Petitioners are to continue praying earnestly. This requires patience, determination and, at times, a willingness to wrestle with God for the desired outcome.

The principle of persistence in prayer
Prayer should be made with patience and perseverance
Ps 40:1 I waited patiently for the Lord; he turned to me and heard my cry.

Ps 88:1 O Lord, the God who saves me, day and night I cry out before you.   *See also* **1 Ch** 16:11; **Ps** 116:2

Jesus Christ taught his disciples to persist in prayer
Lk 18:1–8 Then Jesus told his disciples a parable to show them that they should always pray and not give up. He said: "In a certain town there was a judge who neither feared God nor cared about people. And there was a widow in that town who kept coming to him with the plea, 'Grant me justice against my adversary.' For some time he refused. But finally he said to himself, 'Even though I don't fear God or care about people, yet because this widow keeps bothering me, I will see that she gets justice, so that she won't eventually wear me out with her coming!'" And the Lord said, "Listen to what the unjust judge says . . ."   *See also* **Lk** 11:5–10

Persistence in prayer was exemplified in the early church
Ac 1:14 They all joined together constantly in prayer, along with the women and Mary the mother of Jesus, and with his brothers.   *See also* **Ac** 2:42

Paul exhorted the churches to practise persistent prayer
Eph 6:18 And pray in the Spirit on all occasions with all kinds of prayers and requests. With this in mind, be alert and always keep on praying for all the saints.   *See also* **Ro** 12:12; **1Th** 5:17

Examples of persistence in prayer
Abraham pleads persistently for Sodom
Ge 18:23–33 Then Abraham approached him and said: "Will you sweep away the righteous

with the wicked? What if there are fifty righteous people in the city? Will you really sweep it away and not spare the place for the sake of the fifty righteous people in it? Far be it from you to do such a thing—to kill the righteous with the wicked, treating the righteous and the wicked alike. Far be it from you! Will not the Judge of all the earth do right?" . . .

Jacob persists in wrestling with God
Ge 32:24–32 . . . Then the man said, "Let me go, for it is daybreak." But Jacob replied, "I will not let you go unless you bless me." . . .

Moses persists in interceding for Israel
Dt 9:25–29 . . . "O Sovereign Lord, do not destroy your people, your own inheritance that you redeemed by your great power and brought out of Egypt with a mighty hand. Remember your servants Abraham, Isaac and Jacob. Overlook the stubbornness of this people, their wickedness and their sin . . ."   *See also* **Ex** 32:31–32

Hannah persistently asks for a son
1Sa 1:10–11 In bitterness of soul Hannah wept much and prayed to the Lord. And she made a vow, saying, "O Lord Almighty, if you will only look upon your servant's misery and remember me, and not forget your servant but give her a son, then I will give him to the Lord for all the days of his life, and no razor will ever be used on his head."

Elijah persists in prayer about the rain
Jas 5:17–18 Elijah was human just as we are. He prayed earnestly that it would not rain, and it did not rain on the land for three and a half years. Again he prayed, and the heavens gave rain, and the earth produced its crops.   *See also* **1Ki** 18:36–44

The psalmists persist in calling out to God Ps 88:1–18; 119:147–149; 130:1–6

Jesus Christ persisted in pursuing the Father's will
Lk 22:42–44 "Father, if you are willing, take this cup from me; yet not my will, but yours be done." . . . And being in anguish, he prayed more earnestly, and his sweat was like drops of blood falling to the ground. pp Mt 26:36–43 pp Mk 14:32–40

Persistence in prayer is exemplified in waiting for God

Mic 7:7 But as for me, I watch in hope for the LORD, I wait for God my Saviour; my God will hear me.   *See also* **Ps** 27:14; 33:20; 37:7; 38:15; 40:1; **Isa** 26:8

---

prayer, practicalities

Scripture commends a life of prayer, characterised by simplicity of expression, sincerity of heart and trust in the promises of God. It gives guidance on how, when and where to pray.

Scripture stresses the importance of prayer

1Th 5:16–18 . . . pray continually; give thanks in all circumstances, for this is God's will for you in Christ Jesus.   *See also* **Ac** 6:3–4; **Ro** 12:12

Judgment comes on those who do not pray

Ps 79:6 Pour out your wrath on the nations that do not acknowledge you, on the kingdoms that do not call on your name;   *See also* **Ps** 53:4; **Jer** 10:21; **Zep** 1:4–6; **Jas** 4:2

Prayers should be expressed simply

Mt 6:7–8 "And when you pray, do not keep on babbling like pagans, for they think they will be heard because of their many words. Do not be like them, for your Father knows what you need before you ask him."   *See also* **Ecc** 5:1–3; **Lk** 18:9–14

Prayer should not be ostentatious

Mt 6:5–6 "And when you pray, do not be like the hypocrites, for they love to pray standing in the synagogues and on the street corners to be seen by others. I tell you the truth, they have received their reward in full. But when you pray, go into your room, close the door and pray to your Father, who is unseen. Then your Father, who sees what is done in secret, will reward you."   *See also* **Mt** 14:23 pp **Mk** 6:46; **Lk** 5:16

Physical positions for prayer
Sitting while praying

2Sa 7:18 Then King David went in and sat before the LORD, and he said: "Who am I, O Sovereign LORD, and what is my family, that you have brought me this far?"   *See also* **Jdg** 20:26; **Ne** 1:4

Kneeling while praying

Lk 22:41 He [Jesus] withdrew about a stone's throw beyond them, knelt down and prayed,   *See also* **1Ki** 8:54; **2Ch** 6:13; **Ezr** 9:5; **Ac** 9:40; 21:5; **Eph** 3:14

Standing while praying

1Ki 8:22 Then Solomon stood before the altar of the LORD in front of the whole assembly of Israel . . .   *See also* **1Sa** 1:26; **Mk** 11:25

Lying prostrate while praying

2Ch 20:18 Jehoshaphat bowed with his face to the ground, and all the people of Judah and Jerusalem fell down in worship before the LORD.   *See also* **Ge** 24:52; **Nu** 20:6

Praying with arms outstretched

Ex 9:29 Moses replied, "When I have gone out of the city, I will spread out my hands in prayer to the LORD. The thunder will stop and there will be no more hail, so you may know that the earth is the LORD's."

Isa 1:15 "When you spread out your hands in prayer, I will hide my eyes from you; even if you offer many prayers, I will not listen. Your hands are full of blood;"   *See also* **1Ki** 8:54; **2Ch** 6:13

Praying with hands raised

1Ti 2:8 I want men everywhere to lift up holy hands in prayer, without anger or disputing.   *See also* **Ex** 9:29; **1Ki** 8:22,54; **Ps** 63:4; 77:1–2

Prayer can be offered at any time
Praying several times a day

Da 6:10 Now when Daniel learned that the decree had been published, he went home to his upstairs room where the windows opened towards Jerusalem. Three times a day he got down on his knees and prayed, giving thanks to his God, just as he had done before.   *See also* **Ps** 55:17; 88:1

Praying early in the morning
Mk 1:35 Very early in the morning, while it was still dark, Jesus got up, left the house and went off to a solitary place, where he prayed. *See also* **Ps** 5:3; 119:147

Praying all night
Lk 6:12 One of those days Jesus went out to a mountainside to pray, and spent the night praying to God. *See also* **1Sa** 15:11; **Lk** 2:37

Prayer is not confined to any single place
Jn 4:21–24 Jesus declared, "Believe me, woman, a time is coming when you will worship the Father neither on this mountain nor in Jerusalem . . . Yet a time is coming and has now come when the true worshippers will worship the Father in spirit and truth, for they are the kind of worshippers the Father seeks. God is spirit, and his worshippers must worship in spirit and in truth."

Praying inside a building
Da 6:10 Now when Daniel learned that the decree had been published, he went home to his upstairs room where the windows opened towards Jerusalem. Three times a day he got down on his knees and prayed, giving thanks to his God, just as he had done before.

Mt 6:6 "But when you pray, go into your room, close the door and pray to your Father, who is unseen. Then your Father, who sees what is done in secret, will reward you." *See also* **1Ki** 8:28–30

Praying outside a building
Mk 1:35 Very early in the morning, while it was still dark, Jesus got up, left the house and went off to a solitary place, where he prayed.

Lk 5:16 But Jesus often withdrew to lonely places and prayed. *See also* **Ac** 10:9; 21:5

Prayer may be accompanied by fasting
Ac 13:2–3 While they were worshipping the Lord and fasting, the Holy Spirit said, "Set apart for me Barnabas and Saul for the work to which I have called them." So after they had fasted

and prayed, they placed their hands on them and sent them off. *See also* **Ezr** 8:23; **Ne** 1:4; **Ps** 35:13; **Da** 9:3; **Lk** 2:37; 5:33; **Ac** 14:23; **Mt** 17:21 fn pp Mk 9:29 fn *See also worship, places; worship, times.*

---

prayer, relationship with God

Prayer is based on God's love for believers. Through his grace, he gives them things which they do not deserve, while through his mercy he shields them from those things which they do deserve.

God's children can turn to their Father in prayer
Under the old covenant
Isa 64:8–9 Yet, O LORD, you are our Father. We are the clay, you are the potter; we are all the work of your hand. Do not be angry beyond measure, O LORD; do not remember our sins for ever. Oh, look upon us we pray, for we are all your people. *See also* **Ps** 103:13–14; **Isa** 63:16

Under the new covenant
Mt 6:9–13 "This, then, is how you should pray: 'Our Father in heaven, hallowed be your name . . .'" pp Lk 11:2–4　*See also* **Mt** 6:6; 7:7–11 pp Lk 11:9–13; **Ro** 8:15; **Gal** 4:6

Jesus Christ's prayer life with his Father
Mk 14:36 "*Abba*, Father," he said, "everything is possible for you. Take this cup from me. Yet not what I will, but what you will." pp Mt 26:39 pp Mt 26:42 pp Lk 22:42　*See also* **Jn** 17:1–26

It is possible to approach God in prayer because of Jesus Christ's sacrifice
Heb 10:19–22 Therefore, brothers and sisters, since we have confidence to enter the Most Holy Place by the blood of Jesus, by a new and living way opened for us through the curtain, that is, his body, and since we have a great priest over the house of God, let us draw near to God with a sincere heart in full assurance of faith, having our hearts sprinkled to cleanse us from a guilty conscience and having our bodies washed with pure water. *See also* **Eph** 3:12; **Heb** 7:15–19

Prayer reflects a longing after God

Ps 42:1–2 As the deer pants for streams of water, so my soul pants for you, O God. My soul thirsts for God, for the living God. When can I go and meet with God?

Jer 29:12–13 "Then you will call upon me and come and pray to me, and I will listen to you. You will seek me and find me when you seek me with all your heart." *See also* **Ps** 130:5–6; 145:18–19; **Pr** 8:17; **Isa** 26:9; 33:2; **La** 3:25 *See also knowing God, nature of.*

prayer, response to God

Prayer offers believers a means of acknowledging the character and purposes of God and the opportunity to seek guidance concerning his will for them.

The direction of prayer is upwards towards God

Ps 123:1–2 I [the psalmist] lift up my eyes to you [Lord], to you whose throne is in heaven. As the eyes of slaves look to the hand of their master, as the eyes of a female servant look to the hand of her mistress, so our eyes look to the Lord our God, till he shows us his mercy. *See also* **Ps** 25:1; 86:4; 121:1–2; 143:8–10; 145:15

Fellowship with God through prayer

Ps 73:23–26 . . . I [the psalmist] am always with you [the Lord]; you hold me by my right hand. You guide me with your counsel, and afterwards you will take me into glory. Whom have I in heaven but you? And earth has nothing I desire besides you. My flesh and my heart may fail, but God is the strength of my heart and my portion for ever. *See also* **Ex** 33:11; **1Ki** 8:57–59; **Ps** 16:2; 145:17–20; **Mt** 18:20

The habit of prayer

Lk 5:16 . . . Jesus often withdrew to lonely places and prayed. *See also* **Ne** 2:4; **Da** 6:10–11,13

Contemplative prayer as a response to God's presence

Ps 27:4 One thing I [the psalmist] ask of the Lord, this is what I seek: that I may dwell in the house of the Lord all the days of my life, to gaze upon the beauty of the Lord and to seek him in his temple. *See also* **1Ch** 16:10–11 pp **Ps** 105:3–4; **Ps** 27:8; **Isa** 55:6; **Jer** 29:13; **Ac** 17:27–28; **Heb** 11:6

Prayer of acceptance in response to God's call

1Sa 3:10 The Lord came and stood there, calling as at the other times, "Samuel! Samuel!" Then Samuel said, "Speak, for your servant is listening." *See also* **Isa** 6:8; **Rev** 3:20

Prayer of confession
In response to God's holiness
1Jn 1:5–9 . . . God is light; in him there is no darkness at all . . . If we confess our sins, he is faithful and just and will forgive us our sins and purify us from all unrighteousness. *See also* **Isa** 6:3–7; 55:7–9
In response to sin being exposed
Ps 51:1–2 Have mercy on me, O God, according to your unfailing love; according to your great compassion blot out my transgressions. Wash away all my iniquity and cleanse me from my sin. *See also* **Ps** 51:3–12

Prayer of co-operation in response to God's purposes

Jn 15:7–8 "If you [Jesus' disciples] remain in me [Jesus] and my words remain in you, ask whatever you wish, and it will be given you . . ." *See also* **Ps** 119:105–106; **Lk** 1:38; **Jn** 15:16

Prayer of confidence in response to God's mercy and grace

Heb 4:16 Let us [believers] then approach the throne of grace with confidence, so that we may receive mercy and find grace to help us in our time of need. *See also* **Ne** 1:4–7; **Ps** 123:1–2; **Jas** 1:5–8 *See also fellowship; holiness, of God; repentance.*

preachers and preaching

God declares his word through called and anointed preachers. Preaching is the announcing of the good news of God by his servants through the faithful revelation of God's will, the exposition of God's word and the proclamation of Jesus Christ, the Son of God.

preachers, call

God declares his word through called and anointed preachers. He overcomes their reluctance, helps their weakness, authorises their message and confirms the truth of what they declare.

God's call of preachers
It is not dependent upon background

Am 7:14–15 Amos answered Amaziah, "I was neither a prophet nor a prophet's son, but I was a shepherd, and I also took care of sycamore-fig trees. But the LORD took me from tending the flock and said to me, 'Go, prophesy to my people Israel.'" *See also* **Jer** 1:1–5; **Mt** 4:18–20 pp **Mk** 1:16–19 pp **Lk** 5:1–11; **Ac** 9:10–16

It is not dependent upon ability

Ex 4:10–12 Moses said to the LORD, "O Lord, I have never been eloquent, neither in the past nor since you have spoken to your servant. I am slow of speech and tongue." The LORD said to him, "Who gave human beings their mouths? Who makes them deaf or mute? Who gives them sight or makes them blind? Is it not I, the LORD? Now go; I will help you speak and will teach you what to say." *See also* **Jer** 1:6–9; **Ac** 4:13

It is not dependent upon willingness

Ex 4:13 But Moses said, "O Lord, please send someone else to do it." *See also* **Jnh** 1:1–3; **Ac** 9:1–6

It is a matter of God's sovereign choice

Jer 1:4–5 The word of the LORD came to me, saying, "Before I formed you in the womb I knew you, before you were born I set you apart; I appointed you as a prophet to the nations." *See also* **Isa** 49:1–6; **Eze** 2:1–5; **Am** 7:14–15; **Lk** 4:18–19; **Isa** 61:1–2; **Gal** 1:15

God's commissioning of preachers
They are commissioned to declare God's word

Eze 3:1 And he said to me, "Son of man, eat what is before you, eat this scroll; then go and speak to the house of Israel."

Ro 10:13–15 for, "Everyone who calls on the name of the Lord will be saved." How, then, can they call on the one they have not believed in? And how can they believe in the one of whom they have not heard? And how can they hear without someone preaching to them? And how can they preach unless they are sent? As it is written, "How beautiful are the feet of those who bring good news!" *See also* **Jer** 1:9; **Jnh** 3:1–2; **Mt** 28:18–20

They are to declare God's word with authority

Tit 2:15 These, then, are the things you should teach. Encourage and rebuke with all authority. Do not let anyone despise you. *See also* **Jer** 1:9–10; **Mk** 3:14–15; **Lk** 9:1–2

They are to declare God's word without fear

Jer 1:7–8 But the LORD said to me, "Do not say, 'I am only a child.' You must go to everyone I send you to and say whatever I command you. Do not be afraid of them, for I am with you and will rescue you," declares the LORD. *See also* **Eze** 2:3–7; 3:7–9; **Ac** 5:27–29; **2Ti** 1:6–8

God's constraint upon preachers

1Co 9:16 Yet when I [Paul] preach the gospel, I cannot boast, for I am compelled to preach. Woe to me if I do not preach the gospel! *See also* **Jer** 20:8–9; **Ac** 4:18–20; **Ro** 1:14–15

God's confirmation of his call upon preachers

Ac 14:3 So Paul and Barnabas spent considerable time there [in Iconium], speaking boldly for the Lord, who confirmed the message of his grace by enabling them to do miraculous signs and wonders. *See also* **Ex** 4:1–9; **1Ki** 17:17–24; **Mk** 16:20; **Ac** 4:29–31; **1Co** 2:4 *See also* grace; word of God.

preachers, qualifications

Those entrusted with the task of preaching must ensure that their lives are in line with their message. They must be of good character and conduct, be consistent in all they teach and do and be accountable to others.

Preachers must be of good character

1Ti 4:12 Don't let anyone look down on you because you are young, but set an example for the believers in speech, in life, in love, in faith and in purity.   *See also* **1Th** 2:9–10; **1Ti** 4:16; **2Ti** 2:20–26; **Tit** 2:7–8; **Jas** 3:1

Preachers must practise what they preach

Mt 23:2–4 "The teachers of the law and the Pharisees sit in Moses' seat. So you must obey them and do everything they tell you. But do not do what they do, for they do not practise what they preach. They tie up heavy loads and put them on other people's shoulders, but they themselves are not willing to lift a finger to move them."   *See also* **Ro** 2:21–23; **Gal** 2:11–14

Preachers must be accountable to others and to God

Mk 6:30 The apostles gathered round Jesus and reported to him all they had done and taught. pp Lk 9:10   *See also* **Ac** 14:26–27; 21:17–19; **Gal** 2:1–2

Preachers must not look for honour for themselves

Mk 12:38–40 As he taught, Jesus said, "Watch out for the teachers of the law. They like to walk around in flowing robes and be greeted in the market-places, and have the most important seats in the synagogues and the places of honour at banquets. They devour widows' houses and for a show make lengthy prayers. Such people will be punished most severely." pp Mt 23:5–12 pp Lk 20:45–47   *See also* **Ac** 14:11–15; **1Co** 3:5–6; **1Th** 2:3–6

Preachers must not look for personal gain

2Co 2:17 Unlike so many, we [Paul and Timothy] do not peddle the word of God for profit. On the contrary, in Christ we speak before God with sincerity, as those sent from God.   *See also* **Ac** 20:33–35; **2Co** 11:7–9; **1Th** 2:6–9

Preachers must be people of integrity

2Co 4:2 Rather, we [Paul and Timothy] have renounced secret and shameful ways; we do not use deception, nor do we distort the word of God. On the contrary, by setting forth the truth plainly we commend ourselves to everyone's conscience in the sight of God.   *See also* **2Co** 1:12; **1Th** 2:3–6   *See also holiness.*

preachers, responsibilities

Those entrusted with the responsibility of preaching are to discharge it faithfully, boldly and persistently in the power of the Holy Spirit. The Christian community should honour faithful preachers and challenge those who fail to honour their responsibility.

The responsibilities of preachers

They must be diligent in their preaching
2Ti 2:15 Do your best to present yourself to God as one approved, a worker who does not need to be ashamed and who correctly handles the word of truth.   *See also* **1Ti** 4:13–16; **2Ti** 4:1–5

They must be faithful in their preaching
Ac 20:20 "You know that I [Paul] have not hesitated to preach anything that would be helpful to you but have taught you publicly and from house to house."   *See also* **Jer** 26:1–2; 42:4; **Ac** 20:25–27

They must be persistent in their preaching
2Ti 4:1–5 . . . Preach the Word; be prepared in season and out of season . . .   *See also* **Ac** 18:4–6; 20:31; **1Th** 2:1–2

They must be bold in their preaching
Ac 28:31 Boldly and without hindrance he [Paul] preached the kingdom of God and taught about the Lord Jesus Christ.   *See also* **Jer** 26:7–15; **Am** 7:10–17; **Ac** 4:18–20; 5:27–29; 14:1–3

They must be encouraging in their preaching
Ac 14:21–22 ... Then they [Paul and Barnabas] returned to Lystra, Iconium and Antioch, strengthening the disciples and encouraging them to remain true to the faith ...   *See also* **Ac 15:32; 1Co 14:3–5; 1Th 2:11–12; 2Ti 4:2**
They must be filled with the Holy Spirit
Ac 1:8 "But you [Jesus' disciples] will receive power when the Holy Spirit comes on you; and you will be my witnesses in Jerusalem, and in all Judea and Samaria, and to the ends of the earth."

1Co 2:4 My [Paul's] message and my preaching were not with wise and persuasive words, but with a demonstration of the Spirit's power,   *See also* **Ac 4:31–33; 1Th 1:5; 1Pe 1:12**
They must be compassionate in their preaching
Mk 6:34 When Jesus landed and saw a large crowd, he had compassion on them, because they were like sheep without a shepherd. So he began teaching them many things.   *See also* **Mt 9:35–38**

The responsibilities of the church towards preachers
Faithful preachers should be honoured
1Ti 5:17 The elders who direct the affairs of the church well are worthy of double honour, especially those whose work is preaching and teaching.   *See also* **Mt 13:53–57 pp Mk 6:2–4; Lk 10:3–8; Heb 13:7**
Unfaithful preachers are to be exposed and will be judged
Gal 1:6–9 ... But even if we or an angel from heaven should preach a gospel other than the one we preached to you, let that person be eternally condemned! ...   *See also* **Jer 14:14–16; Eze 13:1–23; 1Ti 1:3–4; 4:1–7; Tit 1:10–11; 2Pe 2:1–3; Rev 2:14–16, 20–23**
See also church; mission.

---

preaching, content

Preaching is centred on the nature and will of God and his claims on all people. Expressed in prophecy, declaration or teaching, it includes the proclamation of the way of salvation to unbelievers and instruction about the faith to believers.

Preaching and the revelation of God's character, word and will
Ac 20:26–27 "Therefore, I [Paul] declare to you today that I am innocent of the blood of everyone. For I have not hesitated to proclaim to you the whole will of God."   *See also* **Ex 8:1; 1Ki 12:21–24; Jer 7:1–11; Eze 2:3–3:4**

Preaching and the declaration of the gospel
Declaring the kingdom
Mk 1:14–15 After John was put in prison, Jesus went into Galilee, proclaiming the good news of God. "The time has come," he said. "The kingdom of God is near. Repent and believe the good news!" pp **Mt 4:17**   *See also* **Mt 4:23 pp Lk 8:1; Ac 19:8; 20:25**
Declaring the person of Jesus Christ and his life
Ac 2:22 "People of Israel, listen to this: Jesus of Nazareth was a man accredited by God to you by miracles, wonders and signs, which God did among you through him, as you yourselves know."   *See also* **Ac 10:36–38; 28:31; 2Co 1:19**
Declaring the facts of the cross and the resurrection
Ac 2:23–24 "This man was handed over to you by God's set purpose and foreknowledge; and you, with the help of wicked people, put him to death by nailing him to the cross. But God raised him from the dead, freeing him from the agony of death, because it was impossible for death to keep its hold on him."   *See also* **Ac 5:30; 10:39–42; 13:28–31; 1Co 1:22–24; 15:12–17**
Declaring the victory and exaltation of Jesus Christ
Ac 2:33–35 "Exalted to the right hand of God, he has received from the Father the promised Holy Spirit and has poured out what you now see and hear ..."   *See also* **Ac 5:31; 1Pe 3:18–22**
Declaring that Jesus is both Messiah (Christ) and Lord
Ac 2:36 "Therefore let all Israel be assured of this: God has made this Jesus, whom you

crucified, both Lord and Christ." *See also* **Ac**
5:42; 8:5; 9:20–22; 10:36; 18:5

Declaring the call to repent
Ac 17:30 "In the past God overlooked such
ignorance, but now he commands all people
everywhere to repent." *See also* **Mk** 1:15 pp **Mt**
4:17; **Ac** 2:38; 3:19; 26:20

Declaring the promise of forgiveness
Ac 13:38 "Therefore, my brothers and sisters, I
[Paul] want you to know that through Jesus the
forgiveness of sins is proclaimed to you."
See also **Lk** 24:46–47; **Ac** 2:38; 5:31; 10:43

Preaching finds expression in the teaching of believers

**The central place of teaching in the lives of
the first Christians**
Ac 2:42 They devoted themselves to the
apostles' teaching . . . *See also* **Ac** 6:2;
11:25–26; 15:35; 18:24–26; 20:20

Teaching from the Scriptures
Ac 18:11 So Paul stayed for a year and a half,
teaching them the word of God. *See also* **2Ch**
17:7–9; **Ne** 8:2–8

Teaching on how to live
Mt 28:19–20 "Therefore go and make
disciples of all nations . . . teaching them to
obey everything I have commanded you . . ."
See also **Eph** 4:20–24; **1Th** 4:1–2; **Tit** 2:1–15

Preaching and the edification of believers

2Ti 4:2 Preach the Word; be prepared in season
and out of season; correct, rebuke and
encourage—with great patience and careful
instruction. *See also* **Ac** 13:42–43; 14:21–22;
20:2; **1Co** 14:26–31

Preaching and the continuation of apostolic doctrine

**Preaching should be rooted in apostolic
doctrine, which is to be faithfully handed on**
2Ti 2:2 And the things you [Timothy] have
heard me [Paul] say in the presence of many
witnesses entrust to reliable people who will also
be qualified to teach others. *See also* **1Co**
11:2; **2Th** 2:15; **2Ti** 1:13–14

**Preaching that does not conform to apostolic
doctrine is to be rejected**
1Ti 1:3–4 . . . command certain persons not
to teach false doctrines any longer nor to devote
themselves to myths and endless genealogies.
These promote controversies rather than God's
work—which is by faith. *See also* **Gal** 1:6–9;
1Ti 4:1–7; **Tit** 1:9–14

Preaching and the rejection of merely human wisdom

1Co 2:1–5 When I [Paul] came to you,
brothers and sisters, I did not come with
eloquence or superior wisdom as I proclaimed to
you the testimony about God . . . My message
and my preaching were not with wise and
persuasive words, but with a demonstration of the
Spirit's power . . . *See also* **1Co** 1:18–25
See also evangelism; gospel, transmission; Scripture.

---

preaching, effects
Faithful preaching leads to, through the grace of
God, the repentance of sinners, the birth of faith
and the nourishment of believers. It can also
evoke hostility from unbelievers.

The basis of effective preaching
It depends upon the grace of God
Ac 4:33 With great power the apostles continued
to testify to the resurrection of the Lord Jesus,
and much grace was upon them all. *See also*
Isa 55:10–11; **Ac** 14:26–27; **1Co** 15:10–11

**It depends upon the power of the cross, not
human wisdom**
1Co 1:17–25 For Christ did not send me
[Paul] to baptise, but to preach the gospel—not
with words of human wisdom, lest the cross of
Christ be emptied of its power . . . *See also*
1Co 2:1–5

It depends upon the power of the Holy Spirit
Lk 4:18–19 "The Spirit of the Lord is on me,
because he has anointed me to preach good news
to the poor. He has sent me to proclaim freedom
for the prisoners and recovery of sight for the
blind, to release the oppressed, to proclaim the
year of the Lord's favour." *See also* **Isa**
61:1–2; **Ac** 2:1–11; 10:44–48; **1Co** 2:4–5

It requires effective, supporting prayer

Col 4:3–4 And pray for us, too, that God may open a door for our message, so that we may proclaim the mystery of Christ . . .   *See also* **Ac** 4:29–31; 6:2–4; 13:1–5; **2Th** 3:1

It needs to be received with faith

Heb 4:2 For we also have had the gospel preached to us, just as they did; but the message they heard was of no value to them, because those who heard did not combine it with faith. *See also* **1Th** 2:13

Preaching and the repentance of sinners

Mt 12:41 "The people of Nineveh will stand up at the judgment with this generation and condemn it; for they repented at the preaching of Jonah . . ." pp **Lk** 11:32   *See also* **Jnh** 3:1–10; **Mt** 3:1–6 pp **Mk** 1:3–5 pp **Lk** 3:3–6

Preaching and the birth of faith

Ac 4:4 But many who heard the message believed, and their number grew to about five thousand.   *See also* **Ac** 2:38–41; 8:9–13; 17:11–12; **1Co** 15:1–2

Preaching and the nourishment of believers

Ac 14:21–22 They [Paul and Barnabas] preached the good news in that city and won a large number of disciples. Then they returned to Lystra, Iconium and Antioch, strengthening the disciples and encouraging them to remain true to the faith. "We must go through many hardships to enter the kingdom of God," they said. *See also* **Ro** 16:25–27; **Eph** 4:11–16; **Col** 2:6–7

Effective preaching and its authentication by miracles

Mk 16:20 Then the disciples went out and preached everywhere, and the Lord worked with them and confirmed his word by the signs that accompanied it.   *See also* **Mt** 4:23–25; **Lk** 9:1–6 pp **Mt** 10:5–14 pp **Mk** 6:7–11; **Ac** 4:29–30; 8:5–8; 14:1–3

Inappropriate responses to preaching
Amazement

Mt 7:28–29 When Jesus had finished saying these things, the crowds were amazed at his teaching, because he taught as one who had authority, and not as their teachers of the law. *See also* **Lk** 4:31–32 pp **Mk** 1:21–22; **Ac** 2:5–12; 4:13–14

Offence

Mk 6:1–6 " . . . Isn't this the carpenter? Isn't this Mary's son and the brother of James, Joseph, Judas and Simon? Aren't his sisters here with us?" And they took offence at him . . . pp **Mt** 13:54–58   *See also* **1Co** 1:22–23

Mere academic interest Ac 17:16–32; 24:22–26

Mockery

Ac 17:32 When they heard about the resurrection of the dead, some of them sneered . . .   *See also* **2Ch** 36:15–16; **Ac** 2:13

Hostility

Ac 17:13 When the Jews in Thessalonica learned that Paul was preaching the word of God at Berea, they went there too, agitating the crowds and stirring them up.   *See also* **Ac** 4:1–3; 5:27–40; 7:54–60; 13:49–51; 17:5–9 *See also* baptism; church; faith; repentance.

---

preaching, importance
Preaching has a central place among God's people and is vital to their life and growth. It is authorised by God, empowered by the Holy Spirit and expressed supremely by Jesus Christ.

Preaching has its origin in God
It is a divine command

Mk 16:15 He [Jesus] said to them, "Go into all the world and preach the good news to all creation." pp **Mt** 28:18–20   *See also* **Jnh** 1:1–2; **Mt** 10:5–7 pp **Mk** 6:7–12 pp **Lk** 9:1–6

It is rooted in God's grace

Eph 3:7–9 I [Paul] became a servant of this gospel by the gift of God's grace given me through the working of his power. Although I am less than the least of all God's people, this grace was given me: to preach to the Gentiles the unsearchable riches of Christ, and to make plain to everyone the administration of this mystery, which for ages past was kept hidden in God, who created all things. *See also* **Isa** 6:1–10; **Ro** 15:15–16

It is empowered by God's Spirit

Ac 1:8 "But you [Jesus' disciples] will receive power when the Holy Spirit comes on you; and you will be my [Jesus'] witnesses in Jerusalem, and in all Judea and Samaria, and to the ends of the earth." *See also* **Isa** 61:1–3; **Lk** 24:46–49; **Ac** 2:1–11; 4:8–12; 10:44; **1Co** 2:4–5

The importance of preaching and Jesus Christ

Jesus Christ himself came to preach

Mk 1:38 Jesus replied, "Let us go somewhere else—to the nearby villages—so that I can preach there also. That is why I have come." pp **Lk** 4:43 *See also* **Eph** 2:17

Jesus Christ's own ministry involved much preaching

Mt 4:23 Jesus went throughout Galilee, teaching in their synagogues, preaching the good news of the kingdom, and healing every disease and sickness among the people. *See also* **Mt** 11:1–5 pp **Lk** 7:18–22

Jesus Christ commissioned his disciples to preach

Mk 3:14–15 He [Jesus] appointed twelve—designating them apostles—that they might be with him and that he might send them out to preach and to have authority to drive out demons. *See also* **Mt** 10:5–7 pp **Lk** 9:1–2

The importance of preaching and the church

It is a natural part of the church's life

Ac 8:4 Those who had been scattered preached the word wherever they went. *See also* **Ac** 3:11–26; 15:35

It is a trust from God

Gal 2:7 . . . they [the apostles] saw that I [Paul] had been entrusted with the task of preaching the gospel to the Gentiles, just as Peter had been to the Jews. *See also* **1Th** 2:4; **1Ti** 1:11; **Tit** 1:3

It is an integral aspect of key ministries in the church

1Ti 3:2 Now the overseer must be . . . able to teach, *See also* **Eph** 4:11–12; **2Ti** 4:2–5; **Tit** 1:7–9

Its importance to Paul

1Co 1:17–18 For Christ did not send me to baptise, but to preach the gospel—not with words of human wisdom, lest the cross of Christ be emptied of its power. For the message of the cross is foolishness to those who are perishing, but to us who are being saved it is the power of God. *See also* **Ac** 9:20–22; 18:5; **Ro** 1:14–15; **1Co** 1:22–25

It is an apostolic command

1Ti 4:13 Until I [Paul] come, devote yourself to the public reading of Scripture, to preaching and to teaching. *See also* **2Ti** 4:2

The importance of preaching for salvation

Ro 10:14–15 How, then, can they call on the one they have not believed in? And how can they believe in the one of whom they have not heard? And how can they hear without someone preaching to them? And how can they preach unless they are sent? As it is written, "How beautiful are the feet of those who bring good news!" *See also* **Isa** 52:7; **Ro** 10:17; **1Co** 1:21

The importance of preaching means preachers and teachers will be judged more strictly

Jas 3:1 Not many of you should presume to be teachers, my brothers and sisters, because you know that we who teach will be judged more strictly. *See also* **Ro** 2:17–24 *See also* prophecy; Scripture; teaching.

predestination

God's foreordination of all events and circumstances for the good of his people and the glory of his name.

Predestination depends on God's sovereignty

He is the Creator of all things

Jer 32:17–19 "Ah, Sovereign LORD, you have made the heavens and the earth by your great power and outstretched arm. Nothing is too hard for you. You show love to thousands but bring the punishment for the parents' sins into the laps of their children after them. O great and powerful God, whose name is the LORD Almighty, great are your purposes and mighty are your deeds . . ." *See also* **Ge** 1:1; **Job** 38:1–4; **Isa** 44:24–28; 45:12–13; 48:12–14

He rules over nature and history

Pr 16:4 The LORD works out everything for his own ends—even the wicked for a day of disaster. *See also* **Ge** 18:10–14; **Ps** 67:4; **Pr** 16:9,33; 21:1; **Mt** 8:23–27 pp **Mk** 4:35–41 pp **Lk** 8:22–25; **Mt** 10:29–30; **Ac** 17:26

His will is perfect

Ge 18:25 "Far be it from you [the LORD] to do such a thing—to kill the righteous with the wicked, treating the righteous and the wicked alike. Far be it from you! Will not the Judge of all the earth do right?" *See also* **Ex** 33:19; **Dt** 32:4; **Job** 8:3; **Ps** 119:137; **Da** 4:37

God's predestined purposes cannot be thwarted

Human beings cannot stand against his will

Ro 9:19–21 One of you will say to me [Paul]: "Then why does God still blame us? For who resists his will?" But you, a mere mortal, who are you to talk back to God? "Shall what is formed say to the one who formed it, 'Why did you make me like this?'" Does not the potter have the right to make out of the same lump of clay some pottery for noble purposes and some for common use? *See also* **Ps** 2:1–4; **Pr** 19:21; 21:30; **Isa** 14:24–27; 46:10–12; **Da** 4:35

False gods are impotent before him

Ps 115:3–8 Our God is in heaven; he does whatever pleases him. But their idols are silver and gold, made by human hands. They have mouths, but cannot speak, eyes, but they cannot see . . . *See also* **Isa** 44:8–20; 45:20; 48:14

He brings good out of evil

Ge 50:20 "You [my brothers] intended to harm me [Joseph], but God intended it for good to accomplish what is now being done, the saving of many lives." *See also* **Ge** 15:13–16; 45:4–8

Predestination undergirds biblical prophecy

It explains the prophets' confidence

1Ki 22:17–28 . . . Micaiah declared, "If you [King Ahab] ever return safely, the LORD has not spoken through me." Then he added, "Mark my words, all you people!" *See also* **1Pe** 1:10–12

It is demonstrated in the fulfilment of prophecy

1Ki 22:29–38 . . . So the king [Ahab] died and was brought to Samaria, and they buried him there. They washed the chariot at a pool in Samaria (where the prostitutes bathed), and the dogs licked up his blood, as the word of the LORD had declared. *See also* **Mt** 1:22; 2:15,23; 4:14; 8:17; 12:17–19; **Ac** 2:17–25; 3:22–25; 13:27–30; 15:15–18

The life and ministry of Jesus Christ was predestined

In that it was predicted by the prophets

Isa 9:6–7 For to us a child is born, to us a son is given, and the government will be on his shoulders. And he will be called Wonderful Counsellor, Mighty God, Everlasting Father, Prince of Peace. Of the increase of his government and peace there will be no end. He will reign on David's throne and over his kingdom, establishing and upholding it with justice and righteousness from that time on and for ever. The zeal of the LORD Almighty will accomplish this. *See also* **Isa** 11:1–10; 52:13–53:12; **Jer** 23:5–6; **Ac** 3:18; **Gal** 4:4–5

In his sufferings and death

Ac 2:23 "This man [Jesus] was handed over to you [Jews] by God's set purpose and foreknowledge; and you, with the help of wicked people, put him to death by nailing him to the cross." *See also* **Mt** 16:21; **Lk** 18:31–32; 22:22; 24:25–27,44–45; **Jn** 13:1; **Ac** 4:27–30

In the outcome it achieved
Ge 3:15 "And I [the Lord] will put enmity
between you [the serpent] and the woman, and
between your offspring and hers; he will crush
your head, and you will strike his heel."

God's purpose in predestination is to bless his people
In the path their lives follow
Ro 8:28 And we know that in all things God
works for the good of those who love him, who
have been called according to his purpose. *See
also* **Ps** 139:14–16; **Jer** 29:11; **Mt** 10:29–31 pp **Lk**
12:6–7
In their salvation
Ro 8:29–30 For those God foreknew he also
predestined to be conformed to the likeness of his
Son, that he might be the firstborn among many
brothers and sisters. And those he predestined, he
also called; those he called, he also justified;
those he justified, he also glorified. *See also* **Ge**
12:1–3; **Mt** 11:25–27; **Mk** 4:11; **Jn** 6:37–44; **Ac**
13:48; **1Th** 5:9
In their assurance of salvation
Ro 8:31–39 . . . Who will bring any charge
against those whom God has chosen? It is God
who justifies. Who then can condemn? . . .
See also **Jn** 10:27–29; 17:2; **Eph** 1:3–14
Regarding final perseverance
Php 1:6 being confident of this, that he [God]
who began a good work in you will carry it on to
completion until the day of Christ Jesus. *See
also* **Ps** 138:8; **Jn** 6:37–40; **Php** 2:12–13; **Jas** 5:11
Regarding God's call to righteousness
Eph 2:10 For we [Paul and all believers] are
God's handiwork, created in Christ Jesus to do
good works, which God prepared in advance for
us to do. *See also* **Jer** 1:4–5; **Ac** 22:10; **Gal**
1:15–17
Regarding future inheritance
Jn 14:2–3 In my Father's house are many
rooms; if it were not so, I [Jesus] would have
told you. I am going there to prepare a place for
you. And if I go and prepare a place for you, I
will come back and take you to be with me that
you also may be where I am. *See also* **Mt**
25:34; **Ro** 8:30

God predestines judgment
Isa 65:11–12 "But as for you who forsake
the Lord and forget my holy mountain, who
spread a table for Fortune and fill bowls of mixed
wine for Destiny, I [the Lord] will destine you for
the sword, and you will all bend down for the
slaughter; for I called but you did not answer, I
spoke but you did not listen. You did evil in my
sight and chose what displeases me." *See also*
Ge 6:17; **Ex** 7:13; 9:13–18; **Jos** 11:20; **2Ki**
19:25–26; **Isa** 14:24–27; 19:12–14; 23:9; **Jer**
49:20; 50:45; **1Pe** 2:6–8; **Isa** 8:14–15

Predestination does not set aside human responsibility
Php 2:12–13 Therefore, my [Paul's] dear
friends, as you have always obeyed—not only in
my presence, but now much more in my
absence—continue to work out your salvation
with fear and trembling, for it is God who works
in you to will and to act according to his good
purpose. *See also* **Jn** 6:37,40; **Ac** 13:48
See also assurance; election; prophecy.

---

promises
Binding offers or commitments on the part of one
person or people to another. The value of such
promises depends upon the reliability and
trustworthiness of the person who makes the
promises. Scripture stresses the total reliability of
God, including his promise to bestow his Spirit,
and urges believers to demonstrate the same
trustworthiness in their dealings with one another.

promises, divine
The promises of God reveal his particular and
eternal purposes to which he is unchangeably
committed and upon which believers can totally
depend. These promises are, however, conditional
upon obedience on the part of believers.

God's promises are irrevocable
He is absolutely trustworthy
Nu 23:19 "God is not human, that he should
lie, nor a human being, that he should change his
mind. Does he speak and then not act? Does he

promise and not fulfil?"   *See also* **Tit** 1:2; **Heb** 6:13–18

He is unchanging Ps 110:4; **Mal** 3:6–7; **Jas** 1:17–18

He has the power and will to fulfil his promises

Isa 55:11 ". . . my [the Lᴏʀᴅ's] word that goes out from my mouth: It will not return to me empty, but will accomplish what I desire and achieve the purpose for which I sent it."   *See also* **Ro** 4:21

He is faithful in keeping all his promises Jos 21:45; 23:14–15; **1Ki** 8:56; **Ps** 145:13; **Heb** 10:23

His promises stem from his goodness and glory 2Pe 1:3–4

God may confirm his promises with an oath

Ge 22:15–18 The angel of the Lᴏʀᴅ called to Abraham from heaven a second time and said, "I swear by myself, declares the Lᴏʀᴅ, that because you have done this and have not withheld your son, your only son, I will surely bless you and make your descendants as numerous as the stars in the sky and as the sand on the seashore. Your descendants will take possession of the cities of their enemies, and through your offspring all nations on earth will be blessed, because you have obeyed me."   *See also* **Ge** 26:3; **Isa** 45:23; **Am** 6:8; 8:7

Examples of God's promises through covenant relationship

Ge 9:8–17

With Abraham: **Ge** 15:9–21; 17:1–22; **Heb** 11:8–9, 17–19

Ge 26:3–4

With Jacob: **Ge** 28:13–15; 46:2–4

With Moses and the Israelites: **Ex** 19:1–6; 24:1–8

Nu 25:10–12

With David: **2Sa** 7:5–16 pp 1Ch 17:4–14; **1Ki** 8:15,24

Jer 31:31–34

The grounding of God's promises in Christ

God's promises are fulfilled in Jesus Christ

2Co 1:18–20 . . . For no matter how many promises God has made, they are "Yes" in Christ.

And so through him the "Amen" is spoken by us to the glory of God.   *See also* **Mt** 5:17; **Lk** 4:16–21; **Ac** 2:29–31; 3:21–26; 7:37; **Dt** 18:15–18; **Ac** 13:23,32–34; 26:6–7; **Ro** 1:2–3; 15:8; **Heb** 9:15

Jesus Christ brings superior promises through the new covenant

Heb 8:6–8 But the ministry Jesus has received is as superior to theirs as the covenant of which he is mediator is superior to the old one, and it is founded on better promises . . .   *See also* **Eph** 1:13–14; **Heb** 7:22; 11:13,39–40; **2Pe** 1:1–4

Jesus Christ has the right to make promises on God's behalf

Jn 3:34–35 "For the one whom God has sent speaks the words of God . . . The Father loves the Son and has placed everything in his hands."   *See also* **Jn** 1:1–2,14; 8:25–29; **Heb** 1:1–3

God's promises must be received by believers

They are received by faith

Gal 3:22 But the Scripture declares that the whole world is a prisoner of sin, so that what was promised, being given through faith in Jesus Christ, might be given to those who believe.   *See also* **Jn** 1:12; **Ro** 4:13–16

They are received by perseverance and obedience

Heb 10:36 You [believers] need to persevere so that when you have done the will of God, you will receive what he has promised.   *See also* **Ro** 4:19–24; **2Co** 7:1; **Heb** 6:12

God's promises unite believing Jews and Gentiles

Eph 3:6 This mystery is that through the gospel the Gentiles are heirs together with Israel, members together of one body, and sharers together in the promise in Christ Jesus.   *See also* **Ac** 2:38–39; **Ro** 9:8; **Gal** 3:29; 4:28; **Eph** 2:11–18; **Heb** 11:39–40

Disaster awaits those who reject God's promises Jos 23:12–16; Jn 3:18–20,36; 2Ti 2:11–13; Heb 6:4–12; 2Pe 3:3–10

Particular promises of God in Christ
The gift of the Holy Spirit Lk 24:49; Ac 1:4; 2:33; Eph 1:13
The fulness of life and eternal life 2Ti 1:1; Heb 12:26–28; Jas 1:12; 2:5; 1Jn 2:25
Resurrection Jn 5:29; 11:25–26; 1Co 15:48–57; 2Co 4:14; 1Th 4:16
The forgiveness of sins 1Jn 1:9
The presence of God Ex 3:12; 33:14; Jos 1:9; Isa 58:9; Mt 28:20; Heb 13:5
The peace of God 1Ch 22:9; Ps 85:8; Isa 9:6–7; Ro 5:1; Php 4:4–9
Joy in God Ps 16:11; 132:16; Jn 16:20–24
The knowledge of God Jer 31:33–34; Jn 17:25–26; 1Jn 5:20   *See also covenant; faith; forgiveness; gospel; promises; obedience; peace; prayer, God's promises; prophecy, concerning Jesus Christ.*

promises, human

Believers must be faithful in keeping promises made to others and to God, because they have been called to live in integrity and truth. False or broken promises are considered as sin.

Examples of promises between people
Ge 14:22–24; 21:22–24; 47:29–31; Nu 30:1–16; Jos 2:12–21

Examples of people making promises to God
Ge 28:20–21; Jdg 11:29–40; 1Sa 1:11–20; 2Sa 15:7–12; Ne 10:28–29

Accompaniments to human promises
Taking an oath
Dt 6:13 Fear the LORD your God, serve him only and take your oaths in his name.   *See also* Ge 14:22; 21:24; 47:31; Jos 2:12–14; Ne 10:29
Declaring a curse
2Sa 3:35 . . . David took an oath, saying, "May God deal with me, be it ever so severely, if I taste bread or anything else before the sun sets!"   *See also* Ru 1:17; 1Sa 14:24; 2Sa 3:9–10; 1Ki 2:23; Mt 26:73–75 pp Mk 14:70–72

Instructions regarding human promises
The importance of keeping promises
Nu 30:1–2 ". . . When a man makes a vow to the LORD or takes an oath to bind himself by a pledge, he must not break his word but must do everything he said."   *See also* Ps 50:14; Pr 5:18–23; Mal 2:14–16; Mt 19:4–9
The sin and peril of false promises
Lev 19:12 " 'Do not swear falsely by my name and so profane the name of your God. I am the LORD.' "   *See also* Ex 20:7; Dt 23:21; Jer 8:11–12; Eze 13:1–7,10–12; Zec 8:17; 2Pe 2:17–19
The danger of making promises rashly, lightly or in ignorance
Ecc 5:1–7 . . . Do not be quick with your mouth, do not be hasty in your heart to utter anything before God. God is in heaven and you are on earth, so let your words be few . . .   *See also* Pr 20:25; Mt 14:1–11 pp Mk 6:21–28; Mt 23:16–22

The call of Jesus Christ to integrity and truth in making promises
Mt 5:33–37 ". . . Simply let your 'Yes' be 'Yes', and your 'No', 'No'; anything beyond this comes from the evil one."   *See also* Dt 23:22–23; Ecc 5:2,5   *See also truth.*

prophecy

The disclosing of the will and purposes of God through inspired or Spirit-filled human beings. The OT emphasises the importance of prophecy as a means of knowing God. Many OT prophecies find their fulfilment in Jesus Christ. The NT sets out the place of prophecy in the life of the church and gives guidance concerning the use of this gift.

prophecy, concerning Jesus Christ

The OT points ahead to the person and ministry of Jesus Christ. Christ's fulfilment of OT prophecy is often noted by NT writers as a demonstration of God's faithfulness to his promises of salvation and as confirmation of the divine authority of Jesus Christ.

Jesus Christ fulfils OT prophecy

He fulfils the OT as a whole

Lk 24:27 . . . beginning with Moses and all the Prophets, he [Jesus] explained to them what was said in all the Scriptures concerning himself.   *See also* **Mt** 5:17; **Lk** 24:44; **2Co** 1:20

He fulfils God's promises to Abraham

Gal 3:14 He [Christ] redeemed us in order that the blessing given to Abraham might come to the Gentiles through Christ Jesus . . .   *See also* **Lk** 1:54–55,72–74; **Gal** 3:16

He fulfils God's promises through the prophets

Ac 10:43 "All the prophets testify about him [Jesus] . . ."   *See also* **Mt** 26:56; **Ac** 3:18,24; 13:27; **Ro** 1:2; **1Pe** 1:10

Prophecies about Jesus Christ's birth

Mt 1:23 "The virgin will be with child and will give birth to a son, and they will call him Immanuel"—which means, "God with us."   *See also* **Isa** 7:14; **Mt** 1:21; **Lk** 1:31–32; **Isa** 9:6; **Mt** 2:6–7; **Mic** 5:2; **Mt** 2:15; **Hos** 11:1

Prophecies about Jesus Christ's ministry

He brings good news

Lk 4:17–19 The scroll of the prophet Isaiah was handed to him [Jesus]. Unrolling it, he found the place where it is written: "The Spirit of the Lord is on me, because he has anointed me to preach good news to the poor . . ."   *See also* **Isa** 61:1–2; **Mt** 4:13–16; **Isa** 9:1–2

He divides people and is rejected

Lk 2:34–35 Then Simeon blessed them and said to Mary, his mother: "This child is destined to cause the falling and rising of many in Israel . . ."   *See also* **Mt** 3:11–12 pp **Mk** 1:7–8 pp **Lk** 3:16–17; **Mt** 21:42 pp **Mk** 12:10–11 pp **Lk** 20:17; **Ps** 118:22–23; **Jn** 13:18; **Ps** 41:9

He teaches in parables

Mt 13:35 So was fulfilled what was spoken through the prophet: "I will open my mouth in parables, I will utter things hidden since the creation of the world."   *See also* **Ps** 78:2; **Mt** 13:13–15 pp **Mk** 4:11–12 pp **Lk** 8:10; **Isa** 6:9–10

Prophecies about Jesus Christ's death

The Lord's Supper

Mt 26:28 "This is my [Jesus'] blood of the covenant, which is poured out for many for the forgiveness of sins." pp **Mk** 14:24 pp **Lk** 22:20   *See also* **Isa** 53:12; **Jer** 31:34

The betrayal

Mt 27:9–10 Then what was spoken by Jeremiah the prophet was fulfilled: "They took the thirty silver coins . . ."
Matthew brings together two prophetic passages fulfilled by this incident: **Jer** 19:1–13; **Zec** 11:12–13
Jn 18:9; 6:39

The cross

Mt 27:46 About the ninth hour Jesus cried out in a loud voice, "*Eloi, Eloi, lama sabachthani?*"—which means, "My God, my God, why have you forsaken me?" pp **Mk** 15:34   *See also* **Ps** 22:1; **Mt** 27:35 fn; **Ps** 22:18; **Lk** 23:46; **Ps** 31:5

Prophecies about Jesus Christ's resurrection and ascension

Mt 12:39–40 He answered, "A wicked and adulterous generation asks for a miraculous sign! But none will be given it except the sign of the prophet Jonah. For as Jonah was three days and three nights in the belly of a huge fish, so the Son of Man will be three days and three nights in the heart of the earth." pp **Lk** 11:29–30   *See also* **Jnh** 1:17; **Ac** 2:25–28; **Ps** 16:8–11; **Ac** 2:31; 13:35; 2:34; **Ps** 110:1; **Eph** 4:8; **Ps** 68:18

Prophecies about Jesus Christ's titles

Jesus Christ as Son of God

Ac 13:32–33 ". . . What God promised our ancestors he has fulfilled for us, their children, by raising up Jesus. As it is written in the second Psalm: 'You are my Son; today I have become your Father.'"   *See also* **Ps** 2:7; **Heb** 1:5; 5:5; **Mt** 22:44 pp **Mk** 12:36 pp **Lk** 20:42; **Ps** 110:1; **Heb** 1:8–9; **Ps** 45:6–7

Jesus Christ as Son of Man

Mt 26:64 . . . "But I [Jesus] say to all of you: In the future you will see the Son of Man sitting at the right hand of the Mighty One and coming on the clouds of heaven." pp **Mk** 14:62

pp Lk 22:69   *See also* Da 7:13–14; Mk 8:31 pp Lk 9:22

Jesus Christ as Son of David
Rev 22:16 "I, Jesus, have sent my angel to give you this testimony for the churches. I am the Root and the Offspring of David, and the bright Morning Star." *See also* 2Sa 7:12–16 pp 1Ch 17:11–14; Lk 1:32–33; Isa 9:7; Ac 13:34; Isa 55:3; Ro 15:12; Isa 11:1

Jesus Christ as the coming Messianic king Mt 26:31 pp Mk 14:27; Zec 13:7; Mt 21:4–5; Zec 9:9

Jesus Christ as the suffering servant
Ac 8:32–35 . . . Then Philip began with that very passage of Scripture and told him the good news about Jesus.   *See also* Isa 53:7–8; Mt 12:17–21; Isa 42:1–4

Jesus Christ as the prophet who is to come
Ac 3:22 "For Moses said, 'The Lord your God will raise up for you a prophet like me from among your own people; you must listen to everything his prophet tells you'." *See also* Dt 18:18; Lk 4:18–19; Isa 61:1–2; Jn 6:14

Jesus Christ as priest
Heb 7:21 . . . he [Jesus] became a priest with an oath when God said to him: "The Lord has sworn and will not change his mind: 'You are a priest for ever.'" *See also* Ps 110:4; Heb 5:5–6; 7:17

---

prophecy, in New Testament
The NT describes the prophetic aspect of the ministry of Jesus Christ, and also recognises that prophetic gifts are given to believers through the Holy Spirit. It provides guidance on how such prophetic gifts are to be used.

Jesus Christ recognised as a prophet
Mt 21:11; Mk 6:4; 8:27–28; Lk 7:16; 24:17–19; Jn 4:19

Prophecy in the church
Prophecy is one among many spiritual gifts
1Co 12:28–29 And in the church God has appointed first of all apostles, second prophets, third teachers, then workers of miracles, also those having gifts of healing, those able to help others, those with gifts of administration, and those speaking in different kinds of tongues. Are all apostles? Are all prophets? Are all teachers? Do all work miracles?   *See also* Ro 12:6; 1Co 12:10; Eph 4:11

Not all are called to be prophets 1Co 12:29; Eph 4:11

Prophecy is valueless without love
1Co 13:1–2 If I speak in human or angelic tongues, but have not love, I am only a resounding gong or a clanging cymbal. If I have the gift of prophecy and can fathom all mysteries and all knowledge, and if I have a faith that can move mountains, but have not love, I am nothing.

Prophecy is for the building up of the church
1Co 14:26 What then shall we say, brothers and sisters? When you come together, everyone has a hymn, or a word of instruction, a revelation, a tongue or an interpretation. All of these must be done for the strengthening of the church.   *See also* Ro 12:3–6; 1Co 14:3–5; 1Pe 4:10

Prophecy superior to speaking in tongues
1Co 14:5 I would like every one of you to speak in tongues, but I would rather have you prophesy. Those who prophesy are greater than those who speak in tongues, unless they interpret, so that the church may be edified.

Prophecy in the early church
Ac 2:17; 11:27–28; 15:32; 21:9   *See also* church; preachers and preaching; revelation, New Testament; spiritual gifts.

---

prophecy, Old Testament fulfilment
All divinely inspired prophecy achieves its purpose. Scripture records the fulfilment of many prophecies.

The principle that all prophecy achieves its purpose
Isa 55:10–11 "As the rain and the snow come down from heaven, and do not return to it without watering the earth and making it bud and flourish, so that it yields seed for the sower and bread for the eater, so is my word that goes out from my mouth: It will not return to me empty,

but will accomplish what I desire and achieve the purpose for which I sent it." *See also* Dt 18:22

Fulfilment of prophecy concerning individuals in the OT

1Ki 20:35–36 By the word of the LORD one of the company of the prophets said to his companion, "Strike me with your weapon," but he refused. So the prophet said, "Because you have not obeyed the LORD, as soon as you leave me a lion will kill you." And after the man went away, a lion found him and killed him. *See also* 1Ki 8:15–21 pp 2Ch 6:4–11; 1Ki 8:23–24 pp 2Ch 6:14–15; 1Ki 13:21–22,24–26; 14:12–13, 17–18; 2Ki 1:6,17; 7:1–2,16–18; 22:15–20; 23:30

Fulfilment of prophecy concerning the nation of Israel

1Ki 12:15 . . . this turn of events was from the LORD, to fulfil the word the LORD had spoken to Jeroboam son of Nebat through Ahijah the Shilonite. *See also* 1Ki 11:29–39

Fulfilment of prophecy concerning the royal house

1Ki 15:29 As soon as he [Baasha] began to reign, he killed Jeroboam's whole family. He did not leave Jeroboam anyone that breathed, but destroyed them all, according to the word of the LORD given through his servant Ahijah the Shilonite— *See also* 1Ki 14:7–11; 16:1–7,12; 21:20–29; 2Ki 9:30–10:11,30; 15:12

Fulfilment of prophecy concerning battles

1Ki 20:13–21 Meanwhile a prophet came to Ahab king of Israel and announced, "This is what the LORD says: 'Do you see this vast army? I will give it into your hand today, and then you will know that I am the LORD.'" . . . At that, the Arameans fled, with the Israelites in pursuit. But Ben-hadad king of Aram escaped on horseback with some of his horsemen. The king of Israel advanced and overpowered the horses and chariots and inflicted heavy losses on the Arameans. *See also* 1Ki 22:17,35–38; 2Ki 19:20–37

Fulfilment of prophecy concerning the Babylonian exile
The rise of the Babylonians
Hab 1:6–11 "I am raising up the Babylonians, that ruthless and impetuous people, who sweep across the whole earth to seize dwelling-places not their own . . ." *See also* 2Ch 36:17
The fall of Jerusalem and exile of the population
2Ki 20:17–18 "The time will surely come when everything in your palace, and all that your predecessors have stored up until this day, will be carried off to Babylon. Nothing will be left, says the LORD. And some of your descendants, your own flesh and blood, that will be born to you, will be taken away, and they will become eunuchs in the palace of the king of Babylon." *See also* 2Ki 21:10–15; 24:2,10–16
The fate of King Zedekiah
Jer 21:3–7 "'. . . After that, declares the LORD, I will hand over Zedekiah king of Judah, his officials and the people in this city who survive the plague, sword and famine, to Nebuchadnezzar king of Babylon and to their enemies who seek their lives. He will put them to the sword; he will show them no mercy or pity or compassion.'" *See also* Jer 32:3–5; Eze 12:12–14; 2Ki 25:1–7; Jer 39:1–7
The length of captivity
Jer 29:10 This is what the LORD says: "When seventy years are completed for Babylon, I will come to you and fulfil my gracious promise to bring you back to this place." *See also* 2Ch 36:21; Da 9:2

Fulfilment of prophecy concerning Jesus Christ
Lk 24:44 He [Jesus] said to them [the disciples], "This is what I told you while I was still with you: Everything must be fulfilled that is written about me in the Law of Moses, the Prophets and the Psalms." *See also* Lk 18:31; Ac 3:18

Fulfilment of other prophecy
Ac 2:14–21 Then Peter stood up with the Eleven, raised his voice and addressed the crowd:

"Fellow Jews and all of you who live in Jerusalem, let me explain this to you; listen carefully to what I say. These people are not drunk, as you suppose. It's only nine in the morning! No, this is what was spoken by the prophet Joel: 'In the last days, God says, I will pour out my Spirit on all people. Your sons and daughters will prophesy, your young men will see visions, your old men will dream dreams. Even on my servants, both men and women, I will pour out my Spirit in those days, and they will prophesy . . .'"   *See also* **Joel** 2:28–32; **Jos** 6:26; **1Ki** 16:34; 13:1–3; **2Ki** 23:16–18; **1Ki** 17:14,16; **Mt** 2:17–18; **Jer** 31:15; **Mt** 3:1–3 pp Mk 1:2–4 pp Lk 3:1–6; **Isa** 40:3

Prophecies modified before fulfilment
1Ki 21:20–26 ". . . 'I am going to bring disaster on you. I will consume your descendants . . . because you have provoked me to anger and have caused Israel to sin.' . . ."

1Ki 21:27–29 . . . Then the word of the LORD came to Elijah the Tishbite: "Have you noticed how Ahab has humbled himself before me? Because he has humbled himself, I will not bring this disaster in his day, but I will bring it on his house in the days of his son."

Isa 38:1 In those days Hezekiah became ill and was at the point of death. The prophet Isaiah son of Amoz went to him and said, "This is what the LORD says: Put your house in order, because you are going to die; you will not recover." pp 2Ki 20:1

Isa 38:4–5 Then the word of the LORD came to Isaiah: "Go and tell Hezekiah, 'This is what the LORD, the God of your father David, says: I have heard your prayer and seen your tears; I will add fifteen years to your life.'" pp 2Ki 20:4–6   *See also* prayer, and faith; prayer, answers.

prophecy, Old Testament inspiration
The prophecies of biblical messengers are acknowledged as being of divine origin, inspired through the activity of the Holy Spirit.

God speaks through his prophets
2Pe 1:20–21 Above all, you must understand that no prophecy of Scripture came about by the prophet's own interpretation. For prophecy never had its origin in the human will, but prophets, though human, spoke from God as they were carried along by the Holy Spirit.   *See also* **Ne** 9:30; **Zec** 7:12; **Heb** 1:1

God is the source of prophecy
Eze 24:20–21 So I [Ezekiel] said to them [the exiles], "The word of the LORD came to me: Say to the house of Israel, 'This is what the Sovereign LORD says . . .'"   *See also* **1Sa** 15:10; **2Sa** 7:4; **1Ki** 13:20; 16:1; 17:2; **2Ki** 20:4; **Jer** 1:2; **Eze** 6:1; **Jnh** 1:1; **Hag** 2:10; **Zec** 1:1

Prophets inspired by God speak the truth
Dt 18:22 If what a prophet proclaims in the name of the LORD does not take place or come true, that is a message the LORD has not spoken . . .   *See also* **Jer** 28:9   *See also revelation, Old Testament; Scripture; word of God.*

propitiation
The satisfaction of the righteous demands of God in relation to human sin and its punishment through the sacrificial death of Jesus Christ upon the cross, by which the penalty of sin is cancelled and the anger of God averted. (The NIV is distinctive at this point, in that it generally translates this term by "atonement" and related words.)

The need for propitiation: God's anger against sin
Ps 7:11 God is a righteous judge, a God who expresses his wrath every day.

Ro 2:5 But because of your stubbornness and your unrepentant heart, you are storing up wrath against yourself for the day of God's wrath, when his righteous judgment will be revealed.   *See also* **Ex** 32:11–14; **Nu** 32:8–15; **Dt** 6:14–15; **2Ki** 23:26; **Ps** 78:38; **Isa** 30:27–31; **Da** 9:16–19;

Hos 11:8–9; Mt 25:41–46; Jn 3:36; Ro 1:18; Eph 5:6

The provision of propitiation: Jesus Christ the atoning sacrifice
The promise in the OT
Isa 53:5–6 But he [God's righteous servant] was pierced for our transgressions, he was crushed for our iniquities; the punishment that brought us peace was upon him, and by his wounds we are healed. We all, like sheep, have gone astray, each of us has turned to our own way; and the Lord has laid on him the iniquity of us all. *See also* Isa 53:10–12
The fulfilment in the NT
Ro 3:21–26 . . . God presented him [Jesus] as a sacrifice of atonement, through faith in his blood . . . *See also* Ro 5:9–10; Col 1:21–22; Heb 2:17; 9:11–14; 1Jn 2:2

The motivation for propitiation: God's love
1Jn 4:10 This is love: not that we loved God, but that he loved us and sent his Son as an atoning sacrifice for our sins. *See also* Ps 85:2–3; 103:8–12; Mic 7:18–19; Ro 5:6–8; 2Co 5:19 *See also* atonement; blood, of Jesus Christ; cross; holiness, of God; mercy; reconciliation; sin.

---

providence
The continuing and often unseen activity of God in sustaining his universe, providing for the needs of every creature, and preparing for the completion of his eternal purposes.

God's general providence
God sustains the created order
Ge 8:22 "As long as the earth endures, seedtime and harvest, cold and heat, summer and winter, day and night will never cease." *See also* Ne 9:6; Isa 40:26; Col 1:17; Heb 1:3
All life is dependent on God
1Ti 6:13 In the sight of God, who gives life to everything . . . *See also* 1Sa 1:27; Job 1:21; Ps 127:3; Ecc 3:2; 9:9; Eze 24:16; Da 5:26; Mt 4:4; 10:29

God controls the elements
Ps 147:8 He [the Lord] covers the sky with clouds; he supplies the earth with rain and makes grass grow on the hills. *See also* Job 37:1–13; Ps 29:3–9; 135:6–7; Mt 5:45; Ac 17:25–28
God provides for the created world
Ps 145:15–16 The eyes of all look to you, and you give them their food at the proper time . . . *See also* Job 38:39–41; Ps 104:27–28; 136:25; 147:9; Lk 12:6–7; Ac 14:17; 1Ti 6:17

God's providence through miraculous means
Job 5:9–10 He [God] performs wonders that cannot be fathomed, miracles that cannot be counted. He bestows rain on the earth; he sends water upon the countryside. *See also* Ex 16:11–14; Nu 16:28–35; Jdg 15:18–19; 1Ki 17:5–6; 2Ki 4:42–44

God's providence in human history
God's control of human intentions
Hab 1:12 O Lord, are you not from everlasting? My God, my Holy One, we will not die. O Lord, you have appointed them [the Babylonians] to execute judgment; O Rock, you have ordained them to punish. *See also* 1Ki 22:19–20; 2Ki 19:27–28 pp Isa 37:28–29; Isa 10:15; Hab 1:6
God's providential actions on behalf of individuals
Ro 8:28 And we know that in all things God works for the good of those who love him, who have been called according to his purpose. *See also* Job 1:12; 2:6; Ps 107:12–14,24–29,33–38; Isa 38:17
God's saving purposes fulfilled through providence
Ge 50:20 "You [Joseph's brothers] intended to harm me, but God intended it for good to accomplish what is now being done, the saving of many lives." *See also* Ge 22:13; 45:5–8; 2Ch 36:22–23 pp Ezr 1:1–3; Ezr 6:14; Isa 44:28–45:1; Ac 2:23; 4:27–28; Gal 4:4–5

God's providence prepares for the completion of his ultimate purpose

God is forming a people for himself

Rev 21:3 And I [John] heard a loud voice from the throne saying, "Now the dwelling of God is with human beings, and he will live with them. They will be his people, and God himself will be with them and be their God."   *See also* **Ex** 6:7; **Jer** 31:33; **2Co** 6:16; **Eph** 2:14–16; **1Pe** 1:3–5; **Rev** 7:9

God will bring all things under Jesus Christ's authority

Eph 1:9–10 And he [God] made known to us the mystery of his will according to his good pleasure, which he purposed in Christ, to be put into effect when the times will have reached their fulfilment—to bring all things in heaven and on earth together under one head, even Christ. *See also* **Isa** 45:22–23; 66:23; **1Co** 15:24–26; **Php** 2:10–11; **Col** 1:20; **Rev** 11:15

God will complete his purpose for creation

Ro 8:20–21 . . . the creation itself will be liberated from its bondage to decay and brought into the glorious freedom of the children of God.   *See also* **Isa** 65:17; 66:22; **2Pe** 3:13; **Rev** 21:1

God directs all things for his glory

Ro 11:36 For from him and through him and to him are all things. To him be the glory for ever! Amen.   *See also* **Ps** 46:10; **Ro** 9:23; 11:36; **Eph** 1:4–6,11–12   *See also creation, and God; life.*

---

reconciliation

The restoration of fellowship between God and humanity and the resulting restoration of human relationships. The NT affirms that the reconciliation of the world to God is only possible on the basis of the work of Jesus Christ.

---

reconciliation, between believers

True reconciliation between people is only possible after they have been reconciled to God through Jesus Christ. Believers are urged to settle differences among themselves in brotherly love.

The cause of the breakdown in relationships is sin

Ge 27:41 Esau held a grudge against Jacob because of the blessing his father had given him. He said to himself, "The days of mourning for my father are near; then I will kill my brother Jacob." The division between Joseph and his brothers: **Ge** 37:4–5,18–20

1Sa 15:12–14; **2Sa** 14:28; **Ac** 15:37–40; **Gal** 2:11

Believers should be reconciled to one another

Mt 5:23–24 "Therefore, if you are offering your gift at the altar and there remember that your brother or sister has something against you, leave your gift there in front of the altar. First go and be reconciled to them; then come and offer your gift"   *See also* **Mt** 5:9,25 pp **Lk** 12:58; **Mt** 5:44; 18:15–17,21–35; **Jn** 17:20–23; **Ro** 12:18–21; **2Th** 3:14–15

The death of Jesus Christ should bring believers together in peace

Eph 2:14–22 For he [Christ] himself is our peace, who has made the two one and has destroyed the barrier, the dividing wall of hostility, by abolishing in his flesh the law with its commandments and regulations. His purpose was to create in himself one new humanity out of the two, thus making peace, and in this one body to reconcile both of them to God through the cross, by which he put to death their hostility. He came and preached peace to you who were far away and peace to those who were near. For through him we both have access to the Father by one Spirit . . .

The church should display reconciliation

Col 3:12–15 . . . Bear with each other and forgive whatever grievances you may have against one another. Forgive as the Lord forgave you. And over all these virtues put on love, which binds them all together in perfect unity. Let the peace of Christ rule in your hearts, since as members of one body you were called to peace . . .   *See also* **Ro** 12:18–21; **Eph** 4:32; **2Th** 3:14–15

Examples of reconciliation between people
Ge 33:4 But Esau ran to meet Jacob and embraced him; he threw his arms around his neck and kissed him. And they [Jacob and Esau] wept.   *See also* **Ge** 45:1–5; **Jos** 22:10–34; **Lk** 23:12; **Jn** 21:15–17; **Ac** 9:26–28; **1Co** 7:11
See also fellowship; forgiveness; love.

reconciliation, world to God
On account of sin, people are alienated from God and cut off from fellowship with him. Through Jesus Christ, God reconciles the world to himself, breaking down the barriers of hostility and estrangement.

A broken relationship through sin brings alienation from God
Isa 59:2 . . . your iniquities have separated you from your God; your sins have hidden his face from you, so that he will not hear.   *See also* **Ge** 3:23–24; 4:13–14; **Isa** 48:22; 64:7; **Jer** 33:5; **Lk** 18:13; **Ro** 5:10; 8:7; **Eph** 2:1–3,12; 4:18; **Col** 1:21; **Jas** 4:4

God takes the initiative in bringing about reconciliation
2Co 5:18–19 All this is from God, who reconciled us to himself through Christ and gave us the ministry of reconciliation: that God was reconciling the world to himself in Christ, not counting people's sins against them . . .   *See also* **Ro** 5:6–8; **Gal** 4:4–5; **Eph** 2:4–5; **1Jn** 4:10

The means of reconciliation is the death of Jesus Christ
Ro 5:6 You see, at just the right time, when we were still powerless, Christ died for the ungodly.   *See also* **2Co** 5:18–19,21; **Eph** 2:13,16; **Col** 1:20

The results of reconciliation are both personal and universal
Peace with God
Ro 5:1 Therefore, since we have been justified through faith, we have peace with God through our Lord Jesus Christ,   *See also* **Ac** 10:36–46;

Eph 2:14–19; **Col** 1:21–22
Access to God
Ro 5:2 through whom we have gained access by faith into this grace in which we now stand . . .   *See also* **Eph** 2:18; 3:12; **Heb** 10:19–22
Adoption as God's children Ro 8:15–16; **Gal** 3:26; 4:4–6; **1Jn** 3:1–2
Peacemaking throughout the universe
Col 1:20 . . . through him [Christ] to reconcile to himself all things, whether things on earth or things in heaven, by making peace through his blood, shed on the cross.   *See also* **Ro** 11:15; **Eph** 1:7–10,22–23

Believers are to be the ambassadors of reconciliation
2Co 5:18–20 All this is from God, who reconciled us to himself through Christ and gave us the ministry of reconciliation: that God was reconciling the world to himself in Christ, not counting people's sins against them. And he has committed to us the message of reconciliation . . .   *See also* atonement; blood, of Jesus Christ; creation, renewal; human race, and redemption; justification; redemption; salvation; sin, effects of; world, redeemed.

redemption
The buying back or release of an object or person. In Scripture redemption refers to God's ransoming of believers only through the death of Jesus Christ upon the cross and to all the benefits that this brings.

redemption, in life
The purchase of a person's freedom or the buying back of an object from the possession of another. Scripture provides illustrations of these everyday meanings of the word.

The OT redemption of property, animals and individuals
Redemption of property
Lev 25:24–28 "'. . . If any of your own people become poor and sell some of their

property, their nearest relative is to come and redeem what they have sold . . .'"   *See also* **Lev 27:15–20; Ru 4:1–6; Jer 32:8**

Redemption of animals

Ex 13:13 "Redeem with a lamb every firstborn donkey, but if you do not redeem it, break its [the donkey's] neck . . ."   *See also* **Ex 34:20; Lev 27:13,27; Nu 18:14–17**

Redemption of individuals

Ex 30:12–16 "When you take a census of the Israelites to count them, each one must pay the LORD a ransom for his life at the time he is counted. Then no plague will come on them when you number them . . ."   *See also* **Ex 13:12–13; 21:8,28–32; 34:19–20; Lev 25:47–55; Nu 3:44–51**

The redemption of the nation of Israel

Ex 6:6 "Therefore, say to the Israelites: 'I am the LORD, and I will bring you out from under the yoke of the Egyptians. I will free you from being slaves to them, and I will redeem you with an outstretched arm and with mighty acts of judgment . . ."   *See also* **Dt 9:26; 2Sa 7:23–24** pp **1Ch 17:21–22; Ne 1:10; Ps 77:15; 78:35; 106:10; Isa 43:1–3; Mic 6:4**

Redemption as release from sin

Ps 130:8 He [the LORD] himself will redeem Israel from all their sins.   *See also* **Isa 40:2**

The role of the redeemer

In helping close relatives regain property or freedom

Lev 25:25 "'If any of your own people become poor and sell some of their property, their nearest relative is to come and redeem what they have sold.'"   *See also* **Lev 25:47–49; 27:15–20; Ru 2:20; 3:9; 4:1–8**

In avenging death **Nu 35:12,19–21**   *See also human race, and redemption.*

---

redemption, in New Testament

The culmination of the OT work of redemption is seen in the cross of Jesus Christ, by which believers are liberated from bondage to sin.

Redemption is achieved through Jesus Christ

Eph 1:7 In him [the Lord Jesus Christ] we have redemption through his blood, the forgiveness of sins, in accordance with the riches of God's grace

Jesus Christ's teaching on redemption

Mk 10:45 "For even the Son of Man did not come to be served, but to serve, and to give his life as a ransom for many." pp **Mt 20:28**   *See also* **Mt 26:26–28** pp **Mk 14:22–25** pp **Lk 22:20–22**

Apostolic teaching on redemption

Jesus Christ is the redemption of believers

1Co 1:30 It is because of him that you are in Christ Jesus, who has become for us wisdom from God—that is, our righteousness, holiness and redemption.   *See also* **1Ti 2:6; Tit 2:14**

Redemption comes through the shedding of the blood of Jesus Christ

Gal 3:13 Christ redeemed us from the curse of the law by becoming a curse for us, for it is written: "Cursed is everyone who is hung on a tree."   *See also* **Ac 20:28; Ro 3:25; 1Co 6:20; 7:23; 11:23–25; 1Pe 1:18–19; Heb 9:12; Rev 1:5–6; 5:9**

The results of redemption

Forgiveness of sin

Col 1:13–14 For he [Christ] has rescued us from the dominion of darkness and brought us into the kingdom of the Son he loves, in whom we have redemption, the forgiveness of sins.

Justification and freedom from the law

Gal 3:8–10 The Scripture foresaw that God would justify the Gentiles by faith, and announced the gospel in advance to Abraham: "All nations will be blessed through you." So those who have faith are blessed along with Abraham, the man of faith. All who rely on observing the law are under a curse, for it is written: "Cursed is everyone who does not continue to do everything written in the Book of the Law."   *See also* **Ro 3:23–25; Gal 4:5**

Inclusion in the covenant

Gal 3:14 He [Christ] redeemed us in order that the blessing given to Abraham might come to the

Gentiles through Christ Jesus, so that by faith we might receive the promise of the Spirit.
See also **Heb** 9:15

Freedom to live a new life
Gal 4:4–7 But when the time had fully come, God sent his Son, born of a woman, born under law, to redeem those under law, that we might receive adoption as God's children. Because you are his children, he sent the Spirit of his Son into our hearts, the Spirit who calls out, "*Abba, Father.*" So you are no longer slaves, but God's children; and since you are his children, he has made you also heirs.   See also **1Co** 6:19–20; 7:22–24; **Col** 1:13; **Tit** 2:14; **Heb** 9:14; **Rev** 1:5–6; 5:9–10

Creation and believers await final redemption
Ro 8:19–23 The creation waits in eager expectation for the children of God to be revealed. For the creation was subjected to frustration, not by its own choice, but by the will of the one who subjected it, in hope that the creation itself will be liberated from its bondage to decay and brought into the glorious freedom of the children of God . . .   See also **Lk** 21:28; **Ac** 3:21; **Eph** 1:14; 4:30   See also blood, of Jesus Christ; forgiveness; gospel; heaven, community of redeemed; justification; Lord's Supper; world, redeemed.

---

redemption, in Old Testament
The act of God by which he delivered his people from bondage. The exodus of Israel from Egypt and the later deliverance of Jerusalem from exile in Babylon are seen as definitive examples of God's redeeming acts.

God is the Redeemer of his people
God redeems his people from captivity out of love
Dt 7:8 But it was because the LORD loved you and kept the oath he swore to your ancestors that he brought you out with a mighty hand and redeemed you from the land of slavery, from the power of Pharaoh king of Egypt.   See also **Ex** 6:6–8; 15:13; **Ps** 130:7–8; **Isa** 43:14; 47:1–4; 63:16; **Jer** 15:21; 31:11; 50:34

His redemption guarantees security
Isa 43:1–4 But now, this is what the LORD says—he who created you, O Jacob, he who formed you, O Israel: "Fear not, for I have redeemed you; I have summoned you by name; you are mine. When you pass through the waters, I will be with you; and when you pass through the rivers, they will not sweep over you. When you walk through the fire, you will not be burned; the flames will not set you ablaze. For I am the LORD, your God, the Holy One of Israel, your Saviour; I give Egypt for your ransom, Cush and Seba in your stead. Since you are precious and honoured in my sight, and because I love you, I will give nations in exchange for you, and peoples in exchange for your life."   See also **Isa** 44:21–28; 48:20; 49:7,22–26; 52:9–12

He redeems from death
Ps 49:15 But God will redeem my life from the grave; he will surely take me to himself . . .
See also **Job** 5:20; 19:25–26; **Hos** 13:14

His redemption is associated with his holiness
Isa 41:14 "Do not be afraid, O worm Jacob, O little Israel, for I myself will help you," declares the LORD, your Redeemer, the Holy One of Israel.   See also **Isa** 43:14; 47:4; 48:17; 49:7; 54:5

He redeems by his mighty arm
Lk 1:51 "He [the LORD] has performed mighty deeds with his arm; he has scattered those who are proud in their inmost thoughts."   See also **Dt** 11:2; **Ps** 89:10; 77:15; **Isa** 62:8   See also holiness, of God.

---

regeneration
The radical renewal of a person's inner being by the work of God's Spirit.

The need for regeneration
Jn 3:3 In reply [to Nicodemus] Jesus declared, "I tell you the truth, no-one can see the kingdom of God without being born again."   See also **Eph** 2:1,5; **Col** 2:13

Regeneration is a work of God
It originates in God the Father
Jn 1:12–13 Yet to all who received him [the Word], to those who believed in his name, he gave the right to become children of God— children born not of natural descent, nor of human decision or a husband's will, but born of God.
It is made possible by the resurrection of Jesus Christ
1Pe 1:3 Praise be to the God and Father of our Lord Jesus Christ! In his great mercy he has given us new birth into a living hope through the resurrection of Jesus Christ from the dead, *See also* **Eph 2:4–5**
It occurs through the hearing of the Christian gospel
Jas 1:18 He chose to give us birth through the word of truth, that we might be a kind of firstfruits of all he created. *See also* **1Pe 1:23–25**
It is effected by God's Spirit
Jn 3:5–8 Jesus answered [Nicodemus], "I tell you the truth, no-one can enter the kingdom of God without being born of water and the Spirit. Flesh gives birth to flesh, but the Spirit gives birth to spirit. You should not be surprised at my saying, 'You must be born again.' The wind blows wherever it pleases. You hear its sound, but you cannot tell where it comes from or where it is going. So it is with everyone born of the Spirit." *See also* **Jn 6:63; Tit 3:5**

Regeneration is given to those who believe in Jesus Christ
1Jn 5:1 Everyone who believes that Jesus is the Christ is born of God, and everyone who loves the father loves his child as well.

Baptism is the sign of regeneration
Jn 3:5 Jesus answered [Nicodemus], "I tell you the truth, no-one can enter the kingdom of God without being born of water and the Spirit." *See also* **Ac 2:38–39; Eph 5:25–26; Tit 3:5**

The results of regeneration
Entry into God's kingdom
Jn 3:5 Jesus answered [Nicodemus], "I tell you the truth, no-one can enter the kingdom of God without being born of water and the Spirit."
A new holiness of life
1Jn 3:9 Those who are born of God will not continue to sin, because God's seed remains in them; they cannot go on sinning, because they have been born of God. *See also* **1Jn 5:18; 1Pe 2:1–2**
Love for other people
1Jn 4:7 Dear friends, let us love one another, for love comes from God. Everyone who loves has been born of God and knows God. *See also* **1Jn 5:2**
Victory over the world's sinful pattern of life
1Jn 5:4 for everyone born of God overcomes the world. This is the victory that has overcome the world, even our faith. *See also* assurance; conversion, nature of; faith, and salvation; forgiveness, divine; repentance, importance; sin.

repentance
A change of mind leading to a change of action. It involves a sincere turning from sin to serve God and includes sorrow for, and confession of, sin and where possible restitution.

repentance, examples
Scripture provides examples to illustrate the importance of repentance for individuals and communities.

The repentance of individuals
The call to personal repentance
Ac 2:38 Peter replied, "Repent and be baptised, every one of you, in the name of Jesus Christ for the forgiveness of your sins. And you will receive the gift of the Holy Spirit." *See also* **2Ti 2:19**
Examples of individual repentance Nu 22:31–35; **2Sa** 24:10 pp 1Ch 21:8; **1Ki** 21:27–29; **2Ki** 22:19; **Job** 42:6; **Ps** 51:1–17; **Lk** 15:21; 18:13; **Mt** 26:75 pp Mk 14:72 pp Lk 22:61–62; **Jn** 21:15–17; **Ac** 8:22–24

Corporate repentance
Examples of corporate repentance
Jer 18:7–8 "If at any time I [the LORD]

announce that a nation or kingdom is to be uprooted, torn down and destroyed, and if that nation I warned repents of its evil, then I will relent and not inflict on it the disaster I had planned."

Mt 3:1–6 . . . People went out to him [John] from Jerusalem and all Judea and the whole region of the Jordan. Confessing their sins, they were baptised by him in the Jordan River. pp Mk 1:1–6 pp Lk 3:1–6   *See also* **Nu** 21:7; **Jdg** 10:15–16; **1Sa** 7:3–4; **Isa** 19:22; **Ac** 9:32–35

Leaders encouraged corporate repentance
Ezr 10:1 While Ezra was praying and confessing, weeping and throwing himself down before the house of God, a large crowd of Israelites—men, women and children—gathered round him. They too wept bitterly.   *See also* **2Ki** 23:1–7; **2Ch** 15:8–15; 30:6–9; **Ezr** 10:10–12; **Jnh** 3:6–8

Corporate repentance within the church
Rev 2:4–5 "Yet I [Jesus] hold this against you [the church in Ephesus]: You have forsaken your first love. Remember the height from which you have fallen! Repent and do the things you did at first. If you do not repent, I will come to you and remove your lampstand from its place."   *See also* **2Co** 7:9–11; **Rev** 2:14–16,20–22; 3:3,19–20

Symbols of repentance
1Ki 21:27 When Ahab heard these words, he tore his clothes, put on sackcloth and fasted. He lay in sackcloth and went around meekly.
Jnh 3:5 The Ninevites believed God. They declared a fast, and all of them, from the greatest to the least, put on sackcloth.   *See also* **1Sa** 7:6; **Ezr** 8:21; **Ne** 9:1; **Jer** 36:9; **Joel** 1:13–14; 2:12   *See also church; conversion; preaching, effects.*

---

repentance, importance

Repentance is of central importance because sin brings God's judgment and fellowship with God is only possible through full and sincere repentance. God, through his servants, calls people to repent as the only way to escape the judgment and receive the forgiveness and restoration which he offers.

The call to repentance
Lk 5:32 "I [Jesus] have not come to call the righteous, but sinners to repentance."

Jas 5:19–20 . . . remember this: Those who turn sinners from the error of their ways will save them from death and cover over a multitude of sins.   *See also* **Jer** 25:4–6; **Eze** 33:7–9; **Mk** 1:4 pp **Lk** 3:3; **Lk** 24:47; **2Ti** 2:24–26

Repentance opens the way for blessing
It is the only way to escape God's judgment
Eze 18:30–32 ". . . Repent! Turn away from all your offences; then sin will not be your downfall. Rid yourselves of all the offences you have committed, and get a new heart and a new spirit. Why will you die, O house of Israel? For I take no pleasure in the death of anyone, declares the Sovereign Lord. Repent and live!"   *See also* **Job** 36:12; **Jer** 18:7–8; 26:3; **Hos** 11:5; **Jnh** 3:10; **Lk** 3:8–9; **Rev** 2:5

It prepares the way for God's kingdom
Mt 4:17 From that time on Jesus began to preach, "Repent, for the kingdom of heaven is near." pp **Mk** 1:14–15   *See also* **Mt** 3:2

It brings forgiveness and restoration
2Ch 7:13–14 ". . . if my people, who are called by my name, will humble themselves and pray and seek my face and turn from their wicked ways, then will I [the Lord] hear from heaven and will forgive their sin and will heal their land."

Isa 55:7 Let the wicked forsake their ways and the unrighteous their thoughts. Let them turn to the Lord, and he will have mercy on them, and to our God, for he will freely pardon.   *See also* **Dt** 30:1–10; **Ne** 1:8–9; **Job** 22:23–25; 36:10–11; **Isa** 44:22; **Ac** 2:38–39; 3:19; 5:31; 11:18

God desires that all people should repent
He wants everyone to be saved
Eze 18:23 "Do I take any pleasure in the death of the wicked? declares the Sovereign Lord. Rather, am I not pleased when they turn from their ways and live?"

His patience with the unrepentant
2Pe 3:9 The Lord is not slow in keeping his promise, as some understand slowness. He is patient with you, not wanting anyone to perish, but everyone to come to repentance.   *See also* **Isa 65:2; Ro 2:4; Rev 2:21**

His discipline encourages repentance
Jer 31:18–20 "I [the LORD] have surely heard Ephraim's moaning: 'You disciplined me like an unruly calf, and I have been disciplined. Restore me, and I will return, because you are the LORD my God . . .'"   *See also* **Isa 10:20–21; 19:22; Hos 2:6–7; 6:1**

Taking God's opportunity for repentance
Isa 55:6 Seek the LORD while he may be found; call on him while he is near.

Ac 17:30–31 "In the past God overlooked such ignorance, but now he commands all people everywhere to repent. For he has set a day when he will judge the world with justice by the man he has appointed . . ."   *See also* **Heb 3:13–15; 4:7; Ps 95:7–8**

Refusing God's opportunity for repentance
Examples of those who refuse to repent
Jer 35:15 " 'Again and again I [the LORD] sent all my servants the prophets to you. They said, "Each of you must turn from your wicked ways and reform your actions; do not follow other gods to serve them. Then you shall live in the land I have given to you and your ancestors." But you have not paid attention or listened to me.'"
See also **Jer 5:3; Mt 11:20; 21:32; Rev 9:20–21; 16:9–11**
God confirms those who refuse to repent in their hardness of heart Mt 13:14–15 pp Mk 4:11–12 pp Lk 8:9–10; Ac 28:25–27; Isa 6:10

Repentance may not remove the effects of human sin
Nu 14:39–45; 1Sa 15:24–26; **2Sa** 12:13–14; **Heb 12:16–17**   *See also forgiveness; gospel, requirements; judgment, God's; kingdom of God; mercy.*

---

repentance, nature of

Scripture stresses the necessity of repentance from sin if individuals and communities are to have full fellowship with God. It also uses the term to refer to God's relenting of sending judgment on his people, usually in response to human repentance.

Repentance is a requirement for fellowship with God

2Ki 17:13 The LORD warned Israel and Judah through all his prophets and seers: "Turn from your evil ways. Observe my commands and decrees, in accordance with the entire Law that I commanded your ancestors to obey and that I delivered to you through my servants the prophets."

1Th 1:9 . . . you turned to God from idols to serve the living and true God,   *See also* **Ps 34:14; Isa 55:7; Ac 14:15; Jas 4:7–10**

Repentance involves turning from sin

Sorrow for sin

Ps 51:17 The sacrifices of God are a broken spirit; a broken and contrite heart, O God, you will not despise.

2Co 7:8–10 . . . your sorrow led you to repentance. For you became sorrowful as God intended . . . Godly sorrow brings repentance that leads to salvation and leaves no regret . . .   *See also* **Job 42:6; Ps 34:18; Isa 57:15; 66:2; Joel 2:12–13; Lk 18:13**

Confession of sin

Lk 15:18–19 ". . . 'I [the prodigal son] will set out and go back to my father and say to him: Father, I have sinned against heaven and against you' . . ."   *See also* **Lev 5:5; Ps 51:1–3; Pr 28:13; Hos 14:1–2**

Forsaking specific sins Ezr 10:10–11; Eze 14:6; Ac 15:19–20

Making appropriate restitution Nu 5:6–7; Lk 19:8

Repentance involves turning to God
Faith in God
Isa 30:15 This is what the Sovereign LORD, the Holy One of Israel, says: "In repentance and rest is your salvation, in quietness and trust is your strength, but you would have none of it." *See also* Lk 22:32; Ac 11:21; 20:21; 26:18
Obedience
Eze 18:21–23 "But if the wicked turn away from all the sins they have committed and keep all my [the LORD's] decrees and do what is just and right, they will surely live; they will not die . . ." *See also* Mal 3:7–10
Repentance demonstrated by actions
Ac 26:20 ". . . I [Paul] preached that they should repent and turn to God and prove their repentance by their deeds." *See also* Isa 1:16–17; Da 4:27; Mt 3:8 pp Lk 3:8; Lk 3:10–14

Repentance must be sincere
Jer 3:10 ". . . Judah did not return to me with all her heart, but only in pretence," declares the LORD.

Jer 24:7 "I will give them a heart to know me, that I am the LORD. They will be my people, and I will be their God, for they will return to me with all their heart.'" *See also* 1Ki 8:46–50 pp 2Ch 6:36–39; Ps 78:34–37; Hos 6:1–4

The repentance of God
Jer 26:3 "Perhaps they [Judah] will listen and each will turn from their evil ways. Then I [the LORD] will relent and not bring on them the disaster I was planning because of the evil they have done." *See also* Ex 32:14; Ps 106:45; Hos 11:8; Joel 2:13; Am 7:1–6 *See also* faith; obedience; sin.

---

resurrection
The raising of Jesus Christ from the dead by God after his suffering and death on the cross. Historical evidence for his resurrection includes the empty tomb and the appearance of the risen Christ to the disciples. It has significance both in relation to the identity of Jesus Christ and the future hope of believers.

---

resurrection, of believers
The future event of finally being raised to glory with Jesus Christ. Believers may rest assured that, on account of their faith, they will share in the resurrection and glory of Christ and be with him for ever.

The nature of the resurrection of believers
A resurrection to eternal life
Jn 11:25–26 . . . "I [Jesus] am the resurrection and the life. Those who believe in me will live, even though they die; and whoever lives and believes in me will never die . . ." *See also* Da 12:3; Lk 20:35–36; Jn 5:24–25
Being completely united to Jesus Christ
Ro 6:5 If we have been united with him like this in his death, we will certainly also be united with him in his resurrection. *See also* Jn 6:39,44; Ac 26:23; Ro 6:8; 1Co 6:14; 15:20–23; 2Co 4:14; Col 3:4; 1Th 4:16; 2Ti 2:11
It leads to becoming like Jesus Christ
1Co 15:49 And just as we have borne the likeness of the earthly, so shall we bear the likeness of the heavenly. *See also* Ps 17:15; Mt 22:24–30 pp Mk 12:18–25; 1Co 15:51–53; Php 3:21; 1Jn 3:2

The resurrection as the future hope of believers
1Co 15:19 If only for this life we have hope in Christ, we are to be pitied more than all people.

1Th 4:13–14 Brothers and sisters, we do not want you to be ignorant about those who fall asleep, or to grieve like the rest, who have no hope. We believe that Jesus died and rose again and so we believe that God will bring with Jesus those who have fallen asleep in him. *See also* Job 19:23–27; Ps 49:15; 71:20; Isa 26:19;

Da 12:3; **Hos** 13:14; **Jn** 11:24; **Ac** 23:6; 24:15; 2Co 5:1–4; **2Ti** 1:10

The resurrection as an incentive to godliness and perseverance

1Co 15:58 Therefore, my dear brothers and sisters, stand firm. Let nothing move you. Always give yourselves fully to the work of the Lord, because you know that your labour in the Lord is not in vain.   *See also* **Lk** 14:12–14; **1Co** 15:30–32; **2Co** 5:6–10; **Php** 1:20–21; **Heb** 11:35; 1Jn 3:3

The resurrection as an incentive to endurance of suffering

Ro 8:17 Now if we are children, then we are heirs—heirs of God and co-heirs with Christ, if indeed we share in his sufferings in order that we may also share in his glory.

2Ti 2:11–12 Here is a trustworthy saying: If we died with him, we will also live with him; if we endure, we will also reign with him . . . *See also* **Jn** 12:24–25; **Ac** 14:22; **1Pe** 4:12–13 *See also heaven, inheritance; hope, as confidence.*

resurrection, of Jesus Christ

The resurrection of Jesus Christ is of central importance to the NT. It affirms the divinity of Jesus Christ, marks the words and deeds of his ministry with God's seal of approval and opens the way to the future resurrection of believers.

Jesus Christ's resurrection was foreshadowed in the OT

In Abraham and Isaac: **Ge** 22:5; **Heb** 11:19
In Jonah: **Jnh** 1:17; 2:10; **Mt** 12:40

Jesus Christ's resurrection was predicted
In the OT

1Co 15:3–4 For what I [Paul] received I passed on to you as of first importance: that Christ died for our sins according to the Scriptures, that he was buried, that he was raised on the third day according to the Scriptures,   *See also* **Isa** 53:11; **Hos** 6:2; **Lk** 24:45–46; **Ac** 2:25–31;

13:35; **Ps** 16:8–11; **Ac** 13:34; 26:22–23
By Jesus Christ himself

Mt 16:21 From that time on Jesus began to explain to his disciples that he must go to Jerusalem and suffer many things at the hands of the elders, chief priests and teachers of the law, and that he must be killed and on the third day be raised to life. pp **Mk** 8:31 pp **Lk** 9:22   *See also* **Mt** 17:9 pp **Mk** 9:9; **Mt** 20:18–19 pp **Mk** 10:32–34 pp **Lk** 18:31–33; **Mt** 26:32 pp **Mk** 14:28; **Jn** 2:19–21

Jesus Christ's resurrection was anticipated by the raising of the dead
In the OT

Heb 11:35 Women received back their dead, raised to life again. Others were tortured and refused to be released, so that they might gain a better resurrection.   *See also* **1Ki** 17:22; **2Ki** 4:35; 13:21
In the miracles of Jesus Christ

Lk 7:22 So he [Jesus] replied to the messengers, "Go back and report to John what you have seen and heard . . . the dead are raised . . ." pp **Mt** 11:4–5   *See also* **Mt** 9:23–25 pp **Mk** 5:38–42; **Mt** 27:52–53; **Lk** 7:14–15; **Jn** 11:43–44

The sequence of events in Jesus Christ's resurrection
It was preceded by suffering and death

Php 2:8–9 And being found in appearance as a human being, he [Jesus] humbled himself and became obedient to death—even death on a cross! Therefore God exalted him to the highest place and gave him the name that is above every name,   *See also* **Jn** 19:28–33; **Heb** 2:9
It took place on the first day of the week **Jn** 20:1–2 pp **Mt** 28:1–2 pp **Mk** 16:2–4 pp **Lk** 24:1–3
It was announced by angels

Mt 28:5–6 The angel said to the women, "Do not be afraid, for I know that you are looking for Jesus, who was crucified. He is not here; he has risen, just as he said. Come and see the place where he lay." pp **Mk** 16:5–6 pp **Lk** 24:4–6 *See also* **Lk** 24:23; **1Ti** 3:16

The disciples were reluctant to believe it
Lk 24:25—26 He [Jesus] said to them, "How
foolish you are, and how slow of heart to believe
all that the prophets have spoken! Did not the
Christ have to suffer these things and then enter
his glory?"   *See also* **Mk** 16:13—14; **Lk** 24:11;
Jn 20:24—25
**The disciples saw the evidence and were
ultimately convinced**
Jn 2:22 After Jesus [Jesus] was raised from the
dead, his disciples recalled what he had said. Then
they believed the Scripture and the words that
Jesus had spoken.   *See also* **Lk** 24:33—35; **Jn**
20:8,18,26—28; **Ac** 2:32; 3:15; 4:33
The risen Christ appeared to many people
Ac 1:3 After his suffering, he [Jesus] showed himself
to them and gave many convincing proofs that he
was alive. He appeared to them over a period of forty
days and spoke about the kingdom of God.
To the disciples: **Mt** 28:16—17; **Mk** 16:14; **Lk**
24:50—52; **Jn** 20:19—23,26—31; 21:1—2; **Ac** 1:9—11
To Mary Magdalene: **Mk** 16:9; **Jn** 20:11—18
Lk 24:13—15
To Peter: **Lk** 24:34; **1Co** 15:5
To Paul: **Ac** 9:3—5 pp Ac 22:6—8 pp Ac 26:12—15;
1Co 15:8
Ac 10:39—41; **1Co** 15:6—7
**The resurrection was followed by Jesus
Christ's entry into glory**
Ro 8:34 . . . Christ Jesus, who died—more
than that, who was raised to life—is at the
right hand of God and is also interceding for
us.   *See also* **1Co** 15:24—29; **Eph** 1:18—21; **1Ti**
3:16; **Heb** 1:3; **Rev** 1:18

**Jesus Christ's resurrection body was
spiritual but not ghostly**
Lk 24:37—39 They [the disciples] were startled
and frightened, thinking they saw a ghost. He
said to them, "Why are you troubled, and why
do doubts rise in your minds? Look at my hands
and my feet. It is I myself! Touch me and see; a
ghost does not have flesh and bones, as you see
I have."   *See also* **Jn** 20:27; **Ac** 1:4; **1Co** 15:50;
Php 3:21   *See also evangelism, nature of; gospel,
foundation; prophecy, concerning Jesus Christ; prophecy,
Old Testament fulfilment.*

resurrection, of the dead

Scripture speaks of a general resurrection of all
people at the end of time, which will be followed
by judgment.

**The resurrection of the dead predicted
in the OT**
Da 12:2 "Multitudes who sleep in the dust of
the earth will awake: some to everlasting life,
others to shame and everlasting contempt."
By Jesus Christ
Jn 5:28—29 "Do not be amazed at this, for a
time is coming when all who are in their graves
will hear his [the Son of God's] voice and come
out—those who have done good will rise to live,
and those who have done evil will rise to be
condemned."

**The resurrection of the dead will occur
at Jesus Christ's return**
Rev 20:12—13 And I [John] saw the dead,
great and small, standing before the throne, and
books were opened. Another book was opened,
which is the book of life. The dead were judged
according to what they had done as recorded in
the books . . .   *See also* **Ac** 17:31; **1Co** 15:52;
1Th 4:16

**The resurrection of the dead includes
both the righteous and wicked**
Ac 24:15 ". . . there will be a resurrection of
both the righteous and the wicked."   *See also*
Mt 25:31—32

**Attitudes to the resurrection of the
dead**
Denial by false teachers
1Co 15:12 But if it is preached that Christ has
been raised from the dead, how can some of you
say that there is no resurrection of the dead?
See also **Mt** 22:23 pp Mk 12:18 pp Lk 20:27; **Ac**
23:8; **2Ti** 2:18
Ridicule from unbelievers Ac 17:18,32
Unbelief
Ac 26:8 "Why should any of you consider it
incredible that God raises the dead?"   *See also*

Mt 22:29–32 pp Mk 12:24–27 pp Lk 20:34–38;
1Co 15:35–44   *See also last things.*

---

resurrection, significance of Jesus Christ's

Jesus Christ's resurrection represents a demonstration of the power of God, the confirmation of the divinity of Jesus Christ and the grounds of hope for Christian believers.

Jesus Christ's resurrection was a demonstration of God's power
The power of God the Father
Eph 1:18–20 I [Paul] pray also that the eyes of your heart may be enlightened in order that you may know . . . his incomparably great power for us who believe. That power is like the working of his mighty strength, which he exerted in Christ when he raised him from the dead . . .   *See also* **Mt** 22:29–32; **Ac** 2:24; 3:15; 10:40; 13:29–30; **Gal** 1:1; **Col** 2:12
The power of the Holy Spirit Ro 1:4; **1Ti** 3:16; **1Pe** 3:18

The resurrection confirmed Jesus Christ as the Son of God
Jn 20:30–31 Jesus did many other miraculous signs . . . But these are written that you may believe that Jesus is the Christ, the Son of God . . .
Ro 1:4 and who through the Spirit of holiness was declared with power to be the Son of God, by his resurrection from the dead: Jesus Christ our Lord.   *See also* **Ps** 2:7; **Ac** 13:33

The centrality of the resurrection of Jesus Christ
As the basis of faith
1Co 15:14–15 And if Christ has not been raised, our preaching is useless and so is your faith. More than that, we are then found to be false witnesses about God, for we have testified about God that he raised Christ from the dead . . .   *See also* **Ac** 3:15; 4:33; 17:18; 24:21; **Ro** 10:9; **2Ti** 2:8; **Heb** 6:1–2

As the basis of believers' justification **Ro** 4:25; 8:34
As the basis of Christian hope **Ac** 24:15; **1Co** 15:19
As the basis of believers' resurrection
1Co 15:20–23 But Christ has indeed been raised from the dead, the firstfruits of those who have fallen asleep. For since death came through a human being, the resurrection of the dead comes also through a human being. For as in Adam all die, so in Christ all will be made alive. But in this order: Christ, the firstfruits; then, when he comes, those who belong to him.   *See also* **Jn** 14:19; **Ac** 26:23; **Ro** 8:11   *See also faith; gospel; hope.*

---

resurrection, spiritual

The gospel brings new life to men and women, who lived in death and darkness until they came to faith. The NT emphasis upon "being made alive in Christ" is closely linked to the resurrection of Jesus Christ.

Being made alive in Christ
Eph 2:1 As for you [Ephesian believers], you were dead in your transgressions and sins,

Eph 2:4–6 But because of his great love for us, God, who is rich in mercy, made us alive with Christ even when we were dead in transgressions—it is by grace you have been saved. And God raised us up with Christ . . .
See also **Eze** 37:1–14

Crossing over from death to life
Jn 5:24–26 "I [Jesus] tell you the truth, those who hear my word and believe him who sent me have eternal life and will not be condemned; they have crossed over from death to life. I tell you the truth, a time is coming and has now come when the dead will hear the voice of the Son of God and those who hear will live. For as the Father has life in himself, so he has granted the Son to have life in himself."   *See also* **Ro** 6:3–5; **1Co** 15:17; **Col** 2:13

Believers continue to live by the power of the risen Christ

Php 4:13 I [Paul] can do everything through him who gives me strength.   *See also* **2Co** 5:17; **Gal** 2:20; **Php** 3:10

Results of being made alive in Christ
Spiritual desires

Col 3:1–2 Since, then, you have been raised with Christ, set your hearts on things above, where Christ is seated at the right hand of God . . .

Spiritual assurance

Col 3:3–4 For you [Colossian believers] died, and your life is now hidden with Christ in God. When Christ, who is your life, appears, then you also will appear with him in glory.   *See also* **Jn** 5:24

Spiritual appetite

1Pe 2:1–3 Therefore, rid yourselves of all malice and all deceit, hypocrisy, envy, and slander of every kind. Like newborn babies, crave pure spiritual milk, so that by it you may grow up in your salvation, now that you have tasted that the Lord is good.   *See also* **Jn** 3:3,6

Commitment to God

Ro 6:13 Do not offer the parts of your body to sin, as instruments of wickedness, but rather offer yourselves to God, as those who have been brought from death to life; and offer the parts of your body to him as instruments of righteousness.

Love for fellow believers

1Jn 3:14 We know that we have passed from death to life, because we love each other . . .

Spiritual character

Ro 7:4 So, my brothers and sisters, you also died to the law through the body of Christ, that you might belong to another, to him who was raised from the dead, in order that we might bear fruit to God.   *See also* **Gal** 5:22–23   *See also assurance, basis of; life; love; regeneration; spiritual growth.*

---

revelation

The making known of God's person, nature and deeds, in Scripture, history and supremely the person of Jesus Christ. God is also made known, to a limited yet important extent, through his creation.

---

revelation, creation

The creation bears witness to the wisdom and power of its creator. This natural knowledge of God is limited in its extent, but is sufficient to convince human beings of the existence of God and the need to respond to him.

The creation bears witness to its creator

Ps 19:1–6 The heavens declare the glory of God; the skies proclaim the work of his hands. Day after day they pour forth speech; night after night they display knowledge. There is no speech or language where their voice is not heard. Their voice goes out into all the earth, their words to the ends of the world . . .   *See also* **Job** 36:22–37:18; **Am** 4:13; **Ac** 14:15–17

All human beings have a natural awareness of God

Ro 2:14–15 . . . when Gentiles, who do not have the law, do by nature things required by the law, they are a law for themselves, even though they do not have the law, since they show that the requirements of the law are written on their hearts, their consciences also bearing witness, and their thoughts now accusing, now even defending them . . .   *See also* **Ac** 17:22–31

The limitations of a natural knowledge of God

Ro 1:18–21 . . . For since the creation of the world God's invisible qualities—his eternal power and divine nature—have been clearly seen, being understood from what has been made, so that they are without excuse. For although they knew God, they neither glorified him as God nor gave thanks to him, but their thinking became futile and their foolish hearts were darkened.   *See also* **Ro** 1:32; **1Co** 1:20–21   *See also knowing God, nature of.*

revelation, necessity

Finiteness and sin make it impossible to gain adequate knowledge of God through human effort alone. God in mercy makes himself known through the incarnation of the Son and the illumination of human minds to understand him.

The impossibility of fully knowing God without revelation

God is beyond unaided human knowing

Jn 1:18 No-one has ever seen God, but God the One and Only, who is at the Father's side, has made him known.   *See also* **Ex** 33:20; **Isa** 55:8–9; **Jn** 6:46; **1Jn** 4:12

The human mind is limited

Job 11:7 "Can you [Job] fathom the mysteries of God? Can you probe the limits of the Almighty?"   *See also* **Job** 9:4,10; 23:3–9; 26:14; 36:26; 37:5,23; **Ps** 139:6; 145:3; **Ecc** 3:11; **Isa** 40:13–14,28; **Ro** 11:33

The human mind cannot discern God of its own accord

2Co 4:4 The god of this age has blinded the minds of unbelievers, so that they cannot see the light of the gospel of the glory of Christ, who is the image of God.   *See also* **Jn** 1:5; **Ro** 1:18–32; **1Co** 1:21; 2:14; **2Co** 3:14; **Eph** 4:17–18

God is known fully only through Jesus Christ

Heb 1:1–2 In the past God spoke to our ancestors through the prophets at many times and in various ways, but in these last days he has spoken to us by his Son, whom he appointed heir of all things, and through whom he made the universe.

1Jn 5:20 We know also that the Son of God has come and has given us understanding, so that we may know him who is true. And we are in him who is true—even in his Son Jesus Christ. He is the true God and eternal life.   *See also* **Jn** 1:14–18; 17:3; **Col** 1:15–20   *See also* **wisdom, source of.**

revelation, New Testament

The NT fulfils and completes the revelation of God which began in the OT. Jesus Christ is the central focus of this self-revelation of God.

The unity and progress of revelation
The unity of OT and NT

Mt 5:17–18 "Do not think that I [Jesus] have come to abolish the Law or the Prophets; I have not come to abolish them but to fulfil them. I tell you the truth, until heaven and earth disappear, not the smallest letter, not the least stroke of a pen, will by any means disappear from the Law until everything is accomplished."   *See also* **Ro** 3:21–22; **2Ti** 3:14–15; **2Pe** 3:15–16; **Rev** 22:18–19

The progress of NT revelation

Heb 1:1–2 In the past God spoke to our ancestors through the prophets at many times and in various ways, but in these last days he has spoken to us by his Son, whom he appointed heir of all things, and through whom he made the universe.   *See also* **Heb** 2:1–4; 12:22–27

The NT fulfils and completes God's revelation of himself

Jesus Christ is the supreme revelation of God

Col 1:25–27 I [Paul] have become its [the church's] servant by the commission God gave me to present to you the word of God in its fulness—the mystery that has been kept hidden for ages and generations, but is now disclosed to the saints. To them God has chosen to make known among the Gentiles the glorious riches of this mystery, which is Christ in you, the hope of glory.   *See also* **Jn** 1:9–18; 14:6; **Ac** 4:12; **Gal** 4:4; **Php** 2:6–8; **Heb** 2:14

Jesus Christ is the image of God

2Co 4:4 The god of this age has blinded the minds of unbelievers, so that they cannot see the light of the gospel of the glory of Christ, who is the image of God.

Col 1:15 He is the image of the invisible God, the firstborn over all creation.

Jesus Christ has the nature of God

Php 2:6 [Christ Jesus] Who; being in very nature God, did not consider equality with God something to be grasped,

Jesus Christ is the exact representation of God

Heb 1:3 The Son is the radiance of God's glory and the exact representation of his being, sustaining all things by his powerful word. After he had provided purification for sins, he sat down at the right hand of the Majesty in heaven.

Jesus Christ is the incarnate Word of God

Jn 1:14 The Word became flesh and made his dwelling among us. We have seen his glory, the glory of the One and Only, who came from the Father, full of grace and truth.

The role of the Holy Spirit in revelation
He is the divine agent of revelation

Jn 16:12–15 ". . . But when he, the Spirit of truth, comes, he will guide you into all truth. He will not speak on his own; he will speak only what he hears, and he will tell you what is yet to come. He will bring glory to me by taking from what is mine and making it known to you. All that belongs to the Father is mine. That is why I said the Spirit will take from what is mine and make it known to you." *See also Jn* 14:16–17; 15:26; 1Jn 4:6; 5:6; **Rev** 2:7,11,17,29; 3:6,13,22

He is the source of revelatory manifestations

1Co 12:7–11 Now to each one the manifestation of the Spirit is given for the common good. To one there is given through the Spirit the message of wisdom, to another the message of knowledge by means of the same Spirit, to another faith by the same Spirit, to another gifts of healing by that one Spirit, to another miraculous powers, to another prophecy, to another distinguishing between spirits, to another speaking in different kinds of tongues, and to still another the interpretation of tongues. All these are the work of one and the same Spirit, and he gives them to each one, just as he determines. *See also* **Ac** 2:1–12; **Ro** 12:6; **1Co** 12:28–30; 13:8–12; 14:1–33; **Eph** 4:11

God's purposes in revelation
To reveal himself in Jesus Christ

Col 1:15–20 . . . For God was pleased to have all his fulness dwell in him, and through him to reconcile to himself all things, whether things on earth or things in heaven, by making peace through his blood, shed on the cross. *See also* **Jn** 1:14; 12:44–45; 14:9; **2Co** 4:4; **Heb** 1:3

To reveal his plan through Jesus Christ

Eph 1:9–10 And he [God] made known to us [believers] the mystery of his will according to his good pleasure, which he purposed in Christ, to be put into effect when the times will have reached their fulfilment—to bring all things in heaven and on earth together under one head, even Christ. *See also* **Ro** 16:25–27; **1Co** 2:7–10; **Eph** 3:3–11; **Col** 1:19–20 *See also prophecy, in New Testament; reconciliation, world to God; salvation; spiritual gifts.*

---

revelation, Old Testament

The OT bears witness to God's revelation in the history of Israel and in the inspired testimony of the prophets and other writers of the period. This knowledge of God prepares the way for the full disclosure of God in Jesus Christ in the NT.

Revelation in Eden and before the flood

Ge 1:3 And God said, "Let there be light," and there was light.

Ge 2:16–18 And the LORD God commanded the man, "You are free to eat from any tree in the garden; but you must not eat from the tree of the knowledge of good and evil, for when you eat of it you will surely die." The LORD God said, "It is not good for the man to be alone. I will make a helper suitable for him." *See also* **Ge** 1:29–30; 3:9–19; 4:6–7,9–15; 6:13–22

The covenant framework of OT revelation after the flood
God's covenant with Noah

Ge 9:8–11 Then God said to Noah and to his sons with him: "I now establish my covenant with you and with your descendants after you . . ." *See also* **Ge** 6:18; 9:12–17

God's covenant with Abraham
Ge 17:7 "I [the LORD] will establish my covenant as an everlasting covenant between me and you [Abraham] and your descendants after you for the generations to come, to be your God and the God of your descendants after you."
See also **Ge** 15:9–21; 17:2,4,10–14; 22:16–18; **Ex** 6:2–6; **1Ch** 16:14–18; **Ps** 105:8–9

God's covenant with Moses at Sinai
Ex 34:27 Then the LORD said to Moses, "Write down these words, for in accordance with these words I have made a covenant with you and with Israel."   *See also* **Ex** 24:3–8; 34:10–14; **Dt** 5:2–4; **Jer** 11:2–5

God's covenant with David
Ps 89:3–4 You [the LORD] said, "I have made a covenant with my chosen one, I have sworn to David my servant, 'I will establish your line for ever and make your throne firm through all generations.'" . . .   *See also* **2Sa** 7:8–16; **Ps** 132:11–12

The promise of a new covenant
Jer 31:31–34 "The time is coming," declares the LORD, "when I will make a new covenant with the house of Israel and with the house of Judah . . ."   *See also* **Isa** 42:6; **Mt** 26:27–28 pp Mk 14:24 pp Lk 22:20 pp 1Co 11:25; **Heb** 8:8–12; 9:15; 10:15–18

The recipients of OT revelation
The people of Israel
Am 3:2 "You only have I chosen of all the families of the earth . . ."   *See also* **Ex** 19:3–6; **Dt** 7:6; **Isa** 65:1; **Eze** 20:5

On occasions God spoke to people outside the covenant community
Da 2:27–28 Daniel replied, "No wise man, enchanter, magician or diviner can explain to the king the mystery he has asked about, but there is a God in heaven who reveals mysteries. He has shown King Nebuchadnezzar what will happen in days to come . . ."   *See also* **Ge** 41:25,28–32; **Da** 4:1–37; 5:17–28

Methods of OT revelation
Direct communication
Dt 18:18 "I [the LORD] will raise up for them

[Israel] a prophet like you from among their people, and I will put my words in that prophet's mouth. My prophet will tell them everything I command."   *See also* **Ex** 4:12; **Nu** 12:8; 23:5; **Isa** 50:4; 51:16; **Jer** 1:9

Visions and dreams
Nu 12:6 he [the LORD] said, "Listen to my words: When there are prophets of the LORD among you, I reveal myself to them in visions, I speak to them in dreams."   *See also* **Ge** 15:1; 28:12; 37:5–7,9; 46:2; **Nu** 24:4; **Dt** 13:1; **Jdg** 7:13–14; **Job** 33:14–15; **Eze** 1:1,26–28

Visible manifestations (theophanies)
Ge 18:1 The LORD appeared to Abraham near the great trees of Mamre while he was sitting at the entrance to his tent in the heat of the day.   *See also* **Ge** 32:24–30; **Ex** 3:1–6; 34:4–7; **Nu** 11:25; 12:5; 14:10–12; **Jos** 5:13–15

Scripture
Dt 31:9 So Moses wrote down this law and gave it to the priests, the sons of Levi, who carried the ark of the covenant of the LORD, and to all the elders of Israel.   *See also* **Ex** 17:14; **Nu** 33:2; **Isa** 30:8; **Jer** 36:2; 51:60

The content of OT revelation
Revelation of God's will and purposes
Ge 17:1–2 When Abram was ninety-nine years old, the LORD appeared to him and said, "I am God Almighty; walk before me and be blameless. I will confirm my covenant between me and you and will greatly increase your numbers."   *See also* **Ge** 12:1–3; 15:1–5; **Ex** 19:5–6; 20:1–17 pp Dt 5:6–21; **Ex** 22:31; **Lev** 11:44–45; 19:1–2; 20:7–8

Revelation of God's plan
Ge 3:15 ". . . I [God] will put enmity between you [the serpent] and the woman, and between your offspring and hers; he will crush your head, and you will strike his heel."   *See also* **Isa** 9:6–7; 11:1–10; 42:1; **Mic** 5:1–5; **Zec** 9:9–13

Revelation of God's character and being
Ex 3:11–15 . . . God said to Moses, "I AM WHO I AM. This is what you are to say to the Israelites: 'I AM has sent me to you.'" God also said to Moses, "Say to the Israelites, 'The LORD, the God of your fathers—the God of Abraham,

the God of Isaac and the God of Jacob—has sent me to you.' This is my name for ever, the name by which I am to be remembered from generation to generation."

God's glory: **Ex** 40:34; **1Ki** 8:11; **Eze** 1:28

God is just and merciful: **Nu** 14:17–19; **Ps** 143:1

God's love: **Dt** 7:7–8; **La** 3:22

God is righteous: **Ps** 72:2; 103:6; **Isa** 59:17

God is the sovereign creator: **Ps** 115:3; 135:5–6

The incompleteness of OT revelation

Heb 11:39–40 These [Old Testament saints] were all commended for their faith, yet none of them received what had been promised. God had planned something better for us so that only together with us would they be made perfect. *See also* **Heb** 1:1–2; **1Pe** 1:10–12   *See also covenant; Scripture, sufficiency; word of God.*

---

revelation, responses

God requires and imparts a frame of mind that receives and responds to what he has made known.

God commands that his word be heeded

Mk 4:3 "Listen! A farmer went out to sow his seed."   *See also* **Isa** 1:10; **Mk** 4:9; **Rev** 2:7

People do not naturally understand what God has revealed

They fail to recognise God's revelation in Jesus Christ

Mt 11:25–27 At that time Jesus said, "I praise you, Father, Lord of heaven and earth, because you have hidden these things from the wise and learned, and revealed them to little children . . . No-one knows the Son except the Father, and no-one knows the Father except the Son and those to whom the Son chooses to reveal him." pp **Lk** 10:21–22   *See also* **Jn** 5:37–40; 6:44–45; 10:24–26; 12:37–41; 14:9; **Ro** 9:31–10:4; **1Co** 1:18–25; 2:8; **2Co** 4:4

They fail to understand God's revelation in general

1Co 2:14 The person without the Spirit does not accept the things that come from the Spirit of

God but considers them foolishness, and cannot understand them because they are spiritually discerned.   *See also* **Mk** 4:11–12 pp **Mt** 13:13–15 pp **Lk** 8:10; **Isa** 6:9–10; **Jn** 8:43–47; **2Co** 3:14–16; **2Th** 2:11–13

God has given his Spirit to illuminate the human mind

He reveals and teaches truth

1Co 2:12–13 We [believers] have not received the spirit of the world but the Spirit who is from God, that we may understand what God has freely given us. This is what we speak, not in words taught us by human wisdom but in words taught by the Spirit, expressing spiritual truths in spiritual words.   *See also* **Jer** 31:31–34; **Mt** 16:17; **Jn** 3:3–10; 14:16–17,25–26; 16:12–15; **Php** 3:15

He reveals through prayer for understanding

Ps 119:18 Open my eyes that I may see wonderful things in your [God's] law.   *See also* **Ps** 119:12,27; **Eph** 1:17–18

Understanding God's revelation carries special responsibility

Lk 12:47–48 ". . . From everyone who has been given much, much will be demanded; and from the one who has been entrusted with much, much more will be asked."   *See also* **Mt** 13:11–12; 25:14–30 pp **Lk** 19:12–27

God's revelation of himself will only be fully understood at the second coming of Jesus Christ

1Co 13:12 Now we [believers] see but a poor reflection as in a mirror; then we shall see face to face. Now I know in part; then I shall know fully, even as I am fully known.   *See also* **1Pe** 1:13; **1Jn** 3:2

The consequences of responding to revelation

Repentance

Ac 2:38 Peter replied, "Repent and be baptised, every one of you, in the name of Jesus Christ for the forgiveness of your sins. And you will receive the gift of the Holy Spirit."   *See also* **Mt** 4:17;

Ac 3:19; 26:20; **2Co** 7:10
Faith
Ro 10:17 Consequently, faith comes from hearing the message, and the message is heard through the word of Christ.   *See also* **Ro** 10:8–10,14–15; **1Co** 2:4–5
Obedience
Ro 1:5 Through him [Jesus Christ] and for his name's sake, we received grace and apostleship to call people from among all the Gentiles to the obedience that comes from faith.   *See also* **Jdg** 2:17; **Phm** 21; **1Pe** 1:2   *See also faith, necessity; gospel, responses; life, spiritual; obedience; repentance.*

righteousness
Scripture identifies a close link between righteousness and faith. Part of "being in a right relationship with God" is believing and trusting in him. The NT does not see faith simply in terms of moral righteousness, but also in terms of a living trusting relationship with God. Scripture affirms the righteousness of God and Jesus Christ in all their activity.

righteousness, as faith
Full faith and trust make a person pleasing in the sight of God.

Human righteousness compared with God's righteousness
Human beings cannot by themselves achieve righteousness in the sight of God
Ecc 7:20 There is not a righteous person on earth who does what is right and never sins.

Isa 64:6 All of us have become like one who is unclean, and all our righteous acts are like filthy rags; we all shrivel up like a leaf, and like the wind our sins sweep us away.

Mt 5:20 "For I [Jesus] tell you that unless your righteousness surpasses that of the Pharisees and the teachers of the law, you will certainly not enter the kingdom of heaven."   *See also* **Pr** 21:2; **Da** 9:18; **Mt** 23:28; **Lk** 16:15; 18:9; **Ro** 3:10,20; **Php** 3:6–7

True righteousness is the result of the action of God
Ro 8:3–4 For what the law was powerless to do in that it was weakened by the sinful nature, God did by sending his own Son in the likeness of sinful humanity to be a sin offering. And so he condemned sin in our sinful nature, in order that the righteous requirements of the law might be fully met in us, who do not live according to the sinful nature but according to the Spirit.

Eph 4:24 . . . put on the new self, created to be like God in true righteousness and holiness.

1Jn 2:29 If you know that he is righteous, you know that everyone who does what is right has been born of him.   *See also* **Ro** 6:13,16–20; 8:10; 14:17; **Gal** 5:5; **Eph** 5:9; **Php** 1:11; **Heb** 12:11; **Jas** 3:18; **1Pe** 2:24; **1Jn** 3:10

Faith pleases God
Ge 15:6 Abram believed the Lord, and he credited it to him as righteousness.

Heb 11:6 And without faith it is impossible to please God, because anyone who comes to him must believe that he exists and that he rewards those who earnestly seek him.   *See also* **1Sa** 26:23; **Ps** 32:10; 40:4; 84:12; 106:30–31; **Jer** 17:7; **Hab** 2:4; **Heb** 10:38; 11:4,7

Righteousness and faith in Jesus Christ
It is God-given and not the result of human effort
Ro 1:17 For in the gospel a righteousness from God is revealed, a righteousness that is by faith from first to last, just as it is written: "The righteous will live by faith."

Php 3:8–9 What is more, I [Paul] consider everything a loss compared to the surpassing greatness of knowing Christ Jesus my Lord, for whose sake I have lost all things. I consider them rubbish, that I may gain Christ and be found in him, not having a righteousness of my own that comes from the law, but that which is through faith in Christ—the righteousness that comes from God and is by faith.   *See also* **Ac** 13:39; **Ro** 3:21,27–28; 4:1–8; 5:17; 9:30–31; **Gal** 3:11–12

Faith is centred on Jesus Christ and what he has accomplished
Ro 5:1–2 Therefore, since we have been justified through faith, we have peace with God through our Lord Jesus Christ, through whom we have gained access by faith into this grace in which we now stand. And we rejoice in the hope of the glory of God.   *See also* **Ro** 3:21–26; 4:18–25; 10:6–10; **Gal** 3:6–9

Saving faith is not mere belief, but acting on the basis of that belief Jas 2:21–24   *See also* *faith; justification.*

---

righteousness, of believers
A sincere desire to please God by keeping his law is both commanded and approved by him. However, human fallibility means that true righteousness must be the product of the Holy Spirit's work in the believer.

Righteousness includes keeping the laws of God
Dt 6:25 "And if we [Israelites] are careful to obey all this law before the LORD our God, as he has commanded us, that will be our righteousness."

Job 27:6 "I will maintain my righteousness and never let go of it; my conscience will not reproach me as long as I live."

1Jn 3:7 Dear children, do not let anyone lead you astray. The one who does what is right is righteous, just as he [God] is righteous.   *See also* **Ge** 6:9; 18:19; **Dt** 6:17–18; **1Ki** 3:6; 15:11; **2Ch** 31:20; **Ps** 7:8; 15:1–5; 17:1; 32:11; 45:7; **Isa** 26:7–9; 48:18; 51:1; **Hos** 14:9; **Lk** 2:25; **Ac** 4:19; **2Co** 6:14; **2Ti** 3:15–16

God requires righteousness of his people
Am 5:24 ". . . let justice roll on like a river, righteousness like a never-failing stream!"

Mt 6:33 ". . . seek first his [God's] kingdom and his righteousness, and all these things will be given to you as well."   *See also* **Isa** 1:16–17; 56:1; **Jer** 22:3; **Hos** 10:12; **Zep** 2:3; **Mt** 5:6; **Eph** 6:14; **1Ti** 6:11; **2Ti** 2:22

God loves those who are righteous
Ps 146:8 the LORD gives sight to the blind, the LORD lifts up those who are bowed down, the LORD loves the righteous.

Pr 15:9 The LORD detests the way of the wicked but he loves those who pursue righteousness.

Jas 1:20 . . . human anger does not bring about the righteous life that God desires.   *See also* **Ps** 1:5–6; 14:5; 33:5; 37:6,28–30; 106:3; **Pr** 10:16

The righteous receive blessing from God
Pr 12:28 In the way of righteousness there is life; along that path is immortality.

Mt 13:43 "Then the righteous will shine like the sun in the kingdom of their Father . . ."   *See also* **Ps** 5:12; 34:15; 37:16–17; 55:22; 92:12; 112:4; **Pr** 10:2–3,6–7,16,29–32; 11:4–6; **Isa** 3:10; 33:15–16; **Da** 12:3; **Jas** 5:16

The righteous may suffer for their faith
Mt 5:10 "Blessed are those who are persecuted because of righteousness, for theirs is the kingdom of heaven."   *See also* **Ps** 94:21; **Isa** 57:1; **Am** 2:6; 5:12; **1Pe** 3:14   *See also* *holiness; law, and gospel; obedience; sanctification.*

---

righteousness, of God
An aspect of God's nature which expresses his unique moral perfection and his readiness to save sinners. It is made known especially through the gospel of Jesus Christ.

God's nature is righteous
Ps 119:137 Righteous are you, O LORD, and

your laws are right.   *See also* **Dt** 32:4; **Ps** 48:10; 97:2; 119:142; 145:17; **Isa** 45:21; **Jer** 12:1; **Jn** 17:25

God's righteousness shows his sovereignty
Ps 71:19 Your righteousness reaches to the skies, O God, you who have done great things. Who, O God, is like you?   *See also* **Job** 37:23; **Ps** 36:6; 97:6; **Isa** 5:16

God's righteousness is eternal
Ps 111:3 Glorious and majestic are his [the LORD's] deeds, and his righteousness endures for ever. *See also* **Ps** 112:3,9; 119:142,160; **Isa** 51:8

God's actions are righteous
Da 9:14 ". . . the LORD our God is righteous in everything he does . . ."   *See also* **Jdg** 5:11; **1Sa** 12:7; **Jer** 9:24; **Rev** 15:3

God's rule is righteous
Ps 9:8 He [the LORD] will judge the world in righteousness; he will govern the peoples with justice.   *See also* **2Sa** 23:3–4; **Ps** 96:13; 99:4; **Jer** 9:23–24

God's righteous acts are saving acts
Ps 65:5 You answer us with awesome deeds of righteousness, O God our Saviour, the hope of all the ends of the earth and of the farthest seas, *See also* **Ps** 40:10; 116:4–6; 129:4; **Isa** 41:10; 46:13; **Da** 9:16; **Mic** 6:5

God's righteousness vindicates his people
Ps 35:24 Vindicate me in your righteousness, O LORD my God; do not let them gloat over me. *See also* **Ps** 4:2–3; 7:9; 9:4; 103:6; **Isa** 50:8; **Mic** 7:9; **Ro** 8:33

God's righteousness shows his faithfulness
Ne 9:8 ". . . You [the LORD God] have kept your promise because you are righteous."   *See also* **Ps** 4:1; **Zep** 3:5; **Zec** 8:8

God's righteousness shows his justice
Jer 11:20 But, O LORD Almighty, you who judge righteously and test the heart and mind . . . *See also* **Ge** 18:25; **Job** 8:3; **Ps** 11:7; 50:6; 51:4; **Pr** 21:12; **Ecc** 3:17; **2Ti** 4:8

God's righteousness is seen in his judgments
Ps 7:11 God is a righteous judge, a God who expresses his wrath every day.   *See also* **2Ch** 12:5–6; **Ezr** 9:15; **Isa** 10:22; 28:17; **La** 1:18; **Mal** 3:5; **Ro** 2:2,5

God's laws show his righteousness
Ps 19:8–9 . . . The ordinances of the LORD are sure and altogether righteous.   *See also* **Dt** 4:8; **Ps** 33:4; 119:7,144; **Ro** 1:32; 7:12; 8:4

God's righteousness contrasts with human unrighteousness
Ro 3:5 But if our unrighteousness brings out God's righteousness more clearly, what shall we say? . . .   *See also* **Ex** 9:27; **Ne** 9:33; **Job** 4:17; 9:2; **Da** 9:7; **Ro** 10:3

God's righteousness is revealed primarily in Jesus Christ
Ro 3:21–22 . . . This righteousness from God comes through faith in Jesus Christ to all who believe . . .   *See also* **Isa** 11:2–5; **Jer** 23:6; **Zec** 9:9; **Ac** 3:14; **Ro** 10:4; **1Co** 1:30; **2Pe** 1:1; **1Jn** 2:1

God's righteousness is revealed in the gospel
Ro 1:17 For in the gospel a righteousness from God is revealed, a righteousness that is by faith from first to last, just as it is written: "The righteous will live by faith."   *See also* **Php** 3:9

God gives his righteousness to believers
Ro 4:22–24 . . . The words "it was credited to him [Abraham]" were written not for him alone, but also for us, to whom God will credit righteousness—for us who believe in him who raised Jesus our Lord from the dead.   *See also* **Ge** 15:6; **Job** 33:26; **Hos** 10:12; **Ro** 3:22; 4:3–8; 5:17; 10:4; **2Co** 5:21

The Holy Spirit reveals God's righteousness
Gal 5:5 But by faith we eagerly await through the Spirit the righteousness for which we hope. *See also* **Jn** 16:8,10; **Ro** 14:17

God's righteousness is to be sought after
Mt 6:33 "But seek first his kingdom and his righteousness, and all these things will be given to you as well."   *See also* **Isa** 51:1; **Zep** 2:3

God's righteousness is a pattern for human living

1Jn 3:7 Dear children, do not let anyone lead you astray. The one who does what is right is righteous, just as he [God] is righteous. *See also* **Ge** 18:19; **Hos** 14:9; **Eph** 4:24; **1Jn** 2:29; 3:12

God's righteousness is worthy of praise

Isa 24:15–16 . . . From the ends of the earth we hear singing: "Glory to the Righteous One." . . . *See also* **Ps** 7:17; 22:31; 35:28; 51:14; 71:15,24; 145:7 *See also holiness, of God; justice, of God; justification; law; propitiation; sin, and God's character.*

---

righteousness, of Jesus Christ

Jesus Christ pleased his Father perfectly in his life on earth and in his death. He now gives believers a new status before God and a new power for living.

The promised Messiah will be righteous

Zec 9:9 Rejoice greatly, O Daughter of Zion! Shout, Daughter of Jerusalem! See, your king comes to you, righteous and having salvation, gentle and riding on a donkey, on a colt, the foal of a donkey. *See also* **Ps** 45:7; **Isa** 53:11; **Jer** 23:5–6; 33:15

The promised Messiah will establish righteousness

Ps 72:1–4; **Isa** 9:7; 11:3–5

Jesus Christ's own righteousness

Righteousness is characteristic of Jesus Christ
Ac 22:14 "Then he [Ananias] said: 'The God of our ancestors has chosen you [Paul] to know his will and to see the Righteous One and to hear words from his mouth.'" *See also* **Ac** 3:14; 7:52; **2Ti** 4:8; **Heb** 1:8–9; **1Jn** 2:1,29; 3:7

Jesus Christ's obedience shows his righteousness
Jn 8:28–29 . . . ". . . I [Jesus] always do what pleases him [the Father]." *See also* **Jn** 4:34; 6:38; 12:49–50; 14:31; **Php** 2:8; **Heb** 5:8–9; 10:9

Jesus Christ judges righteously
Jn 5:30 ". . . my [Jesus'] judgment is just, for I seek not to please myself but him who sent me." *See also* **Rev** 19:11

Jesus Christ is declared not guilty
Lk 23:14–15 . . . ". . . I [Pilate] have examined him [Jesus] in your presence and have found no basis for your charges against him. Neither has Herod, for he sent him back to us; as you can see, he has done nothing to deserve death." *See also* **Lk** 23:4; **Jn** 19:6; **Ac** 3:13

Jesus Christ's righteousness recognised by others
Lk 23:47 The centurion, seeing what had happened, praised God and said, "Surely this was a righteous man." *See also* **Mk** 10:17–18 pp **Lk** 18:18–19; **Lk** 23:41; **Ac** 10:38

Consequences of Jesus Christ's righteousness

God justifies believers on account of the righteousness of Jesus Christ
Ro 5:18–19 . . . just as the result of one trespass was condemnation for all people, so also the result of one act of righteousness was justification that brings life for all people . . . *See also* **Ro** 3:23–26; **1Pe** 3:18; **2Pe** 1:1

All who believe share in the righteousness of Jesus Christ
1Co 1:30 . . . Christ Jesus . . . that is, our righteousness . . . *See also* **Ro** 3:21–22; 4:6,24; 9:30; 10:3–4; **2Co** 5:21

Believers live by and for Jesus Christ's righteousness
Php 1:11 filled with the fruit of righteousness that comes through Jesus Christ . . . *See also* **Ro** 6:18; 8:10; **1Pe** 2:24 *See also faith, origins of; holiness, believers' growth in; holiness, of Jesus Christ; justification; obedience, of Jesus Christ; sanctification.*

Sabbath

The day of rest laid down for the people of God. The OT treated the seventh day of the week (Saturday) as the Sabbath, a custom continued in modern Judaism. The Christian church, in recognition of the importance of the resurrection of Jesus Christ, observed a day of rest on the first day of the week (Sunday).

Sabbath, in New Testament

The NT develops the OT teaching on the Sabbath in three important directions. It declares that the Sabbath should not be observed in a legalistic manner; the Sabbath-rest is treated as an important symbol of the Christian doctrine of salvation; and finally, the NT itself indicates how Sunday, rather than Saturday, came to be seen as the Christian Sabbath.

Gospel incidents connected with the Sabbath

Exorcism Mk 1:21–25 pp Lk 4:31–35

Healing Mt 12:9–14 pp Mk 3:1–6 pp Lk 6:6–11; Mk 1:30–31 pp Lk 4:38–40; Lk 13:10–17; 14:1–6; Jn 5:5–18; 9:1–16

Teaching Mk 6:2 pp Mt 13:54; Lk 4:16

Other references Mt 28:1 pp Mk 16:1; Lk 23:55–56; Jn 12:2

Jesus Christ's teaching regarding the Sabbath

Jesus Christ observes the Sabbath regulation
Lk 4:16 He went to Nazareth, where he had been brought up, and on the Sabbath day he went into the synagogue, as was his custom . . . *See also* Mt 24:20; Ac 1:12

Human well-being is more important than rigid observance of the Law
Mk 2:27–28 Then he [Jesus] said to them [the Pharisees], "The Sabbath was made for people, not people for the Sabbath. So the Son of Man is Lord even of the Sabbath." *See also* Mt 12:3

Ceremonial observance must give way before any higher, or more spiritual, motive
Mt 12:5–6 "Or haven't you read in the Law that on the Sabbath the priests in the temple desecrate the day and yet are innocent? I tell you that one greater than the temple is here." *See also* Lk 6:5

Sabbath reading of Scripture provided an opportunity for reaching the Jews
Ac 17:2 As his custom was, Paul went into the synagogue, and on three Sabbath days he reasoned with them from the Scriptures, *See also* Ac 13:14,27,42,44; 15:21; 16:13; 18:4

Sabbath observance was optional for Gentile Christians
Col 2:16 Therefore do not let anyone judge you by what you eat or drink, or with regard to a religious festival, a New Moon celebration or a Sabbath day.

The Lord's Day
Rev 1:10 On the Lord's Day I was in the Spirit, and I heard behind me a loud voice like a trumpet, *See also* Jn 20:19,26; Ac 20:7; 1Co 16:2

The Sabbath-rest is seen as a symbol of the salvation of the people of God
Heb 4:1 Therefore, since the promise of entering his rest still stands, let us be careful that none of you be found to have fallen short of it.

Heb 3:18–19 And to whom did God swear that they would never enter his rest if not to those who disobeyed? So we see that they were not able to enter, because of their unbelief.

Heb 4:9 There remains, then, a Sabbath-rest for the people of God; *See also* Lord's Day; Scripture.

Sabbath, in Old Testament
The Sabbath of rest is grounded in God's work of creation. Observance of a Sabbath day is distinctive of the people of God.

The Sabbath grounded in creation itself
Ge 2:3 And God blessed the seventh day and made it holy, because on it he rested from all the work of creating that he had done. *See also* Ps 118:24

The purpose of the Sabbath
To remember God's work in creation
Ex 20:8–11 "Remember the Sabbath day by

keeping it holy. Six days you shall labour and do all your work, but the seventh day is a Sabbath to the LORD your God. On it you shall not do any work, neither you, nor your son or daughter, nor your male or female servant, nor your animals, nor the alien within your gates. For in six days the LORD made the heavens and the earth, the sea, and all that is in them, but he rested on the seventh day. Therefore the LORD blessed the Sabbath day and made it holy."   *See also* **Ge** 2:2; **Ex** 35:2

To remember the exodus

Dt 5:12–15 "Observe the Sabbath day by keeping it holy, as the LORD your God has commanded you. Six days you shall labour and do all your work, but the seventh day is a Sabbath to the LORD your God. On it you shall not do any work, neither you, nor your son or daughter, nor your male or female servant, nor your ox, your donkey or any of your animals, nor the alien within your gates, so that your male and female servants may rest, as you do. Remember that you were slaves in Egypt and that the LORD your God brought you out of there with a mighty hand and an outstretched arm. Therefore the LORD your God has commanded you to observe the Sabbath day."   *See also* **Ge** 8:4; **2Sa** 7:1,11; **Ps** 95:10–11; **Heb** 4:9; **Rev** 14:13

To be a sign of the relationship between Israel and God and to give refreshment

Ex 31:17 "'It will be a sign between me and the Israelites for ever, for in six days the LORD made the heavens and the earth, and on the seventh day he abstained from work and rested.'"   *See also* **Dt** 5:12–14

The Law required the Sabbath to be a holy day free from work

Lev 23:3 "'There are six days when you may work, but the seventh day is a Sabbath of rest, a day of sacred assembly. You are not to do any work; wherever you live, it is a Sabbath to the LORD.'"   *See also* **Ex** 34:21; 35:3; **Lev** 23:38; **Isa** 56:2; 58:13

The Sabbath was linked with celebration of the New Moon

2Ki 4:23 "Why go to him [Elisha] today?" he asked. "It's not the New Moon or the Sabbath." . . .   *See also* **Isa** 1:13; **Eze** 46:3; **Hos** 2:11; **Am** 8:5

Abuses of the Sabbath

Ex 16:27–28; **Nu** 15:32; **Ne** 13:15–18 Engaging in commerce: **Ne** 10:31; **Am** 8:5 **Jer** 17:21

Punishments for infringing the Sabbath law

The death penalty Ex 31:14; **Nu** 15:35 **Disaster for Jerusalem Jer** 17:27; **Eze** 20:13; 22:8,15

Sacrifices to be offered on the Sabbath
Bread Lev 24:8; **1Ch** 9:32 **Burnt offerings Nu** 28:9–10; **1Ch** 23:31; **2Ch** 2:4 **Other offerings Eze** 46:4   *See also creation; law, Old Testament.*

---

sacrifice
An important aspect of the relationship between God and humanity but whereas the OT describes many sacrifices, the NT announces the fulfilment of sacrifice in Jesus Christ.

sacrifice, in Old Testament
An act that involved offering to God the life of an animal. It expressed gratitude for God's goodness or acknowledgement of sin. It was also associated with establishing a covenant.

Sacrifice was an integral part of worship
Ge 46:1; **Ex** 10:24–26; **Jdg** 13:19; **1Sa** 1:3; **1Ki** 3:4

Sacrifices were a means of offering thanks to God
Ge 4:4; 8:20; **Ex** 18:12; **Jdg** 11:31; **1Sa** 6:15 The returning exiles: **Ezr** 3:3; 8:35

In response to God's deliverance from danger and sickness: **Ps** 27:6; 54:6; 107:17–22

Sacrifices were offered at regular religious festivals
Lev 23:5–8,18–20,23–25
The Day of Atonement: **Lev** 16:6–10; 23:26–32
Lev 23:33–36

Special occasions were marked by sacrifices
1Ki 8:63; **2Ch** 29:31–33; **Ezr** 3:2–3; 6:17

Sacrifices as signs of individual and national penitence
Lev 4:1–3,13–14; **Jdg** 2:1–5; 20:26; **1Sa** 7:8–9; **2Sa** 24:10–25

The place of sacrifice
It was divinely chosen
Dt 12:13–14 Be careful not to sacrifice your burnt offerings anywhere you please. Offer them only at the place the LORD will choose . . .
See also **Lev** 17:3–5; **Dt** 12:2–6
Rival places of sacrifice caused the Israelites to sin 1Ki 12:28–29,32; **2Ch** 15:17; 31:1

God condemned certain sacrifices
Sacrifices to other gods
1Ki 11:7–8 On a hill east of Jerusalem, Solomon built a high place for Chemosh the detestable god of Moab, and for Molech the detestable god of the Ammonites. He did the same for all his foreign wives, who burned incense and offered sacrifices to their gods. *See also* **Nu** 25:1–3; **2Ki** 16:4,15; **Ps** 106:28; **Isa** 57:7; 65:3,7; **Jer** 19:4
Human sacrifices Lev 18:21; **Dt** 12:31; **1Ki** 16:34; **2Ki** 3:26–27; 16:3; 17:31; 21:6; **Eze** 20:31

Sacrifice to the LORD may be rejected
If it is a substitute for obedience 1Sa 15:20–22; **Jer** 7:21–22; **Hos** 8:11–13; **Am** 4:4; **Mk** 12:33

If it is a substitute for justice and mercy Isa 66:2–3; **Mic** 6:7–8; **Mt** 9:13
If it is imperfect Mal 1:13–14

Blessing is promised when right sacrifices are offered
Ge 22:15–18; **Ps** 4:5; 50:14–15,23; 51:17
See also blood; sin.

---

sacrifice, New Testament fulfilment of
For the people of the new covenant, sacrifice is fulfilled in Jesus Christ. Christians should have nothing to do with other sacrifices but are to bring their own "spiritual" offerings.

The OT points ahead to the fulfilment of sacrifice in Jesus Christ
A new sacrificial system
Isa 56:6–7 "And foreigners who bind themselves to the LORD to serve him, to love the name of the LORD, and to worship him, all who keep the Sabbath without desecrating it and who hold fast to my covenant—these I will bring to my holy mountain and give them joy in my house of prayer. Their burnt offerings and sacrifices will be accepted on my altar; for my house will be called a house of prayer for all nations."
See also **Isa** 19:21
The new people of God Jer 33:18; **Eze** 20:40
The vision of the new temple Eze 40:46

The perfect sacrifice of Jesus Christ
Jesus Christ perceived his death as a sacrifice
Mt 26:28 "This is my blood of the covenant, which is poured out for many for the forgiveness of sins." pp **Mk** 14:24 pp **Lk** 22:20 pp **1Co** 11:25 *See also* **Heb** 5:1
The contrast with the OT sacrificial system
Heb 7:27 Unlike the other high priests, he does not need to offer sacrifices day after day, first for his own sins, and then for the sins of the people. He sacrificed for their sins once for all when he offered himself. *See also* **Heb** 9:23–26; 10:1–3,12

Jesus Christ's sacrifice of a life dedicated to God makes believers holy Tit 2:14; Heb 10:8–10

The sacrifices of Christians
Christians offer themselves as living sacrifices Ro 12:1 Therefore, I urge you, brothers and sisters, in view of God's mercy, to offer your bodies as living sacrifices, holy and pleasing to God—this is your spiritual act of worship.
Paul saw his own death as part of a sacrificial offering: **Php** 2:17; **2Ti** 4:6
The sacrifice of praise and good works
Heb 13:15–16 Through Jesus, therefore, let us continually offer to God a sacrifice of praise—the fruit of lips that confess his name. And do not forget to do good and to share with others, for with such sacrifices God is pleased.

Christian attitudes to pagan sacrifice 1Co 10:18–22,25–26,27–29 *See also atonement; covenant, the new; forgiveness; propitiation.*

---

salvation
The transformation of a person's individual nature and relationship with God as a result of repentance and faith in the atoning death of Jesus Christ on the cross. All humanity stands in need of salvation, which is only possible through faith in Jesus Christ.

---

salvation, nature of
Salvation involves a change in the relationship between God and a person. Salvation includes God's adoption of believers into his family, his acceptance of them as righteous and his forgiveness of their sins. It also includes personal renewal and transformation through the work of the Holy Spirit.

Salvation as a change in status before God
Access to God
Ro 5:1–2 Therefore, since we have been justified through faith, we have peace with God through our Lord Jesus Christ, through whom we have gained access by faith into this grace in which we now stand. And we rejoice in the hope of the glory of God.　*See also* **Eph** 2:13; **Heb** 4:16

Adoption into the family of God Jn 1:12; Ro 8:22–24; Gal 4:4–7

Forgiveness of sin
Ac 5:30–31 "The God of our ancestors raised Jesus from the dead—whom you had killed by hanging him on a tree. God exalted him to his own right hand as Prince and Saviour that he might give repentance and forgiveness of sins to Israel."　*See also* **Ps** 32:1–2; **Mt** 26:28; **Ac** 10:43; 13:38; **Eph** 1:7; **Col** 2:13

Heavenly citizenship
Php 3:20–21 But our citizenship is in heaven. And we eagerly await a Saviour from there, the Lord Jesus Christ, who, by the power that enables him to bring everything under his control, will transform our lowly bodies so that they will be like his glorious body.　*See also* **Eph** 2:19; **Col** 3:1–2; **Heb** 12:22–24

Inheritance from God
Ro 8:17 Now if we are children, then we are heirs—heirs of God and co-heirs with Christ, if indeed we share in his sufferings in order that we may also share in his glory.　*See also* **Col** 1:12; **Rev** 21:7

Peace with God
Eph 2:13–17 But now in Christ Jesus you who once were far away have been brought near through the blood of Christ. For he himself is our peace, who has made the two one and has destroyed the barrier, the dividing wall of hostility, by abolishing in his flesh the law with its commandments and regulations. His purpose was to create in himself one new humanity out of the two, thus making peace, and in this one body to reconcile both of them to God through the cross, by which he put to death their hostility. He came and preached peace to you who were far away and peace to those who were near.　*See also* **Isa** 53:5; **Jn** 16:33; **Ro** 5:1–2; **Col** 3:15

Righteousness in the sight of God
Ro 1:17 For in the gospel a righteousness from God is revealed, a righteousness that is by faith from first to last, just as it is written: "The

righteous will live by faith." *See also* **Isa** 61:10; **Ro** 3:22; 4:3–13,25–5:1; **1Co** 1:30; **2Co** 5:21; **Php** 3:8–9; **2Ti** 4:8; **Heb** 11:7

Salvation as a change in a person's nature

Becoming a new creation
2Co 5:17 Therefore, if anyone is in Christ, there is a new creation: the old has gone, the new has come! *See also* **Ro** 6:4; **Gal** 6:14–15; **Eph** 2:15

Deliverance from God's righteous condemnation
Ro 8:1–2 Therefore, there is now no condemnation for those who are in Christ Jesus, because through Christ Jesus the law of the Spirit of life set me free from the law of sin and death. *See also* **Isa** 50:8; **Ro** 5:15–17; 8:33–39; **Col** 1:22

Deliverance from the power of sin and evil
Gal 1:3–4 Grace and peace to you [Galatian believers] from God our Father and the Lord Jesus Christ, who gave himself for our sins to rescue us from the present evil age, according to the will of our God and Father, *See also* **Ro** 6:14; 7:21–25; 8:2–4; **1Pe** 2:24; **Rev** 1:5

Inner personal renewal
1Jn 1:7 But if we walk in the light, as he is in the light, we have fellowship with one another, and the blood of Jesus, his Son, purifies us from all sin. *See also* **Ps** 51:1–2,7; **Heb** 1:3; 10:19–22

New birth
Jn 3:3–7 . . . Jesus declared, "I tell you the truth, no-one can see the kingdom of God without being born again." "How can anyone be born in old age?" Nicodemus asked. "Surely they cannot enter a second time into their mother's womb to be born!" Jesus answered, "I tell you the truth, no-one can enter the kingdom of God without being born of water and the Spirit. Flesh gives birth to flesh, but the Spirit gives birth to spirit. You should not be surprised at my saying, 'You must be born again.'" *See also* **Jas** 1:18; **1Pe** 1:23; **1Jn** 3:9

The presence of the Holy Spirit
Ro 8:10–11 But if Christ is in you, your body is dead because of sin, yet your spirit is alive because of righteousness. And if the Spirit of him who raised Jesus from the dead is living in you, he who raised Christ from the dead will also give life to your mortal bodies through his Spirit, who lives in you. *See also* **Gal** 5:2–25 *See also* adoption; forgiveness; grace, and salvation; justification; peace; righteousness; sanctification.

---

salvation, necessity of

Scripture stresses that fallen human beings are cut off from God on account of their sin. All need to be saved, if they are to enter into a new relationship with God as their Creator and Redeemer. Salvation is not the result of human achievement, privilege or wisdom, but depends totally upon the graciousness of a loving God, supremely expressed in the cross of Jesus Christ. People must respond in repentance and faith if they are to benefit from God's offer of salvation in Christ.

The necessity of salvation

The universal rule of sin in human nature Isa 64:6; **Ro** 3:19–23; 5:12–18; 7:24; **Eph** 2:3

Sin cuts humanity off from God
Isa 59:1–2 Surely the arm of the LORD is not too short to save, nor his ear too dull to hear. But your iniquities have separated you from your God; your sins have hidden his face from you, so that he will not hear. *See also* **Ge** 3:22–24; **Eph** 2:1–5; 4:18

Sin enslaves humanity to evil Jer 13:23; Hos 5:4; Zec 7:11–12; Ro 7:14–20; 2Pe 2:13–19

Salvation is grounded in the love of God

Salvation is not based on human achievement
Ro 3:28 For we maintain that a person is justified by faith apart from observing the law.

Eph 2:8–9 For it is by grace you have been saved, through faith—and this not from yourselves, it is the gift of God—not by works, so that no-one can boast. *See also* **Ac** 15:7–11; **Ro** 4:1–3; 5:1–2; **Gal** 2:16,21; **2Ti** 1:9

Salvation is grounded in God's love for his people

Eph 2:4–5 But because of his great love for us, God, who is rich in mercy, made us alive with Christ even when we were dead in transgressions—it is by grace you have been saved.   *See also* Dt 7:1–8; Jn 3:16–17; Ro 5:8; 2Th 2:16; 1Jn 4:9–19

Salvation is grounded in God's grace

Ro 3:22–24 This righteousness from God comes through faith in Jesus Christ to all who believe. There is no difference, for all have sinned and fall short of the glory of God, and are justified freely by his grace through the redemption that came by Christ Jesus.   *See also* Jn 1:16; Ac 15:11; Ro 5:15–17; 2Co 6:1–2; Eph 1:5–8; 2:4–10; 1Ti 1:14–15; Tit 2:11; 3:4–7; Heb 2:9

Salvation and the work of Jesus Christ
Salvation is grounded in the work of Jesus Christ

Ac 5:30–31 "The God of our ancestors raised Jesus from the dead—whom you had killed by hanging him on a tree. God exalted him to his own right hand as Prince and Saviour that he might give repentance and forgiveness of sins to Israel."

1Ti 1:15 Here is a trustworthy saying that deserves full acceptance: Christ Jesus came into the world to save sinners—of whom I [Paul] am the worst.   *See also* Jn 4:42; Ac 4:10–12; Ro 5:9–10; Php 3:20–21; 2Ti 1:9–10; Tit 3:5–7; Heb 7:24–25; 1Jn 4:14

Jesus Christ's death was totally sufficient for salvation

1Pe 3:18 For Christ died for sins once for all, the righteous for the unrighteous, to bring you to God. He was put to death in the body but made alive by the Spirit,   *See also* Jn 17:1–4; Ac 4:10–12; Gal 1:3–4; Eph 1:5–10; 1Ti 2:5–6; 2Ti 1:9–10; Heb 10:10; 1Jn 4:9–10; Rev 7:9–10

Salvation demands a human decision

Jn 3:36 "Those who believe in the Son have eternal life, but those who reject the Son will not see life, for God's wrath remains on them."

Ac 3:19 "Repent, then, and turn to God, so that your sins may be wiped out, that times of refreshing may come from the Lord,"   *See also* Mk 1:15; Lk 8:50; Jn 3:17–18; Ac 2:37–39; Heb 12:25; 1Pe 2:4–8; 1Jn 5:10   *See also cross; election, to salvation; faith, and salvation; gospel; human race, and redemption; repentance; sin, deliverance from.*

---

sanctification

The process of becoming consecrated to God, which is an integral aspect of being a member of the people of God. This process of being made holy through the work of the Holy Spirit ultimately rests upon the sacrificial death of Jesus Christ, which the OT anticipates and foreshadows.

---

sanctification, basis of

The process of renewal and consecration by which believers are made holy through the work of the Holy Spirit. Sanctification is the consequence of justification and is dependent upon a person being in a right relationship with God.

Sanctification is grounded in the holiness of God

God is holy

Eze 39:7 " 'I will make known my holy name among my people Israel. I will no longer let my holy name be profaned, and the nations will know that I the LORD am the Holy One in Israel.' "   *See also* Lev 22:32; Jos 24:19; Ps 30:4; Hos 11:9; Isa 6:3; Rev 6:10

God demands that his people should reflect his holiness

Lev 19:2 "Speak to the entire assembly of Israel and say to them: 'Be holy because I, the LORD your God, am holy.' "   *See also* Lev 11:44–45; 20:7–8; Heb 2:11; 1Pe 1:15–16

Sanctification is the will of God for his people

1Th 4:3 It is God's will that you should be sanctified . . .   *See also* Eph 1:4; 2:10; 2Th 2:13; 1Pe 1:1–2

The basis for sanctification

God's election of his people 1Co 1:2; Eph 1:4–11; 1Th 5:9

The atoning death of Jesus Christ

Heb 13:12 And so Jesus also suffered outside the city gate to make the people holy through his own blood.   *See also* Ro 6:11; 7:4; 8:2; 1Co 1:30; 6:11; Eph 5:25–27; Heb 10:10–14; 1Pe 2:5

The grace of God Lk 1:69–75; Php 2:13; 2Ti 1:9; Heb 12:10

The work of the Holy Spirit Ro 15:16; 2Th 2:13; 1Pe 1:2

The word of God Jn 17:17; Eph 5:25–26; 2Ti 3:16

The need for sanctification

The universal sinfulness of humanity

Isa 64:6 All of us have become like one who is unclean, and all our righteous acts are like filthy rags; we all shrivel up like a leaf, and like the wind our sins sweep us away.   *See also* Job 15:14–15; Ps 51:5; Ro 5:12–19; Eph 2:3

Enslavement to evil can only be broken through the death of Jesus Christ

Jn 8:34–36 Jesus replied, "I tell you the truth, everyone who sins is a slave to sin. Now a slave has no permanent place in the family, but a son belongs to it for ever. So if the Son sets you free, you will be free indeed."   *See also* Ro 6:16–18; 8:5–7; Eph 4:17–24

The need for renewal and growth

2Pe 3:18 But grow in the grace and knowledge of our Lord and Saviour Jesus Christ. To him be glory both now and for ever! Amen.   *See also* Ro 12:1–2; Col 1:10; 1Th 4:3–6; Heb 6:1–3

The nature of sanctification

A process which has already been initiated 1Co 1:2; 6:11

A process of growth in holiness Ro 12:1–3; 2Co 3:18; Eph 4:15; 1Th 4:3–7; Heb 12:14; 1Pe 2:1–3; 2Pe 3:18

Consecration to God Ex 32:29; 1Ch 29:5; Pr 23:26; Ro 12:1   *See also grace, and Holy Spirit; holiness; life, spiritual; obedience; righteousness.*

---

sanctification, means and results

Sanctification results from the renewing work of the Holy Spirit and leads to the renewal of believers and their being equipped for ministry in the world.

The means of sanctification

The work of the Holy Spirit

1Co 6:11 . . . you were washed, you were sanctified, you were justified in the name of the Lord Jesus Christ and by the Spirit of our God.   *See also* Ro 8:9–11; 15:15–16; 1Co 12:13; 2Co 1:21–22; Eph 1:13–14; 2Th 2:13; Tit 3:4–7; 1Pe 1:1–2

Meditation on the Scriptures

1Pe 2:2–3 Like newborn babies, crave pure spiritual milk, so that by it you may grow up in your salvation . . .   *See also* Dt 11:18; Ps 119:12–18,48; 143:5–6; Jn 17:17; Col 3:16; Jas 1:25

The active pursuit of holiness and righteousness

1Ti 6:11–12 . . . pursue righteousness, godliness, faith, love, endurance and gentleness. Fight the good fight of the faith. Take hold of the eternal life to which you were called when you made your good confession in the presence of many witnesses.   *See also* 2Co 7:1; Gal 5:24; Eph 4:1; 1Th 5:22; 1Pe 2:9–12; 3Jn 11

Obedience and self-denial Ro 6:19–22; 8:5–14; Gal 2:20; 5:16–24; 1Pe 2:11

Prayer

Ps 145:18 The LORD is near to all who call on him, to all who call on him in truth.   *See also* Mt 7:7–8; Ac 4:31; 1Ti 4:4; Jas 5:16; Jude 20

Confession of sin

1Jn 1:9 If we confess our sins, he is faithful and just and will forgive us our sins and purify us from all unrighteousness.   *See also* Ne 1:6–9; Ps 32:5; 40:11–12; Pr 28:13; Isa 64:5–7; Jer 14:20–22; La 3:40

Obstacles to sanctification
A lack of faith Mt 5:13; **Jn** 15:6; **2Co** 12:20–21; **1Ti** 1:18–19

Rebellion against God
Eze 18:24 "But if the righteous turn from their righteousness and commit sin and do the same detestable things the wicked do, will they live? None of the righteous things they have done will be remembered. Because of the unfaithfulness they are guilty of and because of the sins they have committed, they will die." *See also* **Dt** 32:15–18; **Job** 34:26; **Isa** 65:11–12; **Gal** 1:6–7; 5:7–9; **Heb** 12:15; **Rev** 2:4–5

Satanic temptation
1Pe 5:8–9 Be self-controlled and alert. Your enemy the devil prowls around like a roaring lion looking for someone to devour. Resist him, standing firm in the faith, because you know that your brothers and sisters throughout the world are undergoing the same kind of sufferings.
See also **Ac** 5:3; **2Co** 2:8–11; **Jas** 4:7

Self-indulgence and greed
Lk 12:15 Then he [Jesus] said to them, "Watch out! Be on your guard against all kinds of greed; life does not consist in the abundance of possessions." *See also* **Lk** 21:34; **Ro** 13:13; **2Co** 12:21; **Eph** 4:19

Yielding to sinful desires
1Pe 1:14 As obedient children, do not conform to the evil desires you had when you lived in ignorance. *See also* **Mk** 4:18–19; **1Co** 10:6–8; **1Pe** 2:11; **2Pe** 2:14–18; **1Jn** 2:16–17

The results of sanctification
Good works
2Co 9:8 And God is able to make all grace abound to you, so that in all things at all times, having all that you need, you will abound in every good work. *See also* **Eph** 2:10; **Col** 1:10; 3:15–17; **2Th** 2:16–17; **Heb** 10:24–25; **Jas** 2:14–26

Becoming like Jesus Christ
1Pe 2:21 To this you were called, because Christ suffered for you, leaving you an example, that you should follow in his steps. *See also* **Jn** 13:15; **Ro** 8:28–30; **1Co** 11:1; **2Co** 3:18; **Gal** 3:27; **1Jn** 3:2–3

Becoming like God Mt 5:48; **Eph** 5:1–2; **Col** 1:21–22

Perfection

Mt 5:48 Be perfect, therefore, as your heavenly Father is perfect. *See also* **2Co** 13:11; **Col** 1:28

Blamelessness in the sight of God

2Pe 3:14 . . . make every effort to be found spotless, blameless and at peace with him. *See also* **Eph** 1:4; **Col** 1:21–22; **1Th** 5:23

Being able to see God Heb 12:14 *See also Christlikeness; forgiveness; regeneration; sin, avoidance.*

Satan

The one who opposes the person and purposes of God. Satan is especially associated with deceit, temptation and testing, through which he attempts to deflect believers from obeying God.

Satan, agents of

Satan works in this world through people and through those spiritual beings who acknowledge his authority. His agents oppose God's will and purposes.

Satan works through people

Satan's human agents pursue his evil desires

Jn 8:44 "You belong to your father, the devil, and you want to carry out your father's desire. He was a murderer from the beginning, not holding to the truth, for there is no truth in him . . ." *See also* **Ac** 13:10; **1Jn** 3:8–10,12

Satan works through people to oppose God's purposes **Ac** 5:1–9; **Mt** 16:23 pp **Mk** 8:33

Judas Iscariot: **Lk** 22:3; **Jn** 6:70; 13:2,27

Ac 13:8–10

Examples of people doing Satan's work

False prophets Dt 13:5; Jer 23:26–27; 28:15; 29:21; Eze 13:6–9; Mt 7:15; 24:24; 2Pe 2:1–3
Others who lead people away from God Dt 13:13; 2Ki 21:9–26; Pr 7:21; Isa 3:12; Jer 50:6; 2Pe 2:18–19

Satan works through his spiritual agents
Satan's angels
Mt 25:41 "'. . . the devil and his angels.'"   *See also* 2Pe 2:4; Rev 12:7
Satan's demons
Lk 13:11–16 . . . a woman was there who had been crippled by a spirit for eighteen years . . ." ". . . this woman, a daughter of Abraham, whom Satan has kept bound for eighteen long years . . ."   *See also* Mt 12:22; Lk 11:14–15

Satan's agents are identified by various images and titles
The little horn Da 8:9–12
The prince of Persia Da 10:13
The king of the North Da 11:28
The antichrist 1Jn 4:1–4; 2Jn 7
The man of lawlessness 2Th 2:3–10
The beast Rev 11:7; 13:1–8,11–18; 14:9–11; 16:13; 17:8; 19:20; 20:10
The false prophet Rev 16:13; 19:20
The prostitute or Babylon the Great Rev 14:8; 16:19; 17:1–18; 18:1–10,18; 19:2

Satan, deceiver
Satan's character is deceitful, devious and cunning as in a variety of guises he seeks to influence people for his own ends.

Satan's deceitful character
He is evil
Mt 6:13 ". . . deliver us from the evil one."   *See also* Mt 5:37; 13:19; Jn 17:15; 2Th 3:3; 1Jn 2:13–14; 3:8,12; 5:18
He is a liar
Jn 8:44 ". . . He [the devil] was a murderer from the beginning, not holding to the truth, for

there is no truth in him. When he lies, he speaks his native language, for he is a liar and the father of lies."   *See also* Ge 3:4–5; Job 1:11; 2:5; Rev 3:9
He is devious
2Co 11:14 . . . Satan himself masquerades as an angel of light.   *See also* 2Co 11:3; Eph 6:11; 2Th 2:9; 1Ti 3:7; 2Ti 2:26
He is scheming
Eph 6:11 Put on the full armour of God so that you can take your stand against the devil's schemes.   *See also* 2Co 2:10–11
He is a slanderer
Job 1:9–11 "Does Job fear God for nothing?" Satan replied. "Have you not put a hedge around him and his household and everything he has? . . . But now stretch out your hand and strike everything he has, and he will surely curse you to your face."   *See also* 1Ti 5:14–15; Rev 2:9

Satan's deceitful work
He deceives individuals
1Ti 2:14 . . . it was the woman who was deceived and became a sinner.   *See also* Da 8:25; 2Ti 3:13; Rev 12:9; 20:3,10
He works counterfeit miracles
2Th 2:9–10 The coming of the lawless one will be in accordance with the work of Satan displayed in all kinds of counterfeit miracles, signs and wonders, and in every sort of evil that deceives those who are perishing . . .   *See also* Ex 7:11–12,22; Dt 13:1–2; Mt 24:24 pp Mk 13:22; Rev 13:13–14; 19:20
He appoints false prophets
Mt 7:15 "Watch out for false prophets. They come to you in sheep's clothing, but inwardly they are ferocious wolves."   *See also* Dt 13:5; Jer 23:26; 28:15; 29:21; Eze 13:6–10; 2Pe 2:1–3,18–19
He misuses Scripture Mt 4:6 pp Lk 4:10
He blinds unbelievers
2Co 4:4 The god of this age [Satan] has blinded the minds of unbelievers, so that they cannot see the light of the gospel of the glory of Christ, who is the image of God.   *See also* evil, origins of.

Satan, defeat of

Though defeated on Jesus Christ's cross, Satan is still active in this world, but his final overthrow by God is certain.

Satan is defeated by Jesus Christ
Jesus Christ is stronger than Satan
Jn 14:30 ". . . the prince of this world is coming. He has no hold on me [Jesus]," *See also* **Mt 12:28; Lk 13:16; Ac 10:38; Gal 1:4**
Jesus Christ came to destroy Satan's work
1Jn 3:8 . . . The reason the Son of God appeared was to destroy the devil's work. *See also* **Heb 2:14–15**
Satan is defeated on the cross Col 1:13; Tit 2:14; Rev 3:21
Satan's defeat is foreseen by Jesus Christ
Jn 12:31 ". . . now the prince of this world will be driven out." *See also* **Mt 25:41; Lk 10:18; Jn 16:11**
Satan's agents are also defeated
Col 2:15 And having disarmed the powers and authorities, he [Christ] made a public spectacle of them, triumphing over them by the cross. *See also* **Ro 8:38–39**

Satan is defeated by Christians
Rev 12:11 "They [believers] overcame him by the blood of the Lamb and by the word of their testimony . . ." *See also* **Ac 5:40–42; 1Jn 2:13–14**

Satan's final overthrow
Satan and his agents will be destroyed
Ro 16:20 The God of peace will soon crush Satan under your feet . . . *See also* **Rev 17:14**
Satan's final destiny 1Ti 3:6
Torment: **Rev 20:1–3,10**
Death, the result of Satan's work, will be defeated 1Co 15:26; Rev 20:13–14 *See also cross; evil, victory over; hell, place of punishment; last things.*

Satan, enemy of God

Scripture provides numerous examples of ways in which Satan opposes the presence and purposes of God in his world.

Satan and God's people
Satan opposes believers
1Ch 21:1 Satan rose up against Israel . . . *See also* **Job 2:1–7; Zec 3:1–2; 1Th 2:18**
Satan accuses believers
Rev 12:10 . . . ". . . the accuser of our brothers and sisters [Satan], who accuses them before our God day and night . . ." *See also* **Job 1:8–11; Zec 3:1–2**
Satan slanders believers
1Ti 5:14 . . . give the enemy no opportunity for slander.
Satan tests believers and causes their suffering
Rev 2:10 ". . . the devil will put some of you in prison to test you, and you will suffer persecution . . ." *See also* **Eph 6:11–13,16**
Satan opposes the work of the archangel Michael
Jude 9 But even the archangel Michael, when he was disputing with the devil about the body of Moses . . .
The implication of these verses is that Michael's work is in direct opposition to that of Satan. Michael is the protector of God's people while Satan is their opponent: **Da 10:13,21; 12:1; Rev 12:7**

Satan opposes God
Satan opposes God's purposes
Mt 16:23 Jesus turned and said to Peter, "Get behind me, Satan! You are a stumbling-block to me; you do not have in mind the concerns of God, but human concerns." pp **Mk 8:33**
Satan opposes God's word Mt 13:3–19 pp **Mk 4:3–16** pp **Lk 8:4–12; Mt 13:24–39; Ac 13:8–10**
Satan opposes God's righteousness 1Jn 3:7–10
Satan blasphemes God Rev 13:6

Satan's opposition to God's work will not succeed
Zec 3:2; Lk 10:19

Satan's role as adversary earns him varied titles
The devil
He is the adversary because he deceives: **Rev 12:9; 20:2–3**

Belial
He is the adversary because he is the troublemaker or scoundrel (the same Hebrew word is used in the OT passages as in 2Co 6:15 to describe Satan's work): **Dt 13:13; 1Ki** 21:10; **Pr** 6:12; **2Co** 6:15
The dragon
He is the adversary because he is the enemy: **Rev** 12:4,13–14
The serpent
He is the adversary because he thwarts spiritual insight: **Ge** 3:1–5,13; **2Co** 11:3
The prince of this world
He is the adversary because his rule is temporary, not absolute: **Jn** 12:31; 14:30; 16:11
The angel of the Abyss Rev 9:11

Satan, kingdom of
Satan is depicted as the prince of this world, having power over demons and over godless people. He is, however, subject to God's sovereignty and therefore his power is limited and his rule temporary.

Satan's power
He has power in the world
1Jn 5:19 . . . the whole world is under the control of the evil one. *See also* **Jn** 7:7; 8:44; 14:17; 15:18–19; 16:20; 17:14; **Ac** 26:18; **2Co** 4:4; **Eph** 2:2; **Col** 1:13; **1Jn** 2:15–16; 4:4–5; **Rev** 13:12
He claims power over this world Mt 4:8–9 pp Lk 4:6
He is called the "prince" or the "god" of this world
Jn 12:31 ". . . now the prince of this world will be driven out."
These titles indicate the temporary nature of Satan's rule: **Jn** 14:30; 16:11; **2Co** 4:4
He is responsible for some illnesses
Lk 13:16 ". . . this woman . . . whom Satan has kept bound for eighteen long years . . ."
See also **Job** 2:7; **Ac** 10:38; **2Co** 12:7
He is responsible for death
Heb 2:14 . . . he [Jesus] too shared in their humanity so that by his death he might destroy him who holds the power of death—that is, the devil—

Satan's kingdom
He has a kingdom
Mt 12:26 "If Satan drives out Satan, he is divided against himself. How then can his kingdom stand?" pp Lk 11:18
Col 1:13 For he [the Father] has rescued us from the dominion of darkness and brought us into the kingdom of the Son he loves, *See also* **Ac** 26:18; **Eph** 2:2
He has a throne
Rev 2:13 "I know where you live—where Satan has his throne . . ."
He is the prince of demons
Mt 9:34 . . . "It is by the prince of demons that he [Jesus] drives out demons." *See also* **Mt** 12:24 pp **Mk** 3:22 pp **Lk** 11:15

Satan's authority is limited
He cannot do more than God allows
Job 1:12 The LORD said to Satan, "Very well, then, everything he has is in your hands, but on the man himself do not lay a finger." . . .
See also **Job** 2:6; **1Co** 10:13; **Rev** 12:12; 20:3
His rule is temporary Ro 16:20; **Rev** 20:10
See also kingdom of God; world.

Satan, resistance to
Jesus Christ resisted Satan in his ministry, and believers are commanded to follow his example in this respect. God assists believers in this struggle.

Satan can be resisted
His power is limited Job 1:12; 2:6; **1Co** 10:13; **Rev** 12:12; 20:3
Jesus Christ resists Satan Mt 4:1–11 pp **Lk** 4:1–13; **Jn** 1:5; **Heb** 2:18; 4:15
Christians can resist Satan
Jas 4:7 . . . Resist the devil, and he will flee from you. *See also* **Lk** 10:19; **Ro** 6:13; **Eph** 4:26–27; 6:11–13; **1Pe** 5:8–9; **2Pe** 3:17; **1Jn** 2:13–14

God protects his people from Satan
2Th 3:3 But the Lord is faithful, and he will strengthen and protect you from the evil one.
See also **1Jn** 5:18

God's protection is to be sought in prayer

Jn 17:15 "My [Jesus'] prayer is not that you [Father] take them out of the world but that you protect them from the evil one." *See also* **Mt** 6:13; **Lk** 22:31–32; **Eph** 6:11,18

Jesus Christ has the victory over Satan

Jesus Christ's defeat of Satan on the cross
Col 2:15 And having disarmed the powers and authorities, he [Christ] made a public spectacle of them, triumphing over them by the cross. *See also* **Jn** 12:31; **Rev** 12:11
Jesus Christ's name is powerful against Satan
Php 2:10 . . . at the name of Jesus every knee should bow, in heaven and on earth and under the earth, *See also* **Isa** 45:23; **Ps** 118:10–12; **Mk** 16:17–18; **Lk** 10:17; **Ac** 16:18
God's love cannot be thwarted **Ro** 8:38–39

Resisting Satan brings reward

2Ti 4:7–8 I have fought the good fight, I have finished the race, I have kept the faith. Now there is in store for me the crown of righteousness, which the Lord, the righteous Judge, will award to me on that day . . . *See also* **Jas** 1:12; **Rev** 2:7,17,26; 3:5,12,21 *See also evil, responses to; prayer; sin, avoidance; spiritual warfare.*

Satan, tempter

God's people are incited to evil by Satan. He seeks to exploit their weaknesses in order to deflect them from obedience to God.

Satan incites God's people to evil

Satan exploits human weaknesses
Ge 3:1–5 Now the serpent was more crafty than any of the wild animals the LORD God had made. He said to the woman, "Did God really say, 'You must not eat from any tree in the garden'?" . . . *See also* **Job** 2:4–5; **Eph** 4:26–27
He tempts Christians to fall away
1Th 3:5 . . . I [Paul] was afraid that in some way the tempter might have tempted you and our efforts might have been useless. *See also* **Lk** 22:31; **1Ti** 3:7; **2Ti** 2:26

He inspires people to put God to the test

Ac 5:3–9 Then Peter said, "Ananias, how is it that Satan has so filled your heart that you have lied to the Holy Spirit and have kept for yourself some of the money you received for the land? . . . ". . . Peter said to her [Ananias' wife, Sapphira], "How could you agree to test the Spirit of the Lord? . . ." *See also* **Ps** 78:18,41; 106:14; **Ac** 15:10; **1Co** 10:9
He makes sin attractive
Lack of integrity: **Mt** 5:37; **Ac** 5:3
Sinful desires: **1Co** 7:5; **1Ti** 5:14–15
2Co 2:10–11; **Jas** 3:14–16

Jesus Christ is tempted by Satan

In the wilderness **Mt** 4:1–11 pp **Mk** 1:13 pp **Lk** 4:1–13
Through Simon Peter **Mt** 16:23 pp **Mk** 8:33
Jesus Christ identifies with believers
Heb 4:15 For we do not have a high priest who is unable to sympathise with our weaknesses, but we have one who has been tempted in every way, just as we are—yet was without sin. *See also* **Heb** 2:8

Satan tests Christians

Rev 2:10 ". . . the devil will put some of you in prison to test you, and you will suffer persecution . . ." *See also* **Lk** 22:31; **Rev** 3:10

Satan's temptations can be resisted

By being alert
1Pe 5:8 Be self-controlled and alert. Your enemy the devil prowls around like a roaring lion looking for someone to devour.
By prayer
Mt 26:41 "Watch and pray so that you will not fall into temptation . . ." pp **Mk** 14:38 pp **Lk** 22:40 *See also* **Mt** 6:13 pp **Lk** 11:4; **Lk** 22:32,46
By relying on God's faithfulness
1Co 10:13 No temptation has seized you except what is common among people. And God is faithful; he will not let you be tempted beyond what you can bear. But when you are tempted, he will also provide a way out so that you can stand up under it. *See also* **2Pe** 2:9; **Rev** 3:10

By Jesus Christ's service as high priest Heb 2:18; 4:15

Scripture
The biblical writings, inspired by the Holy Spirit, have been entrusted to the church to remind it of the central teachings of the gospel, to guard it from error and to enable it to grow into holiness. The church is required to be obedient to Scripture and revere it as the Word of God.

Scripture, inspiration and authority
Those writings that are acknowledged to be the word of God to be revered as issuing from him and as having his authority.

Recognition of a body of sacred writings
In the OT
Ne 8:1 all the people assembled with one accord in the square before the Water Gate. They told Ezra the scribe to bring out the Book of the Law of Moses, which the LORD had commanded for Israel. *See also* **Ex** 24:7; **Jos** 8:34; **2Ki** 22:8 pp 2Ch 34:14; **2Ki** 23:2 pp 2Ch 34:30; **2Ch** 35:12; **Ezr** 6:18; **Ne** 8:8; 9:3; 13:1
By Jesus Christ
Mt 22:29 Jesus replied, "You [Sadducees] are in error because you do not know the Scriptures or the power of God." *See also* **Lk** 4:21; 24:27,45
Mt 21:13 "It is written," he [Jesus] said to them, " 'My house will be called a house of prayer,' but you are making it a 'den of robbers'." pp Lk 19:46 *See also* **Isa** 56:7; **Jer** 7:11; **Mt** 4:4 pp Lk 4:4; **Dt** 8:3; **Mt** 4:7 pp Lk 4:12; **Dt** 6:16; **Mt** 4:10 pp Lk 4:8; **Dt** 6:13; **Mt** 21:42 pp Mk 12:10; **Ps** 118:22–23; **Mt** 26:31 pp Mk 14:27; **Zec** 13:7; **Mk** 7:6–7; **Isa** 29:13; **Lk** 7:27; **Mal** 3:1; **Jn** 7:38
By the apostles
2Ti 3:14–15 But as for you [Timothy], continue in what you have learned and have become convinced of, because you know those from whom you learned it, and how from infancy

you have known the holy Scriptures, which are able to make you wise for salvation through faith in Christ Jesus. *See also* **Ac** 1:15–17; **Ro** 1:1–2; 15:4; **1Co** 15:3–4; **2Ti** 3:16–17
By the early church Ac 17:11

The inspiration of Scripture
2Ti 3:16 All Scripture is God-breathed . . .
See also **2Ki** 17:13–14; **Ne** 9:30; **Mt** 22:43–44 pp Mk 12:36; **1Co** 2:13; **Heb** 1:1–2; **1Pe** 1:10–11; **2Pe** 1:20–21

The authority of Scripture recognised in the OT
Ps 119:89 Your word, O LORD, is eternal; it stands firm in the heavens.

Jos 23:6 ". . . be careful to obey all that is written in the Book of the Law of Moses, without turning aside to the right or to the left." *See also* **Jos** 1:8; **2Ki** 22:11; **Ezr** 10:1–4,9–12; **Ne** 13:1–3; **Isa** 40:8

The authority of Scripture recognised in the NT
Jn 10:34–36 ". . . the Scripture cannot be broken . . ." *See also* **Mt** 5:17–19; **Lk** 21:21–23; 16:17; **1Th** 2:13

Jesus Christ claims scriptural authority for his own words
Mt 24:34–35 ". . . Heaven and earth will pass away, but my words will never pass away." pp Mk 13:30–31 *See also* **Jn** 12:47–50; 14:10,23–24 *See also* law, Jesus Christ's attitude; prophecy, Old Testament inspiration; revelation; word of God.

Scripture, purpose
Scripture has been given by God to lead people to faith and salvation. Through Scripture believers are nurtured in faith and led to spiritual maturity.

Scripture is intended to lead people to salvation
2Ti 3:14–15 . . . the holy Scriptures . . . are able to make you wise for salvation through

faith in Christ Jesus.   *See also* **Ps** 19:7–11; **Jn** 20:30–31; **Ro** 10:8

Scripture is intended to lead believers to maturity in faith
By its teaching
2Ti 3:16 All Scripture is God-breathed and is useful for teaching . . .   *See also* **Dt** 6:6–9; **Ps** 19:7–8; 119:9,130; **Col** 3:16
By its rebuke and correction
2Ti 3:16 All Scripture is God-breathed and is useful for . . . rebuking, correcting . . .   *See also* **Ps** 19:11–13; **1Co** 10:11–12; **Heb** 4:12–13
By training in righteousness
2Ti 3:16 All Scripture is God-breathed and is useful for . . . training in righteousness,   *See also* **Dt** 29:29
By its illumination
Ps 119:105 Your [the LORD's] word is a lamp to my feet and a light for my path.

Ps 119:130 The unfolding of your [the LORD's] words gives light; it gives understanding to the simple.   *See also* **2Pe** 1:19; **1Jn** 2:8
By its encouragement and reassurance
Ro 15:4 For everything that was written in the past was written to teach us, so that through endurance and the encouragement of the Scriptures we might have hope.

1Jn 5:13 I write these things to you who believe in the name of the Son of God so that you may know that you have eternal life.   *See also* **Ps** 19:8–9; 119:50–51,76; **Heb** 12:5–6
By its record of God's promises
1Ki 8:56 ". . . Not one word has failed of all the good promises he [the LORD] gave through his servant Moses."

Ps 119:140 Your [the LORD's] promises have been thoroughly tested, and your servant loves them.   *See also* **Eze** 12:25; **Lk** 24:44; **2Co** 1:19–22
By its trustworthiness
1Ki 17:24 Then the woman said to Elijah, "Now I know that you are a man of God and that the word of the LORD from your mouth is the

truth."

Ps 19:7–11 The law of the LORD is perfect, reviving the soul. The statutes of the LORD are trustworthy, making wise the simple . . .

Ps 33:4 For the word of the LORD is right and true; he is faithful in all he does.   *See also* **Ps** 119:151,160; **Jn** 21:24; **Rev** 21:5

Scripture is essential for spiritual growth and maturity
Ps 1:1–3 Blessed are those who do not walk in the counsel of the wicked or stand in the way of sinners or sit in the seat of mockers. But their delight is in the law of the LORD, and on his law they meditate day and night. They are like trees planted by streams of water, which yield their fruit in season and whose leaves do not wither. Whatever they do prospers.   *See also* **Mt** 4:4; **Jn** 15:5–8; 17:17; **Eph** 6:10–17; **2Ti** 3:14–17   *See also faith; righteousness; salvation; teaching.*

Scripture, sufficiency
Scripture is presented as being of itself sufficient for faith and for life.

God's written revelation is sufficient
Dt 4:1–2 Hear now, O Israel, the decrees and laws I [Moses] am about to teach you. Follow them so that you may live and may go in and take possession of the land that the LORD, the God of your ancestors, is giving you. Do not add to what I command you and do not subtract from it, but keep the commands of the LORD your God that I give you.   *See also* **Dt** 12:32; **Jos** 1:7–8; **Pr** 30:5–6; **Jer** 26:2

The NT records the completion and fulfilment of the OT
Heb 1:1–2 In the past God spoke to our ancestors through the prophets at many times and in various ways, but in these last days he has spoken to us by his Son, whom he appointed heir of all things, and through whom he made the universe.   *See also* **Jn** 12:47–50; **Eph** 2:20

Warnings against turning from, or adding to, the apostolic gospel, as set forth in Scripture
Rev 22:18–19 I [Jesus] warn everyone who hears the words of the prophecy of this book: If any one of you adds anything to them, God will add to you the plagues described in this book. And if any one of you takes words away from this book of prophecy, God will take away from you your share in the tree of life and in the holy city, which are described in this book.   *See also* **Gal** 1:6–9; **Col** 1:25–2:8,18,20–23; **2Th** 2:1–2

Descriptions of Scripture point to its sufficiency
Scripture is good
Ro 7:12 So then, the law is holy, and the commandment is holy, righteous and good. *See also* **1Ti** 1:8
Scripture is perfect
Ps 19:7 The law of the LORD is perfect, reviving the soul . . .   *See also* **Ps** 119:142; **Jas** 1:25
Scripture is eternal
Ps 119:89 Your word, O LORD, is eternal; it stands firm in the heavens.   *See also* **Mt** 5:18; 24:35; **1Pe** 1:24–25; **Isa** 40:6–8   *See also gospel; hope, in God; truth.*

Scripture, understanding
God intends his word to be understood and has provided the directions and means for understanding it.

Scripture is intended to be clearly understood
It is accessible to ordinary people
Ps 119:130 The unfolding of your [the LORD's] words gives light; it gives understanding to the simple.   *See also* **Ps** 19:7
Some sections are difficult to understand
2Pe 3:15–16 Bear in mind that our Lord's patience means salvation, just as our dear brother Paul also wrote to you with the wisdom that God gave him. He writes the same way in all his letters, speaking in them of these matters. His letters contain some things that are hard to understand, which ignorant and unstable people distort, as they do the other Scriptures, to their own destruction.   *See also* **Heb** 5:11

God has prescribed the way to understand Scripture
Through public reading
1Ti 4:13 Until I come, devote yourself to the public reading of Scripture, to preaching and to teaching.   *See also* **Ne** 8:2–8; 13:1–3
Through diligent study
2Ti 2:15 Do your best to present yourself to God as one approved, a worker who does not need to be ashamed and who correctly handles the word of truth.   *See also* **Dt** 17:18–20; **Ac** 17:11
Through thoughtful meditation
Ps 1:1–3 . . . their [the righteous] delight is in the law of the LORD, and on his law they meditate day and night . . .   *See also* **Jos** 1:8; **Job** 23:12; **Ps** 119:15,27,48,97,148

Assistance in understanding through the Holy Spirit
1Co 2:9–12 However, as it is written: "No eye has seen, no ear has heard, no mind has conceived what God has prepared for those who love him"—but God has revealed it to us [believers] by his Spirit . . .   *See also* **Isa** 64:4; **Lk** 24:45; **Jn** 14:26; 16:13; **1Jn** 2:27

Assistance in understanding through ministers of the word
Ne 8:2–8 . . . They [the Levites] read from the Book of the Law of God, making it clear and giving the meaning so that the people could understand what was being read.   *See also* **Eph** 4:11–14; **1Ti** 4:11–16; **2Ti** 4:1–5   *See also prayer; preachers and preaching.*

sin
Primarily a wrong relationship with God, which may express itself in wrong attitudes or actions towards God himself, other human beings, possessions or the environment. Scripture stresses that this condition is deeply rooted in human nature, and that only God is able to break its penalty, power and presence.

sin, and God's character

In his righteousness and holiness, God detests sin and its effects upon humanity. In his mercy and grace, he makes available a means of atonement, by the death and resurrection of Jesus Christ.

God's character and sin
God himself is perfect
Hab 1:13 Your eyes are too pure to look on evil; you cannot tolerate wrong . . .

1Jn 1:5 . . . God is light; in him there is no darkness at all.   *See also* **Dt** 32:4; **Jos** 24:19; **Ps** 97:2; **Isa** 6:3
Jesus Christ is sinless
1Pe 2:22 "He committed no sin, and no deceit was found in his mouth."   *See also* **Isa** 53:9; **2Co** 5:21; **Heb** 1:9; 7:26–27; **1Jn** 3:5
God's people are to be holy
1Pe 1:15–16 But just as he who called you is holy, so be holy in all you do; for it is written: "Be holy, because I am holy."   *See also* **Lev** 11:44,45; 19:2; 20:7; **Mt** 5:48; **1Th** 4:7; **1Jn** 3:3

God's attitude to sin
God knows all sin
Jer 16:17 "My eyes are on all their ways; they are not hidden from me, nor is their sin concealed from my eyes."   *See also* **Job** 10:14; **Ps** 139:1–4; **Jer** 2:22; **Hos** 7:2; **Am** 5:12; **Heb** 4:13
God grieves over sin
Ge 6:6 The LORD was grieved that he had made human beings on the earth, and his heart was filled with pain.   *See also* **Isa** 63:10; **Eph** 4:30
God hates sin
Ps 11:5 The LORD examines the righteous, but the wicked and those who love violence his soul hates.   *See also* **Dt** 25:16; **2Sa** 11:27; **Ps** 5:5; **Pr** 6:16–19; **Zec** 8:17; **Lk** 16:15
Sin provokes God's anger
Ro 1:18 The wrath of God is being revealed from heaven against all the godlessness and wickedness of those . . .   *See also* **2Ch** 36:16; **Eze** 20:8; **Am** 1:3; **Jn** 3:36; **Eph** 5:5–6; **Col** 3:5–6
God is also merciful and gracious
Ex 34:6–7 . . . "The LORD, the LORD, the compassionate and gracious God, slow to anger, abounding in love and faithfulness, maintaining love to thousands, and forgiving wickedness, rebellion and sin . . ."   *See also* **Ne** 9:17,31; **Ps** 78:38; 103:8–14; **La** 3:22–23; **Mic** 7:18–19; **Ro** 11:32
God's patience with sinners
2Pe 3:9 . . . He is patient with you, not wanting anyone to perish, but everyone to come to repentance.   *See also* **Ro** 2:4; 9:22; **1Ti** 1:16

Jesus Christ is the supreme revelation of God's love for sinners
Jesus Christ's ministry of forgiveness
1Ti 1:15 . . . Christ Jesus came into the world to save sinners . . .   *See also* **Mt** 9:2 pp **Mk** 2:5 pp **Lk** 5:20–21; **Lk** 7:36–50; 15:1–10; 19:5–10; **Jn** 8:1–11
God's love shown in Jesus Christ's death
Ro 5:8 But God demonstrates his own love for us in this: While we were still sinners, Christ died for us.   *See also* **Jn** 3:16–17; **Eph** 2:4; **1Pe** 3:18; **1Jn** 4:9–10
The risen Christ gives grace to sinful people
1Jn 2:1 . . . But if anybody does sin, we have one who speaks to the Father in our defence— Jesus Christ, the Righteous One.   *See also* **Ro** 8:34; **Heb** 2:17–18; 4:15–5:2   *See also* **grace; holiness, of God; mercy, demonstration of God's; righteousness, of God.**

sin, avoidance

God calls his people to avoid sin, and through Jesus Christ gives them the inner power to be victorious over it.

God's people are to resist sin
1Pe 2:11 Dear friends, I urge you, as aliens and strangers in the world, to abstain from sinful desires, which war against your soul.   *See also* **Ps** 97:10; **Pr** 4:23–27; **1Co** 15:34; **Eph** 4:25–5:20; **Jas** 1:21

The Christian life is a constant struggle against sin
Heb 3:13 . . . so that none of you may be hardened by sin's deceitfulness.   *See also* **Ac** 20:28;

Ro 7:14–25; **Eph** 6:10–18; **1Pe** 5:8–9

God helps his people to resist sin

Release from sin through Jesus Christ's death
1Pe 2:24 He himself bore our sins in his body on the tree, so that we might die to sins and live for righteousness; by his wounds you have been healed.   *See also* **Ro** 6:1–7; **Gal** 2:20; 5:24; **Col** 2:11–12

The avoidance of sin through new life in Jesus Christ
1Jn 3:9 Those who are born of God will not continue to sin, because God's seed remains in them; they cannot go on sinning, because they have been born of God.   *See also* **2Co** 5:17; **1Pe** 1:23; **1Jn** 3:6; 5:18

Believers co-operate with Jesus Christ to avoid sin
Php 2:12–13 . . . continue to work out your salvation with fear and trembling, for it is God who works in you to will and to act according to his good purpose.

Believers are to put to death what is sinful in them
Col 3:5 Put to death, therefore, whatever belongs to your earthly nature: sexual immorality, impurity, lust, evil desires and greed, which is idolatry.   *See also* **Ro** 6:11–14; 8:13

Believers are to exchange sinful for righteous behaviour
Ro 13:12–14 The night is nearly over; the day is almost here. So let us put aside the deeds of darkness and put on the armour of light . . .
See also **Eph** 4:22–24; **Col** 3:7–10; **1Ti** 6:11; **2Ti** 2:22

Believers are to allow the Spirit to inform and direct their conduct
Ro 12:2 Do not conform any longer to the pattern of this world, but be transformed by the renewing of your mind. Then you will be able to test and approve what God's will is—his good, pleasing and perfect will.   *See also* **Ro** 8:5–8; **Gal** 5:16–25

Practical steps for overcoming sin and temptation

Meditation on Scripture
Ps 119:11 I have hidden your word in my heart that I might not sin against you.   *See also* **Ps** 18:22–23; **Mt** 4:1–11 pp **Lk** 4:1–13; **2Ti** 3:16–17

Prayerful dependence upon God
Mt 6:13 " 'And lead us not into temptation, but deliver us from the evil one.' " pp **Lk** 11:4
See also **Ps** 19:13; **Mt** 26:41; **1Co** 10:13; **Heb** 4:15–16

Active seeking of the good
Ro 6:19 . . . Just as you used to offer the parts of your body in slavery to impurity and to ever-increasing wickedness, so now offer them in slavery to righteousness leading to holiness.   *See also* **Ps** 34:14; **Isa** 1:16–17; **Am** 5:14–15; **1Th** 5:22; **3Jn** 11

Incentives for avoiding sin

The fear of God
Pr 16:6 . . . through the fear of the LORD evil is avoided.   *See also* **Ex** 20:20; **Pr** 3:7; 8:13

The holiness of God
1Pe 1:15–16 But just as he who called you is holy, so be holy in all you do; for it is written: "Be holy, because I am holy."   *See also* **Lev** 11:44–45; 19:2; 20:7; **1Co** 6:18–20; **1Th** 4:7

The expectation of Jesus Christ's return
1Pe 4:7 The end of all things is near. Therefore be clear minded and self-controlled so that you can pray.   *See also* **2Co** 5:9–10; **1Th** 5:4–6; **2Pe** 3:10–14

A consideration of the consequences of sin
Gal 6:7–8 Do not be deceived: God cannot be mocked. People reap what they sow. Those who sow to please their sinful nature, from that nature will reap destruction; those who sow to please the Spirit, from the Spirit will reap eternal life.   *See also* **Mk** 9:42–48; **Ro** 6:21–23; **Heb** 6:7–8; 10:26–31

The need to be a good witness to unbelievers
1Pe 2:15 For it is God's will that by doing good you should silence the ignorant talk of foolish people.   *See also* **1Pe** 3:1–2,15–16

The role of others in avoiding sin
Bad company is to be avoided
1Co 15:33 Do not be misled: "Bad company corrupts good character."   *See also* Dt 7:1–4; Ps 1:1; Pr 1:10; 1Co 5:1–13
A good example is to be followed
1Co 11:1 Follow my [Paul's] example, as I follow the example of Christ.   *See also* Php 3:17; 4:9; Heb 12:1–3; 1Pe 4:1–3
Believers are to support one another
Jas 5:19–20 My brothers and sisters, if one of you should wander from the truth and someone should bring that person back, remember this: Those who turn sinners from the error of their ways will save them from death and cover over a multitude of sins.   *See also* Mt 18:15–17; Gal 6:1–2; 1Ti 5:20; Heb 3:12   *See also fellowship; holiness; sanctification.*

---

sin, causes of
Sin is the result of the fall, at which the creation rebels against God its Creator.

Sin as a result of the devil's activity
The devil's instigation of the first sin
Ge 3:13 . . . The woman [Eve] said, "The serpent deceived me, and I ate [the fruit of the tree of knowledge of good and evil]."   *See also* Ge 3:1–6; 2Co 11:3; Rev 12:9
The devil's role as tempter
1Th 3:5 . . . I was afraid that in some way the tempter might have tempted you . . .   *See also* Mt 4:1–11 pp Mk 1:12–13 pp Lk 4:1–13; Mt 6:13
The devil as the source of sinful behaviour
Jn 8:44 "You belong to your father, the devil, and you want to carry out your father's desire. He was a murderer from the beginning, not holding to the truth, for there is no truth in him. When he lies, he speaks his native language, for he is a liar and the father of lies."   *See also* Jn 8:38,41; 1Jn 3:8,10
The sins of angels
2Pe 2:4 For if God did not spare angels when they sinned, but sent them to hell, putting them into gloomy dungeons to be held for judgment;   *See also* Jude 6

Sin as a power in the world
Sin's reign from the time of Adam
Ro 5:12 . . . sin entered the world through one man . . .   *See also* Ge 4:7; Jn 8:34; Ro 5:21; 6:16
Sin uses the law to provoke sinful desires
Ro 7:5 For when we were controlled by the sinful nature, the sinful passions aroused by the law were at work in our bodies, so that we bore fruit for death.   *See also* Ro 7:7–12; 1Co 15:56
The world is under sin's dominion
1Jn 2:16 For everything in the world—the cravings of sinful people, the lust of their eyes and the boasting of what they have and do—comes not from the Father but from the world.   *See also* Lk 21:34; Tit 2:12

Sin is rooted in human nature
The human heart is dominated by sin
Jer 17:9 The heart is deceitful above all things and beyond cure . . .   *See also* Mt 15:19 pp Mk 7:21–22; Ro 1:24; Heb 3:12
Human nature is fundamentally opposed to God
Ro 8:5–8 . . . the sinful mind is hostile to God. It does not submit to God's law, nor can it do so. Those controlled by the sinful nature cannot please God.   *See also* Ro 7:14–25; Gal 5:17–21; Eph 2:3; 2Pe 2:10,18

The act of sinning
Sin results from giving in to evil desires
Jas 1:14–15 . . . each of you is tempted when, by your own evil desire, you are dragged away and enticed. Then, after desire has conceived, it gives birth to sin . . .   *See also* Ro 13:13–14; Jas 4:1; Jude 16
Sin results from the human desire to be like God
Ge 3:5 "For God knows that when you eat of it your eyes will be opened, and you will be like God, knowing good and evil."   *See also* Isa 14:12–14; Eze 28:2
Sin results when the body is placed at sin's disposal
Ro 6:13 Do not offer the parts of your body to sin, as instruments of wickedness . . .   *See also*

Mt 5:29–30; 18:8–9 pp Mk 9:43–47

Sin results from the influence of others
1Co 15:33 . . . "Bad company corrupts good
character." *See also* **Ex** 23:33; **1Ki** 11:3; **Pr**
1:10; 22:24–25

The seriousness of leading others into sin
Mk 9:42 "And if any of you causes one of
these little ones who believe in me to sin, it
would be better for you to be thrown into the
sea with a large millstone tied around your neck."
pp Mt 18:6 pp Lk 17:1–2 *See also* **1Co**
8:9–13 *See also Satan; world.*

---

sin, deliverance from

The gospel reveals the purpose and power of God
to deal with sin and all of its effects. Scripture
uses a range of images to express the
comprehensiveness of salvation.

God's removal of sin
Atonement for sin
Isa 6:7 With it [a live coal] he touched my
mouth and said, "See, this has touched your lips;
your guilt is taken away and your sin atoned
for." *See also* **Ex** 32:30; **Lev** 4:27–31; **Pr** 16:6;
Ro 3:25; **Heb** 2:17

Forgiveness of sin
Mic 7:18 Who is a God like you, who pardons
sin and forgives the transgression of the remnant
of his inheritance? You do not stay angry for ever
but delight to show mercy.

Ac 13:38 "Therefore, my brothers and sisters, I
want you to know that through Jesus the
forgiveness of sins is proclaimed to you." *See
also* **1Ki** 8:35–36; **2Ch** 30:18–20; **Ps** 103:2–3;
Isa 33:24; 55:7; **Joel** 3:21; **Mt** 26:27–28; **Lk**
24:46–47; **Eph** 1:7; **1Jn** 1:9

Cancellation of a debt
Mt 6:12 " 'Forgive us our debts, as we also
have forgiven our debtors.' " *See also* **Mt**
18:21–35; **Lk** 7:41–50

A covering over of sin
1Pe 4:8 Above all, love each other deeply,
because love covers over a multitude of sins.
See also **Ps** 32:1; 85:2; **Jas** 5:20

The taking away of sin
Ps 103:12 as far as the east is from the west,
so far has he removed our transgressions from
us. *See also* **2Sa** 12:13; **Isa** 6:6–7; **Zec** 3:4; **Jn**
1:29; **Heb** 9:28; **1Jn** 3:5

Remembering sin no more
Isa 43:25 "I [the LORD], even I, am he who
blots out your transgressions, for my own sake,
and remembers your sins no more." *See also*
Ps 25:7; **Jer** 31:33–34; **2Co** 5:19

God's deliverance for the sinner
The salvation of the sinner
1Ti 1:15 Here is a trustworthy saying that
deserves full acceptance: Christ Jesus came into
the world to save sinners—of whom I am the
worst. *See also* **Ps** 28:8–9; **Mt** 1:21; **Lk**
19:9–10; **Jn** 3:17; **Heb** 7:25

The image of healing
Lk 5:31–32 Jesus answered them [Pharisees
and teachers of the law], "It is not the healthy
who need a doctor, but the sick. I have not come
to call the righteous, but sinners to repentance."
pp Mt 9:12 pp Mk 2:17 *See also* **2Ch** 7:14;
Isa 53:5; 57:18–19; **Hos** 14:4; **1Pe** 2:24

The image of cleansing
Ps 51:2 Wash away all my iniquity and cleanse
me from my sin. *See also* **Lev** 16:30; **Eze**
36:25; **Jn** 13:1–11; **Heb** 10:22; **Ac** 22:16; **1Jn** 1:9

Redemption by God
Ps 130:8 He himself will redeem Israel from all
their sins. *See also* **Isa** 44:22; **Tit** 2:14; **1Pe**
1:18–19

Justification before God
Gal 2:16 ". . . a person is not justified by
observing the law, but by faith in Jesus Christ. So
we, too, have put our faith in Christ Jesus that
we may be justified by faith in Christ and not by
observing the law, because by observing the law
no-one will be justified." *See also* **Isa** 53:11;
Ro 3:24–26; 4:5,25; 5:16–19; 8:33

Freedom from condemnation
Ro 8:1 Therefore, there is now no condemnation
for those who are in Christ Jesus, *See also* **Jn**
3:18; 8:3–11; **Ro** 8:34

Peace with God
Ro 5:1 Therefore, since we have been justified

through faith, we have peace with God through our Lord Jesus Christ,   *See also* **Isa** 53:5; **Lk** 2:14; **Eph** 2:17

Reconciliation with God
2Co 5:18 All this is from God, who reconciled us to himself through Christ . . .   *See also* **Ro** 5:9–11; **Col** 1:19–20

Sanctification to God
Heb 10:10 And by that will, we have been made holy through the sacrifice of the body of Jesus Christ once for all.   *See also* **1Co** 6:11; **Eph** 5:25–26; **Col** 1:22

Freedom from sin and the sinful nature
Ro 7:24 What a wretched man I am! Who will rescue me from this body of death?

1Pe 2:24 He himself bore our sins in his body on the tree, so that we might die to sins and live for righteousness . . .   *See also* **Ro** 6:1–18; 8:1–9; **Gal** 5:24

A transition from death to life
Col 2:13 When you were dead in your sins and in the uncircumcision of your sinful nature, God made you alive with Christ . . .   *See also* **Lk** 15:22–24; **Eph** 2:4–5

Receiving eternal life
Ro 6:23 For the wages of sin is death, but the gift of God is eternal life in Christ Jesus our Lord.   *See also* **Jn** 3:16,36   *See also justification; peace; reconciliation; redemption; salvation.*

---

sin, effects of
Sin affects every level of human existence, including the sinner's relationship with God, with other human beings and with the environment.

The effects of sin on individuals
Lack of peace of mind
Isa 57:20–21 But the wicked are like the tossing sea, which cannot rest, whose waves cast up mire and mud. "There is no peace," says my God, "for the wicked."   *See also* **Job** 15:20–35; **Ps** 38:5–8; **Pr** 13:15–22; **La** 1:20–21

Bondage to a continuing habit of sin
Jn 8:34 ". . . everyone who sins is a slave to sin."   *See also* **Pr** 5:22; **Ro** 6:16; **2Ti** 2:16

Physical death
1Co 15:56 The sting of death is sin . . .
See also **Ge** 2:17; 3:19; **Pr** 21:16; **Ro** 5:12–14; 6:21–23; **1Co** 15:22; **Jas** 1:15

The sinful life is equivalent to death
Eph 2:1 As for you, you were dead in your transgressions and sins,   *See also* **Ro** 7:9,13; 8:10; **Col** 2:13

The effects of sin on the sinner before God
Uncleanness
Isa 64:6 All of us have become like one who is unclean, and all our righteous acts are like filthy rags . . .   *See also* **Ps** 106:39; **Isa** 6:5; **Jer** 2:22; **La** 1:8; **Mt** 15:18–20 pp **Mk** 7:20–23

Guilt
Ezr 9:6 . . . "O my God, I am too ashamed and disgraced to lift up my face to you, my God, because our sins are higher than our heads and our guilt has reached to the heavens."   *See also* **Ge** 3:10; **Ps** 38:3–4; 44:15; **Isa** 59:12–13; **Jer** 3:25; 14:20

Separation from God
Isa 59:2 But your iniquities have separated you from your God; your sins have hidden his face from you, so that he will not hear.   *See also* **Dt** 31:18; **Isa** 1:15; 64:7; **Eze** 8:6; **Hos** 5:6; **Mic** 3:4; **Eph** 2:12

The effects of sin on Israel
Pr 14:34 Righteousness exalts a nation, but sin is a disgrace to any people.   *See also* **Jos** 7:1–16; **1Ki** 8:33–40; **Isa** 1:4–9; **Ro** 1:21–32

The effects of sin on the world
The ground cursed
Ge 3:17–18 . . . ". . . Cursed is the ground because of you; through painful toil you will eat of it all the days of your life. It will produce thorns and thistles for you, and you will eat the plants of the field."   *See also* **Jer** 12:13; **Ro** 8:20–22

The land polluted
Lev 18:25 " 'Even the land was defiled; so I punished it for its sin, and the land vomited out its inhabitants.' "   *See also* **Ge** 4:10–12; **Nu** 35:33–34; **Ps** 106:38; **Isa** 24:4–6; **Jer** 3:1

sin, forgiveness of

Sinners must respond to God's offer of forgiveness through faith in Jesus Christ.

The conviction of sin

La 1:20 "See, O Lord, how distressed I am! I am in torment within, and in my heart I am disturbed, for I have been most rebellious. Outside, the sword bereaves; inside, there is only death."

Jn 16:8–9 "When he [the Counsellor] comes, he will convict the world of guilt in regard to sin and righteousness and judgment: in regard to sin, because people do not believe in me [Jesus];" *See also* **1Ki** 8:38–40; **Isa** 6:5; **Eze** 33:10–11; **Ac** 16:29

The inward response of faith

Ac 16:31 . . . "Believe in the Lord Jesus, and you will be saved . . ." *See also* **Mk** 1:14–15; **Jn** 3:36; 5:24; **Ac** 13:38–39; 16:25–34; **Ro** 3:22–26; 10:8–10; **Eph** 2:8

The outward response of baptism

Ac 22:16 "'And now what are you waiting for? Get up, be baptised and wash your sins away, calling on his [Jesus'] name.'" *See also* **Mk** 1:4–5 pp **Mt** 3:1–6 pp **Lk** 3:2–6; **Ac** 2:38; 8:36; **Col** 2:11–12; **1Pe** 3:21

Confession of sin

Pr 28:13 Those who conceal their sins do not prosper, but those who confess and renounce them find mercy.

1Jn 1:9 If we confess our sins, he is faithful and just and will forgive us our sins and purify us from all unrighteousness. *See also* **Lev** 16:20–22; 26:40–42; **2Sa** 12:13; **Ps** 32:3–5; **La** 3:40; **Lk** 15:17–20; **Ac** 19:18

Repentance
Turning towards God

Ac 3:19 "Repent, then, and turn to God, so that your sins may be wiped out . . ." *See also* **2Ch** 6:36–39; **Isa** 55:7; **Eze** 18:21; **Mt** 3:1–2 pp **Mk** 1:4 pp **Lk** 3:2; **Ac** 17:30; **2Co** 7:10; **1Th** 1:9

Turning away from sin

Jn 8:11 . . . "Then neither do I condemn you [the woman caught in adultery]," Jesus declared. "Go now and leave your life of sin." *See also* **Jer** 4:3–4; **Lk** 19:1–10; **Jn** 5:14; **Ro** 6:11–14; **1Pe** 2:11

The making of restitution

Lk 19:8 But Zacchaeus stood up and said to the Lord, "Look, Lord! Here and now I give half of my possessions to the poor, and if I have cheated anybody out of anything, I will pay back four times the amount." *See also* **Lev** 6:1–7; **Nu** 5:6–8; **Pr** 6:30–31; **Eze** 33:12–16

The forgiveness of others

Lk 11:4 "'Forgive us our sins, for we also forgive everyone who sins against us . . .'" pp **Mt** 6:12 *See also* **Mt** 6:14–15; 18:21–35; **Mk** 11:25; **Eph** 4:32; **Col** 3:13 *See also baptism; conversion; faith; forgiveness; gospel; repentance.*

---

sin, judgment on

Sin comes under the judgment of God, in that it contradicts his nature and opposes his purposes.

God's judgment on sin
God is the judge of sin

Isa 26:21 See, the Lord is coming out of his dwelling to punish the people of the earth for their sins . . . *See also* **Ps** 99:8; **Isa** 13:11; **Am** 3:14; **Zep** 1:12; **1Th** 4:6

God's judgment is certain

Ro 2:12 All who sin apart from the law will also perish apart from the law, and all who sin under the law will be judged by the law. *See also* **Ps** 37:38; **Pr** 11:21; **Heb** 9:27

God's judgment is in proportion to the seriousness of the sin

Jer 21:14 "'I will punish you as your deeds deserve, declares the Lord . . .'" *See also* **Dt** 25:2; **Isa** 59:18; **Mt** 7:1–5; **Lk** 12:47–48; **Ro** 2:5–6

God's judgment under the Sinaitic covenant

Ex 20:5 ". . . I, the Lord your God, am a jealous God, punishing the children for the sin of

the parents to the third and fourth generation of
those who hate me," pp Dt 5:9
Curses for disobedience formed part of God's covenant
with Israel: **Lev** 26:14–39; **Dt** 28:15–68
Jer 31:29–30; **Eze** 18:1–32
**John the Baptist and Jesus Christ warn of
judgment**
Mt 3:10 "The axe is already at the root of the
trees, and every tree that does not produce good
fruit will be cut down and thrown into the fire."
pp Lk 3:9   *See also* **Mt** 3:12; 7:19; 12:36–37;
Mk 9:42–49

Ways in which God judges sin
God causes sin to bring evil to the sinner
2Ch 6:23 ". . . Judge between your servants,
condemning the guilty and bringing down on their
heads what they have done . . ."   *See also* **Dt**
19:19; **Est** 7:10; **Ps** 7:15–16; **Isa** 30:13
God abandons people
Isa 64:7 . . . for you have hidden your face
from us and made us waste away because of our
sins.   *See also* **Dt** 31:17–18; **Jos** 7:11–12; **La**
4:16; **Eze** 39:23–24
**Unrepentant sinners to be expelled from the
church**
Mt 18:17 "If they refuse to listen to them, tell
it to the church; and if they refuse to listen even
to the church, treat them as you would a pagan
or a tax collector."   *See also* **1Co** 5:1–13
**God exercises judgment through a country's
legal system**
1Pe 2:14 . . . [governors] are sent by him to
punish those who do wrong and to commend
those who do right.   *See also* **Ro** 13:3–4
Untimely death is God's judgment on all sin
Ge 2:17 ". . . but you must not eat from the
tree of the knowledge of good and evil, for when
you eat of it you will surely die."   *See also* **Lev**
20:1–17; **1Ch** 10:13; **Pr** 11:19; **Ro** 1:32; **1Co**
11:29–30
Sinners are excluded from the kingdom of God
Rev 22:15 "Outside are the dogs, those who
practise magic arts, the sexually immoral, the
murderers, the idolaters and everyone who loves
and practises falsehood."   *See also* **1Co** 6:9–10;
Gal 5:9–21; **Rev** 21:27

Occasions of God's judgment on sin
OT examples Ge 3:16–24; 6:1–7:24;
18:20–19:29; **Dt** 9:1–5
The exile of Israel and Judah: **2Ki** 17:7–23; 24:10–20
The destruction of Jerusalem Lk 11:47–51;
13:34–35
God's final judgment of the world
Rev 21:8 "But the cowardly, the unbelieving,
the vile, the murderers, the sexually immoral,
those who practise magic arts, the idolaters and
all liars—their place will be in the fiery lake of
burning sulphur. This is the second death."
See also **Isa** 66:24; **Mt** 25:31–46; **2Th** 1:8–9; **2Pe**
3:7; **Jude** 7   *See also* covenant, at Sinai; hell;
judgment, God's.

sin, nature of
Scripture portrays sin in terms of wrongness before
God in a variety of different ways, such as
uncleanness, guilt or rebellion.

The basic nature of sin
All sin is directed against God
Ps 51:4 Against you, you only, have I sinned
and done what is evil in your sight . . .   *See
also* **Ge** 13:13; **Ex** 10:16; **Jdg** 10:10; **Ps** 41:4; **Lk**
15:18
Sin is essentially a lack of faith in God
Ro 14:23 . . . everything that does not come
from faith is sin.   *See also* **Heb** 11:6

Descriptions of sin
Corruption of God's good purposes
Dt 32:5 They have acted corruptly towards him;
to their shame they are no longer his children,
but a warped and crooked generation.   *See also*
Ge 6:11–12; **Dt** 9:12; 31:29; **Jdg** 2:19
Doing evil in God's sight
Jn 3:19–20 ". . . Light has come into the
world, but people loved darkness instead of light
because their deeds were evil. All those who do
evil hate the light, and will not come into the
light for fear that their deeds will be
exposed."   *See also* **Jdg** 2:11; **Ps** 34:12–16; **Pr**
8:13; **Isa** 59:6–7; **Mt** 12:35 pp **Lk** 6:45
Ungodliness
Jude 14–15 . . . "See, the Lord is coming

with thousands upon thousands of his holy ones to judge everyone, and to convict all the ungodly of all the ungodly acts they have done in the ungodly way, and of all the harsh words ungodly sinners have spoken against him." *See also* **Isa** 9:17; 32:6; **1Ti** 1:9

Rebellion against God's authority
Isa 30:9 These are rebellious people, deceitful children, children unwilling to listen to the Lord's instruction. *See also* **Dt** 9:7; **1Sa** 15:23; **Ps** 78:40,56; **Jer** 3:13; **Hos** 7:13

The breaking or transgression of God's laws
1Jn 3:4 Everyone who sins breaks the law; in fact, sin is lawlessness. *See also* **1Sa** 13:13–14; **1Ch** 10:13; **Ne** 9:29; **Mic** 1:5; 7:18; **Ro** 2:23; 4:15; 5:14–17; **Jas** 2:10–11

Straying from the right path
Isa 53:6 We all, like sheep, have gone astray, each of us has turned to our own way . . .
See also **Ps** 58:3; 95:10; 119:10,21,118

Incurring a debt
Mt 6:12 " 'Forgive us our debts, as we also have forgiven our debtors.' " *See also* **Mt** 18:21–35

Falling short of a standard
Ro 3:23 for all have sinned and fall short of the glory of God,

Uncleanness
Ps 51:2 Wash away all my iniquity and cleanse me from my sin.

Isa 1:16 "wash and make yourselves clean. Take your evil deeds out of my sight! Stop doing wrong," *See also* **Ps** 51:7; **Heb** 9:14

Kinds of sin
Sins of omission
Jas 4:17 So, then, if you know the good you ought to do and don't do it, you sin. *See also* **Mt** 23:23 pp **Lk** 11:42; **Mt** 25:45

Deliberate sins
Lk 12:47 "The servant who knows the master's will and does not get ready or does not do what the master wants will be beaten with many blows." *See also* **Nu** 15:30–31; **Dt** 1:42–43; 17:12; **Ps** 19:13; **Isa** 57:17; **Ro** 1:32

Unintentional sins
Lk 12:48 "But the one who does not know and does things deserving punishment will be beaten with few blows . . ." *See also* **Lev** 4:1–5; **Nu** 15:22–29; **Dt** 4:41–42; **Ac** 3:17; **1Ti** 1:13

Sin against the Holy Spirit
Mk 3:29–30 "But whoever blasphemes against the Holy Spirit will never be forgiven; he is guilty of an eternal sin." He said this because they were saying, "He has an evil spirit." pp **Mt** 12:31–32 pp **Lk** 12:10 *See also* **1Jn** 5:16
See also law.

---

sin, remedy for
Under the old covenant, sin was forgiven through sacrifice, prefiguring the atoning death of Jesus Christ, which brings forgiveness of sins under the new covenant.

Atonement for sins in the OT was through the shedding of blood
Lev 17:11 " 'For the life of a creature is in the blood, and I have given it to you to make atonement for yourselves on the altar; it is the blood that makes atonement for one's life.' "

Kinds of sin offering in the OT
The sin offering was for unintentional sins
Lev 4:1–5:13 The Lord said to Moses, "Say to the Israelites: 'When anyone sins unintentionally and does what is forbidden in any of the Lord's commands . . .' " *See also* **Nu** 15:22–31

The guilt offering was for unintentional sins, where restitution was required
Lev 5:14–6:7 . . . ". . . In this way the priest will make atonement for them before the Lord, and they will be forgiven for any of these things they did that made them guilty." *See also* **Nu** 5:5–10

The annual Day of Atonement cleansed the nation of sin
Lev 16:1–34 . . . ". . . This is to be a lasting ordinance for you: Atonement is to be made once a year for all the sins of the Israelites." . . . *See also* **Ex** 30:11–16; **Lev** 23:26–32; **Heb** 9:7

The priests made atonement on occasions of deliberate national sin Nu 16:46–48; 25:13

Sacrifices of atonement needed to be accompanied by repentance and a willingness to obey

Worshippers recognised the need for repentance and obedience

Pr 21:3 To do what is right and just is more acceptable to the LORD than sacrifice.   *See also* Ps 40:6–8; 51:16–17

The prophets declared the need for obedience

1Sa 15:22 . . . "Does the LORD delight in burnt offerings and sacrifices as much as in obeying the voice of the LORD? To obey is better than sacrifice, and to heed is better than the fat of rams."   *See also* Isa 1:11–17; Jer 7:21–23; Hos 6:6; Mic 6:6–8

The prophets warned of judgment to bring people to repentance

2Ki 17:13 The LORD warned Israel and Judah through all his prophets and seers: "Turn from your evil ways. Observe my commands and decrees, in accordance with the entire Law that I commanded your ancestors to obey and that I delivered to you through my servants the prophets."   *See also* Isa 31:6–7; Jer 4:1–4; 35:15; Eze 3:16–19; Jnh 3:4–10

The death of Jesus Christ brings forgiveness for sin

Jesus Christ died on behalf of sinful humanity

Ro 5:6 . . . when we were still powerless, Christ died for the ungodly.   *See also* Mt 26:26–28; Jn 10:11; 15:13; Gal 2:20

The early church proclaimed that Christ died for the sins of others

1Co 15:3 . . . Christ died for our sins according to the Scriptures.   *See also* Ro 4:25; Gal 1:4; 1Pe 3:18

Jesus Christ bore sin on the cross

2Co 5:21 God made him who had no sin to be sin for us, so that in him we might become the righteousness of God.   *See also* Isa 53:10–12; Heb 9:28; 1Pe 2:24

Jesus Christ has redeemed people by taking their place

Mt 20:28 ". . . the Son of Man did not come to be served, but to serve, and to give his life as a ransom for many." pp Mk 10:45   *See also* Gal 3:13; 1Ti 2:6; Tit 2:14

Jesus Christ's death is sacrificial

Ro 3:25 God presented him as a sacrifice of atonement, through faith in his blood . . . *See also* Ro 8:3; 1Co 5:7; Eph 5:2; Heb 7:27; 10:5–13; 1Jn 2:2; 4:10

The shedding of Jesus Christ's blood brings forgiveness

1Jn 1:7 . . . the blood of Jesus, his Son, purifies us from all sin.   *See also* Jn 1:29; Eph 1:7; Heb 9:12–22; 13:12; 1Pe 1:18–19; Rev 7:14   *See also atonement; blood; forgiveness; propitiation; sacrifice, in Old Testament.*

---

sin, universality

All human beings sin and are guilty in the sight of God on account of an inherently sinful disposition, which can be traced back to Adam. Acts of sin thus arise from a sinful human heart. The basis of cleansing and cancellation of "original sin" is the atoning death of Jesus Christ.

Adam, the cause of universal sin

Ro 5:19 . . . through the disobedience of the one man the many were made sinners . . . *See also* Ge 3:1–24; Ro 5:12; 1Co 15:22

The universe is in subjection to sin

Gal 3:22 . . . the whole world is a prisoner of sin . . .   *See also* Ro 5:21; 11:32

Sin is inherent in human nature

Sinfulness from birth

Ps 51:5 Surely I was sinful at birth, sinful from the time my mother conceived me.   *See also* Job 25:4; Ps 58:3

The sinful heart

Ge 6:5 The LORD saw how great the wickedness of the human race had become on the earth, and that every inclination of the thoughts of their hearts was only evil all the time.   *See also* Ge 8:21; Ecc 9:3; Jer 17:9; Mt 15:19 pp Mk 7:21

The sinful nature

Eph 2:3 All of us also lived among them at one time, gratifying the cravings of our sinful nature and following its desires and thoughts . . . *See also* **Ro** 8:6–8; **Gal** 5:19–21

The universality of sin

No-one is righteous

Ro 3:9–19 What shall we conclude then? Are we any better? Not at all! We have already made the charge that Jews and Gentiles alike are all under sin. As it is written: "There is no-one righteous, not even one; there is no-one who understands, no-one who seeks God. All have turned away, they have together become worthless; there is no-one who does good, not even one." "Their throats are open graves; their tongues practise deceit." "The poison of vipers is on their lips." "Their mouths are full of cursing and bitterness." "Their feet are swift to shed blood; ruin and misery mark their ways, and the way of peace they do not know." "There is no fear of God before their eyes." Now we know that whatever the law says, it says to those who are under the law, so that every mouth may be silenced and the whole world held accountable to God. *See also* **Ps** 5:9; 10:7; 14:1–3 pp Ps 53:1–3; **Ps** 36:1; 140:3; **Isa** 59:7–8

All have sinned

Ro 3:23 for all have sinned and fall short of the glory of God, *See also* **Ge** 6:11–12; **1Ki** 8:46 pp 2Ch 6:36; **Ecc** 7:20; **Isa** 53:6; **Ro** 1:18–32; **Jas** 3:2

Everyone is sinful in God's sight

1Jn 1:8 If we claim to be without sin, we deceive ourselves and the truth is not in us. *See also* **Ps** 130:3; 143:2; **Pr** 20:9; **Isa** 64:6–7; **Mt** 19:17 pp Mk 10:18 pp Lk 18:19; **1Jn** 1:10

Some characters in Scripture are described as being blameless in comparison with their contemporaries
Ge 5:24; 6:9; **1Ki** 15:5

Jesus Christ alone is sinless
Heb 4:15 For we do not have a high priest who is unable to sympathise with our weaknesses, but we have one who has been tempted in every way, just as we are—yet was without sin.

1Pe 2:22 "He [Jesus] committed no sin, and no deceit was found in his mouth." *See also* **Isa** 53:9; **Lk** 23:47; **2Co** 5:21; **Heb** 7:26; **1Jn** 3:5 *See also creation.*

---

spiritual gifts

Although all believers have received the gift of the Holy Spirit, Scripture points to God giving individuals certain special gifts of a spiritual nature for the fulfilling of specific tasks.

---

spiritual gifts, nature of

In both the OT and the NT God graciously pours out gifts on his people. They are to be welcomed and used for the good of all.

OT examples of God giving special gifts

God's gracious provision from above

Joel 2:23–24 Be glad, O people of Zion, rejoice in the LORD your God, for he has given you the autumn rains in righteousness. He sends you abundant showers, both autumn and spring rains, as before. The threshing-floors will be filled with grain; the vats will overflow with new wine and oil. *See also* **Ex** 16:4,8,13–14; **Dt** 11:14; **1Ki** 17:6; **Job** 5:10; **Isa** 55:10

Distribution of land to tribes

Jos 13:6–7 ". . . Be sure to allocate this land to Israel for an inheritance, as I [the LORD] have instructed you, and divide it as an inheritance among the nine tribes and half of the tribe of Manasseh." *See also* **Eze** 47:21

The future promise of spiritual gifts

Joel 2:28–29 "And afterwards I will pour out my Spirit on all people. Your sons and daughters will prophesy, your old men will dream dreams, your young men will see visions. Even on my servants, both men and women, I will pour out my Spirit in those days." *See also* **Ac** 2:17–18

In his earthly ministry Jesus Christ offers supernatural gifts
Mt 11:28 "Come to me, all you who are weary and burdened, and I will give you rest." *See also* **Mt** 16:19; **Lk** 10:19; **Jn** 4:14; 6:51

Spiritual gifts linked with grace
Ro 12:6 We have different gifts, according to the grace given us . . . *See also* **Mt** 10:8; **1Co** 4:7

Specific reference to spiritual gifts
1Co 12:1 Now about spiritual gifts, brothers and sisters, I do not want you to be ignorant. *See also* **Ro** 1:11; **1Co** 14:1,12,37

Diverse gifts, one giver
1Co 12:4–6 There are different kinds of gifts, but the same Spirit. There are different kinds of service, but the same Lord. There are different kinds of working, but the same God works all of them in everyone. *See also* **Ro** 12:6–8; **1Co** 7:7,17; 12:8–11,27; **Eph** 4:11; **Heb** 2:4; **1Pe** 4:10–11

The purpose of spiritual gifts is to build up the church
1Co 14:12 . . . Since you are eager to have spiritual gifts, try to excel in gifts that build up the church. *See also* **1Co** 12:7; 14:2–5,17–19,26,31; **Eph** 4:16
The body of Christ benefits from these varied gifts
1Co 12:12 The body is a unit, though it is made up of many parts; and though all its parts are many, they form one body. So it is with Christ. *See also* **1Co** 12:14–31; **Ro** 12:4–6
Encouragement to aspire to the greater spiritual gifts 1Co 12:31; 14:1

The importance of love in exercising spiritual gifts
1Co 13:1 If I speak in human or angelic tongues, but have not love, I am only a resounding gong or a clanging cymbal. *See also* **Ro** 12:5–9; **1Co** 14:1

Warnings about spiritual gifts
1Co 14:39 Therefore, my brothers and sisters, be eager to prophesy, and do not forbid speaking in tongues. *See also* **1Co** 14:37; **1Th** 5:19–20 *See also church, and Holy Spirit; faith, origins of; prophecy, in New Testament; wisdom.*

spiritual gifts, responsibility
A spiritual gift may be intended to equip its recipient for a specific function or appointment. Those who are equipped in this way need the enabling power of God's spirit to carry out their appointed tasks.

OT examples of God's gifts or appointments
God appoints prophets
Jer 1:5 "Before I formed you [Jeremiah] in the womb I knew you, before you were born I set you apart; I appointed you as a prophet to the nations."
God appoints Israel's kings
1Sa 15:11 "I am grieved that I have made Saul king . . ." *See also* **2Sa** 7:8; 12:7
God appoints the Persian king Cyrus
Isa 45:1 "This is what the LORD says to his anointed, to Cyrus, whose right hand I take hold of . . ." *See also* **Isa** 41:2
God empowers leaders and kings with his Spirit
Nu 27:18 So the LORD said to Moses, "Take Joshua son of Nun, a man in whom is the spirit, and lay your hand on him." *See also* **Jdg** 3:10; 6:34; 11:29; 13:25; 14:6,19; 15:14; **1Sa** 10:6,10; 11:6; 16:13–14
The Spirit is given to the servant of the LORD
Isa 42:1 "Here is my servant, whom I uphold, my chosen one in whom I delight; I will put my Spirit on him and he will bring justice to the nations." *See also* **Isa** 61:1

Jesus Christ is endowed with the Holy Spirit
Mt 3:16–17 As soon as Jesus was baptised, he went up out of the water. At that moment heaven was opened, and he saw the Spirit of God descending like a dove and lighting on him.

And a voice from heaven said, "This is my Son, whom I love; with him I am well pleased." pp Mk 1:10–11 pp Lk 3:21–22   *See also* **Jn** 1:32–33; **Ac** 10:38

The apostles are endowed with the Holy Spirit
Ac 1:8 "But you [the apostles] will receive power when the Holy Spirit comes on you; and you will be my witnesses . . ."

Spiritual gifts given to the church
Eph 4:11 It was he [Christ] who gave some to be apostles, some to be prophets, some to be evangelists, and some to be pastors and teachers,   *See also* **1Co** 12:28
Many functions within the church yet unity is preserved
Eph 4:4–7 There is one body and one Spirit— just as you were called to one hope when you were called—one Lord, one faith, one baptism . . .   *See also* **1Co** 12:4–11
All Christians are appointed to build up the church
Eph 4:15–16 Instead, speaking the truth in love, we will in all things grow up into him who is the Head, that is, Christ. From him the whole body, joined and held together by every supporting ligament, grows and builds itself up in love, as each part does its work.   *See also* **1Co** 12:12

The experience of spiritual gifts
Associated with the laying on of hands
2Ti 1:6–7 For this reason I remind you to fan into flame the gift of God, which is in you through the laying on of my hands. For God did not give us a spirit of timidity, but a spirit of power, of love and of self-discipline.   *See also* **Nu** 8:10; 27:18; **Dt** 34:9; **Ac** 6:6; **1Ti** 4:14; 5:22
Associated with prayer and fasting
Ac 14:23 Paul and Barnabas appointed elders for them [new disciples] in each church and, with prayer and fasting, committed them to the Lord . . .   *See also* **Ac** 13:3

Spiritual gifts must not to be neglected
1Ti 4:14 Do not neglect your gift, which was

given you through a prophetic message when the body of elders laid their hands on you.   *See also* **Lk** 19:11–26   *See also* church, and Holy Spirit; teaching.

spiritual growth
Scripture uses a number of images to emphasise that believers are meant to grow in their faith, understanding, holiness and commitment. It also provides advice on how this may be achieved.

spiritual growth, means of
God has provided various means by which believers may grow spiritually.

God supplies the resources for spiritual growth
Php 2:13 . . . it is God who works in you to will and to act according to his good purpose.

2Pe 1:3 His [Jesus'] divine power has given us everything we need for life and godliness through our knowledge of him who called us by his own glory and goodness.   *See also* **Jn** 1:16; 4:14; 15:2,5; **1Co** 10:13; **2Co** 3:18; 9:10; **Gal** 5:22–23; **Php** 1:6; **Col** 2:19; **Jas** 1:17; 4:6; **Jude** 24

God's people must make efforts to grow spiritually
Php 2:12 . . . continue to work out your salvation with fear and trembling,

2Pe 1:5–9 . . . make every effort to add to your faith goodness; and to goodness, knowledge; and to knowledge, self-control; and to self-control, perseverance; and to perseverance, godliness; and to godliness, mutual affection; and to mutual affection, love . . .   *See also* **Ro** 6:19; **2Co** 7:1; **Gal** 5:16,25; **Eph** 5:15–16; 6:11–13; **1Ti** 4:7; 6:11–12; **2Ti** 1:6; **2Pe** 3:14; **1Jn** 3:3; **Jude** 20

Specific means of spiritual growth
Death to self-interest
Col 3:5 Put to death, therefore, whatever belongs to your earthly nature: sexual immorality, impurity, lust, evil desires and greed, which is

idolatry.   *See also* **Mt** 16:24 pp **Mk** 8:34 pp **Lk** 9:23; **Ro** 6:6,12; 8:13; **Eph** 4:22; **Col** 3:9; **1Pe** 1:14; 2:11

The Scriptures
2Ti 3:16–17 All Scripture is God-breathed and is useful for teaching, rebuking, correcting and training in righteousness, so that God's servant may be thoroughly equipped for every good work.   *See also* **Jos** 1:8; **Ps** 19:7–8; 119:9–11; **Jn** 17:17; **Eph** 6:17; **Col** 3:16; **1Pe** 2:2; **1Jn** 2:14

Prayer
Mt 6:13 " 'And lead us not into temptation, but deliver us from the evil one.' pp **Lk** 11:4
Col 4:2 Devote yourselves to prayer, being watchful and thankful.   *See also* **1Ch** 16:11; **Mt** 7:11 pp **Lk** 11:13; **Mt** 26:41 pp **Mk** 14:38 pp **Lk** 22:46; **Jn** 16:24; **Ac** 4:29–31; **Eph** 6:18; **1Th** 5:17; **Jas** 1:5

Focusing on Jesus Christ
Heb 3:1 Therefore, holy brothers and sisters, who share in the heavenly calling, fix your thoughts on Jesus, the apostle and high priest whom we confess.   *See also* **Mt** 11:29; **Jn** 13:15; **Ro** 15:5; **Php** 2:5; **Heb** 12:2–3; **1Pe** 2:21; **1Jn** 2:6

The role of the Holy Spirit in spiritual growth
Eph 3:16–18 I pray that out of his glorious riches he may strengthen you with power through his Spirit in your inner being, so that Christ may dwell in your hearts through faith. And I pray that you, being rooted and established in love, may have power, together with all the saints, to grasp how wide and long and high and deep is the love of Christ,   *See also* **Eph** 1:13–14,17; 2:19–22

Christian leadership
Eph 4:11–13 It was he [Christ] who gave some to be apostles, some to be prophets, some to be evangelists, and some to be pastors and teachers, to prepare God's people for works of service, so that the body of Christ may be built up until we all reach unity in the faith and in the knowledge of the Son of God and become mature, attaining to the whole measure of the fulness of Christ.   *See also* **1Co** 4:16; 11:1; **Php** 1:25; 3:17; **Heb** 13:7,17; **1Pe** 5:2–3

Faith in God
Eph 6:16 . . . take up the shield of faith, with which you can extinguish all the flaming arrows of the evil one.   *See also* **Heb** 11:6; **1Jn** 5:4

Suffering and testing
Ro 5:3–4 . . . we also rejoice in our sufferings, because we know that suffering produces perseverance; perseverance, character; and character, hope.   *See also* **Job** 23:10; **Ps** 119:67; **Zec** 13:9; **Heb** 12:10–11; **1Pe** 1:6–7; **Jas** 1:2–4

Perseverance
Heb 12:1 . . . let us throw off everything that hinders and the sin that so easily entangles, and let us run with perseverance the race marked out for us.   *See also* **Php** 3:12–14; **1Ti** 4:15

Cultivating wholesome thinking
Php 4:8 Finally, brothers and sisters, whatever is true, whatever is noble, whatever is right, whatever is pure, whatever is lovely, whatever is admirable—if anything is excellent or praiseworthy—think about such things.

God will bring the spiritual growth of believers to completion
1Jn 3:2 Dear friends, now we are children of God, and what we will be has not yet been made known. But we know that when he appears, we shall be like him, for we shall see him as he is.   *See also* **Eph** 5:25–27; **Php** 1:6; **Jude** 24–25; **Rev** 21:2   *See also faith; prayer; Scripture, purpose; spiritual gifts.*

spiritual growth, nature of
Having given spiritual life to his people, God expects them to grow to maturity.

God desires the spiritual growth of his people
Mt 5:48 "Be perfect, therefore, as your heavenly Father is perfect."

Heb 6:1 . . . let us leave the elementary teachings about Christ and go on to maturity, not laying again the foundation of repentance from acts that lead to death, and of faith in God,   *See also* **2Co** 13:9–11; **Eph** 1:4; 2:10; 3:17–19; **Php** 3:12; **1Th** 4:1,7; **2Ti** 1:9

Christlikeness is the goal of spiritual growth

Ro 8:29 . . . those God foreknew he also predestined to be conformed to the likeness of his Son, that he might be the firstborn among many brothers and sisters.   *See also* **Eph** 4:13–15; **Php** 2:5; **1Jn** 3:2–3

Aspects of spiritual growth

Growth in grace

2Pe 3:18 . . . grow in the grace and knowledge of our Lord and Saviour Jesus Christ. To him be glory both now and for ever! Amen.   *See also* **Pr** 4:18; **1Pe** 2:1–3

Growth in faith

2Th 1:3 We [Paul, Silas and Timothy] ought always to thank God for you, brothers and sisters, and rightly so, because your faith is growing more and more, and the love every one of you has for each other is increasing.   *See also* **2Co** 10:15

Growth in love

1Th 3:12 May the Lord make your love increase and overflow for each other and for everyone else, just as ours does for you.   *See also* **Ro** 5:5; **1Co** 14:1; **Php** 1:9; **1Th** 4:9–10; **Heb** 10:24; **1Jn** 4:7–21; 5:1–3

Growth in understanding

Ps 119:27 Let me understand the teaching of your precepts; then I will meditate on your wonders.

1Co 14:20 Brothers and sisters, stop thinking like children. In regard to evil be infants, but in your thinking be adults.   *See also* **Ps** 119:97–99; **Ro** 12:2; 16:19; **1Co** 13:11; **Eph** 1:17–19; **Php** 1:9–10; **Col** 1:9; **Heb** 5:14

Growth in holiness

2Co 7:1 . . . let us purify ourselves from everything that contaminates body and spirit, perfecting holiness out of reverence for God. *See also* **Eph** 5:25–26; **Heb** 2:11; 10:10–14; 12:14; 13:12; **1Pe** 1:15–16

Growth in fruitfulness

Jn 15:16 "You [the disciples] did not choose me [Jesus], but I chose you and appointed you to go and bear fruit—fruit that will last . . ."   *See also* **Mt** 13:23 pp **Mk** 4:20 pp **Lk** 8:15; **Jn** 15:2,8; **Php** 1:11; **Col** 1:10

Growth in contentment

Php 4:11–12 . . . I [Paul] have learned to be content whatever the circumstances . . . *See also* **1Ti** 6:6; **Heb** 13:5

Examples of spiritual growth

In individuals 1Sa 2:26; **Lk** 1:80 Jesus Christ: **Lk** 2:40,52 Paul: **Ac** 9:22; **1Co** 9:26–27; **Php** 3:12–14 **Ac** 18:26; **Phm** 11; **3Jn** 2–3 **In the church Ac** 9:31; 11:26; 16:5; **2Co** 10:15; **Col** 1:6; **1Th** 2:13; **2Th** 1:3   *See also Christlikeness; church, purpose; holiness; sanctification.*

---

spiritual warfare

The struggle against the forces of evil, which is a constant feature of the life of faith. Scripture locates the origins of spiritual warfare in the rebellion of Satan and his angels against God and affirms the hope of God's final victory over such forces through Jesus Christ's death and resurrection.

---

spiritual warfare, armour

The armour of God refers to the resources that Christians possess for defending themselves against the attacks of the world, the flesh and the devil.

God is the believer's strength and shield

Ps 28:7–8 The LORD is my strength and my shield; my heart trusts in him, and I am helped. My heart leaps for joy and I will give thanks to him in song. The LORD is the strength of his people . . .   *See also* **Ge** 15:1; **Dt** 33:29; **Ps** 3:3; 7:10; 119:114

Believers should be rightly clothed for battle

Ro 13:12–14 The night is nearly over; the day is almost here. So let us put aside the deeds of darkness and put on the armour of light. Let us behave decently, as in the daytime, not in orgies and drunkenness, not in sexual immorality and debauchery, not in dissension and jealousy. Rather,

clothe yourselves with the Lord Jesus Christ, and
do not think about how to gratify the desires of
the sinful nature.   *See also* **Eph** 4:22–24; **Col**
3:9,12–14; **1Pe** 4:1

Believers should put on the full armour of God
The belt of truth
Eph 6:14 Stand firm then, with the belt of truth
buckled round your waist . . .
The importance of sound teaching: a good understanding
of God's truth counters Satan's deceit: **Ps** 119:95,116;
Eph 4:14–15; **Col** 2:8; **2Ti** 1:13–14; **1Pe** 1:13
The breastplate of righteousness
Eph 6:14 Stand firm then . . . with the
breastplate of righteousness in place,
Assurance that believers are righteous in God's sight will
counter Satan's accusations: **Pr** 4:23; 13:6; **Isa** 61:10;
Zec 3:1–4
The gospel of peace
Eph 6:15 and with your feet fitted with the
readiness that comes from the gospel of peace.
The peace of God reassures and gives confidence in
times of trouble: **Jn** 14:27; 16:33; **Php** 4:6–7
The shield of faith
Eph 6:16 In addition to all this, take up the
shield of faith, with which you can extinguish all
the flaming arrows of the evil one.
Exercising faith draws strength from God, guards against
deception and helps overcome temptation: **Ro** 1:17;
Hab 2:4; **1Pe** 5:9; **1Jn** 5:4
The helmet of salvation
Eph 6:17 Take the helmet of salvation . . .
The expectation of future glory encourages the Christian
soldier and helps overcome despair: **1Th** 5:8–9; **Tit**
2:11–14; **1Jn** 3:3

The Christian's spiritual weapons
2Co 10:4 The weapons we fight with are not
the weapons of the world. On the contrary, they
have divine power to demolish strongholds.
The sword of the Spirit
Eph 6:17 Take . . . the sword of the Spirit,
which is the word of God.
The Scriptures give readiness and confidence in battle
and a sure defence against the evil one: **Ps** 119:11;
2Ti 3:16–17; **Heb** 4:12

The armour of God is worn with prayer
Eph 6:18 And pray in the Spirit on all occasions
with all kinds of prayers and requests. With this
in mind, be alert and always keep on praying for
all the saints.
Prayer ensures that believers recognise their need to turn
to God and depend on him alone: **Ps** 55:16–18; **Heb**
4:16; **Jas** 5:16   *See also faith; hope, as confidence;
peace, experience; righteousness; Scripture; teaching;
truth.*

spiritual warfare, causes
Spiritual warfare has its origin in a rebellion of
many angels against God. Satan is seen as the
prince of this world, leading an array of forces
opposed to God. Although disarmed by Jesus
Christ on the cross, they remain a powerful threat
to the church and to individual believers.

Satan and his angels fall
2Pe 2:4 . . . God did not spare angels when
they sinned, but sent them to hell, putting them
into gloomy dungeons to be held for judgment;
See also **Isa** 14:12–15; **Eze** 28:12–19; **1Ti** 3:6;
Jude 6

Satan and his angels comprise a well-organised army
Eph 6:12 For our struggle is not against flesh
and blood, but against the rulers, against the
authorities, against the powers of this dark world
and against the spiritual forces of evil in the
heavenly realms.   *See also* **Col** 1:13

Satan and his angels will ultimately be fully disarmed by Jesus Christ
Col 2:15 And having disarmed the powers and
authorities, he [Christ] made a public spectacle of
them, triumphing over them by the cross.

Rev 12:7–9 And there was war in heaven.
Michael and his angels fought against the dragon,
and the dragon and his angels fought back. But
he was not strong enough, and they lost their
place in heaven . . .   *See also* **Mk** 3:27 pp **Mt**
12:29; **Lk** 10:18; **Jn** 12:31; **Heb** 2:14; **1Jn** 3:8

Satan persecutes the church

Rev 12:13 When the dragon saw that he had been hurled to the earth, he pursued the woman who had given birth to the male child.   *See also* **Rev** 2:10; 13:7

Satan opposes the gospel

2Co 4:4 The god of this age has blinded the minds of unbelievers, so that they cannot see the light of the gospel of the glory of Christ, who is the image of God.   *See also* **Mt** 13:19 pp **Mk** 4:15 pp **Lk** 8:12; **Mt** 13:38–39; **1Th** 2:2,18

Examples of opposition to the first Christians
Ac 6:8–14; 7:54–58; 8:1–3

Opposition to Paul and his companions: **Ac** 13:6–12,44–45; 17:13; 18:6,12

Violent hostility to Paul and his companions: **Ac** 9:23; 14:5,19; 16:16–24; 17:5–6; 19:23–29; 20:3; 21:27–36

Jewish plots against Paul in Jerusalem: **Ac** 23:12–15; 25:3

Satan attacks individual believers

Rev 12:17 Then the dragon was enraged at the woman and went off to make war against the rest of her offspring—those who obey God's commandments and hold to the testimony of Jesus.   *See also* **Job** 2:7; **Lk** 22:31–32; **2Ti** 3:12; **1Pe** 5:8   *See also evil, victory over; Satan.*

spiritual warfare, enemies

Christians are at war with the world, the flesh and the devil. Satan empowers the world to attack believers externally, persecuting, deceiving and seducing them. Internally, sinfulness frustrates the efforts of believers to serve God fully.

The world is an enemy

Jas 4:4 You adulterous people, don't you know that friendship with the world is hatred towards God? Anyone who chooses to be a friend of the world becomes an enemy of God.   *See also* **Ro** 12:2; **1Jn** 2:15–17; 5:4

The world hates Christians
Jn 15:19–20 "If you belonged to the world, it would love you as its own. As it is, you do not belong to the world, but I have chosen you out

of the world. That is why the world hates you . . ."   *See also* **Mt** 5:10–12 pp **Lk** 6:22; **Jn** 16:2; 17:14; **1Pe** 4:12–16; **1Jn** 3:13; **Rev** 13:7

The world has its own false teaching and religion
Col 2:8 See to it that no-one takes you captive through hollow and deceptive philosophy, which depends on human tradition and the basic principles of this world rather than on Christ.
See also **1Ti** 4:1; **2Ti** 4:3–4; **1Jn** 4:1; **2Jn** 7–11; **Jude** 3–4; **Rev** 13:11; 19:20

The world seeks to seduce Christians
1Jn 2:16 For everything in the world—the cravings of sinful people, the lust of their eyes and the boasting of what they have and do—comes not from the Father but from the world.
See also **Lk** 12:15,19; **2Ti** 4:10; **Tit** 2:12; **Heb** 11:24–25; **Rev** 17:1–5

Sinful human nature is an enemy

Gal 5:17 For the sinful nature desires what is contrary to the Spirit, and the Spirit what is contrary to the sinful nature. They are in conflict with each other, so that you do not do what you want.

1Pe 2:11 Dear friends, I urge you, as aliens and strangers in the world, to abstain from sinful desires, which war against your soul.   *See also* **Ro** 6:12; 7:14–23; 8:13; **Gal** 5:24; **Col** 3:5; **Heb** 12:4; **Jas** 4:1

The devil is an enemy

1Pe 5:8 . . . Your enemy the devil prowls around like a roaring lion looking for someone to devour.   *See also* **Mt** 13:39 pp **Mk** 4:15 pp **Lk** 8:12; **Jn** 17:15; **2Th** 3:3; **Rev** 2:10; 12:17

He seeks to tempt Christians
1Th 3:5 . . . I was afraid that in some way the tempter might have tempted you and our efforts might have been useless.   *See also* **Ge** 3:1–6; **Heb** 2:18; 4:15

He seeks to deceive
2Co 11:3 But I am afraid that just as Eve was deceived by the serpent's cunning, your minds may somehow be led astray from your sincere and pure devotion to Christ.

Rev 12:9 The great dragon was hurled down—that ancient serpent called the devil, or Satan, who leads the whole world astray . . . *See also* **Ge** 3:13; **2Co** 2:11; 4:4; 11:4; **Rev** 20:3
He constantly seeks to accuse believers
Rev 12:10 . . . ". . . For the accuser of our brothers and sisters, who accuses them before our God day and night, has been hurled down." *See also* **Job** 1:9–11; **Zec** 3:1   *See also* life, spiritual; Satan, enemy of God; sin, avoidance.

---

teaching

The act of instructing in matters of faith and morals, especially in the home or church. The apostles' teaching formed the basis of the instruction given to the first Christians. Parts of the NT draw a distinction between preaching and teaching, seeing the former as a means of converting individuals, and the latter as a means of instructing them after conversion.

The importance of teaching
Ecc 12:11–12 The words of the wise are like goads, their collected sayings like firmly embedded nails—given by one Shepherd. Be warned, my son, of anything in addition to them . . .   *See also* **Pr** 1:8–9; 3:1–2; 4:1–4; 6:20–23; **Mt** 5:19; **1Co** 14:6; **2Ti** 4:2–3

Teaching given by parents
Pr 22:6 Train children in the way they should go, and when they are old they will not turn from it.   *See also* **Dt** 6:6–9; 11:18–19; **Eph** 6:1–4

The apostles' teaching
Ac 2:42 They [converts on the day of Pentecost] devoted themselves to the apostles' teaching and to the fellowship, to the breaking of bread and to prayer.

Tit 1:9 He [the overseer] must hold firmly to the trustworthy message as it has been taught, so that he can encourage others by sound doctrine and refute those who oppose it.   *See also* **Mt** 28:19–20; **Ro** 6:17; 16:17; **1Th** 4:8; **2Th** 2:15;

1Ti 1:10–11; 4:6; 6:3; **2Ti** 1:13–14; 4:3; **Tit** 2:1

The gift of teaching in the church
Ro 12:7 . . . if it is teaching, then teach; *See also* **1Ti** 4:13–14

Ways of teaching believers
Through example
1Th 1:5–6 . . . our gospel came to you not simply with words, but also with power, with the Holy Spirit and with deep conviction. You know how we lived among you for your sake. You became imitators of us and of the Lord; in spite of severe suffering, you welcomed the message with the joy given by the Holy Spirit.   *See also* **1Co** 4:17; 11:1; **Php** 4:9; **1Th** 2:14; **2Ti** 3:10; **Tit** 2:3–7
Through dialogue with the teacher **Ac** 20:7; 19:8–9
Through explanation of ceremonies **Ex** 12:26–27; 13:14–16
Through proverbs **Pr** 1:1–6,20–28
Through the law **Dt** 6:6–9; 11:18–19; 27:1–26; **Ps** 78:5–8
Through mutual edification
Col 3:16 Let the word of Christ dwell in you richly as you teach and admonish one another with all wisdom, and as you sing psalms, hymns and spiritual songs with gratitude in your hearts to God.   *See also* **Ro** 15:14; **1Th** 5:11; **Heb** 5:12
Through the instruction of different groups within the church **Eph** 5:22–6:9; **Col** 3:18–4:1; **Tit** 2:1–10; **1Pe** 2:18–3:7; 5:1–5

The distinction between teaching and preaching
Ac 15:35 But Paul and Barnabas remained in Antioch, where they and many others taught and preached the word of the Lord.   *See also* **Mt** 4:23; 9:35; 11:1; **Lk** 20:1; **Ac** 4:2; 5:42; 28:31

Examples of major themes taught in the NT church
Righteousness from God through faith in Jesus Christ
Ro 3:21–22 But now a righteousness from God, apart from law, has been made known, to

which the Law and the Prophets testify. This righteousness from God comes through faith in Jesus Christ to all who believe . . .   *See also* **Gal** 2:20–21

Freedom in Christ from the demands of the law
Gal 5:1–3 It is for freedom that Christ has set us free. Stand firm, then, and do not let yourselves be burdened again by a yoke of slavery. Mark my words! I, Paul, tell you that if you let yourselves be circumcised, Christ will be of no value to you at all. Again I declare to every man who lets himself be circumcised that he is required to obey the whole law.

The humility of Jesus Christ
Php 2:5–8 Your attitude should be the same as that of Christ Jesus: Who, being in very nature God, did not consider equality with God something to be grasped, but made himself nothing, taking the very nature of a servant, being made in human likeness. And being found in appearance as a human being, he humbled himself and became obedient to death—even death on a cross!
See also **Heb** 13:12–13

The supremacy of Jesus Christ
Col 1:18 And he [Christ] is the head of the body, the church; he is the beginning and the firstborn from among the dead, so that in everything he might have the supremacy.

The superiority of Jesus Christ
Heb 3:3 Jesus has been found worthy of greater honour than Moses . . .

Godly behaviour
Eph 4:22–24 You were taught, with regard to your former way of life, to put off your old self, which is being corrupted by its deceitful desires; to be made new in the attitude of your minds; and to put on the new self, created to be like God in true righteousness and holiness.   *See also* **Ro** 12:1–2; **1Ti** 6:1–2   *See also preachers and preaching.*

---

truth

Truth in Scripture is more than mere veracity. In the OT it is a moral concept, grounded in the being of God himself, which embodies the ideas

of faithfulness and reliability, while in the NT the concept widens to embrace the ideas of reality and completeness.

truth, in New Testament

The NT encompasses the Greek idea of truth as reality, as well as the Hebraic concepts of faithfulness and reliability. Jesus Christ is shown as "the Truth" and the apostles present the gospel as "truth".

Truth as opposed to falsehood and lies
Eph 4:25 Therefore each of you [Ephesian believers] must put off falsehood and speak truthfully to your neighbour, for we are all members of one body.   *See also* **Jn** 3:33; 4:37; 18:23; 19:35; **Ac** 7:1; 21:24; 24:8; 26:25; **Ro** 1:18; 9:1; **1Co** 15:54; **2Co** 7:14; **Gal** 4:16; **Tit** 1:13; **2Pe** 2:22; **1Jn** 2:4; **2Jn** 1–2

Truth as reality
Heb 9:24 For Christ did not enter a man-made sanctuary that was only a copy of the true one; he entered heaven itself, now to appear for us in God's presence.   *See also* **Jn** 1:9; 4:23; 17:3; **Eph** 4:24; **1Th** 1:9; **1Ti** 1:2; 6:19; **Tit** 1:2; 3:2; **Heb** 8:2; 12:8; **1Pe** 5:12; **1Jn** 2:5,8; 5:20; **Rev** 19:9

Truth as trustworthy affirmations
Jn 6:47 "I [Jesus] tell you the truth, whoever believes has everlasting life."   *See also* **Mt** 6:2; 10:23; 16:28; 19:23; 23:36; 26:13; **Mk** 9:41; 11:23; **Lk** 12:44; 21:3; **Jn** 1:51; 5:24–25; 8:34; 10:7; 16:7; **Php** 1:15; **1Ti** 3:9

Truth as faithfulness and reliability
The quality of truth
Php 4:8 Finally, brothers and sisters, whatever is true, whatever is noble, whatever is right, whatever is pure, whatever is lovely, whatever is admirable—if anything is excellent or praiseworthy—think about such things.   *See also* **Jn** 1:17; 3:21; 4:24; 17:17; **Ro** 2:20; **1Co** 5:8; 13:6; **2Co** 13:8; **Eph** 5:9; 6:14; **3Jn** 12

Truth as an aspect of the character of God
Ro 3:3–4 What if some did not have faith? Will their lack of faith nullify God's faithfulness?

Not at all! Let God be true, and every person a liar. As it is written: "So that you may be proved right when you speak and prevail when you judge." *See also* **Ps** 51:4; **Ro** 3:7; 15:8; **1Jn** 5:20; **Rev** 3:7,14; 6:10; 15:3; 16:7; 19:2,11

Truth as a human quality

Ac 11:23 When he [Barnabas] arrived and saw the evidence of the grace of God, he was glad and encouraged them all to remain true to the Lord with all their hearts.

1Jn 1:8 If we claim to be without sin, we deceive ourselves and the truth is not in us. *See also* **Jn** 3:21; 7:18; **Ac** 14:22; **Eph** 4:15; **Php** 1:18; **Rev** 2:13

Jesus Christ as truth

Jn 14:6 Jesus answered, "I am the way and the truth and the life. No-one comes to the Father except through me." *See also* **Jn** 1:14; 15:1; 18:37–38; **1Jn** 5:20

The Spirit of God as truth

Jn 16:13 But when he, the Spirit of truth, comes, he will guide you into all truth. He will not speak on his own; he will speak only what he hears, and he will tell you what is yet to come. *See also* **Jn** 14:16–17; 15:26; **1Jn** 4:6; 5:6

The gospel and the Christian faith as truth

Eph 1:13 And you [Ephesian believers] also were included in Christ when you heard the word of truth, the gospel of your salvation. Having believed, you were marked in him with a seal, the promised Holy Spirit, *See also* **Jn** 8:31–32; **Ac** 20:30; **2Co** 4:2; **Gal** 2:5; **Col** 1:5; **1Ti** 2:3–4; 4:6; **2Ti** 2:18; 4:4; **Tit** 1:1; **Jas** 5:19; **2Pe** 2:2; **1Jn** 3:19 *See also gospel.*

---

truth, nature of

God is the essence of truth and this quality should be reflected in the character of his children. Falsehood is condemned in Scripture, particularly in legal contexts, but truth is praised and advocated. God takes pleasure in truth and honesty, which are marks of an upright person.

Truth originates with God

Ps 43:3 Send forth your [the LORD's] light and your truth, let them guide me; let them bring me to your holy mountain, to the place where you dwell. *See also* **Ps** 25:5; 26:3; 86:11; **Isa** 65:16; **Da** 9:13

Truth is an aspect of God's character
It is demonstrated in his faithfulness and reliability

Nu 23:19 "God is not human, that he should lie, nor a human being, that he should change his mind. Does he speak and then not act? Does he promise and not fulfil?"

Ps 33:4 For the word of the LORD is right and true; he is faithful in all he does. *See also* **1Sa** 15:29; **Ps** 31:5; 40:10–11; 119:160; **Isa** 45:19; **Jer** 10:10; 42:5; **Da** 10:21; **Mic** 7:20
It is demonstrated in his justice and mercy
Ps 96:13 . . . He [the LORD] will judge the world in righteousness and the peoples in his truth. *See also* **Ps** 119:30,43–44,142,151

Truth should be reflected in the character of God's people

Zec 8:16 "These are the things you are to do: Speak the truth to each other, and render true and sound judgment in your courts;" *See also* **1Ki** 17:22–24; **Ps** 15:1–5; 51:6; 145:18; **Pr** 23:23; **Jer** 4:2; 5:1; **Zec** 7:9; 8:3,19; **Mal** 2:6

Absence of truth in the human character displeases God

Isa 59:14–15 So justice is driven back, and righteousness stands at a distance; truth has stumbled in the streets, honesty cannot enter. Truth is nowhere to be found, and whoever shuns evil becomes a prey. The LORD looked and was displeased that there was no justice. *See also* **Isa** 48:1; **Jer** 5:3; 7:28; 9:3

Truth as an abstract quality

Ps 45:4 In your [the king's] majesty ride forth victoriously on behalf of truth, humility and righteousness; let your right hand display awesome deeds. *See also* **Pr** 23:23; **Da** 8:12

Truth is the opposite of falsehood

Pr 16:13 Kings take pleasure in honest lips; they value one who speaks the truth. *See also* **1Ki** 17:24; 22:16 pp 2Ch 18:15; **Ne** 6:6; **Pr** 8:7; 12:17; **Isa** 45:19; **Zec** 8:16

Truth is subject to proof

Ge 42:14–16 . . . ". . . As surely as Pharaoh lives, you [Joseph's brothers] will not leave this place unless your youngest brother comes here. Send one of your number to get your brother; the rest of you will be kept in prison, so that your words may be tested to see if you are telling the truth. If you are not, then as surely as Pharaoh lives, you are spies!" *See also* **Dt** 13:12–15; 17:2–5; 19:16–19; 22:20–21; **1Ki** 10:6–7 pp 2Ch 9:5–6; **Job** 5:27

Truth is commended in Scripture

Pr 12:22 The LORD detests lying lips, but he delights in those who are truthful. *See also* **Ex** 20:16 pp Dt 5:20; **Ex** 23:1,7; **Pr** 12:19; 13:5; 14:25; 19:5,9; **Eph** 4:25; **Rev** 22:14–15

Lack of truth is a characteristic of apostasy

Jer 7:28 ". . . This is the nation that has not obeyed the LORD its God or responded to correction. Truth has perished; it has vanished from their lips.'" *See also* **Ps** 52:1–4; **Isa** 59:12–15; **Jer** 9:5–6; **Am** 5:10

Truth as an expression of affirmation

Da 11:2 "Now then, I [one who looks like a man] tell you [Daniel] the truth: Three more kings will appear in Persia, and then a fourth, who will be far richer than all the others. When he has gained power by his wealth, he will stir up everyone against the kingdom of Greece." *See also* **Jos** 7:20; **Ru** 3:12; **2Ki** 19:17; **Jer** 26:15; **Mt** 5:18; 8:10; 21:21; **Mk** 8:12; 14:30; **Lk** 4:24; 21:32; **Jn** 3:3; 8:51; 21:18

Amen as a liturgical affirmation of truth

Of oaths and curses

Nu 5:22 "'"May this water that brings a curse enter your body so that your abdomen swells and your thigh wastes away." Then the woman is to say, "Amen. So be it."'" *See also* **Dt** 27:15–26; **Ne** 5:13; **Jer** 11:5

Of benedictions and doxologies

1Ch 16:36 Praise be to the LORD, the God of Israel, from everlasting to everlasting. Then all the people said "Amen" and "Praise the LORD." *See also* **Ne** 8:6; **Ps** 41:13; 72:19; 89:52; 106:48

In general use

Jer 28:6 He [Jeremiah] said, "Amen! May the LORD do so! May the LORD fulfil the words you [Hananiah] have prophesied by bringing the articles of the LORD's house and all the exiles back to this place from Babylon." *See also* **1Ki** 1:32–37

In the NT

Ro 1:25 They [unbelievers] exchanged the truth of God for a lie, and worshipped and served created things rather than the Creator—who is for ever praised. Amen. *See also* **Mt** 6:13; **Ro** 9:5; 11:36; **1Co** 14:16; **2Co** 1:20; **Gal** 6:18; **Php** 4:20; **1Ti** 1:17; **Heb** 13:20–21; **2Pe** 3:18; **Jude** 25; **Rev** 1:6–7; 7:12; 22:20 *See also promises.*

wisdom

The quality of knowledge, discernment and understanding characteristic of God himself. True wisdom, seen in the ministry of Jesus Christ, is a gift of the Holy Spirit. Scripture affirms that true human wisdom is a gift from God and points out the folly of trusting in mere human wisdom.

wisdom, human

The human quality which enables the planning and successful achievement of a desired goal. It may be expressed as technical skill, practical instruction and astuteness in political affairs. True wisdom includes spiritual discernment and, above all, the reverence and knowledge of God.

Wisdom as human skill

For work on the tabernacle

Ex 36:1 "So Bezalel, Oholiab and every skilled person to whom the LORD has given skill and ability to know how to carry out all the work of

constructing the sanctuary are to do the work just as the LORD has commanded." *See also* Ex 28:3; 31:2–6 pp Ex 35:30–35; Ex 35:25–26; 36:8
For work on the temple
1Ch 22:15 "You [Solomon] have many workers: stonecutters, masons and carpenters, as well as those skilled in every kind of work" *See also* 1Ch 28:21; 2Ch 2:7,13–14 pp 1Ki 7:13–14
Other skills
Making idols: Isa 40:20; Jer 10:9
Jer 9:17; Eze 27:8–9

Wisdom as instruction in practical living
Pr 14:8 The wisdom of the prudent is to give thought to their ways, but the folly of fools is deception.

Ecc 12:11 The words of the wise are like goads, their collected sayings like firmly embedded nails—given by one Shepherd. *See also* Pr 6:6; 10:5,8–9; 19:11; 20:1; 21:20; 29:11; Ecc 7:7; 10:12

Wisdom as political astuteness
Wisdom brings political success Pr 21:22; Ecc 9:14–15; Isa 10:13; Eze 28:4–5
Wisdom in giving political advice Ge 41:8; Est 1:13; Isa 19:11; Jer 51:57; Da 4:6; 5:8; Ob 8
David's counsellors: 1Ch 26:14; 27:32–33
Wisdom in government Ge 41:33–36; 2Sa 14:20; 1Ki 5:12; Da 2:48

Wisdom associated with mystic arts
Ge 41:8; Ex 7:11; Ps 58:5; Da 2:7; 5:7,11

Wisdom as spiritual discernment
Understanding the plan of God
Ge 41:39 Then Pharaoh said to Joseph, "Since God has made all this known to you, there is no-one so discerning and wise as you." *See also* Jer 9:12; Rev 13:18; 17:9
Understanding God's ways
Hos 14:9 Who are wise? They will realise these things. Who are discerning? They will understand them. The ways of the LORD are right; the

righteous walk in them, but the rebellious stumble in them. *See also* Job 11:6; Ps 107:43; Da 12:10

Wisdom expressed in a right relationship with God
Wisdom as reverent submission to God
Job 28:28 "And he [God] said to all people, 'The fear of the Lord—that is wisdom, and to shun evil is understanding.'" *See also* Ps 111:10; Pr 1:7; 3:7; 9:10; Ecc 12:13; Mic 6:9
Wisdom as the knowledge of God
Pr 30:3 "I have not learned wisdom, nor have I knowledge of the Holy One."

Isa 11:2 The Spirit of the LORD will rest on him [God's Messiah]—the Spirit of wisdom and of understanding, the Spirit of counsel and of power, the Spirit of knowledge and of the fear of the LORD— *See also* Eph 1:17; Col 1:9
Wisdom as obedience to God's command
Dt 4:6 Observe them [the LORD's commands] carefully, for this will show your [Israel's] wisdom and understanding to the nations, who will hear about all these decrees and say, "Surely this great nation is a wise and understanding people." *See also* Ps 119:34,73

Wisdom personified
Wisdom calls out an invitation Pr 8:1–4; 9:1–6
Wisdom teaches what is right Pr 8:5–21
Wisdom existed before creation
Pr 8:22–32 "The LORD brought me [wisdom] forth as the first of his works, before his deeds of old; I was appointed from eternity, from the beginning, before the world began . . ."

Human wisdom can be opposed to God
1Co 1:18–25 For the message of the cross is foolishness to those who are perishing, but to us who are being saved it is the power of God. For it is written: "I will destroy the wisdom of the wise; the intelligence of the intelligent I will frustrate." Where are the wise? Where are the scholars? Where are the philosophers of this age? Has not God made foolish the wisdom of the

world? For since in the wisdom of God the world through its wisdom did not know him, God was pleased through the foolishness of what was preached to save those who believe. Jews demand miraculous signs and Greeks look for wisdom, but we preach Christ crucified: a stumbling-block to Jews and foolishness to Gentiles, but to those whom God has called, both Jews and Greeks, Christ the power of God and the wisdom of God. For the foolishness of God is wiser than human wisdom, and the weakness of God is stronger than human strength.   *See also* **1Co** 4:10

wisdom, importance of

True wisdom may bring material reward but its value far exceeds earthly riches. To those who receive it, it opens a path to life and security and equips for leadership and right conduct.

The supreme value of true wisdom
It is priceless
Pr 4:7 Wisdom is supreme; therefore get wisdom. Though it cost all you have, get understanding.   *See also* **Pr** 3:13; 8:10–11
It leads to life
Pr 15:24 The path of life leads upward for the wise to keep them from going down to the grave.   *See also* **Pr** 11:30; 13:14; 16:22; 24:14; **Da** 12:3
It brings prosperity
Pr 8:18 "With me [wisdom] are riches and honour, enduring wealth and prosperity."   *See also* **Pr** 3:1–2; 19:8,8; 21:20–21; 24:3; **Jer** 10:21
It gives security
Pr 4:6 Do not forsake wisdom, and she will protect you; love her, and she will watch over you.   *See also* **Pr** 1:33; 2:6–11; 14:3; 28:26; **Ecc** 8:5

The application of wisdom
It touches the whole person
1Ki 3:12 "I [the LORD] will do what you [Solomon] have asked. I will give you a wise and discerning heart, so that there will never have been anyone like you, nor will there ever be." *See also* **Job** 38:36; **Ps** 51:6; **Pr** 2:2; 16:23; 22:17

It results in right action
Col 4:5 Be wise in the way you act towards outsiders; make the most of every opportunity.

Jas 3:13 Who are wise and understanding among you? Let them show it by their good life, by deeds done in the humility that comes from wisdom.   *See also* **Ps** 119:34; **Pr** 1:3; 4:11; 15:21; 23:19; **Jer** 4:22; **Hos** 14:9; **Ro** 16:19; **Eph** 5:15; **Col** 1:9–10; **Jas** 3:14–17
It results in watchfulness
Mt 25:1–10 ". . . But while they [the foolish virgins] were on their way to buy the oil, the bridegroom arrived. The virgins who were ready went in with him to the wedding banquet. And the door was shut."   *See also* **Pr** 14:8; 22:3 pp **Pr** 27:12

Wisdom is necessary for leaders
Wisdom to govern
Pr 8:15–16 "By me [wisdom] kings reign and rulers make laws that are just; by me princes govern, and all nobles who rule on earth."

Ac 6:3 "Brothers and sisters, choose seven men from among you who are known to be full of the Spirit and wisdom. We [the apostles] will turn this responsibility [for distributing to the poor] over to them"   *See also* **Dt** 1:13; **1Ki** 5:7; **1Ch** 22:12; **Ps** 2:10; 105:22; **Pr** 28:2; **Ecc** 1:16; **Isa** 56:11; **Jer** 3:15
Wisdom to administer justice
1Ki 3:28 When all Israel heard the verdict the king had given, they held the king in awe, because they saw that he had wisdom from God to administer justice.   *See also* **1Ki** 3:9 pp **2Ch** 1:10; **Ps** 37:30; **Pr** 20:26; 24:23; **Mt** 24:45 pp **Lk** 12:42; **1Co** 6:5

The teaching of wisdom
The wise give instruction
Ecc 12:9 Not only was the Teacher wise, but also he imparted knowledge to the people. He pondered and searched out and set in order many proverbs.   *See also* **Ps** 37:30; 49:3; **Pr** 1:20–21; 5:1; 8:1; 16:21; 31:26; **Da** 11:33; **1Co** 2:6–7; **Col** 1:28; 3:16

The wise listen to instruction
Pr 1:5 let the wise listen and add to their learning, and let the discerning get guidance—

Pr 15:31 Whoever listens to a life-giving rebuke will be at home among the wise. *See also* Pr 4:1; 9:9; 10:8; 13:20; 15:12; 19:20

Examples of those endowed with wisdom
Ac 7:10; **Dt** 1:15; 34:9
David: **2Sa** 14:20; **Ps** 78:72
Solomon: **1Ki** 3:16–28; 4:29–34; 10:4–8 pp 2Ch 9:3–7; **1Ch** 22:12–13; **Mt** 12:42 pp Lk 11:31
Ezr 7:25; **Isa** 11:2; **Da** 1:17
Daniel: **Da** 2:19–23,27–28; 5:11–12
2Pe 3:15

---

wisdom, source of

True wisdom belongs to God and may be given by him alone. It cannot be received by those who put confidence in worldly wisdom which is based upon human cleverness and insight without God's revelation and which will come to nothing.

True wisdom comes from God
It is given by God alone
Job 12:13 "To God belong wisdom and power; counsel and understanding are his." *See also* Ex 28:3; Job 38:36; Ecc 2:26; Jas 3:17
It is received through God's word
Ps 19:7 The law of the LORD is perfect, reviving the soul. The statutes of the LORD are trustworthy, making wise the simple. *See also* Ps 119:99–100,130; Ecc 8:5; Jer 8:8–9; Hos 4:6; Mt 7:24; Col 3:16; 2Ti 3:15
It is received through submission to God
Pr 15:33 The fear of the LORD teaches wisdom, and humility comes before honour. *See also* Isa 33:6
It is imparted by God's Spirit
Eph 1:17 I [Paul] keep asking that the God of our Lord Jesus Christ, the glorious Father, may give you [Ephesian believers] the Spirit of wisdom and revelation, so that you may know him better. *See also* Ex 31:3 pp Ex 35:31; Job 32:8;

Da 4:18; 5:14; Ac 6:3,10; 1Co 12:8; Eph 3:5
It is given in response to prayer
Jas 1:5 If any of you lacks wisdom, you should ask God, who gives generously to all without finding fault, and it will be given to you. *See also* 1Ki 3:9 pp 2Ch 1:10; Pr 2:3–6; Da 10:12; Col 1:9

The emptiness of worldly wisdom
Worldly wisdom is foolishness to God
1Co 3:19–20 For the wisdom of this world is foolishness in God's sight. As it is written: "He catches the wise in their craftiness" . . .
See also Job 5:13; Ps 94:11; Ro 1:21–23
God cannot be known by worldly wisdom
1Co 1:21 For since in the wisdom of God the world through its wisdom did not know him, God was pleased through the foolishness of what was preached to save those who believe. *See also* Ecc 8:16–17; Isa 55:9; Ro 11:33–34; 1Co 1:17; 2:4–5,11–13
Worldly wisdom builds pride and false hope
Isa 47:10 "You [Babylon] have trusted in your wickedness and have said, 'No-one sees me.' Your wisdom and knowledge mislead you when you say to yourself, 'I am, and there is none besides me.'" *See also* Pr 3:7; 26:12; 28:11; Isa 5:21; Jer 9:23; Col 2:23
Paul uses irony to condemn the "wisdom" in which the Corinthians take pride: 1Co 4:10; 2Co 11:18–19
Worldly wisdom will be confounded
Isa 29:14 "Therefore once more I [the LORD] will astound these people [the inhabitants of Jerusalem] with wonder upon wonder; the wisdom of the wise will perish, the intelligence of the intelligent will vanish." *See also* 1Co 1:19–20; Job 5:12–13; Pr 21:30; Isa 19:11; 44:25; Jer 51:57; Eze 28:6–7,17; 1Co 1:25

The revelation of divine wisdom
It is revealed in Jesus Christ
1Co 1:23–24 but we [Paul and Timothy] preach Christ crucified: a stumbling-block to Jews and foolishness to Gentiles, but to those whom God has called, both Jews and Greeks, Christ the power of God and the wisdom of God.
See also 1Co 1:30; 2:6–8; Col 1:15–17

It is rejected by the worldly-wise
1Co 2:14 The person without the Spirit does not accept the things that come from the Spirit of God but considers them foolishness, and cannot understand them because they are spiritually discerned.   *See also* **1Co** 1:18,22–23

It is revealed to the unlearned
Mt 11:25 At that time Jesus said, "I praise you, Father, Lord of heaven and earth, because you have hidden these things from the wise and learned, and revealed them to little children." pp Lk 10:21

1Co 3:18 Do not deceive yourselves. If any of you think you are wise by the standards of this age, you should become "fools" so that you may become wise.   *See also* **1Co** 1:26–27

It is revealed through the church
Eph 3:10 His [God's] intent was that now, through the church, the manifold wisdom of God should be made known to the rulers and authorities in the heavenly realms,

God-given wisdom is superior to worldly wisdom
Lk 21:15 "For I [Jesus] will give you [the disciples] words and wisdom that none of your adversaries will be able to resist or contradict." *See also* **Ge** 41:15; **Ex** 7:11–12; **1Ki** 4:30; **Da** 1:20; 5:7; **Ac** 6:10   *See also revelation.*

---

word of God
The utterances of God, especially as revealed in Scripture. This may take the form of commands or promises. The term can also refer to Jesus Christ as the incarnate Word of God.

The word of God revealed as law
God has made his commands and requirements known
Ps 147:19 He [God] has revealed his word to Jacob, his laws and decrees to Israel.   *See also* **Ex** 20:1–17; 24:3; 34:27–28; **Dt** 5:5; **Isa** 2:3 pp Mic 4:2; **Mt** 15:6 pp Mk 7:13

God's law is to be obeyed
Dt 30:14 . . . the word is very near you; it is in your mouth and in your heart so that you may obey it.   *See also* **Jos** 23:6; **Ps** 119:4; **Lk** 8:21;

11:28; **Jas** 1:22–23

Examples of disobedience and its consequences
Nu 15:31; **1Sa** 15:23–26; **2Sa** 12:9; **1Ch** 10:13; **2Ch** 34:21; **Isa** 5:24; **Jer** 8:9

The word of God as prophecy
The prophets spoke the words of God
Jer 1:9 Then the Lord reached out his hand and touched my mouth and said to me [Jeremiah], "Now, I have put my words in your mouth."

1Sa 3:1 . . . In those days the word of the Lord was rare; there were not many visions.

Jer 25:3 For twenty-three years—from the thirteenth year of Josiah son of Amon king of Judah until this very day—the word of the Lord has come to me [Jeremiah] and I have spoken to you again and again, but you have not listened.   *See also* **1Ki** 17:24; **2Ki** 24:2; **2Ch** 36:12,15; **Isa** 16:13; 24:3; **Jer** 7:1; 14:1; **Am** 8:11–12; **Mal** 1:1

Prophetic introductory formulae
"The word of the Lord came to . . .": **Ge** 15:1; **1Sa** 15:10; **2Sa** 24:11; **1Ki** 6:11; **2Ki** 20:4 pp Isa 38:4; **Jer** 16:1; **Eze** 6:1; **Jnh** 1:1; **Zec** 1:1

"Hear the word of the Lord": **1Ki** 22:19; **2Ki** 20:16 pp Isa 39:5; **Isa** 1:10; **Jer** 2:4; **Hos** 4:1

"This is what the Lord says": **2Sa** 7:5 pp 1Ch 17:4; **2Ki** 1:6; **Isa** 37:6; **Jer** 2:5; **Eze** 2:4; **Am** 1:3; **Hag** 2:11

Prophetic predictions fulfilled
1Ki 12:15 . . . this turn of events was from the Lord, to fulfil the word the Lord had spoken to Jeroboam son of Nebat . . .   *See also* **1Ki** 15:29; 16:12,34; 22:38; **2Ki** 1:17; 9:36; 10:17; 14:25; 15:12; 23:16; **2Ch** 36:21–22

The word "against" a people, indicating judgment Isa 9:8; 37:22; **Jer** 25:30; **Am** 3:1; **Zep** 2:5; **Zec** 9:1

True prophecy is inspired by God
2Pe 1:20–21 Above all, you must understand that no prophecy of Scripture came about by the prophet's own interpretation. For prophecy never had its origin in the human will, but prophets, though human, spoke from God as they were carried along by the Holy Spirit.   *See also* **Ne** 9:30;

Jer 23:16,25–26,30; **Eze** 13:1–3; **Mic** 3:8
A true prophet hears from God **2Ki** 3:12; **Jer**
5:13; 23:18; 27:18
The prophetic word is to be heeded **Ex**
9:20–21; **Jer** 6:10; 25:3; **Zec** 7:12

The word of God as Scripture
Scripture is the written word of God
Da 9:2 . . . I, Daniel, understood from the
Scriptures, according to the word of the Lord
given to Jeremiah the prophet, that the desolation
of Jerusalem would last seventy years.   *See also*
Ro 3:2; 15:4
NT writings are classified as Scripture **1Ti**
5:18; **2Pe** 3:16
Scripture is inspired and true **Jn** 10:35; **2Ti**
3:15
The foundational importance of Scripture
It must not be distorted or changed: **Dt** 4:2; 12:32; **Pr**
30:6; **2Co** 2:17; 4:2; **2Ti** 2:15; **Rev** 22:19
It is to be read publicly: **Ne** 8:1–8; **1Ti** 4:13
It is to be meditated upon: **Ps** 1:2; 119:15,97
It is the test of orthodoxy: **Isa** 8:20; **Ac** 17:11
Mt 22:29 pp **Mk** 12:24
It is the basis for preaching: **Ac** 17:2; 18:28
1Co 4:6

Jesus Christ as the incarnate Word of God
Jesus Christ is God in the flesh
Jn 1:1 In the beginning was the Word, and the
Word was with God, and the Word was God.
See also **Jn** 1:14; 12:45; **Col** 1:15; **Heb** 1:2; **1Jn**
1:1; **Rev** 19:13
Jesus Christ speaks the Father's words
Jn 8:40 " . . . you [the Jews] are determined
to kill me [Jesus], a man who has told you the
truth that I heard from God. Abraham did not do
such things."   *See also* **Mt** 22:16 pp **Mk** 12:14
pp **Lk** 20:21; **Jn** 7:18
Jesus Christ's words have sovereign power
Mt 8:8 pp **Lk** 7:7; **Mt** 8:16; **Heb** 1:3

The gospel as the word of God
It was preached by Jesus Christ
Mk 2:2 . . . he [Jesus] preached the word to
them.   *See also* **Mt** 13:19–23 pp **Mk** 4:14–20 pp

Lk 8:11–15; **Mk** 4:33; **Lk** 4:43 pp **Mk** 1:38; **Lk** 5:1
It was preached by the first Christians
1Th 2:13 . . . when you received the word of
God, which you heard from us [the apostles], you
accepted it not as a human word, but as it
actually is, the word of God . . .   *See also* **Mk**
16:20; **Ac** 6:2; 8:4; 11:1; 13:5; 15:35–36; 17:13;
1Co 14:36; **2Co** 2:17; 4:2; **Php** 1:14; **Col** 1:25;
2Ti 4:2
It leads to numerical and spiritual growth
within the church Ac 6:7; 12:24; 13:49; 19:20;
Col 1:5–6; **1Th** 2:13
It must be preached **Ro** 10:14; **2Ti** 4:2

Descriptions of God's word
It is true: **Ps** 33:4; **Jn** 17:17
It is flawless: **2Sa** 22:31 pp **Ps** 18:30; **Pr** 30:5
It is infallible: **1Ki** 8:56; **2Ki** 10:10
Ps 103:20
It is eternal: **Ps** 119:89,152; **Isa** 40:8; **1Pe** 1:25
Ps 119:103; 138:2; **Isa** 45:23; **Eph** 6:17; **2Ti**
2:9; **Heb** 4:12; **1Pe** 1:23

Comparisons of the word of God with everyday things
Food: **Dt** 8:3; **Job** 23:12; **Ps** 119:103; **Jer** 15:16;
Eze 2:8; 3:1; **1Pe** 2:2
Ps 119:105
Fire: **Jer** 5:14; 20:9; 23:29
Jer 23:29; **Heb** 4:12

The word of God has power
It is active
Isa 55:11 " . . . It [God's word] will not return
to me empty, but will accomplish what I desire
and achieve the purpose for which I sent it."
It brings about creation
Ps 33:6 By the word of the Lord were the
heavens made, their starry host by the breath of
his mouth.   *See also* **2Pe** 3:5
It governs and maintains the created order
Heb 1:3 The Son is the radiance of God's glory
and the exact representation of his being,
sustaining all things by his powerful word . . .
See also **Ps** 147:18
It gives life
Dt 8:3 . . . human beings do not live on bread

alone but on every word that comes from the
mouth of the LORD.   *See also* **Isa** 55:2–3; **Mt**
4:4 pp **Lk** 4:4
It consecrates secular things 1Ti 4:5
It restrains from evil Ps 17:4; 119:11
It heals and rescues Ps 107:20
It has power to save
Jas 1:21 . . . humbly accept the word planted
in you, which can save you.   *See also* **2Ti** 3:15;
1Pe 1:23
**It brings about the growth of the kingdom of
God** Mt 13:23 pp Mk 4:20 pp Lk 8:15
It builds up the saints Ac 20:32   *See also*
*gospel; law; preachers and preaching; prophecy;
revelation; Scripture, inspiration and authority.*

---

world

Scripture understands "the world" in a number of
senses. It initially refers to the world as God's
good creation. However, that same world has now
fallen into sin, with the result that it can be a
threat to believers. Believers are called to live in
the world, maintaining contact with it, while
remaining distinct from it, and avoiding being
contaminated by it.

world, God's creation
The heavens and the earth were created by God,
and ordered by him and for him.

The world was created out of nothing
By the will of God
Ge 1:1 In the beginning God created the
heavens and the earth.   *See also* **Ps** 96:5;
102:25; 148:5; **Isa** 40:28; **Heb** 11:3; **Rev** 4:11;
10:6
By the word of God
Jn 1:1–3 In the beginning was the Word, and
the Word was with God, and the Word was God.
He was with God in the beginning. Through him
all things were made; without him nothing was
made that has been made.   *See also* **Ge** 1:3; **Jn**
1:10; **1Co** 8:6; **Heb** 1:2; **2Pe** 3:5
By the Spirit of God
Ge 1:2 Now the earth was formless and empty,
darkness was over the surface of the deep, and

the Spirit of God was hovering over the
waters.   *See also* **Job** 26:13; 33:4; **Ps** 33:6
By the hand of God
Heb 1:10 . . . "In the beginning, O Lord, you
laid the foundations of the earth, and the heavens
are the work of your hands."   *See also* **Ps** 8:3
By the mind of God
Ps 136:5 who by his [the LORD's]
understanding made the heavens . . .   *See also*
Ps 104:24; **Pr** 3:19–20

The world God created was perfect
Ge 1:31 God saw all that he had made, and it
was very good . . .   *See also* **1Ti** 4:4

God created the world for a purpose
For his glory
Ps 19:1–2 The heavens declare the glory of
God; the skies proclaim the work of his hands.
Day after day they pour forth speech; night after
night they display knowledge.   *See also* **Ps** 50:6;
148:1–4; **Ro** 1:20; 11:36
That people might worship and revere him
Ps 147:4–5 He [the LORD] determines the
number of the stars and calls them each by
name. Great is our Lord and mighty in power; his
understanding has no limit.   *See also* **Ge** 15:5;
Ne 9:6; **Job** 22:12; **Isa** 40:25–26; **Jer** 31:35
For his possession and use
Dt 10:14 To the LORD your God belong the
heavens, even the highest heavens, the earth and
everything in it.

Col 1:16–17 For by him all things were
created: things in heaven and on earth, visible
and invisible, whether thrones or powers or rulers
or authorities; all things were created by him and
for him. He is before all things, and in him all
things hold together.   *See also* **Ps** 24:1–2;
50:12; 89:11; **Ac** 7:49   *See also creation; word of
God.*

---

world, redeemed
Though fallen, the world is offered the hope of
redemption and restoration through Jesus Christ.

This world has an end
It is temporary
1Pe 1:24 . . . "All human beings are like grass, and all their glory is like the flowers of the field; the grass withers and the flowers fall," *See also* **Isa** 40:6–7; **Mt** 5:18; 24:35 pp **Mk** 13:31 pp **Lk** 21:33; **1Co** 7:31; **Heb** 1:10–12; 12:26–27
It is under God's judgment
Isa 13:13 Therefore I [the LORD] will make the heavens tremble; and the earth will shake from its place at the wrath of the LORD Almighty, in the day of his burning anger.   *See also* **Isa** 34:4; 51:6; **Joel** 2:30–31; **2Pe** 3:10; **1Jn** 2:17; **Rev** 20:11

Through Jesus Christ there is redemption and renewal for the world
For humanity
1Jn 2:2 He [Jesus Christ] is the atoning sacrifice for our sins, and not only for ours but also for the sins of the whole world.   *See also* **Mt** 1:21; **Jn** 1:29; 3:16–17; **Ro** 5:18; **2Co** 5:18–19
For creation
Ro 8:19–21 The creation waits in eager expectation for the children of God to be revealed. For the creation was subjected to frustration, not by its own choice, but by the will of the one who subjected it, in hope that the creation itself will be liberated from its bondage to decay . . .   *See also* **Mt** 24:7–8 pp **Mk** 13:8 pp **Lk** 21:10–11; **Col** 1:20
The promise of a new heaven and a new earth
2Pe 3:13 . . . in keeping with his promise we are looking forward to a new heaven and a new earth, the home of righteousness.   *See also* **Isa** 65:17; **1Co** 15:24–28; **Eph** 1:10; **Rev** 21:1–4
See also creation, renewal; heaven; redemption; salvation.

---

worship
The praise, adoration and reverence of God, both in public and private. It is a celebration of the worthiness of God, by which honour is given to his name.

---

worship, acceptable attitudes
True worship is not the mechanical repetition of rituals, but should be wholehearted and reverent. It should be based upon trustful and obedient lives, in that obedience is itself to be seen as an act of worship.

Worship should be in accordance with God's commands
Ge 22:2 Then God said, "Take your son, your only son, Isaac, whom you love, and go to the region of Moriah. Sacrifice him there as a burnt offering on one of the mountains I will tell you about."   *See also* **Ge** 12:1,7–8; **Dt** 30:16–20; **1Sa** 15:22; **Ps** 40:6–8; **Jer** 7:2; **Da** 3:28; **Ac** 13:2; **Ro** 12:1

Worship should not be mechanical
Jn 4:23–24 "Yet a time is coming and has now come when the true worshippers will worship the Father in spirit and truth, for they are the kind of worshippers the Father seeks. God is spirit, and his worshippers must worship in spirit and in truth."   *See also* **Heb** 10:1

Worship should give God the honour due to him
1Ch 16:29 pp **Ps** 96:8–9

Worship of mere human devising is unacceptable
Isa 29:13 The Lord says: "These people come near to me with their mouth and honour me with their lips, but their hearts are far from me. Their worship of me is based on merely human rules which they have been taught."   *See also* **Lev** 10:1; **Mt** 15:7–9 pp **Mk** 7:6–7; **Php** 3:3; **Col** 2:23

Worship should be orderly and reverent
1Co 14:40 But everything should be done in a fitting and orderly way.   *See also* **1Ch** 16:37–42; **1Ki** 18:30–39; **1Co** 14:26

Worship should be grounded in godly and obedient living

Mic 6:6–8 With what shall I come before the LORD and bow down before the exalted God? Shall I come before him with burnt offerings, with calves a year old? Will the LORD be pleased with thousands of rams, with ten thousand rivers of oil? Shall I offer my firstborn for my transgression, the fruit of my body for the sin of my soul? He has showed you, O people, what is good. And what does the LORD require of you? To act justly and to love mercy and to walk humbly with your God.

Ro 12:1 Therefore, I [Paul] urge you, brothers and sisters, in view of God's mercy, to offer your bodies as living sacrifices, holy and pleasing to God—this is your spiritual act of worship. *See also* **Ps** 15:1–5; 24:3–4; **1Ti** 2:10

The proper attitude of worshippers
Preparation for worship

1Co 11:28 We ought to examine ourselves before we eat of the bread and drink of the cup. *See also* **Lev** 16:3–4; **2Sa** 12:20; **2Ch** 7:1; **Mt** 2:11

Wholeheartedness

Dt 6:5 Love the LORD your God with all your heart and with all your soul and with all your strength. *See also* **Ex** 34:14; **Dt** 10:12; **Jos** 22:5; **1Sa** 12:24; **Ps** 27:4; **Mt** 22:37 pp **Mk** 12:30; **Lk** 10:27

Confidence in approaching God

Heb 10:22–23 let us draw near to God with a sincere heart in full assurance of faith, having our hearts sprinkled to cleanse us from a guilty conscience and having our bodies washed with pure water. Let us hold unswervingly to the hope we profess, for he who promised is faithful. *See also* **Ge** 4:4; **Jas** 4:8; **Heb** 7:19; 11:4 *See also holiness; obedience; prayer, practicalities.*

worship, elements

Praise and thankfulness are important elements of worship, which also includes confession of sin, the reading of Scripture and music.

Worship with awe

Dt 10:12 And now, O Israel, what does the LORD your God ask of you but to fear the LORD your God, to walk in all his ways, to love him, to serve the LORD your God with all your heart and with all your soul. *See also* **Lev** 10:1–3; **2Ch** 7:3; **Ps** 2:11; 68:35; 96:9; **Ecc** 5:1

Worship includes trust

Ps 4:5 Offer right sacrifices and trust in the LORD. *See also* **Ps** 37:7; **Heb** 11:6

Worship includes praise

Ps 22:22 I will declare your name to my people; in the congregation I will praise you.

Ps 107:32 Let them exalt him in the assembly of the people and praise him in the council of the elders.

Heb 13:15 Through Jesus, therefore, let us continually offer to God a sacrifice of praise—the fruit of lips that confess his name. *See also* **2Ch** 31:2; **Ne** 9:5–6; **Ps** 150:1–6; **Heb** 2:12; **Rev** 7:11–12

Worship includes thanksgiving

Ps 100:4 Enter his gates with thanksgiving and his courts with praise; give thanks to him and praise his name.

Rev 11:16–17 And the twenty-four elders, who were seated on their thrones before God, fell on their faces and worshipped God, saying: "We give thanks to you, Lord God Almighty, the One who is and who was, because you have taken your great power and have begun to reign." *See also* **2Ch** 7:3; **Ps** 50:14,23; **Eph** 5:19–20; **Php** 4:6; **Rev** 7:11–12

Worship with joy

Ps 95:1 Come, let us sing for joy to the LORD . . . *See also* **Ps** 27:6; 43:4; 100:2; **Lk** 24:52–53; **Ac** 2:46–47

Worship includes the confession of Jesus Christ as Lord
Heb 13:15 Through Jesus, therefore, let us continually offer to God a sacrifice of praise—the fruit of lips that confess his name.

Worship includes confession of sin
Hos 14:2 Take words with you and return to the LORD. Say to him: "Forgive all our sins and receive us graciously, that we may offer the fruit of our lips."   *See also* **Lev** 16:21; **Ne** 9:2; **Ps** 66:18

Worship includes the reading of God's word
Col 3:16 Let the word of Christ dwell in you richly as you teach and admonish one another with all wisdom, and as you sing psalms, hymns and spiritual songs with gratitude in your hearts to God.

1Ti 4:13 Until I come, devote yourself to the public reading of Scripture, to preaching and to teaching.   *See also* **Ne** 8:5–6; 9:3

Worship includes music and song
Ps 95:2–3 Let us come before him [the LORD] with thanksgiving and extol him with music and song. For the LORD is the great God, the great King above all gods.   *See also* **2Sa** 6:5; **Ps** 100:2; **Eph** 5:19–20

Worship includes dance
Ps 149:3 Let them praise his name with dancing and make music to him with tambourine and harp.   *See also* **Ex** 15:20; **Ps** 30:11
See also faith; Scripture.

worship, hindrances
True worship goes beyond mere form and can therefore be hindered by a wrong relationship to God or to others.

Worship that is merely formal is unacceptable
1Sa 15:22 But Samuel replied: "Does the LORD delight in burnt offerings and sacrifices as much as in obeying the voice of the LORD? To obey is better than sacrifice, and to heed is better than the fat of rams."   *See also* **Isa** 1:13; **Eze** 33:31; **Hos** 6:6; **Mt** 6:5; **2Ti** 3:5

Worship is hindered by wrong relationships
To God
Ps 66:18 If I had cherished sin in my heart, the Lord would not have listened;

Mt 15:7–9 ". . . These people honour me with their lips, but their hearts are far from me. They worship me in vain; their teachings are merely human rules.'" pp Mk 7:6–7   *See also* **Isa** 29:13; **Ps** 32:5–6; **Isa** 59:2; 64:7; **Jas** 4:3
To others
Isa 1:11–17 "The multitude of your sacrifices—what are they to me?" says the LORD ". . . Seek justice, encourage the oppressed. Defend the cause of the fatherless, plead the case of the widow."

Mt 5:23–24 "Therefore, if you are offering your gift at the altar and there remember that your brother or sister has something against you, leave your gift there in front of the altar. First go and be reconciled to them; then come and offer your gift."   *See also* **Am** 5:21–24

worship, of God
God alone is worthy of worship; the worship of other gods is forbidden. In the NT worship is offered to the Son of God.

God alone is to be worshipped
He alone is worthy of worship
1Ch 16:25 For great is the LORD and most worthy of praise; he is to be feared above all gods.   *See also* **Ps** 48:1; 96:4–5; 145:3; **2Sa** 22:4
The worship of God the Father
Jn 4:23 "Yet a time is coming and has now come when the true worshippers will worship the Father in spirit and truth, for they are the kind of worshippers the Father seeks."   *See also* **Php** 2:11

The worship of God the Son

Mt 2:11 On coming to the house, they [the Magi] saw the child with his mother Mary, and they bowed down and worshipped him. Then they opened their treasures and presented him with gifts of gold and of incense and of myrrh.

Mt 14:33 Then those who were in the boat worshipped him [Jesus], saying, "Truly you are the Son of God."

Jn 20:28 Thomas said to him [Jesus], "My Lord and my God!"   *See also* **Mt** 28:16–17; **Jn** 9:35–38; **Php** 2:9–11; **Heb** 1:6; **Rev** 5:8–14

Angels worship God

Ps 103:20 Praise the LORD, you his angels, you mighty ones who do his bidding, who obey his word.

Ps 148:1–2 Praise the LORD. Praise the LORD from the heavens, praise him in the heights above. Praise him, all his angels, praise him, all his heavenly hosts.   *See also* **Ps** 29:1–2; **Isa** 6:1–4; **Eze** 10:1–18; **Rev** 4:8–9

The worship of other gods forbidden

Ex 20:3 "You shall have no other gods before me." pp Dt 5:7

2Ki 17:35–36 When the LORD made a covenant with the Israelites, he commanded them: "Do not worship any other gods or bow down to them, serve them or sacrifice to them. But the LORD, who brought you up out of Egypt with mighty power and outstretched arm, is the one you must worship. To him you shall bow down and to him offer sacrifices."   *See also* **Ex** 34:14; **Dt** 6:13–14; **Ne** 9:6; **Ps** 86:9–10; 97:7; **Ac** 10:25–26; 14:13–18

The worship of angels forbidden

Col 2:18 Do not let anyone who delights in false humility and the worship of angels disqualify you for the prize . . .   *See also* **Rev** 19:9–10; 22:8–9

worship, places

Under the old covenant, there were rules governing the places where worship might be offered but under the new covenant the earthly location is of no importance.

Worship at places commemorating some act of God

Ge 12:7 The LORD appeared to Abram and said, "To your offspring I will give this land." So he built an altar there [Shechem] to the LORD, who had appeared to him.   *See also* **Ge** 8:20; 26:23–25; 35:1

Worship at a place chosen by God

Dt 12:13–14 Be careful not to sacrifice your burnt offerings anywhere you please. Offer them only at the place the LORD will choose in one of your tribes, and there observe everything I command you.   *See also* **Ge** 22:2; **Dt** 14:23–25; **1Ch** 21:18–19; **2Ch** 7:15–16

Worship in certain sacred places

Dt 12:5 But you are to seek the place the LORD your God will choose from among all your tribes to put his Name there for his dwelling . . .   *See also* **Ex** 3:12; **Dt** 26:2; **1Sa** 1:3,28; **Isa** 27:13; **Jn** 4:20

Worship at the Tent of Meeting

Ex 25:8–9 "Then have them [the Israelites] make a sanctuary for me [the LORD], and I will dwell among them. Make this tabernacle and all its furnishings exactly like the pattern I will show you [Moses]."   *See also* **Ex** 29:42–43; 33:10; **Lev** 17:1–5

Worship at the temple in Jerusalem

1Ch 22:1 Then David said, "The house of the LORD God is to be here, and also the altar of burnt offering for Israel."   *See also* **2Ch** 7:15–16; 29:27–30; **Ne** 8:6; **Lk** 1:8–10; 2:37; **Ac** 8:27

Worship in a synagogue

Lk 4:16 He [Jesus] went to Nazareth, where he had been brought up, and on the Sabbath day he went into the synagogue, as was his custom. And he stood up to read.　　*See also* **Ac** 13:15; 15:21; 17:2

Worship in the home
Da 6:10 Now when Daniel learned that the decree had been published, he went home to his upstairs room where the windows opened towards Jerusalem. Three times a day he got down on his knees and prayed, giving thanks to his God, just as he had done before.　　*See also* **Mt** 6:6; **Ro** 16:5; **1Co** 16:19; **Col** 4:15; **Phm** 2

The earthly location for worship is unimportant
Jn 4:21–24 Jesus declared, "Believe me, woman, a time is coming when you will worship the Father neither on this mountain nor in Jerusalem . . . a time is coming and has now come when the true worshippers will worship the Father in spirit and truth, for they are the kind of worshippers the Father seeks. God is spirit, and his worshippers must worship in spirit and in truth."　　*See also* **Ge** 24:26; 47:31; **Jdg** 7:15; **Job** 1:20

In heaven worship is perfect
Lk 2:13; **Heb** 12:22; **Rev** 4:9–11; 5:13–14; 7:9–12; 19:4–7　　*See also heaven.*

---

worship, reasons
The supreme reason for human existence is to worship God for his love, greatness and saving deeds.

To worship is a divine command
Mt 4:10 Jesus said to him, "Away from me, Satan! For it is written: 'Worship the Lord your God, and serve him only.'" pp **Lk** 4:8　　*See also* **Dt** 6:13; **Ex** 23:25; **2Ki** 17:36; **1Ch** 16:29; **Ps** 22:23; 29:2; 68:26; 113:1; 117:1; 148:11–13; 150:6; **1Ti** 2:8; **Rev** 14:7

God's people are to be a worshipping people
1Pe 2:9 But you are a chosen people, a royal priesthood, a holy nation, a people belonging to God, that you may declare the praises of him who called you out of darkness into his wonderful light.　　*See also* **Ex** 19:5–6; **Ps** 105:1–6; **Isa** 43:21; **Rev** 1:5–6

Worship is the response of God's people
To God's love
Ex 4:31 . . . And when they [the elders of the Israelites] heard that the LORD was concerned about them and had seen their misery, they bowed down and worshipped.　　*See also* **Dt** 6:5; 12:7; 26:10–11; **2Ch** 7:3; **Ps** 95:6–7; 117:1–2; 138:2
To God's holy presence
1Ch 16:29 . . . Bring an offering and come before him; worship the LORD in the splendour of his holiness. pp **Ps** 96:8–9　　*See also* **Ex** 33:10; **Lev** 10:3; **Jos** 5:13–15; **Ps** 29:2; 99:5; **Rev** 4:8; 15:4
To God's greatness
Ps 95:1–3 Come, let us sing for joy to the LORD; let us shout aloud to the Rock of our salvation. Let us come before him with thanksgiving and extol him with music and song. For the LORD is the great God, the great King above all gods.　　*See also* **Ex** 3:12; **Ps** 22:27–28; 66:1–4; 96:1–3; **Rev** 15:3–4

To the deeds of God
Ge 8:20 Then Noah built an altar to the LORD and, taking some of all the clean animals and clean birds, he sacrificed burnt offerings on it.　　*See also* **Ge** 12:7
The signs and wonders in Egypt and Sinai: **Ex** 4:29–31; 12:27; 15:1,20
Ezr 3:10–11; **Isa** 19:21; **Da** 3:28; **Mt** 9:7–8 pp **Mk** 2:12 pp **Lk** 5:25–26; **Ac** 3:8
To the fear of God
Ps 22:23 You who fear the LORD, praise him! All you descendants of Jacob, honour him! Revere him, all you descendants of Israel!

Heb 12:28 Therefore, since we are receiving a kingdom that cannot be shaken, let us be thankful, and so worship God acceptably with reverence and awe,　　*See also* **Ps** 2:11;

Ac 10:2   *See also holiness, of God; praise; prayer, and worship.*

---

worship, results

Worship not only gives God what is due to him but also results in many benefits for his people.

True worship brings benefits for God's people
Blessing
Ex 23:25–26 "Worship the LORD your God, and his blessing will be on your food and water. I will take away sickness from among you, and none will miscarry or be barren in your land. I will give you a full life span."   *See also Dt 11:13–15*
Guidance
Ac 13:2–3 While they [prophets and teachers in the church at Antioch] were worshipping the Lord and fasting, the Holy Spirit said, "Set apart for me Barnabas and Saul for the work to which I have called them." So after they had fasted and prayed, they placed their hands on them and sent them off.   *See also Isa 58:6–11; Nu 7:89*
Deliverance
Ac 16:25–26 About midnight Paul and Silas were praying and singing hymns to God, and the other prisoners were listening to them. Suddenly there was such a violent earthquake that the foundations of the prison were shaken. At once all the prison doors flew open, and everybody's chains came loose.   *See also Ps 50:14–15*
Joy
1Ch 29:21–22 The next day they [the Israelites] made sacrifices to the LORD . . . They ate and drank with great joy in the presence of the LORD that day . . .   *See also 2Ch 29:30; Ps 43:4; Isa 56:7; Lk 24:52*
A sense of God's presence
2Ch 5:13–14 . . . and the priests could not perform their service because of the cloud, for the glory of the LORD filled the temple of God. pp 1Ki 8:10–11   *See also Ex 40:35*
A deeper sense of Jesus Christ's lordship
Php 2:9–11 Therefore God exalted him [Jesus] to the highest place and gave him the name that is above every name, that at the name of Jesus

every knee should bow, in heaven and on earth and under the earth, and every tongue confess that Jesus Christ is Lord, to the glory of God the Father.   *See also Rev 1:10–18*

Boldness to witness
Ac 4:31 After they [the Jerusalem Christians] prayed, the place where they were meeting was shaken. And they were all filled with the Holy Spirit and spoke the word of God boldly.   *See also Ps 57:9; Ac 18:9–10*

True worship convicts sinners
1Co 14:24–25 But if an unbeliever or someone who does not understand comes in while everybody is prophesying, such people will be convinced by all that they are sinners and will be judged by all, and the secrets of their hearts will be laid bare. So they will fall down and worship God, exclaiming, "God is really among you!"   *See also church, life of.*

---

worship, times

Scripture stresses the importance of regular worship, while at the same time recognising that believers may worship God spontaneously.

Examples of regular worship
On a daily basis
Ac 2:46–47 Every day they [all the believers] continued to meet together in the temple courts. They broke bread in their homes and ate together with glad and sincere hearts, praising God . . .   *See also Ex 29:38–43; Ps 141:2; Eze 46:13–15*
Several times a day
Da 6:10 . . . Three times a day he [Daniel] got down on his knees and prayed, giving thanks to his God, just as he had done before.   *See also 1Ch 16:37; Ps 119:164; Ac 3:1; Heb 10:25*
On holy days
2Ch 8:12–13 On the altar of the LORD that he had built in front of the portico, Solomon sacrificed burnt offerings to the LORD, according to the daily requirement for offerings commanded by Moses for Sabbaths, New Moons and the three annual feasts . . .   *See also Eze 46:3*

At the three annual pilgrim festivals
Dt 16:16 Three times a year all your men must appear before the LORD your God at the place he will choose: at the Feast of Unleavened Bread, the Feast of Weeks and the Feast of Tabernacles . . .
Passover (or the Feast of Unleavened Bread): **Ex** 12:1–20; **Lk** 2:41
Pentecost (or the Feast of Weeks): **Ex** 34:22; **Ac** 2:1
The Feast of Tabernacles (or Ingathering): **Ex** 23:16; **Lev** 23:33–36; **Nu** 29:12–39; **Dt** 16:13–15
On the Day of Atonement
Lev 16:34 "This is to be a lasting ordinance for you: Atonement is to be made once a year for all the sins of the Israelites." And it was done, as the LORD commanded Moses. *See also* **Ex** 30:10; **Lev** 16:3–33; 23:26–32
On Sabbath days
Lk 4:16 He [Jesus] went to Nazareth, where he had been brought up, and on the Sabbath day he went into the synagogue, as was his custom . . . *See also* **Lev** 24:5–8; **Nu** 28:9–10

Examples of spontaneous worship
In response to an awareness of the closeness of God Ex 34:8; Jdg 7:15
In response to the experience of God's mercy
Ex 4:29–31 Moses and Aaron brought together all the elders of the Israelites, and Aaron told them everything the LORD had said to Moses. He also performed the signs before the people, and they believed. And when they heard that the LORD was concerned about them and had seen their misery, they bowed down and worshipped. *See also* **1Sa** 1:19–28
In response to the presence and power of Jesus Christ
Mt 28:8–9 So the women hurried away from the tomb, afraid yet filled with joy, and ran to tell his disciples. Suddenly Jesus met them. "Greetings," he said. They came to him, clasped his feet and worshipped him. *See also* **Mt** 14:33; **Lk** 24:52

Worship should not be dependent on circumstances
Php 4:6 Do not be anxious about anything, but in everything, by prayer and petition, with thanksgiving, present your requests to God. *See also* **Job** 1:20–21; **Da** 6:10; **Ac** 16:25; **1Th** 5:16–18

The continuous worship of God in heaven
Rev 4:10–11; 5:14; 7:11; 11:1; 19:4
See also mercy; Sabbath.

Index

The New International Version

First published in 1979, the NEW INTERNATIONAL VERSION has become the world's most popular modern English Bible translation.

More than 100 scholars from diverse denominational backgrounds worked for 15 years to complete this distinctive translation. Their principal concern was to be faithful to the original texts, and to reflect the literary and stylistic diversity within the Bible.

The result is a Bible eminently suitable both for private study and public reading.

All Popular editions feature:
* topical headings which enhance ease of reading and understanding
* poetic passages printed as poetry
* table of weights and measures
* explanations of original names, measures and phrases in the footnotes
* clear, readable print
* Bible Guide containing
    The Bible at a glance
    The land and people of the Bible
    Well-known events in the life of Jesus
    Plan of the Bible
    Key events in the Bible
    Bible maps

A large range of popular-sized Bibles are available in the NIV:

Red cased	ISBN 0 340 25382 7
Brown cased	ISBN 0 340 26969 3
Paperback	ISBN 0 340 27818 8
Children's, illustrated	ISBN 0 340 26970 7
With Introductory Helps	ISBN 0 340 34601 9

As well as a range of popular-sized **Inclusive Language editions:**
Ideal for Bible study and those interested in the dynamics of Bible translation. Suitable for church use particularly when reading aloud to a mixed congregation.

Blue cased	ISBN 0 340 59140 4
Illustrated cased, green	ISBN 0 340 67134 3
Women's cased, blue	ISBN 0 340 65179 2
Paperback	ISBN 0 340 67136 X

Cased inclusive language editions come with an attractive dust jacket featuring an impressionist painting, making these editions ideal for giving as gifts.

A number of leather editions are also available in both ranges, for more details contact your local bookshop or the publisher.

Original language study tools

Deepen your understanding of Scripture by studying the texts in their original language:

Hebrew-Greek Key Study Bible

Edited by Spiros Zodhiates Th.D   ISBN 0 340 69396 7 US text

Combines the essential study tools for Hebrew and Greek with the NIV translation. Contains a competely new numbering system and lexical aids explaining the meanings and usage of key words.

Interlinear NIV Parallel Old Testament

Edited by John R. Kohlenberger III   ISBN 0 340 42588 1 US text

The Hebrew Old Testament with interlinear translation alongside the NIV text.

Interlinear NRSV-NIV Parallel New Testament in Greek and English

Edited by Alfred Marshall   ISBN 0 340 64299 8 US text

A parallel Bible giving the NRSV and the NIV Bible texts, as well as an interlinear New Testament showing the 21st edition of Nestlé's *Novum Testamentum Graece* Greek and a word-for-word English translation.

A selection of Bible study software with original language tools is also available from Hodder & Stoughton, for more details contact your local bookshop or the publisher.